THE BAPTISM AND FILLING
of the
HOLY SPIRIT
The Unsearchable Riches of Grace

Dr. Lance T. Ketchum

Copyright 2011
Disciple Maker Ministries
Lance T. Ketchum
A.B.S., Th.B., Th.M., Ph.D.

First Printing
April 2012

ISBN 978-0-9860113-0-6

THE BAPTISM AND FILLING
of the
HOLY SPIRIT
The Unsearchable Riches of Grace

List Price: **$39.95 each**
plus postage and handling

Additional copies can be obtained from:

Disciple Maker Ministries

224 Fifth Avenue N.W.
Hutchinson, MN 55350

612-750-5515

LanceKetchum@msn.com
www.disciplemakerministries.org

REVIEWS

"Dr. Lance Ketchum has written another excellent volume in <u>The Unsearchable Riches of Grace</u>. In his usual detailed style, Dr. Ketchum covers the biblical doctrine of Pneumatology thoroughly. The careful Bible student will find in these pages help for questions on the Holy Spirit. More importantly, they will find direction for the challenge of living the Spirit-filled life. The 'how' of demonstrating the supernatural enabling of the indwelling Holy Spirit is detailed. This book will help anyone who desires to be used of God. For the preacher, teacher, or serious Bible student here is help to know the Word and to live the Word in this crucial area. I received help for my own ministry and life through these pages."

Dr. Roger Luiken
Pastor, Liberty Baptist Church
Fremont, NE

"Dr. Ketchum has tackled one of the great themes of the Bible. As I read this book I found myself praising the Lord, awed at His grace, and on my knees in deep thankfulness. <u>Unsearchable Riches of Grace</u> deals with this subject with doctrinal accuracy and yet great devotional heart and passion. Thank you, Dr. Ketchum, for this great addition to the insight of the heart of our great and gracious Heavenly Father."

Dr. Bruce Love
Senior Pastor, Bensalem Baptist Church
Bensalem, PA

"Once again Dr. Ketchum does a very thorough job of expounding the Scriptures concerning the subject of divine grace. Each chapter takes the reader deeper into a more personal reliance on the manifold grace of God rather than on the superficial self-works of modern day Christianity. Dr. Ketchum has done a great job combing multiple Scripture passages with practical Bible lessons that can be easily applied and taught. This book brings to light the untapped power of a Spirit-filled life, made perfect by the finished work of Christ in and through the believer. It will challenge your thinking and the way you have been taught concerning grace. This book is a must read for all who seek more of God and more of His divine grace. Thank you, Brother Lance."

Pastor Rick Sella
West Salem Baptist Church
West Salem, WI

INTRODUCTION

When I began to prepare to preach this series of studies, I had little idea how much they would affect my own life personally. Neither did I understand how shallow my Christian life really was. I understood much of what I was about to teach in an intellectual way. Through the self-examination and personal evaluations of my own life that precedes the preaching of the Word of God if a preacher wants to see God bless what he preaches, God began to reveal Himself. He revealed Himself through His Word in ways I had never experienced before in my 40 years of ministry as a believer. Then, out of this new intimacy with God, He began to show me that He did not merely want to reveal Himself *to* me. God wanted to reveal Himself *through* me. However, before He could, or would, reveal Himself through me, I had to *completely* surrender to His will and to the indwelling Spirit of God. Then, God began to reveal through His Word all the areas of my life that He wanted me to surrender to Him. As He revealed those areas of my life to me, I quickly began to realize just how far *short of the glory of God* my life really was.

I have entitled this series **The Baptism and Filling of the Holy Spirit - The Unsearchable Riches of Grace** because the comprehension of the doctrine of God's grace is really as unfathomable as God is. Like God, the doctrine of Grace can be known, but it can never be fully comprehended for it is as infinite as God is. Yet, God wants us to try to grasp this attribute of His infinite character. Even a small grasp of the knowledge of the grace of God increases the depth of a believer's relationship with God. This happens as God allows a believer to grasp what God wants to do *with* that believer's life and *through* that believer's life. As the knowledge of God's grace increases, the intimacy of the relationship we have with God increases in our prayer life and our devotional life. That intimacy then translates into a partnership in the "work of the ministry" with God Himself, supernaturally empowered by the indwelling Spirit of God.

A special THANK YOU to the members and friends of Shepherd's Fold Baptist Church of Hutchinson, Minnesota for their patience with me in the unfolding and development of the truths contained in this book. You have helped me to grow through these studies and it has been a blessing to see the many decisions that you have made to the glory of God during the preaching of this series. It has also been a blessing to see the increase of spiritual fruit as you began to implement the doctrine of Grace in the practice of your everyday lives. It is my prayer that **The Unsearchable Riches of Grace** will continue to bear fruit through your lives, and the lives of many others as they read these studies and as we all seek to "abide in the Vine."

I also want to thank Mrs. Julie Rydberg for her careful and meticulous proofreading of the manuscript. I pray our Lord will bless you in a special way for your generosity in giving many hours to this work.

To my wife, Patty – thank you for your patience in allowing me almost every free moment of our lives together for the last two years to finish this work. You catered to my every need so as to allow me the time I needed. Your graciousness has exemplified all the truths defined by the doctrine of Grace. Your self-sacrificing love reveals the selflessness that manifests the Spirit-filled life. You are undoubtedly a living definition exemplifying the word "helpmeet."

Your servant in Christ's service,

Lance T. Ketchum

Table of Contents

Chapter One
God's Distribution of Power to Us in the Indwelling Holy Spirit

"[1] Simon Peter, a servant and an apostle of Jesus Christ, to them that have obtained like precious faith with us through the righteousness of God and our Saviour Jesus Christ: [2] Grace and peace be multiplied unto you through the knowledge of God, and of Jesus our Lord, [3] According as his divine power hath given unto us all things that *pertain* unto life and godliness, through the knowledge of him that hath called us to glory and virtue: [4] Whereby are given unto us exceeding great and precious promises: that by these ye might be partakers of the divine nature, having escaped the corruption that is in the world through lust. [5] And beside this, giving all diligence, add to your faith virtue; and to virtue knowledge; [6] And to knowledge temperance; and to temperance patience; and to patience godliness; [7] And to godliness brotherly kindness; and to brotherly kindness charity. [8] For if these things be in you, and abound, they make *you that ye shall* neither *be* barren nor unfruitful in the knowledge of our Lord Jesus Christ. [9] But he that lacketh these things is blind, and cannot see afar off, and hath forgotten that he was purged from his old sins. [10] Wherefore the rather, brethren, give diligence to make your calling and election sure: for if ye do these things, ye shall never fall: [11] For so an entrance shall be ministered unto you abundantly into the everlasting kingdom of our Lord and Saviour Jesus Christ" (II Peter 1:1-11).

I have known many people in my life that the world would consider to be *great Christians*. Yet, in all of those many souls, I believe only a handful of them manifested the power of God in their lives. I am talking about great prayer warriors, great soul winners, and people who really lived and walked in the power of the indwelling Spirit of God. These were people that the Devil knew by name and trembled in fear when they got on their knees before God. These were people who lived their lives in the center of the *spiritual storms* and *battles* of this life. Spiritual difficulties were constant in their lives because they were in the center of the will of God and they daily fought in a warfare most Christians try to avoid at any cost. They experienced the warfare of satanic opposition, but most importantly, they knew the power of the presence of God in their lives and lived in fellowship with Him.

When the believing sinner is "born again" of the Spirit of God "by grace through faith," he is removed from the cursed family of Adam and *baptized* into the family of God. This baptism is referred to theologically as the *baptism with the Spirit*. This once-for-all act of the Spirit of God happens instantaneously and synchronously with a decision of faith to trust in Christ. The believer is baptized *with* the Spirit of God into the *body of Christ*. This *body of Christ* is "the regeneration" (Matthew 19:28) and is what gives the believer a *position* of both great power with God and responsibility "in Christ."

Peter says in II Peter 1:2, "Grace and peace be multiplied unto you through the knowledge of God, and of Jesus our Lord." God's grace is the greatest *treasure* of the Christian life, which is given to us freely and without reservation or limitation. The word "grace" is translated from the Greek word *charis* (khar'-ece).

> Grace refers to *the divine influence upon the heart, and the reflection of that divine influence in a person's life.*

This is a very basic definition of God's grace. Scripturally and theologically, grace is best defined by the *manifestations* of God's power in and through the lives of His people throughout Old Testament books such as Exodus, Joshua, and Judges. Grace is *manifested* and *defined* by the miracles of God in the lives of men like Samuel, Elijah, Elisha, and Ezekiel. These men were *shown* to have power with God. They spoke and God acted in response to their words because they lived in such a union with God, their wills and God's will were almost identical. This is what is necessary to see the power of God in anyone's life. This is what defines revival. Power with God (*synergism*) is nothing more than the manifestation of a right relationship with God. **If you do not see the power, you do not have a right relationship with God. Since God does not change, the conditions for power with God do not change.**

The word "grace" refers to this supernatural *empowering* or *working* of God in and through the lives of believers. The word "multiplied" in II Peter 1:2 is from the Greek word *plethuno* (play-thoo'-no). The Greek word *pletho* (play'-tho) means *to fill*. The Greek word *plethos* (play'-thos) means *fullness* or *multitude*. In Ephesians 5:18, where Paul says, ". . . be not drunk with wine, wherein is excess; but be filled with the Spirit," the word "filled" is the Greek word *pleroo* (play-ro'-o), which means *to cram full*. Whatever God fills, He fills to *abundance*. Whatever God fills, He fills to *overflowing*. King David knew and experienced this multiplied grace of God in his life.

> "[4] Yea, though I walk through the valley of the shadow of death, I will fear no evil: for thou *art* with me; thy rod and thy staff they comfort me. [5] Thou preparest a table before me in the presence of mine enemies: thou anointest my head with oil; <u>my cup runneth over</u>" (Psalm 23:4-5).

Notice that this overflowing, multiplied grace of God is "multiplied unto you through the knowledge of God, and of Jesus our Lord."

The word "knowledge" is not mere intellectual knowledge of facts or theology. The failure to understand the meaning of this word is why so many people fail to see the power of God in their lives. "Knowledge" here is from the Greek word *epignosis* (ep-ig'-no-sis). *Gnosis* is the word used for mere intellectual knowledge. For instance, I *know* the formula $E=MC^2$. However, to *know* it and *understand* the depth of its meaning and significance in the realm of Physics and Quantum Mechanics is another kind of knowledge altogether. *Epignosis* refers to a full, complete, intimate knowledge of something or someone. In regards to people, it is used of the most intimate of relationships. It is this intimate relationship with God that defines the source of *empowering knowledge*.

This is one of the reasons few Christians ever have this overflowing, multiplied grace of God in their lives manifested by power with God in answers to prayer. They do not see power with God in producing the fruit of the Spirit. They do not experience the power with God in seeing souls brought to Christ and discipled to His glory. They are just not yielded to God's will in the way that produces this intimate unity where the power of the Spirit of God simply overflows through their lives. Notice how Paul speaks of this supernatural power of God in I Corinthians 12:1-13.

"[1] Now concerning spiritual *gifts*, brethren, I would not have you ignorant. [2] Ye know that ye were Gentiles, carried away unto these dumb idols, even as ye were led. [3] Wherefore I give you to understand, that no man speaking by the Spirit of God calleth Jesus accursed: and *that* no man can say that Jesus is the Lord, but by the Holy Ghost. [4] Now there are diversities of gifts, but the same Spirit. [5] And there are differences of administrations, but the same Lord. [6] And there are diversities of operations, but it is the same God which worketh all in all. [7] But the manifestation of the Spirit is given to every man to profit withal. [8] For to one is given by the Spirit the word of wisdom; to another the word of knowledge by the same Spirit; [9] To another faith by the same Spirit; to another the gifts of healing by the same Spirit; [10] To another the working of miracles; to another prophecy; to another discerning of spirits; to another *divers* kinds of tongues; to another the interpretation of tongues: [11] But all these worketh that one and the selfsame Spirit, dividing to every man severally as he will. [12] For as the body is one, and hath many members, and all the members of that one body, being many, are one body: so also *is* Christ. [13] For by one Spirit are we all baptized into one body, whether *we be* Jews or Gentiles, whether *we be* bond or free; and have been all made to drink into one Spirit" (I Corinthians 12:1-13).

The word "spiritual" in I Corinthians 12:1 is from the Greek word *pneumatikos* (pnyoo-mat-ik-os'). The word "gifts" is italicized in our KJV, meaning it is not in the original Greek text, but is added for clarification. A literal translation of *pneumatikos* would be simply "concerning spirituals." The word *pneumatikos* refers to something far beyond the normal. It refers to something *supernatural* or *ethereal*. The word *pneumatikos* refers to things, works, or actions that cannot be produced by human wisdom, great talents, or abilities. No matter how good, talented, intelligent, or great a person might be he cannot produce "spirituals" through his life apart from an intimate knowledge/relationship with God.

As I have said, the *baptism with the Holy Spirit* puts the believer into a *new existence* and a *new position* in the "body of Christ" (I Corinthians 12:13). This is not the same as the indwelling of the Holy Spirit. The *baptism with the Holy Spirit* is instantaneous and synchronous with a decision to trust in Christ. The *baptism with the Holy Spirit* provides the potential for all that is involved in the life of Jesus Christ; "[11] And this is the record, that God hath given to us eternal life, and this life is in his Son. [12] He that hath the Son hath life; *and* he that hath not the Son of God hath not life" (I John 5:11-12).

Although this eternal life "in Christ" is already in our possession, the *power* of this eternal life lies in the indwelling Holy Spirit of God. The *power* of this eternal life is the Holy Spirit. When the believer is "filled" with Holy Spirit through practical sanctification, consecration, and yielding his will to God's will, the eternal life that is in us in the Person of the Holy Spirit is released ("multiplied," II Peter 1:2) through the believer's life. This releasing of *power* (the eternal life of God or the *Christ-life*) is manifested through the supernatural *enabling/empowering* of the yielded believer. In looking at this Scripturally, we must be careful to distinguish between *temporary sign gifts* and *continuing service gifts*.

As I have said, the word *pneumatikos*, translated "spiritual *gifts*" in I Corinthians 12:1, refers to something far beyond the normal. It refers to something supernatural or ethereal. The word *pneumatikos* refers to things, works, or actions that cannot be produced by human wisdom, great talents, or abilities.

What is a spiritual *gift* (I Corinthians 12:1)? A spiritual gift is the divine energizing (*empowering*) of a believer's life by the Holy Spirit. The *gift* is the *empowering*. Therefore, when the Spirit of God gives a *spiritual*, it refers to the divine energizing of a believer's knowledge, talents, or abilities that he already has for a special task or purpose.

This spiritual *empowering* is the supernatural working of God in the life of all Spirit-filled (controlled) believers. This *spiritual empowering* is that which is intended to be common to all believers and is what defines the Age of Grace (Church Age Dispensation). This *spiritual empowering* of a believer's knowledge, talents, or abilities is intended to be the common, normal, and everyday *experience* of every Spirit-filled believer.

It is not the baptism with the Holy Spirit that *empowers*. It is the "filling" that *empowers*. The baptism with the Spirit merely places the believer in the *position* of power. The *position* provides the *potential*.

There are two Greek words that define spiritual *gifts*. The first is *pneumatikos* (pnyoo-mat-ik-os') as used in I Corinthians 12:1. It is best translated by the word "spirituals." The idea in the word *pneumatikos* is that the baptism with the Holy Spirit forms the "body of Christ," which "body" is *empowered* (given life and abilities) by the Holy Spirit. The "filling" is the *result* of bringing the human body and its desires under the *control* of the Spirit and is a matter of *yielding* the will (Romans 6:11-13).

The second Greek word that defines spiritual *gifts* is the word *charisma* (khar'-is-mah) that is made up from the Greek word *charis* (khar'-ece), which is usually translated "grace." Therefore, *charisma* refers to the divine *empowering* of the yielded believer by the indwelling Holy Spirit for some *specific task*. Anything any believer seeks to do for the Lord in this life must be done by the *empowering* of the Holy Spirit or it cannot be *blessed of God*; i.e., is not the result of God's power and therefore is not lasting/eternal in its duration. *Charismata* (gifts of *empowering* grace) denote extraordinary and supernatural powers that distinguish certain Christians for special areas of ministry and enables them to serve the Church of Christ (the *body* metaphor).

There "are diversities of gifts" (*charisma,* **or grace empowering I Corinthians 12:4).** "Diversities" is from the Greek word *diairesis* (dee-ah'-ee-res-is), referring to a *distinction arising from a different distribution to different persons.* Not everyone had the same spiritual gift.

> "[29b] *are* all workers of miracles? [30] Have all the gifts of healing? do all speak with tongues? do all interpret" (I Corinthians 12:29b-30)?

There "are differences of administrations" (I Corinthians 12:5; "differences" is from the same Greek word as "diversities" above). "Administrations" is from the Greek word *diakonia* (dee-ak-on-ee'-ah), which can be translated *services* or *ministries.* Not everyone has the same knowledge, talents, or abilities; therefore everyone does not have the same ministry in the local church.

> "[14] For the body is not one member, but many. [15] If the foot shall say, Because I am not the hand, I am not of the body; is it therefore not of the body? [16] And if the ear shall say, Because I am not the eye, I am not of the body; is it therefore not of the body? [17] If the whole body *were* an eye, where *were* the hearing? If the whole *were* hearing, where *were* the smelling? [18] But now hath God set the members every one of them in

WWW.DISCIPLEMAKERMINISTRIES.ORG

the body, as it hath pleased him. [19] And if they were all one member, where *were* the body? [20] But now *are they* many members, yet but one body" (I Corinthians 12:14-20).

The idea of I Corinthians 12:14-20 is that not everyone has the same *job/ministry* (although there are some things everyone is commanded to do). Everyone is not an apostle. Everyone is not a preacher ("prophet"). Everyone is not a pastor/teacher.

"*Are* all apostles? *are* all prophets? *are* all teachers" (I Corinthians 12:29a)?

There "are diversities of operations" (I Corinthians 12:6). "Operations" is from the Greek word *energema* (en-erg'-ay-mah), which means *to display one's activity or work*. Although God never changes (character, nature, or attributes), His *operations* do change. These changes are called *dispensations*.

"For if I do this thing willingly, I have a reward: but if against my will, a dispensation {*stewardship*} *of the gospel* is committed unto me" (I Corinthians 9:17).

"That in the dispensation {*stewardship*} of the fulness of times {*in the New Heaven/Earth*} he might gather together in one all things in Christ, both which are in heaven, and which are on earth; *even* in him:" (Ephesians 1:10).

"If ye have heard of the dispensation {*stewardship*} of the grace of God {*Church Age of Grace*} which is given me to you-ward:" (Ephesians 3:2).

"Whereof I am made a minister, according to the dispensation {*stewardship*} of God which is given to me for you, to fulfil the word of God;" (Colossians 1:25).

The word "dispensation" in each of the above verses is from the Greek word *oikonomia* (oy-kon-om-ee'-ah), which refers to *the management, oversight, and administration of a household or of household affairs*. How God manages His household has changed down through the ages. The word *dispensations* refers mainly to the *stewardship of delegated responsibilities* by God to believers.

The *empowering* by the Spirit is visible in every believer's life for "profit" (bringing forth *spiritual fruit*, I Corinthians 12:7). When the believer produces spiritual fruit, the *empowering* of the Holy Spirit becomes visible. "Manifestation" is from the Greek word *phanerosis* (fan-er'-o-sis), which means to *make manifest* (visible or known) what has been hidden or unknown. The idea here is that, as the Holy Spirit spiritually empowers the believer and as that believer begins to bear fruit, the invisible Holy Spirit is made visible in that believer's life by that fruit.

This leads us to Peter's statement in II Peter 1:3; "According as his divine power hath given unto us all things that *pertain* unto life and godliness, through the knowledge of him that hath called us to glory and virtue." This verse speaks of spiritual *power potential*.

The empowerment cannot take place until the *Tripartite of Power* exists within the believer's life:

1. The Spirit: the supernatural *empowering* of the indwelling Holy Spirit

2. The Word: the *knowledge* of the will of God as revealed by the Word of God

3. The Spirit-filled Believer: the believer yields to the indwelling Spirit **AND** begins to live the Word of God, becoming a "doer of the Word" (James 1:22)

DISCUSSION QUESTIONS

1. The world tends to evaluate the *greatness* of anyone's ministry by pragmatism (results). What do think are God's criteria for defining *greatness of life?*

2. Give an expanded and detailed definition and explanation of the word *grace* as it is used in the context of Scripture.

3. Explain the differences between the *baptism* with the Spirit, the *indwelling* of the Spirit, and the *filling* of the Spirit.

4. Read II Peter 1:2. Discuss how *grace* is *multiplied* in the believer's life and in the life of a local church.

5. Read I Corinthians 12:1-13. What is a spiritual *gift (pneumatikos;* pnyoo-mat-ik-os')?

6. Explain the practical differences between the Baptist with the Spirit and the filling of the Spirit.

7. In what ways is the *empowering* of the Spirit *manifested* in the life of a believer?

Chapter Two
The Essential of Knowing God's Word
(Review Tripartite of Power)

"[8] Remember that Jesus Christ of the seed of David was raised from the dead according to my gospel: [9] Wherein I suffer trouble, as an evil doer, *even* unto bonds; but the word of God is not bound. [10] Therefore I endure all things for the elect's sakes, that they may also obtain the salvation which is in Christ Jesus with eternal glory. [11] *It is* a faithful saying: For **if** we be dead with *him*, we shall also live with *him*: [12] **If** we suffer, we shall also reign with *him*: **if** we deny *him*, he also will deny us: [13] **If** we believe not, *yet* he abideth faithful: he cannot deny himself. [14] Of these things put *them* in remembrance, charging *them* before the Lord that they strive not about words to no profit, *but* to the subverting of the hearers. [15] Study to shew thyself approved unto God, a workman that needeth not to be ashamed, rightly dividing the word of truth. [16] But shun profane *and* vain babblings: for they will increase unto more ungodliness. [17] And their word will eat as doth a canker: of whom is Hymenaeus and Philetus; [18] Who concerning the truth have erred, saying that the resurrection is past already; and overthrow the faith of some. [19] Nevertheless the foundation of God standeth sure, having this seal, The Lord knoweth them that are his. And, Let every one that nameth the name of Christ depart from iniquity. [20] But in a great house there are not only vessels of gold and of silver, but also of wood and of earth; and some to honour, and some to dishonour. [21] **If** a man therefore purge himself from these, he shall be a vessel unto honour, sanctified, and meet for the master's use, *and* prepared unto every good work. [22] Flee also youthful lusts: but follow righteousness, faith, charity, peace, with them that call on the Lord out of a pure heart. [23] But foolish and unlearned questions avoid, knowing that they do gender strifes. [24] And the servant of the Lord must not strive; but be gentle unto all *men*, apt to teach, patient, [25] In meekness instructing those that oppose themselves; **if** God peradventure will give them repentance to the acknowledging of the truth; [26] And *that* they may recover themselves out of the snare of the devil, who are taken captive by him at his will" (II Timothy 2:8-26).

We live in the day of biblical ignorance. Sadly, the ignorance of God's Word is not limited to the lost of the world. Today, most evangelicals have very little interest in the *meat* of doctrine in the study of Scriptures. Many are just not willing to invest the time and effort to know the details of God's *instruction book for living* to His glory.

Sometimes the word *if* is one of the largest words in the Bible. The word *if* is used six (6) different times in II Timothy 2:8-16, detailing six different hypothetical *possibilities* based upon a different *condition* for each of those *possibilities*.

> The word *if* is usually a word of both *condition* and *potential* or *possibility*. The word *if* proposes a hypothetical situation and details the *conditions* necessary for the realization of a hypothetical *possibility*.

1. "For **if** we be dead with *him*, we shall also live with *him*" (II Timothy 2:11; refers to the surety of glorification to the regenerated).

2. "**If** we suffer, we shall also reign with *him*" (II Timothy 2:12; refers to rewards in the Kingdom Age).

3. "[**I**]**f** we deny *him*, he also will deny us" (II Timothy 2:12; refers to the loss of rewards in the Kingdom Age).

4. "**If** we believe not {*are not faithful*}, *yet* he abideth faithful {*to His promises*}: he cannot deny himself" (II Timothy 2:13).

5. "**If** a man therefore purge himself from these, he shall be a vessel unto honour, sanctified, and meet for the master's use, *and* prepared unto every good work" (II Timothy 2:21; conditions for, and promises of, Christ's present blessings upon our ministries and lives).

6. "[25] In meekness instructing those that oppose themselves; **if** God peradventure will give them repentance to the acknowledging of the truth; [26] And *that* they may recover themselves out of the snare of the devil, who are taken captive by him at his will" (II Timothy 2:25-26; refers to the potential of God's supernatural workings through the lives of Spirit-filled believers).

Within the context of these six hypothetical possibilities, we find a command to Timothy regarding his responsibility to all believers within the sound of his voice or within the realm of his influence. This command lies equally within every believer's responsibilities regarding his stewardship of God's indwelling grace; "[14] Of these things put *them* in remembrance, charging *them* before the Lord that they strive not about words to no profit, *but* to the subverting of the hearers. [15] Study to shew thyself approved unto God, a workman that needeth not to be ashamed, rightly dividing the word of truth" (II Timothy 2:14-15).

The enablement of the Holy Spirit that provides us with the understanding of God's Word is called *illumination*. Illumination means *enlightenment* (see Ephesians 1:18). The idea of illumination describes the ministry of the Holy Spirit as He aides the believer in understanding what the Bible is saying.

"[15] Wherefore I also, after I heard of your faith *{the practice or living of what is believed}* in the Lord Jesus, and love unto all the saints, [16] Cease not to give thanks for you, making mention of you in my prayers; [17] That the God of our Lord Jesus Christ, the Father of glory, <u>may give unto you the spirit of wisdom and revelation in the knowledge</u> *{epignosis}* <u>of him:</u> [18] <u>The eyes of your understanding being enlightened</u> *{photizo, to shine light onto something to accurately reveals its details to those living in spiritual darkness, i.e., ignorance of God}* **that** ye may know what is the hope of his calling, and what the riches of the glory of his inheritance in the saints, [19] And what *is* the exceeding greatness of his power to us-ward who believe, according to the working of his mighty power . . ." (Ephesians 1:15-18).

The word "study" in II Timothy 2:15 is translated from the Greek word *spoudazo* (spoo-dad'-zo). It actually means to *give diligence* or *make the necessary effort*. The reason *spoudazo* is translated "study" is its use in the context of the statement "rightly dividing the word of truth." Therefore, the diligence is directed to the intimate *knowledge* and detailed *application* of the Word of God in the everyday *practices* of a person's life (not merely in his *head*). The implication is that a person cannot make the hundreds and thousands of right decisions that are part of each day's spiritual struggle if that person does not have an intricate knowledge of God's Word and of the will of God revealed by God's Word.

The use of the word "study" in II Timothy 2:15 takes the human responsibility far beyond the mere *reading* of the Word of God. The believer is responsible to study and *know* the intimate details of the Word of God so that his life can be lived shamelessly before God. This intimate knowledge of the Word of God is very much connected to the possibility of power with God. We can never live in the *light* of God's revealed will if we do not know the details of the Word of God. Unless we live in the *light* of God's revealed will, we can never live our lives in the power of God's indwelling Spirit. This is a huge *if*. Living in the center of God's will is the central condition for "fellowship" with God and for the enabling power of God in our lives.

Look at what God's Word says regarding this in I John 1:5-10 and noticed the *ifs* in this text.

"[5] This then is the message which we have heard of him, and declare unto you, that God is light, and in him is no darkness at all. [6] **If** we say that we have fellowship with him, and walk in darkness, we lie, and do not the truth: [7] But **if** we walk in the light, as he is in the light, we have fellowship one with another, and the blood of Jesus Christ his Son cleanseth us from all sin. [8] **If** we say that we have no sin, we deceive ourselves, and the truth is not in us. [9] **If** we confess our sins, he is faithful and just to forgive us *our* sins, and to cleanse us from all unrighteousness. [10] **If** we say that we have not sinned, we make him a liar, and his word is not in us" (I John 1:5-10).

The word "fellowship" in I John 1:7 is from the Greek word *koinonia* (koy-nohn-ee'-ah), better translated *partnership*. The idea is in the *communion of shared assets* with each partner in the communion *contributing* something. This does not mean that each partner necessarily contributes equally to the partnership. Obviously, the Lord is the major and primary contributor in this relational partnership in the "work of the ministry." In fact, about all the believer has that he can contribute to this *partnership* is a yielded body and a yielded will (spirit). The key word to this partnership is *yield*.

"[11] Likewise reckon ye also yourselves to be dead indeed unto sin {*your fallen sin nature*}, but alive unto God through Jesus Christ our Lord. [12] Let not sin {*your fallen sin nature*} therefore reign in your mortal body, that ye should obey it in the lusts thereof. [13] Neither yield ye your members *as* instruments of unrighteousness unto sin {*your fallen sin nature*}: but yield yourselves unto God, as those that are alive from the dead, and your members *as* instruments of righteousness unto God. [14] For sin {*your fallen sin nature*} shall not have dominion over you: for ye are not under the law, but under {*the responsibilities of the stewardship of*} grace" (Romans 6:11-14).

There are three reasons given in II Timothy 2:15 for why we should be extremely motivated to study the Word of God.

1. So we can show that our new lives "in Christ" are "approved" (*dokimos*; tested/tried and proven genuine) by God trying of our faith

2. So we can do the work of the ministry ("workmen") and not end up being "ashamed" of what we have done before God presently and at the Judgment Seat of Christ ("ashamed" means not accusable by the "accuser of the brethren," Revelation 12:10) because there is nothing to accuse us of)

3. So we can correctly apply ("rightly dividing" or dissect into the multitude of necessary applications) the truth of God's Word to daily situations of life

> ## We must never forget that faithfulness is always measured by obedience to what God's Word reveals.

Simply because we do not know what God's Word reveals does not in any way minimize our responsibility for obedience or our culpability for disobedience. In other words, we are going to be held accountable for both knowing and living every "jot and tittle" of the Word of God. This certainly defines the intricacy of the knowledge of the Word of God that God expects from every one of His children. There is no excuse for ignorance of God's Word and continuing throughout your lifetime as a "babe."

"[10] {*Jesus*} Called of God an high priest after the order of Melchisedec. [11] Of whom we have many things to say, and hard to be uttered {*difficult to explain and hard to understand*}, seeing ye are dull {*sluggish, slothful, or lazy*} of hearing. [12] For when for the time ye ought to be teachers, ye have need that one teach you again which *be* the first principles {*elementary or rudimentary*} of the oracles of God; and are become such as have need of milk, and not of strong meat {*solid foods*}. [13] For every one that useth milk *is* unskilful in the word of righteousness: for he is a babe. [14] But strong meat belongeth to them that are of full age, *even* those who <u>by reason of use</u> have their senses <u>exercised to discern</u> both good and evil" (Hebrews 5:10-14).

DISCUSSION QUESTIONS

1. The word *if* proposes a hypothetical situation and details the *conditions* necessary to the realization of a hypothetical *possibility*. The word *if* is used six (6) different times in II Timothy 2:8-16, detailing six different hypothetical *possibilities* based upon a different *condition* for each of those *possibilities*. In your own words, explain each of those six (6) uses of the word *if* in that text.

2. The enablement of the Holy Spirit that provides us with the understanding of God's Word is called *illumination*. Explain the meaning of *illumination* and the spiritual dynamic necessary for *illumination* to take place.

3. Give a detailed explanation of what God expects in His command in the word "study" in II Timothy 2:15.

4. Explain the meaning and conditions for the "fellowship" that is mentioned in the context of I John 1:7, especially regarding Romans 6:11-14.

5. What are the three reasons given in II Timothy 2:15 for why we should be extremely motivated to study the Word of God?

6. Faithfulness is always measured by obedience to what God's Word reveals. Discuss the importance of an intimate knowledge of God's Word to faithfulness.

7. Discuss the relation of the statement in Hebrews 5:10-14 to your answer to the discussion of question number six above.

Chapter Three
The Spiritual Dynamic of the Empowerment of a Local Church
(Review Tripartite of Power)

"[12] For as the body is one, and hath many members, and all the members of that one body, being many, are one body: so also *is* Christ. [13] For by one Spirit are we all baptized into one body, whether *we be* Jews or Gentiles, whether *we be* bond or free; and have been all made to drink into one Spirit. [14] For the body is not one member, but many. [15] If the foot shall say, Because I am not the hand, I am not of the body; is it therefore not of the body? [16] And if the ear shall say, Because I am not the eye, I am not of the body; is it therefore not of the body? [17] If the whole body *were* an eye, where *were* the hearing? If the whole *were* hearing, where *were* the smelling? [18] But now hath God set the members every one of them in the body, as it hath pleased him. [19] And if they were all one member, where *were* the body? [20] But now *are they* many members, yet but one body. [21] And the eye cannot say unto the hand, I have no need of thee: nor again the head to the feet, I have no need of you. [22] Nay, much more those members of the body, which seem to be more feeble, are necessary: [23] And those *members* of the body, which we think to be less honourable, upon these we bestow more abundant honour; and our uncomely *parts* have more abundant comeliness. [24] For our comely *parts* have no need: but God hath tempered the body together, having given more abundant honour to that *part* which lacked: [25] That there should be no schism in the body; but *that* the members should have the same care one for another. [26] And whether one member suffer, all the members suffer with it; or one member be honoured, all the members rejoice with it. [27] Now ye are the body of Christ, and members in particular. [28] And God hath set some in the church, first apostles, secondarily prophets, thirdly teachers, after that miracles, then gifts of healings, helps, governments, diversities of tongues. [29] *Are* all apostles? *are* all prophets? *are* all teachers? *are* all workers of miracles? [30] Have all the gifts of healing? do all speak with tongues? do all interpret? [31] But covet earnestly the best gifts: and yet shew I unto you a more excellent way" (I Corinthians 12:12-31).

Modern Bible believing Christianity has become preoccupied with what we are supposed to separate *from*. What we separate *from* is certainly important. However, being separate *from* sin and worldliness is not all that is involved in the believer's practical sanctification. The believer must also realized that there is Someone and something that he is separated *unto*. As the Church ("body of Christ") has progressively become more worldly and carnal over the years, we have seen two phenomena take place within Evangelical Christianity (Liberalism completely abandoned practical sanctification in most part almost a century ago):

1. First, because believers have become so worldly and carnal in their preoccupations with Neo-hedonism (*pleasure seeking*), Church leaders have become preoccupied in dealing with worldliness and carnality as almost an end in itself. This has led the Church into *legalism* (erecting external controls of the "flesh," Galatians 3:1-5); i.e., the false notion that a person is *spiritual* if he keeps away from certain *taboo* sins or practices.
2. Second, there is almost a complete failure to teach WHY believers are to be separate from sin and worldliness; i.e., because this keeps them from being undefiled before God and provides the power of God in their lives to engage the forces of evil in the battle for souls, lives, and produces "fruit" to the glory of God. Until the believer is separated from sin and worldliness, there is really no reason to teach that person what he is separated unto; i.e., to the service of God in doing the "work of the ministry."

"[19] Nevertheless the foundation of God standeth sure, having this seal, The Lord knoweth them that are his. And, Let every one that nameth the name of Christ depart from iniquity. [20] But in a great house there are not only vessels of gold and of silver, but also of wood and of earth; and some to honour, and some to dishonour. [21] **If** a man therefore purge himself from these, he shall be a vessel unto honour, sanctified, and meet for the master's use, *and* prepared unto every good work" (II Timothy 2:19-21).

I Corinthians 12:12-31 is not a text that is filled with truths that are difficult to comprehend. Like the human body, a local church has numerous *body parts* that all serve different purposes. Although there are many different *body parts* that all serve different purposes, they are all under the direction and sovereignty of the one

Head. Because these many body parts have one Head, they do not function independently of one another. Because these many body parts naturally obey the one Head, they work together in a partnership of unity and harmony, each supplying to the body the uniqueness and individuality that each body part possesses as a gift from God.

Why is it then that so few local churches appear to grasp these truths and put them into practice? The answer is equally simple.

> Each *body part* must recognize it has a unique function and must fulfill that function in the power of the indwelling Spirit of God (in grace). Each *body part* must be totally yielded to the Head before the *harmony of the body* can be created. This *harmony* too is a supernatural work of grace in the ministry of the Holy Spirit's enabling.

I once visited a man in the hospital who was comatose. He sat in his chair and stared blankly. I was told they believed he heard people, that his eyes worked fine, and that every part of his body functioned adequately. However, he could not (or did not) feed himself. He could not (or did not) dress himself or clean himself.

Although everything about him physically was fine, he needed someone to do just about everything for him, except the automatic functions of his body. There was a living soul trapped within that body, but his brain was practically disconnected from his body, which in turn disconnected him from being able to accomplish even the simplest of tasks.

Many local churches are *comatose* - meaning many local churches are characterized by *lethargic inertness* and *unresponsiveness to spiritual stimulation.* There are people attending the church services. They seem to be breathing and moving around. They appear to be growing spiritually, but they just never, ever produce any *fruit.* When this is the characteristic of a local church, it is really a symptom of a much more serious spiritual problem. When this describes a local church or an individual Christian, one of the three aspects of the *Tripartite of Power* is missing or *disconnected.* One or more of three failures exists in the majority of the members of such a local church.

1. There is ignorance of the Word of God, and therefore, the will of God, so that the believer is either living in sin or disobedience (any degree of disobedience, commission, or omission is sin).
2. The believer is not yielded to and "filled with" (supernaturally and spiritually empowered by) the indwelling Holy Spirit.
3. The believer is not involved in *doing* the "work of the ministry," praying, and aggressively seeking to win the lost to Christ. Even God cannot bless something you do not do.

Any of these three failures within the membership of a local church will result in a spiritually *dysfunctional* local church. What this means practically, regarding a local church or individual, is that no lasting *fruit* can be produced until this problem is corrected.

According to a number of statements by the Lord Jesus, He has very little tolerance for *fruitless* local churches or *fruitless* Christians.

It is clear from the Lord Jesus' statements that a *fruitless* Christian is a major and unacceptable abnormality.

Before the spiritual *fruit* of souls can be produced, the *Seed* that is God's Word MUST BE SOWN. That means Spirit-filled believers must tell people about the condemnation God has put upon mankind. Spirit-filled believers must tell lost sinners the details of the Gospel of Jesus Christ. Spirit-filled believers must direct souls to repent of sin and "dead works," to trust in Jesus, and to call upon His name to be saved. If Spirit-filled believers do not *sow the Seed*, the *Seed* will not be *sown.*

"[11] Now the parable is this: The seed is the word of God. [12] Those by the way side are they that hear; then cometh the devil, and taketh away the word out of their hearts, lest they should believe and be saved. [13] They on the rock *are they*, which, when they hear, receive the word with joy; and these have no root, which for a while believe, and in time of temptation fall away. [14] And that which fell among thorns are they, which, when they have heard, go forth, and are choked with cares and riches and pleasures of *this* life, and bring no fruit to perfection. [15] But that on the good ground are they, which in an honest and good heart, having heard the word, keep *it*, and bring forth fruit with patience" (Luke 8:11-15).

Yes, much Seed will fall upon *unfruitful ground* and *unproductive soil*, ending the hope of spiritual fruit. However, that is not due to any failure or weakness of the Seed. A good farmer understands that the preparation of the soil PRIOR to sowing the seed is extremely important to producing fruit, if any.

Why does Christ give this parable? He gives this parable because He wants us to understand the believer's responsibility in warning the hearers about these situations. Mostly, the hearers determine what kind of ground their lives are going to be. Therefore, they need to be warned about Satan's tactics that keep the *Seed* from taking *root* and bearing "fruit to perfection."

Secondly, the warning is about faithful believers who "having heard the word, keep *it*" (Luke 8:15). The idea of the word "keep" is to retain, possess, or hold onto. This appears to be a contradiction. How can we *sow the Seed* if we are holding onto it? This is not talking just about *keeping* the Truth of God's Word in our *minds*, but about *living the Truth* of God's Word *in our everyday lives*. The Word of God must become as much a part of us as an arm or a leg. *Keeping* the Word of God is doing everything exactly the way the Word of God directs us. It is ridiculous to think that anyone will give us any credibility in our teaching them the Word of God if we do not love the Word of God enough to live it and do it ourselves.

Although a *fruitless* Christian and a *fruitless* local church is an anomaly that cannot be allowed to exist, Christ is patient with Christians and local churches allowing time to correct their *fruitlessness*.

"[6] He spake also this parable; A certain *man* had a fig tree planted in his vineyard; and he came and sought fruit thereon, and found none. [7] Then said he unto the dresser of his vineyard {*referring to the Pastor or Disciple Maker*} , Behold, these three years I come seeking fruit on this fig tree, and find none: cut it down; why cumbereth it the ground? [8] And he {*the dresser*} answering said unto him, Lord, let it alone this year also, till I shall dig about it, and dung *it*: [9] And if it bear fruit, *well*: and if not, *then* after that thou shalt cut it down" (Luke 13:6-9).

"[4] Abide in me, and I in you. As the branch cannot bear fruit of itself, except it abide in the vine; no more can ye, except ye abide in me. [5] I am the vine, ye *are* the branches: He that abideth in me, and I in him, the same bringeth forth much fruit: for without me ye can do nothing. [6] If a man abide not in me, he is cast forth as a branch, and is withered; and men gather them, and cast *them* into the fire, and they are burned. [7] If ye abide in me, and my words abide in you, ye shall ask what ye will, and it shall be done unto you. [8] Herein is my Father glorified, that ye bear much fruit; so shall ye be my disciples" (John 15:4-8).

Because the vast majority of Christians live under the false belief that the "work of the ministry" (leading souls to Christ, and teaching them to know the Word of God, live the Word of God, and become evangelists themselves) is delegated to pastors, professional evangelists, and certain specially gifted people, they will spend the thousand years of the Kingdom Age on the *Sidelines of Shame* because of their disobedience to the Great Commission.

> To profess to be a Christian and not be actively, boldly, and aggressively involved in bringing souls to Christ and making disciples of Christ is an absolute contradiction, paradox of truth, and an anomaly of everything that defines Christianity.

Failing to be actively involved in evangelism is a complete contradiction to everything that defines the priesthood of all believers who are part of the body of Christ. Because Christ died in our stead, the free gift of salvation comes with an overwhelming obligation to live in "Christ's stead" (II Corinthians 5:20).

"[14] For the love of Christ constraineth {*presses or compels*} us; because we thus judge, that if one died for all, then were all dead: [15] And *that* he died for all, that they which live should not henceforth live unto themselves, but unto him which died for them, and rose again" (II Corinthians 5:14-15).

"I am crucified with Christ: nevertheless I live; yet not I, but Christ liveth in me: and the life which I now live in the flesh I live by the faith of the Son of God, who loved me, and gave himself for me" (Galatians 2:20).

DISCUSSION QUESTIONS

1. Explain the difference between what we are to be separated *from* and what we are to be separated *unto*.

2. Read I Corinthians 12:12-31. From the context of these verses discuss the meaning of the phrase "harmony of the body."

3. Discuss the three common failures of local churches that result in a *comatose body*.

4. According to the Lord Jesus Christ's many statements regarding evangelism and discipleship, what do you think His attitude is toward *fruitless* Christians and/or *fruitless* local churches?

5. Read Luke 8:11-15. What do you think is the relationship between *knowing* the Word of God and *sowing the Seed*, which is the Word of God?

6. Explain the *applicable* meaning of Christ's use of the word "keep" in Luke 8:15.

7. Discuss the following statement; "To profess to be a Christian and not be actively, boldly, and aggressively involved in bringing souls to Christ and making disciples of Christ is an absolute contradiction, paradox of truth, and an anomaly of everything that defines Christianity."

Chapter Four
Living Water Flowing from Living Stones
(Review Tripartite of Power)

"[37] In the last day, that great *day* of the feast, Jesus stood and cried, saying, If any man thirst, let him come unto me, and drink. [38] He that believeth on me, as the scripture hath said, out of his belly shall flow rivers of living water. [39] (But this spake he of the Spirit, which they that believe on him should receive: for the Holy Ghost was not yet *given*; because that Jesus was not yet glorified.)" (John 7:37-39).

The work of the Spirit of God through the lives of yielded believers is a supernatural work of God involving constant acts of re-creation. In other words, in God's work of re-creation, He takes something that already exists in a broken or fallen state of existence, makes it new (unbroken and unfallen), and then begins to supernaturally multiply that *new creation* through the operations of His indwelling Spirit. God produces *spiritual fruit*, not physical fruit, through the lives of yielded believers by His operations of grace. *Spiritual fruit* is eternal fruit. This is what Christ is speaking about in John 7:38 regarding the "living waters" that *flow* from within the new creation of a "born again" believer. The *flow* happens as individuals live within the spiritual dynamic of the Tripartite of Power.

We cannot grasp the depth of what Christ is saying in John 7:37-39 if we do not understand the historical context of the Feast of Tabernacles and the events of that Jewish feast. This feast contains a number of prophetic types within its practices. The Feast of Tabernacles was instituted as part of the Mosaic Covenant shortly after of the Exodus.

"The seventh and final Feast of the Jewish calendar year is the Feast of Tabernacles. It occurs five days after the Day of Atonement on the fifteenth of Tishri (October). This feast is also called the Feast of Ingathering (Exodus 23:16; 34:22), the Feast to the Lord (Leviticus 23:3[4]; Judges 21:[19]), the Feast of Booths, or simply 'the feast' (Leviticus 23:36; Deuteronomy 16:13; I Kings 8:2; II Chronicles 5:3, 7:8; Nehemiah 8:14; Isaiah 30:29; Ezekiel

45:23,25) because it was so well-known [reference number in brackets corrected].

On the eighth and final day of the feast, the high priest of Israel, in a great processional made up of priests and tens of thousands of worshipers, descended from the Temple Mount to pause briefly at the Pool of Siloam. A pitcher was filled with water, and the procession continued via a different route back to the Temple Mount. Here, in the midst of great ceremony, the high priest poured the water out of the pitcher onto the altar.

Since in Israel the rains normally stop in March, there is no rain for almost seven months! If God does not provide the 'early' rains in October and November, there will be no spring crop, and famine is at the doorstep. This ceremony, then, was intended to invoke God's blessing on the nation by providing life-giving water."[1]

The Pool of Siloam was filled by a stream (the stream of Siloah) that flowed from under the Temple Mount (The Mount of the Rock). Many believed this pool had healing qualities because they believed that it was filled from the *water from the Rock*. They believed that this water and the Temple Mount which was built upon the threshing floor of Ornan (I Chronicles 21:23) were the fulfillment of the prophetic type of the *water from the rock* in the wilderness (Exodus 17:6).

"[1] Moreover, brethren, I would not that ye should be ignorant, how that all our fathers were under the cloud, and all passed through the sea; [2] And were all baptized unto Moses in the cloud and in the sea; [3] And did all eat the same spiritual meat; [4] And did all drink the same spiritual drink: for they drank of that spiritual Rock that followed them: and that Rock was Christ. [5] But with many of them God was not well pleased: for they were overthrown in the wilderness. [6] Now these things were our examples, to the intent we should not lust after evil things, as they also lusted. [7] Neither be ye idolaters, as *were* some of them; as it is written, The people sat down to eat and drink, and rose up to play" (I Corinthians 10:1-7).

Of course, Christ is the *Rock* from which that *living water* flows. Today, the local church is the *body of Christ* from which the *living waters* flow. The local church is the fulfillment of this prophetic type through God's work of grace. The New Covenant Church is *embodied* through the baptism with the Holy Spirit into the *body of Christ* of all born again believers. The New Covenant

---

[1] http://www.christcenteredmall.com/teachings/feasts/tabernacles.htm

Church is *empowered* through the indwelling and filling of believers with the Holy Spirit. In John 7:37-39, Christ is saying that the prophetic typology of the Feast of Tabernacles, or Ingathering, was about to be fulfilled and that the fulfillment was not going to be water flowing from the Jewish Temple into the Pool of Siloam. The actual fulfillment was going to be the *living water* of the Holy Spirit flowing from the new Living Temple of the *body* of all believers. The actual fulfillment happens when all believers are united together in a local church, yielded to the Spirit of God, being living translations of the Word of God, and doing the "work of the ministry" as sanctified and consecrated priests before God.

In the Jewish Feast of the Tabernacles, the emphasis was on God's work of grace in providing the harvests and the water that nourished those crops to their completion or maturity. Without the water from God there would be no fruit. All the sacrifices, fastings, and cries of repentance before God were for national sanctification so that the life giving water from God could and would flow freely.

Another important point here; Christ is saying is that the water that was gathered from the Pool of Siloam was carried/transported by the thousands of worshippers to the Temple to be poured out before the Altar of God. Israel understood that all the blessings of God (His operations of grace) were connected directly to the altar.

In fact, it was probably at the very moment when these thousands of worshippers stood before the Altar of God pouring out their individual pitchers of water from the Pool of Siloam that "Jesus stood and cried, saying, If any man thirst, let him come unto me, and drink. [38] He that believeth on me, as the scripture hath said, out of his belly shall flow rivers of living water." (John 7:37b-38).

"[4] To whom coming {*Jesus*}, *as unto* a living stone, disallowed indeed of men, but chosen of God, *and* precious, [5] Ye also, as lively stones, are built up a spiritual house, an holy priesthood, to offer up spiritual sacrifices, acceptable to God by Jesus Christ. [6] Wherefore also it is contained in the scripture, Behold, I lay in Sion a chief corner stone, elect, precious {*upon which each lively stone is laid to build the living Temple*}: and he that believeth on him shall not be confounded {*brought to shame or disgrace as was the Mosaic Covenant priesthood*}. [7] Unto you therefore which believe *he is* precious: but unto them which be disobedient, the stone which the builders (*the Christ rejecting Jews*} disallowed, the same is made the head of the corner, [8] And a stone of stumbling, and a rock of offence, *even to them* which stumble at the word, being disobedient: whereunto also they were appointed. [9] But ye {*Church Age believers collectively*} *are* a chosen generation, a royal priesthood, an holy nation, a peculiar people; that ye should shew forth the praises of him who hath called you out of darkness into his marvellous light: [10] Which in time past *were* not a people, but *are* now the people of God: which had not obtained mercy, but now have obtained mercy. [11] Dearly beloved, I beseech *you* as strangers and pilgrims, abstain from fleshly lusts, which war against the soul; [12] Having your conversation honest among the Gentiles: that, whereas they speak against you as evildoers, they may by *your* good works, which they shall behold, glorify God in the day of visitation" (I Peter 2:4-12).

> Yes, every individual believer is a "lively stone" and each individual body is the Temple of the Holy Spirit of God. However, as a "lively stone," God never intended you to be a *Lone Ranger brick* wandering around alone.

God intended you to be part of the something much larger than yourself; i.e. one born again believer working independently of others. God made you a "lively stone" to build a *living temple* from which the His "living water" could freely flow. The Seed is the Word of God *in the believer*. The Word of God in the believer is how Christ sows the Seed into the world. The Water is the Spirit of God. The Sower of the Seed is Jesus through the Spirit-filled, "born again" believer *overflowing* with "living water," "sanctified, and meet for the Master's use, *and* prepared unto every good work" (II Timothy 2:21).

The spiritual dynamic in the reality of the praxis of the filling of the Holy Spirit is that every "lively stone" is to be built into the wall of the Living Temple of God upon the Head Stone ("Cornerstone") of the New Creation in Jesus Christ. The Living Temple is the Church. Every "lively stone" built upon the "Living Stone" has the potential to produce a stream of "living water" from their midst.

When the world comes to that local church (either gathered or dispersed in everyday life), they ought to be able to come expecting the flow of "living water" from each of us individually, and, especially, all of us corporately as a local church.

It is equally important for people to know that the source of the "living water" is not us personally. The source of the "living water" is the Living God who dwells within us. "Living water" flowing from a *rock* is a supernatural work of grace manifesting the continuing work of God in constant re-creation. This *Living Temple* metaphor made up of Jesus Christ and all "born again" believers united together within the context of a local church assembly is what Paul is talking about in I Corinthians 3:9-16.

"[9] For we are <u>labourers together with God</u>: ye are God's husbandry, *ye are* God's building {*oikodome, domed temple*}. [10] According to the grace of God {*the supernatural operations and workings of the Holy Spirit*} which is given unto me, as a wise masterbuilder, I have laid the foundation {*faith in Christ that begins the regeneration*} and another {*other believers of succeeding generations by winning souls and making disciples*} buildeth thereon. But let every man take heed how he buildeth thereupon. [11] For other foundation can no man lay than that is laid, which is Jesus Christ. [12] Now if any man build upon this foundation gold, silver, precious stones, wood, hay, stubble; [13] Every man's work shall be made manifest: for the day {*Judgment Seat of Christ*} shall declare it, because it shall be revealed by fire; and the fire shall try every man's work of what sort it is. [14] If any man's work abide which he hath built thereupon, he shall receive a reward. [15] If any man's work shall be burned, he shall suffer loss: but he himself shall be saved; yet so as by fire. [16] Know ye not that ye are {*este, second person plural present indicative*; *collectively belong*; i.e., *the local church*} the temple of God, and *that* the Spirit of God dwelleth in you? [17] If any man defile the temple of God, him shall God destroy; for the temple of God is holy, which *temple* ye are" (I Corinthians 3:9-17).

The Church of Christ, as a Living Temple of God, is NOT to be merely the *house of God's dwelling place*. The Church of the Living Temple (gathered or scattered) is to be the source of "living waters."

Therefore, now get this, every local church (believers united together formally by a common salvation, a common doctrine, and a common purpose) are to be God's DISTRIBUTION CENTERS OF GRACE. God wants to do His work of re-creation in and through our lives.

What is the "living water"? The "living water" is the water of eternal life flowing through the yielded believer's life.

"[11] And this is the record, that God <u>hath given to us eternal life, and this life is in his Son</u>. [12] <u>He that hath the Son hath life</u>; *and* he that hath not the Son of God hath not life" (I John 5:11-12).

God never intended us to be merely *bags of bones* that have eternal life as some future promise for us that we call *pie in the sky*. Eternal life is already the possession of every "born again" believer. The greatest present aspect of the miracle of the regeneration is that when we are sanctified, separated from worldliness and unto God's use, and sowing God's Seed, we become the *vehicles of this grace* and the *distribution centers* for the miracles of the indwelling Creator.

DISCUSSION QUESTIONS

1. Within the context of a proper understanding of the doctrine of grace enabling, discuss the following statement: "In God's work of re-creation, He takes something that already exists in a broken or fallen state of existence, makes it new (unbroken and unfallen), and then begins to supernaturally multiply that *new creation* through the operations of His indwelling Spirit."

2. Explain John 7:37-39 in the context of a proper understanding of the Feast of Tabernacles.

3. Read I Corinthians 10:1-7 and explain verse 4 from a proper understanding of John 7:37-39. Discuss how these portions of Scripture *complement* one another.

4. Read I Peter 2:4-12 and explain this from a proper understanding of John 7:37-39 and I Corinthians 10:1-7.

5. Discuss the statement, "God never intended you to be a *Lone Ranger brick* wandering around alone" as it relates to you being a living stone as part of a living Temple or local church.

6. Explain I Corinthians 3:9-16 from your understanding of all of the above truths regarding your personal responsibilities in being filled with the Spirit of God as part of a local church.

7. Expand upon the following statement, "God never intended us to be merely *bags of bones* that have eternal life as some future promise for us that we call *pie in the sky*."

Chapter Five
Discipleship and the Actualization of One's Christianity
(Review Tripartite of Power)

"[35] Again the next day after John stood, and two of his disciples; [36] And looking upon Jesus as he walked, he saith, Behold the Lamb of God! [37] And the two disciples heard him speak, and they followed Jesus. [38] Then Jesus turned, and saw them following, and saith unto them, What seek ye? They said unto him, Rabbi, (which is to say, being interpreted, Master,) where dwellest thou? [39] He saith unto them, Come and see. They came and saw where he dwelt, and abode with him that day: for it was about the tenth hour. [40] One of the two which heard John *speak*, and followed him, was Andrew, Simon Peter's brother. [41] He first findeth his own brother Simon, and saith unto him, We have found the Messias, which is, being interpreted, the Christ. [42] And he brought him to Jesus. And when Jesus beheld him, he said, Thou art Simon the son of Jona: thou shalt be called Cephas, which is by interpretation, A stone. [43] The day following Jesus would go forth into Galilee, and findeth Philip, and saith unto him, Follow me. [44] Now Philip was of Bethsaida, the city of Andrew and Peter. [45] Philip findeth Nathanael, and saith unto him, We have found him, of whom Moses in the law, and the prophets, did write, Jesus of Nazareth, the son of Joseph. [46] And Nathanael said unto him, Can there any good thing come out of Nazareth? Philip saith unto him, Come and see. [47] Jesus saw Nathanael coming to him, and saith of him, Behold an Israelite indeed, in whom is no guile! [48] Nathanael saith unto him, Whence knowest thou me? Jesus answered and said unto him, Before that Philip called thee, when thou wast under the fig tree, I saw thee. [49] Nathanael answered and saith unto him, Rabbi, thou art the Son of God; thou art the King of Israel. [50] Jesus answered and said unto him, Because I said unto thee, I saw thee under the fig tree, believest thou? thou shalt see greater things than these. [51] And he saith unto him, Verily, verily, I say unto you, Hereafter ye shall see heaven open, and the angels of God ascending and descending upon the Son of man" (John 1:35-51).

A person's Christianity is a history of thousands upon thousands of personal decisions of the will. One's Christianity begins with a decision to believe that Jesus died for our sins, propitiated God's wrath for the "sins of the whole world" (I John

2:2), that He was buried, was resurrected and ascended victorious over death opening a "door" (Himself; John 10:1-9) into the *New Genesis* for "whosoever" that is willing to believe the gospel, confess Him as Lord (God) and call on His Name to save him (Romans 10:9-13). However, there is also a vocational call to all believers. That call is to become a DISCIPLE; a learner and doer of the Word.

Throughout Scripture, water baptism is primarily connected to formal local church membership and accountability to become a disciple (follower or doer) of the teachings/doctrine of Jesus Christ.

The next decision after salvation that the believer is to be lead to make is the decision to be baptized by immersion. **This is the decision to become a disciple of Jesus Christ.** This is the decision to be a committed student of Truth and a consecrated, sanctified follower of Jesus Christ. Baptism involved a decision to begin dying to the old, carnal way of life led by the "old man," and a commitment to "walk in the newness of life" (Romans 6:1-13) as led by the indwelling Spirit of God.

Decisional Christianity is clearly the pattern of orthopraxy that we find in the gospels, the book of Acts, and in the New Covenant Epistles. In simple words, we find this pattern of incremental *decisional Christianity* portrayed by Christ in His preaching and teaching ministry over and over again in the gospels. Christ took people through numerous *incremental levels of decisions,* leading them to higher degrees of faith and increased levels of commitment to serve Him at each level.

We find this same type of *incremental decisional Christianity* portrayed by the Apostles over and over again in the book of Acts. We also find this *incremental decisional Christianity* portrayed over and over again throughout the Epistles and even the book of Revelation.

Incremental decisional Christianity **is normal Christianity.**

Therefore, any Christian who is not regularly making *incremental decisions* that brings him/her to a closer walk with God, a higher degree of trust in God, an increased dependency on God in prayer, and a higher level of commitment to God in reaching the lost and making disciples to His glory is probably *backslidden*.

John 1:35 begins the first day of the three year discipleship ministry of Jesus Christ. From this point forward, it is a count-down to Golgotha. Jesus has three years to create a continuum of discipleship by training twelve men and leading them through a number of progressive decisions (progressive sanctification).

It is critically important to understand that the disciples Jesus chose to train, as the disciples to be the Apostles, were already saved disciples of John the Baptist (1:35). That means they were already saved according to the Old Covenant. They were believers in the promised Messiah and were looking for His coming (1:41). This is important in order to understand what is taking place in this portion of Scripture. These men are not getting saved and leading others to salvation. All those they brought to Jesus were already saved like they were saved. **This text is about becoming disciples of Jesus and the commitment involved in becoming a *follower* of Jesus.**

Many people get saved who never become *Christians*. Being a *Christian* is defined by practicing or *following* the teachings of Jesus (Scripture). Granted, a person professing to be saved and never becoming a follower of Jesus as taught in the Word of God should really question the reality of his/her salvation. This kind of so called *Christianity* is not Christianity at all. In fact, the profession of a person who says he is a believer, but who never lives like a believer by actually following (living) the teachings of Jesus Christ, is most probably a false profession of someone who is living under an *illusion* of salvation.

> "[3] And hereby we do know that we know him, if we keep his commandments. [4] He that saith, I know him, and keepeth not his commandments, is a liar, and the truth is not in him. [5] But whoso keepeth his word, in him verily is the love of God perfected: hereby know we that we are in him. [6] He that saith he abideth in him ought himself also so to walk, even as he walked" (I John 2:3-6).

The whole of the *body* of Scriptural teaching is referred to as "the faith." Once a person is truly and really saved by trusting in the finished sacrifice of Christ Jesus in His full payment of the death sentence substitutionally for all mankind, that person is eternally secure in that salvation. Getting saved is the easy part. It costs the believer nothing. It is a gift. Getting saved is a simple matter.

"[8] For by grace are ye saved through faith; and that not of yourselves: *it is* the gift of God: [9] Not of works, lest any man should boast" (Ephesians 2:8-9).

On the other hand, *being* a disciple of Jesus (Christian) is a very costly process of numerous decisions. Becoming a disciple begins with a decision to follow Jesus and live according to His teachings. Salvation is a new creation and a new beginning. Salvation is becoming a "born again" child of God. Discipleship is parenting that newborn babe in Christ to full spiritual maturity.

"For we are his workmanship, created in Christ Jesus unto good works, which God hath before ordained that we should walk in them" (Ephesians 2:10).

What does it mean to be a disciple? The following are a few questions every Christian should regularly ask himself:

1. How committed am I about winning souls, making disciples, and walking with the Lord in separation from worldliness and dedication to ministry?
2. Do I live for Jesus because of peer pressure, because I want to project an image of spirituality to my own glory, or because I really know what I believe and because I really want to live those beliefs to the glory of God?
3. Do I understand my *spiritual gifts* and am I utilizing those *spiritual gifts* in the power of the indwelling Holy Spirit to my fullest potential?
4. How many people's lives am I intimately involved in by praying specifically for the salvation of both their souls and their lives and what people's lives am I actually engaged in through personal witness and personal discipleship process?

How you answer these four questions determines to what degree you are either *faithful* or *backslidden*. When Jesus called these men to become disciples, He was calling them to two things. He was calling them to <u>training</u> for work and He was calling them to the <u>work</u> of evangelism (becoming "fishers of men;" Mark 1:17).

Making disciples of these men meant a long, slow process of training them to be *soul winning disciple makers*.

41

This is why Christ planned for the establishment of local churches. They were to be training centers for disciples to do the work of evangelism and to maintain the continuum of disciple makers. Formal membership in a local church is like enrollment in a Bible college where you are expected to attend all the classes, do the homework, take the tests, graduate, and ultimately begin to do the work you were trained to do. Water Baptism and formal church membership are directly connected to a commitment to the *discipleship process* to be *perfected* (*equipped* or *matured* spiritually in the Tripartite of Power) "for the work of the ministry."

"[11] And he gave some, apostles; and some, prophets; and some, evangelists; and some, pastors and teachers; [12] For the perfecting of the saints, for the work of the ministry, for the edifying of the body of Christ: [13] Till we all come in the unity of the faith, and of the knowledge of the Son of God, unto a perfect man, unto the measure of the stature of the fulness of Christ: [14] That we *henceforth* be no more children, tossed to and fro, and carried about with every wind of doctrine, by the sleight of men, *and* cunning craftiness, whereby they lie in wait to deceive; [15] But speaking the truth in love, may grow up into him in all things, which is the head, *even* Christ: [16] From whom the whole body fitly joined together and compacted by that which every joint supplieth, according to the effectual working in the measure of every part, maketh increase of the body unto the edifying of itself in love" (Ephesians 4:11-16).

When Jesus chose these twelve men to be His disciples, He committed three years of almost twenty-four hours a day of His short life to training them to know and live the Word of God. When He began with them, they were weak in their faith, undependable, unfaithful in their prayer life, ignorant, slow to learn, and pretty selfish in their thinking.

Over three years of time, Christ took eleven of these twelve men from a group of self-absorbed men in pursuit of prominent positions in the Kingdom (that they thought was going to come into existence any day), to a level of understanding of the reality of God's existence that brought them to a faith that was willing to risk everything they owned, and even their lives, for the cause of Christ. Christ took them from being men in selfish pursuit of power and position to become men willing to be servants to the degree they were willing to die in the attempt to bring the very people that sought to kill them to faith in Christ.

The vast majority of today's professing Christians never become disciples, let alone arrive at this final destination of absolute and total commitment to serve the one and only True and Living God.

> The purpose for getting saved believers into the local church is not to *institutionalize* them (meaning all ministry and worship done within the walls of the *institution*). The purpose for getting saved believers into the local church is to *actualize* them (to help them become *actually* what they only presently profess to be).

That cannot, and will not, happen apart from a real, living relationship with the Real, Living God. Neither will it happen apart from a supernatural work from within by the indwelling Holy Spirit of God.

Sadly, the vast majority of professing Christians prefer to be *institutionalized* rather than *actualized*. Being *institutionalized* does not make any demands on your life. Being *institutionalized* allows you the false notion that church attendance carries with it no real accountability to learn or any culpability before God. For the *institutionalized* believer, church attendance is merely the fulfillment of some pseudo-notion of worship obligations. What a façade of real Christianity.

The goal of every local church, which is true to both the Word of God and to the God of the Word, is *actualization*. In *actualization,* a believer can never be said to be *actualized* until he is equipped for the work of the ministry through the *actualization* of the Tripartite of Power and begins to actually do the "work of the ministry."

DISCUSSION QUESTIONS

1. Define what it means and what is involved in *being* a disciple of Jesus Christ.

2. Read Romans 6:1-13. Discuss how a decision to be water baptized relates to the *process discipleship*, formal local church membership, and an ongoing life of *decisional Christianity*.

3. Define and expand upon *Decisional Christianity* and how it relates to the process of discipleship and the preaching/teaching of the Word of God.

4. Explain what it means to *create a continuum of discipleship* and how this relates to your own discipleship process and the depth of your discipleship regarding both knowing and living the Word of God.

5. Discuss the difference between *getting saved* and actually becoming a *Christian*.

6. Discuss your answers to the four questions regarding defining and determining the reality of your commitment to *being* a disciple of Jesus Christ. Be transparent.

7. Read Ephesians 4:11-16. According to this text, what is the primary *missional purpose* in the establishment of a local church and God's purpose in giving gifted men to a local church? Be detailed in that your answer to this defines your Ecclesiology and the missions' statement of a local church in a *practical sense*.

Chapter Six
Becoming Fructiferous
The Outcome of the Actualization of a Disciple

"[1] Simon Peter, a servant and an apostle of Jesus Christ, to them that have obtained like precious faith with us through the righteousness of God and our Saviour Jesus Christ: [2] <u>Grace</u> and <u>peace</u> be multiplied unto you through the <u>knowledge</u> of God, and of Jesus our Lord, [3] According as his <u>divine power</u> hath given unto us all things that *pertain* unto life and godliness, through the knowledge of him that hath called us to glory and virtue: [4] Whereby are given unto us exceeding great and precious promises: that by these ye might be partakers of the divine nature, having escaped the corruption that is in the world through lust. [5] And beside this, giving all diligence, add to your faith virtue; and to virtue knowledge; [6] And to knowledge temperance; and to temperance patience; and to patience godliness; [7] And to godliness brotherly kindness; and to brotherly kindness charity. [8] <u>For if these things be in you, and abound, they make *you that ye shall* neither *be* barren nor unfruitful in the knowledge of our Lord Jesus Christ</u>" (II Peter 1:1-8).

Christ considered a Christian or local church that did not win souls and make disciples an anomaly that was wasting His *blood investment* in the redemption of their souls. **Fruit bearing is expected!**

"[6] He spake also this parable; A certain *man* had a fig tree planted in his vineyard; and he came and sought fruit thereon, and found none. [7] Then said he unto the dresser of his vineyard, Behold, these three years I come seeking fruit on this fig tree, and find none: cut it down; <u>why cumbereth it the ground?</u> [8] And he answering said unto him, Lord, let it alone this year also, till I shall dig about it, and dung *it*: [9] And if it bear fruit, *well*: and if not, *then* after that thou shalt cut it down" (Luke 13:6-9).

Within the text of II Peter 1:1-8, we find a trinity for *fruit production*. This trinity comes all wrapped up for us in the word "faith" in II Peter 1:1. This trinity rapidly unfolds in the next seven verses in the key words "grace," "peace," "knowledge," and "divine power" ultimately ending in *fruitfulness* (fruit bearing). This trinity involves three spiritual dynamics (the Tripartite of Power):

1. Knowledge (illumination) of God's will through His Word
2. The supernatural enabling of the Holy Spirit of God in the *illumination* and the *application* of God's Word
3. Translating the Word of God into the *language of living* (becoming "doers of the Word")

Training in these three areas is really what defines "the perfecting of the saints, for the work of the ministry" (Ephesians 4:12). Herein is where most local churches fail so often in their discipleship ("perfecting") ministry. This is also what makes *preaching* different than *teaching.* Teaching primarily appeals to the head while preaching primarily appeals to the heart.

> Preaching is the dogmatic presentation of the truths of God's Word in the power of the Spirit of God ("unction") resulting in the confrontation of our *Will Gates* with the intent of bringing our living into harmony with the Word of God (*living/doing* faith).

Knowing **faith is not the same as** *living* **faith.** We see very few real life changing decisions today in our invitations at the conclusion of preaching services. The lack of these decisions is even more evident in the reality of the lack of any real change in how people live out their professed faith in the everyday living of their lives. If spiritual decisions are genuine, that genuineness will manifest itself by these people engaging their *corporate ethic* with the gospel of Jesus Christ. It is almost as if people think they can live the Christian life (*living* faith) covertly. This kind of thinking must be confronted and eradicated before true *living* faith can become a reality. *Living* faith is a public faith that stands on the highest ground of a person's corporate and individual influence with a living testimony of a life that points to Jesus Christ.

"[25] It is enough for the disciple that he be as his master, and the servant as his lord. If they have called the master of the house Beelzebub, how much more *shall they call* them of his household? [26] Fear them not therefore: for there is nothing covered, that shall not be revealed; and hid, that shall not be known. [27] What I tell you in darkness, *that* speak ye in light: and what ye hear in the ear, *that* preach ye upon the housetops. [28] And fear not them which kill the body, but are not able to kill the soul: but rather fear him which is able to destroy both soul and body in hell" (Matthew 10:25-28).

"Let your light so shine before men, that they may see your good works, and glorify your Father which is in heaven" (Matthew 5:16).

Orthodoxy must always result in orthopraxy. Orthodoxy involves knowing correct doctrine. Orthopraxy is accurately living correct doctrine (truth) to the degree that it reflects and restores the image of who God is in our lives resulting in manifesting His communicable attributes to the world. This is known as *bringing God glory*. Glorifying God (manifesting who He is through the way we live) is the primary purpose of Bible study and the pursuit of orthodoxy. Without orthodoxy we can never achieve orthopraxy and we can never truly glorify the Lord. The focal purpose of orthodoxy is always doxological or it is not orthodox.

Obtaining "Like Precious Faith"

The word "faith" is used of both *saving* faith and *living* faith in the Word of God. The context of use must determine which of these meanings are being referred too. These two meanings of faith can be found together in Romans 1:17.

"[16] For I am not ashamed of the gospel of Christ: for it is the power of God unto salvation to every one that believeth; to the Jew first, and also to the Greek. [17] For therein is the righteousness of God revealed from {*saving*} faith to {*living*} faith: as it is written, The just shall live by faith" (Romans 1:16-17).

The context of II Peter is referring to Christian service (ministry). Therefore, the meaning of the word "faith" here is *living* faith.

> In this context the word "faith" refers to putting some *muscle* upon the *theological bones* of Bible doctrine.

It is not that the believer puts *life* to the Word of God (it is inherently *living*). The idea is that the indwelling Holy Spirit of God puts life to our bodies, dead in trespasses and sin and still possessing a *sin nature*, through the transforming, cleansing power of the Living Word of God. This happens when the believer yields to the indwelling Holy Spirit of God and begins to live the truths of God's Word through the Spirit's supernatural enabling (grace).

47

However, this miraculous work of the indwelling Spirit does not take place until a believer yields to the indwelling Spirit AND begins to live the Word of God (*living faith*).

Biblical faith is not merely what we *choose* to believe. Biblical faith is *Sola Scriptura*. *Sola Scriptura* means our beliefs are what the Word of God teaches; nothing more and nothing less. This is what the Word of God means when God speaks of "like precious faith" and "the faith." Biblical faith is not about man's opinions, traditions, or philosophies. Biblical faith is not about our observations of human behavior patterns (psychology). Biblical faith is not discovered by rationalism or human logic. Biblical faith comes by the supernatural illumination of *Sola Scriptura*. This is an absolute necessity in the spiritual dynamic of *faith building* in both the life of the preacher/teacher and in the life of the disciple.

> "[1] Now therefore hearken, O Israel, unto the statutes and unto the judgments, which I teach you, for to do *them*, that ye may live, and go in and possess the land which the LORD God of your fathers giveth you. [2] Ye shall not add unto the word which I command you, neither shall ye diminish *ought* from it, that ye may keep the commandments of the LORD your God which I command you" (Deuteronomy 4:1-2).

Therefore, the second aspect of the Tripartite of Power necessary to fruit bearing is the fact that Theology (knowing who God is) is intricately connected to Pneumatology (knowing who the Spirit of God is and what He is doing in our lives). This is the connecting link in II Peter 1:1-8 between *saving* faith and *living* faith. This is communicated in this text by the words "grace," "divine power," and "partakers of the divine nature." If we miss this truth, we miss the primary distinctive characteristic of what defines the Age of Grace or the Church Age.

> "[18] I will not leave you comfortless: I will come to you. [19] Yet a little while, and the world seeth me no more; but ye see me: because I live, ye shall live also. [20] At that day ye shall know that I *am* in my Father, and ye in me, and I in you . . . [26] But the Comforter, *which is* the Holy Ghost, whom the Father will send in my name, he shall teach you all things, and bring all things to your remembrance, whatsoever I have said unto you" (John 14:18-20, 26).

The third aspect of the trinity necessary to fruit bearing is that Pneumatology (knowing who the Spirit of God is and what He is doing in our lives) is the connecting link to translating the Word of God into the language of living (becoming "doers of the Word and not hears only").

Anything less than living supernaturally enabled by the indwelling Holy Spirit of God will be nothing more than carnal legalism.

"[1] O foolish Galatians, who hath bewitched you, that ye should not obey the truth, before whose eyes Jesus Christ hath been evidently set forth, crucified among you? [2] This only would I learn of you, Received ye the Spirit by the works of the law, or by the hearing of faith? [3] Are ye so foolish? having begun in the Spirit, are ye now made perfect by the flesh? [4] Have ye suffered so many things in vain? if *it be* yet in vain. [5] He therefore that ministereth to you the Spirit, and worketh miracles among you, *doeth he it* by the works of the law, or by the hearing of faith" (Galatians 3:1-5)?

The Christian life (*living faith*) is supernaturally produced. Apart from the supernatural enabling of the Holy Spirit of God, the Christian life is completely beyond our realization. The Spirit of God produces the Christian life (the *Christ-life*) in us when we yield our will gate to Him as He reveals His will to us through the illumination of the Word of God.

"[1] Therefore being justified by faith, we have peace with God through our Lord Jesus Christ: [2] By whom also we have access by faith into this grace wherein we stand, and rejoice in hope of the glory of God. [3] And not only *so*, but we glory in tribulations also: knowing that tribulation worketh patience; [4] And patience, experience; and experience, hope: [5] And hope maketh not ashamed; because the love of God is shed abroad in our hearts by the Holy Ghost which is given unto us" (Romans 5:1-5).

In II Peter 1:5-8, the Christian life is described by seven tangible, evidentiary realities that are added to faith through *incremental decisions* intended to make a believer's life fertile soil for *fruit bearing* to the glory of God. The word "add" is from the Greek word *epichoregeo* (ep-ee-khor-ayg-eh'-o). It literally means *to nourish* or *to aid*. The context would imply that the seven attributes listed bring faith to its fullest potential; i.e. fruit bearing. As these seven qualities are built one *upon* another (the word "to" should actually be translated *upon*) and are connected one *to* the other, they will nourish faith to its fullest stature and potential.

1. Virtue: from *arete* (ar-et'-ay), manliness or valor and probably refers to moral strength of character

2. Knowledge: from *gnosis* (gno'-sis), most commentators agree that the context implies this to mean *applied knowledge* for discerning the will of God and therefore knowing the will of God with assurance dogmatically

3. Temperance: from *egkrateia* (eng-krat'-i-ah), self-control or self-restraint; refers to *holding oneself in*

4. Patience: from *hupomone* (hoop-om-on-ay'), meaning constancy; enduring under trials or difficulties

5. Godliness: from *eusebeia* (yoo-seb'-i-ah), holiness or separation from worldliness and unto ministry (loving self-sacrifice)

6. Brotherly kindness: *philadelphia* (fil-ad-el-fee'-ah), kindness and generosity to other believers

7. Charity: *agape* (ag-ah'-pay), sacrificial benevolence to the benefit of others. This kind of love does not happen apart from GIVING of <u>self</u> sacrificially. It is the kind of love that God is.

These seven character qualities are the essentials of grace to produce fruit through the empowering of the indwelling Holy Spirit. In other words, there are some very tangible aspects of Christian character that we must possess before the power of the indwelling Spirit of God can be released through our lives. The Word of God does not tell us to what extent we must have added these qualities, but I would surmise that the more of these qualities we possess the more eternal fruit will be produced through our ministry by the Holy Spirit.

> These are the attributes of a *living faith* forged in the foundry of spiritual growth intent upon production of eternal fruit.

These attributes forge a *chain* that connects the supernatural existence of God to the temporal existence of mankind. The believer with these qualities added to his/her faith becomes that *connecting link*. The outcome of that supernatural connection is that "if these things be in you, and abound, they make *you that ye shall* neither *be* barren nor unfruitful in the knowledge of our Lord Jesus Christ" (II Peter 1:8).

Central to a local church's failure in fulfilling the Great Commission is the failure of people who have not forged a real world faith in their lives and who are not living in the Tripartite of Power.

> *Wilderness Christians* remain in the barren wilderness of fruitlessness because they have a superficial knowledge of God, a superficial knowledge of the ministry of His indwelling Spirit, and a superficial faith that never connects them to the spiritual warfare that living in the Promised Land necessitates.

DISCUSSION QUESTIONS

1. Read Luke 13:6-9. Discuss why Christ considers a *fruitless* Christian or local church an *anomaly*.

2. What is the *trinity for fruit production*?

3. Discuss the difference between *preaching* and *teaching*.

4. Discuss the differences between *knowing faith* and *living faith* as these terms relate to a *decisional Christianity* and a true measurement of spiritual growth.

5. Explain in detail the phrase *orthodoxy must always result in orthopraxy* as this phrase relates to the differences between *knowing faith* and *living faith*.

6. Discuss why Theology (knowing who God is) is intricately connected to Pneumatology (knowing who the Spirit of God is and what He is doing in our lives) regarding *fruit bearing*.

7. Discuss why Pneumatology (knowing who the Spirit of God is and what He is doing in our lives) is the connecting link to translating the Word of God into the language of living (becoming "doers of the Word and not hears only") regarding *fruit bearing*.

Chapter Seven

Doing: Ministry and the Manifestation of Power

"[7] But the end of all things is at hand: be ye therefore sober, and watch unto prayer. [8] And above all things have fervent charity among yourselves: for charity shall cover the multitude of sins. [9] Use hospitality one to another without grudging. [10] As every man hath received the gift, *even so* minister the same one to another, as good stewards of the manifold grace of God. [11] If any man speak, *let him speak* as the oracles of God; if any man minister, *let him do it* as of the ability which God giveth: that God in all things may be glorified through Jesus Christ, to whom be praise and dominion for ever and ever. Amen" (I Peter 4:7-11).

In I Peter 4:7-9, God gives an admonition to believers within a local church *union* about living during the *last days*. The Church Age Dispensation will end with the death of every lost soul on the face of planet earth. Only the lost who enter into the Tribulation and who repent of sin and trust in the finished work of Christ for their redemption during the seven year Tribulation will enter into the Kingdom Age Dispensation alive. Every other person who has received *the mark of the Beast* will be destroyed by the glory of the coming of Christ. With this view in mind, the believer should carefully follow the admonitions of I Peter 4:7-9.

Along with what we are told in Revelation chapters four through nineteen and numerous other prophecies, this is the world view of every Christian who believes in the imminent (any moment) second coming of Jesus Christ. This is the looming *dark cloud* of God's promise of His unleashed wrath in His judgment of the nations. This is the theological foundation in the any moment pending reality to which the words: "[7] But the end of all things is at hand: be ye therefore sober, and watch unto prayer. [8] And above all things have fervent charity among yourselves: for charity shall cover the multitude of sins. [9] Use hospitality one to another without grudging" (I Peter 4:7-9) are addressed. Perhaps if we truly understood this *any moment* pending reality, we might begin to take these words seriously.

The word "end" in I Peter 4:7 is from the Greek word *telos* (tel'-os). This word refers to *the point aimed at as a limit* or *the point of termination*. The Church Age Dispensation is the next to the last age of God's longsuffering grace upon this fallen creation. Then comes the "day of wrath" that Paul speaks of in Romans 2:5: "But after thy hardness and impenitent heart treasurest up unto thyself wrath against the day of wrath and revelation of the righteous judgment of God. . ." This is the future *horizon* of which all Church Age believers must be constantly reminded. We must keep this prophecy as part of *today's* possible realities.

Shortly after the Vietnam War, there was an extensive influx of Hmong people to the United States. After a while, many of them, especially their elderly, were going to emergency medical centers for treatment of malnutrition. They were living almost completely on blanched white rice manufactured in the United States. The fact is, there were not enough nutrients left in the processed rice to sustain them. Even though they increased the amounts they were eating, they were starving to death.

I believe this scenario is equally true of local churches where the "meat" of Bible doctrine has been removed. Take the definitive Truths of God's Word away from the admonitions to a local church and you take away the spiritual nutrients that lead us to power with God. Although that local church may look like and act like it is growing, it is dying of malnutrition at the same time.

Have you ever gone to a restaurant and ordered a cup of coffee expecting a rich, robust flavor to fill your mouth only to find nothing more than a cup of warm, brown water? Have you ever sat down at a table with someone where the food looks wonderful, but there just seems to be a lack of titillating odors and when you taste the food you realize why? It is tasteless. Have you ever gone to a sports activity expecting to see exciting competition between some very skilled athletes only to find mediocre performances with almost a complete lack of enthusiasm? What is common to each of these scenarios? We come to each of these events in life expecting something that just wasn't there. No matter how much we wanted it to be there, it just was not there.

Vapid means flat, tasteless, or dull. The coffee was vapid, because it was made from poor coffee, there was not enough coffee in the mix, or the coffee was just poorly prepared. The food was vapid, because it had no seasonings, or it was not prepared properly.

I do not get too excited about going to someone's house for a steak if I know that their method of preparation is boiling it. Sports activities are vapid if the participants do not put in the necessary effort to perfect their skills and if they do not play with a passion to win.

> The biblical word for vapid is "lukewarm." It is the word Christ uses to describe the plastic, tasteless, pretentious, lifeless local church of Laodicea in Revelation 3:14-22. He spewed it out!

Every Christian is commanded to be both "salt" and "light" in this world. Yet, the Christian that is not empowered by the indwelling Holy Spirit will be *savorless salt* and *hidden* or *covered* "light." The point is that we are going to be "lukewarm" if we are not willing to make some extreme, radical changes in our priorities and how we live this new life we have "in Christ." Before we fool ourselves into thinking that we have achieved some type of success because we have convinced a large group of people to *join* our multitude, we better examine what kind of multitude we *really are* and what we are *trying to become.*

"[25] And there went great multitudes with him: and he turned, and said unto them, [26] If any *man* come to me, and hate not his father, and mother, and wife, and children, and brethren, and sisters, yea, and his own life also, he cannot be my disciple. [27] And whosoever doth not bear his cross, and come after me, cannot be my disciple. [28] For which of you, intending to build a tower, sitteth not down first, and counteth the cost, whether he have *sufficient* to finish *it*? [29] Lest haply, after he hath laid the foundation, and is not able to finish *it*, all that behold *it* begin to mock him, [30] Saying, This man began to build, and was not able to finish. [31] Or what king, going to make war against another king, sitteth not down first, and consulteth whether he be able with ten thousand to meet him that cometh against him with twenty thousand? [32] Or else, while the other is yet a great way off, he sendeth an ambassage, and desireth conditions of peace. [33] So likewise, whosoever he be of you that forsaketh not all that he hath, he cannot be my disciple. [34] Salt *is* good: but if the salt have lost his savour, wherewith shall it be seasoned? [35] It is neither fit for the land, nor yet for the dunghill; *but* men cast it out. He that hath ears to hear, let him hear" (Luke 14:25-35).

I Peter 4:7-11 gives us a *spiritual recipe* to avoid being a *vapid* local church. In I Peter 4:7-11 we see a number of words that describe the overflow of the Spirit of God that manifest His indwelling power flowing through our lives. There are seven ministry areas of the Christian life that are intimately and intricately connected to having a right **working** relationship with the Lord. Understanding these words is critical to understanding the how God releases His power through our lives in ministry to one another.

1. Sobriety: from the word *sophroneo* (so-fron-eh'-o), meaning sound of mind or thinking. Sound mindedness comes from *thinking things through* and taking into consideration all the Truths of God's Word as they weigh upon any given subject or situation. *Sophroneo* was a word that described a person who did not allow his mind to come under the influence of alcohol.

2. Watch unto prayer: the word "watch" is from the word *nepho* (nay'-fo), meaning to abstain from wine drinking and connecting sobriety (right mindedness) with prayer (God-dependency) in power with God in all matters of life. Contradistinctively, failure in *nepho* (abstaining from wine drinking or any similar worldly practice) would disconnect the believer from power with God. Worldly desires manifest a *weak mind* (the opposite of a *strong* or *sound mind*).

3. Fervent charity: literally, unceasing sacrificial (parenting kind of) love for other true believers. The idea is the willingness to make extreme sacrifices for one another, to help one another grow in grace, and to escape the *shackles* of our own selfishness. The words "charity shall cover the multitude of sins" in I Peter 4:8 is a quote from Proverbs 10:12. "Hatred stirreth up strifes: but love covereth all sins." The idea is that our love is not constantly stirring up the *dunghill* of a fellow Christian's past failures of which he has confessed and that have been forgiven.

4. Use hospitality: from the word *philoxenos* (fil-ox'-en-os), it simply means *being fond of guests*. Christians ought to enjoy the company of other Christians and "use hospitality" to encourage one another. Notice this comes with the qualifier, "one to another without grudging" (grumbling or complaining about having to do it). Remember, "God loveth a cheerful giver" (II Corinthians 9:7). Hospitality costs both time and money. If love does not cost us something, we have not loved.

5. Minister "the gift:" "gift" is from *charisma* and "minister" is from *diakoneo* (dee-ak-on-eh'-o). In other words, God did not give us the supernatural gift of spiritual enablement to consume upon ourselves. He has *gifted* us with the intent we will use that "gift" and spread it as a resource to the widest possible scale of our influence "as good stewards of the manifold grace of God." Notice, there is a *stewardship* involved. Stewardship means we will be held accountable for this "manifold grace of God." This accountability defines the Dispensation (stewardship) of Grace. Salvation is a free gift of grace, but with it comes overwhelming spiritual responsibilities for which we are accountable to God. He expects "fruit."

6. Speech: "If any man speak, *let him speak* as the oracles of God" (I Peter 4:11). The word "the" is not in the Greek text in front of the word "oracles." It should read, "Speak as oracles of God." The idea is the "thus sayeth the LORD" proclamation of the Old Testament prophets. The idea is that you are not communicating some philosophical idea or some great thought from your own mind. There is no option for debate or dissension. Truth is to come forth from the mouth of the prophet of God, as if God is speaking Himself. Therefore, when you are speaking forth the Word of God, you are to do so with the authority of its Author.

7. Ministry to the glory of God: "If any man minister, *let him do it* as of the ability which God giveth: that God in all things may be glorified through Jesus Christ, to whom be praise and dominion for ever and ever. Amen" (I Peter 4:11b). We often hear the word *charismatic* used to describe people who can attract large crowds. They are like fly paper. The fly was just looking for a place to land to get something to eat and then he found himself *stuck*.

When God uses the word *charisma*, He uses it in the context of His supernatural enabling of a believer for the "work of the ministry." This gift of grace is never to be used for some guy to build himself an empire of loyal followers. God's gift of grace should be used to make followers of Jesus Christ where all that we do is intent upon bringing God glory - revealing Him in all of His wondrous attributes to a blind, cursed, and dying world of sinners. Sometimes there is a narrow line between a man building himself a kingdom or a man working to win souls and make disciples for the Kingdom of God. That line is sometimes difficult to discern.

DISCUSSION QUESTIONS

1. Explain the significance of the use of the word "therefore" in I Peter 4:7 in the context of I Peter 4:7-11.

2. Read Revelation 3:14-22 and explain the meaning of the word "lukewarm" as it relates to being a true disciple of Jesus Christ.

3. Discuss how being "salt" and "light" is contradicted by being "lukewarm."

4. List and define the seven ministry areas given in I Peter 4:7-11 that will spiritually enable you to avoid becoming a "lukewarm" Christian.

5. Discuss the phrase "this gift of grace is never to be used for some guy to build himself an empire of loyal followers" as it relates to *manufactured blessings* through the pragmatism of *Empire Building* in the Emergent Church philosophy of the Church Growth movement.

6. Discuss the difference between *gathering a crowd* and *building a local church.*

7. Since true *spiritual growth* is directly connected to genuine *fruit production*, discuss why carnally and pragmatically manufactured Church Growth is nothing more than *plastic.*

Chapter Eight
The Four Leavens of the Defilement of Spiritual Empowerment

"Another parable spake he unto them; The kingdom of heaven is like unto leaven, which a woman took, and hid in three measures of meal, till the whole was leavened" (Matthew 13:33).

"[5] And when his disciples were come to the other side, they had forgotten to take bread. [6] Then Jesus said unto them, Take heed and beware of the leaven of the Pharisees and of the Sadducees. [7] And they reasoned among themselves, saying, *It is* because we have taken no bread. [8] *Which* when Jesus perceived, he said unto them, O ye of little faith, why reason ye among yourselves, because ye have brought no bread? [9] Do ye not yet understand, neither remember the five loaves of the five thousand, and how many baskets ye took up? [10] Neither the seven loaves of the four thousand, and how many baskets ye took up? [11] How is it that ye do not understand that I spake *it* not to you concerning bread, that ye should beware of the leaven of the Pharisees and of the Sadducees? [12] Then understood they how that he bade *them* not beware of the leaven of bread, but of the doctrine of the Pharisees and of the Sadducees" (Matthew 16:5-12).

"[14] Now *the disciples* had forgotten to take bread, neither had they in the ship with them more than one loaf. [15] And he charged them, saying, Take heed, beware of the leaven of the Pharisees, and *of* the leaven of Herod. [16] And they reasoned among themselves, saying, *It is* because we have no bread. [17] And when Jesus knew *it*, he saith unto them, Why reason ye, because ye have no bread? perceive ye not yet, neither understand? have ye your heart yet hardened? [18] Having eyes, see ye not? and having ears, hear ye not? and do ye not remember? [19] When I brake the five loaves among five thousand, how many baskets full of fragments took ye up? They say unto him, Twelve. [20] And when the seven among four thousand, how many baskets full of fragments took ye up? And they said, Seven. [21] And he said unto them, How is it that ye do not understand" (Mark 8:14-21)?

The word "leaven" in the Word of God is always used to represent some form of *spiritual corruption* (defilement or uncleanness before God). Any form of *leaven* must be removed or *cleansed* from our lives before God can use us or empower us spiritually. The first instance of *spiritual corruption* began with the fall of Lucifer due to his own corruption through arrogance and pride.

> "[12] How art thou fallen from heaven, O Lucifer, son of the morning! *how* art thou cut down to the ground, which didst weaken the nations! [13] For thou hast said in thine heart, I will ascend into heaven, I will exalt my throne above the stars of God: I will sit also upon the mount of the congregation, in the sides of the north: [14] I will ascend above the heights of the clouds; I will be like the most High" (Isaiah 14:12-14).

However, like all fallen beings, misery loves company. Lucifer, once fallen, set out to corrupt or "leaven" all of God's creation. In his fall, he led one third of the angelic host into his rebellion against God's appointed order and against God plan of redemption.

> "And his tail drew the third part of the stars of heaven {*angels*}, and did cast them to the earth: and the dragon {*Satan*} stood before the woman {*Israel*} which was ready to be delivered, for to devour her child {*Messiah*} as soon as it was born" (Revelation 12:4).

Then Satan introduced the "leaven" of his sin to mankind through the deception of Eve by using the attribute of love *against* mankind. In Satan's deception of Eve, he introduced even more spiritual death to mankind.

> Adam loved Eve more than he loved God and willfully sinned against God by passing the "leaven" of the corruption of sin into mankind seminally (Romans 5:12).

However, God had a plan of redemption and reconciliation in place before the "foundation of the world." He would become a man to die in the sinner's place and to pay the death penalty of the curse that His holiness necessitated. This was God's promise to mankind in the words of God's curse upon Satan and his forces of evil.

> "[14] And the LORD God said unto the serpent, Because thou hast done this, thou *art* cursed above all cattle, and above every beast of the field; upon thy belly shalt thou go, and dust shalt thou eat all the days of thy life: [15] And I will put enmity between thee and the

woman, and between thy seed and her seed; it shall bruise thy head, and thou shalt bruise his heel" (Genesis 3:14-15).

In Genesis 3:15, we have the *Protevangeli*um; the first mention of the *good news* of the promised coming One. This was the gospel in the Promised One in which Adam and Eve trusted to be saved. Immediately, Satan sought to instill the "leaven" of corruption to distort the simple message of redemption and reconciliation through the coming Promised One. Very shortly after the fall, we find Cain and Abel. Cain rises up in insurrection, rebellion, and jealousy against his brother Abel because Abel offered an acceptable sacrifice of a Lamb while Cain offered the work of his own hands to God. Cain believed Satan's "leaven" of *spiritual corruption* of the good news - any avenue to restored fellowship with God is acceptable as long as we are *sincere*. In Cain's deception, Satan introduced the "leaven" of the corruption of false doctrine regarding a way to restored fellowship with God through "works" rather than "by grace through faith."

We must never forget that this world has two *gods*.

There is *thee* One and Only True God with a capital "G" and there is the "god of this world" (II Corinthians 4:4) with a small, tiny, *itsy-bitsy* "g." The "god of this world" is the "god" and author of the *leaven of spiritual corruption*, intent upon defiling everything and everyone before God. For the believer, any defilement equals the loss of spiritual empowerment.

There are four types of "leaven" (spiritual corruption) mentioned in these three portions of Scripture. Satan's "leaven" of defilement comes from many different angles, taking numerous avenues of subtleness. If he can infect us with any one of these forms of leaven, we will be defiled before God and unusable for the purposes for which God has saved us.

1. The Leaven of Sin (the corruption of spiritual seduction)
2. The Leaven of the Pharisees (the corruption of spiritual hypocrisy)
3. The Leaven of the Sadducees (the corruption of spiritual existence)
4. The Leaven of the Herodians (the corruption of Politicalism)

First, let's talk about the corruption of the leaven of sin. Sin is more than acts contrary to the will of God in either disobedience or rebellion. Sin is really the very essence of our existence apart from the inward supernatural enabling of the indwelling Spirit of God.

> Sin is descriptive of our very nature of thought, desires, and actions apart from God's supernatural inward workings. Sin is a *fountain* that corrupts everything that comes from our lives.

"[10] And he called the multitude, and said unto them, Hear, and understand: [11] Not that which goeth into the mouth defileth a man; but <u>that which cometh out of the mouth, this defileth a man</u>. [12] Then came his disciples, and said unto him, Knowest thou that the Pharisees were offended, after they heard this saying? [13] But he answered and said, Every plant, which my heavenly Father hath not planted, shall be rooted up. [14] Let them alone: they be blind leaders of the blind. And if the blind lead the blind, both shall fall into the ditch. [15] Then answered Peter and said unto him, Declare unto us this parable. [16] And Jesus said, Are ye also yet without understanding? [17] Do not ye yet understand, that whatsoever entereth in at the mouth goeth into the belly, and is cast out into the draught? [18] But <u>those things which proceed out of the mouth come forth from the heart; and they defile the man</u>. [19] For out of the heart proceed evil thoughts, murders, adulteries, fornications, thefts, false witness, blasphemies: [20] These are *the things* which defile a man: but to eat with unwashen hands defileth not a man" (Matthew 15:10-20).

The "leaven of the Pharisees" is the hypocrisy of religious externalism and spiritual pretentiousness. This comes in the form of self-righteousness manifested primarily through contempt for sinners. The defiling leaven of spiritual hypocrisy looks at others in their sinfulness and presumptuously passes a sentence upon them. The spiritual hypocrite infected with the leaven of pretense creates a level of expectation for others that he knows he does not even keep. He does not even consider the sins of the heart and the sins of the thought life. Nonetheless, he is defiled before God (and maybe not even saved).

"In the mean time, when there were gathered together an innumerable multitude of people, insomuch that they trode one upon another, he began to say unto his disciples first of all, Beware ye of the leaven of the Pharisees, which is hypocrisy" (Luke 12:1).

"[14] Woe unto you, scribes and Pharisees, hypocrites! for ye devour widows' houses, and <u>for a pretence</u> make long prayer: therefore ye shall receive the greater damnation. . . [16] Woe unto you, ye blind guides which say, Whosoever shall swear by the temple, it is nothing; but whosoever shall swear by the gold of the temple, he is a debtor. . . [18] And, Whosoever shall swear by the altar, it is nothing; but whosoever sweareth by the gift that is upon it, he is guilty" (Matthew 23:14, 16, 18).

The "leaven of the Sadducees" is the denial of supernatural powers or an eternal state of existence for believers (Heaven or Hell). This is the "leaven" of false theology through human rationalism. The Sadducees denied the resurrection from the dead, and the eternal state of existence of those resurrected. The Sadducees were one of the earliest forms of Deism because of the influence of the Greek culture upon them (Hellenization). They did not believe that God interfered in the world in any supernatural way. The simplest way to explain Deism is the idea that God's creation was like a man *throwing a bowling ball down the lane*. Once the ball has left his hand, he does not interfere in any way. In Deism, God is always transcendent (separate from and completely independent of the physical existence) and never immanent (meaning to *remain* within). The point of the "leaven of the Sadducees" is that bad theology or false beliefs about God's involvement within His creation certainly is contradictory to synergism with God in spiritual empowerment of a believer.

"[23] The same day came to him the Sadducees, which say that there is no resurrection, and asked him, [24] Saying, Master, Moses said, If a man die, having no children, his brother shall marry his wife, and raise up seed unto his brother. [25] Now there were with us seven brethren: and the first, when he had married a wife, deceased, and, having no issue, left his wife unto his brother: [26] Likewise the second also, and the third, unto the seventh. [27] And last of all the woman died also. [28] Therefore in the resurrection whose wife shall she be of the seven? for they all had her. [29] Jesus answered and said unto them, Ye do err, not knowing the scriptures, nor the power of God. [30] For in the resurrection they neither marry, nor are given in marriage, but are as the angels of God in heaven. [31] But as touching the resurrection of the dead, have ye not read that which was spoken unto you by God, saying, [32] I am the God of Abraham, and the God of Isaac, and the God of Jacob? God is not the God of the dead, but of the living. [33] And when the multitude heard *this*, they were astonished at his doctrine" (Matthew 22:23).

The "leaven of the Herodians" is a worldly compromise of absolutes for political and sociological advancements through political activism. The Herodians sought to integrate Roman political policies and culture into the nation of Israel. However, there is a more serious heresy in the "leaven of the Herodians. They looked to the Herods: Herod the Great, Antipas, and Agrippa successively - as their *Messiah*. Therefore, they were in alignment with the Sadducees regarding Deism and the Kingdom being merely temporal and earthly. They merely placated the Pharisees regarding Jewish government polity, doing all they could to gain acceptance from Rome. Their compromises mirror the philosophy of today's Emerging Church. We must always remember that the words *politics* and *compromise* are directly connected and almost synonymous practically.

"[15] Then went the Pharisees, and took counsel how they might entangle him in *his* talk. [16] And they sent out unto him their disciples with the Herodians, saying, Master, we know that thou art true, and teachest the way of God in truth, neither carest thou for any *man*: for thou regardest not the person of men. [17] Tell us therefore, What thinkest thou? Is it lawful to give tribute unto Caesar, or not? [18] But Jesus perceived their wickedness, and said, Why tempt ye me, *ye* hypocrites? [19] Shew me the tribute money. And they brought unto him a penny. [20] And he saith unto them, Whose *is* this image and superscription? [21] They say unto him, Caesar's. Then saith he unto them, Render therefore unto Caesar the things which are Caesar's; and unto God the things that are God's. [22] When they had heard *these words*, they marvelled, and left him, and went their way" (Matthew 22:16-22).

> "Leaven" is any form of false doctrine (*heterodoxy*) or false practices (*heteropraxy*) that result in false allegiances, alliances, and practices.

The outcome of any one of these forms of "leaven" in a believer's life is the breech of fellowship (synergism) with God. When this happens there is no possibility for spiritual empowerment until the believer is restored to fellowship with God by repentance of the sin, of pretentiousness/hypocrisy/self-righteousness, of false doctrine, and/or of false allegiances that compromises a believer's separation from worldliness and unto God.

"Thou shalt not offer the blood of my sacrifice with leaven; neither shall the sacrifice of the feast of the passover be left unto the morning" (Exodus 34:25).

"No meat-offering, which ye shall bring unto the LORD, shall be made with leaven: for ye shall burn no leaven, nor any honey, in any offering of the LORD made by fire" (Leviticus 2:11).

DISCUSSION QUESTIONS

1. Define the meaning of the word "leaven" as it regards your personal sanctity before the Lord Jesus Christ.

2. Discuss Satan's *leavening* of all of God's creation and the impact of that *leavening* upon God's blessings.

3. Discuss how Satan used the attribute of love to corrupt mankind.

4. Explain Satan's methodology and the ramifications of the *leaven of sin*.

5. Explain Satan's methodology and the ramifications of the *leaven of the Pharisees*.

6. Explain Satan's methodology and the ramifications of the *leaven of the Sadducees*.

7. Explain Satan's methodology and the ramifications of the *leaven of the Herodians*.

Chapter Nine
The Impact of Spiritual Defilement (Uncleanness) Upon Prayer

> Let your heart soar on the wings of prayer to places your hands cannot reach.

Seldom do Christians ever consider the broad spiritual ramifications of the impact of sin in their lives and the defilement before God that sin causes. Any sin that is not repented of, abandoned, confessed to God, and cleansed by the Blood of Christ (I John 1:9) makes that Christian unclean and defiled before God. Until that *uncleanness* is *cleansed*, that believer is out of "fellowship" with God and all spiritual blessing upon his life is lost. In our salvation, God creates a new *union* with the believer, which provides all believers with the possibility/potential for spiritual empowerment. However, *unity* with the believer, through which empowerment flows, is dependent upon the believer's being *clean* before God and living in "fellowship" with Him.

"[1] That which was from the beginning, which we have heard, which we have seen with our eyes, which we have looked upon, and our hands have handled, of the Word {*Logos*} of life {*the "Word of life" is used here to refer to the Gospel of Jesus Christ as equal to the "breath of life;" Gen. 2:7*}; [2] (For the life was manifested, and we have seen *it*, and bear witness, and shew unto you that eternal life, which was with the Father, and was manifested unto us;) [3] That which we have seen and heard declare we unto you, <u>that ye also may have fellowship</u> {*koinonia, a working partnership in the work of the ministry*} with us: and truly our fellowship *is* with the Father, and with his Son Jesus Christ. [4] And these things write we unto you, that your joy may be full. [5] This then is the message which we have heard of him, and declare unto you, that God is light, and in him is no darkness at all. [6] If we say that we have fellowship {*koinonia, a working partnership in the work of the ministry*} with him, and walk in darkness, we lie, and do not the truth: [7] But if we walk in the light, as he is in the light, we have fellowship one with another, and the blood of Jesus Christ his Son cleanseth us from all sin. [8] If we say that we have no sin, we deceive ourselves, and the truth is not in us. [9] If we confess our sins, he is faithful and just to forgive us *our* sins, and to cleanse us from all unrighteousness. [10] If we say that we have not sinned, we make him a liar, and his word is not in us" (I John 1:1-9).

We must consider the practical aspects of each person in a local church as we are *networked* together in the "work of the ministry" through the omnipresence of God. In this network we must ask, what are some absolute essentials necessary for us to see the supernatural working of God through the Spirit-filled lives of His individual distribution centers of grace? The first *mission* (goal) in evangelism/disciple making is always SUBMISSION!

1. Absolutely no *spiritual fruit* can be produced apart from "abiding in Christ."

"[4] Abide in me, and I in you. As the branch <u>cannot</u> bear fruit of itself, except it abide in the vine; no more can ye, except ye abide in me. [5] I am the vine, ye *are* the branches: He that abideth in me, and I in him, the same bringeth forth much fruit: for <u>without me ye can do nothing</u>" (John 15:4-5).

Since this is an emphatic truth, how should this truth prompt us to pray one for another in our everyday, moment-by-moment walk with God "in light" (I John 1:7)?

2. We must understand that there are two *gods*; there is a big "G" God and a little "g" *god*. Believers partner in prayer with the big "G" God to thwart the workings of the little "g" *god*.

"[1] And you *hath he quickened*, who were dead in trespasses and sins; [2] Wherein <u>in time past ye walked according to the course of this world, according to the prince of the power of the air</u>, the spirit that now worketh in the children of disobedience: [3] Among whom also we all had our conversation in times past in the lusts of our flesh, fulfilling the desires of the flesh and of the mind; and were by nature the children of wrath, even as others" (Ephesians 2:1-3).

"[10] Finally, my brethren, be strong in the Lord, and in the power of his might. [11] Put on the whole armour of God, that ye may be able to <u>stand against the wiles of the devil</u>. [12] For we wrestle not against flesh and blood, but against principalities, against powers, against the rulers of the darkness of this world, against spiritual wickedness in high *places*. [13] Wherefore take unto you the whole armour of

God, <u>that ye may be able to withstand in the evil day, and having done all, to stand</u>" (Ephesians 6:10-13).

"[1] Therefore seeing we have this ministry, as we have received mercy, we faint not; [2] But have renounced the hidden things of dishonesty, not walking in craftiness, nor handling the word of God deceitfully; but by manifestation of the truth commending ourselves to every man's conscience in the sight of God. [3] But if our gospel be hid, it is hid to them that are lost: [4] In whom the <u>god of this world hath blinded the minds of them which believe not</u>, lest the light of the glorious gospel of Christ, who is the image of God, should shine unto them. [5] For we preach not ourselves, but Christ Jesus the Lord; and ourselves your servants for Jesus' sake. [6] For God, who commanded the light to shine out of darkness, hath shined in our hearts, to *give* the light of the knowledge of the glory of God in the face of Jesus Christ. [7] But we have this treasure in earthen vessels, that the excellency of the power may be of God, and not of us" (II Corinthians 4:1-7).

Understanding the spiritual reality of these two supernatural beings, how should the Truths from these three texts prompt us to pray one for another in our everyday, moment-by-moment walk with God? Make a list of prayer needs prompted by your knowledge of the truths in these three texts.

> Although Satan is a powerful enemy, he is still just a created being whose power is very limited compared to God's power.

"Ye are of God, little children, and have overcome them: because greater is he that is in you, than he that is in the world" (I John 4:4).

How should this knowledge impact your boldness in prayer & witness?

3. The "grace of God" is the supernatural enabling of a believer's life, ministry, witness, and prayer through the indwelling Holy Spirit of God. Anything attempted for the Lord apart from that supernatural enabling is an attempt to do God's work in the power of the "flesh."

"[7] But the end of all things is at hand: be ye therefore sober, and watch unto prayer. [8] And above all things have fervent charity among yourselves: for charity shall cover the multitude of sins. [9]

Use hospitality one to another without grudging. [10] As every man hath received the gift {*charisma*}, *even so* minister the same one to another, as good stewards of the manifold grace {*charis*} of God. [11] If any man speak, *let him speak* as the oracles of God; if any man minister, *let him do it* as of the ability which God giveth: that God in all things may be glorified through Jesus Christ, to whom be praise and dominion for ever and ever. Amen" (I Peter 4:7-11).

"[2] Continue in prayer, and watch in the same with thanksgiving; [3] Withal praying also for us, that God would open unto us a door of utterance, to speak the mystery of Christ, for which I am also in bonds: [4] That I may make it manifest, as I ought to speak. [5] Walk in wisdom toward them that are without, redeeming the time. [6] Let your speech *be* alway with grace {*charis*}, seasoned with salt, that ye may know how ye ought to answer every man" (Colossians 4:2-6).

4. Sin defiles the believer, his ministry, and his prayer life before God.

> Sin is any **action, thought,** or **emotion** that is out of alignment with the will (Word) of God. We tend to minimalized *thought* sins and *emotion* sins.

For instance, pride is a sin that defiles a believer just as much as adultery. Remember, "pride made a devil out of an angel."[2]

"If I regard iniquity in my heart, the Lord will not hear *me*" (Psalm 66:18).

"[3] For though we walk in the flesh, we do not war after the flesh: [4] (For the weapons of our warfare *are* not carnal, but mighty through God to the pulling down of strong holds;) [5] Casting down imaginations, and every high thing that exalteth itself against the knowledge of God, and bringing into captivity every thought to the obedience of Christ; [6] And having in a readiness to revenge all disobedience, when your obedience is fulfilled" (II Corinthians 10:3-6).

"[1] If ye then be risen with Christ, seek those things which are above, where Christ sitteth on the right hand of God. [2] Set your affection on things above, not on things on the earth. [3] For ye are dead, and your life is hid with Christ in God. [4] When Christ, *who is* our life, shall appear, then shall ye also appear with him in glory. [5] Mortify

---

[2] Statement heard in a sermon from Evangelist Tom Ferrell

therefore your members which are upon the earth; fornication, uncleanness, inordinate affection, evil concupiscence {*desire for the forbidden*}, and covetousness, which is idolatry: [6] For which things' sake the wrath of God cometh on the children of disobedience: [7] In the which ye also walked some time, when ye lived in them. [8] But now ye also put off all these; anger, wrath, malice, blasphemy, filthy communication out of your mouth. [9] Lie not one to another, seeing that ye have put off the old man with his deeds; [10] And have put on the new *man*, which is renewed in knowledge after the image of him that created him: [11] Where there is neither Greek nor Jew, circumcision nor uncircumcision, Barbarian, Scythian, bond *nor* free: but Christ *is* all, and in all" (Colossians 3:1-11).

5. Perhaps the most wasted and abused resource of God's grace in the Christian's life is the amount of time we waste trying to do God's work in our own strength. We cannot do God's work when defiled before God because our attempts at missions ("the work of the ministry") are not bathed in the prayerful declaration of our own absolute dependency upon His empowerment.

Power *from* God flows from prayer *to* God that comes from a heart that is pure *with* God.

"[16] Confess *your* faults one to another, and pray one for another, that ye may be healed. The effectual fervent prayer of a righteous man availeth much. [17] Elias was a man subject to like passions as we are, and he prayed earnestly that it might not rain: and it rained not on the earth by the space of three years and six months. [18] And he prayed again, and the heaven gave rain, and the earth brought forth her fruit" (James 5:16-18).

Understanding the necessary condition of personal righteousness before God in practical sanctification is essential before our prayer life can be either "effectual" or "fervent." How should this knowledge preface the priority of our prayer life before we begin to make our requests known unto God through prayer?

"But sanctify the Lord God in your hearts: and *be* ready always to *give* an answer to every man that asketh you a reason of the hope that is in you with meekness and fear" (I Peter 3:15).

6. The primary purpose in prayer is that God will be glorified (revealed in all His wondrous attributes) through answered prayer.

The primary purpose in prayer is NOT to have our prayers answered.

"[12] Verily, verily, I say unto you, He that believeth on me, the works that I do shall he do also; and greater *works* than these shall he do; because I go unto my Father. [13] And whatsoever ye shall ask in my name, that will I do, <u>that the Father may be glorified in the Son</u>. [14] If ye shall ask any thing in my name, I will do *it*" (John 14:12-14).

If our desire for answered prayer is truly motivated by the desire to see God glorified, how critical is it that this *attitude* and *desire* become the prefix to prayer and how should this truth be communicated through our prayer?

7. Prayer that moves God is prayer that keeps the eternal Kingdom of God at the forefront of all that we ask God to do. Although God's provision of the material needs of this physical life are important, we must be careful that they must never be given priority over things that have eternal consequences. If the Christian is living in "fellowship" (synergism) with the Holy Spirit, God has promised that material needs will be provided. Therefore, the believer who "lives by faith" does not need to constantly be asking God for these provisions. Instead, he should be BELIEVING God for these provisions.

When our spiritual *priorities* are in order, God takes care of our *minorities*.

"[25] Therefore I say unto you, Take no thought for your life, what ye shall eat, or what ye shall drink; nor yet for your body, what ye shall put on. Is not the life more than meat, and the body than raiment? [26] Behold the fowls of the air: for they sow not, neither do they reap, nor gather into barns; yet your heavenly Father feedeth them. Are ye not much better than they? [27] Which of you by taking thought can add one cubit unto his stature? [28] And why take ye thought for raiment? Consider the lilies of the field, how they grow; they toil not, neither do they spin: [29] And yet I say unto you, That even Solomon in all his glory was not arrayed like one of these. [30] Wherefore, if God so clothe the grass of the field, which to day is, and to morrow is cast into the oven, *shall he* not much more *clothe* you, O ye of little faith? [31] Therefore take no thought, saying, What

72

shall we eat? or, What shall we drink? or, Wherewithal shall we be clothed? [32] (For after all these things do the Gentiles seek:) for your heavenly Father knoweth that ye have need of all these things. [33] But seek ye first the kingdom of God, and his righteousness; and all these things shall be added unto you. [34] Take therefore no thought for the morrow: for the morrow shall take thought for the things of itself. Sufficient unto the day *is* the evil thereof" (Matthew 6:25-34).

> Certainly, the moment a Spirit-filled believer engages God in prayer, Satan engages that believer in spiritual warfare.

The priorities of our prayer life should be preoccupied with the supernatural, spiritual workings of God. Satan wants to keep you from being spiritually empowered by the indwelling Spirit of God through tempting you into sin, or by misdirecting the priorities of your life away from prayer, witnessing, and making disciples. If he can accomplish any of this, he does not need to worry about anything you do because it will be spiritually powerless anyway.

Understanding these matters should greatly direct how we pray one for another and about what we should be praying. Understanding these matters helps us grasp the reality of spiritual warfare and helps us understand that we should expect sharp, hostile opposition to the things we attempt for God's.

DISCUSSION QUESTIONS

"Let your heart soar on the wings of prayer to places your hands cannot reach."[3]

Discuss and formulate a theology of prayer that encompasses all the truths from this short study. Discuss and list specifics that we need to pray about and pray for both for ourselves, our local church ministries, and for missionaries throughout the world.

_____

_____

_____

_____

_____

_____

_____

_____

_____

_____

_____

_____

_____

_____

_____

_____

_____

_____

_____

_____

_____

_____

_____

_____

_____

_____

_____

_____

_____

_____

_____

[3] Lance Ketchum

Chapter Ten
Making Sure We Possess Unfeigned Faith

"[1] Paul, an apostle of Jesus Christ by the commandment of God our Saviour, and Lord Jesus Christ, *which is* our hope; [2] Unto Timothy, *my* own son in the faith: Grace, mercy, *and* peace, from God our Father and Jesus Christ our Lord. [3] As I besought thee to abide still at Ephesus, when I went into Macedonia, that thou mightest charge some that they teach no other doctrine, [4] Neither give heed to fables and endless genealogies, which minister questions, rather than godly edifying which is in faith: *so do.* [5] Now the end of the commandment is charity out of a pure heart, and *of* a good conscience, and *of* <u>faith unfeigned</u>: [6] From which some having swerved have turned aside unto vain jangling; [7] Desiring to be teachers of the law; understanding neither what they say, nor whereof they affirm. [8] But we know that the law *is* good, if a man use it lawfully; [9] Knowing this, that the law is not made for a righteous man, but for the lawless and disobedient, for the ungodly and for sinners, for unholy and profane, for murderers of fathers and murderers of mothers, for manslayers, [10] For whoremongers, for them that defile themselves with mankind, for menstealers, for liars, for perjured persons, and if there be <u>any other thing that is contrary to sound doctrine</u>; [11] According to the glorious gospel of the blessed God, which was committed to my trust. [12] And I thank Christ Jesus our Lord, <u>who hath enabled me</u>, for that he counted me faithful, putting me into the ministry; [13] Who was before a blasphemer, and a persecutor, and injurious: but I obtained mercy, because I did *it* ignorantly in unbelief. [14] And the grace of our Lord was exceeding abundant with faith and love which is in Christ Jesus. [15] This *is* a faithful saying, and worthy of all acceptation, that Christ Jesus came into the world to save sinners; of whom I am chief. [16] Howbeit for this cause I obtained mercy, that in me first Jesus Christ might shew forth all longsuffering, for a pattern to them which should hereafter believe on him to life everlasting. [17] Now unto the King eternal, immortal, invisible, the only wise God, *be* honour and glory for ever and ever. Amen" (I Timothy 1:1-16).

Apart from the supernatural working of the indwelling Holy Spirit of God, we are all what Paul describes in verses 9 and 10; "[9] Knowing this, that the law is not made for a righteous man, but for the lawless and disobedient, for the ungodly and for sinners, for unholy and profane, for murderers of fathers and murderers of mothers, for manslayers, [10] For whoremongers, for them that defile themselves with mankind, for menstealers, for liars, for perjured persons, and if there be <u>any other thing that is contrary to sound doctrine</u>." These are the words God uses to describe those who live in the carnality of the defilement of the "flesh."

We will not be preoccupied with these words that describe our corruption apart from the inward working of the indwelling Spirit of God. Instead, let us examine what is necessary to insure that these defiling characteristics do not flow from our lives; particularly what "unfeigned faith" is. The word "unfeigned" comes from the Greek word *anupokritos* (an-oo-pok'-ree-tos). This word refers to something that is not dissembled, undisguised, without pretense, real, genuine, or without hypocrisy.

> **"Unfeigned faith" is an apparent faith. It is a faith that is openly visible and easily distinguished from the counterfeit.**

With unpretentious faith there is no attempt to manipulate people or to get them to follow Christ through deceit or hidden agendas. This kind of faith is open and transparent about both its intentions and objectives. This is not true of the false teacher who seeks to make *merchandise* out of people.

> "[1] But there were false prophets also among the people, even as there shall be false teachers among you, who privily shall bring in damnable heresies, even denying the Lord that bought them, and bring upon themselves swift destruction. [2] And many shall follow their pernicious ways; by reason of whom the way of truth shall be evil spoken of. [3] And through covetousness shall they <u>with feigned words make merchandise of you</u>: whose judgment now of a long time lingereth not, and their damnation slumbereth not" (II Peter 2:1-3).

The word "feigned" in II Peter 2:3 is from the Greek word *plastos* (plas-tos'), meaning *artificial* or *molded*. God's intent here is condemning the use of words to manipulate. Words are carefully chosen by the deceiver to fit the individual. This is an excellent description of *Positivism*. *Positivism* tells a person what he *wants* to hear, not what he *needs* to hear. Positivism talks *around* sin, not *about* sin. Positivism never confronts the problem head on, but seeks a *painless pathway* (this is an impossibility in the extraction of sin from our characters).

Positivism sees people and treats people as *merchandise.*

Since the Church is dependent upon the voluntary benevolent giving, the *Positivist's* agenda is focused upon keeping people benevolent (wanting to give). In such a scenario, there can be no genuine confrontation in the *Plastic Church* of disingenuousness with what is genuine ("unfeigned faith"). In the scenario of the *Plastic Church*, definitive doctrine (indoctrination) must be deemphasized and personal relationships (socialization) must be emphasized. In the *Plastic Church* scenario, people do not attend because they are learning definitive Truths that help them with their personal relationship with God, their practical sanctification before God, and their supernatural enablement by God in doing the work of the ministry. Instead, the *Plastic Church* scenario, a person comes once a week to get *stroked, coddled, tickled behind the ears*, and made to *feel good* about his life even though his faith is *plastic* and his life is *plastic.*

Today's evangelical Christianity has an abnormal, dysfunctional passivity when it comes to truth ("unfeigned faith").

Therefore, almost all professing Christians are caught somewhere between *empty faith* (unbelief) and *full faith*. Full faith rests completely upon the knowledge of God as revealed by His Word. To truly and intimately know God is to truly and genuinely trust God.

"So then faith *cometh* by hearing, and hearing by the word of God" (Romans 10:17).

"[9] The LORD also will be a refuge for the oppressed, a refuge in times of trouble. [10] And <u>they that know thy name</u> will put their trust in thee: for thou, LORD, hast not forsaken them that seek thee" (Psalm 9:9-10).

Yet, "unfeigned faith" is careful not to make knowledge of God's Word a substitute for a faithful relationship with God. Those with "unfeigned faith" will not easily be led astray by the deception of false emotions. Those with "unfeigned faith" will have spiritual discernment to discern between good and evil.

"[10] Called of God an high priest after the order of Melchisedec. [11] Of whom we have many things to say, and hard to be uttered, seeing ye are dull of hearing. [12] For when for the time ye ought to be teachers, ye have need that one teach you again which *be* the first principles of the oracles of God; and are become such as have need of milk, and not of strong meat. [13] For every one that useth milk *is* unskilful in the word of righteousness: for he is a babe. [14] But strong meat belongeth to them that are of full age, *even* those who by reason of use have their senses exercised to discern both good and evil" (Hebrews 5:10-14).

Christians need to know and to be told that they will stand before God and be accountable for their superficial knowledge of God's Word and for their superficial knowledge of the God of the Word. God will even hold people accountable for their own deception by the false teachers who are able to use *plastic words* to be manipulated into accepting and producing a *plastic faith.* God is only going to be satisfied with the *real thing* - "unfeigned faith."

> Real faith causes us to act upon what we believe. Faith is not in knowledge. Our faith is not even in the Word of God. "Unfeigned faith" leads us to rest in the Person of God and to live our lives to His glory according to the principles and precepts of His Instruction Book.

There is great defilement in religion without relationship. There is great defilement and self-deception in *knowing*, but not *doing* what God's Word teaches us. There is great defilement in doing what God's Word teaches us because we want acceptance from our peers rather than because we genuinely love the LORD and want to please Him with all of our heart, soul, and mind. *Plastic faith* is always a defiling and a corrupting kind of pseudo-faith.

The Hebrew word that is translated "faith" in the Old Testament books is the word *emuwnah* (em-oo-naw'). It literally means *firmness.* However, the *stability* or *firmness* depends upon the surety of the foundation of the Truth upon which faith is structured.

The word "believe" in the Old Testament is usually translated from the Hebrew word *aman* (aw-man'). The English word *amen* is a transliteration of this Hebrew word. It literally means *to build something up* or *support it*. When a truth about God or from God is believed, that truth literally becomes a foundation upon which one builds his life and upon which a person lives and walks each day. Therefore, the phrase "walk in the light" is to literally walk upon the pathway that is the truths that one *amen's*.

> To declare an *amen* to a truth read or proclaimed is in essence to publicly declare before God that you believe that truth to be *sure/solid* and is now part of your *foundation* for living.

This kind of faith is "unfeigned faith." Anything else is just *plastic faith*. In fact, *plastic faith* is not faith at all. *Plastic faith* is a deceptive faith. *Plastic faith* defiles a person possessed by it before God (people do not possess this kind of faith, it possesses them).

Faithful means *full of faith*. A faithful life is a life filled with living the detailed knowledge of God's Word. A person who believes that the Word of God is the Word of God will "labour in the word and doctrine" (I Timothy 5:17). A life empty of real faith is a life empty of the intimate knowledge of the Word of God. Show me a person who is not interested in knowing the details of the Word of God and I will show you a person with *vain* faith. Real faith is always anchored to the promises of God revealed in His Word.

"[12] Now if Christ be preached that he rose from the dead, how say some among you that there is no resurrection of the dead? [13] But if there be no resurrection of the dead, then is Christ not risen: [14] And if Christ be not risen, then *is* our preaching vain, and your faith *is* also vain. [15] Yea, and we are found false witnesses of God; because we have testified of God that he raised up Christ: whom he raised not up, if so be that the dead rise not. [16] For if the dead rise not, then is not Christ raised: [17] And if Christ be not raised, your faith *is* vain; ye are yet in your sins. [18] Then they also which are fallen asleep in Christ are perished. [19] If in this life only we have hope in Christ, we are of all men most miserable" (I Corinthians 15:12-19).

A life full of faith acts upon the truths believed. The Spirit - filled believer who prays for the salvation of a friend or neighbor then begins to move in the *direction of expectation*. If that believer never moves in the *direction of his expectation*, his faith is in vain.

"[14] What *doth it* profit, my brethren, though a man say he hath faith, and have not works? can faith save him? [15] If a brother or sister be naked, and destitute of daily food, [16] And one of you say unto them, Depart in peace, be *ye* warmed and filled; notwithstanding ye give them not those things which are needful to the body; what *doth it* profit? [17] Even so faith, if it hath not works, is dead, being alone. [18] Yea, a man may say, Thou hast faith, and I have works: shew me thy faith without thy works, and I will shew thee my faith by my works. [19] Thou believest that there is one God; thou doest well: the devils also believe, and tremble. [20] But wilt thou know, O vain man, that <u>faith without works is dead</u>" (James 2:14-20)?

In the next verse, James 2:21, the Word of God gives us the example of faith that moves in the *direction of its expectation* - "[21] Was not Abraham our father justified by works, when he had offered Isaac his son upon the altar? [22] Seest thou how faith wrought with his works, and by works was faith made perfect? [23] And the scripture was fulfilled which saith, Abraham believed God, and it was imputed unto him for righteousness: and he was called the Friend of God." If Abraham would not have actually been willing to offer Isaac, would God have accepted a mere declaration of faith?

> Real faith is always tested and proven faith. If your declaration of belief never moves in the *direction of its expectation,* your faith is in vain (it is empty).

"Vain" Faith is Empty of Two Necessities

1. Intimate and detailed knowledge of the Word of God
2. The failure to move in the *direction of our expectations* of God

If those two necessities are not intricate parts of your Christian life, you are living in the power of your own carnal "flesh." What that means in practical language is that you are spiritually powerless to engage the forces of evil and Satan will "sift you as wheat." Unless you are honest about this evaluation of your faith, you will spend your life in denial. You will deny the actuality of your own unbelief and, in doing so, will continually deny the LORD.

"[31] And the Lord said, Simon, Simon, behold, Satan hath desired *to have* you, that he may sift *you* as wheat: [32] But I have prayed for thee, <u>that thy faith fail not</u>: and when thou art converted, strengthen thy brethren. [33] And he said unto him, Lord, <u>I am ready to go with thee, both into prison, and to death</u> {*a proclamation of faith is not the same as an action of faith; Peter was not willing to move in the direction of his expectation*}. [34] And he said, I tell thee, Peter, the cock shall not crow this day, before that thou shalt thrice deny that thou knowest me" (Luke 22:31-34).

Now, before we get too haughty about Peter's failure, we must remember that only Peter had enough faith to get out of that boat to attempt to meet Christ on the stormy sea. He may not have gotten far, but at least he *moved in the direction of his expectation.* Beginning on the Day of Pentecost, Peter *moved in the direction of his expectation* many more times.

DISCUSSION QUESTIONS

1. Read I Timothy 1:9-10. What is Paul describing in these verses of Scripture?

2. What is the meaning of the words "faith unfeigned" in I Timothy 1:5 and what is the significance of these words to spiritual empowerment?

3. What is the idea behind the use of the word "feigned" in II Peter 2:3?

4. What is *Positivism* and how does it relate to *plastic faith*?

5. Explain the significance of the declaration of an *Amen* to reading or hearing Truth.

6. How would you evaluate a *declaration of faith* (an Amen!) that never moves in the *direction of the expectation* of the Truth that is declared to be true?

7. List and discuss the two necessities of which *vain faith* is empty.

Chapter Eleven
The Relationship of Faith to Spiritual Empowerment

"[4] By faith Abel offered unto God a more excellent sacrifice than Cain, by which he obtained witness that he was righteous, God testifying of his gifts: and by it he being dead yet speaketh. [5] By faith Enoch was translated that he should not see death; and was not found, because God had translated him: for before his translation he had this testimony, that he pleased God. [6] But without faith *it is* impossible to please *him*: for he that cometh to God must believe that he is, and *that* he is a rewarder of them that diligently seek him" (Hebrews 11:4-6).

Faith is a decision that grasps intangible realities. Faith is a blind man staring blankly into the darkness listening for the still small voice of God in the whisper of the wind. Faith smells the scent of God through the fragrance of a flower carried gently upon a breeze. Faith sees that which is invisible to his eye knowing with surety that God is real and that there must be a Creator if there is a creation. However, although we are all spiritually blind to God's existence, real faith is not content with a mere intellectual assent to a *probability*. Real faith must, and will, reach out to try and grasp the intangible transcendence of God - to touch God or to be touched by His immanency.

We must lay some historical background here to understand what is being emphasized in this text. Jesus said He would come again. Many believers assumed it would be during the first century of the Church. In II Timothy 2:17-18 we read of two men - Hymenaeus and Philetus, "who concerning the truth have erred, saying that the resurrection is past already; overthrowing the faith of some." False teaching already existed by 67 A.D. that led people to believe they had missed the second coming.

In I Thessalonians 4:13, Paul prefaces his statements regarding the rapture of the Church and the second coming of Christ intending to correct an abnormality in doctrine – ignorance. "But I would not have thou ignorant, brethren, concerning them which are asleep, that ye sorrow not, even as others which no hope."

Christ and the apostles taught the imminent (any moment) return of Christ for his Church. By the time of the epistle to the Hebrews (about 68 A.D.), most of the first Christians were growing old. Christ had not returned and many of the Jewish believers were giving up hope and returning to Old Covenant Temple practices. (The Temple was not destroyed until 70 A.D.).

> Hebrews 11:4-13 gives an important message to the professing Christians of this era in the example of the four patriarchs - true faith does not give up hope.

"These all died in faith, not having received the promises" (Hebrews 11:13a). This theme will continue through all the examples of faith in Hebrews chapter eleven.

"And these all, having obtained a good report through faith, received not the promise" (Hebrews 11:39).

In Hebrews 11:4-13, we have the examples of four men and one woman who saw eternity through the eyes of faith and "embraced" the "promise" that God offered for them to possess. These five people saw certainty ("substance") sustained in God's immutability and rested their eternal hope in God's promises (Hebrews 11:1). These are five examples of people whose faith became the proof ("evidence") of the reality of the invisible things of God. **They all moved in the direction of their expectations of God.**

1. Abel's continuing testimony of faith was that he maintained pure worship according to God's ordained pattern (Hebrews 11:4).

We are told in Genesis 4:2b that "Abel was a keeper of sheep, but Cain was a tiller of the ground." God had already established that man's approachability to Him must be preceded by faith in the death of a substitute. Abel maintained purity of this faith/belief and worship by strictly following this pattern directed by God. This pattern has never changed.

"Jesus saith unto him, I am the way, the truth, and the life: no man cometh unto the Father, but by me" (John 14:6).

Cain on the other hand abandoned this idea. Cain tried to approach God with the fruit of the cursed ground and the produce of his cursed hands. Why was Abel's offering "more excellent"? It was "more excellent" because it was offered based upon continuing faith through strict application of God's instruction.

This is the continual warning of Hebrews: "How shall we escape if we neglect so great salvation (2:3). Abel is the positive example of continual faith. Cain is the negative example of reprobation in abandonment of God's ordained way and thereby exemplifies falling away from true faith.

"If they shall fall away, to renew them again unto repentance; seeing they crucify to themselves the Son of God afresh, and put *him* to an open shame" (Hebrews 6:6).

By Abel's continuation in the practice of faith, manifested by the sacrifice he offered, he obtained witness (God's testimony) "that he was righteous" in the Substitute portrayed by his offering (Hebrews 11:4).

"[21] But now the righteousness of God without the law is manifested, being witnessed by the law and the prophets; [22] Even the righteousness of God *which is* by faith of Jesus Christ unto all and upon all them that believe: for there is no difference: [23] For all have sinned, and come short of the glory of God; [24] Being justified freely by his grace through the redemption that is in Christ Jesus: [25] Whom God hath set forth *to be* a propitiation through faith in his blood, to declare his righteousness for the remission of sins that are past, through the forbearance of God; [26] To declare, *I say*, at this time his righteousness: that he might be just, and the justifier of him which believeth in Jesus" (Romans 3:21-26).

There was no difference between Abel and Cain in relation to their being sinners (Romans 3:22-23). The difference was in their faith. Real faith never gives up on the promises of God. Real faith sees those promises as certainty (Hebrews 11:1).

The word "testifying" is from the Greek word *martureo* (mar-too-reh'-o). The interesting thing about this word is that it is in the present tense. In other words, God is still giving witness to the superiority of the sacrifices ("gifts") of Abel, and by that continuing witness of God, Abel, though now dead, continues to speak to us as well (Hebrews 11:4). Abel was righteous, not on the basis of his character, but based on his gifts or sacrifices manifesting the *object of his faith.* God keeps that kind of testimony alive, even though the original testifier has died.

"And by it" (his continual faith) Abel continues, even after death, to bear witness to the "certainty of God's promises" (Hebrews 11:1). Abel continues to witness, because he did not quit at any time in his life as did Cain. After Cain had his offering rejected, he "went out from the presence of the Lord" (Genesis 4:16). If Abel had done that, He would bear no continuing witness. The idea of the text continues the emphasis that the only way to approach God is found in and through Jesus Christ as the substitute *sin bearer.*

2. Abel is our example of continuing faith in the *purity of worship* of God, while Enoch is our example of continuing faith in the *purity of walk* in fellowship with God (Hebrews 11:5-6).

> "[21] And Enoch lived sixty and five years, and begat Methuselah: [22] And Enoch walked with God after he begat Methuselah three hundred years, and begat sons and daughters: [23] And all the days of Enoch were three hundred sixty and five years: [24] And Enoch walked with God: and he *was* not; for God took him" (Genesis 5:21-24).

Enoch walked with God for 365 years of his life and God took him home without death. Why did God bless Enoch with a blessing with which no one else in history has ever been blessed? The answer is because he "pleased God" by maintaining perfect fellowship with God; he "walked with God." "He pleased God" (Hebrews 11:4). This is the testimony God gives about Enoch.

We often speak of giving testimony for God. Telling people about Who God is and what He is doing is what people of faith do for the God we love and serve. Yet, how often do we consider the fact that God bears testimony about us - glory!

Hebrews 11:6 continues to exemplify the faith of Enoch with the all-encompassing, time transcending statement, "But without faith it is impossible to please God." Was Enoch sinless (Romans 3:23; 5:12)? So what made the difference? God says his faith made the difference. Enoch, like all after him that wanted to please God, "came to God." He believed God was who He said He was. By faith Enoch believed God would reward those "that diligently seek him." The example then is in the answer to the question, what do you suppose Enoch (a man of faith) did as the result of that belief? He diligently sought God until God was so pleased with him that God translated him right off of the face of the earth.

The words "diligently seek" are from the Greek word *ekzeteo* (ek-zay-teh'-o). It refers to *an insatiable craving to know God.* Perhaps this definition is why only one man in the history of the world has the testimony of Enoch.

3. Noah is our example of continuing faith in the purity of work or service (Hebrews 11:7).

God continues to maintain the testimony of real people of faith. In Genesis 5:29, God says of Noah, "And he called his name Noah, saying, This *same* shall comfort us concerning our work and toil of our hands, because of the ground which the LORD hath cursed." The word "Noah" means *rest* or *comfort.*

In Genesis 6:9, God says of Noah, "These *are* the generations of Noah: Noah was a just man *and* perfect in his generations, *and* Noah walked with God." Like Enoch, Noah "walked with God." In Genesis 6:22, God says of Noah, "Thus did Noah; according to all that God commanded him, so did he."

According to Hebrews 11:7, God tells us that Noah, "moved with fear" of God, did what God told him to do. Why was Noah's service of faith so great an example of continuation in service? In Genesis 7:4, God said to Noah, "I will cause it to rain upon the earth." That does not seem like such a remarkable statement to us today. What makes this statement remarkable is to understand that, according to Genesis 2:5, it had never rained before. Here we have a man building a giant ark for a *floating zoo* and preaching that God was going to destroy mankind by causing it to rain.

"[5] And every plant of the field before it was in the earth, and every herb of the field before it grew: for the LORD God had not caused it to rain upon the earth, and *there was* not a man to till the ground. [6] But there went up a mist from the earth, and watered the whole face of the ground" (Genesis 2:5-6).

Can you imagine the ridicule Noah got during the 100 years he spent building this *giant circus boat*? Yet he did not quit "according to all that God commanded him, so did he" (Genesis 6:22).

4. Abraham is our example of continuing testimony of faith in the purity of witness (Hebrews 11:8-19).

God had given him the promise of a land and a people (nation). Can you imagine stopping Abraham after he had left his home and family at Haran? You: Where are you going Abraham? Abraham: I don't know, I am going someplace where I will receive an inheritance. You: Who told you that and how will you find it if you don't know where it is? Abraham: God told me! He will show me! You: Which God do you worship Abraham? Abraham: I worship *my* God!

The world would shake their heads in amazement over a man wondering around in the desert looking for a land he does not know where it is, believing in an *unknown* God. Yet Abraham continued looking (vs. 9). Why? Because faith saw certainty in the promise of God (Hebrews 11:10).

Abraham's continuing testimony of faith in purity of his witness is twofold - land and people (Hebrews 11:11-12). Did Abraham quit believing God for the son he was promised?

Abraham waned but never quit.

Abraham was ninety-nine years old and Sarah was ninety years old when Isaac was born. Jacob would be Isaac's son sixty years later. By faith, the land of promise was Abraham's possession (Hebrews 11:9), although he never possessed it except by faith.

DISCUSSION QUESTIONS

1. Explain the phrase "faith is a decision that grasps intangible realities."

2. In what practical ways does a real faith reveal itself within the historical context of belief in the imminent (any moment) return of Christ?

3. Discuss and detail the perimeters of Abel's continuing testimony of faith.

4. Discuss and detail the perimeters of Enoch's continuing testimony of faith.

5. Discuss and detail the perimeters of Noah's continuing testimony of faith.

6. Discuss and detail the perimeters of Abraham's continuing testimony of faith.

7. Discuss and detail the perimeters of your continuing testimony of faith.

Chapter Twelve
Looking for the Manifestation of God in All the Wrong Places

As stated previously, real faith is always tested and proven faith. If our declaration of belief never moves in the *direction of its expectation*, our faith is in *vain* (it is empty). **Therefore, "vain" faith is empty of two necessities.**

1. Intimate and detailed knowledge of the Word of God
2. The failure to move in the direction of our expectations of God

However, sometimes our expectations of God are distorted due to our misunderstanding of doctrine. Because we fail to see dispensational transitions and God's purposes in certain aspects of what He does, we tend to expect that the operations of God within time/space/matter will always be the same. This is just not so. God's operations change. We have already seen this from I Corinthians chapter 12.

"[1] Now concerning spiritual *gifts*, brethren, I would not have you ignorant. [2] Ye know that ye were Gentiles, carried away unto these dumb idols *{by deception through pseudo and demonic spiritual manifestations}*, even as ye were led. [3] Wherefore I give you to understand *{so this demonic deception can no longer be accomplished}*, that no man speaking by the Spirit of God calleth Jesus accursed: and *that* no man can say that Jesus is the Lord, but by the Holy Ghost. [4] Now there are diversities *{differences or varieties}* of gifts, but the same Spirit. [5] And there are differences *{varieties}* of administrations, but the same Lord. [6] And there are diversities *{differences or varieties}* of operations *{energema, workings}*, but it is the same God which worketh all in all. [7] But the manifestation *{phanerosis, the means of exhibition}* of the Spirit is given to every man to profit withal" (I Corinthians 12:1-7).

What does this all mean regarding the believer's expectation of the manifestations of God's power through his life? This means *possibility is not equal to probability.* In other words, although God answered the prayer of Elijah causing it not to rain "on the earth by the space of three years and six months" (James 5:17), that was not a *common* answer to prayer. Although such a manifestation is a *possible* manifestation of God's power through our lives, and we can pray with confidence that God is able to do that again at any time, that *possibility is not necessarily a probability.* If we pray for such a manifestation (for whatever purpose it might be God's will to do such a thing), we should then begin to move in the direction of our expectation (begin storing up water).

What God *can do* is not necessarily what God *will do.*

"[18] Now in the morning as he returned into the city, he hungered. [19] And when he saw a fig tree in the way, he came to it, and found nothing thereon, but leaves only, and said unto it, Let no fruit grow on thee henceforward for ever. And presently the fig tree withered away. [20] And when the disciples saw *it*, they marvelled, saying, How soon is the fig tree withered away! [21] Jesus answered and said unto them, Verily I say unto you, If ye have faith, and doubt not, ye shall not only do this *which is done* to the fig tree, but also if ye shall say unto this mountain, Be thou removed, and be thou cast into the sea; it shall be done. [22] And all things, whatsoever ye shall ask in prayer, believing, ye shall receive" (Matthew 21:18-22).

As we can obviously see from this text, full faith *opens a door* for the potential for some amazing possibilities in the manifestation of the operations of God through our lives. We know that the Apostles experienced miraculous workings of God through their lives. God healed physical sicknesses, physical blindness, restored wholeness to those crippled, and cast out demons through the faith of the Apostles.

"[1] Now Peter and John went up together into the temple at the hour of prayer, *being* the ninth *hour*. [2] And a certain man lame from his mother's womb was carried, whom they laid daily at the gate of the temple which is called Beautiful, to ask alms of them that entered into the temple; [3] Who seeing Peter and John about to go into the temple asked an alms. [4] And Peter, fastening his eyes upon him with John, said, Look on us. [5] And he gave heed unto them, expecting to receive something of them. [6] Then Peter said, Silver and gold have I none; but such as I have give I thee: In the name of Jesus Christ of Nazareth rise up and walk. [7] And he took him by the right hand, and lifted *him* up: and immediately his feet and ankle bones received strength. [8] And he leaping up stood, and walked, and entered with them into the temple, walking, and leaping, and praising God. [9] And all the people saw him walking and praising God: [10] And they knew that it was he which sat for alms at the Beautiful gate of the temple: and they were filled with wonder and amazement at that which had happened unto him. [11] And as the lame man which was healed held Peter and John, all the people ran together unto them in the porch that is called Solomon's, greatly wondering" (Acts 3:1-11).

We could look at numerous texts of similar miracles in the book of the Acts of the Apostles. In most part, these kinds of miracles through the Apostles were "signs" to the Jews that the Apostles were men of God, blessed of God, and that they spoke with the authority of God. The intent of these "sign gifts" was to show the Jews that the Apostles were the *new* prophets of God and the words that they spoke were the Words of God.

It is important to understand that these miracles were temporary *signs*. After this transitional period of time, and the completion of the transcription of the new revelation that came through the Apostles was complete, the need for these kinds of *sign* miracles was finished. After that, believers were to "walk by faith, not by sight" (II Corinthians 5:7, or *signs*).

"[38] Then certain of the scribes and of the Pharisees answered, saying, Master, we would see a sign {*a supernatural proof or wonder*} from thee. [39] But he answered and said unto them, An evil and adulterous generation seeketh after a sign; and there shall no sign be given to it, but the sign of the prophet Jonas: [40] For as Jonas was three days and three nights in the whale's belly; so shall the Son of man be three days and three nights in the heart of the earth. [41] The men of Nineveh shall rise in judgment with this generation, and shall condemn it: because they repented at the preaching of Jonas; and, behold, a greater than Jonas *is* here. [42] The queen of the south {*I Kings 10:1; Sheba, II Chronicles 9:1*} shall rise up in the judgment with this generation, and shall condemn it: for she came from the uttermost parts of the earth to hear the wisdom of Solomon; and, behold, a greater than Solomon *is* here. [43] When the unclean spirit is gone out of a man, he walketh through dry places, seeking rest, and findeth none. [44] Then he saith, I will return into my house from whence I came out; and when he is come, he findeth *it* empty, swept, and garnished. [45] Then goeth he, and taketh with himself seven other spirits more wicked than himself, and they enter in and dwell there: and the last *state* of that man is worse than the first. Even so shall it be also unto this wicked generation {*that seeks a sign instead of believing the Word*}" (Matthew 12:38-45).

Therefore, we should understand that these statements of Christ to His disciples regarding *mountain moving faith* are not intended to be the kind of manifestations with which Christians should be preoccupied. These *sign gifts* are no longer God's way of manifesting His miraculous moving through the lives of believers.

> As amazing as it might be to see someone command a mountain to move and to see it actually moving, that is not the way God wants sinners to accept His existence and believe in who He is. That is not faith. That is empiricism (sense experience).

God cannot be experienced or known through the natural senses (sight, touch, smell, hearing, taste; II Corinthians 2:9-14). Supernatural (or unexplainable) events, happening within the natural realm of existence, reveal nothing about the supernatural except its possibility.

God has revealed Himself through the inspiration of the Holy Scriptures and we are supposed to accept Him as He reveals Himself in the details of His inspired Words. Miraculous events are not the answer to unbelief. Faith in the revelation of the Word of God is the answer to unbelief. Faith is a decision and a choice to believe and act upon what God's Word says. The Word of God leads us to faith in the God of the Word.

"[19] There was a certain rich man, which was clothed in purple and fine linen, and fared sumptuously every day: [20] And there was a certain beggar named Lazarus, which was laid at his gate, full of sores, [21] And desiring to be fed with the crumbs which fell from the rich man's table: moreover the dogs came and licked his sores. [22] And it came to pass, that the beggar died, and was carried by the angels into Abraham's bosom: the rich man also died, and was buried; [23] And in hell he lift up his eyes, being in torments, and seeth Abraham afar off, and Lazarus in his bosom. [24] And he cried and said, Father Abraham, have mercy on me, and send Lazarus, that he may dip the tip of his finger in water, and cool my tongue; for I am tormented in this flame. [25] But Abraham said, Son, remember that thou in thy lifetime receivedst thy good things, and likewise Lazarus evil things: but now he is comforted, and thou art tormented. [26] And beside all this, between us and you there is a great gulf fixed: so that they which would pass from hence to you cannot;

neither can they pass to us, that *would come* from thence. [27] Then he said, I pray thee therefore, father, that thou wouldest send him to my father's house: [28] For I have five brethren; that he may testify unto them, lest they also come into this place of torment. [29] Abraham saith unto him, <u>They have Moses and the prophets; let them hear them.</u> [30] And he said, Nay, father Abraham: but if one went unto them from the dead, they will repent. [31] And he said unto him, <u>If they hear not Moses and the prophets, neither will they be persuaded, though one rose from the dead</u>" (Luke 16:19-31).

Luke 16:19-31 is not a parable. This is a Scriptural testimony from God of an actual historical account that took place in the invisible, spiritual realm of existence. Notice that God expects people to be "persuaded" to believe by the witness of the Word of God and act according to the instructions of the Word of God to be saved. God expects people to be "persuaded" by His Word to believe and live the truths of His Word.

How many miracles would you need to witness in order to confirm a belief in the God of the Bible?

Simply because something happens that you cannot explain, does that confirm that there is a *God* that caused it? Even if you somehow come to believe in some miracle producing *God*, does the miracle define Him beyond the perimeters of the miracle? Can you know God's will in any way through some unexplainable miracle? Can your witnessing of something fantastic or unexplainable miracle define what sin before God is? Can you somehow know what that miraculous God requires in order for you to be saved from His wrath because you witness Him doing something fantastic? How do you know that the *signs and wonders* you have witnessed were not produced by the great Deceiver and how do you know that you are not being led astray by false doctrine? In fact, we are told in Scripture that the Antichrist will use "signs and wonders" to deceive millions during the Tribulation.

"[21] For then shall be great tribulation, such as was not since the beginning of the world to this time, no, nor ever shall be. [22] And except those days {*the Tribulation*} should be shortened, there should no flesh be saved: but for the elect's sake {*natural Israel*} those days shall be shortened. [23] Then if any man shall say unto you, Lo, here *is* Christ, or there; believe *it* not. [24] For there shall arise false Christs, and false prophets, and <u>shall shew great signs and wonders</u>; insomuch that, if *it were* possible, <u>they shall deceive</u> the very elect" (Matthew 24:21-24).

"[7] For the mystery of iniquity doth already work: only he who now letteth *will let*, until he be taken out of the way. [8] And then shall that Wicked be revealed, whom the Lord shall consume with the spirit of his mouth, and shall destroy with the brightness of his coming: [9] *Even him*, whose coming is after the working of Satan <u>with all power and signs and lying wonders</u>, [10] And with all deceivableness of unrighteousness in them that perish; <u>because they received not the love of the truth, that they might be saved</u>. [11] And for this cause God shall send them strong delusion, that they should believe a lie: [12] That they <u>all might be damned who believed not the truth</u>, but had pleasure in unrighteousness" (II Thessalonians 2:7-12).

We must be careful that we do not confuse knowing the Word of God with actually believing the Word of God. ". . . [F]aith *cometh* by hearing, and hearing by the word of God" (Romans 10:17). Simply because we *hear* the Word of God, or even *understand* and *know* the Word of God, does not mean that we *believe* the Word of God. Neither does mere legalistic obedience of the Word of God bring with it spiritual/supernatural empowerment.

> Faith has no power in itself to produce supernatural empowerment. God produces supernatural empowerment.

Therefore, supernatural empowerment is produced through the believer's life when that believer is brought into *spiritual unity* with God through illumination of God's Word. Then the believer must be *Spirit-filled* through repentance and confession of all that the Word of God calls sin, whereby that cleansed believer is brought into "fellowship" (synergism) with God. Once the believer is cleansed, he can yield his body to the indwelling Spirit of God and be supernaturally enabled to serve God in the power of the Spirit.

When God's Word is understood by the illumination of the Holy Spirit, and then lived through the believer's life through yielding to the Holy Spirit and enabling by the Holy Spirit, that believer's life will be a manifestation of the Spirit. This happens as the believer begins to move in the direction of the expectation of his faith. Unless all three aspects of this *tripartite of faith* exist, the believer's life will not be a manifestation of the Spirit in producing *fruit* to the glory of God.

DISCUSSION QUESTIONS

1. Vain" faith is empty of what two necessities?

2. Read I Corinthians 12:1-7. Explain what is meant by the statement, "God's operations change."

3. Discuss the significance of the statement, "What God *can do* is not necessarily what God *will do*."

4. Discuss the danger of Empiricism (*sight faith*) as a priority source of *true* faith.

5. Read Luke 16:19-31 and discuss the theological importance of the statement in verse 31 to the priority source of *true* and *pure* faith.

6. Discuss the relationship of *pure* and *true* faith to the manifestation of the power of God through the life of a Spirit-filled believer.

7. Discuss the relationship between *knowing* truth and *living* truth to the manifestation of the power of God through the life of a Spirit-filled believer.

Chapter Thirteen
The Defilement of Doubt and Double Mindedness
to Spiritual Empowerment

"[18] Now in the morning as he returned into the city, he hungered. [19] And when he saw a fig tree in the way, he came to it, and found nothing thereon, but leaves only, and said unto it, Let no fruit grow on thee henceforward for ever. And presently the fig tree withered away. [20] And when the disciples saw *it*, they marvelled, saying, How soon is the fig tree withered away! [21] Jesus answered and said unto them, Verily I say unto you, <u>If ye have faith, and doubt not</u>, ye shall not only do this *which is done* to the fig tree, but also if ye shall say unto this mountain, Be thou removed, and be thou cast into the sea; it shall be done. [22] And all things, whatsoever ye shall ask in prayer, believing, ye shall receive" (Matthew 21:18-22).

The Emerging Church is an evolving pseudo-Christianity that is more *New Age* and *Hindu* than it is *Christian*. The philosophy that drives the Emerging Church is the attempt to make *Christianity/religion* attractive by incorporating dominant and accepted cultural mores into the worship and culture of the Church. For these heretics, Christianity should not look nor feel radically different than the culture in which the Church exists. In other words, the *Seeker* should be able to feel as comfortable in a *church* assembly as he does at a rock festival, a ball game, or at a county fair. In fact, many of the practices from these events are incorporated into the Emerging Church in order to make the *church* assembly *relevant* to the culture and people to which it seeks to *minister* (meaning *merchandise*). Worshippers are viewed as *customers* and catering to their carnality is requisite to *attracting* them and *holding* them long enough to indoctrinate them in this doctrinally watered-down, pseudo-Christianity. This is a form of *seduction*, not evangelism.

In the Emergent Church philosophy, dogmatic doctrines are *minimalized* and *marginalized* in order to *maximize* numbers (attendance and offerings).

In fact, the Emerging Church goes beyond *minimalizing* and *marginalizing* dogmatic, definitive doctrine. The Emerging Church *glorifies* doubt, as opposed to substantiating absolutes through doctrinal dogmatisms in the in-depth study of God's Word. What happens in the dynamic of discussion among those involved in the Emerging Church is the constant distorting, blending, and merging of a wide diversity of religious beliefs. This is nothing more than the satanic obfuscation of biblical Truth. It is a perversion and a *smoke screen* of diversion. The person who does not have a thorough, detailed, intimate knowledge of God's Word will be deceived and captured by this philosophy. It is a subtle, slimy, and slippery form of deception that is becoming Satan's methodology in leading the vast majority of the evangelical church into deception and apostasy. It also leads to the perversion of the gospel of Jesus Christ. The Emerging Church is the Laodicean Church of Revelation 3:14-22. An example of this is the teaching of the heretic Tony Campolo. He says:

> "When it comes to what is ultimately important, the Muslim community's sense of commitment to the poor is exactly in tune with where Jesus is in the 25th chapter of Matthew. That is the description of judgment day. And if that is the description of judgment day what can I say to <u>an Islamic brother</u> who has fed the hungry, and clothed the naked? You say, 'But he hasn't a personal relationship with Christ.' I would argue with that. And I would say from a Christian perspective, in as much as you did it to the least of these you did it unto Christ. You did have a personal relationship with Christ, you just didn't know it. And Jesus himself says: 'On that day there will be many people who will say, when did we have this wonderful relationship with you, we don't even know who you are . . .' 'Well, you didn't know it was me, but when you did it to the least of these it was doing it to me'"[4] *Underlining added*

The tool of Satan in his obfuscation of doctrine is his ancient practice of *questioning* and *distorting* God's Word. The purpose of Satan's questioning and distorting God's Word is to simply cast doubt on our *understanding* of what God has said. It is not to completely deny that God has said what He has said.

---

[4] "On Evangelicals and Interfaith Cooperation," Crosscurrents, Spring 2005, http://findarticles.com/p/articles/mi_m2096/is_1_55/ai_n13798048

"[1] Now the serpent was more subtil than any beast of the field which the LORD God had made. And he said unto the woman, Yea, <u>hath God said</u> {*questioning what God said*}, Ye shall not eat of every tree of the garden? [2] And the woman said unto the serpent, We may eat of the fruit of the trees of the garden: [3] But of the fruit of the tree which *is* in the midst of the garden, God hath said, Ye shall not eat of it, neither shall ye touch it, lest ye die. [4] And the serpent said unto the woman, <u>Ye shall not surely die</u> {*a distortion; she would die spiritually immediately, but she would not die physically immediately*}: [5] For God doth know that in the day ye eat thereof, then your eyes shall be opened, and ye shall be as gods, knowing good and evil {*accusing God of selfish motives*}" (Genesis 3:1-5).

The reason this satanic tactic can be so successful in our lives is because God has created us with the ability to *rationalize* and *reason*. These abilities are intended to help us make the everyday decisions of life. However, truth about God and His will is to be understood and obeyed. It is not to be questioned and rationalized into obscurity and doubt through human reason. When we rationalize, we tend to render our understanding of truth in favor of our desires or in favor of a more permissive allowance regarding God's commandment. The result of giving *rationalism/reason* a place of prominence regarding truth is that the outcome often leads to *doubt* rather than dogmatism. Real (true or full) faith is built from the dogmatic understanding of Scripture, not doubt.

> Real faith always moves in the direction of the extreme when it comes to any doubt of God's will. Shallow faith always moves in the direction of permissiveness when it comes to any doubt of God's will.

Satan counts on this latter aspect of the spiritual dynamic of *reason* and *rationalism* when it comes to truth that is not understood. When truth is understood to the point of dogmatism, there is no question regarding God's will in a matter. Wisdom comes from the thorough, complete understanding of God's will whereby the human will is brought into perfect unity with God's will. Although temptation will still exist due to the sinner's fallen nature, full, mature faith will consistently choose unity with God's will by always siding with the extreme over anything questionable that might lead to permissiveness. True, mature faith will always avoid anything that might be considered questionable regarding God's will.

It is God's intent that all believers be perfected (completely equipped) through the thorough explanation and understanding of the details of God's Word (Ephesians 4:12): "Till we all come in the unity {oneness} of the {one; see 4:5} faith, and of the knowledge of the Son of God, unto a perfect man, unto the measure of the stature of the fulness of Christ" (Ephesians 4:13).

"2 My brethren, count it all joy when ye fall into divers temptations {putting to proof; i.e., testings}; 3 Knowing this, that the trying {testing as to genuineness} of your faith worketh patience {enduring under or continuance}. 4 But let patience {enduring under or continuance} have her perfect {maturing} work, that ye may be perfect {brought to full maturity} and entire {complete in every way}, wanting {lacking} nothing. 5 If any of you lack {same Greek word as "wanting"} wisdom {life experience; discernment in decision making}, let him ask of God, that giveth to all men liberally, and upbraideth not; and it shall be given him. 6 But let him ask in faith, nothing {not even the smallest} wavering {without hesitation or doubt}. For he that wavereth {hesitates about God's will or doubts what God's will is} is like a wave of the sea driven with the wind and tossed {easily led astray}. 7 For let not that man think that he shall receive any thing of the Lord. 8 A double minded {dipsuchos, a two willed man who vacillates between two opinions} man is unstable {lacking consistency or constancy} in all his ways {roadways; i.e., walk or practices}" (James 1:2-8).

Double mindedness is a complete contradiction of full faith. A *double minded* person is a person that is unsure of God's will about a matter. Single mindedness is a person that simply pursues knowing God's will in a matter. Single mindedness is intent upon doing that will regardless of the outcome of that action as it relates to the opinions or actions of others toward us personally. Double mindedness can also result from a shallowness of faith in God. Double mindedness is unwilling to trust one's destiny in any situation to God by a willingness to obey God's revealed will regardless of the possible consequences to us personally.

Double mindedness is the person who thinks in two directions at the same time - the *temporal* and the *eternal*. When a person has perfect (matured) faith, that person has trained his mind to think only in the direction of God's will. The person with matured faith asks only one question in any matter - what is God's will? That person than seeks to discover that single mindedness from the revelation of God's Word.

Double minded people seek to please both men and God.

The very notion of such vacillation is an abomination to God. Single mindedness thinks only in the direction of being approved by God and about pleasing God.

"Study {*make every effort*} to shew {*to stand as an exhibition*} thyself approved {*tried, proven, & accepted*} unto God, a workman {*laborer or doer of Truth*} that needeth not to be ashamed {*disgraced before God, angels, and other believers*}, rightly dividing {*cutting a straight line to walk on or follow, turning neither to the left or right through compromise*} the word of truth" (II Timothy 2:15).

This was Peter's problem at Galatia (Galatians 2:11-21). Peter was compromising the Gospel by tolerating false teaching to keep peace. Paul referred to that compromise as seeking "to please men" (Galatians 1:10). There were Jews who had made a profession of faith in Christ as Messiah, but who were mixing the necessity of "works" (the Moralism and Ritualism of the Law) with the gospel, thereby perverting the gospel and leading people into misplaced faith. To "seek to please men" immediately disqualified such as person as a "servant of Christ" (Galatians 1:10).

"[6] I marvel that ye are so soon removed from him that called you into the grace of Christ unto another gospel: [7] Which is not another; but there be some that trouble you, and would pervert the gospel of Christ. [8] But though we, or an angel from heaven, preach any other gospel unto you than that which we have preached unto you, let him be accursed. [9] As we said before, so say I now again, If any *man* preach any other gospel unto you than that ye have received, let him be accursed. [10] For do I now persuade men, or God? or do I seek to please men? for if I yet pleased men, I should not be the servant of Christ" (Galatians 1:6-10).

This kind of double mindedness that Paul refers to, as he deals with the outcome of Peter's and Barnabas's hypocrisy, defiles us before God for spiritual empowerment. When we are willing to even consider compromising truth to please men, we are already defiled before God. This kind of thinking is treacherous and traitorous to the cause of Christ and it bears negative eternal consequences.

Paul exemplified this *single mindedness* when it came to preaching and teaching truth. His pattern and model for us was to always think and speak in one direction - PLEASING GOD. This was the model of ministry he established for all believers to follow.

"[1] For yourselves, brethren, know our entrance in *{coming}* unto you, that it was not in vain *{empty of purpose or results}*: [2] But even after that we had suffered before, and were shamefully entreated *{violently abused}*, as ye know, at Philippi, we were bold *{frank in utterance, or confident in spirit and demeanor}* in our God to speak unto you the gospel of God with much contention *{agon, opposing conflict}*. [3] For our exhortation *{to call near; i.e., invitation by invocation of truth}* was not of deceit, nor of uncleanness, nor in guile: [4] But as we were allowed of God to be put in trust with the gospel, even so *{because of that entrusting by Christ}* we speak; not as pleasing men, but God, which trieth *{to test with the intent of approving}* our hearts *{objectives and motives}*. [5] For neither at any time used we flattering *{feel good}* words, as ye know, nor a cloke *{disguise}* of covetousness *{fraudulent greediness}*; God *is* witness: [6] Nor of men sought we glory *{praise or fame}*, neither of you, nor yet of others, when we might have been burdensome *{to hold down or back because of weight; weighed you down instead of building you up}*, as the apostles of Christ" (I Thessalonians 2:1-6).

DISCUSSION QUESTIONS

1. Discuss defining reasons why the Emergent Church is an evolving pseudo-Christianity.

2. Discuss the issues of *minimalizing* and *marginalizing* dogmatic, definitive doctrine to replace dogmatism in the Emergent Church by *glorifying* doubt.

3. Discuss the statement quoted from the heretic Tony Campolo.

4. Expand upon the statement, "The tool of Satan in his obfuscation of doctrine is his ancient practice of *questioning* and *distorting* God's Word."

5. Apply the statement, "Real faith always moves in the direction of the extreme when it comes to any doubt of God's will. Apply the statement, "Shallow faith always moves in the direction of permissiveness when it comes to any doubt of God's will," to give yourself a proper understanding of Romans chapter 14.

6. Discuss and define "double-mindedness" as an anomaly of true faith.

7. Discuss and define "single-mindedness" as the pattern of true faith.

Chapter Fourteen

Lite Christians or Light Christians?

We live in the age of *body worship* (actually the worship of *sexuality*) where the idea of a *good food* is one that has all the nutrients we need to sustain us physically but has very few calories. This is the age of *lite* everything. The first thing people look for on the packaging, or in the advertising of anything, is the word *lite*. In fact, the word *lite* is a recent invention. *Lite* means *having less substance or weight or fewer calories than something else.* It is an alteration of the word *light*. I think the word *lite* accurately describes the vast majority of *Post Modern Christianity* and aptly summarizes the *lukewarm* professing *Christian* of the Laodicean Church in Revelation 3:14-22. How does Christ describe these *lite Christians*? Notice Christ's criticism of them has to do with the superficiality of their *substance* as professing Christians. This is a pseudo-Christianity that promotes *image* over substance. Christ hates it!

"[15] I know thy works, that thou art neither cold nor hot: I would thou wert cold or hot. [16] So then because thou art lukewarm, and neither cold nor hot, I will spue thee out of my mouth. [17] Because thou <u>sayest</u>, I am rich, and increased with goods, and have need of nothing; and <u>knowest not</u> that thou art wretched, and miserable, and poor, and blind, and naked; [18] I counsel thee to buy of me gold tried in the fire, that thou mayest be rich; and white raiment, that thou mayest be clothed, and *that* the shame of thy nakedness do not appear; and anoint thine eyes with eyesalve, that thou mayest see" (Revelation 3:15-18).

God is holy! That means God is completely separate from sin of any kind. God is separate from attitude sins, emotional sins (out of control anger, vengeance desires, etc.), and acts of sins (anything contrary to His revealed will through His Word). However, that does not mean God has separated Himself from the presence of sin. It means sin is in no way part of who God is and that sin in no way corrupts Him.

God's holiness necessitates that He cannot *fill* and empower believers who do not live in "fellowship" (Synergism) with Him.

> God's children must be cleansed, forgiven, and practically sanctified before God can bless their service and bring forth fruit through their lives.

In order for this cleansing, forgiveness, and practical sanctification to be accomplished in the life of a believer, the believer must be brought to recognition, conviction, and repentance of any sin in his life. He must then come to God seeking forgiveness and cleansing in order to be filled with the Spirit of God. He can then be spiritually empowered for spiritual service (the "work of the ministry"). Satan is doing all he can within the realm of his dominion ("the prince of the power of the air" and the "god of this world") to keep believers "worldly" (carnally minded) and defiled before God.

"[5] This then is the message which we have heard of him, and declare unto you, that God is light, and in him is no darkness at all. [6] If we say that we have fellowship with him, and walk in darkness, we lie, and do not the truth: [7] But if we walk in the light, as he is in the light, we have fellowship one with another, and the blood of Jesus Christ his Son cleanseth us from all sin. [8] If we say that we have no sin, we deceive ourselves, and the truth is not in us. [9] If we confess our sins, he is faithful and just to forgive us *our* sins, and to cleanse us from all unrighteousness. [10] If we say that we have not sinned, we make him a liar, and his word is not in us" (I John 1:5-10).

This *formula* for "fellowship" (revival) seems simple enough. *All* we need to do is understand the extreme holiness of God, that He hates sin, that there is absolutely "no darkness at all" in Him *and that there can be "no darkness at all" in us.* In other words, we must "walk {*live*} in the light, as He is in the light." Secondly, Christ said, "without me ye can do nothing" (John 15:5b). This *paradox of possibilities* would be very discouraging to us if I John 1:5-10 did not continue into I John chapter two. The great truth is that this "walking in the light" must be done in *partnership* with the indwelling Holy Spirit. In fact, this is the ONLY way a sinner will be able to "walk in the light, as He is in the light." This *paradox of possibilities* is actually an *impossibility* in our own power and is a supernatural work that requires the supernatural enabling of God, the Creator.

Before we look at the first eleven verses of I John chapter two, let's look at the last two verses. These two verses provide us with the motivation for the constant pursuit of spiritual revival in our own lives and in our local church. The normal focus (actually an *abnormal focus*) is the production of "fruit" or the desire to see the local church *grow* in size.

Local church growth is merely the normal outcome of revival. Local church growth should be desired by every true Christian, but growth is not the primary reason why we should constantly seek to be revived. Every true Christian should be working at *body building* (Church growth), but having a *large* body does not mean we have a *healthy* body. There is a big difference between a large, healthy, muscular body and a fat body. A *healthy body* is a local church filled with people who are filled with the Spirit and walking in the depth (doctrinal substance) of their understanding of the Word of God. The modern *church growth* movement is content with having a *large body* (fat and really useless to God).

> "[28] And now, little children, abide in him; that, when he shall appear, we may have confidence, and not be ashamed before him at his coming. [29] If ye know that he is righteous, ye know that every one that doeth righteousness is born of him" (I John 2:28-29).

There are consequences for living outside of "fellowship" with God (*abiding* "in him"). The word "abide" (*meno*) in I John 2:28 means there is an expectancy of faithfulness in the life of the believer. This expectancy of faith is to be prioritized with staying in a given place or relationship, or continuing and enduring in a struggle. The struggle or *battle* of the Christian's life is the struggle for a real, vibrant, living faith through which the Spirit of God can bless, produce eternal spiritual fruit, and grow the local church. The critical truth regarding this command to "abide in Him" is that these consequences (good or bad outcomes) are *eternal* in their scope, influence, and results - not merely *temporal*.

Notice that this relates to the time we stand "before him at his coming." This is the Judgment Seat of Christ. Here the believer's "works" (or ministry) will be judged according to our faithfulness with the "gifts" of the Spirit of God during the time of the *dispensation of grace* to all believers. We are all stewards of this grace and we will all be held accountable for the minute details of our faithfulness in the stewardship of this *dispensation of grace.*

Notice also the possibility and potential for being "ashamed before Him." Remember II Timothy 2:15, "Study to shew thyself approved unto God, a workman that needeth not to be ashamed, rightly dividing the word of truth." What Paul says in II Timothy 2:15 is very close in its intent to what John says in I John 2:28, "And now, little children, abide in him; that, when he shall appear, we may have confidence, and not be ashamed before him at his coming."

The admonition in both these two texts is that we *should* be able to stand before Christ in the judgment of our works and be bold and outspoken as our life's work is brought into evaluation and judgment. Perhaps the idea is that we will have to defend before Jesus Christ what we did with our lives. We will have to defend how we invested ourselves in the cause of Christ as His Ambassadors of Reconciliation. Perhaps we will have to defend ourselves for all our self-deception regarding our own faithfulness in being "doers of the Word, and not hearers only" (James 1:22).

The fact that we can possibly present our life's work before Jesus and "not be ashamed" certainly expresses the possibility and potential for the opposite - being ashamed.

> We will be required to answer in defense of our decisions for every wasted, ruined, fruitless moment that is not lived in "fellowship" with God (revival).

Simply put, God expects believers, "born again" of the Spirit of God, to seek to live each and every moment of our lives in the empowering of the indwelling Spirit of God.

This *filling of the Spirit* is a *resource* for which we will be held accountable according to the microseconds of our existence on earth as believers. We will not be allowed to give mere *lip service* to our faithfulness within this *resource* of God's "unspeakable gift" (II Corinthians 9:14-15) and the "unsearchable riches of His grace" (Ephesians 3:8) to us in our regeneration (see Ephesians chapter three). There is an overwhelming *investment* by God both in our redemption and in our practical sanctification. God is going to hold us accountable for this *investment* at the Judgment Seat of Christ. With that in mind, let's read I John 2:1-11.

"¹ My little children, these things write I unto you, that ye sin not. And if any man sin, we have an advocate {*parakletos, intercessor or one who stands between in defense*} with the Father, Jesus Christ the righteous {*as our representative High Priest Who is innocent of any wrong doing*}: ² And he is the propitiation for our sins {*Jesus has satisfied God's wrath on our sins substitutionally and provided the complete remission of the penalty upon ALL our sins*}: and not for ours only, but also for *the sins of* the whole world. ³ And hereby {*by this reality*} we do know {*resulting in assurance; I John 3:19*} that we know him {*are "born again" of the Spirit*}, if we keep his commandments. ⁴ He that saith, I know him, and keepeth not his commandments, is a liar {*falsifier; i.e. has a false testimony or witness*}, and the truth {*Jesus is the Personification of Truth; John 14:6*} is not in him {*therefore, Jesus is not in him*}. ⁵ But whoso keepeth his word, in him verily is the love of God perfected {*finished or brought to full maturity*}: hereby {*our self-sacrifice coming to full maturity in its expression of God's indwelling*} know we that we are in him. ⁶ He that saith he abideth {I John 2:28} in him ought himself also so to walk {*as the outcome of Him "in us" and us "in Him"*}, <u>even as he walked</u>" (I John 2:1-6).

Now, let's pause here for a moment and look at this phrase "even as He walked." The word "as" here does not mean that we must accomplish this reality *in order* to be saved or even *in order* to be blessed of God. The word "as" establishes the God ordained pattern, or model, for how we will live our lives when we are revived by the filling of the Spirit and walk in empowerment. It is by this pattern/model of Christ's actual life that we can measure our spiritual maturity and our spiritual growth. The idea is that if living (walking in "the light") is really the priority of our lives, we can be assured of our having been "born again." Then, in I John 2:7-11, God *raises the bar* of expectation.

"⁷ Brethren, I write <u>no</u> new {*kahee-nos', new in kind, not neos; new in time*} commandment unto you, but an old {*ancient*} commandment which ye had from the beginning. The old commandment {*since Cain killed his brother Abel*} is the word which ye have heard from the beginning {*John 13:34; "love one another <u>as I have loved you</u>"*}. ⁸ Again, a new commandment {*old in teaching, but new and greatly increased in its expectations*} I write unto you, which thing {*this new living definition of this new* *kind of extreme self-sacrificing love}* is true *{actualized or fully exposed or revealed}* in him *{Jesus}* <u>and</u> in you: because the darkness is past *{present tense, middle voice, indicative mood, i.e., is passing; refers to the fallen state of the original creation; see I John 2:17}* and the true light now *{already}* shineth *{the morning Sun of the dawn of the regeneration is on the horizon}*. [9] He that saith he is in the light *{part of the new genesis "in Christ"}*, and hateth his brother, is in darkness *{the fallen state of the original creation}* even until now. [10] He that loveth his brother abideth in the light *{as part of the new genesis "in Christ"}*, and there is none occasion of stumbling in him. [11] But he that hateth his brother is in darkness *{the fallen state of the original creation}*, and walketh in darkness, and knoweth not whither he goeth, because that darkness hath blinded his eyes" (I John 2:7-11).

God is not content with a mere *desire* for unity with Him. Neither is He content with the mere *declaration* of communion and love among believers. God expects us to move in the direction of His expectations as well. God expects *actual* unity with Him.

> God expects *actual* unity in doctrine, purpose, and ministry among believers within a local church. Before God can truly bless a local church with true, deep spiritual growth, each member of that local church must be *actualizing* the tripartite of faith.

In other words, God is not content with the revival of individuals within a local church. God wants and expects all members of a local church to be fervently and diligently pursuing spiritual empowerment through practical sanctification. To think that we might be part of the "light" (the dawning New Genesis "in Christ") when we have hate for a brother or sister "in Christ" manifests the Cain/Abel relationship of the fall (I John 2:11). It always amazes me how easily believers can justify their dislike or distaste for another believer in a local church without even giving consideration to the defilement of spiritual empowerment that such an attitude creates.

Satan is in the business of *delusion* and *illusion*. He is the Deceiver. That is not the business of the Church. Our ministries need to be holy, particular, peculiar, and distinct from anything that even has the *smell* of worldliness. Any degree of worldliness is parcel and portioned in the "darkness" and corruption of the curse. Worldliness may merely begin with an attitude of compromise, or a momentary covetous look in the direction of desire/lust for the world's enticement, but it always ends leaving you in the "darkness" of spiritual corruption and out of the realm of God's blessings.

DISCUSSION QUESTIONS

1. According to Revelation 3:15-18, what are some characteristics of a *lite Christian*?

2. Explain what God means in His Word when He says He is *holy*.

3. Explain what is involved in God's commandment to believers to be "holy as He is holy."

4. Explain and elaborate on the statement, "Local church growth is merely the normal outcome of revival."

5. Discuss what is necessary for any believer to be able to stand before the Judgment Seat of Christ and not be ashamed before Him for the way we lived our lives.

6. Discuss the *filling* of the Spirit of God as a *resource provision* of grace for which we will be held accountable?

7. Read I John 2:1-6 and explain the phrase in verse six, "He that saith he abideth in him ought himself also so to walk, <u>even as he walked.</u>"

Chapter Fifteen
The Dangers of the Subtlety of
Satanic Deception to Empowerment

God continues to be immanent in the midst of sin although He is transcendent regarding its impact upon Him. For instance, Satan still has access to God's presence as the "accuser of the brethren."

"[1] Now the serpent was more subtil than any beast of the field which the LORD God had made. And he said unto the woman, Yea, hath God said, Ye shall not eat of every tree of the garden? [2] And the woman said unto the serpent, We may eat of the fruit of the trees of the garden: [3] But of the fruit of the tree which *is* in the midst of the garden, God hath said, Ye shall not eat of it, neither shall ye touch it, lest ye die. [4] And the serpent said unto the woman, Ye shall not surely die: [5] For God doth know that in the day ye eat thereof, then your eyes shall be opened, and ye shall be as gods, knowing good and evil" (Genesis 3:1-5).

We have all read of the biblical account of the deception of Eve and Adam's willful sin on many occasions. I would often to ask myself how they could have been led astray so easily. I did so until I took a hard look at my own self-righteousness and came away with contempt for my own hypocrisy.

If you are like me (and I know you are), when I look back on my many failures before God and my own unfaithfulness to God, I am amazed at how easily Satan is able to trick me, deceive me, and how quickly I have rationalized myself into sin. I believe that the only reason I do not live in sinfulness constantly is the grace of God in my life that keeps me from temptation. Without constant yielding to God's indwelling presence, I immediately begin to lean in the direction of sin. Therefore, yielding is about learning to control the direction in which I lean (and let's be clear, our natural tendency is to lean in the direction of sin). "But every man is tempted, when he is drawn away of his own lust, and enticed" (James 1:14). Let's admit it. The "lust" (desire) for sin is in us. We *naturally* lean in that direction. We *want* what Satan offers.

Satan uses many tactics to defile believers before God. He does this to hinder the spiritual empowerment of believers by the indwelling Holy Spirit in order to render them useless for the "work of the ministry."

Satan seldom comes at mature believers with a frontal attack. His attacks are subtle.

Satan is a *trickster*, but not a *funny/joker* kind of *trickster*. Satan is a treacherous kind of *trickster*. His trickery is treachery. His intent is always destructive intent upon death to spiritual life and fellowship with God. His deceptions are intent upon seducing believers with any kind of worldliness that might defile them for God's empowerment.

"[10] Finally, my brethren, be strong in the Lord, and in the power of his might. [11] Put on the whole armour of God, that ye may be able to stand against the wiles {*methods of trickery*} of the devil. [12] For we wrestle not against flesh and blood, but against principalities, against powers, against the rulers of the darkness of this world, against spiritual wickedness in high *places*" (Ephesians 6:10-12).

The word "subtil" in Genesis 3:1 is from the Hebrew `aruwm (aw-room'). It means *cunning* and is usually used in the sense of a negative character trait. It carries the idea of being crafty in a deceptive sort of way. Deception is a central characteristic of Satan and the people who are used by him. In fact, a synonym for Satan is the Deceiver. He is a con artist, a manipulator of circumstances and thinking, and a perpetrator of shams. He is the *god* of the *sleight of hand*, the use of shadows disguised as light, and the use of half-truths disguised as whole truth. He is able to talk around issues while constantly providing new nuances of questionings and doubt. Enter into dialogue with one of his emissaries and you often come away confused and belittled, shamefully realizing you may just have betrayed all that you say you believe and hold dear. This subtle deception begins with the *giving of an ear* or an *innocent lean in the wrong direction*.

On the other hand, God's Word is intended to instruct us in wisdom so that the believer can avoid Satan's subtle deceptions and seduction into sin. The Greek word *planos* (plan'-os) can be translated either *deceiver* or *seducer*. We find *planos* translated "seducing" in I Timothy 4:1 and "deceiver" in II John 1:7. As we read these two texts, notice that *planos* is not used to speak of Satan directly, but indirectly. The word is used of false teachers who deceive others because they have been deceived themselves. Human deceivers merely become the vehicles of deception who voice the same heresies to others by which they themselves were deceived. In doing so, they become the *ambassadors of deception* intent upon perverting and corrupting true believers who are ambassadors of reconciliation.

"[1] Now the Spirit speaketh expressly, that in the latter times some shall depart from the faith, giving heed to seducing {*planos*} spirits, and doctrines of devils; [2] Speaking lies in hypocrisy; having their conscience seared with a hot iron; [3] Forbidding to marry, *and commanding* to abstain from meats, which God hath created to be received with thanksgiving of them which believe and know the truth. [4] For every creature of God *is* good, and nothing to be refused, if it be received with thanksgiving: [5] For it is sanctified by the word of God and prayer" (I Timothy 4:1-5).

> Why will the last days before the catching away of the Bride be characterized as a time of great departure "from the faith"?

I Timothy 4:1 says this will happen because many people with give "heed to seducing spirits, and doctrines of devils." In other words, people who SHOULD know better will give an ear to false philosophies that will lead them astray "from the faith" through false theology. This can only happen to those who are doctrinally *weak*. Doctrinal weakness almost always results in a lack of wisdom regarding spiritual discernment in making spiritual decisions. Apathy towards learning and knowing the Word of God (doctrine; i.e., "the faith") will result in the atrophy of spiritual strength. "The faith" (correct doctrine) is one of God's central weapons against Satan's "fiery darts" of deception.

"Above all, taking the shield of faith, wherewith ye shall be able to quench all the fiery darts of the wicked" (Ephesians 6:16).

How does faith (belief in right doctrine or orthodoxy) become a "shield" that extinguishes "fiery darts"? In ancient times, two armies would arrange themselves about a half mile apart. As they prepared to charge one another in battle, two lone flaming arrows, one from each side, would stream through the air and stick in the ground. This arrow was a *distance maker*. When the opposing army reached where that arrow landed, a rainbow of thousands of arrows would arch through the sky. Each warrior carried a wooden shield covered in a thin layer of brass/bronze that he would raise over his shoulders like an umbrella against the rain of arrows that had been oil-soaked. If the opponent's shield was held at a slight angle to the falling arrows, the arrows would glance off, stick harmlessly in the earth, and be quickly extinguished. This is what right doctrine is intended to provide for us. Failure to learn right doctrine is a foolish, irresponsible, dereliction of duty as a "good soldier of Jesus Christ" (II Timothy 2:3b).

We must never forget that faith is not merely the willingness to believe in something or *someone* we cannot see.

Faith is the acceptance of the revelation of God and His promises that come to us through the inspired Words of God.

"[16] But they have not all obeyed the gospel. For Esaias saith, Lord, who hath believed our report? [17] So then faith *cometh* by hearing, and hearing by the word of God" (Romans 10:16-17).

The Word of God tells us that a tactic of Satan is to take away the Word of God from the hearing of those who need its confirming and *faith increasing* truths. He does this in local churches where the *meat* of doctrine is never taught and where it could never be expected that people would be willing to invest the time necessary to learn and assimilate *meat*. Pastors tend to condescend to the wishes of the people in this area instead of taking *oversight* and being the leaders they need to be. In doing so, they actually become a subtle partner with Satan who uses doctrinal ignorance as a weapon of destruction.

"[9] And his disciples asked him, saying, What might this parable be? [10] And he said, Unto you it is given to know the mysteries of the kingdom of God: but to others in parables; that seeing they might not see, and hearing they might not understand. [11] Now the parable is this: The seed is the word of God. [12] Those by the way side are they that hear; then cometh the devil, and <u>taketh away the word out of their hearts,</u> lest they should believe and be saved" (Luke 8:9-13).

This is what is happening in the *market driven* churches where doctrine is both minimalized and marginalized. This kind of *ministry* (used in a very deceptive way) is about *gathering a crowd* by creating a carnival atmosphere of carnal excitement and pseudo-spirituality. There is one predominant characteristic in this philosophy; Satan has "taketh away the word out of their hearts."

The minimalizing of doctrine is the central characteristic of many false teachers who actually deny the teaching of the Word of God regarding the Person and Work of Jesus Christ. The Word of God refers to these false teachers as "antichrists" in II John 1:7. John's intent, by the inspiration of God, is to provide a serious warning regarding pertinent characteristics of false teachers who profess to be *Christians*.

"[7] For many deceivers {*planos*} are entered into the world, who confess not that Jesus Christ is come in the flesh. This is a deceiver {*planos*} and an antichrist. [8] Look {*take heed*} to yourselves, that we lose not those things which we have wrought {*earned rewards*}, but that we receive a full reward. [9] Whosoever transgresseth {*violates a command*}, and abideth {*continues to dwell or to stand firm*} not in the doctrine of {*not about, but of*} Christ {*i.e., Christ's teaching is not evolving or more than what God's inspired Word gives us*}, hath not God. He that abideth {*dwells or stands firm*} in the doctrine of Christ, he hath both the Father and the Son. [10] If there come any unto you, and bring not this doctrine, receive him not into *your* house, neither bid him God speed: [11] For he that biddeth him God speed is partaker of his evil deeds" (II John 1:7-11).

A critical point regarding the subtlety of satanic deception is that once a believer has been deceived, he then becomes a partner in deception when he begins to teach or live according to that deception.

According to II John 1:7, this individual now becomes one of the many *antichrists* in partnership with the ultimate Antichrist - Satan. This is a serious issue for someone who professes to be a "born again" child of God. The point of the text (especially verse nine) is that such a person is not manifesting the life of a "born again" believer. The high probability is that such a person "hath not God."

Sinful indulgences are a contradiction against the model that Christ puts before us. Although we will fall into sin often and fail regularly, true believers will *begin again*. God is the God of *new beginnings*. True believers will not deface the model that Christ puts before us by compromising His doctrine, or minimizing His expectations of us as His disciples. True believers will "press towards the mark" until the day they are called to glory. It should be noted that those compromising His doctrine, or minimizing His expectations, has taken the *mark* of the Deceiver according to II John 1:7-11.

"[8] Yea doubtless, and I count all things *but* loss for the excellency of the knowledge of Christ Jesus my Lord: for whom I have suffered the loss of all things, and do count them *but* dung, that I may win Christ, [9] And be found in him, not having mine own righteousness, which is of the law, but that which is through the faith of Christ, the righteousness which is of God by faith: [10] That I may know him, and the power of his resurrection, and the fellowship of his sufferings, being made conformable unto his death; [11] If by any means I might attain unto the resurrection of the dead. [12] Not as though I had already attained, either were already perfect: but I follow after, if that I may apprehend that for which also I am apprehended of Christ Jesus. [13] Brethren, I count not myself to have apprehended: but *this one thing I do*, forgetting those things which are behind, and reaching forth unto those things which are before, [14] I press toward the mark for the prize of the high calling of God in Christ Jesus" (Philippians 3:8-14).

Spiritual infants remain as such because they have believed Satan's subtle deception whispered into their ears. They believe they have *arrived*. They believe they know everything they need to know and now it is their mission in life to pull everyone else up to the level they have achieved. Satan's subtle deception is that these people have just made themselves the *model of Christianity* instead of Christ. The reality is that instead of pulling everyone else up to a higher level, they will end up doing just the opposite. They will one day fail and destroy the faith of many. When you think you have *arrived*, you are stuck and will stop growing.

There is a tedious process involved in true spiritual growth. The process involves many unpleasant realities of the Christian life. The process involves personal rejection by friends and family members. The process involves public and private persecutions. The process involves endless failures coupled with occasional and momentary successes. God and the world will bring before us hundreds of very complex decisions that will need to be made every day. The more mature we become, the more complex those decisions will become. The process of spiritual growth involves hundreds of hours of Bible study, prayer, work in personal evangelism, and the discipleship of individuals. There will be blessings and chastisement, and we will need to praise God for both those streams of love into our lives. Deep spiritual growth is painful and expensive!

DISCUSSION QUESTIONS

1. Why do you think Satan can so easily lead us astray and deceive us?

2. Once you are saved from Hell, why does Satan still want to deceive you and lead you astray and why is it important that you understand both his devices and purpose?

3. From your understanding of the word "subtil" in Genesis 3:1, explain the phrase, "Satan is the *god* of the *sleight of hand.*"

4. Discuss the practical application of the militancy of *spiritual warfare* in Ephesians 6:10-12 in light of your understanding of the fact that Satan is a deceiver and seducer.

5. According to I Timothy 4:1, why will the last days before the catching away of the Bride be characterized as a time of great departure "from the faith"?

6. How does faith (belief in right doctrine or orthodoxy) become a "shield" that extinguishes "fiery darts"?

7. Read Luke 8:9-13 and discuss some of the ways Satan uses deceived people to take away the Word out of the hearts of people.

Chapter Sixteen
Satan as the Tempter

Once a person is saved and "born again" of the Spirit of God, that person will see increased attacks by Satan and his emissaries who are intent upon keeping that believer from being spiritually empowered by the indwelling Holy Spirit of God. If Satan and his emissaries can get the believer to defile himself (Satan cannot defile us or anyone else) before God, that person is rendered useless as a vessel of God's grace and as a *distribution center* of His supernatural workings. Satan will attempt to get a believer to defile himself before God through the means of his world system and through various avenues of temptation that his world system provides.

The Word of God uses the Greek word *kosmos* to distinguish Satan's vast network of sinful influence and temptation.

> The word "world," when used in Scripture, "refers to the 'order,' 'arrangement,' under which Satan has organized the world of unbelieving mankind upon his cosmic principle of force, greed, selfishness, ambition, and pleasure." [5]

The word "worldly" is never used in a good or moral sense. Within that *kosmos*, there are three basic avenues through which Satan tempts people.

"[15] Love not the world, neither the things *that are* in the world. If any man love the world, the love of the Father is not in him. [16] For all that *is* in the world, <u>the lust of the flesh</u>, and <u>the lust of the eyes</u>, and <u>the pride of life</u>, is not of the Father, but is of the world. [17] And the world passeth away, and the lust thereof: but he that doeth the will of God abideth for ever" (I John 2:15-17).

---

[5] Scofield Reference Bible notes on Revelation 13:8

The lust of the flesh involves temptation in the areas of our appetites (taste, pleasure/fun, drink, sexuality, etc.). The lust of the eyes involves covetousness desires. The pride of life involves the desire for fame/self-glory, power, dominance, and riches. These were the three areas in which Christ was tempted. If Satan had been successful in any temptation of Christ, Jesus would have defiled Himself before God and would have rendered His death at Calvary worthless for the substitutionary propitiation of God.

"For he hath made him *to be* sin for us, who knew no sin; that we might be made the righteousness of God in him" (II Corinthians 5:21).

Jesus' success in overcoming temptation is absolutely critical to the doctrine of salvation. If He sinned in the least way, He was defiled before God and all that He did on the Cross was in vain.

Jesus' life sets the new standard by which God determines His blessing of empowerment upon the believer's life today. The believer must be cleansed of unrighteousness, free from sin, and yielded to the indwelling Spirit of God.

"[1] Then was Jesus led up of the Spirit into the wilderness to be tempted of the devil. [2] And when he had fasted forty days and forty nights, he was afterward an hungred. [3] And when the tempter came to him, he said, If thou be the Son of God, command that these stones be made bread. [4] But he answered and said, It is written, Man shall not live by bread alone, but by every word that proceedeth out of the mouth of God. [5] Then the devil taketh him up into the holy city, and setteth him on a pinnacle of the temple, [6] And saith unto him, If thou be the Son of God, cast thyself down: for it is written, He shall give his angels charge concerning thee: and in *their* hands they shall bear thee up, lest at any time thou dash thy foot against a stone. [7] Jesus said unto him, It is written again, Thou shalt not tempt the Lord thy God. [8] Again, the devil taketh him up into an exceeding high mountain, and sheweth him all the kingdoms of the world, and the glory of them; [9] And saith unto him, All these things will I give thee, if thou wilt fall down and worship me. [10] Then saith Jesus unto him, Get thee hence, Satan: for it is written, Thou shalt worship the Lord thy God, and him only shalt thou serve. [11] Then the devil leaveth him, and, behold, angels came and ministered unto him" (Matthew 4:1-11).

If we know (and understand) the avenues of temptation for sin to enter our lives, why is it that we do not guard against attack at these avenues? The problem lies in the fact that all three of these arenas for temptation are also necessities for our existence. God has given us appetites to alert us to when we are hungry and need nourishment, when we are thirsty and need fluids, and sexual attraction for one another to encourage procreation. God has given us eyes to see the things He has provided to fulfill all of these desires of the flesh. The desire for acceptance, recognition, or praise when we do good things (glory) are a part of our being created in God's image. None of these desires are sinful in themselves. They become sinful when we yield to temptation to fulfill them in ways God forbids. It is the desire for these forbidden temptations that turn these normal desires into sinful "lust," and then the "lust" alone defiles us before God.

We tend to take our sin so lightly and make forgiveness such a cheapened resource because it is so easy to ask for forgiveness and so easy to receive forgiveness. This attitude needs to be radically changed. God has some strong language for believers who love the *world*. Since all believers, as the Church, are the Bride of Christ, worldliness is viewed as *equal* to sexual unfaithfulness to the Bridegroom. Worldliness is spiritual adultery. God even views "friendship {*a fondness*} of the world" as aggressive, hostel, hatefulness against Him. Even *flirting* with the world is sin.

> "[4] Ye adulterers and adulteresses, know ye not that the friendship {*fondness*} of the world is enmity with God? whosoever therefore will be a friend (*associate*} of the world is {*lit. makes himself*} the enemy of God. [5] Do ye think that the scripture saith in vain, The spirit that dwelleth in us lusteth to envy? [6] But he giveth more grace. Wherefore he saith, God resisteth the proud, but giveth grace unto the humble. [7] Submit yourselves therefore to God. Resist the devil, and he will flee from you. [8] Draw nigh to God, and he will draw nigh to you. Cleanse *your* hands, *ye* sinners; and purify *your* hearts, *ye* double minded. [9] Be afflicted, and mourn, and weep: let your laughter be turned to mourning, and *your* joy to heaviness. [10] Humble yourselves in the sight of the Lord, and he shall lift you up" (James 4:4-10).

When a person genuinely repents of sin and worldliness, that act is accompanied with a number of *actions* and *attitudes* that are detailed in James 4:7-10. These *actions* and *attitudes* manifest a complete change in mind and heart regarding the issues of sin and the innate *lusts* of our "spirit" (vs. 5; "spirit that dwelleth in us"). God's solution to this innate *lust* is that "he giveth more grace."

However, the giving of this supernatural, *overcoming grace* is conditioned on certain actions and attitudes regarding sin and our innate *lusts*. Without the reality of these actions and attitudes there will be no habitual victory over temptations.

1. The believer must "humble" himself before God.

2. The believer must "submit" himself "to God."

3. The believer must "resist" (stand against or oppose) the temptations of "the devil" in the power of the supernatural enabling (grace) given by God. This enabling is given to the "humble" and submissive (yielded) believer. This resistance is to be expressed first by the believer in his own life. At the same time and equally, the believer is to resist the sin that corrupts society. This is the person who has relegated his life to be the servant of God by the dedication to living for God and to doing the "work of the ministry."

4. The believer must "draw nigh to God." The idea is to be cautious against *drifting*. Staying near God in the intimacy of a devotional relationship requires constant and continual effort.

5. The believer must "cleanse" his "hands" (from the contaminations of the filth with which we come in contact) and "purify" his heart (from the desires and corrupt emotions of carnality).

6. The believer must "be afflicted, and mourn, and weep" (James 4:9) about sin and for souls.

7. The believer must insure that his "laughter be turned to mourning, and his "joy to heaviness." There needs to be seriousness, gravity, and somberness about the way a Christian views the world, mankind's lost state, and his purpose in it all. The Christian life is not about skipping through life from social events, to recreational events, or involvement in endless pursuit of entertainment.

> I regularly hear Christians pray and ask that God would reveal Himself to them. That is a prayer of unbelief.

God has already revealed Himself to us. We have sixty-six books of inspired Scripture giving us detailed revelation of God. How much more revelation do we need? We need to be praying God will reveal Himself THROUGH us. For this to happen, we need to read His Word, believe His Word, and live His Word in the supernatural empowerment of the indwelling Spirit of God. Read it! Believe it! Live it!

Above we read: "[15] Love not the world, neither the things *that are* in the world. If any man love the world, the love of the Father is not in him. [16] For all that *is* in the world, the lust of the flesh, and the lust of the eyes, and the pride of life, is not of the Father, but is of the world. [17] And the world passeth away, and the lust thereof: but he that doeth the will of God abideth for ever" (I John 2:15-17). Here we saw the three main avenues of temptation for sin into our lives.

We also saw in James 4:4: "Ye adulterers and adulteresses, know ye not that the friendship of the world is enmity with God? whosoever therefore will be a friend of the world is the enemy of God." Here we see that even a *fondness* for Satan's *cosmic influence* will bring you into the realm of God's opposition against your life. The reason a mere *fondness* for Satan's *cosmic influence* brings us into the realm of God's opposition (the opposite of *blessings*) is because, in that *fondness* for the world, we actually become an *associate of Satan* in his opposition against the work and purpose of God. That reality ought to give us a radical perspective against any *shadow* of *worldliness*. It ought to amaze and disgust Christians about just how much *mileage* Satan is able to get out of God's Spirit indwelled *vehicles of grace*. As James 4:4 tells us, when we allow this, or are seduced into being an associate of Satan, we involve ourselves in *spiritual adultery*. We become unfaithful to our promised Bridegroom.

"[12] All things {*that are not immoral such as foods, participation in Feast Days, etc.*} are lawful unto me, but all things are not expedient: all things are lawful for me, but I will not be brought under the power of any. [13] Meats for the belly, and the belly for meats: but God shall destroy both it and them. Now the body *is* not for fornication, but for the Lord; and the Lord for the body. [14] And God hath both raised up the Lord, and will also raise up us by his own power. [15] Know ye not that your bodies are the members of Christ? shall I then take the members of Christ, and make *them* the members of an harlot? God forbid. [16] What? know ye not that he which is joined to an harlot is one body? for two, saith he, shall be one flesh. [17] But he that is joined unto the Lord is one spirit. [18] Flee fornication. Every sin that a man doeth is without the body; but he that committeth fornication sinneth against his own body. [19] What?

know ye not that your body is the temple of the Holy Ghost *which is in you*, which ye have of God, and ye are not your own? [20] For ye are bought with a price: therefore glorify God in your body, and in your spirit, which are God's" (I Corinthians 6:12-20).

> As the "god of this world" and the "prince of the power of the air," Satan is also the *god of doubt*.

What that means is that he is the creator of doubt. Since he is invisible, he creates doubt by whispering questions into our ears. This is the subtlety he used with Eve: "Hath God said?" These questions may not always come directly from Satan. In fact, they seldom come directly from him. These questions, intent upon breeding doubt, usually come to us through someone who has already been deceived. They think they are manifesting great intelligence and depth of spirituality by asking questions to which someone might not know the answer. Their purpose in asking the question is not to find an answer. Their purpose is Satan's deception through the avenue of the "pride of life."

To avoid being used of Satan to create doubt in someone's life, never ask a question for which you do not know a Bible answer. Never ask a question you are not desirous to have answered, and for which you are willing to receive a Bible answer. In other words, do not ask questions with a desire to merely cause doubt about someone's beliefs unless you are willing to provide a solid answer to your own question from the Word of God.

Part of Satan's *cosmic influence* in temptation (the "world") is a network of false teachers and deceived sinners (many who have been "born again") who are being used by Satan to entice people into various levels of sinful, destructive, and addictive practices. These temptations come at people from every possible level of our existence within a society. The more corrupt a society becomes, the more corrupting that society will be in its influences. This is especially true in the *shadows* and *secret places* of a person's life where no one else might know about it. That is, no one else know about secret sins except God. God frequently warns believers to avoid the enticements found in the *secret places* of concealment. These *secret places* of concealment are where Satan is the most effective in temptations. In Psalm 10:1-11, "the wicked" are those deceived and used by Satan as tools of corruption. The "wicked" become an intricate part of Satan's network of deception, defilement, and corruption.

"¹ Why standest thou afar off, O LORD? *why* hidest thou *thyself* in times of trouble? ² The wicked in *his* pride doth persecute the poor: let them be taken in the devices that they have imagined. ³ For the wicked boasteth of his heart's desire, and blesseth the covetous, *whom* the LORD abhorreth. ⁴ The wicked, through the pride of his countenance, will not seek *after God*: God *is* not in all his thoughts. ⁵ His ways are always grievous; thy judgments *are* far above out of his sight: *as for* all his enemies, he puffeth at them. ⁶ He hath said in his heart, I shall not be moved: for *I shall* never *be* in adversity. ⁷ His mouth is full of cursing and deceit and fraud: under his tongue *is* mischief and vanity. ⁸ He sitteth in the lurking places of the villages: in the secret places doth he murder the innocent: his eyes are privily set against the poor. ⁹ He lieth in wait secretly as a lion in his den: he lieth in wait to catch the poor: he doth catch the poor, when he draweth him into his net. ¹⁰ He croucheth, *and* humbleth himself, that the poor may fall by his strong ones. ¹¹ He hath said in his heart, God hath forgotten: he hideth his face; he will never see *it*" (Psalm 10:1-11).

Many professing Christian women are often used of Satan in his network of deception, defilement, and corruption that the Word of God refers to as "the world." Our society is satanically corrupted. Women are taught from early childhood (*Barbie Doll Syndrome*) to dress seductively in order to be sensually attractive to men (*sexy*). Although they may not realize it (most do), by appealing to the sensuality of men, they are inviting men to lust after them and have joined in association with the *wicked* described in Psalm 10:1-11.

Let me interject here that I believe women can be *feminine* and *attractive* without purposefully trying to be sexy and attract the lust of men. In fact, mothers should teach their daughters how to dress *femininely* without trying to be *sexy*. This training (both by word and modeling) should be a major aspect of a mother's parenting of her daughters. The defining issue in this is when a woman purposely emphasizes various parts of her anatomy to attract the lust of men (*sexual attraction*). The Word of God refers to this as "the attire of an harlot" and to the woman who does this as being "subtil of heart" (in other words, *seductive* and *deceptive*). **God warns men about this type of woman.**

"[1] My son, **keep my words**, and lay up my commandments with thee. [2] Keep my commandments, and live; and my law as the apple of thine eye. [3] Bind them upon thy fingers, write them upon the table of thine heart. [4] Say unto wisdom, Thou *art* my sister; and call understanding *thy* kinswoman: [5] That **they may keep thee from** the strange woman, from the stranger *which* flattereth with her words. [6] For at the window of my house I looked through my casement, [7] And beheld among the simple ones, I discerned among the youths, a young man void of understanding, [8] Passing through the street near her corner; and he went the way to her house, [9] In the twilight, in the evening, in the black and dark night: [10] And, behold, there met him a woman *with* the attire of an harlot, and subtil of heart. [11] (She *is* loud and stubborn; her feet abide not in her house: [12] Now *is she* without, now in the streets, and lieth in wait at every corner.) [13] So she caught him, and kissed him, *and* with an impudent face said unto him, [14] *I have* peace offerings with me; this day have I payed my vows. [15] Therefore came I forth to meet thee, diligently to seek thy face, and I have found thee. [16] I have decked my bed with coverings of tapestry, with carved *works*, with fine linen of Egypt. [17] I have perfumed my bed with myrrh, aloes, and cinnamon. [18] Come, let us take our fill of love until the morning: let us solace ourselves with loves. [19] For the goodman *is* not at home, he is gone a long journey: [20] He hath taken a bag of money with him, *and* will come home at the day appointed. [21] With her much fair speech she caused him to yield, with the flattering of her lips she forced him. [22] He goeth after her straightway, as an ox goeth to the slaughter, or as a fool to the correction of the stocks; [23] Till a dart strike through his liver; as a bird hasteth to the snare, and knoweth not that it *is* for his life" (Proverbs 7:1-23).

> The Christian should become a *radical* when it comes to insuring that he/she does not become part of Satan's *network of temptations.*

Yet, sadly, many Christian women wear "the attire of an harlot" and are involved in the very worldly tactics of *sexual enticement* and *seduction.* We recently had a Miss USA contestant who paraded around in front of millions of people in her underwear (they call it a *bikini* these days) and was lauded and praised for her *Christian convictions* against homosexual marriages. I applaud her for her convictions in one area, but rebuke her for her lack of them in the other. We call that *hypocrisy.* She condemns one kind of sin while being an associate of Satan's network of seduction in another area of sin (the "lust of the eyes").

"As an ox goeth to the slaughter," men are lured and seduced into spiritual corruption by women being *sexy*. That is the modern term for the *seductress*. Men and women are naturally attracted to one another. However, when either gender emphasizes their sexuality to attract, they have joined with Satan's "world" of temptation and defilement. They have become *worldly*.

As the Tempter, Satan tempts people into immorality. However, Satan's subtle deception is that he has convinced people that sin does not occur if the person does not actually commit an act of immorality. If he can accomplish this subtle deception, you will accept the false notion that lust (wanting the immorality with which we are tempted) is not sin. When we accept that false idea, we will still be defiled by the lust. However, we will not be aware of our defilement and loss of empowerment. We will also fail to repent, confess, seek forgiveness, and be cleansed and restored to fellowship with God.

If we really want the empowerment of God in our lives, we will not be content with confessing the obvious sins in our lives. We will BECOME aware of the subtle sins in our lives by which we have allowed ourselves to be deceived. If we are really serious about our relationship with God, we will look to the Word of God for the exposure of our deception.

"[7] The law of the LORD *is* perfect, converting the soul: the testimony of the LORD *is* sure, making wise the simple. [8] The statutes of the LORD *are* right, rejoicing the heart: the commandment of the LORD *is* pure, enlightening the eyes. [9] The fear of the LORD *is* clean, enduring for ever: the judgments of the LORD *are* true *and* righteous altogether. [10] More to be desired *are they* than gold, yea, than much fine gold: sweeter also than honey and the honeycomb. [11] Moreover by them is thy servant warned: *and* in keeping of them *there is* great reward. [12] Who can understand *his* errors? cleanse thou me from secret {*hidden or concealed*} *faults*" (Psalm 19:7-12).

DISCUSSION QUESTIONS

1. Why would Satan and his emissaries want to defile believers before God?

2. Read I John 2:15-17 and give a detail explanation of what God means in His use of the word "world" (*kosmos*).

3. List and discuss the three main avenues of sin in our lives.

4. If we know (and understand) the avenues of temptation for sin to enter our lives, why is it so difficult to against attack at these avenues?

5. Read James 4:4-10 and discuss what defines spiritual adultery with the world.

6. List and discuss the seven actions and attitudes that accompany genuine repentance of sin and of worldliness that are detailed in James 4:7-10.

7. Explain the meaning of the statement, "Satan is also the *god of doubt.*"

Chapter Seventeen
The Danger of Turning Aside

Next to the doctrine of salvation and the doctrine of grace, perhaps one of the most misunderstood doctrines in the Bible is the doctrine of the Law. Because of this misunderstanding, there is also a misunderstanding of the doctrine of Grace. The Law is not merely misunderstood in its purpose today, but it has been misunderstood for millennia. Satan deceived the Jewish Levitical priesthood about God's purpose in giving the Law and the priesthood and false prophets propagated this satanic deception for centuries. A great deal of deception continues today regarding the purpose of the Law.

"[32] Ye shall observe to do therefore as the LORD your God hath commanded you: ye shall not turn aside to the right hand or to the left. [33] Ye shall walk in all the ways which the LORD your God hath commanded you, that ye may live, and *that it may be* well with you, and *that* ye may prolong *your* days in the land which ye shall possess" (Deuteronomy 5:32-33).

"[26] Behold, I set before you this day a blessing and a curse; [27] A blessing, if ye obey the commandments of the LORD your God, which I command you this day: [28] And a curse, if ye will not obey the commandments of the LORD your God, but turn aside out of the way which I command you this day, to go after other gods, which ye have not known. [29] And it shall come to pass, when the LORD thy God hath brought thee in unto the land whither thou goest to possess it, that thou shalt put the blessing upon mount Gerizim, and the curse upon mount Ebal. [30] *Are* they not on the other side Jordan, by the way where the sun goeth down, in the land of the Canaanites, which dwell in the champaign over against Gilgal, beside the plains of Moreh? [31] For ye shall pass over Jordan to go in to possess the land which the LORD your God giveth you, and ye shall possess it, and dwell therein. [32] And ye shall observe to do all the statutes and judgments which I set before you this day" (Deuteronomy 11:26-32).

"Turn not aside." These are simple words giving a simple warning from God. Yet, the warning involves very severe consequences if it is not heeded. The "turn not aside" warning is connected to the "blessing and a curse" promise of God upon national Israel regarding their faithfulness to enforce the conditions of the Mosaic Covenant (the Law) nationally upon the residents of the nation of Israel.

The "blessing and a curse," along with the warning to "turn not aside," refers to the *jot and tittles* of the "statutes and judgments" defined in detail in the Law. To "keep" these "statutes and judgments" meant to preserve the Truths by teaching them and by enforcing the penalties ("judgments") upon those disobeying a "statute" (an individual Law).

The intent in all of this was to manifest to the children of Israel the importance of *justice* in the plan and program of God. Sin (disobedience) *must* bear a penalty and that penalty *must* be adjudicated justly. Although God does show mercy through grace, the penalty ("judgment") for sin MUST be paid.

Christians have a tendency to minimize God's attitude regarding sin and justice. We have a tendency to categorize sins by the degrees they hurt or affect us and those we love. Although the "judgments" of God bore varying degrees of penalties upon those that broke certain "statutes," we must remember that anything short of death is a measure of the grace and mercy of a holy God upon any sin. Adam merely chose to make one decision based upon false information, based upon self-interests. That choice brought a death sentence upon the whole of God's original creation "under heaven," upon himself, and upon all of humanity born seminally as Adam's descendants (Romans 5:12). This gives us the context of God's warning to "turn not aside."

Secondly, Christians have a tendency to give themselves some *leeway* or *liberty* when it comes to the command to "turn not aside." There is no *leeway* or *liberty* given in this warning. ANY deviation away from God's command is a *turning away* from that command. Because Israel took the same kind of liberties with God's "statutes," God needed to explain and reiterate the "turn not aside" warning over and over again throughout Israel's history by the faithful prophets. For a king of Israel to govern his people according to the "statutes and judgments" of God, and to insure that he turned "not aside" from them, he was required to handwrite his own personal copy of the Word of God.

"[14] When thou art come unto the land which the LORD thy God giveth thee, and shalt possess it, and shalt dwell therein, and shalt say, I will set a king over me, like as all the nations that *are* about me; [15] Thou shalt in any wise set *him* king over thee, whom the LORD thy God shall choose: *one* from among thy brethren shalt thou set king over thee: thou mayest not set a stranger over thee, which *is* not thy brother. . . [18] And it shall be, when he sitteth upon the throne of his kingdom, that he shall write him a copy of this law in a book out of *that which is* before the priests the Levites: [19] And it shall be with him, and he shall read therein all the days of his life: that he may learn to fear the LORD his God, to keep all the words of this law and these statutes, to do them: [20] That his heart be not lifted up above his brethren, and <u>that he turn not aside from the commandment, *to* the right hand, or *to* the left</u>: to the end that he may prolong *his* days in his kingdom, he, and his children, in the midst of Israel" (Deuteronomy 17:14-15 and 18-20).

During the time of Israel's partial occupation of the land and just prior to Joshua's death, Joshua reiterates the "turn not aside" warning. He reminds them that all of God's blessings in bringing them into the land were part of His promise for their faithfulness in keeping the "statutes and judgments."

"[6] Be ye therefore very courageous to keep and to do all that is written in the book of the law of Moses, <u>that ye turn not aside therefrom *to* the right hand or *to* the left</u>; [7] That ye come not among these nations, these that remain among you; neither make mention of the name of their gods, nor cause to swear *by them*, neither serve them, nor bow yourselves unto them: [8] But cleave unto the LORD your God, as ye have done unto this day. [9] For the LORD hath driven out from before you great nations and strong: but *as for* you, no man hath been able to stand before you unto this day. [10] One man of you shall chase a thousand: for the LORD your God, he *it is* that fighteth for you, <u>as he hath promised you</u>" (Joshua 23:6-10).

It is important to understand that the "blessing and a curse" Mosaic Covenant was not about conditions for individual salvation. These were God's conditions for *blessing* upon an already redeemed people. Therefore, the "blessing and curse" are connected to the practical sanctification of Israel. We certainly cannot assume that God has made this promise to all nations. He has not. We must be careful that we do not misrepresent God's promises and apply them to other nations other than Israel.

However, the *pathway to fellowship* is frequently spoken of as a "way" in the Word of God. The idea is that you staying on a certain pathway will naturally lead you to the destination to which that pathway is connected.

> The believer who seeks the face of God cannot stray to the left or to the right from God's pathway for us. In other words, we cannot "turn aside" in any direction and stay on the pathway to God's present and eternal blessings.

"[7] Hear, O LORD, *when* I cry with my voice: have mercy also upon me, and answer me. [8] *When thou saidst*, Seek ye my face; my heart said unto thee, Thy face, LORD, will I seek. [9] Hide not thy face *far* from me; put not thy servant away in anger: thou hast been my help; leave me not, neither forsake me, O God of my salvation. [10] When my father and my mother forsake me, then the LORD will take me up. [11] Teach me thy way, O LORD, and lead me in a plain path, because of mine enemies" (Psalm 27:7-11).

This should be a major part of the substance of our prayer life as exemplified in Psalm 119. The Christian should be preoccupied with knowing and living God's Word. The word "blessed" establishes a condition.

"[1] Blessed *are* the undefiled in the way, who walk in the law of the LORD. [2] Blessed *are* they that keep his testimonies, *and that* seek him with the whole heart. [3] They also do no iniquity: they walk in his ways. [4] Thou hast commanded *us* to keep thy precepts diligently. [5] O that my ways were directed to keep thy statutes! [6] Then shall I not be ashamed, when I have respect unto all thy commandments. [7] I will praise thee with uprightness of heart, when I shall have learned thy righteous judgments. [8] I will keep thy statutes: O forsake me not utterly" (Psalm 119:1-8).

"[33] Teach me, O LORD, the way of thy statutes; and I shall keep it *unto* the end. [34] Give me understanding, and I shall keep thy law; yea, I shall observe it with *my* whole heart. [35] Make me to go in the path of thy commandments; for therein do I delight" (Psalm 119:33-35).

The sins with which parents allow themselves to be *scarred* will almost always be the sins that will *scar* their children, only more deeply and more severely. When parents misunderstand God's purpose of giving the Law, they will not take its warnings serious and they will become the vehicles of satanic deception and permissiveness into the lives of their children. They will be associates of Satan's corrupting influence (the "world") upon their own children and they will be the very tools Satan will use to *cut* and *scar* their children spiritually.

> However, we should remember that Cain and Abel were raised by the same parents.

Even when parents are faithful in living separated from the world and trying to limit the negative influence of their corporate ethic upon their children's lives, children are still free moral agents with their own corrupted wills. We know Eve had a propensity for rationalizing truth and allowing her own emotions to re-interpret what God said.

Rationalizing truth is an open door to corrupting truth and taking liberties with truth that are very spiritually dangerous. Yet, this is exactly what Cain did regarding the sacrifice he offered to God. The fact is that Cain brought to God a testimony of his own accomplishment rather than a declaration of dependency upon God's promised profession in the Promised Seed. When he took that liberty with the way of salvation and redemption, it was a declaration to God of his own rejection of God's way and an accusation of unfairness against God.

Abel did not offer the sacrifice of a lamb just because he had raised it. Abel offered a lamb because it was what God's Word dictated as the only way of approaching God and the only way to restored fellowship with God. Christ Jesus declared that His own death, burial, and resurrection/glorification were a fulfillment of the *way of the Lamb* promise to both salvation and to restored fellowship with God.

"[1] Let not your heart be troubled: ye believe in God, believe also in me. [2] In my Father's house are many mansions: if *it were* not *so*, I would have told you. I go to prepare a place for you. [3] And if I go and prepare a place for you, I will come again, and receive you unto myself; that where I am, *there* ye may be also. [4] And whither I go ye know, and the way ye know. [5] Thomas saith unto him, Lord, we know not whither thou goest; and how can we know the way? [6] Jesus saith unto him, I am the way, the truth, and the life: no man cometh unto the Father, but by me" (John 14:1-6).

DISCUSSION QUESTIONS

1. Discuss the many reasons why it is important to understand the doctrine of the Law.

2. Explain what you think God means by the statement, "ye shall not turn aside to the right hand or to the left" in Deuteronomy 5:32.

3. Explain the practical significance of understanding that the Mosaic Covenant, the Law, was "a blessing and a curse" covenant (Deuteronomy 11:26).

4. Discuss why it is so important to never minimize God's attitude regarding sin and justice.

5. Since the "turn not aside" warning was such an emphatic part of the Mosaic Covenant, why do you think Joshua had to reiterate that warning in Joshua 23:6-10?

6. Expand upon the statement, "the *pathway to fellowship* is frequently spoken of as a *way* in the Word of God" as it relates to the warning to "turn not aside."

7. Discuss why it is important to remember that Cain and Abel were raised by the same parents.

Chapter Eighteen
Cultivating Personal Devotion to Christ

"[1] If thou wilt return, O Israel, saith the LORD, return unto me: and if thou wilt put away thine abominations out of my sight, then shalt thou not remove. [2] And thou shalt swear, The LORD liveth, in truth, in judgment, and in righteousness; and the nations shall bless themselves in him, and in him shall they glory. [3] For thus saith the LORD to the men of Judah and Jerusalem, <u>Break up your fallow ground, and sow not among thorns.</u> [4] Circumcise yourselves to the LORD, and take away the foreskins of your heart, ye men of Judah and inhabitants of Jerusalem: lest my fury come forth like fire, and burn that none can quench *it*, because of the evil of your doings" (Jeremiah 4:1-4).

The nation of Israel had progressively become worldly and was almost completely paganized. The prophecies of Jeremiah (626-580 B.C.) began in the thirteenth year of the reign of king Josiah in 626 B.C. His early ministry was in conjunction with the prophecies of both Zephaniah (630-620 B.C.) and Habakkuk (627-586 B.C.). Jeremiah was called of God to preach to Israel regarding God's judgment of the pending captivity of Israel and the destruction of Jerusalem. He was sent to Israel with this proclamation and with the mission to call Israel to repentance of their worldliness and paganism and return to the worship of Jehovah in "spirit and in Truth." The transgressions of Israel are summed up in a few verses in Jeremiah chapter two:

"[4] Hear ye the word of the LORD, O house of Jacob, and all the families of the house of Israel: [5] Thus saith the LORD, What iniquity have your fathers found in me, that they are gone far from me, and have walked after vanity, and are become vain? [6] Neither said they, <u>Where *is* the LORD</u> *{they forgot Jehovah}* that brought us up out of the land of Egypt, that led us through the wilderness, through a land of deserts and of pits, through a land of drought, and of the shadow of death, through a land that no man passed through, and where no man dwelt? [7] And I brought you into a plentiful country, to eat the fruit thereof and the goodness thereof; but when ye entered, ye defiled my land, and made mine heritage *{Israel's* *children}* an abomination. [8] The priests said not, <u>Where *is* the LORD?</u> and they that handle the law knew me not: the pastors also transgressed against me, and the prophets prophesied by Baal, and walked after *things that* do not profit. [9] Wherefore *{because of this}* I will yet plead with you *{the people and children of Israel}*, saith the LORD, and with your children's children will I plead *{God's longsuffering mercy}*. [10] For pass over the isles of Chittim *{the heathens to the West}*, and see; and send unto Kedar *{the heathens to the East}*, and consider diligently, and see if there be such a thing. [11] Hath a nation changed *their* gods, which *are* yet no gods? but my people have changed their glory for *that which* doth not profit. [12] Be astonished, O ye heavens, at this, and be horribly afraid, be ye very desolate, saith the LORD. [13] For my people have committed two evils; they have forsaken me *{the One and Only True God}* the fountain of living waters *{ever renewing fresh supply}*, *and* hewed them out cisterns, broken cisterns (*pagan idols; earthen cisterns leak and soak up the water that is provided; they have no source of supply in themselves, therefore they TAKE, they do not GIVE}*, that can hold no water" (Jeremiah 2:4-13).

Jeremiah's ministry was to warn and call the children of Israel to "return," which is a plea for repentance (Jeremiah 4:1).

> The instruction of Jeremiah 4:3 regarding the command "break up your fallow ground," is a call to Israel to remember Jehovah and cultivate devotion to Him in prayer, service, and worship.

"Fallow ground" is ground that is tillable, but that has never been cultivated. "Fallow ground" is ground that is overgrown with weeds because of neglect. "Fallow ground" is the normal consequences of the corruption of the *curse* when God's people do not fulfill their responsibilities of cultivating and maintenance. In this text, it refers to a believer's personal relationship with the LORD. The maintenance of a believer's relationship with God is critical to the ongoing reality of that relationship. The Jews were to quote the *Shema* three times daily to be a constant testimony of their faith and a constant reminder of their relationship responsibilities before God. The *Shema* was the summary responsibility of the Mosaic Covenant (the Law).

"[4] Hear, O Israel: The LORD our God *is* one LORD: [5] And thou shalt love the LORD thy God with all thine heart, and with all thy soul, and with all thy might. [6] And these words, which I command thee this day, shall be in thine heart: [7] And thou shalt teach them diligently unto thy children, and shalt talk of them when thou sittest in thine house, and when thou walkest by the way, and when thou liest down, and when thou risest up. [8] And thou shalt bind them for a sign upon thine hand, and they shall be as frontlets between thine eyes. [9] And thou shalt write them upon the posts of thy house, and on thy gates" (Deuteronomy 6:4-9).

Pastors frequently try to convince God's children of the importance of setting aside some time each day for personal devotions. Having personal devotions involves a short time of reading Scripture, meditating on what God wants us to do, and spending some time with the Lord in prayer. Every true Christian realizes he should have daily personal devotions, yet it is something very few of us regularly do.

Why is that? We are busy people. We are too busy when we are too busy to spend time with the Lord. The word *devotion* comes from the word *devoted*. We have *devotion to* what we are *devoted*. To what we willing give our time, and for what we are willing to find time, reveals where our devotion is.

> The word *devoted* refers to a purpose, cause, or person to which someone is <u>wholly</u> given or dedicated.

We will have personal devotions when we are devoted to the Lord. The believer is commanded to love the Lord "with all thy heart, and with all thy soul, and with all thy strength, and with all thy mind; and thy neighbour as thyself" (Luke 10:27). This statement defines the word *devoted* from which daily personal devotions should result. **One reason most Christians do not have daily personal devotions is because we really do not love the Lord the way we should.**

To truly know the Lord is to love the Lord. A person cannot know Him and not love Him. There is a paradox in all of this. Most Christians do not love the Lord the way they should because they do not have the personal devotions involving them in learning about Him and knowing Him personally. Because they do not know Him personally, they do not have personal devotions.

What are the purposes of having personal devotions?

1. To develop and build a personal, intimate relationship with Jesus Christ

2. To understand that Jesus is <u>personally</u> our Lord

3. To understand that Jesus is <u>personally</u> our Saviour

Why is having personal devotions important?

"³ <u>Now ye are clean</u> {*purged or purified; i.e., practical sanctification*} <u>through the word</u> {*doing or obedience is presumed*} <u>which I have spoken unto you.</u> ⁴ Abide in me {*work to remain in this place of practical sanctification*}, and I in you {*the intimacy of the unity of the Spirit*}. As the branch cannot bear fruit of itself, except it abide in the vine; no more can ye, except ye abide in me. ⁵ I am the vine, ye *are* the branches: He that abideth in me, and I in him, the same bringeth forth much fruit: for without me ye can do nothing" (John 15:3-5).

1. Through personal devotions we are cleansed of unscriptural thinking through learning and applying the Word of God to our lives (through the empowering of the indwelling Spirit, v. 3).

2. The believer cannot "bear fruit" unless he is devoted to Christ (v. 4, as defined by the word "abide").

3. The believer will not achieve spiritual victories or be able to live victorious over temptation and sin (v. 5, "without me ye can do nothing").

4. With devotion to Christ comes the promise of "much fruit" (v. 5). Without devotion to Christ comes the promise of *no fruit* and a wasted life.

5. Only the devoted are "filled" with the Spirit of God and empowered. Only those filled will do what God wants them to do in the power of the Spirit out of love for the Lord.

> "Then Peter, <u>filled with</u> {*spiritual unity with God is achieved when filled*} the Holy Ghost, said unto them . . ." (Acts 4:8a).

> "And when they had prayed, the place was shaken where they were assembled together; and they were all filled with the Holy Ghost, and they spake the word of God with boldness" (Acts 4:31).

6. The central qualification for any ministry is to be filled with the Spirit, which comes from being to devoted to Christ. Only the devoted will serve the Lord out of a spirit of self-sacrifice regardless of the cost to them personally.

"Wherefore, brethren, look ye out among you seven men of honest report, full of the Holy Ghost and wisdom, whom we may appoint over this business" (Acts 6:3).

"But he {*Stephen*}, being full of the Holy Ghost, looked up stedfastly into heaven, and saw the glory of God, and Jesus standing on the right hand of God" (Acts 7:55).

Out of this cultivation of a personal devotion to Christ (breaking up our "fallow ground") will grow a <u>real</u> prayer life, a <u>real</u> purpose for the study of the Word of God, and <u>real</u> ministry *from the heart* for all the right reasons.

"[46] And he said unto them, Set your hearts unto all the words which I testify among you this day, which ye shall command your children to observe to do, all the words of this law. [47] For it *is* not a vain thing for you; because it *is* your life: and through this thing ye shall prolong *your* days in the land, whither ye go over Jordan to possess it" (Deuteronomy 32:46-47).

The implication of the words "set your hearts unto all the words" (v. 46) is the integration of those truths into your life. That will not happen apart from being devoted to Christ. Cultivating a personal devotion to Christ is "not a vain thing" (v. 47). It is **not** an empty, time consuming exercise without any real value. Cultivating personal devotion to Christ "is your life" (v. 47).

It is through the *conduit* of personal devotion to Christ that the *Christ-life* flows to the believer as he studies and applies the Word of God. It is "through this thing" (v. 47, the cultivation of personal devotion to Christ through Bible study and prayer) that all of God's blessings flow (spiritual and material).

The primary focus of personal devotions is not on <u>what</u> we do or <u>how</u> we do it. The primary focus is to spend personal and intimate time with the Lord Jesus and to allow Him access to every aspect of our lives. True ministry and true holiness will never happen in our lives until we are truly devoted to Christ.

"[8] Yea doubtless, and I count all things *but* loss for the excellency of the knowledge of Christ Jesus my Lord: for whom I have suffered the loss of all things, and do count them *but* dung, that I may win

Christ, [9] And be found in him, not having mine own righteousness, which is of the law, but that which is through the faith of Christ, the righteousness which is of God by faith: [10] That I may know him, and the power of his resurrection, and the fellowship of his sufferings, being made conformable unto his death; [11] If by any means I might attain unto the resurrection of the dead. [12] Not as though I had already attained, either were already perfect: but I follow after, if that I may apprehend that for which also I am apprehended of Christ Jesus. [13] Brethren, I count not myself to have apprehended: but *this* one thing *I do*, forgetting those things which are behind, and reaching forth unto those things which are before, [14] I press toward the mark for the prize of the high calling of God in Christ Jesus" (Philippians 3:8-14).

Paul understood the effort required of him to maintain his "fellowship" with God. He appeals to believers (he pleads with them) to make the same effort. Israel did not listen to Zephaniah, Habakkuk, or Jeremiah. Therefore, the captivity came just as God warned.

Judgment (chastisement) is always immanent with disobedience (inherent or within). The only way to remove the immanency of chastisement is repentance, i.e., removing the disobedience by forsaking the sin, confessing, and receiving the cleansing of forgiveness through the blood of Christ.

DISCUSSION QUESTIONS

1. Explain the phrase, "Break up your fallow ground, and sow not among thorns" in Jeremiah 4:3.

2. In Jeremiah 2:6, the prophet Jeremiah says of the children of Israel that they never ask "where is the LORD?" Discuss the practical significance of that statement and how such a tragic thing could ever happen in any believer's life.

3. How does the term "fallow ground" relate to the apathetic kind of Christianity that we see so much of at present?

4. To truly know the Lord is to love the Lord. A person cannot know Him and not love Him. Discuss the paradox between knowing and loving and why the paradox exists.

5. Read John 15:3-5. List and discuss the six reasons why believers should have regular personal devotions.

6. Explain and discuss the practical significance of the words "set your hearts unto all the words" in Deuteronomy 32:46.

7. Read Philippians 3:8-14. Discuss the primary purpose of spending personal time with the LORD in Bible study and prayer.

Chapter Nineteen
Holiness and the Priesthood of the Believer

"[5] Ye also, as lively stones, are built up a spiritual house, an holy priesthood, to offer up spiritual sacrifices, acceptable to God by Jesus Christ. [6] Wherefore also it is contained in the scripture, Behold, I lay in Sion a chief corner stone, elect, precious: and he that believeth on him shall not be confounded. [7] Unto you therefore which believe *he is* precious: but unto them which be disobedient, the stone which the builders disallowed, the same is made the head of the corner, [8] And a stone of stumbling, and a rock of offence, *even to them* which stumble at the word, being disobedient: whereunto also they were appointed. [9] But ye *are* a chosen generation, a royal priesthood, an holy nation, a peculiar people; that ye should shew forth the praises of him who hath called you out of darkness into his marvellous light" (I Peter 2:5-9).

"And hath made us kings and priests unto God and his Father; to him *be* glory and dominion for ever and ever. Amen" (Revelation 1:6).

Holiness is the practical responsibility of our position in Christ. Every truly "born again" believer is a "saint" before God. The word "saint" is from the Greek word *hagios* (hag'-ee-os). It is a word that describes a most holy and sacred thing. It refers to something or someone that has been *set apart* for God's use and God's use alone. As it refers to believers, it refers to their particular calling as servants of God. It refers to their position "in Christ." It refers to the Priesthood of all believers. All "born again" believers from the Day of Pentecost forward makeup a new priesthood. We are to be faithful where the Levitical priesthood failed in the preservation and proclamation (discipleship and evangelism) of the Word of God.

The Priesthood of the believer refers to the ministry that is common to all believers. The word *ministry* defines God's work. The word "priesthood" describes both the believer's position in this world and his responsibility. The word "priesthood" is associated with a *job description* and the responsibilities of that *job description*. Any time a believer fails to fulfill his *job description* as a priest before God, in any way, that individual believer is living in sin.

Every true believer is a Sanctified One. All believers are God's representatives before lost mankind. They are representatives of the *character* of God to restore His image and bring Him glory by being living embodiments of the Word of God. They are to represent God by working to replicate His *character* in their lives.

When the Word of God says, "for all have sinned and come short of the glory of God" (Romans 3:23), He is saying that we come short of replicating the *character* of God in our lives and therefore, do not deserve His blessings or praise. The *character* of God is what distinguishes Him from every other being.

> The central and foremost responsibility of every Believer Priest is to replicate the *character* of God in our lives through the enabling power of the indwelling Holy Spirit.

Therefore, a major part of the "work of the ministry" relates to this issue of personal holiness. Again, we must remind ourselves that the word *holy* does not refer to moral perfection or personal piety. These realities may be achieved to some *degree* by personal holiness. The twofold reality of personal holiness is defined on two spiritual battlefronts:

1. Separation from worldliness
2. Separation unto God

These two realities are essential to the "work of the ministry" of the Believer Priest. The "work of the ministry" refers to the "spiritual sacrifices" that the Believer Priest offers to the Lord. In order for the Lord to accept these "spiritual sacrifices," a believer's holiness is absolutely essential.

"[10] In the four and twentieth *day* of the ninth *month*, in the second year of Darius, came the word of the LORD by Haggai the prophet, saying, [11] Thus saith the LORD of hosts; Ask now the priests *concerning* the law, saying, [12] If one bear holy flesh in the skirt of his garment, and with his skirt do touch bread, or pottage, or wine, or oil, or any meat, shall it be holy? And the priests answered and said, No. [13] Then said Haggai, If *one that is* unclean by a dead body touch any of these, shall it be unclean? And the priests answered and said, It shall be unclean. [14] Then answered Haggai, and said, So

145

is this people, and so *is* this nation before me, saith the LORD; and so *is* every work of their hands; and that which they offer there *is* unclean" (Haggai 2:10-14).

The "work of the ministry" is spiritual work. It is unlike any other kind of work.

> Spiritual work is a supernatural endeavor that brings the physical world into contact with the supernatural world. Anytime that happens, like metal in a microwave oven, *sparks* start to fly.

The separated Believer Priest becomes the *spiritual conduit* through which God works. Before a Believer Priest can become that *spiritual conduit*, all that he is and can be must be absolutely and completely given to the Lord. He must be separated from worldliness. In the Old Testament, this relationship was expressed by the words "perfect heart." To understand this idea is to understand that there can be no difference between the will and desires of a person and the will and desires of God. They become one.

"[1] I beseech you therefore, brethren, by the mercies of God, that ye present your bodies a living sacrifice, holy, acceptable unto God, *which is* your reasonable service. [2] And be not conformed to this world: but be ye transformed by the renewing of your mind, that ye may prove what *is* that good, and acceptable, and perfect, will of God" (Romans 12:1-2).

When a Believer Priest sins in any way, he defiles himself before God and makes himself "unclean." What are some of things that defile the Priesthood of a believer? Any sin defiles the Priesthood of a believer. However, there are certain practices which are common that many Christians do not consider defiling. Worldliness comes in many forms and is usually evidenced by the presence of any one of the "works of the flesh."

"[16] *This* I say then, Walk in the Spirit, and ye shall not fulfil the lust of the flesh. [17] For the flesh lusteth against the Spirit, and the Spirit against the flesh: and these are contrary the one to the other: so that ye cannot do the things that ye would. [18] But if ye be led of the Spirit, ye are not under the law. [19] Now the works of the flesh are manifest, which are *these*; Adultery, fornication, uncleanness, lasciviousness, [20] Idolatry, witchcraft, hatred, variance, emulations, wrath, strife, seditions, heresies, [21] Envyings, murders, drunkenness, revellings, and such like: of the which I tell you before, as I have also told *you* in time past, that they which do such things shall not inherit the kingdom of God" (Galatians 5:16-21).

None of us would have any problem with identifying the first seven things listed (adultery, fornication, uncleanness, lasciviousness, idolatry, witchcraft, hatred) and understanding that they would defile a Believer Priest from being used of God. However, many Christians do not see that the next seven things listed are equally defiling (variance, emulations, wrath, strife, seditions, heresies, envyings).

The word "variance" is from the Greek word *eris* (er'-is). It refers to a spirit of contention and strife. It refers to the wrangling that goes on behind the scenes when someone wants to get their way or force their opinion on others. Bitterness results from self-focus and a high self-opinion that believes a person does not get what he deserves. This contentious spirit is absolutely defiling and almost always generates factions and bitterness between believers.

"[14] Follow peace with all *men*, and holiness, without which no man shall see the Lord: [15] Looking diligently lest any man fail of the grace of God; lest any root of bitterness springing up trouble *you*, and thereby many be defiled" (Hebrews 12:14-15).

The word "emulations" in Galatians 5:20 is equally defiling. It is from the Greek word *zelos* (dzay'-los). It refers to an angry, contentious rivalry of a person or group of people that seek to punish or banish anyone that is not willing to bow down to their opinion. It refers to a selfish, misdirected zeal. "Variance" and "emulation" are almost always the inseparable twin sisters of carnality. They are defiling sins.

The next defiling sin listed is the sin of "wrath." It is from the Greek word *thumos* (thoo-mos'). It refers to fierce anger that blows up and vents itself against the person with which someone disagrees. It comes from the Greek word *thuo* (thoo'-o), which means to sacrifice or slaughter. Although this wicked spirit may not seek to kill a person, it almost always seeks to sacrifice another person to *get its way*.

The word "strife" is from the Greek word *eritheia* (er-ith-i'-ah). It refers to the person who practices electioneering to gain power or position. This is almost always done secretly through gossip. I call this *politicking*. It is probably one of the most destructive defiling practices, destroying more local churches and individual lives than any other sin. God condemns it on numerous occasions in Scripture.

> "*Let* nothing *be done* through strife or vainglory; but in lowliness of mind let each esteem other better than themselves" (Philippians 2:3).

> "[13] Who *is* a wise man and endued with knowledge among you? let him shew out of a good conversation his works with meekness of wisdom. [14] But if ye have bitter envying and strife in your hearts, glory not, and lie not against the truth. [15] This wisdom descendeth not from above, but *is* earthly, sensual, devilish. [16] For where envying and strife *is*, there *is* confusion and every evil work" (James 3:13-16).

The word "seditions" is from the Greek word *dichostasia* (dee-khos-tas-ee'-ah). The word *dis* (dece) means twice or again and *stasis* (stas'-is), which refers to insurrection. In other words, "seditions" refers to an ongoing, standing insurrection against authority - a continuous work (not just a single act) of rebellion. Before God can use a Believer Priest, or a local church of Believer Priests, this spirit of insurrection must be removed.

The next defiling sin that destroys the usefulness of individual Believer Priests is "heresies." "Heresies" is from the Greek word *hairesis* (hah'-ee-res-is). It refers to the act of taking a captive. A false teacher leads people astray from the right way (righteousness) by false teaching. A heresy is anything that generates wrong practices. These wrong practices can come through the perversion of biblical truth or through a practice of life. This type of person always tries to *gather a following*. He captures a person when that person does what he does (usually sedition). Any one of the "works of the flesh" can generate "heresies."

The last of these defiling sins in this passage is "envyings." It is from the Greek word *phthonos* (fthon'-os). Although it simply means to envy, it probably relates more to its root word, which is *phtheiro* (fthi'-ro). This root word means to corrupt or to destroy. In the opinion of the Jews, the temple was corrupted or destroyed when anyone defiled it or damaged anything in it to the slightest degree. In the context of Galatians 5:21, it refers to a selfish, prideful attitude that results in leading a church away from knowledge and holiness.

As Believer Priests, every Christian needs to regularly examine and cleanse his heart from these corrupting, defiling sins of "variance, emulations, wrath, strife, seditions, heresies, and envyings." We need to understand that God not only puts them in the same category as "adultery, fornication, uncleanness, lasciviousness, idolatry, witchcraft, hatred, murders, drunkenness, and revellings, but that God presents them as *equals*. They render a Believer Priest unclean and useless to God.

> Pride keeps a person from acknowledging the wickedness of these particular "works of the flesh."

Pride will keep a believer from even looking at his heart and seeing the corrupting influences of these sins in his own life and in the lives of others. Pride will keep a heart closed to the *pointing finger* of conviction as the Holy Spirit directs us all to repentance and commitment to change.

"Pride *goeth* before destruction, and an haughty spirit before a fall" (Proverbs 16:18). **Pride not only produces the "works of the flesh," pride keeps feeding them.** Without pride they will die. But pride will also keep a person from seeing his sin, acknowledging it as sin and repenting.

DISCUSSION QUESTIONS

1. As a Believer-Priest and a "saint," discuss why holiness is the practical responsibility of our position in Christ.

2. Discuss the importance of understanding that being a Believer-Priest is more than a position, but that it defines a ministry/work with a *job description.*

3. Discuss what is involved in seeking to replicate the character of God in our lives.

4. Explain Haggai 2:10-14 in the light of your new position as a Believer-Priest before God.

5. Discuss the meaning and significance in understanding that, as a Believer-Priest, you are a *spiritual conduit* for God's supernatural workings of grace.

6. Explain what it means to have a *perfect heart.*

7. In Galatians 5:16-21, God gives us the "works of the flesh." Define each of these and discuss why any one of them defiles us and our ministry before God.

Chapter Twenty
The Constant Need of the Renewal of Vision and Purpose

"[17] This I say therefore, and testify in the Lord, that ye henceforth walk not as other Gentiles walk, in the vanity of their mind, [18] Having the understanding darkened, being alienated from the life of God through the ignorance that is in them, because of the blindness of their heart: [19] Who being past feeling have given themselves over unto lasciviousness, to work all uncleanness with greediness. [20] But ye have not so learned Christ; [21] If so be that ye have heard him, and have been taught by him, as the truth is in Jesus: [22] That ye put off concerning the former conversation the old man, which is corrupt according to the deceitful lusts; [23] And be renewed {rejuvenated} in the spirit of your mind {by your new spiritual nature; II Peter 1:4}; [24] And that ye put on the new man {the imparted new nature of the indwelling Holy Spirit}, which after God is created in righteousness and true holiness. [25] Wherefore putting away lying, speak every man truth with his neighbour: for we are members one of another. [26] Be ye angry, and sin not: let not the sun go down upon your wrath: [27] Neither give place to the devil. [28] Let him that stole steal no more: but rather let him labour, working with his hands the thing which is good, that he may have to give to him that needeth. [29] Let no corrupt communication proceed out of your mouth, but that which is good to the use of edifying, that it may minister grace unto the hearers. [30] And grieve not the holy Spirit of God, whereby ye are sealed unto the day of redemption. [31] Let all bitterness, and wrath, and anger, and clamour, and evil speaking, be put away from you, with all malice: [32] And be ye kind one to another, tenderhearted, forgiving one another, even as God for Christ's sake hath forgiven you" (Ephesians 4:17-32).

The longer I live, the more I realize the truths of what the Apostle Paul speaks in Romans chapter seven: "[21] I find then a law {a primary governing principle of my nature}, that, when I would do good, evil {of his own fallen nature} is present with me. [22] For I delight in the law of God after the inward man: [23] But I see another law in my members, warring against the law of my mind, and bringing me into captivity to the law of sin which is in my members. [24] O wretched man that I am! who shall deliver me from the body of this death? [25] I thank God through Jesus Christ our Lord. So then with the mind I myself serve the law of God; but with the flesh the law of sin."

There is an old hymn written by C. Austin Miles entitled **"A New Name in Glory"** that begins with the words, "I was once a sinner, but I came. . . " I often shrug my head in amazement as these words are sung by Christians. I change these words when I sing this hymn. I sing, "I am still a sinner, but I came . . ." I have no illusions, or delusions, about what I am. I am a sinner saved by the wonderful, amazing, and incomprehensible grace of God.

I, like the Apostle Paul and ALL Christians, struggle with the issues of sin. I struggle with keeping my priorities in order. I struggle with issues of pride, selfishness, personal ambitions, self-protection, and the lusts of the flesh. If we are honest and transparent, we would all admit this is the reality of the daily struggle of our Christian lives. Some days we do well and some days we fail miserably. Sadly, one of the most subtle forms of spiritual deception is our own self-deception. We seldom recognize how poorly we are doing in this spiritual battle to maintain intimacy with God and complete selflessness in our own Christian lives. We all like to think more highly of ourselves than we ought.

The truth is, no matter how much effort we make to restore the image of Christ in our lives, we will always "come short of the glory of God." That is a fact of life. However, it is not a fact of life that should somehow keep us from making the effort, because God is measuring our spirituality by measuring the effort we put into being Christ-like in the enabling power of the indwelling Holy Spirit.

"[13] Brethren, I count not myself to have apprehended {*grasped onto, achieved or attained to what I pursue*}: but *this* one thing *I do*, forgetting those things which are behind, and reaching forth unto those things which are before, [14] I press toward the mark for the prize of the high calling of God in Christ Jesus" (Philippians 3:13-14).

The picture before us in this text is of a Christian in pursuit of godliness. He is chasing after it and pursuing it with every ounce of strength in his body. No matter how much effort he exerts, it is always just out of his grasp. Yet, he does not give up. He continues to "press toward the mark" (the *goal* of Christ-likeness). Herein lays the truth regarding the *renewal* of which Paul speaks in

Ephesians 4:23. We need to be constantly "renewed {*rejuvenated*} in the spirit of your mind." This constant spirit of *renewal* must be the spirit that drives every local church in every aspect of its ministry. This constant spirit of *renewal* must be the spirit that drives every individual Christian every day of our lives.

Our great tragedy of the failure in maintaining our efforts for constant *renewal* is the issue of *Distanciation*.

Distanciation simply refers to the *distance* that grows between us and Christ-likeness when we fail to maintain our focus upon being totally yielded to the indwelling Holy Spirit in every pursuit or ambition in life.

This is the only way we can truly measure our own spiritual growth. This is the *measuring stick* of practical sanctification. It certainly is the *measuring stick* of true spirituality. More importantly, it is a true *measuring stick* of true church growth (not pragmatically by *numbers*, but in spiritual depth).

Although local churches are made up of *living stones* (born again believers), God's blessing upon the organism of any local church is conditioned upon the reality of intimacy with Him and the local church's unity in spirit, doctrine, and purpose.

"[1] Wherefore laying aside all malice, and all guile, and hypocrisies, and envies, and all evil speakings, [2] As newborn babes, desire the sincere milk of the word, that ye may grow thereby: [3] If so be ye have tasted that the Lord *is* gracious. [4] To whom coming, *as unto* a living stone, disallowed indeed of men, but chosen of God, *and* precious, [5] Ye also, as lively stones, are built up a spiritual house, an holy priesthood, to offer up spiritual sacrifices, acceptable to God by Jesus Christ. . . [9] But ye *are* a chosen generation, a royal priesthood, an holy nation, a peculiar people; that ye should shew forth the praises of him who hath called you out of darkness into his marvellous light: [10] Which in time past *were* not a people, but *are* now the people of God: which had not obtained mercy, but now have obtained mercy. [11] Dearly beloved, I beseech *you* as strangers and pilgrims, abstain from fleshly lusts, which war against the soul; [12] Having your conversation honest among the Gentiles: that, whereas they speak against you as evildoers, they may by *your* good works, which they shall behold, glorify God in the day of visitation" (I Peter 2:1-5 and 9-12).

The continued blessings of God upon a local church will not be appropriated because we dedicate a *physical building* to be a *lighthouse* in a community. God does not *shine* (reveal His glory) through physical structures today. God reveals His glory through the lives of sanctified and consecrated believers in local churches made up of *living stones* united together in Spirit, doctrine, and purpose. If this is going to be the ongoing and continuing testimony of any local church, that local church must constantly and continually "be renewed {*rejuvenated*} in the spirit of your mind." This spirit of constant renewal must constantly be maintained in our consciousness. **We must belabor this truth.**

> Bringing the *light* of the reality of radically changed lives to testify to the Person of God is to what every local church is to be dedicated. Apart from this reality, every local church loses both its purpose for existence and its right to exist.

"[14] Ye are the light of the world. A city that is set on an hill cannot be hid. [15] Neither do men light a candle, and put it under a bushel, but on a candlestick; and it giveth light unto all that are in the house. [16] Let your light so shine before men, that they may see your good works, and glorify your Father which is in heaven" (Matthew 5:14-16).

There is a natural digression from true (normal) Christianity to a pseudo (abnormal) Christianity in every local church or organization. A loss of "vision" and the failure to maintain constant renewal is almost always the direct cause of this digression.

The six stages from life to the death of a church or organization are:

Stage One: Missional, as characterized by spiritual immaturity and theological foundation laying, faith building and learning to "walk" with the Lord

Stage Two: Maturation, as characterized by personal evangelistic vibrancy and fervency for the things of God among the vast majority of a congregation (This is normalcy. Each stage after this is moving away from normalcy by degrees.)

Stage Three: Man Centered, as characterized by *programs*

centered in *professionalism* intent on *gathering crowds* and by *catering to the carnal* eliminating the necessity of *personal involvement* in evangelism (it is at the point where *renewal* is critical)

Stage Four: Maintenance, as characterized by minimizing controversial doctrines and maintaining *numbers,* avoiding conflict at any cost in order to maintain *unity* (falsely so called)

Stage Five: Mechanical, as characterized by extensive structuring (Committees, Prayer Bands, Small Groups, etc.) that lack any real personal evangelistic vision and whose emphasis is mainly *knowing* truth rather than *doing* truth

Stage Six: Monumental (as in *gravestone*), as characterized by an elderly congregation *hanging on by the skin of their teeth* with both the organization and the people just waiting to die (This kind of local church is actually already dead.)

Sadly, many local churches are in varying stages of self-deception regarding the reality of realizing their purpose for existence. **A simple test is to ask and answer two questions:**

1. What is our purpose for existence?
2. Where are we in fulfilling our purpose for existence?

DISCUSSION QUESTIONS

1. Explain what Paul means in Ephesians 4:23 when he says, "And be renewed in the spirit of your mind."

2. According to Romans 7:21-25, do you think any Christian will ever progress beyond a continual struggle with the *sin nature* in this present life? Explain your answer.

3. Explain what Paul means by his statement in Philippians 3:13-14 and discuss why Paul's statement should be the goal of every true Christian.

4. Explain *Distanciation.*

5. Discuss the following statement: "Bringing the *light* of the reality of radically changed lives to testify to the Person of God is to what every local church is to be dedicated."

6. List and explain the six *stages* from life to the death of a church or an organization.

7. Evaluate your own Christian life and the effectiveness of your local church by answering the two questions:

   A. What is our purpose for existence?
   B. Where are we in fulfilling our purpose for existence?

Chapter Twenty-one
Living unto Jesus

"[1] For we know that if our earthly house of *this* tabernacle were dissolved, we have a building of God, an house not made with hands, eternal in the heavens. [2] For in this we groan, earnestly desiring to be clothed upon with our house which is from heaven: [3] If so be that being clothed we shall not be found naked. [4] For we that are in *this* tabernacle do groan, being burdened: not for that we would be unclothed, but clothed upon, that mortality might be swallowed up of life. [5] Now he that hath wrought us for the selfsame thing *is* God, who also hath given unto us the earnest of the Spirit. [6] Therefore *we are* always confident, knowing that, whilst we are at home in the body, we are absent from the Lord: [7] (For we walk by faith, not by sight:) [8] We are confident, *I say*, and willing rather to be absent from the body, and to be present with the Lord. [9] Wherefore we labour, that, whether present or absent, we may be accepted of him. [10] For we must all appear before the judgment seat of Christ; that every one may receive the things *done* in *his* body, according to that he hath done, whether *it be* good or bad. [11] Knowing therefore the terror of the Lord, we persuade men; but we are made manifest unto God; and I trust also are made manifest in your consciences. [12] For we commend not ourselves again unto you, but give you occasion to glory on our behalf, that ye may have somewhat to *answer* them which glory in appearance, and not in heart. [13] For whether we be beside ourselves, *it is* to God: or whether we be sober, *it is* for your cause. [14] For the love of Christ constraineth us; because we thus judge, that if one died for all, then were all dead: [15] And *that* he died for all, that they which live should not henceforth live unto themselves, but unto him which died for them, and rose again. [16] Wherefore henceforth know we no man after the flesh: yea, though we have known Christ after the flesh, yet now henceforth know we *him* no more. [17] Therefore if any man *be* in Christ, *he is* a new creature: old things are passed away; behold, all things are become new. [18] And all things *are* of God, who hath reconciled us to himself by Jesus Christ, and hath given to us the ministry of reconciliation; [19] To wit, that God was in Christ, reconciling the world unto himself, not imputing their trespasses unto them; and hath committed unto us the word of reconciliation. [20] Now then we are ambassadors for Christ, as though God did beseech *you* by us: we pray *you* in Christ's stead, be ye reconciled to God. [21] For he hath made him *to be* sin for us, who knew no sin; that we might be made the righteousness of God in him" (II Corinthians 5:1-21).

Heaven is mentioned often in the Word of God. However, there is little definitive teaching about where Heaven is or what it will be like. The word "heaven" in the New Testament books is translated from the Greek word *ouranos* (o-ran-os'). In the simplistic sense, the word simply carries the idea of *elevation*. In most cases, people simply define that to mean *in the sky, in the air,* or *up*. The meaning is probably more related to an elevation of existence or a higher dimension of existence. This certainly appears to be the meaning from the context of II Corinthians 5:1-21.

Another word that many people have a lot of trouble understanding is the word "eternal" as used in II Corinthians 5:1. The word "eternal" is translated from the Greek word *aionios* (ahee-o'-nee-os). Many tend to understand the meaning of this word to be *ageless* or *timeless*. The real meaning is actually *perpetual* or *never ending*.

> The word *eternal* is usually used to relate just to a person's physical existence. However, we should not forget that all that we are, say, and do results in eternal consequences. Therefore, the results of our influence (good or bad) are also eternal or self-perpetuating.

The results of our influence will continue forever unless it is stopped by God by some form of annihilation. Even after death, there are consequences for our influence upon the souls of others that continue beyond this existence into Heaven or Hell (two different planes of eternal existence). Heaven is a higher plane of existence and Hell is a lower plane of existence. Therefore, there is a little *taste* of Heaven in our present existence and a little *taste* of Hell.

Holiness is an existence within an existence. Holiness is not just moral purity. Holiness involves a *moral peculiarity* and a separation of our lives from all that is *common*. It is this distinctiveness that differentiates the true believer and is what makes this person *peculiar* to everyone else. This is what Paul is addressing in II Corinthians 5:1-21. The emphasis of the text is to encourage believers to keep our lives and ministry focused upon our future existence in Heaven and to live in this existence as if we already possessed the glories of Heaven.

The reality of being part of this higher existence should change the way a true believer *walks* (lives his daily life). The issue here is that God does not want to merely rescue our souls from Hell. God wants to rescue the eternal *influence* of our lives as well.

"[17] Brethren, be followers together of me, and mark them which walk so as ye have us for an ensample. [18] (For many walk, of whom I have told you often, and now tell you even weeping, *that they are* the enemies of the cross of Christ: [19] Whose end *is* destruction, whose God *is their* belly, and *whose* glory *is* in their shame, who mind earthly things *{preoccupied with the things of this earth or existence}*.) [20] For our conversation is in heaven; from whence also we look for the Saviour, the Lord Jesus Christ: [21] Who shall change our vile body, that it may be fashioned like unto his glorious body, according to the working whereby he is able even to subdue all things unto himself" (Philippians 3:17-21).

The believer's "conversation" (*politeuma, i.e., citizenship*) is already (presently) "in heaven, from whence also we look for the Saviour, the Lord Jesus Christ" (Philippians 3:20). There is an aspect of this that goes beyond a mere *positional* reality to an *actual* reality. As God is both transcendent (being beyond the limits of all possible experience and knowledge within the material existence) and immanent (being within the limits of possible experience or knowledge within the material existence; i.e. God can be known), so is eternal life.

> The transcendency and immanency of eternal life cannot be understood apart from our understanding the unfolding nature of "the regeneration" within our material existence into eternity.

The Lord Jesus' death, burial, and resurrection became the "door" into "the regeneration" (the eternal, perpetual existence) and the believer enters "through" (Ephesians 2:8-9) that "door" "by grace through faith." However, there is an aspect of that eternal, perpetual existence that enters into the material existence positionally in the promises of God. This happens *actually* in the believer's reception of the indwelling of the Holy Spirit when that believer receives Jesus Christ as Lord through an act of faith. The moment this happens, the believer has passed from death unto life *positionally* and, to a degree, *actually*.

> "⁴ Therefore we are buried with him by baptism {*the baptism of the Holy Spirit into the body of Christ; i.e. "the regeneration," I Cor. 12:13*} into death: that like as Christ was raised up from the dead by the glory of the Father, even so we also should walk in newness of life. ⁵ For if we have been planted together in the likeness of his death, we shall be also *in the likeness* of *his* resurrection: ⁶ Knowing this, that our old man is crucified with *him*, that the body of sin {*the Sin Nature*} might be destroyed, that henceforth we should not serve sin {*the Sin Nature*}. ⁷ For he that is dead is freed from {*the condemnation of the*} sin {*the Sin Nature*}. ⁸ Now if we be dead with Christ, we believe that we shall also live with him: ⁹ Knowing that Christ being raised from the dead dieth no more; death hath no more dominion over him {*He is no longer under the dominion of death*}. ¹⁰ For in that he {*Jesus*} died, he {*Jesus*} died unto sin once: but in that he {*Jesus*} liveth, he {*Jesus*} liveth unto God" (Romans 6:4-10).

When Satan deceived Eve, and Adam willfully sinned, sin brought God's judgment of death upon the first Creation. That creation's existence ceased to be *perpetual* in the state of its original creation. Satan had won a victory, but God would not allow that victory to continue without correcting it. Satan's victory made death a doorway into eternal (perpetual) death (which is perpetual separation from God). God overruled that victory "by grace through faith" in the promised "Seed" (Genesis 3:15) by making death a door into eternal (perpetual) life. Death, for the believer, became a doorway to God's eternal (perpetual) existence.

> "⁸ But God commendeth his love toward us, in that, while we were yet sinners, Christ died for us. ⁹ Much more then, being now justified by his blood, we shall be saved from wrath through him. ¹⁰ For if, when we were enemies, we were reconciled to God by the death of his Son, much more, being reconciled, we shall be saved by his life. ¹¹ And not only *so*, but we also joy in God through our Lord Jesus Christ, by whom we have now received the atonement. ¹² Wherefore, as by one man sin entered into the world, and death by sin; and so death passed upon all men, for that all have sinned: ¹³ (For until the law sin was in the world: but sin is not imputed when there is no law. ¹⁴ Nevertheless death reigned from Adam to Moses, even over them that had not sinned after the similitude of Adam's transgression, who is the figure of him that was to come. ¹⁵ But not as the offence, so also *is* the free gift. For if through the offence of one many be dead,

much more the grace of God, and the gift by grace, *which is* by one man, Jesus Christ, hath abounded unto many. [16] And not as *it was* by one that sinned, *so is* the gift: for the judgment *was* by one to condemnation, but the free gift *is* of many offences unto justification. [17] For if by one man's offence death reigned by one; much more they which receive abundance of grace and of the gift of righteousness shall reign in life by one, Jesus Christ.) [18] Therefore as by the offence of one *judgment came* upon all men to condemnation; even so by the righteousness of one *the free gift came* upon all men unto justification of life" (Romans 5:8-18).

What was a paradox to the world existing in unbelief and spiritual blindness, became a wonderful vision of another eternal existence beyond the curse of this material existence. What was that paradox? For those saved "by grace through faith," death was, in *actuality*, life! Satan had infected the world with the fear of death. God had provided an inoculation against that lifetime of bondage. God provided salvation "by grace through faith," revealing death as merely a *doorway* to eternal (perpetual) life.

"[14] Forasmuch then as the children are partakers of flesh and blood, he also himself likewise took part of the same; that through death he might destroy him that had the power of death, that is, the devil; [15] And deliver them who through fear of death were all their lifetime subject to bondage" (Hebrews 2:14-15).

The life of Jesus was human and divine; temporal and eternal. Yet, in His death, burial, and resurrection, Jesus opened the "door" from *temporal* life into *eternal* life. The resurrection for believers means our lives are *inextinguishable*; the "light" that is in us can NEVER be put out. Eternal (perpetual) life has taken residence in our bodies through the indwelling of the Holy Spirit of God even within the realm of the *temporal*.

"[20] But now is Christ risen from the dead, *and* become the firstfruits of them that slept. [21] For since by man *came* death, by man *came* also the resurrection of the dead. [22] For as in Adam all die, even so in Christ shall all be made alive. [23] But every man in his own order: Christ the firstfruits; afterward they that are Christ's at his coming. [24] Then *cometh* the end, when he shall have delivered up the kingdom to God, even the Father; when he shall have put down all rule and all authority and power. [25] For he must reign, till he hath put all enemies under his feet. [26] The last enemy *that* shall be destroyed *is* death. . . [54] So when this corruptible shall have put on incorruption, and this mortal shall have put on immortality, then shall be brought to pass the saying that is written, Death is swallowed up in victory. [55] O death, where *is* thy sting? O grave, where *is* thy victory? [56] The sting of death *is* sin; and the strength of sin *is* the law. [57] But thanks *be* to God, which giveth us the victory through our Lord Jesus Christ" (I Corinthians 15:20-26, 54-57).

> If we then truly believe these wonderful truths, how then should we live our lives within this transcendent, but immanent reality?

We are being beaten, persecuted, and threatened by this temporal world (existence). The weight of the world's problems and God's pending judgment falls, to some degree, upon us as well. God gives us simple instructions for living within this temporal existence in II Corinthians chapter five.

"[14] For the love of Christ constraineth us; because we thus judge, that if one died for all, then were all dead: [15] And *that* he died for all, that they which live **should** not henceforth live unto themselves, but unto him which died for them, and rose again" (II Corinthians 5:14-15).

"[W]ere all dead" in II Corinthians 5:14 is in the aorist tense. Usually, the aorist tense is merely rendered in the past tense in our English translations. However, that is not always an accurate way to translate the aorist tense. Another way the aorist tense is described is as something having happened at some point in time, usually in the past, with continuing and ongoing results. However, a more distinct and definitive understanding of the aorist tense is the concept of the verb as considered *without regard for past, present, or future time*. Therefore, we might say that the aorist tense is the *outcome* of some event or decision with *eternally, perpetuating results*. Therefore, the statement "were all dead" renders an action that "should" (if that action was real and actual) bare continuing and perpetuating results. The one decision regarding what Christ has accomplished for us positionally and actually through His death, burial, and resurrection "should" result in the ongoing, moment by moment decision of living "unto" that new reality and that new existence "in Christ." The idea is that these two realities "should" not be separated in *actuality*. They may be separated in *practice*, but they "should" not be. The true believer NOW has only ONE

EXISTENCE. The believer is NOW (presently in this world) in eternal life.

Notice that it is "the love of Christ" that "constraineth us." Interestingly, "constraineth" is in the present tense. In other words, this is not referring to a past action of Christ, but a present and ongoing action. This is not referring to the love of Christ expressed on the Cross. This refers to the love of Christ given to the believer in the indwelling of the Holy Spirit. That love is intended to be constantly being released through the "filling" (to overflow) of the Holy Spirit.

> The Christian is not intended to be a mere vessel to contain God's love, but a *distribution center* of God's grace to the whole world.

"[1] Therefore being justified by faith, we have peace with God through our Lord Jesus Christ: [2] By whom also we have access by faith into this grace wherein we stand, and rejoice in hope of the glory of God. [3] And not only *so*, but we glory in tribulations also: knowing that tribulation worketh patience; [4] And patience, experience; and experience, hope: [5] And hope maketh not ashamed; because the love of God is shed abroad in our hearts by the Holy Ghost which is given unto us" (Romans 5:1-5).

Love is a central aspect of God's immutable attributes. Also, love is one of God's communicable attributes that is given to the believer in the indwelling Holy Spirit. However, until we "live unto" Christ as living sacrifices to God, this communicable attribute of God's love will lie dormant and wasted in a *vessel of clay*. There must be a yielding of our wills to the Holy Spirit (Romans 6:11-13) before the "love of God" in us can be released in the self-sacrificial way God intends.

The word "constraineth" is from the Greek word *sunecho* (soon-ekh'-o). It means to hold in place, like grabbing someone by both ears and holding the head in place. It is this love of Christ in the indwelling Holy Spirit of God, as we yield our will to Him, that *holds us* or *presses us* into a pattern of a self-sacrificial lifestyle. The reason we need this supernatural activity is because we are, by nature, self-protective. It is not natural for us to put everything we are and have in this world at risk for the benefit of someone else.

However, doing this is what defines normal (but supernatural) Christianity.

To what the indwelling love of Christ constrains us is the reality of our new existence in Christ. Notice that the word "were" in the phrase "then were all dead" in II Corinthians 5:14 is not "we're" (third person possessive) as most people read it. It is "were" in the English translation and is intended to reflect the past tense. In other words, at some point in time, you made a decision to trust in Christ and His death, burial, and resurrection for your salvation. At that moment in time (not the same as God's foreknowledge), you entered into "the regeneration," or the realm of God's eternal existence (eternal life). At that moment, your life became perpetual life (as opposed to perpetual death). Living our lives in that new reality is where the "love of Christ" intends to hold us.

This leads us to the admonition found in II Corinthians 5:15: "And *that* he died for all, that they which live **should** not henceforth live unto themselves, but unto him which died for them, and rose again." Paul said the same thing on one other occasion in a little different way that really explains this statement in II Corinthians 5:15.

"[19] For I through the law am dead to the law, that I might live unto God. [20] I am crucified with Christ: nevertheless I live; yet not I, but Christ liveth in me: and the life which I now live in the flesh I live by the faith of the Son of God, who loved me, and gave himself for me. [21] I do not frustrate the grace of God: for if righteousness *come* by the law, then Christ is dead in vain" (Galatians 2:19-21).

It is the "love of Christ" that should constrain the yielded believer, not merely the "terror" of Christ (II Corinthians 5:10-11a); "[10] For we must all appear before the judgment seat of Christ; that every one may receive the things *done* in *his* body, according to that he hath done, whether *it be* good or bad. [11] Knowing therefore the terror of the Lord, we persuade men . . ." Although salvation is a free gift of God's grace to the believing sinner, it does come with some responsibilities and obligations. We do not need to fulfill these responsibilities and obligations to be saved, or even keep our salvation. However, these responsibilities and obligations are inseparably connected to the eternal (perpetual) life we receive as a gift of salvation.

Therefore, Paul says, "And *that* he died for all, that they which live **should** not henceforth live unto themselves, but unto him which died for them, and rose again" (II Corinthians 5:15).

The idea here is the transition from the *positional* reality of the believer's death with Christ to the *practical* reality of the believer's death (separation) to worldliness. The latter SHOULD follow the former.

"Died" is in the aorist tense, meaning an action from some point in time with perpetual results. Part of the perpetual (eternal) results of Christ's death for those "born again" of the Spirit of God is that they "**should** not henceforth live unto themselves, but unto him which died for them, and rose again." If our eternal life is born out of faith in Christ's death, burial, and resurrection, that new reality should manifest itself in the presence of that eternal life in the believer's life. The "born again" believer "**should** not henceforth live unto themselves, but unto him which died for them, and rose again." In other words, the eternal (perpetual) life given the believer is not a *pie in the sky* promise that we receive after we die. Eternal (perpetual) life is our present possession and it should manifest itself in the manner we live our lives NOW in this temporal existence. If there is a change in our existence, that change should manifest itself in a major change in our practices (the way we live and even a change in the motivation for doing what we do).

"[1] Forasmuch then as Christ hath suffered for us in the flesh, arm *{Aorist Imperative; this is an absolute command}* yourselves likewise with the same mind: for he that hath suffered in the flesh hath ceased from sin; [2] That he no longer should live the rest of *his* time in the flesh to the lusts of men, but to the will of God" (I Peter 4:1-2).

This leads us to the direction of this new, eternal life that is our present possession along with it new responsibilities and obligations. With this new *possession* comes a new *position*.

"[17] Therefore if any man be in Christ, *he is* a new creature: old things are passed away; behold, all things are become new. [18] And all things *are* of God, who hath reconciled us to himself by Jesus Christ, and hath given to us the ministry of reconciliation; [19] To wit, that God was in Christ, reconciling the world unto himself, not imputing their trespasses unto them; and hath committed unto us the word of reconciliation. [20] Now then we are ambassadors for Christ, as though God did beseech *you* by us: we pray *you* in Christ's stead, be ye reconciled to God. [21] For he hath made him *to be* sin for us, who knew no sin; that we might be made the righteousness of God in him" (II Corinthians 5:17-21).

DISCUSSION QUESTIONS

1. Discuss where and what you think Heaven is from Scripture.

2. Discuss the meaning of the word *eternal* from the perspective of *existence*.

3. Discuss the issue of your *perpetual influence*.

4. Discuss the "unfolding nature of 'the regeneration' within our material existence into eternity."

5. What was a paradox to the world of unbelief and spiritual blindness became a wonderful vision of another eternal existence beyond the curse of this material existence. What was that paradox?

6. Read I Corinthians 15:20-26, 54-57. If we then truly believe these wonderful truths, how then should we live our lives within this transcendent, but immanent, reality?

7. Thoroughly explain the statement found in II Corinthians 5:15: "And *that* he died for all, that they which live **should** not henceforth live unto themselves, but unto him which died for them, and rose again."

Chapter Twenty-two
I. Transitioning Between the Possession of Eternal Life and Its Manifestation

There is overwhelming Scriptural evidence that eternal life is not merely something believers will receive after they die. The fact is, they died "with Christ" positionally and were given eternal life through the indwelling Holy Spirit of God the very instant they were "born again" "by grace through faith." If we understand the doctrine of grace from the Word of God, eternal life dwells within the believer and is released through the "filling" (to overflow) of the believer by the Holy Spirit. This "filling" is referred to in the Word of God as being in "fellowship" with God. This "fellowship" with God is a spiritual *union* and *unity* whereby the eternal life of God that is in us in the Person of the Holy Spirit is released through our lives. That "filling" is manifested by the visible, communicable attributes of God through our lives. These visible, communicable attributes of God are referred to in the Word of God as the "fruit of the Spirit" (Galatians 5:22-26).

"[1] Whosoever believeth that Jesus is the Christ is born of God: and every one that loveth him that begat loveth him also that is begotten of him. [2] By this we know that we love the children of God, when we love God, and keep his commandments. [3] For this is the love of God, that we keep his commandments: and his commandments are not grievous. [4] For whatsoever is born of God overcometh the world: and this is the victory that overcometh the world, *even* our faith. [5] Who is he that overcometh the world, but he that believeth that Jesus is the Son of God? [6] This is he that came by water and blood, *even* Jesus Christ; not by water only, but by water and blood. And it is the Spirit that beareth witness, because the Spirit is truth. [7] For there are three that bear record in heaven, the Father, the Word, and the Holy Ghost: and these three are one. [8] And there are three that bear witness in earth, the Spirit, and the water, and the blood: and these three agree in one. [9] If we receive the witness of men, the witness of God is greater: for this is the witness of God which he hath testified of his Son. [10] He that believeth on the Son of God hath the witness in himself: he that believeth not God hath made him a liar; because he believeth not the record that God gave of his Son. [11] And this is the record, that God hath given to us eternal life, and this life is in his Son. [12] He that hath the Son hath life; *and* he that hath not the Son of God hath not life. [13] These things have I written unto you that believe on the name of the Son of God; that ye may know that ye have eternal life, and that ye may believe on the name of the Son of God" (I John 5:1-13).

The epistle of I John is a difficult epistle for many to understand. Understanding the epistle is difficult because many miss its central theme.

> The epistle of I John is primarily about empirical evidences of having been "born again" of the Spirit of God. These evidences exist so that the believer might "assure" himself of his regeneration.

It is not that doing these *works* saves anyone, or even contributes in any way to someone's salvation, but that IF (the word "if" is used twenty-one times in the little epistle of I John) a person is "born again" of the Spirit of God there ought to be a visible, tangible expression, and manifestation (evidence) of that new life from the believer's life within this temporal existence. The issue of the use of the word "if" is to transition from the *indefinite* (doubt) to the *definite* (assurance).

Assurance of salvation (having been "born again") is not the same as the doctrine of eternal security. Assurance of salvation is about *definite evidence* that you have (perfect tense) "passed from death unto life." Assurance of salvation does not merely return to a moment when we repented of sin and "dead works," put our trust in the objective facts of the Gospel of Jesus Christ, confessed Jesus as Jehovah, called on His Name to save us, and received His indwelling presence in the Person of the Holy Spirit. The epistle of I John tells us that there ought to be *manifest evidences* that we presently possess eternal life and that the Spirit of God is actually producing practical righteousness in us.

"[14] We know {*perfect active of eido, perceive with the eyes or any of the other senses of the body; visible or sensatory evidences*} that we have passed {*perfect active*} from death unto life, because we love the brethren {*those who are truly "born again" people*}. He that loveth not his brother abideth in death. [15] Whosoever hateth his brother is a murderer: and ye know that no murderer hath eternal life *{personified in the indwelling Holy Spirit}* abiding in him. [16] Hereby perceive *{ginosko; i.e., definitively know absolutely}* we the love of God *{what God means to love someone}*, because he laid down his life for us: and we ought to lay down our lives for the brethren *{this extreme sacrificial Spirit defines what it means to "love the brethren"}*. [17] But whoso hath this world's good *{a foundational example of love dealing with material resources}*, and seeth his brother have need *{of material resources}*, and shutteth up his bowels of compassion from him *{does not give sacrificially of those material resources}*, how dwelleth the love of God *{personified in the indwelling Holy Spirit}* in him? [18] My little children, let us not love in word *{not just talk about love}*, neither in tongue *{not just say we will love}*; but in deed and in truth *{actually love by giving sacrificially of ourselves}*. [19] And hereby *{because we are willing to make extreme sacrifices for other believers, even die for them if necessary}* we know *{ginosko; i.e., know absolutely}* that we are of the truth *{personified in the indwelling Holy Spirit; i.e. & therefore "born again"}*, and shall assure our hearts before him" (I John 3:14-19).

God expands upon this statement in I John chapter four. In chapter four, God expands upon the ultimate expression of Christian love regarding the Christian's responsibility in evangelism of the lost.

> We do not love God, or love our neighbors, the way God loves us if we are not willing to make extreme sacrifices and take extreme personal risks to bring them to Christ and disciple them.

Yet, the emphasis of the text is that such an unloving "spirit" is not the manifestation of the presence of new life in Christ. An unloving "spirit" is, in fact, the manifestation of the selfish "*spirit* of antichrist" that is preoccupied with the things of this temporal existence and that person's status within this temporal existence. The reason this last issue is important is that many people, who discover they do not sacrificially love people through evangelism and discipleship, think they merely need to begin doing those things. However, the problem is that this is a manifestation that they have not been "born again."

To simply begin doing something to give yourself a false assurance of salvation is *legalism* in its most subtle form of self-deception. Look closely at I John chapter four.

"[1] Beloved, believe not every spirit, but try the spirits whether they are of God: because many false prophets are gone out into the world. [2] Hereby know ye the Spirit of God: Every spirit that confesseth {*present tense and active voice; is openly/publicly declaring*} that Jesus Christ is come in the flesh is of God: [3] And every spirit that confesseth not {*present tense and active voice; is not openly/publicly declaring*} that Jesus Christ is come in the flesh is not of God {*not "born again" and is, in fact, a "false prophet"*}: and this is that *spirit* of antichrist, whereof ye have heard that it should come; and even now already is it in the world.[4] Ye are of God, little children, and have overcome {*perfect tense; there is a positional completeness already in our new life in Christ*} them {*the Satanic, worldly influence of the "false prophets" or "antichrists"*}: because greater is he that is in you, than he that is in the world. [5] They {*the "false prophets"*} are of the world {*Satan's dominion and under his lordship*}: therefore speak they of the world {*they are preoccupied with talking about temporal things rather than eternal things*}, and the world {*those under Satan's dominion and under his lordship*} heareth them {*are listening to and believing what they are teaching*}. [6] We are of God: he that knoweth God {*those who are truly "born again" people; i.e., brethren "in Christ"*} heareth us {*are listening to and believing what we are teaching*}; he that is not of God heareth not us {*are not listening to and believing what we are teaching*}. Hereby {*by what people are listening to and believing that determines how they will live their lives*} know we the spirit of truth, and the spirit of error. [7] Beloved, let us love one another: for love is of God {*God is the supernatural source of true love and apart from "fellowship" or spiritual union with Him, no one can produce the kind of love that God is*}; and every one that loveth {*present, active, participle; is persistently and consistently loving others the way God loves us*} is born of God {*'born again'*}, and knoweth {*present tense; is having a personal relationship with*} God. [8] He that loveth not (*present, active, articular, participle; continues to not live sacrificially*} knoweth not God {*timeless aorist, has never, ever had a personal relationship with God*}; for God is love. [9] In this {*the sacrificial way in which Jehovah became man and died for our sins*} was manifested {*made physically visible in this temporal existence*} the love of God toward us, because that God sent his only begotten Son into the world {*to die in our place to satisfy God's judgment of wrath upon sin*}, that we might live through him {*through His*} *indwelling presence; Galatians 2:20*}. [10] Herein is love {*the kind of love that God is manifested, exemplified, and defined*}, not that we loved God, but that he loved us, and sent his Son *to be* the propitiation for our sins. [11] Beloved, if God so loved us, we ought also to love one another. [12] No man hath seen God at any time. If we love one another, God dwelleth in us, and his love is perfected in us. [13] Hereby know we that we dwell in him, and he in us, because he hath given us of his Spirit" (I John 4:4-13).

There is a very serious issue before us in these verses of Scripture to which every Christian should give careful consideration. There are two sides to the issue of assurance that every believer MUST understand.

1. Before we are genuinely "born again" of the Spirit of God, Satan wants to gives us a *false assurance* of salvation. He wants us to trust in a false gospel or in something we have done. Any such thing will produce a *false assurance* (Galatians 5:4, 9).

2. After the believer is genuinely "born again" of the Spirit of God, Satan wants to constantly cause doubt to preoccupy the believer with the issues of his own salvation and to keep us from involving ourselves in "the work of the ministry."

These two sides of the issue of assurance lead us to the necessity of a serious study of I John chapter five. In this desire for assurance, we need to ask ourselves a number of questions.

1. Have I genuinely repented of sin and "dead works"?

2. Do I have an understanding of the Gospel of Jesus Christ -what He has accomplished on the sinner's behalf in His death, burial, and resurrection?

3. Am I believing/trusting/resting in what Jesus has accomplished and NOTHING ELSE?

4. Do I truly believe that Jesus Christ is God (Jehovah incarnate) and have I publicly declared my belief in Him as LORD (Jehovah)?

5. Have I called on the name of the incarnate Jehovah (Jesus) to save me?

6. Have I received the indwelling Holy Spirit of God. There is manifest (empirical) evidence of His abiding presence through my spiritual growth, and chastisement when I sin. There is illumination of, desire for, and understanding of the Word of God that is regularly producing spiritual fruit through my life?

In laying the foundation for the exegesis of I John chapter five, we see the need to ask ourselves these six question regarding the issue of assurance of salvation. Someone has said, "Circumstances do not make a man. They only reveal what he is." If there are no external evidences of eternal life in our daily walk with God, we need to make a serious, contemplative examination of the reality of our professed *new birth*.

Often, trying to help someone find assurance of salvation is like propping up a building that is falling apart because it does not have a foundation. The issue of the reality of someone's salvation must be built upon the *reality* of a real faith decision *event* in their understanding of who Jesus is and what He has accomplished on the sinner's behalf. Just as the understanding of all this must be real, so must the sinner's faith be real and a salvation *event* (spiritual new birth) be real. If the profession/confession of faith is real, the possession of eternal life is real. If the possession of eternal life is real, eternal life will manifest itself in the communicable attributes of God as the believing sinner yields his will to God's will as led by the indwelling Spirit of God.

"[37] In the last day, that great *day* of the feast, Jesus stood and cried, saying, If any man thirst, let him come unto me, and drink. [38] He that believeth on me, as the scripture hath said, out of his belly shall flow rivers of living water. [39] (But this spake he of the Spirit, which they that believe on him should receive: for the Holy Ghost was not yet *given*; because that Jesus was not yet glorified.)" (John 7:37-39).

The "feast" of John 7:37 is critical to our understanding of what Christ is saying in verses 37-39. This "feast" was the Feast of the Tabernacles or the Feast of the Firstfruits. This "feast" lasted seven weeks and the "last day" (the day after the seventh Sabbath) was the Day of Pentecost. There is an important theological distinction regarding dispensational transitions that needs to be noted in this text as detailed by Henry W. Soltau's comments on Leviticus 9:1 regarding the "eight day."

"The next chapter of Leviticus, the 9th, opens with '*the eight day.*' This is a singular expression, because it is an additional day to a week already ended. And this *eight day* would necessarily be the *first day* of a new week. Thus we have a type of resurrection. For resurrection could not be unless there has been a preceding creation, which had failed, having been ruined by sin. Resurrection is something entirely new, and yet it comes in upon that which is old.

The only feast which had an eighth day was the feast of Tabernacles. Lev. xxiii. 36, 39; Num. xxix. 35. . . . Circumcision was on the eighth day. Lev. xii. 3. In this rite there was evidently a shadow of what resurrection effects. The true circumcision; 'the putting off the body of the sins of the flesh.' Col. ii. 11-13. 'We are the circumcision, which worship God in the Spirit, and rejoice in Christ Jesus, and have no confidence in the flesh.' Phil. iii.3. As the man-child was on the eighth day circumcised, so on that day the firstling of the oxen and sheep were given to God. Exod. xxii.30; Lev. xxii.27. Another shadow of death and resurrection. It is also deeply interesting to observe that the leper, when healed of his disease of leprosy, and fulfilling the ritual appointed for his ceremonial cleansing, had an eighth day service, which in many respects approached very nearly to the ritual appointed for the consecration of the priests. . . . A cleansed leper obtained that to which no ordinary Israelite who had never suffered under the fearful disease of leprosy, was entitled. **A saved sinner is raised by the grace of God to an infinitely higher position, and is a far higher being in the scale of existence, than was Adam before his fall.**"[6]

Therefore, in John 7:37-39 Christ is referring to the fulfillment of the Old Testament type found within the Feast of the Tabernacles (or the Feast of the Firstfruits). This was fulfilled in His resurrection and the seven week and one day (the eighth day and the first actual day of "the regeneration") span after His resurrection that would be the Day of Pentecost and the coming of the Holy Spirit to indwell all "born again" believers. "(But this spake he of the Spirit, which they that believe on him should receive: for the Holy Ghost was not yet *given*; because that Jesus was not yet glorified.)" (John 7:39). The resurrection AND glorification of Jesus would mark a new historical paradigm in the unfolding dispensational plan of God. Jesus became the "firstborn" of humanity into the "new creation" opening a "door" for "whosoever" and the creation of the "church of the firstborn."

The importance of this *special day* marking the coming of the Holy Spirit to indwell believers lifts the doctrine of Grace and the believer to an extremely higher new level of existence (this is the substance of Christ's remarks regarding the future *hypostatic union*

---

[6] Henry. W. Soltau, **The Tabernacle, the Priesthood, and the Offerings**, Kregal Publications, Grand Rapids, Michigan, Pages 403-404

of the believer through the indwelling). God would be working with believers in a new way never before experienced by mankind since the fall of Adam. Once the believer was indwelled by the Holy Spirit, the indwelling moved the believing sinner from mere positional righteousness to the potential for the supernatural production of God-kind righteousness through the believer's life. This happens when that believer yields his will to God and is "filled" with the Spirit of God.

Both the words "come" and "drink" in John 7:37 are present imperatives (essential commands). In other words, a person MUST both "come" and "drink" before the "living water" will flow from his life. The sinner must be both SAVED and habitually coming to *drink* of the Holy Spirit ("be ye being filled" with; Ephesians 5:18). "Believeth" in verse 38 is a present, active, participle, better translated "is believing."

> Although there must be a salvation event (a new beginning) before this "living water" can begin to flow, there must also be *continuity* to this *believing.*

The potential for the flow of "living water" comes from a salvation event. The actual flow is supernaturally produced by the indwelling Holy Spirit through the *continuity of a living faith* that continues living in belief. This continuation is being filled in the moment-by-moment of each day. Real belief is manifested in this continuity of living what we believe (James 1:22).

The Spirit-filled believer is intended to be the medium of the distribution of this "living water." We have three critical components to the evangelization of the world to the glory of God (Matthew 13:18-23).

1. The Seed (the objective facts of the Gospel of Jesus Christ)
2. The Spirit-filled Sower of the Seed
3. The Soils (the Spirit *conditioned*, cultivated, convicted and *watered* heart of the sinner brought to "understanding" of both his need and God's provision for that need. This *conditioning* of the hearts or "soil" of lost souls should be the substance of the prayers for the lost by Spirit-filled believers. Only the Spirit of God can *condition* hearts.

All three of these components flow through the Spirit-filled believer.

> Although God's Spirit works *apart* from the believer (He is in the world), the Seed and the Spirit-filled Sower are God's ordained and primary means *through which* the Holy Spirit operates.

The "go ye" command of the Great Commission is to literally be the *distribution center* of God's grace (the workings of the Spirit of God) everywhere believers move. The Spirit-filled believer becomes the primary *transportation vehicle* for the work of the Spirit of God. It is in this dynamic that the Spirit-filled believer becomes a "well of water springing up into everlasting life" (John 4:14). Paul describes this intended spiritual dynamic in Romans 10:14-17:

> "[14] How then shall they call on him in whom they have not believed? and how shall they believe in him of whom they have not heard? and how shall they hear without a preacher? [15] And how shall they preach, except they be sent? as it is written, How beautiful are the feet of them that preach the gospel of peace, and bring glad tidings of good things! [16] But they have not all obeyed the gospel. For Esaias saith, Lord, who hath believed our report? [17] So then faith *cometh* by hearing, and hearing by the word of God" (Romans 10:14-17).

The statement of Christ in John 7:38 ("He that believeth on me, as the scripture hath said, out of his belly shall flow rivers of living water.") is a statement that speaks of the fulfillment of two prophetic types given to Israel by Moses while in the wilderness. (Unfortunately, Moses seriously distorted the second type by smiting the rock the seconded time instead of speaking to the rock.) The smiting of the rock (Exodus 17:6) refers to the death, burial, and resurrection of Jesus from which the "living water" of eternal life would find its source. The second prophetic type (Numbers 20:8) refers to the continual presence of Christ and His provision of spiritual sustenance in the "living water" that was available for *the asking* after the crucifixion through the ministry of the Holy Spirit of God (the *Shekinah presence*).

"[1] Moreover, brethren, I would not that ye should be ignorant, how that all our fathers were under the cloud, and all passed through the sea; [2] And were all baptized unto Moses in the cloud and in the sea; [3] And did all eat the same spiritual meat; [4] And did all drink the same spiritual drink: for they drank of that spiritual Rock that followed them: and that Rock was Christ" (I Corinthians 10:1-4).

Another critical issue regarding the statement of Jesus is found in the words, "let him come unto me" in John 7:37. On the "last day of the feast" (the Day of Pentecost), water was gathered from the Pool of Siloam, whose source was believed to be from below the Temple Mount. We have looked at this previously, but it needs to be repeated here.

We cannot grasp the depth of what Christ is saying in John 7:37-39 if we do not understand the historical context of the Feast of the Tabernacles and the events of that Jewish Feast. It contains a number of prophetic types within its practices. The Feast of Tabernacles was instituted as part of the Mosaic Covenant shortly after of the Exodus.

"The seventh and final Feast of the Jewish calendar year is the Feast of Tabernacles. It occurs five days after the Day of Atonement on the fifteenth of Tishri (October). This feast is also called the Feast of Ingathering (Exodus 23:16; 34:22), the Feast to the Lord (Leviticus 23:3[4]; Judges 21:[19]), the Feast of Booths, or simply 'the feast' (Leviticus 23:36; Deuteronomy 16:13; I Kings 8:2; II Chronicles 5:3, 7:8; Nehemiah 8:14; Isaiah 30:29; Ezekiel 45:23,25) because it was so well-known [Quote corrected].

On the eighth and final day of the feast, the high priest of Israel, in a great processional made up of priests and tens of thousands of worshipers, descended from the Temple Mount to pause briefly at the Pool of Siloam. A pitcher was filled with water, and the procession continued via a different route back to the Temple Mount. Here, in the midst of great ceremony, the high priest poured the water out of the pitcher onto the altar."[7]

The Pool of Siloam was filled by a stream (the stream of Siloah) that flowed from underneath the Temple Mount (the Mount of the Rock). Many believed this pool had healing qualities because of the belief that it was filled from the water from the Rock. They believed that this water and the Temple Mount built upon the

---

[7] http://www.christcenteredmall.com/teachings/feasts/tabernacles.htm

threshing floor of Ornan (I Chronicles 21:23) was the fulfillment of the prophetic type of the *water from the rock* in the wilderness (Exodus 17:6). Of course, this was an erroneous understanding of the type.

Therefore, in Jesus' statement, "let him come unto me" in John 7:37, He is saying that neither the Mosaic Covenant Temple, nor the Mosaic Covenant Priesthood and its sacrifices were the *actual* source of the "water of life." Jesus Himself was the fulfillment of that prophetic type. Secondly, the Mosaic Covenant Temple was to be replaced with the *actual* source of "living water" through the indwelling of the believer by the Holy Spirit of God.

> The believer's body would become the "Temple" of God's dwelling place and the means through which the Shekinah would be revealed through the filling (to overflow) of the Spirit filled believer.

God's intent was that the flow of "living water" would be continual and abundant. The source of this "living water" is "Christ in you, the hope of glory" (Colossians 1:27). "Christ in you" is the indwelling Holy Spirit. This indwelling creates a *continuum of the incarnation* as the believer ministers in Christ's stead (II Corinthians 5:16-21).

In the indwelling of the Holy Spirit, there is a *hypostatic union* (describing the presence of both human and Divine natures) of God and man, but not a *hypostatic unity*. The "living water" does not flow until there is *unity* of the human and divine natures. *Unity* of these two natures is achieved when the believer yields his will to the will of God in the indwelling Holy Spirit. The Bible word for this *unity* is "fellowship."

"[1] I therefore, the prisoner of the Lord, beseech you that ye walk worthy of the vocation wherewith ye are called, [2] With all lowliness and meekness, with longsuffering, forbearing one another in love; [3] Endeavouring {*working eagerly, promptly, speedily*} to keep {*watch or guard*} the unity of the Spirit in the bond of peace. [4] *There is* one body, and one Spirit, even as ye are called in one hope of your calling; [5] One Lord, one faith, one baptism, [6] One God and Father of all, who *is* above all, and through all, and in you all. [7] But unto every one of us is given grace according to the measure of the gift of Christ" (Ephesians 4:1-7).

The unity of the Godhead is to be maintained in the "unity of the Spirit" in the hypostatic union created by the indwelling of the Spirit. The prioritizing of maintaining this *unity* is the primary responsibility of all believers, all local churches, and is an absolute essential before the "living water" can flow through us. Salvation is not the most important outcome of the work of Christ. Salvation is merely an *open door* to a new existence that brings the believing sinner into *positional union* with God. It also brings the believer into the potential for *practical unity* with Him so that we can become the vehicles to reveal Him in all of His wondrous attributes (glorify Him). God deserves every believer living in such harmony with Him that we glorify Him.

DISCUSSION QUESTIONS

1. Explain the significance of having died *with* Christ positionally and the practical significance of how that relates to your present possession of eternal life.

2. Discuss the central theme of I John and why it is important to understand that theme.

3. Discuss the statement, "The issue of the use of the word 'if' is to transition from the *indefinite* (doubt) to the *definite* (assurance)."

4. From your understanding of I John chapter four, explain the statement, "We do not love God, or love our neighbors, the way God loves us if we are not willing to make extreme sacrifices and take extreme personal risks to bring them to Christ and disciple them."

5. Define the two sides to the issue of assurance and discuss why it is important to understand the two sides to the issue of assurance.

6. Give the six questions regarding assurance of salvation and discuss why these questions are important.

7. Explain John 7:37-39 from your understanding of the Feast of the Tabernacles and discuss how this truth should be fleshed out in the reality of your life each day.

Chapter Twenty-three

II. Transitioning Between the Possession
of Eternal Life and Its Manifestation

"And hereby we know that we are of the truth, and shall assure our hearts before him" (I John 3:19).

The transition between the *hypostatic union* and *hypostatic unity* (Ephesians 4:1-7) is a critical empirical evidence to assure that there was a salvation event (new birth) in our lives. Until we honestly evaluate our salvation decision (the reality of our faith; i.e., what we have believed and done with the Gospel of Jesus Christ and the Person of Jesus Christ), we cannot receive from I John chapter five what God intends for this text to give us (I John 3:19). After we have honestly answered the six questions from the last chapter, we can break down I John chapter five into some spiritually digestible parts.

"[1] Whosoever believeth *{present participle; i.e., is believing}* that Jesus is the Christ *{incarnate Jehovah}* is born *{perfect tense; describes an action which is viewed as having been completed in the past, once and for all, not needing to be repeated; passive voice; represents the subject as being the recipient of the action, not the doer of the action}* of God: and every one that loveth *{present participle; i.e., is loving}* Him that begat loveth *{present participle; i.e., is loving}* him *{all other true believers}* also that is begotten *{"born again"}* of Him. [2] By this we know that we love the children of God, when we love God, and keep his commandments *{a circular proposition; we cannot love other believers if we live contrary to the Word of God}*" (I John 5:1-2).

Immediately, we are confronted with the spiritual reality of genuine faith and a genuine new life "in Christ." There is a radical supernatural outcome of having been "born again." The genuine family of God loves every other genuine member of the family. This means much more than merely wanting to be with them (although that is true). It means a willingness to make enormous personal sacrifices in order to benefit them both materially and spiritually. There is an extreme supernatural *sacrificiality* of personal relationship with other true believers when *hypostatic unity* exists through the filling of the Spirit.

Secondly, we cannot say we truly love other "children of God" (vs. 2) when we live in duplicity (double mindedness. i.e., *spiritually* and *worldly* at the same time). Such a thing is both a contradiction to a genuine testimony of salvation and genuine love for anyone. We cannot love someone and lead that person away from the center of God's will by permissively modeling a contradiction to that will.

Thirdly, "love" cannot exist apart from the medium of truth (His "commandments"). Truth is the medium through which "love" is expressed. Therefore, truth is greater than love. Although truth exists apart from love, genuine "love" does not, and cannot, exist apart from the medium of living and teaching truth. Love is the expression of truth. Therefore, love cannot contradict truth.

> "[3] For this is {*the visible expression of*} the love of God, that we keep {*keep on keeping*} his commandments: and his commandments are not grievous {*heavy or a great burden*}. [4] For whatsoever is born {*perfect participle; has been born*} of God overcometh {*present active; keeps on conquering*} the world {*Satan's realm of influence and temptations*}: and this is the victory that overcometh {*continually is overcoming, aorist, active, participle; indicates an individual experience that began some point in time and continues in the practice of our lives throughout our lifetimes and into eternity*} the world, even our faith {*by living our beliefs as shown by our confessing/proclaiming Christ (verse 1) and living Christ like (verse 2)*}. [5] Who is he that overcometh {*present, active, participle; is overcoming or conquering*} the world, but he that believeth {*present, active, participle; is believing*} that Jesus is the Son of God {*incarnate*}" (I John 5:3-5)?

God does not leave our understanding of loving Him up to our rationalization by allowing "love" to be defined as some ambiguous *emotion*. "Love" is defined in very tangible terms and with some very measureable qualities. These verses define a major transition from the life of the believer prior to Pentecost and the indwelling of the Holy Spirit of God. Now, after Pentecost and the indwelling, the believer has an intimacy with God never before experienced by mankind before the fall. Like marriage, an actual *union* has been generated.

"[30] For we are members of his body, of his flesh, and of his bones. [31] For this cause shall a man leave his father and mother, and shall be joined unto his wife, and they two shall be one flesh. [32] This is a great mystery: but I speak concerning Christ and the church" (Ephesians 5:30-32).

Fear is a juvenile motivation for obedience/faithfulness. Love is the adult/mature motivation for obedience/faithfulness. When loving someone is our motivation for obedience/faithfulness, our obedience/faithfulness will not be a burden. Being obedient/faithful will be a joy because we know that our obedience/faithfulness will bring joy to the One we love. Therefore, living in obedience/faithfulness (continually overcoming) will be a constant priority of the true believer's life because he does not merely want to PROCLAIM his love for God. That believer wants to LIVE his love for God.

Before we can assure our hearts that a salvation event has taken place, there must be evidence of *continuity of living* that which we profess to believe. Although true believers will fail in their Christian lives often, they will ALWAYS repent, confess, be cleansed, and begin again. That is what defines the "victory that overcometh {*continually is overcoming*} the world" (I John 5:4).

The *hypostatic union* can never be broken, but every time the *hypostatic unity* is broken by failure/sin, the believer seeks to restore that unity through repentance, confession, and forgiveness/cleansing. We are not to fight wounded. We fight restored and reconciled.

"[6] This is he that came by {*through or by the means of*} water and blood, even Jesus Christ; not by water only, but by water and blood. And it is the Spirit that beareth witness, because the Spirit is truth. [7] For there are three that bear record {*present, active, participle; are witnessing or testifying*} in heaven, the Father, the Word, and the Holy Ghost: and these three are one. [8] And there are three that bear witness {*present, active, participle; are witnessing or testifying*}in earth, the Spirit, and the water, and the blood: and these three agree in one" (I John 5:6-8).

This is an extremely difficult text. It has been the subject of debate since the ninth century of Christianity. Part of the debate is over the authenticity of what is known as the Johannine Comma (verses 7-8, see footnote for excellent answer to this debate[8]). If you have a marginal reference in your Bible that I John 5:7-8 is "not in the best manuscripts," reject that statement.

For me, the subject of I John 5:6 is plainly understood to refer to two existences and how Jesus in His humanity enters into those two existences. The "water" does not refer to the baptism of Jesus. "Water" refers to His physical birth. This is what Jesus spoke about in John chapter three in His conversation with Dr. Nicodemus.

> "[3] Jesus answered and said unto him, Verily, verily, I say unto thee, Except a man be born again, he cannot see the kingdom of God. [4] Nicodemus saith unto him, How can a man be born when he is old? can he enter the second time into his mother's womb, and be born? [5] Jesus answered, Verily, verily, I say unto thee, Except a man be born of water {womb birth} and of the Spirit, he cannot enter into the kingdom of God. [6] That which is born of the flesh {womb birth} is flesh; and that which is born of the Spirit is spirit. [7] Marvel not that I said unto thee, Ye must be born again" (John 3:3-7).

"Blood" refers to the means of redemption and the propitiation of God's wrath. The new birth is through faith in His blood. Therefore, the "blood" refers to the doorway of reconciliation with God into both salvation (hypostatic union) and fellowship (hypostatic unity).

> "[8] But God commendeth his love toward us, in that, while we were yet sinners, Christ died for us. [9] Much more then, being now justified by his blood, we shall be saved from wrath through him. [10] For if, when we were enemies, we were reconciled to God by the death of his Son, much more, being reconciled, we shall be saved by his life" (Romans 5:8-10).

> "[12] Giving thanks unto the Father, which hath made us meet to be partakers of the inheritance of the saints in light: [13] Who hath delivered us from the power of darkness, and hath translated us into the kingdom of his dear Son: [14] In whom we have redemption through his blood, even the forgiveness {aphesis; remission} of sins: [15] Who is the image of the invisible God, the firstborn {primogeniture} of every {all} creature {creation}: [16] For by him

---

[8] Maynard, Michael , M.L.S.; A History of the Debate Over I John 5:7-8. (Tempe, AZ: Comma Publications, 1995).

were all things created, that are in heaven, and that are in earth, visible and invisible, whether *they be* thrones, or dominions, or principalities, or powers: all things were created by him, and for him: [17] And he is before all things, and by him all things consist. [18] And he is the head of the body, the church: who is the beginning, the firstborn from the dead; that in all *things* he might have the preeminence" (Colossians 1:12-18).

"[11] But Christ being come an high priest of good things to come, by a greater and more perfect tabernacle, not made with hands, that is to say, not of this building; [12] Neither by the blood of goats and calves, but by his own blood he entered in once into the holy place, having obtained eternal redemption *for us*" (Hebrews 9:11-12).

The "Spirit . . . beareth witness, because the Spirit is truth" (I John 5:4) to both the humanity of Jesus as the incarnate Jehovah and the resurrection/glorification of that same Jesus into "the regeneration." This is why the *bodily* resurrection/glorification of Jesus is a critical truth to our faith decision and a genuine salvation event. However, this statement also relates to the empirical evidence of the *hypostatic union* and *hypostatic unity* in the life of a believer.

"[7] Nevertheless I tell you the truth; It is expedient for you that I go away: for if I go not away, the Comforter will not come unto you; but if I depart, I will send him unto you. [8] And when he is come, he will reprove the world of sin, and of righteousness, and of judgment: [9] Of sin, because they believe not on me; [10] Of righteousness, because I go to my Father, and ye see me no more; [11] Of judgment, because the prince of this world is judged. [12] I have yet many things to say unto you, but ye cannot bear them now. [13] Howbeit when he, the Spirit of truth, is come, he will guide you into all truth: for he shall not speak of himself; but whatsoever he shall hear, *that* shall he speak: and he will shew you things to come. [14] He shall glorify me: for he shall receive of mine, and shall shew *it* unto you. [15] All things that the Father hath are mine: therefore said I, that he shall take of mine, and shall shew *it* unto you" (John 16:7-15).

The statement, "Spirit . . . beareth witness, because the Spirit is truth" (I John 5:4) relates to WHAT the Spirit of God will do through our lives WHEN *hypostatic unity* ("fellowship" or "abiding in Christ") has happened. This "witness" about who Jesus is and what He has accomplished will be part of the *flow* of "living water." This "witness" will not need to be *forced.* It will be the supernatural outcome of *hypostatic unity.* By this supernatural "witness," the inward reality (*hypostatic union and unity*) will manifest itself in the outward reality.

This leads us to the next statement regarding the spiritual continuity of the *hypostatic union:* "[7] For there are three that bear record {*present, participle; are bearing witness*} in heaven, the Father, the Word, and the Holy Ghost: and these three are one {*referring to unity in essence*}. [8] And there are three that bear witness {*present, participle; are bearing witness*} in earth, the Spirit, and the water, and the blood: and these three agree {*third person, present, indicative; lit., "they are"*} in one {*the incarnate Jehovah; i.e., the hypostatic union of Christ*}" (I John 5:7-8). The issue of these two verses of Scriptures is that of perfect unity in the *testimony* ("witness") of the Tri-unity of God in both eternity (*perpetuity*) and in this cursed existence called "earth." This perfect unity of witness also lies within the *hypostatic union* of the believer and is released through the believer's life when *hypostatic unity* ("fellowship") exists. This is almost exactly what Paul says in Ephesians 4:1-7.

"[1] I therefore, the prisoner of the Lord, beseech you that ye walk worthy of the vocation wherewith ye are called, [2] With all lowliness and meekness, with longsuffering, forbearing one another in love; [3] Endeavouring {*working eagerly, promptly, speedily*} to keep {*watch or guard*} the unity of the Spirit in the bond of peace. [4] *There is* one body {*of Christ in "the regeneration" made up of all born again believers since the Day of Pentecost*}, and one Spirit {*who empowers the "one body" for ministry and service; the only source for hypostatic union and hypostatic unity*}, even as ye are called in one hope {*the believer's future glorification*} of your calling {*to glorify God through the hypostatic union and hypostatic unity*}; [5] One Lord {*referring to the incarnation of Jehovah in Jesus as the Redeemer of both the souls of lost men and of lost Adamic dominion*}, one faith {*refers to the inscripturalized revelation of biblical truth from which we establish our knowledge of God, of God's will, and what we are to believe and practice providing believers the medium for hypostatic union "in Christ" and hypostatic unity with God and with one another*}, one {*efficacious*} baptism {*referring to the baptism with the Holy Spirit into the "body" of Christ, the "last Adam," and contradistinctively, the removal from the cursed family of Adam; I Corinthians 12:13*}, [6] One God and Father of all, who *is* above all, and through all, and in you all. [7] But unto every one of us is given grace {*in that this supernatural enabling of the indwelling Holy Spirit is given to every believer, every believer is equally responsible and culpable for the spiritual resources of the hypostatic union demanding that we live our lives in the continuity of hypostatic unity both with God and one another*} according {*referring to culpability for the various spiritual service gifts; Romans 12:3-8*} to the measure of the gift of Christ" (Ephesians 4:1-7).

"[9] If we receive the witness of men, the witness of God is greater: for this is the witness of God which he hath testified of his Son. [10] He that believeth on the Son of God hath the witness in himself {*referring to the hypostatic union*}: he that believeth {*present, active, participle; is not believing and, therefore, is not loving 'the world,' 2:15, and is not habitually and regularly overcoming 'the world,' 5:4*} not God {*the Scriptural witness of God about the coming of His Son, His death, burial, and resurrection, and what that would accomplish; believing refers to the issue of faith or resting in those truths*} hath made {*perfect, active, indicative; a once for all completed action resulting in a permanent state*} him a liar; because he believeth {*perfect, active, indicative; a once for all completed action resulting in a permanent state; i.e., complete rejection and, therefore, reprobation*} not the record {*same Greek word as 'witness' in verses 9 and 10*} that God gave {*perfect, active, indicative; a once for all completed action resulting in a permanent state*} of his Son. [11] And this is the record {*same Greek word as 'witness' in verses 9 and 10*}, that God hath given {*aorist, active, indicative; an action from some point in time with continuing and perpetual/eternal results*} to us eternal {*perpetual*} life {*perfect, full, complete, abundant life/existence*}, and this {*perfect, full, complete, abundant life/existence*} life is in his Son {*in the hypostatic union of 'the regeneration' and hypostatic unity through yielding to the indwelling Holy Spirit*}. [12] He that hath {*present, active, participle; is having*} the Son hath {*present, active, indicative*} life {*the life; definite article is in the Greek text*}; and he that hath not {*present, active, participle; is not having*} the Son of God hath {*present, active, indicative*} not life {*the idea is that if there is not hypostatic union through a faith decision to receive the indwelling Holy Spirit, there is no possibility for hypostatic unity and the manifestation of 'the life' of the 'new creation'*}. [13] These things have I written unto you that believe {*present, active, participle; are believing*} on the name of the Son of God; that ye may know {*perfect, active, subjunctive; i.e., possibility or that you may know with full assurance or without doubt*} that ye have eternal life {*by the manifestation of the hypostatic union through hypostatic*} *unity*}, and that ye may believe {*present, active, subjunctive; the idea is a continuation in the assurance of your faith decision and the accompanying overcoming eternal life within you*} on {*indicating the point reached or entered; i.e. the point where you began*} the name of the Son of God" (I John 5:9-13).

When the believer receives Jesus Christ as LORD (as the incarnate Jehovah), the believer is also receiving this triune inner Witness that exists both in "heaven" and in the "earth."

"[14] For as many as are led by the Spirit of God, they are the sons of God. [15] For ye have not received the spirit of bondage again to fear; but ye have received the Spirit of adoption, whereby we cry, Abba, Father. [16] The Spirit itself beareth witness with our {*hemon*, hay-mone'; *from our or of our*} spirit, that we are the children of God:" (Romans 8:14-16).

This inner Witness is the supernatural workings of the indwelling Holy Spirit of God. If this supernatural inner Witness exists (the hypostatic union), there WILL BE (not ought to be or might be) empirical, tangible, external evidences of new existence. The believer has become a "new creature" (II Corinthians 5:17; new creation; see also Galatians 6:15). He has been radically changed in both his position and his spiritual makeup from what he was before he was "born again."

> Although the believer's *transfiguration* is not yet complete (he is not yet glorified to be like Christ is presently), he is BEING *transfigured*.

This *transfiguration* to become more and more like Christ in our beliefs and practices (the "one faith") is the way spiritual growth is measured and what defines practical sanctification. Assurance comes from the evidences of progressive spiritual growth.

DISCUSSION QUESTIONS

1. Explain the theological difference between *hypostatic union* and *hypostatic unity.*

2. From I John 5:1-2, discuss the radical supernatural outcome of having been "born again."

3. Discuss why it can be said that truth is greater than love.

4. Discuss the following two statements: "Fear is a juvenile motivation for obedience/faithfulness. Love is the adult/mature motivation for obedience/faithfulness."

5. How is the evidence of continuity of living what we profess to believe manifested?

6. Discuss this statement, "The issue of these two verses of Scriptures is that of perfect unity in the *testimony* ("witness") of the Tri-unity of God in both eternity (*perpetuity*) and in this cursed existence called 'earth.' This perfect unity of witness also lies within the *hypostatic union* of the believer and is released through the believer's life when *hypostatic unity* ('fellowship') exists."

7. Discuss the following statement regarding progressive sanctification, "Although the believer's *transfiguration* is not yet complete (he is not yet glorified to be like Christ is presently), he is BEING *transfigured.*

Chapter Twenty-four
Out of Control Christians!

"[1] Simon Peter, a servant and an apostle of Jesus Christ, to them that have obtained like precious faith with us through the righteousness of God and our Saviour Jesus Christ: [2] Grace and peace be multiplied unto you through the knowledge of God, and of Jesus our Lord, [3] According as his divine power hath given unto us all things that pertain unto life and godliness, through the knowledge of him that hath called us to glory and virtue: [4] Whereby are given unto us exceeding great and precious promises: that by these ye might be partakers of the divine nature, having escaped the corruption that is in the world through lust. [5] And beside this, giving all diligence, add to your faith virtue; and to virtue knowledge; [6] And to knowledge temperance; and to temperance patience; and to patience godliness; [7] And to godliness brotherly kindness; and to brotherly kindness charity. [8] For if these things be in you, and abound, they make you that ye shall neither be barren nor unfruitful in the knowledge of our Lord Jesus Christ. [9] But he that lacketh these things is blind, and cannot see afar off, and hath forgotten that he was purged from his old sins. [10] Wherefore the rather, brethren, give diligence to make your calling and election sure: for if ye do these things, ye shall never fall: [11] For so an entrance shall be ministered unto you abundantly into the everlasting kingdom of our Lord and Saviour Jesus Christ" (II Peter 1:1-11).

Christians (like everyone) have problems with sin. The difference should be that Christians recognize their failures as sin, repent, and begin to do what is right. However, there seems to be an increasing number of Christians who refuse to recognize their un-Scriptural behavior as sin. As a result, we see more and more Christian children in rebellion against their parents. Teenagers, young adults, and adults are involved in worldly practices, carnal life styles, fornication, and adultery.

Divorce among Christians has become common. This problem is due people's *hardness of hearts* to the will of God for their lives, refusing to forgive, and out of control lusts and anger. It would appear that like the world, Christians are *out of control*. II Peter 1:1-11 tells us why Christians are *out of control*.

In II Peter 1:3, Peter begins this epistle about living in the last days with a reminder that believers have been given "all things" that are necessary for a life of "godliness" because they each have received God's "divine power."

"Divine" is the Greek word *theios*. It refers to something that belongs to the Godhead. Here it refers to the "power" that the Godhead possesses. It refers to the indwelling Holy Spirit who will empower (*enable*) the believer to be the type of person described in verses 5-8.

According to II Peter 1:4, because we have trusted in Jesus Christ for our salvation, we rest in the wonderful promises of God. One of these promises is that when Christ left, another Comforter would come to aid believers to live the way Christ had taught them to live. This is what is meant by "that we might be partakers of the divine nature." Because we have received the indwelling Holy Spirit to enable us to live the way Christ taught, we can also participate in the "nature" that belongs to the Godhead. *Don't run by this at a hundred miles an hour.* Stop here for a moment.

When we see Christians out of control and living carnally, it is because they fail (or refuse) to utilize one of the most precious gifts of their salvation - the indwelling presence of the Holy Spirit of God. You have the "divine nature" living in you. When Christians refuse to recognize sin, they "quench" His enabling power and "grieve" Him. The effect of that quenching upon their lives and upon the cause of Christ is overwhelmingly devastating.

In II Peter 1:4 we are told that the Spirit of God is given to us that we might "escape the corruption that is in the world through lust." When we refuse to recognize the sin of which He convicts us, we "quench" His work in our lives. He is the only means by which the believer can be supernaturally enabled to habitually escape the corrupting influences of this world and the corrupting influences of our own carnal natures/spirits. The Spirit of God gives us the strength to say *no* to sin (and *mean it from the heart*). He gives us the strength to say yes to righteousness (and *mean it from the heart*). Both of these things require the enabling power of the Holy Spirit. This is what *"grace"* means.

"Faith" in Christ for salvation is just a new beginning (II Peter 1:5). In salvation we are assured of spending eternity with God. We have a *new birth*. However, new babies are expected to grow. Read II Peter 3:17-18.

Growth results when we work in cooperation with the Holy Spirit to "add" certain characteristics to our new life in Christ. It is impossible for a person to succeed in *"escaping the corruption that is in the world through lusts"* while refusing to recognize the Holy Spirit's conviction of sin. This recognition then must be followed by seeking His empowering to live victorious over the flesh.

Go to II Peter 1:6 and *camp* **for a while on "temperance." It means self-control.** Why are so many Christians *out of control*? They are *out of co*ntrol because they have never added *self-control* to their salvation (control of self). They are not working to bring self (the sin nature, lusts, and emotions) under the control of the Holy Spirit. When I say a person is *out of control*, I mean he is out of the Holy Spirit's control and *in the flesh*. When you are *in the flesh*, you are always *out of control* and carnal. A spiritual person is *spiritual* because he is under the control of the Spirit and begins to bear the *"fruit of the Spirit"* in his life.

Being *out of control* is most evident in our emotions.

What you are emotionally is a visible manifestation of what you are as a person and your level of spiritual growth. Remember, spiritual growth is measured by the degree our lives are yielded to the Holy Spirit and the percentage of time that *yielding* exists. When our emotions are *out of control*, we are out of the control of the Holy Spirit. In other words, we are living carnally/fleshly and are in sin.

Bringing our emotions under the Spirit's control will bring our lives under His control. The majority of people do not control their emotions. Their emotions control them. They are *out of control*. At best, they merely *suppress* their emotions. We must always remember that recognizing the evident characteristic of the flesh as sin is the first step in bringing it under control.

The majority of the decisions we make are greatly influenced by our emotions. However, when decisions are made based solely upon emotions, they are almost always wrong

decisions. For instance, how many people choose a husband or wife based upon strong *feelings* (that they call *love*) that they have for that person? How many relationships have been destroyed because of out of control anger? How many people have quit on a marriage because they have a *feeling* of lost hope?

> **We can usually trace every bad decision back to one of three out of control emotions. It is what I call the *triangle of failure*. These emotions are ANGER, FEAR, and DESIRE (more commonly known as *lusts*).**

Self-focus (selfishness or self-first) will result in each of these three things being out of control. Read Ephesians 4:26-32.

"[26] Be ye angry, and sin not: let not the sun go down upon your wrath: [27] Neither give place to the devil. [28] Let him that stole steal no more: but rather let him labour, working with his hands the thing which is good, that he may have to give to him that needeth. [29] Let no corrupt communication proceed out of your mouth, but that which is good to the use of edifying, that it may minister grace unto the hearers. [30] And grieve not the holy Spirit of God, whereby ye are sealed unto the day of redemption. [31] Let all bitterness, and wrath, and anger, and clamour, and evil speaking, be put away from you, with all malice: [32] And be ye kind one to another, tenderhearted, forgiving one another, even as God for Christ's sake hath forgiven you."

When anger is out of the control of the Holy Spirit, anger turns to wrath. This results in a number of other out of control *emotions*. Each of these is an *evidence/manifestation* of out of control anger.

1. Bitterness
2. Resentment
3. Intolerance
4. Vengeance or malice
5. A critical spirit (gossip and slander)
6. Unforgiveness

When fear is out of the control of the Holy Spirit, it also manifests itself in a number of ways. These are all evidences of out of control fear. Most fears stem from a fear of one of two things: *failure* or *rejection*.

1. Worry or anxiety
2. Withdrawal resulting in loneliness
3. Paranoia (suspicions)
4. Defensiveness
5. Indecision
6. Shyness
7. Moodiness

When desires are out of the control of the Holy Spirit they result in the following:

1. Covetousness
2. Idolatry (especially *idols of the heart*)
3. Addictions
4. Impulsiveness
5. Fornication and adultery

Anytime we recognize one of these characteristics of out of control anger, fear, or desires, we need to immediately recognize that we are in the *flesh* and out of control of the Holy Spirit. The longer we stay out of control, the more damage will be done. When this *triangle of emotions* is not brought under the control of the Holy Spirit, a person will be completely crippled in doing anything, or being anything for the cause of Christ. As a result, this person's Christianity will be empty and unfulfilling.

When anger and fear remain out of control, a person almost always ends up at a *pity pa*rty attended by just one person, himself. No one else is allowed, because he knows that no one else wants to be there. **Self-pity opens the door to depression (the *black hole*).** Depression has become a serious problem in our society because of the continual emphasis on self- focus. When anger, fear, or desires dominate a person's life, other emotions take control, and it is a downward slide into the *black hole*.

If we want to have successful relationships that bring honor and glory to God, we must learn to bring our lives and our emotions under the control of the Spirit. Unless we do that, all of our relationships are doomed to failure, misery, and (ultimately) destruction. Secondly, our testimony will be habitually destroyed. We can spend months of intense spiritual work to rebuild a destroyed testimony only to rip it all apart in a few seconds of out of control emotions. We must remember that whenever we destroy our own testimony and try to rebuild it, in the eyes of those who have seen the destruction, we are merely re-building with the *rubble* of our own failures. There will always be the *ghost* of that past failure underneath the rebuilt and recovered testimony in the memory of those involved, even if they have forgiven the past failure.

1. Will you recognize those emotions, which are manifested in your life, as evidence that you are/were out of control and in sin?
2. Will you confess your failures to God and to the others that they have affected?
3. Will you repent, meaning that you will promise to work at change, and begin to work at doing what is right? It will take consistency over a long span of time to remove of *ghost* of the memory of you destroying your own testimony in a moment of **ANGER, FEAR, or DESIRES (more commonly known as** *lusts*).

DISCUSSION QUESTIONS

1. According to II Peter 1:3, what has every believer received that enables him to live a life of "godliness? Discuss how and when this was received.

2. Explain the phrase "that we might be partakers of the divine nature" in II Peter 1:4, specifically focusing on the word "partakers."

3. Explain what it means in the spiritual sense to be *out of control*. Be thorough.

4. List and discuss the three emotions that, when they are out of control, define the *Triangle of Failure*.

5. List and define the six *evidences/manifestations* of out of control anger.

6. List and define the seven *evidences/manifestations* of out of control fear.

7. List and define the five *evidences/manifestations* of out of control desires/lusts.

Chapter Twenty-five
Transfiguring Grace in Hypostatic Unity

The vast majority of Bible believing Christians are taught a list of *do's and don'ts*. They are taught that as long as they do the *do's*, and don't do the *don'ts*, they will be in God's good graces and be blessed. I do not have a problem with the list of *do's and don'ts*. I do have a problem with the false teaching that merely trying to obey this list of *do's and don'ts* will make you a spiritual person and right with God. It will not. Thinking this way and living in this mindset is what defines legalism. We got saved by "grace through faith." We trusted in the death, burial, and resurrection of the Lord Jesus Christ and were immediately translated into the realm of God's grace (Romans 5:2; supernatural empowering). Once regenerated, we simply must yield to the indwelling Spirit of God who will begin to *transform/transfigure* us with His filling. This *transforming/transfiguring* is an inward supernatural work of God that manifests itself in outward characteristics referred to as the "fruit of the Spirit."

Most Christians claim to believe in the resurrection from the dead. After all, the resurrection from the dead is a fundamental doctrine of Christianity. However, we must admit that the vast majority of professing Christians have an inaccurate view of the resurrection from the dead, or a very superficial view at best. Most Christians view the resurrection from the dead to be a resurrection to a body very much like the one we presently have, except it will not get old, sick, or fat. The reality of the resurrection is that the believer will be completely transfigured into another essence of existence altogether. Yes, there will be some similarities to our old bodies, but those similarities will be superficial compared to our "new creation."

"[1] And he said unto them, Verily I say unto you, That there be some of them that stand here, which shall not taste of death, till they have seen the kingdom of God {*refers to "the regeneration"*} come with power. [2] And after six days Jesus taketh *with him* Peter, and James, and John, and leadeth them up into an high mountain apart by themselves: and he was transfigured before them. [3] And his raiment became shining, exceeding white as snow; so as no fuller on earth can white them. [4] And there appeared unto them Elias with Moses: and they were talking with Jesus. [5] And Peter answered and said to Jesus, Master, it is good for us to be here: and let us make three tabernacles; one for thee, and one for Moses, and one for Elias. [6] For he wist not what to say; for they were sore afraid. [7] And there was a cloud that overshadowed them: and a voice came out of the cloud, saying, This is my beloved Son: hear him. [8] And suddenly, when they had looked round about, they saw no man any more, save Jesus only with themselves. [9] And as they came down from the mountain, he charged them that they should tell no man what things they had seen, till the Son of man were risen from the dead. [10] And they kept that saying with themselves, questioning one with another what the rising from the dead should mean. [11] And they asked him, saying, Why say the scribes that Elias must first come? [12] And he answered and told them, Elias verily cometh first, and restoreth all things; and how it is written of the Son of man, that he must suffer many things, and be set at nought. [13] But I say unto you, That Elias is indeed come, and they have done unto him whatsoever they listed, as it is written of him" (Mark 9:1-13).

The Jewish understanding of the Kingdom Age fell completely short of the magnificence of the spiritual reality that it will actually be. The Jews saw the Kingdom Age as the coming of a Messianic *political deliverer* who would lead the nation of Israel to be the next world-wide empire on the earth. This was both a superficial view of the promised Messiah and a false view.

The incident of the transfiguration recorded in Mark 9:1-13 is intended to correct this false view of the Kingdom Age, address the superficiality of the spiritual understanding of this false view, and expose the supernatural transitional aspects of the eternal/perpetual "new creation" merging together with the temporal creation during the Kingdom Age. During the Kingdom Age, Christ and all believers of the Church Age, will be fully transfigured (glorified) and will dwell within this temporal creation as *kings and priests* over the non-glorified. This reality exists presently, during the Church Age, in an embryonic sense of *transfiguration*. Spiritual growth in the areas of practical sanctification is, in fact, progressive *transfiguration*. **This *progressive transfiguration* is empirical evidence that a believer has been "born again."**

"[1] Behold {*aorist imperative; a command to continue to perceive with the eyes*}, what manner of love the Father hath bestowed {*perfect tense*} upon us, that we should be called the sons of God {*John 1:11-12*}: therefore the world knoweth us not, because it knew him not. [2] Beloved, now are we the sons of God, and it doth not yet {*as of yet* or *right now*} appear {*aorist, passive; fully apparent*} what we shall be: but we know that, <u>when he shall appear, we shall be like him; for we shall see him as he is.</u> [3] And every man that hath this hope in him purifieth {*present, active*} himself, even as he {*Jesus*} is pure {*sacred; physically pure, morally blameless, and/or completely consecrated*}" (I John 3:1-3).

The focus of I John 3:1-3 is transitional in nature.

Although the believer is presently a child of God by *new birth*, he is not yet *glorified*. However, the present position of the believer "in Christ" carries with it the moral obligation of progressive transfiguration through progressive sanctification. According to verse two, all believers are presently ("now") the "sons {*teknon, a child as produced*} of God." Although we cannot fully comprehend what our glorification will look like, we can grasp the reality of the truth that, when it happens, we will look like Jesus looked when He was transfigured before Peter, James, and John. Therefore, this understanding of our future transfiguration and glorification carries with it the responsibility of being *purified*. The word "purified" is from the Greek word *hagnizo* (hag-nid'-zo). The word means *to make clean*. The idea is to remove from our lives and persons any defiling influence from the satanic realm of darkness (*worldliness*). The person who understands and has the "hope" of future glorification will make any sacrifice necessary to insure that he has completely separated his life and ambitions from any degree of *worldliness* (world-like-ness, I John 2:15). The failure to do so is a manifestation of unbelief and a failure to really understand what it means to *love* God.

"[1] Do we begin again to commend ourselves? or need we, as some *others*, epistles of commendation to you, or *letters* of commendation from you? [2] Ye are our epistle written in our hearts, known and read of all men: [3] *Forasmuch as ye are* manifestly declared to be the epistle of Christ ministered by us, written not with ink, but with the Spirit of the living God; not in tables of stone, but in fleshy tables of the heart. [4] And such trust have we through Christ to God-ward: [5] Not that we are sufficient of ourselves to think any thing as of ourselves; but our sufficiency *is* of God; [6] Who also hath made us able ministers of the new testament; not of the letter, but of the spirit: for the letter killeth, but the spirit giveth life. [7] But if the ministration of death, written *and* engraven in stones, was glorious, so that the children of Israel could not stedfastly behold the face of Moses for the glory of his countenance; which *glory* was to be done away: [8] How shall not the ministration of the spirit be rather glorious? [9] For if the ministration of condemnation *be* glory, much more doth the ministration of righteousness exceed in glory. [10] For even that which was made glorious had no glory in this respect, by reason of the glory that excelleth. [11] For if that which is done away *was* glorious, much more that which remaineth *is* glorious. [12] Seeing then that we have such hope, we use great plainness of speech: [13] And not as Moses, *which* put a vail over his face, that the children of Israel could not stedfastly look to the end of that which is abolished: [14] But their minds were blinded: for until this day remaineth the same vail untaken away in the reading of the old testament; which *vail* is done away in Christ. [15] But even unto this day, when Moses is read, the vail is upon their heart. [16] Nevertheless when it shall turn to the Lord, the vail shall be taken away. [17] Now the Lord is that Spirit: and where the Spirit of the Lord *is*, there *is* liberty. [18] But we all, with open face beholding as in a glass the glory of the Lord, are changed *{present, passive; i.e., are being changed}* into the same image from glory to glory *{from varying degrees of partial transfiguration to final and complete transfiguration/glorification}*, *even* as by the Spirit of the Lord" (II Corinthians 3:1-18).

The word "changed" in II Corinthians 3:18 is from the Greek word *metamorphoo* (met-am-or-fo'-o). This is the same word translated "transfigured" in Mark 9:2. In Romans 12:2, this same Greek word is translated "transformed." The word in Romans 12:2 should also be translated *transfigured* as it is used in the same context as it is used in II Corinthians 3:18. In Romans 12:2, the Greek word *metamorphoo* (met-am-or-fo'-o) is a present, passive, imperative. The important aspect of the use of this word in Romans 12:2 and II Corinthians 3:18 is that the uses are in the present passive; *i.e., are being transfigured.* The passive aspect of the verb conveys the absolute dependency upon the indwelling Holy Spirit to accomplish this progressive transfiguration in our lives as we yield our wills to Him. We cannot *transfigure* ourselves. This is a supernatural work of God. Yet, in Romans 12:2, the verb is used as an imperative - i.e., *a command*. Although we cannot accomplish this progressive transfiguration, we are commanded to be transfigured.

"[1] I beseech you therefore, brethren, by the mercies of God, that ye present your bodies a living sacrifice, holy, acceptable unto God, *which is* your reasonable service. [2] And be not conformed to this world: but be ye transformed by the renewing of your mind, that ye may prove what *is* that good, and acceptable, and perfect, will of God. [3] For I say, through the grace given unto me, to every man that is among you, not to think *of himself* more highly than he ought to think; but to think soberly, according as God hath dealt to every man the measure of faith" (Romans 12:1-3).

Chafer's Systematic Theology[9] gives us some great insight into defining God's intent in the believer's progressive transfiguration through progressive sanctification.

"It is evident that a thing is transformed by influences from without while a thing is transfigured by the outshining of a light or vitality which is resident within. Christ's essential glory was veiled while here upon the earth, but in the moment of transfiguration His intrinsic Shekinah glory was allowed to break forth. He was not merely assuming a glory or standing in the radiance of an outward glory which fell upon Him. The glory was His own, and originated in Him and emanated from Him. It is a truth which lends so much importance to the two passages wherein transfiguration is related to believers – Romans 12:2; 2 Corinthians 3:18. The believer is subject to transfiguration and not to mere transformation. The divine Presence within is as a light, and this is to have its normal outshining and will work great changes within the heart where that Nature dwells."

The significance of this is that the indwelling Holy Spirit is doing a progressive work of *creation* within us as we habitually yield our wills to Him. This work of *creation* that progressively transfigures us is the supernatural empowerment that takes place when the *Tripartite of Power* exists within the believer's life. In this *Tripartite of Power,* the glory of God within the believer is released and the believer manifests a *partial* transfiguration (i.e., "light"

---

[9] Chafer, Lewis Sperry. *Systematic Theology, Volume V,* 9 Dallas, Texas :Dallas Seminary Press, Thirteenth Printing, June, 1976), 86.

shines, Matthew 5:16). Full transfiguration does occur until the believer's ultimate and final glorification.

The Tripartite of Spiritual Power

1. The Spirit: the supernatural *empowering* of the indwelling Holy Spirit

2. The Word: the *knowledge* of the will of God as revealed by the Word of God

3. The Spirit-filled believer: as the believer yields to the indwelling Spirit **AND** begins to live the Word of God, becoming a "doer of the Word" (James 1:22)

The believer's progressive transfiguration will progress only during those times when the believer is Spirit "filled." Progressive transfiguration will progress only when hypostatic unity is achieved by repentance, confession of sin, and cleansing of defilement (I John 1:7-9) AND when the believer is fully consecrated to DOING what God's Word commands in the empowering of the Spirit.

DISCUSSION QUESTIONS

1. Discuss why merely keeping and trying to obey a list of *do's and don'ts* cannot and will not make you a spiritual person.

2. Explain the resurrection of the Redeemed from the perspective of the "new creation" and glorification. What will the resurrected and glorified believer be like and not be like?

3. Discuss I John 3:1-3 as it relates progressive transfiguration in the use of the command to be "purified."

4. Explain the following text as it relates to your responsibilities in progressive transfiguration. "[18] But we all, with open face beholding as in a glass the glory of the Lord, are changed {*present, passive; i.e., are being changed*} into the same image from glory to glory {*from varying degrees of partial transfiguration to final and complete transfiguration/glorification*}, *even* as by the Spirit of the Lord" (II Corinthians 3:18).

5. Explain Romans 12:1-3 as it relates to the spiritual dynamic of progressive transfiguration of your responsibilities in this spiritual dynamic.

6. Read the comment from Chafer's Systematic Theology on page 201 and discuss this statement as it relates to progressive transfiguration.

7. List and define the *Tripartite of Spiritual Power* and discuss how these three entities work together to create progressive transfiguration.

Chapter Twenty-six
Legalism: Doing All the Right Things for the Wrong Reasons

Legalism is a contradiction of the doctrine of grace. However, legalism is much more subtle than we might imagine regarding its spiritual deception. We are all *by nature* legalists. When I say we are legalists *by nature,* I mean legalism is part of our fallen nature. We think that if we try hard and do our best, we can stand before God and be accepted by Him. We think that as long as we are trying our best to do what God's Word commands, we are being *spiritual.* Simply defined, legalism is the religion of *will power.* God hates it!

> "[1] O foolish Galatians, who hath bewitched you, that ye should not obey the truth, before whose eyes Jesus Christ hath been evidently set forth, crucified among you? [2] This only would I learn of you, Received ye the Spirit by the works of the law, or by the hearing of faith? [3] Are ye so foolish? having begun in the Spirit, are ye now made perfect by the flesh? [4] Have ye suffered so many things in vain? if *it be* yet in vain. [5] He therefore that ministereth to you the Spirit, and worketh miracles among you, *doeth he it* by the works of the law, or by the hearing of faith" (Galatians 3:1-5)?

Spirituality cannot be produced by fallen beings. Also, just because we are saved does not mean that salvation is a *magic wand* waved over our lives that changes our fallen heart (spirit). The sin nature has not been eradicated by our salvation. Yes, it was "crucified with Christ" (Romans 6:6), but we must, as Scripture tells us, "reckon ye also yourselves to be dead indeed unto sin, but alive unto God through Jesus Christ our Lord" (Romans 6:11). This is what Christ referred to in John 15:5 when He said, "without me ye can do nothing."

This is a truth that we MUST grasp by faith. If we have grasped the Truth that our sin natures were "crucified with Christ," then we will understand our new *position* in Christ. We will understand our new *potential* for spirituality through the indwelling of the Holy Spirit as we yield our hearts (wills) to Him. Salvation saves our souls from eternal damnation (Romans 8:1), but it does not change our hearts in any way. Our hearts (spirits) are still carnal and corrupt. There is still no good thing in our hearts. Even though we might want (will) to do good, we cannot produce God-kind righteousness or spirituality through our corrupt flesh. Even though our souls are saved by grace, our hearts (spirits) are dead apart from the inner workings of the *Parakletos* (John 14:26). Growing in grace is the moment-by- moment process of being transfigured from within. This is a progressive act of creation by the indwelling Holy Spirit as we yield our wills to Him. You cannot change yourself apart from the supernatural workings of the indwelling Creator.

> "Can the Ethiopian change his skin, or the leopard his spots? *then* may ye also do good, that are accustomed to do evil" (Jeremiah 13:23; compare II Corinthians 3:18; 4:1-2 and 6-7).

The questions of Jeremiah 13:23 are rhetorical. No, the black man cannot change the color of his skin. No, the leopard cannot change his spots. Either of these situations would require a *new creation* or a *re-creation*. Their DNA would need to be changed before these things could be effected. In salvation, the death sentence upon sin has been satisfied (God is propitiated). The baptism with the Holy Spirit has removed the saved sinner from the condemned realm of the first and cursed creation and translated the believer's soul into "the regeneration . . . in Christ." However, the saved sinner still has the same old heart problem.

> "[5] Thus saith the LORD; Cursed *be* the man that trusteth in man, and maketh flesh his arm, and whose heart departeth from the LORD. [6] For he shall be like the heath {*naked and destitute*} in the desert, and shall not see when good cometh; but shall inhabit the parched places in the wilderness, *in* a salt land and not inhabited. [7] Blessed *is* the man that trusteth in the LORD, and whose hope the LORD is. [8] For he shall be as a tree planted by the waters, and *that* spreadeth out her roots by the river, and shall not see when heat cometh, but her leaf shall be green; and shall not be careful in the year of drought, neither shall cease from yielding fruit. [9] The heart *is* deceitful {*incurably sick or corrupted; i.e., it cannot be healed or repaired*} above all *things*, and desperately wicked: who can know it? [10] I the LORD search the heart, *I* try the reins, even to give every man according to his ways {*chosen pathways of life*}, *and* according to the fruit of his doings" (Jeremiah 17:5-10).

Although the sinner's soul has been delivered from condemnation, our hearts are still corrupt and cannot produce God-kind righteousness apart from a supernatural partnership ("fellowship") with the indwelling Spirit of God (the "divine nature;" II Peter 1:4).

Legalism is when we try to do God's will apart from supernatural partnership ("fellowship") with the indwelling Spirit of God. Paul tells us in many places in the Scriptures that this supernatural partnership ("fellowship") with the indwelling Spirit of God is what defines allowing Christ to live through us.

"[19] For I through the law am dead to the law, that I might live unto God. [20] I am crucified with Christ: nevertheless I live; yet not I, but Christ liveth in me: and the life which I now live in the flesh I live by the faith of the Son of God, who loved me, and gave himself for me. [21] I do not frustrate {*atheteo, ath-et-eh'-o, i.e., set aside or neutralize/nullify*} the grace of God: for if righteousness *come* by the law, then Christ is dead in vain" (Galatians 2:19-21).

Legalism is trying to live the Christian life through your own *will power*, through the *self-life* controlled by your own *will power*. Legalism produces a sad state of affairs. Legalism produces enormous frustration in the lives of those seeking to live this way. This frustration is shown in Romans chapter seven as Paul gives us the scenario of his own life under the Law (Mosaic Covenant) as he tried to live for Jehovah through the *self-life* of *will power*.

"[1] Know ye not, brethren, (for I speak to them that know the law,) how that the law hath dominion over a man as long as he liveth? [2] For the woman which hath an husband is bound by the law to *her* husband so long as he liveth; but if the husband be dead, she is loosed from the law of *her* husband. [3] So then if, while *her* husband liveth, she be married to another man, she shall be called an adulteress: but if her husband be dead, she is free from that law; so that she is no adulteress, though she be married to another man. [4] Wherefore, my brethren, ye also are become dead to the law by the body of Christ; that ye should be married to another, *even* to him who is raised from the dead, that we should bring forth fruit unto God. [5] For when we were in the flesh, the motions of sins, which were by the law, did work in our members to bring forth fruit unto death. [6] But now we are delivered from the law, that being dead

206

wherein we were held; that we should serve in newness of spirit, and not *in* the oldness of the letter" (Romans 7:1-6).

The text continues in the context of "dominion" from Romans 6:14. The two unions (*marriages*) refer metaphorically to the Old Covenant in Adam under the governance (dispensation) of Law and the New Covenant "in Christ" under the governance (dispensation) of Grace. In Adam and under the Law, the believer did not have the indwelling of the Holy Spirit. The Law was limited in what it could accomplish. The Law only provided external benefits through the external leading and guidance of the Holy Spirit. The Law was a *child-leader*, constantly pointing and directing the believer to faith in the Coming One (Messiah) through endless sacrifices. The Law sought to keep the believer from the destruction of sin through *building fences* that externally restrained the believer's life, producing an outward form of righteousness. No matter how great a relationship the Law provided to the Old Covenant believer in the external workings of the Spirit of God *upon* the believer's life, the Law could never enable a believer to produce the *fruit* of God-kind righteousness *through* the believer's life.

Romans 7:1 actually begins with the Greek word *e* (ay). It can be translated *and, but,* or *or.* I believe the context (the sentence is a question) demands the translation *or.* William R. Newell translates it; "Or are ye ignorant, brethren. . . "[10] The beginning word "or" of Romans 7:1 is critical because it connects the context of Romans seven with Paul's statement in Romans 6:14; "For sin shall not have dominion over you: for ye are not under the law, but under grace." Without this context connection, we would lose much of what Romans chapter seven is teaching.

In the *fall* the whole first creation was infected with a *spiritual virus* called sin. That *spiritual virus* was genetically passed on through procreation to every descendant of Adam. Sin corrupted each individual from within corrupting our *hearts* (wills or spirits). To be a descendant of Adam means to be born "in sin." David said it like this: "Behold, I was shapen in iniquity; and in sin did my mother conceive me" (Psalm 51:5). The word "iniquity" in this verse is from the Hebrew word `avon (aw-vone'), meaning *perversity* or *the punishment of sin* (i.e., condemnation), referring to

---

[10] Newell, William R. **Romans Verse by Verse**; Moody Press, SwordSearcher Software 6.0.

the medium in which his body grew and was formed in the womb of his mother. The words "in sin" are from the Hebrew word *chet'* (khate), meaning the *penalty of a crime*. David acknowledges that all descendants of Adam (including himself) are both formed in the womb in condemnation and conceived in condemnation. This will be critical to understand in the *contextual continuity* that leads to Romans 8:1: "There is, therefore, NOW no condemnation to them who are **in** Christ Jesus . . ."

> The *spiritual virus* with which Satan infected the whole first creation brought immediate spiritual death (separation from God, meaning the opportunity for *fellowship* with God) to everything it infected.

The effect of that was not immediately apparent. Adam and Eve knew they were naked, revealing *moral consciousness* in their spiritual death. The empirical evidence of their separation from God was not yet apparent in that they continued to be alive physically. The fact that they did not immediately die physically reveals the continuing realm of God's grace allowing them time and opportunity to repent and receive the *gift* of God's redemption, forgiveness and salvation through faith in the Promised One of Genesis 3:15 (see Revelation 13:8). Although all human beings are born spiritually dead, they too are given the *grace of time and opportunity* to repent and be saved.

Every contact of God with the fallen human race is an act of His wondrous, abounding grace. The question of Romans 6:1 is referring to the *infected* realm of sin. "Shall we continue {*living our lives*} in {*the realm of*} sin, that grace may abound?" Or, should we move our new lives into the realm of the *New Creation* "in Christ" where "we have access by faith into this *new realm of* grace in which we stand" (Romans 5:2)? Just as we are saved by grace through faith, we must practically *move* our new lives "in Christ" into the realm of Grace "by faith" ("the just*ified* shall live by faith," Romans 1:17) in order to produce God-kind righteousness through our new lives "in Christ."

"[20] Moreover the law entered, that the offence might abound. But where sin abounded, grace did much more abound: [21] That as sin hath reigned unto death, even so might grace reign through righteousness unto eternal life by Jesus Christ our Lord" (Romans 5:20-21).

Today, very few people can grasp Paul's attitude toward the Law. They do not understand the ramifications of what he is saying because few people today have grown up under the Law as he did. Paul does not speak of the Law as a bad thing. In fact just the opposite is true.

"Wherefore the law *is* holy, and the commandment holy, and just, and good" (Romans 7:12).

"[7] The law of the LORD *is* perfect, converting the soul: the testimony of the LORD *is* sure, making wise the simple. [8] The statutes of the LORD *are* right, rejoicing the heart: the commandment of the LORD *is* pure, enlightening the eyes. [9] The fear of the LORD *is* clean, enduring for ever: the judgments of the LORD *are* true *and* righteous altogether. [10] More to be desired *are they* than gold, yea, than much fine gold: sweeter also than honey and the honeycomb. [11] Moreover by them is thy servant warned: *and* in keeping of them *there is* great reward" (Psalm 19:7-11).

When Paul speaks of the Law with a negative connotation, he is referring to the Law *as a religion in itself* (the *self-life* or *righteousness by will power*) as taught and practiced by Judaism (particularly Phariseeism; i.e., legalism). This is the Law Paul knew and under which he grew to adulthood. He addresses Romans 7:1 to people with which he had a similar experience and knowledge of the Law as did he. Today, this would also apply to the vast majority of professing Christians living under liturgical/sacramental/sacerdotal *Christianity*. Although different than Judaism in its practices, this type of *Christianity* is the same in its legalism.

We hear a verse of Scripture like, "If I regard iniquity in my heart, the Lord will not hear *me*" (Psalm 66:18), and we simply decide we won't "regard iniquity in" our hearts *so that* God will hear our prayers. Of course, the reality of our fallen natures is that we "regard iniquity in" our hearts as part of our fallen natures. Therefore, repentance and humbling ourselves before God goes far beyond what we do in acts of disobedience. Repentance and humbling ourselves before God is constantly acknowledging to ourselves and then to God that we CANNOT be what God wants us to be. Until we grasp that spiritual reality, we are doomed to live a life of legalism and to producing nothing through our lives but "wood, hay, and stubble" (I Corinthians 3:12).

If this is true (that we are at best, due to our fallen nature, legalists and can never obey God's commands "from the heart"), why then did God give the Law? The answer is found in Romans chapter six.

DISCUSSION QUESTIONS

1. Discuss why legalism is a contradiction against the doctrine of grace. Also discuss why it can be said that legalism is the religion of *will power*.

2. Discuss the difference between the fact that your sin nature has been crucified with Christ (Romans 6:6) and what is often referred to as the *eradication of the sin nature*.

3. Discuss the questions of Jeremiah 13:23 in the context of attempting to *change yourself*. Discuss the only way this *change* can be accomplished.

4. Explain Romans 7:1-6 from the context of "dominion" as referred to in Romans 6:14.

5. Discuss the use of the metaphor of a *spiritual virus* regarding the *infection* of sin, how sin is *spread* from one generation to the next, why this virus is *incurable*, and how the *application* of grace is the only way to overcome it.

6. According to Romans 7:12 and Psalm 19:7-11, the Law is not a bad thing. Discuss how false teaching regarding the doctrine of grace denigrates the Law. Discuss why such false teaching is inherently evil.

7. When Paul speaks of the Law with a negative connotation, he is referring to the Law *as a religion in itself* (the *self-life* or *righteousness by will power*) as taught and practiced by Judaism (particularly Phariseeism; i.e., legalism). In what ways does liturgical Christianity with its sacerdotalism and sacramentalism compare to Paul's negative connotations regarding legalism?

Chapter Twenty-seven
Dealing with the Errant Definitions of Legalism and Liberalism

The term *legalism* is used nowadays (errantly) to refer to a strict interpretation and application of the Word of God. The argument against strict interpretation is errantly justified by a *liberal* interpretation of what *grace* means in the Word of God.

For many today, *liberalism* is understood to be a good thing. In some ways, it is good to be *liberal*. Generosity is good and means a person is liberal in his giving of money and time to help to meet physical needs as well as liberally giving love, forgiveness, mercy, and compassion to others. However, liberalism can also mean open-minded, tolerant, or not bound by traditional or conventional ideas and values. A libertarian is a person who is favorable to, or in accord with, concepts of the maximum of individual freedom that is possible, especially as guaranteed by law and secured by governmental protection of civil liberties. Regarding biblical interpretation, *liberalism* is basically defined as opposing strict or rigorous interpretations while favoring a more free approach of allegory as opposed to literalism. Extreme forms of *liberalism* have great distain for those who hold to literal interpretations of Scripture. *Liberalism* is not stark unbelief. *Liberalism* is merely varying degrees of *broader* interpretation of the Word of God than intended in arguing *grace liberty* to the point of *license* to do whatever one wants to do. In other words, *liberalism broadens* the definitions of what the Word commands in less restrictive, more liberating ways.

Understanding that both *legalism* and *liberalism* are condemned in Scripture, we must find out from Scripture what differentiates between the terms. First, *legalism* is NOT merely too strict an interpretation and application of the Word of God. God commands a strict interpretation and application of His Word. **Therefore, a broader more liberal/loose/liberating interpretation of Scripture is actually contrary to Christ's teachings**.

"[17] Think not that I am come to destroy the law, or the prophets: I am not come to destroy, but to fulfil. [18] For verily I say unto you, Till heaven and earth pass, one jot or one tittle shall in no wise pass from the law, till all be fulfilled. [19] Whosoever therefore shall break *{luo loo'-o, literally loosen; the idea is to teach a more relaxed, broader, more liberal interpretation}* one of these least *{in size or importance; i.e.; seemingly insignificant}* commandments, and shall teach men so, he shall be called the least in the kingdom of heaven: but whosoever shall do and teach *them*, the same shall be called great in the kingdom of heaven. [20] For I say unto you, That except your righteousness shall exceed *the righteousness* of the scribes and Pharisees, ye shall in no case *{double negative in Greek text; not at all or not by any means}* enter into the kingdom of heaven *{this is not referring to the final eternal state of existence, but is referring to the Kingdom Age because God-kind righteousness is required; i.e., justification 'by grace through faith'}*" (Matthew 5:17-20).

Before dealing with the theological substance of Christ's teachings in Matthew chapters five through seven, understand that those who teach that Christ's teachings in these three chapters is for the Kingdom Age believers, and not for Church Age believers, completely miss the point of what Christ is teaching. The Jewish Levitical priesthood had perverted the Mosaic Covenant. They perverted both the moral Law and ceremonial Law of God making them the means of salvation and fellowship with God through which the blessings of God would flow. To some degree they were correct regarding the issues of fellowship with God, but where they were in error in their interpretation and application of the moral Law (the commandments) and ceremonial Law (the sacrifices, Priesthood, holy days) was so subtle that the error completely perverted (leavened) the whole (Galatians 5:9) and was a complete perversion of God's intended *faith way* ("the just shall live by faith;" Habakkuk 2:4, Romans 1:17, Galatians 3:11, and Hebrews 10:38). Granted, no believer can keep the Law the way Matthew chapters five through seven detail until they are fully glorified/transfigured. However, that is exactly what the text teaches. During the Church Age there is *progressive transfiguration* through the supernatural workings of the indwelling Holy Spirit through *hypostatic unity* ("fellowship"). This progressive transfiguration happens as the Spirit works within the yielded, saved sinner. When the believer comes to understand that reality, then, and only then, will he seek to discover what the *faith way* is: i.e., living by grace enabling.

First, we can clearly see from Matthew 5:17-20 and the two following chapters, that *liberalism* is not what defines Christian *liberty*. In other words, the restrictions of the Law are not *loosened* or *lessened* under the dispensation of grace (supernatural enabling from within, i.e. "from the heart"). In fact, according to what Christ teaches in what follows Matthew 5:17-20, in the rest of chapters five, six, and seven, the restrictions of the moral obligations of the Law are defined in a much more strict and definitive way, not a looser, less restrictive way.

Second, the text is not talking about a *performance based salvation* that requires a person to live sinless to be saved. The text is talking to saved believers about the outcome of their salvation "by grace through faith." Only those "born again" of the Spirit of God, indwelled by the Spirit of God, and supernaturally enabled by the indwelling Spirit would be enabled to produce God-kind righteousness in their lives. Only these individuals will be enabled to live the expectations of this extremely more strict and definitive way that Christ interprets the Law and the Prophets. It is this extremely more strict and definitive way in which Christ interprets the Law and the Prophets that is referred to elsewhere in Scripture as the *spirit* of the Law as opposed to the *letter* of the Law. The *letter* of the Law is the mere legalistic external application of Law keeping. The *spirit* of the Law applies to the desires of the heart regarding Law keeping. Acceptable obedience MUST be preceded with the right motivation/desire/attitude about the person we are, what we are, and about who and what God is before that obedience can be blessed of God.

"[23] Thou that makest thy boast of the law, through breaking the law dishonourest thou God? [24] For the name of God is blasphemed among the Gentiles through you, as it is written. [25] For circumcision verily profiteth, if thou keep the law: but if thou be a breaker of the law, thy circumcision is made uncircumcision. [26] Therefore if the uncircumcision keep the righteousness of the law, shall not his uncircumcision be counted for circumcision? [27] And shall not uncircumcision which is by nature, if it fulfil the law, judge thee, who by the letter and circumcision dost transgress the law? [28] For he is not a Jew, which is one outwardly; neither is that circumcision, which is outward in the flesh: [29] But he is a Jew, which is one inwardly; and circumcision is that of the heart, in the spirit, and not in the letter; whose praise is not of men, but of God" (Romans 2:23-29).

"^{6} Who also hath made us {*hikanoo, hik-an-o'-o; enabled or fitted with all necessities*} able ministers of the new testament; <u>not of the letter, but of the spirit</u>: for the letter killeth, but the spirit giveth life. ^{7} But if the ministration of death, written *and* engraven in stones, was glorious, so that the children of Israel could not stedfastly behold the face of Moses for the glory of his countenance; which *glory* was to be done away: ^{8} How shall not the ministration of the spirit be rather glorious? ^{9} For if the ministration of condemnation *be* glory, much more doth the ministration of righteousness exceed in glory. ^{10} For even that which was made glorious had no glory in this respect, by reason of the glory that excelleth. ^{11} For if that which is done away *was* glorious, much more that which remaineth *is* glorious" (II Corinthians 3:6-11).

> Those who hold the *spirit* of the Law *in their hearts* do not view the Law as merely *restrictive*. Those who hold the "spirit" of the Law *in their hearts* view the Law as *liberating*.

The Law exposes the *invisible chains of the bondage* of what sin is that imprison us to our fallen natures and to satanic temptations of our corrupted desires. If we only see the "letter" of the Law, we only see the symptoms of sin and only deal with, and externally try to correct, those symptoms. The *spirit* of the Law reveals to us the corruption of our own fallen natures. It reveals the external symptoms revealed by sinful acts. These failures cannot be dealt with merely by eternally ceasing or restraining the acts of sin, like taking an aspirin for a headache caused by a brain tumor. Then, the person never deals with the root issue of sin. The root issue is the very desire for sin in the first place.

Until practical sanctification through *hypostatic union* (the indwelling of the Spirit) and *hypostatic unity* (the "filling" with the Spirit as the believer yields his will to the indwelling Spirit) are a practical reality in an individual's life; the very best that person ever can do is *try* to fulfill the *letter* of the Law externally. However, he will never fulfill the *spirit* (inward obligations) of the Law, which exponentially increases God's expectations compared to the *letter* (external obligations) of the Law.

The *spirit* of the Law is the *inward desire* for perfect holiness both inwardly AND outwardly that brings about

intimate knowledge and fellowship with God. If a believer has the *spirit* of the Law *in his heart*, this *spirit* is what dominates his thinking and every decision that comes before him. His thinking is dominated with what will be pleasing to God and acceptable before God. He certainly is not thinking liberally regarding a looser, less restrictive interpretation of God's expectations. Instead, when he holds the *spirit* of the Law *in his heart,* he will be thinking more definitively. Whenever there might be doubt about something being unacceptable, he will ALWAYS abstain from doubtful things or practices. That is one liberating aspect of the *spirit* of the Law *in his heart.* It immediately removes from the discussion, or equation of decision making, anything that might be defined as "doubtful disputations" (Romans 14:1).

  What then is the Word of God's instruction regarding *Law keeping* **as a means of practical sanctification before God?** Certainly we can see that Law keeping cannot save anyone because keeping the Law requires we inwardly keep the *spirit* (inward obligations) of the Law. That means we must eradicate even our desire for sin. If the desire to sin is there, we have broken the *spirit* of the Law. This extreme expectation of the *spirit* (inward obligations) of the Law is an absolute impossibility. This expectation of the *spirit* (inward obligations) of the Law demands that we cry out to God in hopeless despair for deliverance from the guilt and judgment that comes along with the failure to keep the *spirit* (inward obligations) of the Law. This is *exactly* God's intent in giving the Law.

  "[9] What then? are we better *than they*? No, in no wise: for we have before proved both Jews and Gentiles, that they are all under sin; [10] As it is written, There is none righteous, no, not one: [11] There is none that understandeth, there is none that seeketh after God. [12] They are all gone out of the way, they are together become unprofitable; there is none that doeth good, no, not one. [13] Their throat *is* an open sepulchre; with their tongues they have used deceit; the poison of asps *is* under their lips: [14] Whose mouth *is* full of cursing and bitterness: [15] Their feet *are* swift to shed blood: [16] Destruction and misery *are* in their ways: [17] And the way of peace have they not known: [18] There is no fear of God before their eyes. [19] Now we know that what things soever the law saith, it saith to them who are under the law: that every mouth may be stopped, and all the world may become guilty before God. [20] Therefore by the deeds of the law {*Law keeping*} there shall no flesh be justified {*referring to salvation by self-justification through Law keeping}* <u>in his sight: for</u> <u>by the law *is* the knowledge of sin.</u> [21] But now the righteousness of God without the law is manifested, being witnessed by the law and the prophets; [22] Even the righteousness of God *which is* by faith *{fullness}* of Jesus Christ <u>unto all and upon all them that believe</u> *{imputation and impartation}*: for there is no difference: [23] For all have sinned, and come short of the glory of God; [24] Being justified freely by his grace through the redemption that is in Christ Jesus: [25] Whom God hath set forth *to be* a propitiation through faith in his blood, to declare his righteousness for the remission of sins that are past, through the forbearance of God; [26] To declare, *I say*, at this time his righteousness: that he might be just, and the justifier of him which believeth in Jesus" (Romans 3:9-26).

Salvation cannot come to us by Law keeping because we cannot keep the *spirit* of the Law in the strength of our own corrupt nature, no matter how much we may desire to do so. That is why repentance of "dead works" is so critical to salvation and is a primary manifestation of an understanding of the doctrine of condemnation.

"[1] Therefore leaving the principles of the doctrine of Christ, let us go on unto perfection; not laying again the foundation of repentance from dead works, and of faith toward God, [2] Of the doctrine of baptisms, and of laying on of hands, and of resurrection of the dead, and of eternal judgment" (Hebrews 6:1-2).

Secondly, once we are saved "by grace through faith," we must keep the *spirit* of the Law to be practically sanctified before God. Here again we find another impossibility apart from God's enabling grace through yielding to the indwelling Holy Spirit of God. This is what Paul was referring to in Galatians 3:1-5 and also in II Corinthians 3:6 when he said by inspiration of the Spirit of God, "Who also hath made us *{hikanoo, hik-an-o'-o; enabled or fitted with all necessities}* able ministers of the new testament; <u>not</u> <u>of the letter, but of the spirit</u>: for the letter killeth, but the spirit giveth life."

Matthew 5:1-7:29 are critical verses defining God's expectations in the interpretation and application of the Law and the Prophets (what we call the Old Testament books). It is clear from Matthew 5:17-20 that Jesus commanded a strict and narrow interpretation of the Law and the Prophets. In fact, we can dogmatically say that what Christ Jesus teaches in Matthew 5:1-7:29

is a much more strict interpretation and application of the Law and the Prophets than what was previously applied by the *legalistic* Pharisees. This is what Christ is talking about in the phrase "except your righteousness shall exceed *the righteousness* of the scribes and Pharisees" in Matthew 5:20.

After the statement in Matthew 5:17-20, Jesus goes on in detail explaining His stricter, narrower interpretation and application of the Law and the Prophets. Jesus is defining the differences between the *spirit* of the Law and the *letter* of the law. The Pharisees only sought to keep the *letter* of the Law externally. They never even gave consideration to the necessity of first obeying the *spirit* of the Law inwardly. The *spirit* of the Law was the desire to please God more than anything else and glorify Him through our lives. This motivating *attitude* (spirit) is what defines true faithfulness and true obedience "from the heart."

> Christ is giving a stricter interpretation and more definitive description of God's expectations regarding the application of the Law and the Prophets. This is NOT resolved by a MORE *legalistic* approach to the Law and the Prophets.

The Jews could not obey *from the heart* the less stringent, more liberal interpretation and application. Why then would anyone think Christ was teaching that they needed to be MORE legalistic? **The solution to legalism is not liberalism (in any degree) and the answer to liberalism is not increased legalism.** Christ was seeking to bring these legalistic Jews to the place of hopeless despair regarding their own ability to keep the Law in any real and practical way *from the heart.* Christ was seeking to reveal to the legalists that the purpose of the Law was to reveal man's hopelessly lost, guilty, and condemned condition before God. Christ was seeking to bring the legalist before God to cry out to Him in hopeless despair: I cannot do and I cannot be what you expect of me! I need your grace! I need your supernatural enabling! Until we see that purpose in Matthew chapters five through seven, we will miss Christ's intent regarding this serious instruction, correcting perverted teaching regarding the purpose of the Law. The answer is not found in either liberalism or legalism, but in God's grace.

As we look at a number of these examples that Jesus gives in the strict interpretation and application regarding God's higher expectation of obedience, one dominant theme runs throughout - obedience must be an inward desire before the outward action can be either controlled or accepted by God. This principle of obedience is not new to the Gospels or the New Covenant epistles. There must be a genuine desire to obey the Law *from the heart.* This genuine desire must go beyond pleasing God merely so that the sinner can *get God to do* what he wants God to do. The Law and the Prophets detail this expectation over and over again.

"Praise ye the LORD. Blessed *is* the man *that* feareth {*reverential awe of*} the LORD, *that* <u>delighteth greatly</u> {*finds obeying God exceedingly pleasureful*} <u>in his commandments</u>" (Psalm 112:1).

"Thy words were found, and I did eat them; and thy word was unto me the joy and rejoicing of mine heart: for I am called by thy name, O LORD God of hosts" (Jeremiah 15:16).

"[8] Behold, I go forward, but he *is* not *there*; and backward, but I cannot perceive him: [9] On the left hand, where he doth work, but I cannot behold *him*: he hideth himself on the right hand, that I cannot see *him*: [10] But he knoweth the way that I take: *when* he hath tried me, I shall come forth as gold. [11] My foot hath held his steps, his way have I kept, and not declined. [12] Neither have I gone back from the commandment of his lips; I have esteemed {*hoarded, saved, or treasured*} the words of his mouth more than my necessary *food*" (Job 23:8-12).

"[1] My son, if thou wilt receive my words, and hide my commandments with thee; [2] So that thou incline thine ear unto wisdom, *and* apply thine heart to understanding; [3] Yea, if thou criest after knowledge, *and* liftest up thy voice for understanding; [4] If thou seekest her as silver, and searchest for her as *for* hid treasures; [5] Then shalt thou understand the fear of the LORD, and find the knowledge of God" (Proverbs 2:1-5).

"[30] The mouth of the righteous speaketh wisdom, and his tongue talketh of judgment. [31] The law of his God *is* in his heart; none of his steps shall slide" (Psalm 37:30-31).

"[1] My son, forget not my law; but let thine heart keep my commandments: [2] For length of days, and long life, and peace, shall they add to thee. [3] Let not mercy and truth forsake thee: bind them about thy neck; write them upon the table of thine heart: [4] So shalt thou find favour and good understanding in the sight of God and man. [5] Trust in the LORD with all thine heart; and lean not unto thine own understanding. [6] In all thy ways acknowledge him, and he shall direct thy paths" (Proverbs 3:1-6).

There is no reason for the Jews (or deceived Christians today) to think that God could be pleased with the mere external, legalistic obedience of His commandments. In fact, we can go beyond the fact that God merely is NOT pleased with such nonsense. We can unequivocally state that God is displeased with the very idea of legalistic externalism and hates it; He loathes it.

"[10] Hear the word of the LORD, ye rulers of Sodom; give ear unto the law of our God, ye people of Gomorrah. [11] To what purpose *is* the multitude of your sacrifices unto me? saith the LORD: I am full of the burnt offerings of rams, and the fat of fed beasts; and I delight not in the blood of bullocks, or of lambs, or of he goats. [12] When ye come to appear before me, who hath required this at your hand, to tread my courts? [13] <u>Bring no more vain oblations; incense is an abomination unto me; the new moons and sabbaths, the calling of assemblies, I cannot away with; *it is* iniquity, even the solemn meeting.</u> [14] <u>Your new moons and your appointed feasts my soul hateth: they are a trouble unto me; I am weary to bear *them*.</u> [15] And when ye spread forth your hands, I will hide mine eyes from you: yea, when ye make many prayers, I will not hear: your hands are full of blood. [16] Wash you, make you clean; put away the evil of your doings from before mine eyes; cease to do evil; [17] Learn to do well; seek judgment, relieve the oppressed, judge the fatherless, plead for the widow. [18] Come now, and let us reason together, saith the LORD: though your sins be as scarlet, they shall be as white as snow; though they be red like crimson, they shall be as wool. [19] If ye be willing and obedient, ye shall eat the good of the land: [20] But if ye refuse and rebel, ye shall be devoured with the sword: for the mouth of the LORD hath spoken *it*" (Isaiah 1:10-20).

Most English translations (including the KJV) do not do a good job with Matthew 5:17. "Think not that I am come to destroy the law, or the prophets: I am not come to destroy, but to fulfil." Critical to understanding the whole of Matthew chapters five through seven, is our understanding of the two Greek words translated "destroy" and "fulfill" in Matthew 5:17. The word "destroy" is from the Greek word *kataluo* (kat-al-oo'-o). It means to *loosen downwardly, to take apart, disintegrate, or dissolve.* Christ said, do not think that He came to do such a thing. Instead, understand that He came to *fulfill* the Law. Many have offered numerous explanations regarding Christ's meaning of this statement. However, I think the best meaning is simply in the context of the grammar of the statement.

The word *fulfill* is translated from the Greek word *pleroo* (play-ro'-o). The word means to *fill to the fullest extent*, to *cram full*. Granted, Jesus did fulfill the Law in both the sense of living it in its fullest intent *from the heart* and substitutionally satisfying its sentence upon the guilty offender through His death, burial, and resurrection thereby propitiating God's wrath upon sin (I John 2:2). We know Jesus fulfilled the Law in this way from numerous Scriptural testimonies.

"[1] Brethren, my heart's desire and prayer to God for Israel is, that they might be saved. [2] For I bear them record that they have a zeal of God, but not according to knowledge. [3] For they being ignorant of God's righteousness, and going about to establish their own righteousness *{through legalistic Law keeping}*, have not submitted themselves unto the righteousness of God *{justification by grace through faith}*. [4] For Christ *is* the end of the law <u>for righteousness</u> to every one that believeth" (Romans 10:1-4).

As Romans 10:4 says, Christ came to end the false teaching of apostate Israel that Law keeping could bring them the God-kind righteousness necessary to either salvation or "fellowship" with God. However, this is not the context of Matthew 5:17. The context is that Jesus did not come to *lessen* or *loosen* God's expectations of sinners regarding Law keeping.

Jesus came to restore the extreme, fullest extent of God's expectations in perfect Law keeping both inwardly and outwardly, i.e. *from the heart*.

Law and Grace do not oppose one another as enemies. They are cooperating partners. Neither do they exist apart from one another. They are inseparable partners of truth that must walk hand-in-hand if mankind is to be restored both in salvation and sanctification. An old poem by an unknown author states:

To run and work the Law commands,
Yet gives me neither feet nor hands;
But better news the gospel brings:
It bids me fly and gives me wings.

The Law by itself brings nothing but guilt, failure, despair, hopelessness, and condemnation. Until we understand the doctrine of Grace, there is little wonder why we hate the Law and its outcomes. When all we see of God is the Law, we can find little about God that would cause us to love Him. However, this scene of life is rapidly changed from a cloud of doom and despair to a rainbow of hope and blessings in God's wondrous love, mercy, forgiveness, and eternal promises. This scenario chances once we add a proper understanding of the doctrine of Grace. The Law by itself is a portrait of destruction and ruin. Add an understanding of the doctrine of Grace to it and the portrait begins to progressively unfold into the present potentials of this life and the eternal blessings of progressive unfolding of "the regeneration." Grace saves us "through faith" and begins to progressively transfigure us through sanctification as we actively work in partnership with the indwelling Holy Spirit of God.

Secondly, this union of Law and Grace is an indestructible, eternal union. Matthew 5:18 says, "For verily I say unto you, Till heaven and earth {*referring to the final stage of God's judgment in the dissolution of the original creation*} pass, one jot or one tittle shall in no wise pass from the law, till all be fulfilled." When will this union of Law and Grace be dissolved by God in that it will no longer be necessary? This will happen at the end of the world! The necessity of the marriage of Law and Grace-enabling will be dissolved when the world is dissolved and redeemed mankind is glorified and delivered from the very presence of sin.

"[9] The Lord is not slack concerning his promise, as some men count slackness; but is longsuffering to us-ward, not willing that any should perish, but that all should come to repentance. [10] But the day of the Lord will come as a thief in the night; in the which the heavens shall pass away with a great noise, and the elements shall melt with fervent heat, the earth also and the works that are therein shall be burned up. [11] *Seeing* then *that* all these things shall be dissolved, what manner *of persons* ought ye to be in *all* holy conversation and godliness, [12] Looking for and hasting unto the coming of the day of God, wherein the heavens being on fire shall be dissolved, and the elements shall melt with fervent heat? [13] Nevertheless we, according to his promise, look for new heavens and a new earth, wherein dwelleth righteousness. [14] Wherefore, beloved, seeing that ye look for such things, be diligent that ye may be found of him in peace, without spot, and blameless" (II Peter 3:9-14).

The word "fulfilled" in Matthew 5:18 is not from the same Greek word translated "fulfil" in Matthew 5:17. The word "all" in the phrase "all be fulfilled" in Matthew 5:18 is most probably not merely referring to the Law, but to all *eschatological promises* of the Law and the Prophets. In other words, "all be fulfilled" refers to the final completion of the New Genesis, i.e., "the regeneration" in God's creation of the "new heaven and earth" (Revelation 21:1).

It is a serious spiritual abuse to teach people the necessity of keeping the moral requirements of the Law before God without also accurately and practically teaching the doctrine of Grace. Christ spoke of this with great disdain when describing the Pharisees.

"[1] Then spake Jesus to the multitude, and to his disciples, [2] Saying, The scribes and the Pharisees sit in Moses' seat: [3] All therefore whatsoever they bid you observe, *that* observe and do; but do not ye after their works: for they say, and do not. [4] For they bind heavy burdens and grievous to be borne, and lay *them* on men's shoulders; but they *themselves* will not move them with one of their fingers. [5] But all their works they do for to be seen of men: they make broad their phylacteries, and enlarge the borders of their garments, [6] And love the uppermost rooms at feasts, and the chief seats in the synagogues, [7] And greetings in the markets, and to be called of men, Rabbi, Rabbi. [8] But be not ye called Rabbi: for one is your Master, *even* Christ; and all ye are brethren. [9] And call no *man* your father upon the earth: for one is your Father, which is in heaven. [10] Neither be ye called masters: for one is your Master, *even* Christ. [11] But he that is greatest among you shall be your servant. [12] And whosoever shall exalt himself shall be abased; and he that shall humble himself shall be exalted" (Matthew 23:1-12).

Some interpret this text to say Christ is rejecting the strict interpretation of the Law by the Pharisees and rebuking them for this strict interpretation. As we have already seen from Matthew 5:17-20, this is certainly NOT what Christ is saying. Christ is rebuking the Pharisees for legalism, i.e., teaching the moral obligations of the

Law without teaching the doctrine of Grace. Christ is rebuking the Pharisees for exacting definitive obligations regarding Law-keeping while understanding that they themselves were not even able to obey from the heart those exacting interpretations and applications (even if those interpretations and applications were less strict than God's intent). Christ is rebuking the Pharisees for their motivation in exacting their strict interpretations and applications of the Law for their own personal promotions, giving them prominent positions of leadership *over* God's people where the people of Israel looked to them for their authoritarian interpretations of the Law. Their interpretations had become equal in authority to the Law, even replacing the Law in its original intent.

These interpretations of the Law were written down in a scroll called the Talmud. The Talmud incorporates the *Mishnah* and the rabbinical discussions of the *Mishnah*, known as the *Gemara*. These interpretations of the Law began to be defined and compiled about 200 B.C. and continued to be developed for the next 700 years. Eventually they came to be treated as equal in authority to the Scriptures themselves. The dynamic of this scenario has been repeated down through the years of Church history in giving authority to the interpretations of Scripture in systematic theologies equal to the Scriptures themselves. In other words, the Talmud (like systematic theologies) was a constantly growing and evolving document referred to in Scripture by the Apostle Peter as the "traditions of men" and by Paul as "the works of the Law."

"[13] Wherefore gird up the loins of your mind, be sober, and hope to the end for the grace that is to be brought unto you at the revelation of Jesus Christ; [14] As obedient children, not fashioning yourselves according to the former lusts in your ignorance: [15] But as he which hath called you is holy, so be ye holy in all manner of conversation; [16] Because it is written, Be ye holy; for I am holy. [17] And if ye call on the Father, who without respect of persons judgeth according to every man's work, pass the time of your sojourning *here* in fear: [18] Forasmuch as ye know that ye were not redeemed with corruptible things, *as* silver and gold, from your vain conversation {*the Gemara*} *received* by tradition {*the Mishnah*} from your fathers; [19] But with the precious blood of Christ, as of a lamb without blemish and without spot: [20] Who verily was foreordained before the foundation of the world, but was manifest in these last times for you, [21] Who by him do believe in God, that raised him up from the dead, and gave him glory; that your faith and hope might be in God.

[22] Seeing ye have purified your souls in obeying the truth through the Spirit unto unfeigned love of the brethren, *see that ye* love one another with a pure heart fervently: [23] Being born again, not of corruptible seed, but of incorruptible, by the word of God, which liveth and abideth for ever" (I Peter 1:13-23).

Although teaching the moral obligations of the Law without teaching the doctrine of Grace (*legalism*) is serious spiritual abuse, teaching the doctrine of Grace without teaching moral obligations defined by the Law, and even more strictly defined by Christ and His life, *which is liberalism*, is an aberration of all that Christ teaches regarding the Christian life.

The Law of God is not abrogated in Christ. The Law of God is increased (*crammed full*) in Christ. Christ's life (the Spirit-filled life or the anointed life) became available to all believers with new definitions and increased expectations regarding the believer's moral obligations during the Age of Grace.

Christ, in Matthew chapters five through seven, is not giving a new definition of the moral Laws given by Moses, but a *restoration* of their original intent in obedience *from the heart*. Christ is correcting the false notion that the moral obligations could be *fulfilled* (fully obeyed *from the heart*) by fallen sinners. The solution to this false notion was not a less strict interpretation of the Law, but a more intense, stricter interpretation. The resulting conclusion in all of the five examples Christ gives is hopeless despair of finding acceptance before God for self-produced righteousness through externalism (*legalism*).

Neither legalism nor liberalism, in any degree, is the solution to the problem of sin and mankind's corrupt inward desires/lusts for sin. At the time of Christ's first advent, there were three basic sects within Judaism (of course, each of these three sects had numerous divisions within themselves).

1. Sadducees (liberals)
2. Pharisees (very strict interpretations of the Law with varying degrees of legalism)

3. Essenes or Qumran Covenanters (even stricter interpretations of the Law than the Pharisees with varying degrees of legalism)

Within these three sects there were two main corruptions of the doctrine of grace (although the vast majority of the Essenes, Qumran Covenanters, or the Damascus Zadokites believed in justification by faith). John the Baptist was most likely connected with this sect.

1. There was the heresy of salvation by Law keeping (moral Law and ceremonial Law).
2. There was also the heresy of sanctification, and being right with God, by the mere externals of Law keeping.

Matthew chapters five through seven deal with these failures in the various ways and degrees of each of these three sects and seeks to establish God's answer to the interpretation and application of the Law through *grace-living* ("Christ in you the hope of glory;" Romans 5:2 and Colossians 1:27). The *life of Christ* is the new standard of righteousness above and beyond the Law and the only way to live that *Christ-life* is "Christ in you, the hope of glory" (Colossians 1:27).

"[1] Therefore being justified by faith, we have peace with God through our Lord Jesus Christ: [2] By whom also we have access by faith into this grace wherein we stand, and rejoice in hope of the glory of God. [3] And not only *so*, but we glory in tribulations also: knowing that tribulation worketh patience; [4] And patience, experience; and experience, hope: [5] And hope maketh not ashamed; because the love of God is shed abroad in our hearts by the Holy Ghost which is given unto us" (Romans 5:1-5).

"[25] Whereof I am made a minister, according to the dispensation of God which is given to me for you, to fulfil the word of God; [26] *Even* the mystery which hath been hid from ages and from generations, but now is made manifest to his saints: [27] To whom God would make known what *is* the riches of the glory of this mystery among the Gentiles; which is Christ in you, the hope of glory: [28] Whom we preach, warning every man, and teaching every man in all wisdom; that we may present every man perfect in Christ Jesus: [29] Whereunto I also labour, striving according to his working, which worketh in me mightily" (Colossians 1:25-29).

DISCUSSION QUESTIONS

1. Discuss the differences between legalism and liberalism as they apply to the way Scriptures are interpreted.

2. Explain the word "break" in Matthew 5:19 from the meaning of the original Greek word *luo*. Discuss why this is important as it relates to the way liberalism interprets the Law.

3. Many today teach that Christ's Sermon on the Mount, including the Beatitudes, is not for Church Age believers. Discuss why this is a false view of these texts.

4. Thoroughly explain the difference between the *letter* of the Law and the *spirit* of the Law.

5. Define and explain the differences between *hypostatic union* and *hypostatic unity*. Discuss also why understanding the dynamic of these two spiritual realities is essential to ever living in a way that might be pleasing to God.

6. Why is it essential to understand the hopeless despair regarding our own ability to keep the Law *from the heart* in any real and practical way and for us to truly understand and seek God's only solution to that dilemma?

7. Explain the meaning of the Greek words translated "fulfill" and "destroy" in Matthew 5:17. Explain the significance of these meanings to understanding all that Christ teaches in Matthew chapters five through seven.

Chapter Twenty-eight
The River of Eternal Influence

I was standing on a bridge over a small river at a family camp where I was preaching. I was praying as I waited for the upcoming chapel hour. I watched as the water flowed from two separate streams to join just before it flowed under the bridge. I thought of a saying that I have often heard people say about past failures: "That's water under the bridge." The saying simply means we cannot do anything to erase yesterday's failures and there is no sense dwelling upon it. They are partially right! We cannot erase the influence of our past failures. I thought about the water that flowed under that bridge. It did not stop once it went under the bridge. It went on and on and on. That is the way the influence of our lives is. The influence of our lives will go on into eternity either for good or for evil, either for edification or destruction.

This is why *Grace-living* is so critical. *Grace-living* is the manifestation of the *Christ-life* that is within all believers in the indwelling of the Holy Spirit. *Grace-living* is also *faith-living* in that it is the continual action of faith in God's *Word Promises* regarding Spiritual empowering. *Grace-living* leads the believer to habitually yield his will to the will of God as revealed by His Word ("the just shall live by faith"). It is upon this continuing action of faith ("be ye being filled," Ephesians 5:18) that God releases the *Christ-life* through *overflow* (filling) and into the world. It is through this *overflow* that the believer becomes both "salt" and "light" in the world (Matthew 5:13-16). Bringing glory to God through our lives is the central purpose in the doctrine of *Grace-living*. In fact, *Grace-living* is the only way the sinner can truly reflect the *Christ-life* that is in us. This is what Christ addresses in Matthew 5:13-16.

"[13] **Ye are the salt of the earth**: but if the salt have lost his savour, wherewith shall it be salted? it is thenceforth good for nothing, but to be cast out, and to be trodden under foot of men. [14] **Ye are the light of the world**. A city that is set on an hill cannot be hid. [15] Neither do men light a candle, and put it under a bushel, but on a candlestick; and it giveth light unto all that are in the house. [16] Let your light so shine before men, that they may see your good works, and glorify your Father which is in heaven" (Matthew 5:13-16).

Salt has two purposes; it brings "savour" to food and it is used to preserve food by inhibiting the growth of bacteria. The use in Matthew 5:13 is defined as "savour." The idea behind the metaphor is that individual Christians lose their intended spiritual influence when they become like the *world*. We must choose to be **distinctively** *salty* (spiritual) rather than **commonly** *worldly* (carnal or world-like, dirty salt loses its flavor). To be *salt*, the believer is to be "in the world," while at the same time keeping the world out of us.

Every Christian is to be the *embodiment of Christ.*

Every local church is to become the corporate "body of Christ." True Christianity is defined as the *embodiment of Christ.* As the *embodiment of Christ* through the indwelling and filling of the Holy Spirit, Christians individually and Christianity corporately through local churches are to render godly influence upon the world. The *world* is composed of those spiritually blinded by the satanic obfuscation of truth. Believers are to render the influence that Christ would have rendered had He not died in our "stead." Because He died in our "stead," He left His redeemed on earth to serve in His "stead." Paul spoke in the place of Christ as the voice of God in II Corinthians 5:20.

When the believer is filled with the Spirit of God, the Spirit of God literally moves and speaks through us with the *authority* and *power* of God. It is through this supernatural dynamic that God exerts His spiritual influence upon those within the reach of our influence. They in turn extend the reach of that influence into their own realm of influence.

"[17] Therefore if any man *be* in Christ, *he is* a new creature: old things are passed away; behold, all things are become new. [18] And all things *are* of God, who hath reconciled us to himself by Jesus Christ, and <u>hath given to us the ministry of reconciliation;</u> [19] To wit, that God was in Christ, reconciling the world unto himself, not imputing their trespasses unto them; and hath committed unto us the word of reconciliation. [20] Now then we are ambassadors for Christ, <u>as though God did beseech *you* by us: we pray *you* in Christ's stead,</u>

be ye reconciled to God. [21] For he hath made him *to be* sin for us, who knew no sin; that we might be made the righteousness of God in him" (II Corinthians 5:17-21)

"[10] As every man hath received the gift, *even so* minister the same one to another, as good stewards of the manifold grace of God. [11] If any man speak, *let him speak* as the oracles {*logion, log'-ee-on; as the voice*} of God; if any man minister, *let him do it* as of the ability which God giveth: that God in all things may be glorified through Jesus Christ, to whom be praise and dominion for ever and ever. Amen" (I Peter 4:10-11).

Christ spoke of this potential of the exponential reproduction of Himself in the lives of true, dead-to-self believers in the metaphor of a seed of wheat falling into the ground, dying, and bringing forth fruit exponentially. Every believer possesses this same potential in the indwelling and filling of the Holy Spirit of God. Each believer becomes a continuation of the incarnation in the indwelling (*hypostatic union*) and a potential for the continuation of this spiritual dynamic of *fruit production* through the filling of the Holy Spirit (*hypostatic unity*; Ephesians 4:1-32).

"[23] And Jesus answered them, saying, The hour is come, that the Son of man should be glorified. [24] Verily, verily, I say unto you, **Except a corn {*seed*} of wheat fall into the ground and die, it abideth alone: but if it die, it bringeth forth much fruit**. [25] He that loveth his life shall lose it; and he that hateth his life in this world shall keep it unto life eternal. [26] If any man serve me, let him follow me; and where I am, there shall also my servant be: if any man serve me, him will *my* Father honour" (John 12:23-26).

If the believer wants to bear fruit in the way Christ mentions in John 12:24, the prerequisite to that taking place is patterned for us by Christ Himself. Unless we are willing to die to self and to the world, we will abide alone without any fruit from our lives. If we are willing to die to self and to the world, we have the promise of bringing "forth much fruit." This refers to the exponential potential of eternal influence that extends itself with every soul saved and discipled to produce a continuum to the glory of God. It is this potential for this continuum of exponential increase that Christ refers to in the metaphors of "salt" and "light' in Matthew chapter five. This is also what Christ addresses in the next few verses in John chapter twelve.

"[27] Now is my soul troubled; and what shall I say? Father, save me from this hour: but for this cause came I unto this hour. [28] Father, glorify thy name. Then came there a voice from heaven, *saying*, I have both glorified *it*, and will glorify *it* again. [29] The people therefore, that stood by, and heard *it*, said that it thundered: others said, An angel spake to him. [30] Jesus answered and said, This voice came not because of me, but for your sakes. [31] Now is the judgment of this world: now shall the prince of this world be cast out. [32] And I, **if I be lifted up** from the earth, will draw all *men* unto me. [33] **This he said, signifying what death he should die.** [34] The people answered him, We have heard out of the law that Christ abideth for ever: and how sayest thou, The Son of man must be lifted up? who is this Son of man? [35] Then Jesus said unto them, Yet a little while is the light with you. Walk while ye have the light, lest darkness come upon you: for he that walketh in darkness knoweth not whither he goeth. [36] **While ye have light, believe in the light** {*in Jesus as the Messiah and living revelation of God's righteousness and grace*}, **that ye may be** {*ginomai, ghin'-om-ahee; i.e., to cause to be or generated, referring to the believer's regeneration by the "breath of life" by the indwelling Holy Spirit*} **the children of light.** These things spake Jesus, and departed, and did hide himself from them" (John 12:27-36).

> The "light" is the *eternal life* of the *Christ-life* that dwells within every believer in the indwelling of the Holy Spirit.

When the believer is filled with the Holy Spirit through death to self and death to this world, this *light of life* is released through the believer's life. This light is released into the world to supernaturally impact that believer's realm of influence in exponential ways. This goes far beyond mere spiritual *enlightenment* (understanding). This refers to the actual revelation of the image of God in our present bodies and through our lives presently.

"[1] In the beginning was the Word, and the Word was with God, and the Word was God. [2] The same was in the beginning with God. [3] All things were made by him; and without him was not any thing made that was made. [4] **In him was life; and the life was the light of men**" (John 1:1-4).

"Then spake Jesus again unto them, saying, I am the light of the world: **he that followeth me** {*conditional*} shall not walk in darkness, but shall have the **light of life**" (John 8:12).

Paul details this release of the *Christ-life* ("salt" and "light") through three *unities* in Ephesians chapter four.

"[1] I therefore, the prisoner of the Lord, beseech you that ye walk worthy of the vocation wherewith ye are called, [2] With all lowliness and meekness, with longsuffering, forbearing one another in love; [3] Endeavouring to keep the **unity of the Spirit** {*hypostatic unity*} in the bond of peace. [4] *There is* one body, and **one Spirit**, even as ye are called in one hope of your calling; [5] **One Lord**, one faith, one baptism, [6] **One God and Father** of all {*oneness in this Tri-unity equals the unity of the Godhead to which the believer is united upon hypostatic unity through the filling of the Spirit*}, who *is* above all, and through all, and **in you all** {*hypostatic union*}. [7] But unto every {*each*} one of us is given grace {*the divine influence upon the heart through the supernatural workings of the Holy Spirit and the potential for the release of that divine influence through the filling of the Holy Spirit*} according to the measure {*the degree, which is actually limitless in its potential in that it is the omnipotent power that spoke the world into existence*} of the gift of Christ. [8] Wherefore he saith, When he ascended up on high, he led captivity captive, and gave gifts {*the gifted men spoken of in v. 11 for the purpose spoken of in vs. 12-13*} unto men. [9] (Now that he ascended, what is it but that he also descended first into the lower parts of the earth? [10] He that descended is the same also that ascended up far above all heavens, that he might fill {*pleroo, play-ro'-o; cram full or fill to the fullest*} all things.) [11] And he gave some, apostles; and some, prophets; and some, evangelists; and some, pastors and teachers; [12] For the perfecting of the saints, for the work of the ministry, for the edifying of the body of Christ: [13] Till we all come in the **unity of the faith**, and of the {*unity of the*} **knowledge** {*epignosis, ep-ig'-no-sis*} of the Son of God, unto a perfect man, unto the measure {*degree*} of the stature of the fulness of Christ: [14] That we *henceforth* be no more children, tossed to and fro, and carried about with every wind of doctrine, by the sleight of men, *and* cunning craftiness, whereby they lie in wait to deceive; [15] But speaking the truth in love, may grow up into him in all things, which is the head, *even* Christ: [16] From whom the whole body {*the local church*} fitly joined together and compacted by that which every joint {*individual believer*} supplieth {*contributes*}, according to the effectual working {*referring to the supernatural power of the* *indwelling Spirit*} in the measure of every part, maketh increase of the body {*of Christ in the local church*} unto the edifying of itself in love" (Ephesians 4:1-16).

The purpose of God's *lighting* believers is that through their intimate knowledge of Him and through the synergistic union with Him (*hypostatic unity*), those believers can reveal God to those *blinded* by satanic deception and the obfuscation of theological revelation. This means God has designed regeneration as the means for man to glorify Him. This revelation of God goes beyond the mere inspiration of written Scripture (as wondrous as that reality is). God has also chosen to reveal Himself through the medium of *living Scripture* through the lives of believers who are being filled to overflow with the indwelling, living Word of God; "Christ in you, the hope of glory" (Colossians 1:27). Paul goes on in Ephesians 4:17-6:20 to detail what exactly is involved in dying to self and to the world so that this "light of life" can be released and the potential for the exponential production of fruit can be produced through that *death*.

"[17] This I say therefore, and testify in the Lord, that ye henceforth walk not as other Gentiles walk, in the vanity {*moral depravity*} of their mind {*thought life*}, [18] Having the understanding darkened, being alienated from the life of God through the ignorance that is in them, because of the blindness {*hardness of unbelief*} of their heart: [19] Who being past feeling {*an I could care less attitude*} have given themselves over unto lasciviousness {*giving one's self over to fulfilling all lusts of the flesh; pure Hedonism*}, to work {*to be occupied*} all uncleanness {*moral impurity*} with greediness {*self-serving covetousness*}. [20] But ye have not so learned Christ; [21] If so be that ye have heard him, and have been taught by him, as the truth is in Jesus: [22] That ye put off {*cast away*} concerning the former conversation {*behavior; i.e. ungodly behavior*} the old man, which is corrupt {*depraved and defiled before God*} according to the deceitful lusts; [23] And be renewed in the spirit of your mind; [24] And that ye put on the new man, which after God is created in righteousness and true holiness. [25] Wherefore putting away lying, speak every man truth with his neighbour: for we are members one of another. [26] Be ye angry, and sin not: let not the sun go down upon your wrath: [27] Neither give place to the devil. [28] Let him that stole steal no more: but rather let him labour, working with *his* hands the thing which is good, that he may have to give to him that needeth. [29] Let {*allow*} no corrupt {*morally worthless*} communication {*logos;*

i.e., words} proceed out of your mouth, but that which is good to the use of edifying {*building up spiritually*}, that it {*the communication of the mouth*} may minister {*deliver or give*} grace {*divine influence upon the heart*} unto the hearers. [30] And grieve {*sorrow*} not the holy Spirit of God, whereby {*His indwelling as the seal*} ye are sealed unto the day of redemption. [31] Let all bitterness, and wrath, and anger, and clamour, and evil speaking, be put away from you, with all malice: [32] And be ye kind {*gracious or overflowing with graciousness*} one to another, tenderhearted, forgiving one another, even as God for Christ's sake hath forgiven you" (Ephesians 4:17-32).

DISCUSSION QUESTIONS

1. Discuss why it is absolutely critical for every Christian to understand that our spiritual influence, good or bad, goes on into eternity with eternal consequences and that God's forgiveness of those consequences in no way removes them.

2. From the context of your answer above, discuss what *Grace-living* is and why it is absolutely critical.

3. Explain the *outcomes* of *Grace-living* in the metaphors of "light" and "salt" in Matthew 5:13-16.

4. Discuss the practical meaning of being the *embodiment of Christ* as an individual and as it applies to you and your local church.

5. Explain the practical application of the following text: "[10] As every man hath received the gift, *even so* minister the same one to another, as good stewards of the manifold grace of God. [11] If any man speak, *let him speak* as the oracles {*logion; log'-ee-on; as the voice*} of God; if any man minister, *let him do it* as of the ability which God giveth: that God in all things may be glorified through Jesus Christ, to whom be praise and dominion for ever and ever. Amen" (I Peter 4:10-11).

6. Read John 12:24. The prerequisite to fruit production is patterned for us by Christ Himself as defined by this verse. Expand upon this in a practical application in your own life.

7. Read John 12:27-36. The "light" is the *eternal life* of the *Christ-life* that dwells within every believer in the indwelling Holy Spirit. Discuss how you personally can become a revelation of the image of God through your life.

Chapter Twenty-nine
The Fragility of Grace Enablement

In Ephesians chapter four, we saw three potential unities available to the believer through the supernatural enabling of the indwelling Spirit of God (in the believer's *hypostatic union*, or the doctrine of grace).

1. **"Unity of the Spirit in the bond {*uniting principle*} of peace {*peace with God through reconciliation and hypostatic union*}"** (Ephesians 4:3). The word "endeavoring" is a present, active, participle; meaning that the *keeping* (literally guarding or protecting) of the "unity of the Spirit" must be a constant and continual priority of a believer's focus in life. The emphasis of the word "endeavoring" is that keeping the "unity of the Spirit" is the responsibility of each believer and of every local church.

2. **The "unity of the faith" (Ephesians 4:13):** "The faith" refers to doctrinal unity, not to unity in our ability to trust God (although our ability to trust God is an outcome of correct doctrine).

3. **The unity "of the knowledge of the Son of God" (Ephesians 4:13):** "Knowledge" is relational knowledge that is the outcome of a real, personal relationship with Christ. This "knowledge" is the foundation of real service, real prayer, and real devotion to Christ (i.e., faithfulness). The unity of believers within a local church then share in this foundation of relational intimacy with Christ. This relational intimacy with Christ expands into all the rest of a believer's relationships detailed beginning in Ephesians 5:21. This patterned is established by *submission* (yielding; Romans 6:11-13) to the Lordship of Christ in and through the unity "of the knowledge of the Son of God," by the words "submitting yourselves one to another in the fear of God." The words "submitting yourselves one to another in the fear of God" carry the meaning: be under obedience (*in submission to the LORDSHIP of Christ*), reduplicating yourselves (*i.e., in the image of Christ*) in the fear of God (*in that you we will be held accountable at the Judgment seat*).

Once these three unities are established, they are to be manifested and lived out practically within and through five levels of relationships defined by four action words (verbs; one is used twice). These action verbs are consistent with the character of God ten revealed through the character of a believer yielded to the indwelling Spirit of God.

1. Wives "**submit** . . . unto your own husbands <u>as</u> unto the Lord"
2. Husbands "**love** your wives, <u>even as</u> Christ also loved the church, and gave himself for it"
3. Children "**obey**" {*hupakouo, meaning to heed or to conform to a command or authority*} and "**honour** {*hold in reverence or highly value*} thy father and mother"
4. Servants (or employees) "**be obedient** {*subservient*};" from the Greek word *hupakouo* (hoop-ak-oo'-o) meaning *to heed or to conform to a command or authority*
5. Masters (or employers) have no "**respect of persons**" (*be fair, just, and do not administrate according to favoritism*)

> Within the *contextual continuity* of the epistle to the Ephesians, we see the fragility of the supernatural enabling of the believer as to the very narrow boundaries of living truth necessary to this enabling. Apart from this *grace* (supernatural enabling) there can be no real spiritual blessing and there can be no real spiritual fruit produced.

This certainly helps us understand what Christ said in Matthew 5:17, "Think not that I am come to destroy the law, or the prophets: I am not come to destroy, but to fulfil." The word "destroy" is from the Greek word *kataluo* (kat-al-oo'-o). It means to *loosen downwardly, to take apart, disintegrate, or dissolve.* Christ said: *do not think that He came to do such a thing.* Instead, understand that He came to "fulfil" the Law. The word "fulfil" is translated from the Greek word *pleroo* (play-ro'-o). The word means to *fill to the fullest extent*, to *cram full*. The fragility of the supernatural enabling (grace) of the believer is exemplified by the understanding of this verse. Christ expects an inward obedience ("from the heart") of the "Spirit of the Law," not just mere *lip service* or mere external conformity by the strength of human *will power*.

Spiritual growth is measured essentially within two mediums; "grace . . . and the knowledge of our Lord and Saviour

Jesus Christ." The means of this spiritual growth is through the knowledge of the Word of God and yielding to the indwelling Spirit of God to be enabled to live "from the heart" the truths that are known.

"[11] *Seeing* then *that* all these things shall be dissolved, what manner *of persons* ought ye to be in *all* holy conversation and godliness, [12] Looking for and hasting unto the coming of the day of God, wherein the heavens being on fire shall be dissolved, and the elements shall melt with fervent heat? [13] Nevertheless we, according to his promise, look for new heavens and a new earth, wherein dwelleth righteousness. [14] Wherefore, beloved, seeing that ye look for such things, be diligent that ye may be found of him in peace {*practice*}, without spot, and blameless. [15] And account *that* the longsuffering of our Lord *is* salvation; even as our beloved brother Paul also according to the wisdom given unto him hath written unto you; [16] As also in all *his* epistles, speaking in them of these things; in which are some things hard to be understood, which they that are unlearned and unstable wrest, as *they do* also the other scriptures, unto their own destruction. [17] Ye therefore, beloved, seeing ye know *these things* before, beware lest ye also, being led away with the error of the wicked, fall from your own stedfastness. [18] But **grow in grace, and in the knowledge of our Lord and Saviour Jesus Christ**. To him *be* glory both now and for ever. Amen" (II Peter 3:11-18).

"[1] Wherefore laying aside all malice, and all guile, and hypocrisies, and envies, and all evil speakings, [2] As newborn babes, desire the sincere milk of the word, that ye may grow thereby: [3] If so be ye have tasted {*personally experienced*} that the Lord *is* gracious {*a quote from Psalm 34:8; "O taste and see that the LORD is good: blessed is the man that trusteth in him."*}" (I Peter 2:1-3).

Therefore, the fragility of grace enablement explains why we seldom see the supernatural enabling of believers in modern Christianity. In most part, doctrine is minimized, interpretations of God's will are liberalized, obedience is legalized, and Pneumatology is marginalized.

The context of this supernatural enabling of the believer's life by the indwelling Holy Spirit through *hypostatic unity* ("the unity of the Spirit," Ephesians 4:3), and the essentials for this all to take place, goes through chapter five and then into chapter six of Ephesians. In continues in Paul's concluding statement detailing seven spiritual necessities provided by grace for spiritual warfare.

Again, the necessity of these seven spiritual realities reveals the fragility of grace even though they are all provided without limit to the believer to be received by grace through faith. Ephesians 6:10-20 details why the believer's "work of the ministry" requires supernatural enabling. Apart from this supernatural work of grace in our lives, every believer is vulnerable and defenseless. We do not have the ability to *fight* ("stand") against the archenemy of mankind and his minions of evil in our own strength.

"[10] Finally, my brethren, be strong *{empowered}* in the Lord, and in the power *{dominion; referring to the spiritual realm}* of his might *{ischus, is-khoos'; His ability or strength}*. [11] Put on the whole armour of God, that ye may be able to stand *{the idea is to stand in opposition}* against the wiles *{deceptive methods}* of the devil. [12] For we wrestle not against flesh and blood *{other human beings}*, but against principalities *{chief or very high, very powerful beings}*, against powers *{superhuman strength and abilities}*, against the rulers *{the force of evil that imprisons the world}* of the darkness *{spiritual obscurity}* of this world, against spiritual wickedness *{depravity}* in high *places {above or beyond the sky; outside of the realm of our existence in another dimension}*. [13] Wherefore *{because of this}* take unto you the whole armour of God *{of what God's grace provides because you will not be able to stand if you do not}*, that ye may be able to withstand in the evil day, and having done all, to stand *{as the victor}*. [14] *{Take your}* Stand therefore, having your **loins girt about with truth**, and having on the **breastplate of righteousness**; [15] And your **feet shod with the preparation of the gospel of peace**; [16] Above all, taking the **shield of faith**, wherewith ye shall be able to quench all the fiery darts of the wicked. [17] And take the **helmet of salvation**, and the **sword of the Spirit, which is the word of God**: [18] **Praying always with all prayer and supplication in the Spirit**, and **watching thereunto** with all perseverance and supplication for all saints; [19] And for me, that utterance may be given unto me, that I may open my mouth boldly, to make known the mystery of the gospel, [20] For which I am an ambassador in bonds: that therein I may speak boldly, as I ought to speak" (Ephesians 6:10-20).

Christians have a formidable enemy in Satan and his many minions of evil. These are fallen angels with powers and abilities that exceed even our vain human imaginations. Although these fallen creatures are not as powerful as God, they are far beyond our capabilities to engage and oppose. These fallen creatures exert their corrupting influence within the realm of the fallen creation that the Word of God refers to as "the world." Satan is the "god of this world" (II Corinthians 4:4) and the "prince and power of the air" (Ephesians 2:2). He is a superhuman being that knows the intricacies of the Word of God and the frailties of mankind, manipulating both to accomplish as much defilement and destruction as possible. His warfare against humankind is to lead them into self-destruction because he does not have the authority to take a life. His warfare against Christians is to discourage them to distrust God's motives. He wants to defeat them spiritually by overwhelming their lives with difficulties. He wants to get them to defile themselves by yielding to his temptations by preoccupying themselves with the vanities of this world and by corrupting themselves with many forms and degrees of worldliness. Yet, the average Christian is so ignorant of his devices that he seldom even considers this *realm of evil influence* upon himself and the degree to which he has already succumbed.

In the eightfold instruction regarding the believer's *spiritual armor* for spiritual warfare against the satanic forces of evil that the Word of God calls "the world," the verb tenses, voice, and mood are critical to understanding meaning. The words "take unto you" in the phrase "take unto you the whole armour of God" in Ephesians 6:13 are in the Aorist tense. The aorist tense is the outcome of some event or decision with eternally, perpetuating results. The idea is that we entered into this *spiritual warfare* the moment we received Christ and, in receiving Christ in the indwelling Holy Spirit," **we began something that must be continued**. Although we have all the items of the *spiritual armor* as our eternal possession, we must continually be aware of the necessity of taking that armor and putting it on - i.e., appropriating the spiritual significance of each piece in our moment-by-moment struggle against the demonic forces of evil in "the world."

1. "Having your loins girt about with truth" (Ephesians 6:14). This is aorist tense, again communicating the idea of the outcome of some event or decision with eternally, perpetuating results regarding something begun sometime in the past that must be continued. The believer has already "girded" his "loins . . . about with truth." The girdle was the *cloth* or *leather belt* that held all of a soldiers' armor in place. **The first level of truth** necessary to binding all our armor together is a thorough *understanding* (Matthew 13:23) of the theological details of the gospel of Jesus Christ. **The second level of truth** necessary to binding all our armor together is the "unity of the faith" spoken of in Ephesians 4:13; "the faith" refers to doctrinal unity.

2. "Having on the breastplate of righteousness" (Ephesians 6:14). Again, this is aorist tense and middle voice. Literally translated, this would be "having put the breastplate of righteousness upon *you*." This "righteousness" is the constant and continuing awareness of the believer's new standing before God "in Christ" through the baptism with the Spirit into the "body of Christ" (I Corinthians 12:13; i.e. "the regeneration" in the "last Adam"). Every individual believer that is "born again" of the Spirit of God stands before God positionally and appositionally (*side-by-side with Christ*) in the perfect, God-kind righteousness of our High Priest and Intercessor - the risen Lord Jesus Christ. Therefore, the believer's adversary (Satan), as the "accuser of the brethren" (Revelation 12:10) has absolutely nothing to accuse the believer. God has ALREADY been propitiated for every sin or failure we have committed, or ever will commit. This "breastplate of righteousness" is fastened securely with the *girdle of truth*. The *Christ-life* in our hearts is protected against satanic threat by the continuing knowledge of the believer's God-kind righteousness "in Christ." Therefore, even though we may fail occasionally, we are secure in our God-kind righteousness "in Christ" for that surety is *already* anchored (Hebrews 6:19) "within the veil" in heaven.

3. "And your feet shod with the preparation of the gospel of peace" (Ephesians 6:15). Again, "your feet shod" is aorist tense, middle voice, and participle mood. Literally translated it would be *having bound-up your feet with the sandals of the readiness to preach the gospel of peace {or the word of reconciliation; II Corinthians 5:18-19}.* This metaphor reminds us of the LORD's command to the Israelites in the eating of the Passover. "And thus shall ye eat it; *with* your loins girded, your shoes on your feet, and your staff in your hand; and ye shall eat it in haste: it *is* the LORD'S Passover" (Exodus 12:11). The intent in the Passover instruction was *to be ready* at any moment for the Lord's leading. I believe this is the intent in the meaning of the metaphor *having shod your feet with the preparation of the* *gospel of peace* in Ephesians 6:15. Peter said this same thing is another way.

"^{12} For the eyes of the Lord *are* over the righteous, and his ears *are open* unto their prayers: but the face of the Lord *is* against them that do evil. ^{13} And who *is* he that will harm you, if ye be followers of that which is good? ^{14} But and if ye suffer for righteousness' sake, happy *are ye*: and be not afraid of their terror, neither be troubled; ^{15} But sanctify the Lord God in your hearts: and *be* ready always to *give* an answer to every man that asketh you a reason of the hope that is in you with meekness and fear:" (I Peter 3:12-15).

4. "Above all, taking the shield of faith, wherewith ye shall be able to quench all the fiery darts of the wicked" (Ephesians 6:16). The word "taking" is aorist tense. The believer has already taken this "shield of faith" in his salvation decision. However, how we began our life as a Christian is how we must continue living that life; "the just shall live by faith" (Habakkuk 2:4, Romans 1:17, Galatians 3:11, and Hebrews 10:38). The warrior's shield was a body length oblong wooden shield behind which the warrior could stand.

A primary means of attack against a marching army was to have thousands of archers shoot a volley of arrows that literally rained down upon those advancing against them, killing or wounding thousands. These arrows were often set on fire with oil that would start the clothing and wooden shields on fire. Therefore, the metaphor is twofold. The "shield of faith" protects against the attack of the arrows and, at the same time, is able to extinguish the collateral damage of the "fire" of doubt and discouragement.

Faith believes *in* God, but also faith *believes* God. Through faith we "know that all things work together for good to them that love God, to them who are the called according to *his* purpose" (Romans 8:28). Through faith we know that, "Being confident of this very thing, that he which hath begun a good work in you will perform *it* until the day of Jesus Christ" (Philippians 1:6). Doubting God's love, grace, or mercy defiles us before God. Real faith is anchored in the knowledge of God's promises. Real faith understands Satan's devices to defile us. Real faith simply extinguishes those devices by yielding to the Holy Spirit and obeying God's commands regardless of the temporal consequences. Therefore, faith allows us to face the difficulties of the threat of the "fire darts of the wicked with the resolution of faith to: "[5] *Let your* conversation *be* without covetousness; *and be* content with such things as ye have: for he hath said, I will never leave thee, nor forsake thee. [6] So that we may boldly say, The Lord *is* my helper, and I will not fear what man shall do unto me" (Hebrews 13:5-6).

5. "And take the helmet of salvation" (Ephesians 6:17a). "Take" here (and into the context of the next phrase regarding the "sword of the Spirit") is aorist tense, middle voice, and imperative mood. The meaning would be *"having taken the {hope of the; I Thessalonians 5:8} helmet of salvation upon yourselves, continue living in that hope."* The "hope of salvation" is the surety of what God begins in us will ultimately end in what He promises, i.e., our glorification. Our regeneration is positionally complete "in Christ," but is practically unfolding.

"[21] And you, that were sometime *{being before or being at some time in the past}* alienated *{living in the continual state of estrangement from God}* and enemies *{living in the continual state of hateful hostility toward God}* in your mind by wicked works *{of Hedonism and Heathenism}*, yet now *{in the new order of the new dispensation of grace, i.e., the operations of the Spirit in His indwelling and baptism}* hath he reconciled *{Aorist; having a beginning with continuing, eternal results or outcomes}* [22] In the body of his flesh through death, to present you *{to place beside Christ appositionally}* holy and unblameable *{without a blemish}* and unreproveable *{without anything to be accused}* in his sight *{'in Christ' as our representative High Priest}*: [23] If ye continue *{those who have truly believed and understood the gospel will never abandon its eternal promise and the surety of the hope of their future glorification}* in the faith *{all the teaching of the Scriptures}* grounded *{foundationalized in "the faith"}* and settled *{the idea is to sit at rest implying a steadfastness in "the faith"}*, and be not moved away from the hope of the gospel *{which is ultimately our glorification}*, which ye have heard, and which was preached to every creature which is under heaven; whereof I Paul am made a minister; [24] Who now rejoice in my sufferings for you, and fill up that which is behind of the afflictions of Christ in my flesh for his body's sake, which is the church: [25] Whereof I am made a minister, according to the dispensation of God which is given to me for you, to fulfil the word of God *{to cram every aspect of his life to the* *fullest extent of his influence through being a living translation of the Word of God as empowered by the indwelling Spirit of God*}; [26] Even the mystery {*Christ in you*} which hath been hid from ages and from generations, but now is made manifest {*brought into open view and understanding*} to his saints: [27] To whom God would make known what is the riches of the glory of this mystery among the Gentiles; <u>which is Christ in you</u>, the {*surety of the*} hope {*confident expectation or anticipation*} of glory: [28] Whom we preach, warning every man, and teaching every man in all wisdom; that we may present {*appositionally; Paul beside those he discipled being an instrument of God's grace and as a testimony to God's grace through him and in those he discipled*} every man perfect {*spiritually matured and living by grace*} in Christ Jesus {the *last Adam and Head of the New Genesis*}: [29] Whereunto I also labour, <u>striving according to his working, which worketh in me mightily. . .</u>

<u>.</u> [1] For I would that ye knew what great conflict {*agony, both in his external struggles of persecution and internal anxieties*} I have for you, and for them at Laodicea, and for as many as have not seen my face in the flesh; [2] That their hearts might be comforted, being knit together in love, and unto all riches of the <u>full assurance of understanding</u>, to the acknowledgement of the mystery of God {*of the unsearchable riches of Christ in you*}, and of the Father, and of Christ; [3] In whom {*Christ in you*} are hid all the treasures of wisdom and knowledge. [4] And this I say, lest any man should beguile you with enticing words. [5] For though I be absent in the flesh, yet am I with you in the spirit, joying and beholding your order, and the stedfastness of your faith in Christ. [6] As ye have therefore received Christ Jesus the Lord {*by grace through faith*}, so walk ye in him {*by grace through faith*}: [7] Rooted and built up in him, and stablished in the faith, as ye have been taught, abounding therein with thanksgiving. [8] Beware lest any man spoil you through philosophy and vain deceit, after the tradition of men, after the rudiments of the world, and not after Christ. [9] For in him dwelleth {*is permanently house*} all the fulness {*pleroma, play'-ro-mah; in the fullest sense of full, packed or crammed full*} of the Godhead bodily. [10] And ye are complete {*pleroo, play-ro'-o; i.e., equally full of the Godhead*} in him {*in His indwelling in you*}, which is the head {*the seizing of the head as the primary control of the body; i.e., therefore taking dominion*} of all principality {*arche ar-khay', the first or primary position of rank; i.e., Lordship*} and power {*absolute, unlimited judicial authority as Lord*}: [11] In whom {*Jesus as the believer's representative High Priest*} also ye are circumcised with the circumcision made without hands, in putting off the body of the sins of the flesh by the circumcision of Christ: [12]

Buried with him in baptism, wherein also ye are risen with him through the faith of the operation of God, who hath raised him from the dead. [13] And you, being dead in your sins and the uncircumcision of your flesh, hath he quickened together with him, having forgiven you all trespasses; [14] Blotting out the handwriting of ordinances that was against us, which was contrary to us, and took it out of the way, nailing it to his cross; [15] And having spoiled principalities and powers, he made a shew of them openly, triumphing over them in it" (Colossians 1:21-2:15).

This is the "helmet of *{the hope of}* salvation" by which Paul tells the believer to continue living in Ephesians 6:17. There is no persecution, threat to us physically, or failure in life that can give Satan and his minions of evil a moment of victory in our lives. He has no victory when we live within the realm of the surety of the hope of salvation and the fulfillment of all that is ours in the *unsearchable riches of grace in Christ Jesus.* That is why it is important to understand the aorist tense of the word "take." To be victorious, we must continue to live by grace through faith in the promises of the Gospel. When we fail or falter in life, we must quickly return to the promises of the Gospel.

6. "[And] *{take}* the sword of the Spirit, which is the word of God" (Ephesians 6:17b). Again, the Aorist Tense would lead us to understand this to say, *having taken the sword of the Spirit, which is the {promises} of the word of God; continue learning and living in the reality of these promises.* A central ministry of the indwelling Spirit in the operations of grace (the supernatural enablement of the yielded believer) is the translation of the living promises of God's Word into the language of living. This translation is through obedience in the life of the believer. Therefore taking "the sword of the Spirit, which is the word of God" is much more than a mere intellectual *understanding* or *knowing.* Taking "the sword of the Spirit, which is the word of God" is the *appropriation* of the eternal promises of the Word of God applicable to the eternal realm of God's existence (the spiritual) applied in a very practical sense here in the realm of the fall (i.e., the world).

When we live the Word of God through the supernatural enabling of the Spirit of God, we create a *bubble* of the eternal existence within this present temporal existence of the fall. This new *bubble* of existence (whether just one Christian or a group of Christians in a local church) becomes a "light to shine out of darkness" as long as he, or the local church, remains separate from the "world."

"[6] For God, who commanded the light to shine out of darkness {*in the first creation*}, hath shined in our hearts {*in the new Creation*}, to {*for the purpose of giving*} give the light of the knowledge of the glory of God {*God's perfect righteousness or goodness*} in the face of Jesus Christ. [7] But we have this treasure in earthen vessels, that the excellency of the power may be of God, and not of us" (II Corinthians 4:6-7).

7. "Praying always with all prayer and supplication in the Spirit" (Ephesians 6:18a). Prayer is the believer's *declaration of dependence.* It springs forth from the depth of spiritually understanding two truths. When we truly understand these two truths then, and only then, will we understand the utmost importance of prayer. Then, and only then, will we understand our absolute dependence upon God to be victorious over our sin nature from within, temptations from without. Then, and only then, will we understand the impossibility of producing moral goodness or spiritual fruit apart from His enabling grace.

A. "[4] Abide in me, and I in you. As the branch cannot bear fruit of itself, except it abide in the vine; no more can ye, except ye abide in me. [5] I am the vine, ye *are* the branches: He that abideth in me, and I in him, the same bringeth forth much fruit: for without me ye can do nothing" (John 15:4-5).

B. "I can do all things through Christ which strengtheneth {*present, participle, is strengthening*} me" (Philippians 4:13).

> Prayer is not part of the believer's "armour." Prayer is what the believer does when he has put on his "armour."

Satan and his minions of evil quake in fear when a Spirit-filled believer is fully *armored* and when that believer gets on his knees before God. At the same time, Satan and his minions of evil laugh in derision at the foolish human who thinks he can accomplish anything spiritual when he lives in sin or in the strength of his own will power. Prayer that comes forth from the believer to engage the spiritual forces of evil in the world must come forth from the overflow of the Spirit-filled life of a believer, armored with the truths of Ephesians 6:13-17. This is the spiritual dynamic of grace enablement through which the believer resists "the devil" (the archenemy of all that is good and righteous) causing him to "flee from you" in fear (James 4:7). Satan cannot stand in the face of the glory of God (His moral goodness) and neither can he stand in opposition to the prayer of a Spirit-filled and truth *armored* believer through whose life the glory of God shines. Satan's strength of evil melts under the onslaught of manifestation of the glory of God.

8. "[A]nd watching thereunto with all perseverance and supplication for all saints" (Ephesians 6:18b).

Prayer engages the enemy. Then, true prayer dependency always moves in the direction of its expectation.

What we pray for in the power of the Spirit of God believing, we watch for God to do in expectancy. The word "watching" simply means to *stay awake*. The implication is to be alert and aware of your environment and what is happening within that environment. Then we are given to attitudes of this spiritual alertness in the words "perseverance and supplication." The word "perseverance" refers to *a persistency in our expectations of answered prayer*. We are not to forget about what we asked God to do. Our persistency in our expectation is a measurement of the reality of our expectation.

The word "supplication" refers to the persistence in making strong pleadings to God. When we look in the direction of our expectation and see no form of response from God upon the horizon, we should examine our lives for sin or contradiction and ask again, and again, and again. The word "supplication" is connected to the phrase "for all saints" (or other believers). Prayer is not to be merely occupied with the realm of one's own interests, but also for the needs, weaknesses, and interests of other believers. This communion of interest is part of the *body principle* of Christianity.

"[21] And the eye cannot say unto the hand, I have no need of thee: nor again the head to the feet, I have no need of you. [22] Nay, much more those members of the body, which seem to be more feeble, are necessary: [23] And those *members* of the body, which we think to be less honourable, upon these we bestow more abundant honour; and our uncomely *parts* have more abundant comeliness. [24] For our comely *parts* have no need: but God hath tempered the body together, having given more abundant honour to that *part* which lacked: [25] That there should be no schism in the body; but *that* the members should have the same care one for another. [26] And whether one member suffer, all the members suffer with it; or one member be honoured, all the members rejoice with it" (I Corinthians 12:21-26).

We need to understand that Satan need not defile every member of the *body* to defile the *body*. If he is successful in infecting/corrupting any member of the *body*, the *body* is infected and defiled. Therefore, we should each carefully watch out for one another "with all perseverance and supplication" (Ephesians 6:18b).

> Your business is my business and my business is your business.

In our *independence,* we must never forget our *co-dependence* on one another and especially upon Christ "in us." *Church discipline* within the Age of Grace (Church Age) is administrated differently in the New Covenant than under the Mosaic Covenant. We do not stone or execute the sinner. Instead, we seek to restore the sinner through repentance and discipleship. Nonetheless, the principle of *body defilement* of a local church before God by any church member is a consistent truth. It is a truth that transcends all dispensations. We find the foundation for the *body principle* in Joshua chapter seven:

"[1] But the children of Israel committed a trespass in the accursed thing: for Achan, the son of Carmi, the son of Zabdi, the son of Zerah, of the tribe of Judah, took of the accursed thing: and the anger of the LORD was kindled against the children of Israel. [2] And Joshua sent men from Jericho to Ai, which *is* beside Bethaven, on the east side of Bethel, and spake unto them, saying, Go up and view the country. And the men went up and viewed Ai. [3] And they returned to Joshua, and said unto him, Let not all the people go up; but let about two or three thousand men go up and smite Ai; *and* make not all the people to labour thither; for they *are but* few. [4] So there went up thither of the people about three thousand men: and they fled before the men of Ai. [5] And the men of Ai smote of them about thirty and six men: for they chased them *from* before the gate *even* unto Shebarim, and smote them in the going down: wherefore the hearts of the people melted, and became as water. [6] And Joshua rent his clothes, and fell to the earth upon his face before the ark of the LORD until the eventide, he and the elders of Israel, and put dust upon their heads. [7] And Joshua said, Alas, O Lord GOD, wherefore hast thou at all brought this people over Jordan, to deliver us into the hand of the Amorites, to destroy us? would to God we had been content, and dwelt on the other side Jordan! [8] O Lord, what shall I say, when Israel turneth their backs before their enemies! [9] For the Canaanites and all the inhabitants of the land shall hear *of it*, and shall environ us round, and cut off our name from the earth: and what wilt thou do unto thy great name? [10] And the LORD said unto Joshua, Get thee up; wherefore liest thou thus upon thy face? [11] Israel hath sinned, and they have also transgressed my covenant which I commanded them: for they have even taken of the accursed thing, and have also stolen, and dissembled also, and they have put *it* even among their own stuff. [12] Therefore the children of Israel could not stand before their enemies, *but* turned *their* backs before their enemies, because they were accursed: neither will I be with you any more, except ye destroy the accursed from among you. [13] Up, sanctify the people, and say, Sanctify yourselves against to morrow: for thus saith the LORD God of Israel, *There is* an accursed thing in the midst of thee, O Israel: thou canst not stand before thine enemies, until ye take away the accursed thing from among you. [14] In the morning therefore ye shall be brought according to your tribes: and it shall be, *that* the tribe which the LORD taketh shall come according to the families *thereof*; and the family which the LORD shall take shall come by households; and the household which the LORD shall take shall come man by man. [15] And it shall be, *that* he that is taken with the accursed thing shall be burnt with fire, he and all that he hath: because he hath transgressed the covenant of the LORD, and because he hath wrought folly in Israel. [16] So Joshua rose up early in the morning, and brought Israel by their tribes; and the tribe of Judah was taken: [17] And he brought the family of Judah; and he took the family of the Zarhites: and he brought the family of the Zarhites man by man; and Zabdi was taken: [18] And he brought his household man by man; and Achan, the son of Carmi, the son of Zabdi, the son of Zerah, of the tribe of Judah, was taken. [19] And Joshua said unto Achan, My son, give, I pray thee, glory to the LORD God of Israel, and make confession unto him; and tell me now what thou hast done; hide *it* not from me. [20] And Achan answered Joshua, and said, Indeed I have sinned against the LORD God of Israel, and thus and thus have I done: [21] When I saw among the spoils a goodly Babylonish garment, and two hundred shekels of silver, and a wedge of gold of fifty shekels weight, then I coveted them, and took them; and, behold, they *are* hid in the earth in the midst of my tent, and the silver under it. [22] So Joshua sent messengers, and they ran unto the tent; and, behold, *it was* hid in his tent, and the silver under it. [23] And they took them out of the midst of the tent, and brought them unto Joshua, and unto all the children of Israel, and laid them out before the LORD. [24] <u>And Joshua, and all Israel with him, took Achan the son of Zerah, and the silver, and the garment, and the wedge of gold, and his sons, and his daughters, and his oxen, and his asses, and his sheep, and his tent, and all that he had: and they brought them unto the valley of Achor.</u> [25] And Joshua said, Why hast thou <u>troubled</u> us? the LORD shall trouble thee this day. And <u>all Israel</u> <u>stoned him with stones</u>, and <u>burned them with fire</u>, after they had <u>stoned them with stones</u> {*because they all knew about the stolen items hidden in their tent and became party to the sin in the concealment of the sin; 36 men died at Ai because of this sin and its concealment*}. [26] And they raised over him a great heap of stones unto this day. So the LORD turned from the fierceness of his anger. Wherefore the name of that place was called, The valley of Achor {*troubled*}, unto this day" (Joshua 7:1-26).

Although God detailed the judgment for the offense, the congregation of Israel was responsible for executing that judgment. This is also true of the Church Age. Although Church Age believers do not execute people by stoning, congregational polity is still responsible to execute God's detailed judgment upon unrepentant offenders.

"[1] It is reported commonly *that there is* fornication among you, and such fornication as is not so much as named among the Gentiles, that one should have his father's wife. [2] And ye are puffed up, and have not rather mourned, that he that hath done this deed might be taken away from among you. [3] For I verily, as absent in body, but present in spirit, have judged already, as though I were present, *concerning* him that hath so done this deed, [4] In the name of our Lord Jesus Christ, when ye are gathered together, and my spirit, with the power of our Lord Jesus Christ, [5] To deliver such an one unto Satan for the destruction of the flesh, that the spirit may be saved in the day of the Lord Jesus. [6] Your glorying *is* not good.

Know ye not that a little leaven leaveneth the whole lump? [7] Purge out therefore the old leaven, that ye may be a new lump, as ye are unleavened. For even Christ our passover is sacrificed for us: [8] Therefore let us keep the feast, not with old leaven, neither with the leaven of malice and wickedness; but with the unleavened *bread* of sincerity and truth. [9] I wrote unto you in an epistle not to company with fornicators: [10] Yet not altogether with the fornicators of this world, or with the covetous, or extortioners, or with idolaters; for then must ye needs go out of the world. [11] But now I have written unto you not to keep company {*getting mixed up*}, if any man that is called a brother be a fornicator, or covetous, or an idolater, or a railer, or a drunkard, or an extortioner; with such an one no not to eat. [12] For what have I to do to judge them also that are without? do not ye judge them that are within? [13] But them that are without God judgeth. Therefore put away from among yourselves that wicked person" (I Corinthians 5:1-13).

DISCUSSION QUESTIONS

1. List and define the three potential *unities* available to the believer through the supernatural enabling of the indwelling Spirit of God detailed in Ephesians 4:1-13.

2. In Ephesians 5:21 through 6:9, we are given five levels of relationships defined by four action words (verbs - one is used twice) that are consistent with the character of God. List each of these five levels of relationships and discuss the application of each of the four action words (verbs) as they apply to personal responsibilities regarding these relationships.

3. Expand upon and discuss the fact that spiritual growth is measured essentially from within two mediums: "grace . . . and the knowledge of our Lord and Saviour Jesus Christ."

4. Discuss the *fragility of grace enablement* and how this fragility can be overcome.

5. Thoroughly discuss the eightfold instruction regarding the believer's *spiritual armor* for spiritual warfare against the satanic forces of evil that the Word of God calls "the world." Discuss this along with the verb tenses, voice, and mood in Ephesians 6:10-18.

6. Thoroughly explain Colossians 1:21-2:15 in the context of the *fragility of grace enablement*.

7. Read Joshua 7:1-26 and thoroughly discuss the *Body Principle*. Discuss the potential for defilement of a local church by any individual that is formally united to that local church and how local church discipline is intended to *purge the body* of unrepentant defilement.

Chapter Thirty
Kingdom Rewards for Grace-living

God speaks often of rewards for faithful service in His Word. Christ gives us considerable detail regarding rewards for the faithful in the parable of the "talents" in Matthew 25:14-30. Uniquely, the context takes on both the sense of an encouragement and a warning. The Apostle Paul uses similar language in II Corinthians 5:1-11 as he speaks about the 'judgment seat of Christ," concluding with the statement in verse eleven; "Knowing therefore the terror of the Lord, we persuade men."

God inspires the use of metaphors relating to the ancient Greek Olympic games/contests to refer to the spiritual rewards from the Lord Jesus at the Bema/Judgment Seat of the "King of kings and LORD of lords." These are awarded to His faithful servants at the beginning of the Kingdom Age. One of those is in II Timothy 2:1-7 and another is in I Corinthians 9:24-27. If we look at all of these texts inductively, we see that these "crowns," or rewards for faithful service, will determine the prominence of the positions of Church Age believers as "kings and priests" during the Kingdom Age.

"[1] Thou therefore, my son, be strong in the grace that is in Christ Jesus. [2] And the things that thou hast heard of me among many witnesses, the same commit thou to faithful men, who shall be able to teach others also. [3] Thou therefore endure hardness, as a good soldier of Jesus Christ. [4] No man that warreth entangleth himself with the affairs of *this* life; that he may please him who hath chosen him to be a soldier. [5] And if a man also strive {*athleo; ath-leh'-o; compete*} for masteries {*lit., the victor's crown*}, yet is he not crowned, except he strive lawfully {*legitimately or according to the rules*}. [6] The husbandman {*God, John 15:1*} that laboureth must be first partaker of the fruits {*the firstfruits of glory belong to God*}. [7] Consider what I say; and the Lord give thee understanding {*spiritual comprehension*} in all things" (II Timothy 2:1-7).

In the metaphor of II Timothy 2:5, the Word of God tells us essentially that a person might appear to have won a *victory*, but will yet not be "crowned" as a victor if that person does not compete according to the exact specifications regarding the competition that is entered. The critical statement defining the specifications for being "crowned" is actually found in II Timothy 2:1 in the phrase - "be strong in the grace that is in Christ Jesus." Therefore, the believer's ministry that brings spiritual reward MUST be done within the confines of a strict interpretation and application of what the Word of God. In other words, what the Word of God teaches regarding the doctrine of Grace (the supernatural enabling of the believer who has yielded his will to the indwelling Holy Spirit of God; Romans 6:11-13). Because there is such errant teaching regarding the doctrine of Grace by many from both the legalists and the liberals within professing Christianity, the vast majority of professing believers will be found looking for crowns at the Bema Seat, but will instead find themselves in shame before the Lord.

Sadly, many Christians have lived their Christian lives in the power of the flesh (legalism). They think they have been faithful and they think that they will receive rewards at the Bema Seat. Instead, they will discover that they have spent their lives building up a pile of *kindling* for the Judgment Seat. The kindling of "wood, hay, and stubble," from ministries lived in the power of the *flesh*, will bring much shame at the Bema Seat. Carnality is more than living *sinfully* and *worldly*. Carnality exists anytime we live in the power of the *flesh*.

"[1] And I, brethren {*writing to believers*}, could not speak unto you as unto spiritual {*supernaturally enabled, Spirit-filled, yielded to the will of God in the Word of God, and producing eternal influence to the glory of God through the indwelling Spirit*}, but as unto carnal {*fleshly; i.e., producing temporal results either to man's eternal shame, or for man's personal glory*}, even as unto babes in Christ {*implying spiritual immaturity in living by grace*}. [2] I have fed you with milk, and not with meat: for hitherto ye were not able to bear it, neither yet now are ye able. [3] For ye are yet carnal: for whereas there is among you envying, and strife, and divisions {*manifesting spiritual immaturity in living by grace*}, are ye not carnal, and walk as men {*the implication is that such behavior is part of the natural existence, rather than supernatural, regenerate man*}? [4] For while one saith, I am of Paul; and another, I am of Apollos {*glorifying men thereby denying the supernatural working of the indwelling Spirit*}; are ye not carnal? [5] Who then is Paul, and who is Apollos, but ministers by whom {*by their ministry of the Word in the power of the Spirit of God*} ye believed, even as the Lord gave {*this same*} *enabling grace; see v. 10}* to every man *{for ministry}*? [6] I have planted, Apollos watered; but God gave the increase *{God works with the believer's hands}*. [7] So then neither is he that planteth any thing, neither he that watereth; but God that giveth the increase *{The miracle is in the 'increase.' So this is where the glory is to be directed; i.e., don't give glory to men for what God has done and men should not take the glory that only God deserves.}*. [8] Now he that planteth and he that watereth are one *{in our ministry and purpose of glorifying God}*: and every man shall receive his own reward *{from God, not men}* according to his own labour. [9] For we *{all believers corporately and individually}* are labourers together with God *{the synergism created with God within this supernatural spiritual dynamic of grace enabling that the Bible calls "fellowship"}*: ye *{the local church}* are God's husbandry *{cultivated field from which God would produce fruit through the lives and "work of the ministry" of perfected/spiritually equipped believers}*, ye are God's building *{All believers are the ministering servants who are both the 'building,' or spiritual, living Temple/'stones,' and the builders of the living Temple/'stones' as well; think stone masonry in layers or generations.}*. [10] According to the grace of God which is given unto me, as a wise masterbuilder, I have laid the foundation, and another *{referring to all that follow him down through the generations}* buildeth thereon *{lay the next level of 'living stones'}*. But let every man take heed how he buildeth thereupon *{a warning to his successors}*. [11] For other foundation can no man lay than that is laid, which is Jesus Christ *{salvation always must precede discipleship and the shaping of the 'living stone'}*. [12] Now if any man build upon this foundation gold, silver, precious stones, wood, hay, stubble; [13] Every man's work shall be made manifest: for the day *{the Bema/Judgment Seat}* shall declare it, because it shall be revealed by fire; and the fire shall try every man's work of what sort it is. [14] If any man's work abide *{if it is 'gold, silver, and precious stones' it will survive the trial by 'fire'}* which he hath built thereupon, he shall receive a reward. [15] If any man's work shall be burned *{if it is 'wood, hay, and stubble' it will not survive the trial by 'fire'}*, he shall suffer loss *{of rewards and perhaps suffer shame}*: but he himself shall be saved; yet so as by *{through}* fire (I Corinthians 3:1-15).

Preachers have a tendency to speak in platitudes (including myself) without considering the Scriptural correctness of those platitudes. One such platitude is that we should work for spiritual rewards or crowns so *that we might cast them at Jesus' feet, for He alone deserves the glory for what is done through the believer's life.*

This is certainly true, but the statement misses the whole purpose of Christ's giving of these visible "crown" rewards. They are not given for the "works" we have done. They are given for the "works" *God has done through our surrender to Him* (Ephesians 2:10). These "crowns" are the believer's testimony to what God has done through that believer's life. This is to what Peter speaks in I Peter 5:1 and 4.

> "[1] The elders which are among you I exhort, who am also an elder, and a witness of the sufferings of Christ, and also a partaker *{koinonos; koy-no-nos'}* of the glory that shall be revealed: . . [4] And when the chief Shepherd shall appear, ye shall receive a crown of glory that fadeth not away *{that is literally fadeless}*" (I Peter 5:1 and 4).

A believer's rewards are going to be at least a 1,000 year long testimony to how much glory he brought to God. Glorifying God comes through the supernatural enabling of the Holy Spirit of God upon his life's ministry in winning souls to Christ and making disciples.

Therefore, the *crowns* given to believers for their ministry will really be a *continuing* testimony of their lives to the "unsearchable riches" (Ephesians 3:8) of God's grace throughout the Kingdom Age. This the testimony of what God's enabling-grace can do through a believer's life when he is willing to live yielded to the Holy Spirit and allow the Christ-life to be *released* through ministry. This revelation of God, through being a "living stone" from which flows the "rivers of living water" to reveal the wondrous attributes of God through our lives, is the ultimate purpose in a sinner's salvation.

> "[10] As every man hath received the gift *{charisma, the spiritual or grace endowment}* *even so* minister the same one to another, as good <u>stewards of the manifold grace</u> of God. [11] If any man speak, *let him speak* as the oracles *{logion, log'-ee-on; lit., as the voice}* of God; if any man minister, *let him do it* <u>as of the ability which God giveth</u>: <u>that God in all things may be glorified through Jesus Christ,</u> to whom be praise and dominion for ever and ever. Amen. [12] Beloved, think it not strange concerning the fiery trial which is to try you, as though some strange thing happened unto you: [13] But

rejoice, inasmuch as ye are partakers {*koinoneo*} of Christ's sufferings; that, when his glory shall be revealed, ye may be glad also with exceeding joy. [14] If ye be reproached for the name of Christ, happy *are ye*; for the spirit of glory and of God resteth upon you: on their part he is evil spoken of, but on your part he is glorified" (I Peter 4:10-14).

The words "stewards of . . . grace" in I Peter 4:10 translates into the practical reality of **accountability** for this supernatural spiritual endowment of power that is given to all true believers "born again" of the Spirit of God. The eyes of faith see every task or difficulty in life through the possibility of grace enablement. This translates into two great spiritual realities that we MUST understand.

"[4] Abide in me, and I in you. As the branch cannot bear fruit of itself, except it abide in the vine; no more can ye, except ye abide in me. [5] I am the vine, ye *are* the branches: He that abideth in me, and I in him, the same bringeth forth much fruit: for without me ye can do nothing" (John 15:4-5).

"I can do all things through Christ which strengtheneth me" (*endunamoo; en-doo-nam-o'-o = endowment of power or empowers; this is the same word used in II Timothy 2:1; "be strong in the grace,"* Philippians 4:13).

The wearing of these "crowns" will be necessary because these believers will be in glorified bodies, ruling as "kings and priests" under their Great High Priest, Jesus Christ. Jesus will be on earth as the "King of kings and LORD of lords." I believe the purpose of this *testimony* of the *crown rewards* is directed towards those in the Kingdom Age living in fleshly bodies as to their own spiritual potential when fully surrendered to the indwelling Spirit of God. Paul details the necessities of spiritual discipline again in I Corinthians 9:24-27:

"[24] Know ye not that they which run in a race run all, but one receiveth the prize? So run, that ye may obtain. [25] And every man that striveth for the mastery is temperate in all things. Now they *do it* to obtain a corruptible crown; but we an incorruptible. [26] I therefore so run, not as uncertainly; so fight I, not as one that beateth the air: [27] But I keep under my body, and bring *it* into subjection: lest that by any means, when I have preached to others, I myself should be a castaway" (I Corinthians 9:24-27).

The great tragedy is that millions have been misled by the heresy that Paul was indorsing the legalistic teaching known as Asceticism in I Corinthians 9:27. Nothing could be further from the truth. If we look at what Paul taught inductively, we see that he warned against any form of the false doctrine of legalism over and over again. What then is this defiling legalism that will cause millions to lose rewards at the Bema due to the false teaching regarding *spirituality* through legalism ("touch not, taste not, handle not" - Colossians 2:21 and Galatians 3:1-5). What then is this defiling legalism that will cause millions of millions more to suffer under an illusion of salvation because of Soteriological legalism (Galatians 1:6-9)? First, *legalism* is NOT merely too strict an interpretation and application of the Word of God. God commands a strict interpretation and application of His Word. **Therefore, a broader more liberal/loose/liberating interpretation of Scripture is actually contrary to Christ's teachings**.

"[17] Think not that I am come to destroy the law, or the prophets: I am not come to destroy, but to fulfil. [18] For verily I say unto you, Till heaven and earth pass, one jot or one tittle shall in no wise pass from the law, till all be fulfilled. [19] Whosoever therefore shall break *{luo loo'-o; literally loosen; the idea is to teach a more relaxed, broader, more liberal interpretation}* one of these least *{in size or importance; i.e.; seemingly insignificant}* commandments, and shall teach men so, he shall be called the least in the kingdom of heaven: but whosoever shall do and teach *them*, the same shall be called great in the kingdom of heaven. [20] For I say unto you, That except your righteousness shall exceed *the righteousness* of the scribes and Pharisees, ye shall in no case *{double negative in Greek text; not at all or not by any means}* enter into the kingdom of heaven *{this is not referring to the final eternal state of existence, but is referring to the Kingdom Age because God-kind righteousness is required; i.e., justification "by grace through faith"}*" (Matthew 5:17-20).

What decisions do we need to make regarding these truths?

1. Salvation is a gift, but rewards are earned for faithful service in the "work of the ministry.
2. God has not lowered or lessen His standard of righteousness. In fact, He has redefined His expectations to His own communicable attributes.
3. We have already been given everything we need to live the Christ-life in the Person of the indwelling Holy Spirit of God.

4. The believer will ONLY be rewarded for the "fruit" produced through the supernatural enabling of the Holy Spirit (Grace).

5. We are individual stewards of this supernatural enabling of the Holy Spirit (Grace), meaning we will be held accountable for how we use it and for the "fruit" God desires to produce through our lives.

6. Our positions in the Kingdom Age will be determined by the degree of our faithfulness to the stewardship of Grace. This is what the parable of the "talents" details in Matthew 25:14-30. Some will live in glorified bodies throughout the Kingdom Age, but live in disgrace and shame because they were irresponsible "stewards of grace."

7. The believer must decide each day, and each moment of each day, to allow Christ to live through us, completely and totally yielded to doing God's will in every moment of life to win souls and make disciples to the glory of God.

DISCUSSION QUESTIONS

1. Discuss why Matthew 25:14-30 gives the believer both a message of encouragement and a warning.

2. Explain the essential confines of spiritual work that is necessary before any believer can expect to be rewarded for such work.

3. Thoroughly explain the text of I Corinthians 3:1-15 as these verses relate to spiritual responsibilities lived "according to the grace of God."

4. Explain why the platitude that says we should work for spiritual rewards or crowns so *that we might cast them at Jesus' feet for He alone deserves the glory for what is done through the believer's life* is a false platitude. Explain the real purpose of these Crown rewards.

5. Read John 15:4-5 and Philippians 4:13. What are the two great spiritual realities that we MUST understand regarding *grace enablement* from these two texts?

6. What then is this defiling legalism that will cause millions to lose rewards at the Bema due to the false teaching regarding *spirituality* through legalism ("touch not, taste not, handle not;" Colossians 2:21 and Galatians 3:1-5)? What then is this defiling legalism that will cause millions of millions more to suffer under an illusion of salvation because of Soteriological legalism (Galatians 1:6-9)?

7. List and define in your own words the seven decisions given that every believer needs to make regarding *grace enablement* and rewards for Christian ministry.

Chapter Thirty-one

The Five Crown Rewards for Grace-living (the Christ-life)

Perhaps one of the greatest misnomers of Christianity is that Christians will receive rewards in the Kingdom Age for merely being *good little boys and girls* (because they do not *live in sin*). The fact is, Christians will receive rewards for *fruit produced* (souls won and disciples made) to the glory of God. They will receive these rewards because they yielded their bodies to the indwelling Holy Spirit of God, Who then creates the *Christ-life* in their lives. This is what the Apostle Paul referred to in Galatians 2:20, Romans 6:11-13, and 12:1-2.

"[17] Think not that I am come to destroy the law, or the prophets: I am not come to destroy, but to fulfil. [18] For verily I say unto you, Till heaven and earth pass, one jot or one tittle shall in no wise pass from the law, till all be fulfilled. [19] Whosoever therefore shall break *{luo loo'-o; literally loosen; the idea is to teach a more relaxed, broader, more liberal interpretation}* one of these least *{in size or importance; i.e.; seemingly insignificant}* commandments, and shall teach men so, he shall be called the least in the kingdom of heaven: but whosoever shall do and teach *them*, the same shall be called great in the kingdom of heaven. [20] For I say unto you, That except your righteousness shall exceed *the righteousness* of the scribes and Pharisees, ye shall in no case *{double negative in Greek text; not at all or not by any means}* enter into the kingdom of heaven *{this is not referring to the final eternal state of existence, but is referring to the Kingdom Age because God-kind righteousness is required; i.e., justification "by grace through faith"}*" (Matthew 5:17-20).

Notice, in Matthew 5:19-20, that there are three divisions of people divided according to their proper understanding and application of the union of Law and Grace. "[19] Whosoever therefore shall break one of these least commandments, and shall teach men so, he shall be called the least in the kingdom of heaven: but whosoever shall do **and** teach *them*, the same shall be called great in the kingdom of heaven. [20] For I say unto you, That except your righteousness shall exceed *the righteousness* of the scribes and Pharisees, ye shall in no case enter into the kingdom of heaven."

1. Those who will be "least" in the Kingdom Age (v. 19a, the unfaithful; i.e., the spiritual legalist and liberal)
2. Those who will be "great" in the Kingdom Age (v. 19b, the faithful believer who lives in the supernatural enabling of the Spirit and produces "fruit" to God's glory)
3. Those who will not even "enter into the" the Kingdom Age (v. 20, the lost)

The "kingdom of heaven" is the Kingdom Age, not the *final eternal state of existence*. The *final eternal state of existence* is called the Kingdom of God in the Word of God. There is a difference between these two *kingdoms*. The "kingdom of heaven," or the Kingdom Age, will still be part of the first and fallen creation. However, *dominion* will be restored to mankind through the reign of the Lord Jesus Christ. Rewards will determine the *positions* that glorified Church Age believers will hold for these thousand years of Christ's rule on Earth.

The parable of the "talents" in Matthew 25:14-30 explains that these positions will be determined solely on the basis of the *fruit* (or gain). This is the *fruit* that the yielding of our lives to Christ produces as the indwelling Spirit of God creates the *Christ-life* through us. Christ precedes His teaching on the parable of the "talents" with His parable of the ten virgins (five "wise" and five "foolish") in Matthew 25:1-13. Which group of "five" do you think REALLY believed that the Bridegroom was coming for them?

Secondly, the "kingdom of heaven" will last one millennium, or a thousand years. It has events defining its beginning and events defining its ending. Part of the events defining its beginning is the Judgment (Bema) Seat of Christ where Christ will evaluate the ministry/service of believers during the Church Age. The faithful will be given "crowns" for various areas of faithful service. These rewards will also translate into varying degrees of responsibility of positions in the Kingdom Age as they rule and reign with Christ as His *kings and priests*. Matthew 5:19-20 is addressing these faithful individuals from the Church Age, their positions, and how the degrees of power or greatness of those positions will be determined.

The Word of God speaks of five different "crowns" given to *faithful* believers as *rewards*. All five crowns are determined by how faithfully a believer lives the *grace-life* (Christ-life) in the enabling power of the indwelling Christ.

1. The Crown of Life

"Blessed is the man that endureth {*faithfully continues under*} temptation {the trying or testing of the reality of faith, James 1:2}: for when he is tried {*dokimos ginomai, i.e., proven to be a regenerated person by his faithfulness to his love for the Lord*} he shall receive the <u>crown of life</u>, which the Lord hath promised **to them that love him**" (James 1:12).

"Fear none of those things which thou shalt suffer: behold, the devil shall cast some of you into prison, that ye may be tried; and ye shall have tribulation ten days: be thou faithful unto death, and I will give thee a <u>crown of life</u>" (Revelation 2:10).

The "crown of life" is NOT salvation. Salvation is not a reward for faithful service to Christ. Salvation is the salvation of our souls "by grace through faith." The "crown of life" is the crown for living the *Christ-life*. The "crown of life" is Christ's reward to the believer for being "salt" and "light" by living the *Christ-life* "by grace through faith." The believer lives the *Christ-life* by yielding his body to the indwelling Holy Spirit. Therefore the "crown of life" is the Crown of the *Christ-life* habitually lived through the life of the yielded believer as described in Galatians 2:20. The "crown of life" is Christ's reward to the faithful believer for the salvation of our *lives* (not our souls). This involves yielding our ambitions, abilities, and resources to the cause of Christ in evangelizing the world and in bringing glory to God.

"[19] For I through the law am dead to the law, that I might live unto God. [20] I am crucified with Christ: nevertheless I live; yet not I, but Christ liveth in me: and the life which I now live in the flesh I live by the faith of the Son of God, who loved me, and gave himself for me" (Galatians 2:19-20).

The "crown of life" (the *Christ-life*) is given as a reward to the believer who truly lives out the testimony of his water baptism. This translates into practically dying daily to self and the commitment to live life in the resurrection power of the indwelling Christ.

Failure to keep the promise of daily dying to self and being filled with the Spirit (putting on the *Christ-life*) that was made in water baptism will result in the loss of this reward and the position of ruling "over cities" that comes with the reward (Luke 19:11-17). Those who are not faithful in living the *grace-life/Christ-life* during the Church Age will hold a position of shame as a castaway servant (this is not referring to loss of salvation) during the Kingdom Age. The degree of rewards (greatness in positions of rule) during the Kingdom Age for glorified Church Age saints will be determined solely because of the spiritual fruit produced by the Holy Spirit through our lives habitually yielded to Him.

2. The Incorruptible Crown

"[24] Know ye not that they which run in a race run all, but one receiveth the prize? So run, that ye may obtain. [25] And every man that striveth for the mastery is temperate in all things. Now they do it to obtain a corruptible crown; but we an incorruptible. [26] I therefore so run, not as uncertainly; so fight I, not as one that beateth the air: [27] But I keep under my body, and bring it into subjection: lest that by any means, when I have preached to others, I myself should be a castaway" (I Corinthians 9:24-27).

The crowns awarded at the Greek Olympic Games were *laurel wreaths*. They would quickly wilt, turn brown, and crumble into dust. They were intended to be very temporal because they represented who was the champion in that particular event at that *particular moment*. On any other day, another of the competitors may win that crown. However, the "incorruptible crown" is an eternal crown because it is not given for one race. The "incorruptible crown" is given to a Christian based upon Christ's evaluation of a believer's whole life. The key to this reward are the words "temperate in all things" (I Corinthians 9:25).

The word "temperate" is from the Greek word *egkrateuomai* (eng-krat-yoo'-om-ahee) and refers to the self-control of human appetites, carnal lusts, and/or worldly desires or ambitions. There are six things that God "hates." Either the seventh, or having all seven, is an "abomination" (disgusting or abhorrent) to Him.

"[16] These six *things* doth the LORD hate: yea, seven *are* an abomination unto him: [17] A proud look, a lying tongue, and hands

264

that shed innocent blood, [18] An heart that deviseth wicked imaginations, feet that be swift in running to mischief, [19] A false witness *that* speaketh lies, and he that soweth discord among brethren" (Proverbs 6:16-19).

One sin connects to another that connects to another that connects to another. For instance, in David's sin with Bathsheba, we see all seven of these abominations referred to in Proverbs 6:16-19. Pride led to lying that led to cover-up that created a situation of urgency that plotted to do evil that led to murder that brought God's chastisement upon David, his family, and ultimately upon the nation of Israel. David's sin gave his children permission to do the same and the seed of spiritual discord was sown.

God does not leave us guessing about what constitutes intemperance or the failure in the self-control of the "flesh." In Galatians chapter five, God tells us exactly how intemperance will manifest itself through a person's life.

"[13] For, brethren, ye have been called unto liberty; only *use* not liberty for an occasion to the flesh, but by love serve one another. [14] For all the law is fulfilled in one word, *even* in this; Thou shalt love thy neighbour as thyself. [15] But if ye bite and devour one another, take heed that ye be not consumed one of another. [16] *This* I say then, Walk in the Spirit, and ye shall not fulfil the lust of the flesh. [17] For the flesh lusteth against the Spirit, and the Spirit against the flesh: and these are contrary the one to the other: so that ye cannot do the things that ye would. [18] But if ye be led of the Spirit, ye are not under the law. [19] Now the works of the flesh are manifest, which are *these*; Adultery, fornication, uncleanness, lasciviousness, [20] Idolatry, witchcraft, hatred, variance, emulations, wrath, strife, seditions, heresies, [21] Envyings, murders, drunkenness, revellings, and such like: of the which I tell you before, as I have also told *you* in time past, that they which do {*present, active, participle; i.e. are doing as the regular practice of their life*} such things shall not inherit the kingdom of God" (Galatians 5:13-21).

The "kingdom of God" is the *final eternal state of existence* provided only to those "born again" into God's family "by grace through faith." All true believers receive this *inheritance*. Therefore, the issue of unrepentant, habitual living in the "flesh" is also a manifestation of still being lost in spite of a profession of faith in Christ.

The third crown reward for living the *Christ-life* builds upon the previous two. We cannot earn the third crown reward apart from having earned the first two. Producing a true disciple of Jesus Christ must be done in the power of the indwelling Spirit of God. Discipleship is a supernatural work involving progressive transfiguration (Romans 12:2).

3. The Crown of Joy or Rejoicing (the disciple maker's crown)

"[17] But we, brethren, being taken from you for a short time in presence, not in heart, endeavoured the more abundantly to see your face with great desire. [18] Wherefore we would have come unto you, even I Paul, once and again; but Satan hindered us. [19] For what *is* our hope, or joy, or crown of rejoicing? *Are* not even ye in the presence of our Lord Jesus Christ at his coming? [20] For ye are our glory and joy" (I Thessalonians 2:17-20).

This "crown" is often referred to as the soul winner's crown. However, I like to refer to it as the disciple maker's crown because there are *three phases* in the evangelization of a soul. These *three phases* (or *steps,* because they must follow in *order* or *succession* to one another) of evangelism are detailed in the Great Commission given by Christ to His Church (all "born again" believers).

"[16] Then the eleven disciples went away into Galilee, into a mountain where Jesus had appointed them. [17] And when they saw him, they worshipped him: but <u>some doubted.</u> [18] And Jesus came and spake unto them, saying, All power is given unto me in heaven and in earth. [19] Go ye therefore, and teach all nations, baptizing them in the name of the Father, and of the Son, and of the Holy Ghost: [20] Teaching them to observe all things whatsoever I have commanded you: and, lo, I am with you alway, *even* unto the end of the world. Amen" (Matthew 28:16-20).

A. The first phase of evangelism is preaching the gospel and leading a soul to a faith decision to be "born again."
B. The second phase of evangelism is leading a "born again" believer to become a disciple of Jesus in daily dying to the "old man" and yielding himself to the indwelling Holy Spirit. The beginning of this second phase of evangelism is leading a person to be water baptized, which is a physical/outward portrayal of this spiritual/inward commitment. In this step, we lead the newly

"born again" believer to the local church for discipleship. Water baptism is intricately connected to formal local membership and accountability to other members of the local body in living the Christ-life. There is no such thing in Scripture as a *lone ranger Christian* outside of formal membership to a local body of believers. Scripturally, such a person would be considered an anomaly and to be living contrary to the commands of God.

C. The third phase is teaching the "born again" believer, now committed to live the *Christ-life*, the Word of God and how to become a "doer of the Word" and not just a "hearer only." The emphasis in the words "teaching them to observe all things whatsoever I have commanded you" in Matthew 28:20 is upon the word "observe." The idea of the word "observe" is to *preserve* or *guard*. The natural tendency is to lower or lessen God's expectations. The believer is to live in such a way as to never let this happen. The high expectations of righteousness (and therefore righteous living) must be carefully guarded and passed on from one generation of Christians to the next with exacting specificity. This involves teaching the specificity of Bible doctrine and living the specificity of what we know.

This *three-fold mission* is what defines the ministry/purpose of the *Christ-life* and is what should define the life of the believer who hopes for the "crown of rejoicing." **Christ died for this purpose.** This crown of rejoicing is the reward of rejoicing for the souls won to Christ and made disciples through YOUR "work of the ministry." In His resurrection and ascension to the Father, Jesus sowed the seed of the Holy Spirit of God into the bodies of every "born again" believer with the hope they each would begin to live His purpose; i.e., God-kind righteousness being miraculously produced through the lives of "born again" sinners. This same purpose must become the disciple maker's sole purpose for living. When this "fruit of the Spirit" is produced inwardly in the believer, it will produce the *fruit of souls* won to Christ and disciples made of Christ to the glory of God. This crown is the actual believers who are saved and discipled through your ministry.

"Therefore, my brethren dearly beloved and longed for, my joy and crown, so stand fast in the Lord, *my* dearly beloved" (Philippians 4:1).

"[19] For what *is* our hope, or joy, or crown of rejoicing? <u>*Are* not even ye in the presence of our Lord Jesus Christ at his coming?</u> [20] For <u>ye are our glory and joy</u>" (I Thessalonians 2:19-20).

4. The Crown of Righteousness (the crown for keeping "the faith")

"[1] I charge *thee* therefore before God, and the Lord Jesus Christ, who shall judge the quick and the dead at his appearing and his kingdom; [2] Preach the word; be instant in season, out of season; reprove, rebuke, exhort with all longsuffering and doctrine. [3] For the time will come when they will not endure sound doctrine; but after their own lusts shall they heap to themselves teachers, having itching ears; [4] And they shall turn away *their* ears from the truth, and shall be turned unto fables. [5] But watch thou in all things, endure afflictions, do the work of an evangelist, make full proof of thy ministry. [6] For I am now ready to be offered, and the time of my departure is at hand. [7] I have fought a good fight, I have finished *my* course, I have kept {*to guard against loss by teaching and living*} the faith {*the jot and tittles of the Word of God*}: [8] Henceforth there is laid up for me a crown of righteousness, which the Lord, the righteous judge, shall give me at that day: and not to me only, but unto all them also that love his appearing" (II Timothy 4:1-8).

The local church (made up of individual believers saved by "grace through faith," discipled, and "perfect[ed] for the work of the ministry") is the "pillar and ground of the Truth." Every local church and every individual believer will be judged at the Judgment Seat of Christ according to two criteria regarding how we *kept* "the faith."

A. The effort we put into learning the Word of God and the effort we made to teach the Word of God to others.
B. The effort we made to translate the Word of God into the *language of living* ("be ye doers of the Word, and not hearers only").

The *crown of righteousness* is for learning, living, and teaching the Word of God to others so that they might do the same (creating a continuum of "the faith"). Living the Word of God cannot be separated from teaching the doctrine of Grace, because no one can live the Word of God (be righteous) apart from the supernatural inner workings of the indwelling Spirit of God.

"[1] O foolish Galatians, who hath bewitched you, that ye should not obey the truth, before whose eyes Jesus Christ hath been evidently set forth, crucified among you? [2] This only would I learn of you, Received ye the Spirit by the works of the law, or by the hearing of faith? [3] Are ye so foolish? having begun in the Spirit, are ye now made perfect by the flesh" (Galatians 3:1-6)?

The *crown of righteousness* is the reward for yielding to the indwelling Holy Spirit, who then produces God-kind righteousness through our lives. Apart from this work of Grace, the believer can never be anything but a sinner. The Spirit of God is the inner source of "living water" (God-kind righteousness).

"[17] Therefore if any man *be* in Christ, *he is* a new creature: old things are passed away; behold, all things are become new. [18] And all things *are* of God, who hath reconciled us to himself by Jesus Christ, and hath given to us the ministry of reconciliation; [19] To wit, that God was in Christ, reconciling the world unto himself, not imputing their trespasses unto them; and hath committed unto us the word of reconciliation. [20] Now then we are ambassadors for Christ, as though God did beseech *you* by us: we pray *you* in Christ's stead, be ye reconciled to God. [21] For he hath made him *to be* sin for us, who knew no sin; that we might be made the righteousness of God in him" (II Corinthians 5:17-21).

II Corinthians 5:21 refers to practical God-kind righteousness supernaturally produced by the Spirit of God through the regenerated believer. Christ having been "made . . . sin for us" opens the *spiritual door* for the Spirit of God to indwell the believer. "Made" in II Corinthians 5:21 is from the Greek word *ginomai* (ghin'-om-ahee). The idea is *to become.* I believe this goes beyond the imputation of righteousness "in Christ" to the potential of practical God-kind righteousness supernaturally produced through the believer's life by the indwelling Spirit of God.

This is exactly what Paul is saying in Romans 8:4; "That the righteousness of the law might be fulfilled in us, who walk not after the flesh, but after the Spirit." This was never even a possibility prior to the indwelling of the Holy Spirit and the Age of Grace. "Now . . . in Christ Jesus" the fulfillment of "the righteousness of the law" is a possibility in the regenerated believer's life if that believer will "walk not after the flesh, but after the Spirit." This of course refers back to what Paul has already said in Romans 6:11-13.

5. The Crown of Glory (the faithful pastor's crown)

"[1] The elders which are among you I exhort, who am also an elder, and a witness of the sufferings of Christ, and also a partaker of the glory that shall be revealed: [2] Feed the flock of God which is among you, taking the oversight *thereof*, not by constraint, but willingly; not for filthy lucre, but of a ready mind; [3] Neither as being lords over *God's* heritage, but being ensamples to the flock. [4] And when the chief Shepherd shall appear, ye shall receive a crown of glory that fadeth not away" (I Peter 5:1-4).

The crown of glory is possibly the highest ranking crown of all. Christ gives rewards for faithfulness according to levels of responsibility of ministry He has given to people. We must remember that pastors will be held accountable for the lives under their ministry. They will lose rewards if they have not taught people properly and/or administrated the local church under their charge according to the directives given to us in the Word by the Chief Shepherd.

"[7] Remember them which have the rule over you, who have spoken unto you the word of God: whose faith follow, considering the end of *their* conversation. [8] Jesus Christ the same yesterday, and to day, and for ever. [9] Be not carried about with divers and strange doctrines. For *it is* a good thing that the heart be established with grace; not with meats, which have not profited them that have been occupied therein. [10] We have an altar {*the Lord's Supper*}, whereof they have no right to eat which serve the tabernacle. [11] For the bodies of those beasts, whose blood is brought into the sanctuary by the high priest for sin, are burned without the camp. [12] Wherefore Jesus also, that he might sanctify the people with his own blood, suffered without the gate. [13] Let us go forth therefore unto him without the camp, bearing his reproach. [14] For here have we no continuing city, but we seek one to come. [15] By him therefore let us offer the sacrifice of praise to God continually, that is, the fruit of *our* lips giving thanks to his name. [16] But to do good and to communicate forget not: for with such sacrifices God is well pleased. [17] Obey them that have the rule over you, and submit yourselves: for <u>they watch for your souls, as they that must give account, that they may do it with joy, and not with grief: for that *is* unprofitable for you</u>" (Hebrews 13:7-17).

All Five Crowns are referred to as "a full reward."

"[7] For many deceivers are entered into the world, who confess not that Jesus Christ is come in the flesh. This is a deceiver and an antichrist. [8] Look to yourselves, that we lose not those things which we have wrought, but that we receive a full reward. [9] Whosoever transgresseth, and abideth not in the doctrine of Christ, hath not God. He that abideth in the doctrine of Christ, he hath both the Father and the Son" (II John 1:7-9).

DISCUSSION QUESTIONS

1. Discuss why one of the greatest misnomers of Christianity is that Christians will receive rewards in the Kingdom Age for merely being *good little boys and girls* (because they do not *live in sin*).

2. List and define the three divisions of people, divided according to their proper understanding and application of the *union* of Law and Grace in Matthew 5:19-20.

3. Discuss the differences between the *Kingdom of Heaven* and the *Kingdom of God*.

4. List and define each of the five crown rewards with Scripture references also defining the qualifications for earning these rewards.

5. Explain the following statement, "Sin is like a spider web. Seldom is there but one strand."

6. List and define the three phases (steps) of evangelism according to Matthew 28:16-20.

7. Every local church and every individual believer will be judged at the Judgment Seat of Christ according to two criteria regarding how we *kept* "the faith." Give and explain these two criteria.

Chapter Thirty-two
Fulfilling the Grace Commission

"[1] The former treatise have I made, O Theophilus, of all that Jesus began both to do and teach, [2] Until the day in which he was taken up, after that he through the Holy Ghost had given commandments unto the apostles whom he had chosen: [3] To whom also he shewed himself alive after his passion by many infallible proofs, being seen of them forty days, and speaking of the things pertaining to the kingdom of God: [4] And, being assembled together with *them*, commanded them that they should not depart from Jerusalem, but wait for the promise of the Father, which, *saith he*, ye have heard of me. [5] For John truly baptized with water; but ye shall be baptized with the Holy Ghost not many days hence. [6] When they therefore were come together, they asked of him, saying, Lord, wilt thou at this time restore again the kingdom to Israel? [7] And he said unto them, It is not for you to know the times or the seasons, which the Father hath put in his own power. [8] But ye shall receive power, after that the Holy Ghost is come upon you: and ye shall be witnesses unto me both in Jerusalem, and in all Judaea, and in Samaria, and unto the uttermost part of the earth. [9] And when he had spoken these things, while they beheld, he was taken up; and a cloud received him out of their sight. [10] And while they looked stedfastly toward heaven as he went up, behold, two men stood by them in white apparel; [11] Which also said, Ye men of Galilee, why stand ye gazing up into heaven? this same Jesus, which is taken up from you into heaven, shall so come in like manner as ye have seen him go into heaven" (Acts 1:1-11).

The book of Acts is often referred to as the *Fifth Gospel*. It was written by Luke and it continues where he left off in the Gospel of Luke. The Gospel of Luke is what Luke is referring to in Acts 1:1 by the statement, "[t]he former treatise have I made."

Secondly, the book of Acts is directed to someone named "Theophilus." The Greek word "theophilus" simply means *friend of God*. I believe the word "theophilus" is used as a general term addressing this narrative to those who consider themselves *friends of God*, or *Christians*. The term *friend of God* is used to describe *faithful* believers who live "the faith." It was first used to describe Abraham.

"[17] Even so faith, if it hath not works, is dead, being alone. [18] Yea, a man may say, Thou hast faith, and I have works: shew me thy faith without thy works, and I will shew thee my faith by my works. [19] Thou believest that there is one God; thou doest well: the devils also believe, and tremble. [20] But wilt thou know, O vain man, that faith without works is dead? [21] Was not Abraham our father justified by works, when he had offered Isaac his son upon the altar? [22] Seest thou how faith wrought with his works, and by works was faith made perfect? [23] And the scripture was fulfilled which saith, Abraham believed God, and it was imputed unto him for righteousness: and <u>he was called the Friend of God</u>" (James 2:17-22).

Later, in the Epistle of James, he would extend this *friendship* terminology into a contradistinction in teaching that anyone who was a *friend of the world* was not a friend of God, but an enemy of God.

"[1] From whence *come* wars and fightings among you? *come they* not hence, *even* of your lusts that war in your members? [2] Ye lust, and have not: ye kill, and desire to have, and cannot obtain: ye fight and war, yet ye have not, because ye ask not. [3] Ye ask, and receive not, because ye ask amiss, that ye may consume *it* upon your lusts. [4] Ye adulterers and adulteresses, know ye not that the <u>friendship of the world is enmity with God? whosoever therefore will be a friend of the world is the enemy of God.</u> [5] Do ye think that the scripture saith in vain, The spirit that dwelleth in us lusteth to envy? [6] But he giveth more grace. Wherefore he saith, God resisteth the proud, but giveth grace unto the humble. [7] Submit yourselves therefore to God. Resist the devil, and he will flee from you. [8] <u>Draw nigh to God, and he will draw nigh to you</u>. Cleanse *your* hands, *ye* sinners; and purify *your* hearts, *ye* double minded. [9] Be afflicted, and mourn, and weep: let your laughter be turned to mourning, and *your* joy to heaviness. [10] Humble yourselves in the sight of the Lord, and he shall lift you up" (James 4:1-10).

There is simplicity to *grace-living* and, yet, there is complexity to it. *Grace-living* is simply yielding all that we are, all that we can be, and all our desires to the indwelling Spirit of God. If the quality of our faith in the reality of God's existence and our understanding of the scope of His existence was where it ought to be, the simplicity of yielding to Him and allowing Him to live through us would not be so complex. That is what James is dealing with in his epistle - the reality of our faith in God.

Luke is dealing with the reality of our faith in God in his introduction to his continuation of the Gospel of Luke that we have come to call the Acts of the Apostles. The title *Acts of the Apostles* is a man-made title. That title does not accurately reflect the scope of the intent of this historical account of the first generation of the Age of Grace. This purpose is given to us in the first two verses of Acts chapter one, "[1b] all that Jesus began both to do and teach, [2] Until the day in which he was taken up, after that he through the Holy Ghost had given commandments unto the apostles whom he had chosen." **Do not rush by this statement.**

In this statement, we have the whole Church Age defined as well as the scope of the "work of the ministry" as a continuum of the *Christ-life* through every Spirit enabled believer of the Church Age.

This historical account would be better entitled the *Acts of Jesus Christ Lived through the Priesthood of All Believers*. David Thomas gives us the following note on the statement "all that Jesus began both to do and teach:"

" . . . from the arrangement of these words in the original Greek, two things are plain which escape the English reader: First, there is an emphasis on the verb '*began*;' secondly, there is none on the word '*Jesus*.' The contrast is not that the former treatise related what *Jesus* began, and this relates what some other person or persons continued; but it is that the former treatise related what Jesus *began* to do and teach: and this relates what He, the same Jesus, *continued* to do and teach."[11]

The question immediately then is raised, how could Jesus continue to "do and teach" after He was dead? Answering this question gives us the supernatural nature of God's intent beyond salvation from Hell. This deals with what we see *fleshed out* in the

---

[11] Thomas, David. *Acts of the Apostles Expository and Homiletical*. (Grand Rapids, MI: Kregel Publications. (Reprint of the 1870 ed. published by R.D. Dickinson, London, under title: *Homiletic Commentary on the Acts of the Apostles*.)

lives of those recorded in the book of Acts. The answer is simple: Christ lives supernaturally through the yielded life of the believer indwelled and "filled" with the Spirit of God. What Jesus began to do on the Day of Pentecost was something the world had never seen. Jesus would supernaturally live THROUGH those "born again" of the Spirit of God and who were completely yielded to Him.

> This understanding of the historical record of the book of Acts gives us the supernatural perspective that must be included in our perspective of the history of the Church. This history began to be written in the book of Acts and *is being written* each day through the historical events of the lives of believers.

The work of evangelism and the teaching that Jesus began in His incarnation is continued through the *hypostatic union* of God in all believers. That work is divinely energized when *hypostatic unity* (Ephesians 4:1-7) is supernaturally created in the life of a believer completely yielded to the indwelling Christ. The history of the book of Acts is the record of what Jesus did as He lived His life THROUGH the life of His disciples. ALL THAT HAPPEN IN THEM IS POTENTIALLY STILL AVAILABLE TO ALL BELIEVERS!

The willingness of these believers to risk everything, even life itself, to completely yield themselves to Christ was based upon the reality of their faith in the resurrection of Jesus Christ. It was based upon the reality of their faith in their own glorification and exaltation in the coming Kingdom Age. This is the central reason we have ten recorded appearances of the resurrected Jesus to His disciples.

"[3] To whom also he shewed himself alive after his passion by <u>many infallible proofs</u>, being seen of them forty days, and speaking of the things pertaining to the kingdom of God: [4] And, <u>being assembled together with *them*,</u> commanded them that they should not depart from Jerusalem, but wait for the promise of the Father {*referring to the indwelling, John 15:26-27*}, which, *saith he*, ye have heard of me. [5] For John truly baptized with water; but ye shall be baptized with the Holy Ghost not many days hence" (Acts 1:3-5).

The words "infallible proofs" are translated from the Greek word *tekmerion* (tek-may'-ree-on), which simply means *criteria for certainty*. There was no doubt, none whatsoever, about the resurrection and glorification of Jesus. For the early Christians, this was an established FACT. This established fact gave them a living FAITH. Their living faith trusted in the promises of God regarding yielding their lives to the supernatural workings of God. That did not mean that their lives would be without persecutions, difficulties, spiritual warfare, temptations, trials, hunger, pain, or sufferings. In fact, all of these types of things would increase in their lives. They increased because of opposition in Satan's attempt to discourage and corrupt/defile them for God's supernatural workings through their lives. The only way these early believers would be able to survive the horrendous onslaught of satanic opposition would be a real, living faith in the reality of their own resurrection/glorification.

Another important aspect of Christ's post resurrection appearances that David Thomas points out is that Jesus never speaks to the lost multitudes in any of those ten different appearances. Jesus appeared and communicated only with His disciples after His resurrection (with the exception of His call of the Apostle Paul). The emphasis in this fact is that after the Day of Pentecost and the indwelling of, and baptism with, the Holy Spirit, Jesus would from that time forward in the Church Age speak TO His disciples through His inspired Word and TO the lost world THROUGH His disciples. That is why we can truly call the Great Commission the GRACE COMMISSION.

"[26] But when the Comforter is come, whom I will send unto you from the Father, *even* the Spirit of truth, which proceedeth from the Father, he shall testify of me: [27] And ye also shall bear witness, because ye have been with me from the beginning" (John 15:26-27).

"[7] Nevertheless I tell you the truth; It is expedient for you that I go away: for if I go not away, the Comforter will not come unto you; but if I depart, I will send him unto you. [8] And when he is come, he will reprove the world of sin, and of righteousness, and of judgment: [9] Of sin, because they believe not on me; [10] Of righteousness, because I go to my Father, and ye see me no more; [11] Of judgment, because the prince of this world is judged. [12] I have yet many things to say unto you, but ye cannot bear them now. [13] Howbeit when he, the Spirit of truth, is come, he will guide you into all truth: for he shall not speak of himself; but whatsoever he shall hear, *that* shall he speak: and he will shew you things to come. [14] He shall glorify me: for he shall receive of mine, and shall shew *it* unto you. [15] All things that the Father hath are mine: therefore said I, that he shall take of mine, and shall shew *it* unto you" (John 16:7-15).

After the Day of Pentecost (which was the beginning of the Church Age or the Age of Grace), reaching the lost would become the sole responsibility of local churches and individual, faithful believers making up those local churches. Believers individually, and local churches (believers corporately), were to be the *distribution centers* of truth through the supernatural enabling of the indwelling Holy Spirit (II Corinthians 5:17-21). The Great Commission required that reaching the world with the Gospel of Jesus Christ become the accepted and lived responsibility of the Church and every individual Christian "born again" of the Spirit of God.

Yet, the Great Commission was not to be, and could not be, accomplished through human will power, strength/might, or through human wisdom. Fulfilling the Great Commission would need to be a cooperative, supernatural work done in synergism with the indwelling Holy Spirit of God. It would require a network of other believers of like precious faith in various local churches. Fulfilling the Great Commission requires an in-depth knowledge of the Word of God, an intimate relationship with the God of the Word, and a living, vibrant faith that is willing to make enormous personal sacrifices and take enormous personal risks to insure that the Gospel of Jesus Christ is proclaimed throughout the world.

"[15] Wherefore I also, after I heard of your faith in the Lord Jesus, and love unto all the saints, [16] Cease not to give thanks for you, making mention of you in my prayers; [17] That the God of our Lord Jesus Christ, the Father of glory, may give unto you the spirit of wisdom and revelation in the knowledge of him: [18] The eyes of your understanding being enlightened; that ye may know what is the hope of his calling, and what the riches of the glory of his inheritance in the saints, [19] And what *is* the exceeding greatness of his power to us-ward who believe, according to the working of his mighty power, [20] Which he wrought in Christ, when he raised him from the dead, and set *him* at his own right hand in the heavenly *places*, [21] Far above all principality, and power, and might, and dominion, and every name that is named, not only in this world, but also in that which is to come: [22] And hath put all *things* under his feet, and gave him *to be* the head over all *things* to the church, [23] Which is his body, the fulness of him that filleth all in all" (Ephesians 1:15-23).

> Fulfilling the Great Commission would require a *partnership* with God in "the work of the ministry." This *partnership* is available to every believer and is communicated by the word "fellowship" in our English Bibles.

The availability of this *partnership* to every believer is communicated in the last phrase of the Great Commission: "and, lo, <u>I am with you alway</u>, *even* unto the end of the world. Amen" (Matthew 28:20). This "work of the ministry" was never intended to be done apart from a partnership with the indwelling Christ. Yet, the "work of the ministry" is the Great Commission and is commanded to every believer.

DISCUSSION QUESTIONS

1. Explain why the book of Acts is often referred to as the *Fifth Gospel*.

2. Explain why there is a simplicity to *grace-living* and, yet, there is a complexity to it.

3. Discuss why the Book of Acts would be better entitled the *Acts of Jesus Christ Lived through the Priesthood of All Believers*.

4. David Thomas gives us the following note on the statement "all that Jesus began both to do and teach:"

> ". . . from the arrangement of these words in the original Greek, two things are plain which escape the English reader: First, there is an emphasis on the verb '*began*;' secondly, there is none on the word '*Jesus.*' The contrast is not that the former treatise related what *Jesus* began, and this relates what some other person or persons continued; but it is that the former treatise related what Jesus *began* to do and teach: and this relates what He, the same Jesus, *continued* to do and teach."[12]

How could Jesus continue to "do and teach" after He was dead?

5. After the Day of Pentecost (beginning the Church Age or the Age of Grace), reaching the lost would become the sole responsibility of local churches and individual, faithful believers making up those local churches. Discuss the role of the "born again" human agent through Grace enabled evangelism.

6. Explain Ephesians 1:15-23 in the light of your answer to your answer above.

7. How does the last phrase of the Great Commission, "and, lo, I am with you alway, *even* unto the end of the world. Amen" (Matthew 28:20), communicate the ongoing availability of Christ's *grace enabling* presence throughout the Church Age.

---

[12] Ibid., page 2.

Chapter Thirty-three

The Servant Vision of the Christ-life

Undoubtedly, the greatest example of being a servant is the example given us in the incarnate, eternal Son of God. The Creator of heaven and earth was willing to become a man in order to pay the "wages of sin" for our redemption. The Son of God came in the form of the Son of man and took on Himself the "form of a servant." What is important for us to see in this is that this servant aspect of Christ's character flows supernaturally from His Divine Nature.

"[3] Let nothing be done through strife or vainglory; but in lowliness of mind let each esteem other better than themselves. [4] Look not every man on his own things, but every man also on the things of others. [5] Let this mind be in you, which was also in Christ Jesus: [6] Who, being in the form of God, thought it not robbery to be equal with God: [7] But made himself of no reputation, and took upon him the form of a servant, and was made in the likeness of men: [8] And being found in fashion as a man, he humbled himself, and became obedient unto death, even the death of the cross. [9] Wherefore God also hath highly exalted him, and given him a name which is above every name: [10] That at the name of Jesus every knee should bow, of things in heaven, and things in earth, and things under the earth; [11] And that every tongue should confess that Jesus Christ is Lord, to the glory of God the Father" (Philippians 2:3-11).

The disciples had an ongoing struggle with being servants to others. This was something contrary to everything they had ever been taught in life. Their parents began to engrain in them *prominence thinking. Prominence thinking* continued to be taught by everything aspect of the Jewish culture. Culturally, people works hard to become *people of importance* and to hold positions of prominence in the world. Although faithful Christians will receive great prominence and be exalted to be ruling kings and priests with Christ in the Kingdom Age, they were not to live or work motivated by that future position. An integral aspect of the Divine Nature (II Peter 1:4) that indwells the believer is the character of a servant.

Christ addresses this as He answers the question of the disciples in Acts 1:6 regarding when the Kingdom would be *restored.*

The disciples were preoccupied with the prominence of their future positions in the Kingdom rather than being preoccupied with the ministry they had been trained to perform. They struggled with being the servants (*bond slaves*) Christ had exemplified and prepared them to become. The *greatness* (the degree of exaltation) of their Kingdom positions would be determined proportionately to the degree they were willing to set aside the *pride of life* (desire for prominence) to become the servants of both God and their fellowman.

"[20] Then came to him the mother of Zebedee's children with her sons, worshipping *him*, and desiring a certain thing of him. [21] And he said unto her, What wilt thou? She saith unto him, Grant that these my two sons may sit, the one on thy right hand, and the other on the left, in thy kingdom. [22] But Jesus answered and said, Ye know not what ye ask. Are ye able to drink of the cup that I shall drink of {*referring to the kind of death He would suffer*}, and to be baptized with the baptism that I am baptized with {*referring to the baptism with the Spirit into the death of Christ and the resurrected life of Christ*}? They say unto him, We are able. [23] And he saith unto them, Ye shall drink indeed of my cup, and be baptized with the baptism that I am baptized with: but to sit on my right hand, and on my left, is not mine to give, but *it shall be given to them* for whom it is prepared of my Father. [24] <u>And when the ten heard *it*, they were moved with indignation against the two brethren.</u> [25] But Jesus called them *unto him* {*reproving or correcting their false thinking; Christ is condemning their attitudes of pride, self-glorification, and personal ambitions for power and position*}, and said, Ye know that the princes {*rulers*} of the Gentiles exercise dominion over them, and they that are great {*megas, higher in authority*} exercise authority upon them {*the lower rulers*}. [26] But it shall not be so among you {*will not be in the Kingdom Age and should not be in your present mindset; you should not be thinking like this because it is a carnal way to think*}: but whosoever will be great {*megas, foremost in authority*} among you, let him be your minister {*diakonos, literally one who runs errands, does menial tasks, or waits upon others to serve them*} [27] And whosoever will be chief {*protos, first*} among you, let him be your servant {*doulos, literally bondman or bond servant*} : [28] Even as the Son of man came not to be ministered {*diakoneo*} unto {*literally, to be waited upon*}, but to minister {*diakoneo, literally to wait upon others*}, and to give his life {*the extreme degree and example of this servant mentality to which all believers are to aspire*} a ransom for many" (Matthew 20:20-28).

Critical to our understanding of this text and its practical application for our lives is that this *servant mentality* must be maintained throughout our lives. The reason why the *servant mentality* must be maintained is because we are by nature selfish, prideful, self-promoting, power-hungry, and carnally ambitious in our desires for personal recognition. Our fallen natures lust for prominence and we are by nature competitive in order to achieve status among our peers. In our carnal thinking, it does not make much difference if we find acceptance and extreme self-worth in a righteous relationship with our Heavenly Father and our position of prominence as His sons. That spiritual position is an invisible position of prominence. We want (lust for) a visible, recognizable, acknowledge position of prominence among our peers. This is carnal and worldly!

> Although the faithful, Spirit-filled believer will achieve extreme exaltation in the coming Kingdom Age, the condition for that exaltation is humility and selflessness in our present existence.

We find this admonition in two major Bible texts referring to this condition of humility for exaltation. In other words, those who meet the conditions will be exalted before men, but that exaltation should not be what motivates us to be servants.

"[5] Do ye think that the scripture saith in vain, The spirit that dwelleth in us lusteth to envy? [6] But he giveth more grace. Wherefore he saith, God resisteth the proud, but giveth grace unto the humble. [7] Submit yourselves therefore to God. Resist the devil, and he will flee from you. [8] Draw nigh to God, and he will draw nigh to you. Cleanse *your* hands, *ye* sinners; and purify *your* hearts, *ye* double minded. [9] Be afflicted, and mourn, and weep: let your laughter be turned to mourning, and *your* joy to heaviness. [10] Humble yourselves {*the idea is to reflect an attitude in your living of an accurate opinion of what you really deserve*} in the sight of the Lord, and he shall lift {*hupsoo, elevate or exalt*} you up" (James 4:5-10).

How easily we forget from whence we have come. How easily we achieve a false sense of self-importance. As soon as we begin to see some spiritual growth in our lives and begin to have a spiritual walk with God, we must guard against the false notion of self-righteousness and spiritual superiority. Self-righteousness and spiritual superiority will raise their *ugly heads* in our lives. This will be manifested by contempt for sinners (rather than contempt for their sin). This will be manifested by casting people aside because we view them unworthy to be in our presence or incapable of ever achieving our degree of spirituality. When that becomes your spirit, look out friend! God is going to give you a wakeup call to reality. That attitude is part of our fallen natures. It is carnal and worldly!

"[1] The elders which are among you I exhort, who am also an elder, and a witness of the sufferings of Christ, and also a partaker of the glory that shall be revealed: [2] Feed the flock of God which is among you, taking the oversight *thereof*, not by constraint, but willingly; not for filthy lucre, but of a ready mind; [3] Neither as being lords over *God's* heritage, but being ensamples to the flock. [4] And when the chief Shepherd shall appear, ye shall receive a crown of glory that fadeth not away. [5] Likewise, ye younger {*neos; i.e., new, referring to new believers who are still spiritually immature*}, submit {*subordinate, put yourself under*} yourselves unto the elder {*presbuteros, referring to the pastor*}. Yea, all *of you* be subject {*subordinate, put yourself under*} one to another, and be clothed with humility: for God resisteth {*opposes*} the proud, and giveth grace to the humble. [6] Humble yourselves therefore under the mighty hand of God, that he may exalt you in due time: [7] Casting all your care upon him; for he careth for you" (I Peter 5:1-7).

In I Peter 5:7, believers are commanded to "humble yourselves therefore under the mighty hand of God." That which defines this submissive spirit of humility is not left up to our imaginations. Neither is it merely defined linguistically. In fact, Jesus defined it by giving an example in Matthew 18:4. With this example, He gives a serious warning regarding corrupting children in their thinking and living. This warning is about the issues of pride and self-importance. For the lost, these are the kinds of things that keep people from the humility of genuine repentance, leading to genuine salvation and an honest evaluation of what they really are apart from God's workings of grace in their lives. For the "born again" believer, these are the kinds of things that keep people from being filled with the Spirit of God and experiencing the abundance of the *Christ-life*.

"[1] At the same time came the disciples unto Jesus, saying, Who is the greatest in the kingdom of heaven? [2] And Jesus called a little child unto him, and set him in the midst of them *{as an example of humility and submissiveness; when the child was summoned to come, he obeyed immediately and submissively}*, [3] And said, Verily I say unto you, Except ye be converted, and become as little children, ye shall not enter into the kingdom of heaven. [4] Whosoever therefore shall humble himself as this little child, the same is greatest in the kingdom of heaven. [5] And whoso shall receive one such little child in my name receiveth me. [6] But whoso shall offend *{skandalizo, to trip up or lead astray}* one of these little ones which believe in me, it were better for him that a millstone *{a huge grinding stone for crushing grain}* were hanged about his neck, and *that* he were drowned in the depth *{the deepest part}* of the sea" (Matthew 18:1-6).

Obviously Christ considered any person leading someone astray in the area of self-promotion/exaltation by a failure to be humble and submissive, especially a child, to be a serious offense. Such an offense merited a punishment that was used upon those who committed crimes against a whole society, rather than merely another individual. Hanging a huge stone around the neck and casting the person into the depth of the sea was a unique death sentence. It was a sentence put upon those committing either *parricide* (killing a parent) or *infanticide* (killing one's own child). This means of execution was an extreme form of dishonor and shame. This means of execution portrayed the just dessert of casting away the soul of such a person. This kind of crime was so degenerate that the judgment upon such corruption of the life of an *innocent* falls now upon their own eternal destiny.

This is a serious warning. It is a warning about a crime that should result in careful consideration about corrupting a child through selfish living. This is expanded upon in Matthew 18:7-14. This continues in the context of the warning regarding leading a child astray in the area of humility or self-aggrandizing. **Do not lose the context of this warning regarding living an exemplary life of humility as servants to others.** Notice, Christ's instruction defines the extreme measures a person should go in order to avoid corrupting a little child in these motivating behavioral attitudes.

"[7] Woe unto the world because of offences! for it must needs be that offences come; but woe to that man by whom the offence cometh! [8] Wherefore if thy hand or thy foot offend thee, cut them off, and cast *them* from thee: it is better for thee to enter into life halt or maimed, rather than having two hands or two feet to be cast into everlasting fire. [9] And if thine eye offend thee, pluck it out, and cast *it* from thee: it is better for thee to enter into life with one eye, rather than having two eyes to be cast into hell fire. [10] Take heed that ye despise not one of these little ones; for I say unto you, That in heaven their angels do always behold the face of my Father which is in heaven. [11] For the Son of man is come to save that which was lost. [12] How think ye? if a man have an hundred sheep, and one of them be gone astray, doth he not leave the ninety and nine, and goeth into the mountains, and seeketh that which is gone astray? [13] And if so be that he find it, verily I say unto you, he rejoiceth more of that *sheep*, than of the ninety and nine which went not astray. [14] <u>Even so it is not the will of your Father which is in heaven, that one of these little ones should perish</u>" (Matthew 18:7-14).

Why is it that so many children of professing believers grow up to reject Christ and to live in sin as unbelievers? It is not that they reject the God of the Bible or the love of God manifested in the death, burial, and resurrection of Christ. They do not begin as reprobate unbelievers. Unbelief is progressive in children's lives as they WATCH the adults around them live like unbelievers.

A genuine life of faith is manifested to children through a genuine life of faithfulness (submissive obedience to God's commands and instructions for living).

Like Lot's children, who could not take their father's warning of God's pending judgment upon Sodom and Gomorrah seriously because of their father's hypocrisy and spiritual inconsistencies, our children are *hindered* (offended) by our duplicities. We tell them to do one thing while we live in contradiction to the principles we are trying to establish in them. This is the sin of hypocrisy and it is a sin against society as a whole and the individuals within our immediate influence specifically.

DISCUSSION QUESTIONS

1. Discuss why it is important to see that the servant aspect of Christ's character flows supernaturally from His Divine Nature.

2. Discuss why most of us are *preoccupied* with our own *prominence* and *preeminence* in life.

3. Discuss how being *preoccupied* with our own *prominence* and *preeminence* will be hindrances to *promotion* (exaltation) in the Kingdom Age.

4. Discuss why many Christians so easily succumb to having achieved a false sense of self-importance.

5. Discuss in what ways genuine humility continually overcomes the deception of having achieved a false sense of self-importance.

6. Discuss some of the ways that adults gender self-promotion and self-exaltation in children through emphasis on such things as sports or seeking the praise of others.

7. Expand upon the following statement, "A genuine life of faith is manifested to children through a genuine life of faithfulness (submissive obedience to God's commands and instructions for living)."

Chapter Thirty-four

The New Beginning

"[1] The former treatise have I made, O Theophilus, of all that Jesus began both to do and teach, [2] Until the day in which he was taken up, after that he through the Holy Ghost had given commandments unto the apostles whom he had chosen: [3] To whom also he shewed himself alive after his passion by many infallible proofs, being seen of them forty days, and speaking of the things pertaining to the kingdom of God: [4] And, being assembled together with *them*, commanded them that they should not depart from Jerusalem, but wait for the promise of the Father, which, *saith he*, ye have heard of me. [5] For John truly baptized with water; but ye shall be baptized with the Holy Ghost not many days hence. [6] When they therefore were come together, they asked of him, saying, Lord, wilt thou at this time restore again the kingdom to Israel? [7] And he said unto them, It is not for you to know the times or the seasons, which the Father hath put in his own power. [8] But ye shall receive power, after that the Holy Ghost is come upon you: and ye shall be witnesses unto me both in Jerusalem, and in all Judaea, and in Samaria, and unto the uttermost part of the earth. [9] And when he had spoken these things, while they beheld, he was taken up; and a cloud received him out of their sight. [10] And while they looked stedfastly toward heaven as he went up, behold, two men stood by them in white apparel; [11] Which also said, Ye men of Galilee, why stand ye gazing up into heaven? this same Jesus, which is taken up from you into heaven, shall so come in like manner as ye have seen him go into heaven" (Acts 1:1-11).

Acts chapter one takes place in the ten days between the ascension of Christ and the coming of the Holy Spirit. The Holy Spirit came to indwell all those who trusted in the finished work of the death, burial, and resurrection of Jesus. Acts chapter one records the final occasion of Christ's post resurrection appearances to His disciples (this does not include His appearance to the Apostle Paul). The most important aspect of Acts chapter one is that it records the last events transitioning from the Mosaic Covenant to the beginning of the New Covenant in Christ's blood (I Corinthians 11:25). These events are recorded in Acts chapter two on the Day of Pentecost in the celebration of the Feast of the Firstfruits and the beginning of the Church Age in the "church of the firstborn" (Hebrews 12:23).

These ten days transition us to the Day of Pentecost and the Day of the New Beginnings.

The vast majority of teaching that I have heard on Acts chapter two focuses upon the numbers of souls saved and the miracle of the disciples speaking in tongues. Although these are important, they are not the emphasis of the transition. On the Day of Pentecost, Christ would create a new order of *human existence* where there would be *full union* with the Divine Nature and the human nature in the body of "born again" believers. The New Creation ("the regeneration") was directly connected with the Divine through the indwelling of believers with the Holy Spirit of God. **This New Beginning made Spirit-filled believers the *conduit* through which God would supernaturally work.**

The Apostle Paul refers to this new order of *human existence* as the "new creature" (II Corinthians 5:17). This new order of *human existence* is the foundational truth for New Covenant believers becoming the "ambassadors for Christ." Jesus has "committed unto us the "word {*Logos*} of reconciliation {*restoration to Divine favor*}. This connects every believer to the *responsibility* of the "ministry of reconciliation." This ministry is the *responsibility* of the servant to the ministry of the restoration of souls to Divine favor through the Gospel of Jesus Christ in the salvation and discipleship of individuals. This "ministry of reconciliation" is to become the occupation of every "born again" believer as we remain in this world.

We pick up in Acts 1:8, with the emphasis of the Holy Spirit's supernatural ministry through the yielded believer. After the Day of Pentecost, the glorified Christ Jesus would be able to literally live His Life through the body of the yielded believer (Romans 6:11-13, 12:1-2, and Galatians 2:20). We are told clearly that "ye shall receive power, after that the Holy Ghost is come upon you: and ye shall be witnesses unto me both in Jerusalem, and in all Judaea, and in Samaria, and unto the uttermost part of the earth." Christ had already taught the disciples this purpose earlier in their discipleship. Christians today do not need to *tarry for* the Spirit or *wait for* the

Spirit after the Day of Pentecost. He has already come and is now *waiting on us* to yield to Him so He can accomplish His purpose *through* us. We simply need to be *filled* and then *move in the direction of our expectation.*

"[13] Howbeit when he, the Spirit of truth, is come, <u>he will guide you into all truth</u>: for <u>he shall not speak of himself</u>; but whatsoever he shall hear, *that* shall he speak: and <u>he will shew you things to come</u>. [14] He shall glorify me: for he shall receive of mine, and shall shew *it* unto you. [15] All things that the Father hath are mine: therefore said I, that he shall take of mine, and shall shew *it* unto you" (John 16:13-15).

Clearly, according to John 16:13-15, the indwelling Spirit of God is the *conduit* through which the *Christ-life* is intended to flow. The *Christ-life* flows through the life of the Spirit-filled believer and into the world. The indwelling of believers with Spirit of God became a new *direct link* of the spiritual realm of God with the physical/material world of mankind. The primary purpose of God in establishing this *conduit of Grace* was so that God could be glorified within His fallen creation (meaning that God could be known and experienced in all of His wondrous attributes and character as a Person and could interact directly with humanity through the lives of Spirit-filled believers). The believer was expected to so thoroughly know the Word of God that the Spirit of God could literally speak the Word of God through the mouth of the believer to reach the lost and disciple believers. The Spirit of God would supernaturally bring to the remembrance of the Spirit-filled believer those things that believer had learned from the Word of God.

> The great truth of Christ's resurrection transcends the mere restoration of what He was before His resurrection exponentially. Jesus was resurrected in His glorified humanity and, in His glorification, created a *New Existence/Creation* within the fallen first creation. The intent of this *New Existence* for all believers "in Christ" is that there is the availability to us presently, in this existence, a portion of the New Life that is ours in this *New Creation* "in Christ."

The connecting link to this supernatural aspect of our New Life "in Christ" is the indwelling Holy Spirit of God and the filling with the Spirit of God. Through this connecting Link, every believer could become the *conduit* through which the power of God could flow directly into the fallen creation in a supernatural way.

"[15] Wherefore I also, after I heard of your faith in the Lord Jesus, and love unto all the saints, [16] Cease not to give thanks for you, making mention of you in my prayers; [17] That the God of our Lord Jesus Christ, the Father of glory, may give unto you the spirit of wisdom and revelation in the knowledge of him: [18] The eyes of your understanding being enlightened; that ye may know what is the hope of his calling, and what the riches of the glory of his inheritance in the saints, [19] And what *is* the exceeding greatness of his power to us-ward who believe, according to the working of his mighty power, [20] Which he wrought in Christ, when he raised him from the dead, and set *him* at his own right hand in the heavenly *places*, [21] Far above all principality, and power, and might, and dominion, and every name that is named, not only in this world, but also in that which is to come: [22] And hath put all *things* under his feet, and gave him *to be* the head over all *things* to the church, [23] Which is his body, the fulness of him that filleth all in all" (Ephesians 1:15-23).

The means of the appropriation of "the working {*energeia, the supernatural energy of God*} of His mighty power" is the filling of the Spirit of the indwelling resurrected, glorified Jesus Christ, "the fulness of Him that filleth all in all." The resurrection power of Jesus is that *New Life* that now flows through the "Vine" to the "branches" that Christ speaks of in John chapter fifteen. Whatever "branch" that receives that power by being connected to the "vine" WILL PRODUCE FRUIT.

We might call this *Pneumatological Kinesis. Kinesis is the movement of an organism or cell in response to a stimulus, the rate of movement being dependent on the strength of the stimulus.*

The *stimulus* is the filling with the Spirit of God conditioned on total yielding (Romans 6:11-13 and 12:1-2). The potential in the power of God that is released through this *kinesis* is communicated in Ephesians 1:19 by the words "exceeding greatness of his power to us-ward who believe." The words "exceeding greatness" intend to convey an immeasurable and infinite resource in the power of God. This resource is given to believers through the resurrection and glorification of Jesus Christ. It is available to us, and through us, in the *conduit* of being filled with the indwelling Spirit (similar in scope to the "unsearchable riches of Christ" in Ephesians 3:8b).

In his Epistle to the Ephesians, Paul refers to this "fulness of him that filleth all in all" (Ephesians 1:23). He does so in terms that correct the false doctrine of other *mediums* or *mediators* through which the believer is, or can be, connected to the Divine Person, Power, and Potential of God's creative power.

> "[19] For it pleased *the Father* that in him {*Jesus*} should all fulness dwell; [20] And, having made peace through the blood of his cross, by him to reconcile all things unto himself; by him, *I say*, whether *they be* things in earth, or things in heaven. [21] And you, that were sometime alienated and enemies in *your* mind by wicked works, yet now hath he reconciled [22] In the body of his flesh through death, to present you holy and unblameable and unreproveable in his sight: [23] If ye continue in the faith grounded and settled, and *be* not moved away from the hope of the gospel, which ye have heard, *and* which was preached to every creature which is under heaven; whereof I Paul am made a minister" (Colossians 1:19-23).

In verse nineteen, the Greek word translated "fullness" (*pleroma*) was understood and used by the Gnostics to denote various *mediatorial images*, angels, or *spirit beings* that were each believed to give a *partial* revelation of God. Therefore it was necessary to have "knowledge" of all these *mediators* in order to have a FULL knowledge of God.

When Paul told Timothy (I Timothy 2:5) that Christ was the only "mediator between God and men," he was denying the whole foundation of Gnostic beliefs. Some continue a form of Gnosticism in *praying to saints* (invoking them to act on their behalf), angels, the dead, and to Mary. There are two primary characteristics of the "fullness" of the Godhead in Christ.

1. In Jesus we find the totality of Divine powers and attributes. Everything that God is, Jesus is.

2. The "fullness of the Godhead" dwells "in Christ." That "fullness" is permanently at home in Christ Jesus. Christ Jesus is the permanent residence of the fullness of the Godhead. The idea conveys the permanency of the *union of God and man in the Person of Jesus*.

> Beginning on the day of Pentecost in the indwelling of the believer with the Holy Spirit, the "fullness" of the Godhead that resides in Christ also resides in the believer's body. This "fullness" is released through the overflow of the *filling* of the Spirit. This *filling* is what defines and triggers *Pneumatological Kinesis*.

The fullness of the Godhead "in Christ" is a provision for mankind's benefit (Colossians 1:20-23). Again the Gnostics taught that there could only be a partial completion of the work of salvation. Therefore a person could never be fully saved, because the angelic mediators could only provide a partial reconciliation. The emphasis of verses 20-23 is that the security of a believer's salvation is based upon an already accomplished reality. Jesus has provided complete reconciliation to God.

DISCUSSION QUESTIONS

1. Discuss why the events of Day of Pentecost as recorded in Acts chapter two should be understood as the *Day of New Beginnings*.

2. On the Day of Pentecost, Christ would create a new order of *human existence* where there would be *full union* with the Divine Nature and the human nature in the body of "born again" believers. Discuss how this *full union* would make a believer a *conduit* through which God would supernaturally work.

3. Explain the phrase "ye shall receive power, after that the Holy Ghost is come upon you: and ye shall be witnesses unto me both in Jerusalem, and in all Judaea, and in Samaria, and unto the uttermost part of the earth" from the theological context of your discussion from the above two questions.

4. Expand upon the idea of the Spirit-filled believer as a *conduit of Grace*.

5. Discuss the practical reality of the fact that Jesus created a *New Existence/Creation* within the fallen first creation as it regards your own ministry of reconciliation.

6. Define and practically explain *Pneumatological Kinesis*.

7. Thoroughly explain how the "fulness of him that filleth all in all" (Ephesians 1:23) relates to you personally as a *conduit of Grace*.

Chapter Thirty-five
The Coming of the Indwelling Spirit

"[1] And when the day of Pentecost was fully come {*being completely fulfilled in its type*}, they were all with one accord in one place. [2] And suddenly {*in such a manner as to be startling*} there came a sound from heaven as {*like the sound*} of a rushing mighty wind, and it filled all the house where they were sitting. [3] And there appeared unto them cloven tongues like as of fire {*so that they could know this was more than just a rushing wind*}, and it sat upon each of them. [4] And they were all filled with the Holy Ghost, and began to speak with other tongues, as the Spirit gave them utterance" (Acts 2:1-4).

People lacking a comprehension of the Old Testament types in the Feast Days and sacrifices are prone to miss the great truths regarding dispensational transitional issues when we see these types fulfilled. This is the case with the Day of Pentecost. Before time itself was created, the Godhead covenanted together in a three-fold plan of redemption and a New Genesis. Lewis Sperry Chafer refers to this as the "before time covenant."[13] This Covenant of the Regeneration (promise of a new, eternal Genesis) is spoken of in II Timothy 1:9 and Titus 1:2. It is the primary Covenant of God to which all other Covenants find their source in Grace and in God's longsuffering with fallen mankind. It is to this ultimate "blessed hope" that the believer's citizenship in Heaven is connected and to which the Day of Pentecost, in both the giving of the Law at Sinai and the beginning of the Church Age on this day in Acts 2, connects believers and our service/ministry to the LORD and His eternal purpose and creation.

"[6] Wherefore I put thee in remembrance that thou stir up the gift of God, which is in thee by the putting on of my hands. [7] For God hath not given us the spirit of fear; but of power, and of love, and of a sound mind. [8] Be not thou therefore ashamed of the testimony of our Lord, nor of me his prisoner: but be thou partaker of the afflictions

---

[13] Lewis Sperry Chafer; *Systematic Theology; Vol. V*. (Dallas, Texas: Dallas Seminary Press, Thirteenth Printing, June, 1976) page 27.

of the gospel according to the power of God; [9] Who hath saved us, and called _us_ with an holy calling, not according to our works, but according to his own purpose and grace, which was given us in Christ Jesus before the world began, [10] But is now made manifest by the appearing of our Saviour Jesus Christ, who hath abolished death, and hath brought life and immortality to light through the gospel: [11] Whereunto I am appointed a preacher, and an apostle, and a teacher of the Gentiles. [12] For the which cause I also suffer these things: nevertheless I am not ashamed: for I know whom I have believed, and am persuaded that he is able to keep that which I have committed unto him against that day. [13] Hold fast the form of sound words, which thou hast heard of me, in faith and love which is in Christ Jesus. [14] That good thing which was committed unto thee keep by the Holy Ghost which dwelleth in us" (II Timothy 1:6-14).

Therefore, the critical truth for us to see here is that the New Genesis began "in Christ Jesus" in the plan of God "before the world began." **Secondly**, the New Genesis "in Christ Jesus" is an ongoing WORK of creation. Jesus referred to this continual work of the New Creation in John 5:17: "But Jesus answered them, My Father worketh hitherto, and I work." **Thirdly**, believers join themselves to this continual, ongoing work of the New Creation "in Christ" as they live the Word of God and proclaim the Good News of redemption.

Finally, "born again" believers (those entering the New Creation by being _born again_ spiritually) are elected/chosen _vocationally_ to become partners with Christ in this _vocation_ (Ephesians 1:4 and 4:1; _vocationally_ "chosen in Him" as our High Priest). They are vocationally elected to reach the lost through the supernatural work of the Holy Spirit in bringing the lost to conviction of their sin, God's righteousness, the coming eternal judgment, repentance towards God, and faith towards the Lord Jesus Christ (Acts 20:21). They then are convicted of _actually_ beginning to be "doers of the Word, and not hearers only." In other words, the free gift of salvation comes with a moral obligation to be the ambassadors (servants) of Christ and actually DOING the "ministry of reconciliation" (II Corinthians 5:17-21).

"[1] Paul, a servant of God, and an apostle of Jesus Christ, according to the faith {_faithfulness or fidelity to our responsibilities to God as His "born again" children_} of God's elect {_vocational Priests_}, and the acknowledging of the truth which is after godliness; [2] In hope of eternal life, which God, that cannot lie, promised before the world began; [3] But hath in due times manifested his word through preaching, which is committed {*pisteuo, entrusted to my faithfulness*} unto me according to the commandment of God our Saviour; [4] To Titus, *mine* own son after the common faith: Grace, mercy, *and* peace, from God the Father and the Lord Jesus Christ our Saviour" (Titus 1:1-4).

> The Day of Pentecost typified this promised new, everlasting, eternal Day initially existing only in the Plan and Purpose of God. This existed through the promise of the birth, holy life, death, burial, resurrection, and glorification of the promised God/Man (the "last Adam") extending from eternity past into eternity future.

The original Day of Pentecost fell on the fiftieth day after a seven week period (there are seven Dispensations or *Days of New Beginnings* revealed throughout Scripture), with each week ending on a Sabbath Day. This was the *day* God gave Israel the Law through Moses on Mount Sinai. The Day of Pentecost, as part of the Feast of Weeks (also called the Feast of Firstfruits), then always fell on the first day of a *new week* after this seven week cycle. It typified the *New Eternal/Everlasting Day* of "the regeneration." Although all believers of all Ages (Dispensations) have been POSITIONALLY integrated into this New Genesis, Christ Jesus was the first human being who ACTUALLY became part of this *Eternal Genesis* through His resurrection/glorification (the "Firstborn").

In Acts 2:1-4, we find God's record of the *first day* of this *New Beginn*ing of the New Covenant as manifested in the release of the Holy Spirit of God. He was released to indwell believers, baptize those believers into the "body of Christ" (the *New Creation*), and be released through the lives of yielded believers. This would happen as those believers were supernaturally enabled in their priestly vocations as bold witnesses of the Lord Jesus Christ. The baptism with the Spirit and the indwelling of the Spirit is a partial fulfillment of the believer's future glorification/transfiguration. Therefore, the baptism with the Spirit and the indwelling of the Spirit partially fulfill the believer's glorification/transfiguration.

The believer is progressively being transfigured (becoming Christ-like) through progressive sanctification (Romans 12:2, "be ye transformed" - lit., *transfigured*; *present, passive, imperative*). Practically then, if the disciples had not been obedient to Christ's command to wait those ten days between His ascension and the coming of the Spirit they would not have experienced the events of the Day of Pentecost. After the Spirit of God came and they were "filled" with the Spirit of God (meaning they yielded their wills to Him), they spoke the Gospel message. If they failed to be where God appointed them to be, because they were afraid of being killed by the Jews, none of the miraculous *outcomes* of the Day of Pentecost would have happened. What then do we need to learn from Acts 2:1-4?

1. According to Matthew 5:17-48, we each need to strictly interpret the Word of God to discover God's expectations of us before we can seek to live those expectations. Lowering God's standards of expectation by a liberal/loose interpretation of the Word of God, or a distortion/perversion of the doctrine of Grace, will not release the power of God through our lives.

2. "They were ALL in ONE ACCORD in one place *{assembled where they were supposed to be}*. We must obey what God tells us to do (and not to do) and we must do so through the supernatural enabling of the indwelling Holy Spirit (in "fellowship" or in the "unity of the Spirit").

3. We must understand that no one can be saved apart from HEARING, UNDERSTANDING the details of the Gospel of Jesus Christ, and BELIEVING *(resting faith)* in the Person of Jesus Christ (Matthew 13:18-23 - notice the word "understandeth"). Therefore, we must understand that this is a supernatural work and we will not attempt it in the mere strength of our own human resources of knowledge, intellect, art of persuasion, or appeals to human carnality.

4. "They were all filled with the Holy Ghost, and began to speak with other tongues, as the Spirit gave them utterance." We must *actually* unite ourselves in the eternal purpose of the Godhead in the plan of redemption. We do this by uniting ourselves to the Godhead in "fellowship" (partnership in "the work of the ministry") and by becoming living translations of the Word of God. Then we become the literal *voices* of the Holy Spirit of God in the proclamation of the Gospel of Jesus Christ. The "other tongues" was to reveal the supernatural nature of the Spirit of God in bringing UNDERSTANDING to the hearers of the message. People are amazed by, and often foolishly become preoccupied with, miracles without seeing the supernatural purpose in the miracles. Real faith merely sees God supernaturally working in everything that is "good" (Romans 8:28) and then seeks to be joined with God ("fellowship") in that supernatural work ("the work of the ministry").

The visible result, or spiritual outcome, of this *new operation* of the Spirit (the "fruit"), beginning on the Day of Pentecost, was that thousands of people believed, were baptized, and were added to the Church ("of the firstborn").

This was a literal fulfillment of what Christ spoke of in John chapter 15:5, "I am the vine, ye *are* the branches: He that abideth in me, and I in him, the same bringeth forth much fruit: for without me ye can do nothing."

As we read the book of Acts, we need to keep in mind that it records transitional issues moving from the *operations of God* in the Dispensation of Law (the Mosaic Covenant) into the Dispensation of Grace (the *New Covenant* or the *New Creation*). As we come to understand that the Day of Pentecost was a fulfillment of an Old Covenant type fulfilled at the time recorded in Acts chapter 2:1-4, we understand that this event recorded the coming of the Holy Spirit. He came to begin a *new way* in which God would operate *through* ALL believers during the Dispensation of Grace regarding the fourfold ministry of the Holy Spirit in the lives of believers:

1. To indwell all believers the moment they trust in Christ and are "born again"
2. To move those believers positionally from the fallen family of Adam and into the family of God (the baptism with the Holy Spirit)
3. To fill to *overflowing* all believers who are completely yielded to, and in unity with, the indwelling Spirit of God, thereby supernaturally producing the *overflowing Christ-life*
4. To continue God's ongoing work of the New Creation that began "before the world began in Christ Jesus" through a synergism with Him in a constantly growing network (local churches) of Spirit-filled and supernaturally empowered believers supernaturally enabled to do "the work of the ministry"

DISCUSSION QUESTIONS

1. Explain the Old Testament type in the Day of Pentecost and the *already, not yet* aspects of its fulfillment in Acts chapter two.

2. Explain the *Before Time Covenant* as detailed in II Timothy 1:9 and Titus 1:2 and why it is critical to understand this if you are going to understand the *New Covenant* and the *New Creation* "in Christ."

3. List and discuss the four critical truths that define the practical reality of the unfolding of the *Before Time Covenant* as detailed in II Timothy 1:6-14.

4. Explain Titus 1:1-4 from the context of election being vocational rather than salvational.

5. Explain the *New Eternal/Everlasting Day* of "the regeneration."

6. List and discuss the four things given that we need to learn from Acts 2:1-4?

7. List and discuss the four things given that relate to the indwelling of the Holy Spirit. Discuss His beginning a *new way* in which God would operate *through* ALL believers during the Dispensation of Grace regarding the fourfold ministry of the Holy Spirit in the lives of believers.

Chapter Thirty-six
Some Temporary Aspects of the Coming of the Spirit

"[1] And when the day of Pentecost was fully come {*being completely fulfilled in its type*}, they were all with one accord in one place. [2] And suddenly {*in such a manner as to be startling*} there came a sound from heaven as {*like the sound*} of a rushing mighty wind, and it filled all the house where they were sitting. [3] And there appeared unto them cloven tongues like as of fire {*so that they could know this by more than just a rushing wind*}, and it sat upon each of them. [4] And they were all filled with the Holy Ghost, and began to speak with other tongues, as the Spirit gave them utterance" (Acts 2:1-4).

In coming to an understanding of the transitional nature of the historical record of Acts 2:1-4, there are some aspects of this event that were unique to the transition and should not be expected to be seen afterwards. **First, this records a one-time (on *one day in history*) event and believers afterward should not expect a similar *experience*.**

Although we find two other occurrences of some visible ("sign") evidences of this new ministry of the Holy Spirit, even these two occurrences were transitional in nature and not the same as on the Day of Pentecost. **The second record is found in Acts 8:5-25 and it records the miracles of Philip at Samaria in 34 A.D.** (This is not a *Samaritan Pentecost*; there were no *cloven tongues of fire* or *sound of mighty rushing of wind*.). The coming of the Holy Spirit and the beginning of the New Covenant was made evident to the Samaritans (a group of *half breed* Jews, II Kings 17:24), who had not believed on Jesus before Philip came. This was to visibly reveal God's union of believers from these two groups (which had hitherto despised one another) after the Day of Pentecost into the *body of Christ*. The reason for waiting for the Apostles and the laying on of their hands was to show that the authority of truth was centered in what the Apostles taught (and no one else). This is significant because God did not, and does not, want a *sectarian Christianity*.

When the Apostles passed out of history (historical transition), their authority was established in the written and inspired Word of God (inscripturalized). The *laying on of hands*, that signified the giving of the Holy Spirit, ended with them (according to Scripture). This practice did not even continue throughout their lifetimes.

The third record found is in Acts 10:1-48 (verses 44-48, 41 A.D.) and records the visible evidence ("sign") to the Jews (Acts 10:45) that the Gentile believers were united with the Jews and Samaritans into the "body" of Christ (This was not a *Gentile Pentecost*. There were no *cloven tongues of fire* or *sound of mighty rushing of wind.*).

Cornelius was a Gentile believer in the Old Testament sense (Acts 10:1-2). Therefore, he was a Gentile proselyte to Judaism. However, the central reason for what took place at Caesarea was to show the Jews that Gentiles were joined with them in the *body of Christ* in the Church Age dispensation (Acts 10:45).

This coming of the Spirit of God on the Day of Pentecost was a *spiritual phenomenon*. Those present would not normally be aware (through their physical senses, I Corinthians 2:9) of what was taking place. Therefore, this *spiritual phenomenon* required some physical (sensatory) aspects of this supernatural occurrence for the Jews to know that this was a fulfillment of prophecy, although an *already, not yet* fulfillment; i.e. it was not a complete fulfillment.

Therefore, the *sensatory aspects* of this event were threefold. There was the "sound from heaven." There were the "cloven tongues of fire" resting upon each of the disciples (to visibly show who it was that was receiving these new supernatural *operations* of the Spirit). There was the speaking "with other tongues." These all were *temporary* "signs" **to the Jews** to reveal this new ministry of the Spirit.

In the Old Covenant, God revealed Himself and His operations (workings) in the midst of Israel through "signs and wonders" (Exodus 4:1-9, 17, Numbers 14:11, Deuteronomy 4:34, 6:22, 7:19, 29:3, Joshua 24:17, Daniel 4:2-3, 6:27; Mark 16:17-20). "Signs and wonders" were an historical constant in the history of God's manifestations of His workings to the children of Israel beginning with their deliverance from Egyptian bondage. The Jews expected that these miraculous manifestations would continue to be God's way of revealing His operations among them.

"[18] Then answered the Jews and said unto him, <u>What sign shewest thou unto us</u>, seeing that thou doest these things? [19] Jesus answered and said unto them, Destroy this temple, and in three days I will raise it up. [20] Then said the Jews, Forty and six years was this temple in building, and wilt thou rear it up in three days? [21] But he spake of the temple of his body. [22] When therefore he was risen from the dead, his disciples remembered that he had said this unto them; and they believed the scripture, and the word which Jesus had said" (John 2:18-21).

"Then said Jesus unto him {*the nobleman from Capernaum*}, Except ye see signs and wonders, ye will not believe" (John 4:48).

"[14] But Peter, standing up with the eleven, lifted up his voice, and said unto them, Ye men of Judaea, and all *ye* that dwell at Jerusalem, be this known unto you, and hearken to my words: [15] For these are not drunken, as ye suppose, seeing it is *but* the third hour of the day. [16] <u>But this is that which was spoken by the prophet Joel;</u> [17] And it shall come to pass in the last days, saith God, I will pour out of my Spirit upon all flesh: and your sons and your daughters shall prophesy, and your young men shall see visions, and your old men shall dream dreams: [18] And on my servants and on my handmaidens I will pour out in those days of my Spirit; and they shall prophesy: [19] And I will shew wonders in heaven above, and signs in the earth beneath; blood, and fire, and vapour of smoke: [20] The sun shall be turned into darkness, and the moon into blood, before that great and notable day of the Lord come: [21] And it shall come to pass, *that* whosoever shall call on the name of the Lord shall be saved. [22] Ye men of Israel, hear these words; Jesus of Nazareth, <u>a man approved of God among you by miracles and wonders and signs</u>, which God did by him in the midst of you, as ye yourselves also know" (Acts 2:14-22).

"[21] For after that in the wisdom of God the world by wisdom knew not God, it pleased God by the foolishness of preaching to save them that believe. [22] <u>For the Jews require a sign</u> {*a miraculous event before they would believe that God was involved*}, and the Greeks seek after wisdom: [23] But we preach Christ crucified {*see John 2:18-21 above*}, unto the Jews a stumblingblock, and unto the Greeks foolishness; [24] But unto them which are called, both Jews and Greeks, Christ the power of God, and the wisdom of God" (I Corinthians 1:21-24).

The Gentiles, on the other hand, had a different perspective that came from their religious practices. They were saved out of demonically influenced paganism. When it came to the issue of miraculous things such as *tongues,* the saved pagans understood *tongues* from their pagan experiences. We must **understand that Paul was dealing with these "signs and wonders" at Corinth from this historical context.** The majority of those in the church at Corinth were Gentiles who were saved out of the pagan mystery religions (I Corinthians 12:2). These people were incorporating some of the religious practices of the pagan mystery religions with their Christianity.

Whatever God does, Satan is quick to counterfeit. Then, Satan subverts people by bringing their focus upon the counterfeit and manufacturing a *religion* based upon the pursuit of what he has counterfeited. This is what Satan did within what came to be known as the mystery religions of paganism. These mystery religions became preoccupied with the spiritual miraculous and seeking the miracles rather than seeking the Person of God. Because of this satanic misdirection, people were easily led astray to follow false religious leaders.

> "Ye know that ye were Gentiles, carried away unto these dumb idols, even as ye were led" (I Corinthians 12:2).

Most of these mystery religions *evolved* out of Babylon from the occult practices of Nimrod. These pagan views resulted in the building of the Tower of Babel and God's confounding of the languages ending in the dispersal of the people into different nations (*language groups*). The origin and evolution of these mystery religions was demonic. Therefore, the supernatural happenings of the mystery religions were also of demonic sources.

Common to the mystery religions was the practice of *Ecstasism* and *Enthusiasm.* S. Angus, details these two practices.

> ". . . Ecstasy (*ekstasis*) and Enthusiasm (*enthusiasmos*), both of which might be induced by vigil and fasting, tense religious expectancy, whirling dances, physical stimuli, the contemplation of sacred objects, the effect of stirring music, inhalation of fumes, revivalistic contagion (such as happened in the church at Corinth), hallucination, suggestion, and other means belonging to the apparatus of the Mysteries."[14]

Both *Ecstasy* and *Enthusiasm* were used to promote a

---

[14] Angus, S. *The Mystery Religions.* (New York: Dover Publications, 1975).

heightened sense of euphoria and human experience. In this euphoric state, the participant experiences a feeling of having *communed with deity.* His involvement has been with the supernatural realm, but not the divine. *Ecstasism* and *Enthusiasm* were satanic in origin.

From our historical understanding of all of this, we can understand that Paul is dealing with two types of tongues in I Corinthians 14. Since Paul would not be present to discern every *tongues experience,* and the *gift of tongues* was still a viable reality at this juncture in the historical transition between dispensations, he seeks to *regulate* them by the *process of elimination.*

The first *(false)* type of tongues is *ecstatic tongues* which are denoted by the italicized word "unknown." The King James translators understood the HISTORICAL CONTEXT of what Paul was addressing and added the word *unknown* to distinguish this kind of *tongues,* from the kind of *tongues* recorded in the book of Acts. This is the tongues experience Paul seeks to eliminate. Genuine "tongues" (which were always *known* languages) were used to communicate truth to someone who would not be able to otherwise understand.

If God is communicating, He will always do so with the intent of edification and understanding (I Corinthians 14:1-22). In the only three examples of *tongues* in the book of Acts (Acts 2:4-11, Acts 8:5-25, and Acts 10:44-46), the *communication* came with *understanding* by the hearers. The miracle (*Grace-gift*) of tongues was not in the speaking, but in the hearing.

"[4] And they were all filled with the Holy Ghost, and began to speak with other tongues, as the Spirit gave them utterance. [5] And there were dwelling at Jerusalem Jews, devout men, out of every nation under heaven. [6] Now when this was noised abroad, the multitude came together, and were confounded, <u>because that every man heard them speak in his own language.</u> [7] And they were all amazed and marvelled, saying one to another, Behold, are not all these which speak Galilaeans? [8] And <u>how hear we every man in our own tongue,</u> wherein we were born? [9] Parthians, and Medes, and Elamites, and the dwellers in Mesopotamia, and in Judaea, and Cappadocia, in Pontus, and Asia, [10] Phrygia, and Pamphylia, in Egypt, and in the parts of Libya about Cyrene, and strangers of Rome, Jews and proselytes, [11] Cretes and Arabians, <u>we do hear them speak in our tongues the wonderful works of God</u>" (Acts 2:4-11).

Clearly from I Corinthians 14:27, we can see the scope of the miracle of "tongues" is in the *hearing* and not in the *speaking*. Even though the one speaking needed to be "filled" with the Spirit before the miracle could take place, this was a supernatural work that flowed *through* the Spirit-filled believer to the lost.

It is also important for us to understand from I Corinthians 14:27 that God tells us that He is only going to perform this miracle of "tongues" *one-at-a-time* ("by course," one after the other). Therefore, the miracle of "tongues" must be understood from the *hearing perspective*. As *one* of the disciples was speaking, either in Hebrew or maybe Greek, each person in the crowd heard what that *one* person was saying, but each person heard the speaker in his own native *tongue* (language). The speaker might not even have been aware that the miracle was taking place.

What is described in Acts 2:4-11 may have been the common experience of the Apostle Paul (see I Corinthians 14:18) as he preached throughout his missionary journeys. I doubt very much if Paul was able to speak all the languages of all the countries in which he started churches.

Why is understanding all of this important to us today? It is important to understand all of this so that the believer is not looking for, or pursuing after, something the Spirit of God is not going to do. There are three important truths from I Corinthians chapter twelve that we must understand.

1. There "are diversities of gifts" (*charisma*). Not everyone had the same spiritual gifts. It should not be expected that everyone possess each gift. In fact, that expectation would be unscriptural.

"*29b are* all workers of miracles? {*No!*} ³⁰ Have all the gifts of healing? {*No!*} do all speak with tongues? {*No!*} do all interpret" {*No!*} (I Corinthians 12:29b-30; *I have added the word No! after each question to show the rhetorical intent of the questions.*)?

2. According to I Corinthians 12:5, there "are differences of administrations." Not everyone had the same ministry in the local church. The idea is that not everyone has the same job (although there are some things everyone is commanded to do). Everyone is not an Apostle. Everyone is not a preacher ("prophet"). Everyone is not a pastor/teacher.

"*Are* all apostles? *are* all prophets? *are* all teachers" (I Corinthians 12:29a)?

3. According to I Corinthians 12:6, there "are diversities of operations." Although God never changes (in His character, nature, and attributes), He does change His *operations*. These changes are called "dispensations." This is what the focus is on in I Corinthians chapter thirteen. It is known as the doctrine of *historical transition.*

Sign gifts were for this time of *historical transition* between the Dispensation of Law and the Dispensation of Grace. Each of these dispensations is one of God's "diversities of operations." There were a number of changes in *operations* between these two dispensations. Sign gifts were to make this time of transition evident and to prove that what was being done was of God.

There are at least six major dispensational transitional changes in God's *operations* in the transition from the Mosaic Covenant and the Dispensation of Law to the New Covenant and the Dispensation of Grace (the Church Age).

1. Old Testament believers looking forward to the coming of Messiah needed to know of Jesus and trust in His once for all sacrifice in order to become a formal member of a local church.
2. There was a transition from the local synagogue to the local church.
3. There was the transition from government of the Old Testament priesthood to congregational polity administrated by local pastors called by God.
4. There was a transition from the Temple sacrifices that looked forward to the coming Messiah, now abrogated in that the sacrifice of Jesus fulfilled them "once *for all*."
5. There was the abrogation of Temple worship in that the believer's body becomes the Temple of the Holy Spirit (a living Temple) and the believer is given direct access to the Throne of Grace because of the mediatorial work of Christ.
6. There was a transition in the Passover celebration. The Passover looked forward in *anticipation* to the coming of the incarnate Lamb of God to the Lord's Supper. The Lord's Supper looks backward in *remembrance* of the completed sacrifice of the Lamb of God.

This New Dispensation and the beginning of the New Covenant (beginning *actually* in time, not merely promised) is expressed by the words "under grace" in the Bible. The Dispensation of the Law is expressed by the words "under Law." The believer is now under the New Covenant and the Dispensation of Grace (God's supernatural enabling of the yielded believer through the indwelling Spirit).

The focus of I Corinthians chapter thirteen is on what will continue in the *operations* of God through the Holy Spirit beyond this *historical transition* and what will not. "Charity" (love, that from which all "fruit of the Spirit" comes) is the one *operation* of the Spirit of God that encompasses all of His workings and characterizes all genuine spiritually "born again" children of God. Therefore, the continuing sign or evidence of the New Covenant relationship with God will be this characteristic of love (self-sacrifice, I Corinthians 13:1-7), not "prophecies," not "tongues," and/or not special revelatory "knowledge."

DISCUSSION QUESTIONS

1. Discuss why it is critical to understand the transitional nature of the historical record of Acts 2:1-4.

2. List and describe the two other occurrences of the visible ("sign") evidences of this new ministry of the Holy Spirit. Discuss what it is about these two other occurrences that reveals their purpose and why they were temporary.

3. Discuss why this special miracle of tongues and the coming of the Holy Spirit on the Day of Pentecost was *sensatory* (sight and sound).

4. Discuss the importance of "signs and wonders" to the Jews and why the *sensatory* aspects of the miraculous revelation of the coming of the Holy Spirit were necessary particularly for the Jews.

5. Discuss the difference in the Gentile pagan view of tongues from the perspective of those deceived by the mystery religions and Paul's dealing with these "sign" gifts in I Corinthians chapters 12-14. Explain what Paul is doing in these texts.

6. Explain what is meant by the statement that true tongues were *hearing miracles* rather than *speaking miracles*.

7. List and explain the three important truths from I Corinthians chapter twelve that we must understand.

Chapter Thirty-seven

The Indwelling Spirit and the Foolishness of Preaching

"[14] But Peter, standing up with the eleven, lifted up his voice, and said unto them, Ye men of Judaea, and all *ye* that dwell at Jerusalem, be this known unto you, and hearken to my words: [15] For these are not drunken, as ye suppose, seeing it is *but* the third hour of the day. [16] But this is that which was spoken by the prophet Joel; [17] And it shall come to pass in the last days, saith God, I will pour out of my Spirit upon all flesh: and your sons and your daughters shall prophesy, and your young men shall see visions, and your old men shall dream dreams: [18] And on my servants and on my handmaidens I will pour out in those days of my Spirit; and they shall prophesy: [19] And I will shew wonders in heaven above, and signs in the earth beneath; blood, and fire, and vapour of smoke: [20] The sun shall be turned into darkness, and the moon into blood, before that great and notable day of the Lord come: [21] And it shall come to pass, *that* whosoever shall call on the name of the Lord shall be saved. [22] Ye men of Israel, hear these words; Jesus of Nazareth, a man approved of God among you by miracles and wonders and signs, which God did by him in the midst of you, as ye yourselves also know: [23] Him, being delivered by the determinate counsel and foreknowledge of God, ye have taken, and by wicked hands have crucified and slain: [24] Whom God hath raised up, having loosed the pains of death: because it was not possible that he should be holden of it. [25] For David speaketh concerning him, I foresaw the Lord always before my face, for he is on my right hand, that I should not be moved: [26] Therefore did my heart rejoice, and my tongue was glad; moreover also my flesh shall rest in hope: [27] Because thou wilt not leave my soul in hell, neither wilt thou suffer thine Holy One to see corruption. [28] Thou hast made known to me the ways of life; thou shalt make me full of joy with thy countenance. [29] Men *and* brethren, let me freely speak unto you of the patriarch David, that he is both dead and buried, and his sepulchre is with us unto this day. [30] Therefore being a prophet, and knowing that God had sworn with an oath to him, that of the fruit of his loins, according to the flesh, he would raise up Christ to sit on his throne; [31] He seeing this before spake of the resurrection of Christ, that his soul was not left in hell, neither his flesh did see corruption. [32] This Jesus hath God raised up, whereof we all are witnesses. [33] Therefore being by the right hand of God exalted, and having received of the Father the promise of the Holy Ghost, he hath shed forth this, which ye now see and hear. [34] For David is not ascended into the heavens: but he saith himself, The LORD said unto my Lord, Sit thou on my right hand, [35] Until I make thy foes thy footstool. [36] Therefore let all the house of Israel know assuredly, that God hath made that same Jesus, whom ye have crucified, both Lord and Christ. [37] Now when they heard *this*, they were pricked in their heart, and said unto Peter and to the rest of the apostles, Men *and* brethren, what shall we do? [38] Then Peter said unto them, Repent, and be baptized every one of you in the name of Jesus Christ for the remission of sins, and ye shall receive the gift of the Holy Ghost. [39] For the promise is unto you, and to your children, and to all that are afar off, *even* as many as the Lord our God shall call. [40] And with many other words did he testify and exhort, saying, Save yourselves from this untoward generation. [41] Then they that gladly received his word were baptized: and the same day there were added *unto them* about three thousand souls" (Acts 2:14-41).

Ten days after the ascension of Jesus Christ to the *right hand* of the Father in glory, the Person of the Holy Spirit of God was *released* into the world. However, He was not merely *released* into the atmosphere. In God's omnipresence, the Spirit of God already filled the atmosphere of the world. On the Day of Pentecost, the Person of the Spirit of God was *released* into those believers who had trusted in the death, burial, and resurrection/glorification of the Lord Jesus Christ for their salvation and redemption.

Upon Christ's resurrection/glorification, He created a *New Genesis* and a *New Existence.* In this *New Genesis* and a *New Existence,* God would once again dwell within His creation, although only within those "born again" of the Spirit into this *New Genesis.* The intent of this new *spiritual dynamic* was for the ongoing work of God in the New Creation. This new *spiritual dynamic* that began in Christ "before the world began" (II Timothy 1:9 and Titus 1:2), would now continue through a supernatural *partnership* ("fellowship") with "born again" believers. These are the "born again" Church Age believers indwelled by, and filled with, the Person of the Holy Spirit of God.

The Spirit of God indwelling believers is *conditioned* upon their salvation. It is the outcome of a person's faith decision to repent of sin, to believe the Gospel, to confess Christ to be JEHOVAH (LORD), to call on the Name of Jesus to save us from eternal separation from God ("death"), and to receive the Person of Christ in the Person of the indwelling Spirit of God.

The indwelling is a one-time (*once-for-all*) occurrence that never needs to be repeated in that God's promise is that He "[5b] will never leave thee, nor forsake thee. [6] So that we may boldly say, The Lord *is* my helper, and I will not fear what man shall do unto me" (Hebrews 13:5b-6).

The filling of the Spirit of God is the releasing of the *creative power* of God through the *ministry* of the life of the Spirit indwelled believer. The intent of this release of the *creative power* of God through the "work of the ministry" in the life of a believer is for spiritual "fruit." This spiritual "fruit" is to be produced to God's glory. Spiritual "fruit" refers specifically to souls being saved by the Spirit-filled believer's proclamation of the Gospel of Jesus Christ. Spiritual "fruit" refers to a sinner being brought to conviction of sin, righteousness, and judgment. Spiritual "fruit" refers to that same sinner making a faith decision to repent, believe, confess, call upon the Name of Jesus, and receive the indwelling Holy Spirit. This whole spiritual dynamic of the work of the indwelling Holy Spirit through the life of a Spirit-filled believer is that which defines "by grace through faith" in Ephesians 2:8-9. The word "grace" defines the supernatural operations of God in every dispensation. In the Age of Grace, the supernatural operations of God are done through the lives of Spirit-filled believers.

The believer's filling of the Spirit of God is conditioned upon a believer's total surrender of his will, emotions, actions, and ambitions to the indwelling Christ. In the filling of the surrendered believer by the Holy Spirit, that believer is literally physically, emotionally, and spiritually being transfigured to be Christ-like.

When a believer is filled with the Spirit of God, that believer will be preoccupied with the same things that preoccupy the Spirit of God. In other words, there are spiritual outcomes that manifest a believer's being filled with the Spirit. If the outcomes do not exist, neither does the filling exist. When a believer is truly filled with the Spirit of God, the *Christ-life* will be produced. The presence of the *Christ-life* will be manifested through seven *outcome realities* in that believer's life. The Spirit-filled believer will be:

1. Preoccupied with being separated from worldliness
2. Preoccupied with being holy in that separation from worldliness and living in holiness are two essentials for our ministry being acceptable unto God and, therefore, blessed of God (for "fruit" to be produced)
3. Preoccupied with the in-depth study of God's Word to be equipped to do the "work of the ministry" in persuading sinners of truth
4. Preoccupied with maintaining unbroken fellowship with the Godhead through total surrender of our wills and absolute obedience to God's will
5. Preoccupied with seeking the lost and proclaiming the Gospel of Jesus Christ
6. Preoccupied with leading the people who get saved to become part of a local church where they can be discipled and be sent "into all the world." (Authority to minister always comes through a local church.)
7. Preoccupied with discipleship. This involves teaching people the *doctrine of grace* and the spiritual essentials necessary to create a continuum of "fruit" producers.

Throughout the history of Christianity, these seven *outcome realities* have preoccupied the lives of those we have come to know as truly great Christians. The *light* of their lives shined so brightly in the darkness of the world's evil corruption that they could not be ignored. Their lives drew the attention of the world upon them and that attention was almost always accompanied by great persecution: "Yea, and all that will live godly in Christ Jesus shall suffer persecution" (II Timothy 3:12). As their lives moved through the history of this spiritual tension, thousands upon thousands came to trust in Christ for salvation, were added to the membership of local churches, and were discipled to create a continuum of what really defines *true* Christianity or *remnant* Christianity. In every case they brought forth *much fruit.*

Clearly, this is the spiritual dynamic we see in Acts chapter two. This is the historical record of the beginning of the New Covenant in the Acts of Jesus Christ. This happens through the *indwelling* and *filling* of believers by the Holy Spirit (the real subject matter of what is commonly referred to as the Acts of the Apostles). Truth that is known, but never lived, is more dangerous to the believer than complete ignorance in that the believer, at the point of that knowledge, immediately becomes responsible to live what he knows. The difference between the truth we know and the truth we live is the measurement of the degree of our own hypocrisy.

Prior to the ministry of John the Baptist and the beginning of the ministry of Jesus Christ, there were four-hundred *years of silence.* For four-hundred years God's voice through a prophet was silent to the people of Israel. There were many false prophets and false Messiahs that came on the scene of history over those four-hundred years, but God did not speak through them. The coming of Jesus Christ and the proclamation of the message of redemption broke through this darkness of silence like a bright morning sunrise after a long, dark night.

"[1] God, who at sundry times and in divers manners spake in time past unto the fathers by the prophets, [2] Hath in these last days spoken unto us by *his* Son, whom he hath appointed heir of all things, by whom also he made the worlds; [3] Who being the brightness of *his* glory, and the express image of his person, and upholding all things by the word of his power, when he had by himself purged our sins, sat down on the right hand of the Majesty on high" (Hebrews 1:1-3).

The last act of Christ before His ascension unto the Father was to delegate the responsibility of the proclamation of the Gospel and of making disciples to Church Age believers. "[8] But ye shall receive power {*dunamis; i.e., mighty force implying, miraculous, creative, explosive power*}, after that the Holy Ghost is come upon you: and {*the outcome of this power is that*} ye shall be witnesses unto me both in Jerusalem, and in all Judaea, and in Samaria, and unto the uttermost part of the earth. [9] And when he had spoken these things, while they beheld, he was taken up; and a cloud received him out of their sight" (Acts 1:8-9). The filling of the Spirit of God is almost always accompanied by the manifestation of the powerful proclamation of the Gospel in producing/creating "fruit."

Preaching: the Preoccupation with the Ministry of Proclamation

> Never in the book of Acts is the filling of the Spirit separated from the *proclamation* of the Gospel of Jesus Christ as a primary outcome of that filling.

"[1] And Saul was consenting unto his death. And at that time there was a great persecution against the church which was at Jerusalem; and they were all scattered abroad throughout the regions of Judaea and Samaria, except the apostles. [2] And devout men carried Stephen *to his burial*, and made great lamentation over him. [3] As for Saul, he made havock of the church, entering into every house, and haling men and women committed *them* to prison. [4] Therefore *{due to Saul's persecution of the believers before he was saved}* they that were scattered abroad <u>went every where preaching the word</u>" (Acts 8:1-4).

"[19] Now they which were scattered abroad upon the persecution that arose about Stephen travelled as far as Phenice, and Cyprus, and Antioch, preaching the word to none but unto the Jews only. [20] And some of them were men of Cyprus and Cyrene, which, when they were come to Antioch, spake unto the Grecians, preaching the Lord Jesus. [21] And the hand of the Lord was with them: and a great number believed, and turned unto the Lord" (Acts 11:19-21).

Perhaps one of Satan's greatest deceptions and perversions of moral responsibility is the deception that preaching is only the responsibility of a select, special group of people that would come to be known as *clergymen*. The etymology of the meaning of the word *clergy* is that of *higher learning* or in the noun form, a *very learned person*. This evolved into referring to someone with high theological training as a *clergyman*.

The second greatest deception and perversion of the Great Commission was that preaching was to be done by *clergymen* in a *building* called the *church*. This made the *church* (whatever that term came to mean at that point in history) a *place* where people came to hear the *clergyman preach* (in most cases that meant whatever perversion of the Gospel that *clergyman* believed).

Although the pastor of a local church is responsible to proclaim the "whole counsel" of God, the preaching of the Gospel is the responsibility of every Christian in every venue, place, and opportunity of their everyday lives. Certainly, this proclamation of the Gospel and Christ's expectations of the redeemed is not to be segregated from our everyday lives and it is not to be relegated to within the *church house* walls.

> "[17] For Christ sent me not to baptize, but to preach the gospel: not with wisdom of words, lest the cross of Christ should be made of none effect. [18] For the preaching of the cross is to them that perish foolishness; but unto us which are saved it is the power of God. [19] For it is written, I will destroy the wisdom of the wise, and will bring to nothing the understanding of the prudent. [20] Where *is* the wise? where *is* the scribe? where *is* the disputer of this world? hath not God made foolish the wisdom of this world? [21] For after that in the wisdom of God the world by wisdom knew not God, it pleased God by the foolishness of preaching to save them that believe" (I Corinthians 1:17-21).

The Scriptural pattern of preaching found in the book of Acts is not that of a handful of specially trained men, but that of every "born again" believer telling others about what happened to them personally and what Christ will do for others if they will believe. This Scriptural pattern of preaching found in the book of Acts defines what normal, Spirit-filled Christianity should *look like* and with what it should be occupied.

This radical transitional change of responsibility between the thousands of years of recorded history of the Old Covenant and the first sixty years of the beginning of the New Covenant on the day of Pentecost in Acts chapter two is exemplified by the fact that "preaching is referred to twenty times in the Old testament and two-hundred and fifty times in the New testament."[15] This preaching of the Gospel of Jesus Christ and creating disciples of Jesus Christ is what defines the "work of the ministry" that all believers are to be brought to spiritual maturity so as to be equipped to do.

---

[15] Chafer, Lewis Sperry. *Systematic Theology; Vol. VII*, (Dallas, Texas: Dallas seminary Press, Thirteenth Printing, June, 1976) page 254.

Discipleship should be the occupation of every local church as it assembles. Evangelism (preaching the Gospel) should be the occupation of a local church as it leaves the assembly and goes into the world.

Local church membership, personal and corporate Bible study, personal and corporate prayer, and the preaching/teaching ministry in the assembly CANNOT be separated from this ultimate responsibility to preach the Gospel *in the world* and make disciples. In Ephesians 4:1-16, the Apostle Paul details the moral responsibility to the grace of God in the local church and sets before us an outline of necessities to the outcome of true local church growth ("for the edifying of the body of Christ," v. 12b).

"[1] I therefore, the prisoner of the Lord, beseech you that ye **walk worthy** of the vocation wherewith ye are called, [2] *{the worthy walk now defined}* With all lowliness and meekness, with longsuffering, forbearing one another in love; [3] Endeavouring to keep the unity of the Spirit in the bond of peace. [4] *{unity now defined} There is* one body, and one Spirit, even as ye are called in one hope of your calling; [5] One Lord, one faith, one baptism, [6] One God and Father of all, who *is* above all, and through all, and in you all. [7] But unto every one *{every individual, signifying individual responsibility}* of us is given grace *{the inner supernatural enabling}* according to the measure of the gift of Christ. [8] Wherefore he saith, When he ascended up on high, he led captivity captive, and gave gifts *{the gifted men of verse 11}* unto men. [9] (Now that he ascended, what is it but that he also descended first into the lower parts of the earth? [10] He that descended is the same also that ascended up far above all heavens, that he might fill *{referring to the filling of the Spirit}* all things.) [11] And he gave some, apostles; and some, prophets; and some, evangelists; and some, pastors and teachers *{those that preach and teach in the assembly of local churches}*; [12] For the perfecting *{to completely furnish all that is necessary to complete a task or purpose}* of the saints, for the work of the ministry *{to take what they have been taught by the apostles, prophets, evangelists, and pastors and teachers and proclaim it in the world}*, for the edifying *{referring to the construction of the living Temple organism through evangelism/discipleship)* of the body of Christ *{local churches}*" (Ephesians 4:1-12).

Ephesians 4:12 clearly lays the responsibility for *preparing* ALL believers upon the gifted men that Christ gives to local churches. This preparation is done within a local assembly. Believers are to be prepared to preach/teach/speak about the Lord Jesus Christ. They should also be prepared to speak about His provision of salvation "by grace through faith," and His definitive expectations of those who profess to be "born again" of the Spirit of God. However, if the *gifted men* that Christ gives to local churches have done what they are commissioned to do, the responsibility for reaching the world with the Gospel and making disciples of every nation (ethnicity or language group) becomes the responsibility of the members of the "body of Christ." This understanding radically impacts how each individual establishes his/her own missional vision regarding personal responsibility through the ministry of a local church and how that local church extends its ministries into "all the world."

Ephesians 4:13-16 continues to define and develop the missional vision of a local church. This text continues to define individual members of a local church in their accountability to the Lord Jesus Christ and to one another in some very specific details. As we read the text, notice that there is an ultimate and definitive goal in the spiritual maturity that is prepared to engage the world with the Gospel of Jesus Christ.

I believe in these few verses we can find why individual Christians and most local churches are really ineffective in confronting the world with the doctrine of condemnation and becoming part of the *rescue mission* of Christ - SPIRITUAL IMMATURITY. This spiritual immaturity can be credited to one of two causes (or both). People either refuse to learn and obey or God's gifted men are not teaching the "whole counsel of God." In the first case, there is little a pastor can do but to *shake off the dust from his feet* and move on to another locality where his ministry might be received. In the second case, where the pastor is failing to teach the whole counsel of God, the people need to cry out for the teaching they need. Or, they need to find a local church where the pastor is fulfilling his obligations to try to bring the people to spiritual maturity. Look at Ephesians 4:13-16 and see the perimeters of Christ's expectations regarding this.

"[13] Till we all come {*attain to or arrive at*} in the unity {*oneness*} of the {*one*} faith, and of the knowledge {*intimate, relational*} *knowledge, not mere intellectual knowledge}* of the Son of God, unto a perfect *{teleios, completed in spiritual maturity in living the Christ-life}* man, unto the measure of the stature of the fulness of Christ *{i.e., maturity compared to Christ and His teachings}*: [14] That we *henceforth* be no more children, tossed to and fro, and carried about with every wind of doctrine, by the sleight of men, *and* cunning craftiness, whereby they lie in wait to deceive; [15] But speaking the truth in love, may grow up into him in all things, which is the head, *even* Christ: [16] From whom the whole body fitly joined together and compacted by that which every joint supplieth, according to the effectual working in the measure of every part, maketh increase of the body unto the edifying of itself in love" (Ephesians 4:13-16).

According to Ephesians 4:13-16, we are clearly given a measureable standard by which we can compare where we are, and where we ought to be, both individually and corporately as a local assembly. Every individual member within a local assembly is an integral part of the mechanism of *church growth*. Each of us is uniformly accountable for one another's spiritual growth towards spiritual maturity. To divorce ourselves from that responsibility is a serious manifestation of either ignorance or willful disobedience. In either case, it is still SIN! Surely we can understand that even God cannot bless something we do not do. Surely we can understand that our failure to work towards spiritual maturity is a gross abuse of the grace of God.

DISCUSSION QUESTIONS

1. Thoroughly and specifically explain in what new way the Person of the Holy Spirit of God was released into the world on the day of Pentecost.

2. Explain what is meant by the statement, "the filling of the Spirit of God is the releasing of the *creative* power of God through the *ministry* of the life of the Spirit-indwelled believer."

3. Thoroughly expand upon all that is involved in surrender to the Holy Spirit for His filling.

4. List and explain the seven outcome realities in the believer's life that is filled with the Holy Spirit.

5. List and discuss the one common outcome throughout the book of Acts that always accompanied the Spirit.

6. List and discuss the two greatest satanic deceptions and perversions of the Great Commission.

7. Explain Ephesians 4:1-16 according to your understanding of the previous question.

Chapter Thirty-eight
The Self-Deception of the Fallen Nature
Lying to the Holy Spirit

"[1] But a certain man named Ananias, with Sapphira his wife, sold a possession, [2] And kept back *part* of the price, his wife also being privy *to it*, and brought a certain part, and laid *it* at the apostles' feet. [3] But Peter said, Ananias, why hath Satan filled thine heart to lie to the Holy Ghost, and to keep back *part* of the price of the land? [4] Whiles it remained, was it not thine own? and after it was sold, was it not in thine own power? why hast thou conceived this thing in thine heart? thou hast not lied unto men, but unto God. [5] And Ananias hearing these words fell down, and gave up the ghost: and great fear came on all them that heard these things. [6] And the young men arose, wound him up, and carried *him* out, and buried *him*. [7] And it was about the space of three hours after, when his wife, not knowing what was done, came in. [8] And Peter answered unto her, Tell me whether ye sold the land for so much? And she said, Yea, for so much. [9] Then Peter said unto her, How is it that ye have agreed together to tempt the Spirit of the Lord? behold, the feet of them which have buried thy husband *are* at the door, and shall carry thee out. [10] Then fell she down straightway at his feet, and yielded up the ghost: and the young men came in, and found her dead, and, carrying *her* forth, buried *her* by her husband. [11] And great fear came upon all the church, and upon as many as heard these things" (Acts 5:1-11).

How easily we slip into the façade of pretense for purposes of *self-promotion*. How quickly we enable ourselves to justify deception for *self-aggrandizing*. How often we use pseudo-spirituality to exalt ourselves in the eyes of others to *steal God's glory*. This mentality promotes a secret sin-life and an idolatrous promotion of self-worship and glory seeking. However, the lies we manufacture in the hidden darkness of the fallen natures of our own corruption to deceive others, cannot deceive God. There are no sinful actions, thoughts, emotions, or motives to which He is not aware. The wise Christian will also maintain his own awareness of God's awareness and be constantly guarding his motives and his thought life before God.

Perhaps there is no greater manifestation of *pretense Christianity* and its accompanying manifestation of unbelief than to somehow, in any way, think we can *pull a fast one* and deceive God. *Pretense Christianity* always is accompanied with a *secret sin-life*. Why would anyone live in this kind of pretense before others while having a *secret sin-life* that walks in pursuit of the fulfillment of the lusts of their flesh? This is carnality at its highest level of existence! Paul deals with this in his second epistle to the Corinthian church after this local church had already dealt with the *externals* of their carnality. In his second epistle, Paul deals with the *internal* issues of carnality. The carnal man wants to think of himself more "highly than he ought" (Romans 12:3). The carnal man wants others to hold the same, false high opinion. In that motivation, the carnal man is willing to manufacture his own spirituality, but manufactured spirituality will always be empty of any real spiritual fruit.

"[1] Now I Paul myself beseech you by the meekness and gentleness of Christ, who in presence *am* base among you, but being absent am bold toward you: [2] But I beseech *you*, that I may not be bold when I am present with that confidence, wherewith I think to be bold against some, which think of us as if we walked according to the flesh. [3] For though we walk in the flesh, we do not war after the flesh: [4] (For the weapons of our warfare *are* not carnal, but mighty through God to the pulling down of strong holds;) [5] Casting down imaginations, and every high thing that exalteth itself against the knowledge of God, and bringing into captivity every thought to the obedience of Christ; [6] And having in a readiness to revenge all disobedience, when your obedience is fulfilled. [7] Do ye look on things after the outward appearance" (II Corinthians 10:1-7)?

The concluding question of II Corinthians 10:7 is critical to our evaluation of the reality of our own filling of the Spirit and our own spirituality. "Do ye look on things after the outward appearance?" This is how carnal people measure their own spirituality. Of course, the externals can all *look* great and a person can be doing all the religious stuff that mere *religion without relationship* asks of us and that person can still be as carnal as carnal can be. The only way anyone would ever know that such a person has merely *manufactured spirituality* is when their *secret sin-life* is exposed in some way. This exposure of the *secret sin-life* is merely a manifestation of this deep seated carnality and the façade of religiosity. However, merely dealing with the symptoms of an externalistic, manufactured religiosity, without dealing with the façade of pretense that lies at the heart of the lie, will just create a continuum of externalism and reinforce the pretense with more pretense.

Paul's admonition to the carnal believers at Corinth is a basic rebuke. It is GET REAL! Why did they need the rebuke? They needed the rebuke because they were measuring spirituality by "the outward appearance." Christ challenges the façade of the religious externalism in the religious leaders of the Jews by telling them to stop looking at how beautiful the tree is and start looking at the fruit the tree produces.

"[15] Beware of false prophets {*pseudoprophetes, a pretending prophet or religious imposter*}, which come to you in sheep's clothing {*outward appearance of genuineness*}, but inwardly they are ravening wolves {*pursuing the selfish satisfaction of their own appetites*}. [16] Ye shall know them by their fruits. Do men gather grapes of thorns {*do you gather grapes from a thorn bush*}, or figs of thistles {*do you gather figs from a thistle bush*}? [17] Even so every good tree bringeth forth good fruit; but a corrupt tree bringeth forth evil fruit. [18] A good tree cannot bring forth evil fruit, neither *can* a corrupt tree bring forth good fruit. [19] Every tree that bringeth not forth good fruit is hewn down, and cast into the fire. [20] Wherefore by their fruits ye shall know them" (Matthew 7:15-20).

Notice the unity of the Spirit that existed in the local church at Jerusalem. It is into this unity of the Spirit that Satan introduces this defiling selfishness of glory seeking in the hearts of Ananias and Sapphira his wife. If this defiling corruption would have been left unexposed, it would have defiled the whole church. The credit for the miraculous work of the ministry of the Holy Spirit through their lives and the spiritual revival would have been given to men. As a result, the fruit produced through this revival would have immediately ceased.

"[32] And the multitude of them that believed were of one heart and of one soul: neither said any *of them* that ought of the things which he possessed was his own; but they had all things common. [33] And with great power gave the apostles witness of the resurrection of the Lord Jesus: and great grace was upon them all. [34] Neither was there any among them that lacked: for as many as were possessors of lands or houses sold them, and brought the prices of the things that were sold, [35] And laid *them* down at the apostles' feet: and distribution was made unto every man according as he had need. [36] And Joses, who by the apostles was surnamed Barnabas, (which is, being interpreted, The son of consolation,) a Levite, *and* of the country of Cyprus, [37] Having land, sold *it*, and brought the money, and laid *it* at the apostles' feet" (Acts 4:32-37).

Notice in Acts 5:3-4 where this self-deception of Ananias and Sapphira originated. It was a purely selfish acts of self-aggrandizing motivation that originated by the suggestion of the king of selfishness - Satan himself. "[3] But Peter said, Ananias, why hath Satan filled thine heart to lie to the Holy Ghost, and to keep back *part* of the price of the land? [4] Whiles it remained, was it not thine own? and after it was sold, was it not in thine own power? why hast thou conceived this thing in thine heart? thou hast not lied unto men, but unto God." Although Satan sowed the seed of selfishness in their hearts, the conception and birth of sin did not happen until they consented and allowed the seed of selfishness to join with their own carnal lust. We cannot correct serious heart issues by merely changing eternal circumstances. **We MUST deal with the corrupting issues of the heart!**

"[13] Let no man say when he is tempted, I am tempted of God: for God cannot be tempted with evil, neither tempteth he any man: [14] But every man is tempted, when he is drawn away of his own lust, and enticed. [15] Then when lust hath conceived, it bringeth forth sin: and sin, when it is finished, bringeth forth death. [16] Do not err, my beloved brethren. [17] Every good gift and every perfect gift is from above, and cometh down {*is coming down*} from the Father of lights {*illumination*}, with whom is no variableness {*God is constant*}, neither shadow of turning {*not even a shade of variation in His character and attributes*}. [18] Of his own will begat he us with the word of truth, that we should be a kind of firstfruits of his creatures" (James 1:13-18).

Another sad aspect of the story of Ananias and Sapphira is that they enabled each other to *conspire to deceive*.

Instead of one of them say to the other, "this is not right," they consented together to raise the opinions about themselves in the minds of others through deception in order to get themselves *spiritual status*. God addresses this kind of thinking in Proverbs

4:14-27 and refers to it as entering "into the path of the wicked." What is this subtle form of self-deception? It is the desire to get something of value, such as a good testimony or a good reputation, without really doing what is necessary to deserve it. They saw the praise, admiration, and gratefulness given to many others for their sacrificial giving as recorded in Acts 4:32-37. They decided they would get some of that for themselves. So they conceived a plan of deception whereby they could get it all at a *discount price*. There is no such thing in the eyes of God as *discount spirituality*. It will always cost more than we can afford.

The issues of the heart refer to what *issues* or *flows* from the heart. The heart refers to the seat of the human will or the spirit of man. The human will is corrupt, deceitful, defiled, and wicked. This corrupt issue is all that will come from our lives if we do not guard the heart against its own corruption and the outcomes of that corruption.

"[14] Enter not into the path of the wicked, and go not in the way of evil *men*. [15] Avoid it, pass not by it, turn from it, and pass away. [16] For they sleep not, except they have done mischief; and their sleep is taken away, unless they cause *some* to fall. [17] For they eat the bread of wickedness, and drink the wine of violence. [18] But the path *{the direction and purpose of life existence as a testimony to the Truth}* of the just *{the justified or saved}* is as the shining light, that shineth more and more *{as the sunrise fills the morning with increasing light}* unto the perfect day. [19] The way *{the direction and purpose of life existence}* of the wicked *is* as darkness *{as the sunset that begins to fill the night with increasing darkness due to the absence of light}*: they know not at what they stumble. [20] My son, attend *{prick up your ears; listen up}* to my words; incline *{lean towards}* thine ear unto my sayings. [21] Let them *{God's Words}* not depart from thine eyes; keep them *{God's Words}* in the midst of thine heart. [22] For they *{God's Words}* are life unto those that find them, and health to all their flesh. [23] Keep *{guard or protect}* thy heart *{against outward temptations and against attack by inward corruption}* with all diligence; for out of it *{the heart or inward man}* are the issues of life. [24] Put away from thee a froward mouth *{distortion of God's Word}*, and perverse lips *{language of departure from God's Word}* put far from thee. [25] Let thine eyes *{of inward desires that lead you in outward pursuits}* look right on *{straight ahead with the same unchanging consistency manifested of God in God's Word}*, and let thine eyelids *{every time you open your eyes to see* *anything}* look straight before thee. [26] Ponder {*prepare or roll out flat}* the path of thy feet, and let all thy ways {*chosen pathways of life}* be established {*fixed or anchored; i.e., to the Words of God}.* [27] Turn not to the right hand nor to the left: remove thy foot from evil" (Proverbs 4:14-27).

As we can see from Acts chapter five in God's response to Ananias' and Sapphira's attempt to deceive the Holy Spirit by trying to deceive the local church about their spirituality, God will not tolerate this kind of sin in the church. Perhaps the reason why God acts so promptly and severely upon this secret, covert attempt at spiritual deception is the consequences of such deception. People would have been deceived about His blessing upon the whole of work of the ministry in the filling and overflow of the Spirit. God had to deal with the sin, just like He dealt with the sin of Achan in Joshua chapter seven. God needed to deal with Achan's sin before His *overflowing presence* could go before them in the many, many spiritual battles that lay before them. God cannot, and will not, bless pretense. Christ spoke to the hypocrisy of externalism over and over again as recorded in the Gospels (especially in Matthew chapter 23).

What was the sin of Ananias and Sapphira? Yes, the sin conceived in their hearts came forth, or was born, as a lie to the Holy Spirit and to the local church, but the sin itself was the sin of hypocrisy. Hypocrisy is *manufactured spirituality.*

True spirituality is a supernatural act of ongoing creation that progressively transfigures the outward life of a believer by the inward "renewing" of the mind (Romans 12:2).

This is like the little child that dresses up in daddy's or mommy's cloths and shoes and pretends to be daddy or mommy. This is *pretending.* However living in the pretense of hypocrisy is deception. It is the attempt to present yourself as the person you are pretending to be for personal gain. That was the sin of Ananias and Sapphira.

The sin of pretentious hypocrisy is a sin each of us needs to confront in our lives. Although God may not kill us on the spot for such wickedness today, we need to understand that the outcome, or *fruit,* of such hypocrisy is always death.

Living *fruit* cannot be *born* from the *womb* of dead hypocrisy.

"[11] Woe unto them! for they have gone in the way of Cain {*selfishness*}, and ran greedily after the error of Balaam for reward {*selfishness*}, and perished in the gainsaying of Core {*selfishness*}. [12] These are {*defiling*} spots in your feasts of charity {*the Lord's Supper*}, when they feast with you, feeding themselves without fear: clouds *they are* without water, carried about of winds; trees whose fruit withereth, without fruit, twice dead, plucked up by the roots; [13] Raging waves of the sea, foaming out their own shame; wandering stars, to whom is reserved the blackness of darkness for ever" (Jude 1:11-13).

The vanity of hypocrisy is always trying to make God into our own image in order to transfer to ourselves worship that belongs only to God. That is a wickedness that encompasses the very essence of the sin of selfishness in that selfishness seeks to establish a false image of God with our name on it. Oh, what covert wickedness! Perhaps the greater trespass is justifying such an abominable act. Herein we see the moral depravation of the fallen nature of humankind. Carnality tries to get a *discount good testimony* before men through deception. The carnal believer does not consider that the only testimony that really matters is our testimony before an omniscient God, manifesting that he really does not believe in Him.

"[10] He that is faithful in that which is least {*Mammon*} is faithful also in much: and he that is unjust in the least is unjust also in much. [11] If therefore ye have not been faithful in the unrighteous mammon, who will commit to your trust the true *riches* {*spiritual responsibilities regarding unlimited spiritual resources*}? [12] And if ye have not been faithful in that which is another man's, who shall give you that which is your own? [13] No servant can serve two masters: for either he will hate the one, and love the other; or else he will hold to the one, and despise the other. Ye cannot serve God and mammon. [14] And the Pharisees also, who were covetous, heard all these things: and they derided him. [15] And he {*Jesus*} said unto them {*the self-righteous Pharisees*}, Ye are they which justify yourselves before men; but God knoweth your hearts: for that which is highly esteemed among men {*for the hypocrisy of self-righteousness*} is abomination {*as idolatry is detested by God*} in the sight of God" (Luke 16:10-15).

We can be quite sure that Ananias and Sapphira enabled one another in this deception by justifying themselves to one another. We can almost hear their conversation; "After all, who is it going to hurt? No one will ever know. It is not a big deal. We are giving a lot. No one needs to know how much we got for the property. What others think is their problem, not ours." Oh, the subtlety of self-deception.

Those who pursue a genuine testimony understand that it will be expensive and in ways they will not be able to anticipate. King David understood this, especially after he had destroyed his testimony before God, his family, and the nation of Israel. We find King David individually in Psalm 19 communicating truths that reveal to us why it was said of him that he was *a man after God's own heart*. It was not about his pursuit of God's love for him. He already had that. David wanted his heart to be genuinely like God's heart, because David genuinely loved the Lord and genuinely regretted his own human failures and frailties. David was primarily concerned about his testimony *before God's eyes*, not just before men.

"[7] The law of the LORD *is* perfect, converting the soul: the testimony of the LORD *is* sure, making wise the simple. [8] The statutes of the LORD *are* right, rejoicing the heart: the commandment of the LORD *is* pure, enlightening the eyes. [9] The fear of the LORD *is* clean, enduring for ever: the judgments of the LORD *are* true *and* righteous altogether. [10] More to be desired *are* *they* than gold, yea, than much fine gold: sweeter also than honey and the honeycomb. [11] Moreover by them is thy servant warned: *and* in keeping of them *there is* great reward. [12] Who can understand *his* errors? cleanse thou me from secret *faults*. [13] Keep back thy servant also from presumptuous *sins*; let them not have dominion over me: then shall I be upright, and I shall be innocent from the great transgression. [14] Let the words of my mouth, and the meditation of my heart, be acceptable in thy sight, O LORD, my strength, and my redeemer" (Psalm 19:7-14).

Seldom is there a household where degrees of worldliness are tolerated. Seldom is there a household where the husband and wife are not also complicit in the sin of tempting God similar to that of Ananias and Sapphira. They just never consider that God would care about something they deem to be a *small thing* or a *little lie*. Christian households all around the world are guilty of the same sin that Ananias and Sapphira committed. They have one life they live before the church and another *secret-life* that they somehow have convinced themselves that no one will ever know. What does this self-deception reveal about these people? What are they cultivating in the lives of their children who live with them in their secret sin? The answer is they are cultivating UNBELIEF and husbands and wives are being complicit in this wickedness!

Granted, God's response to the sin of Ananias and Sapphira is one of those instances of something that was transitional in nature in the early beginnings of the Church Age. A temporal response to the duplicity is so apparent in the lives of so many who profess Christ as Savior and Lord. If we did not understand this, we would not understand the foolishness of the pragmatism of the *carnival nature* of the Emerging Church movement as it advances its deception of people in these last days.

What we would see if God's immediate judgment fell upon hypocrisy, as it did upon Ananias and Sapphira, is that most people who profess Christ as Lord would start getting real serious about the reality of their spiritual relationship with the Lord. In God's immediate judgment upon the hypocrisy of Ananias and Sapphira, we simply see God's attitude towards this kind of thinking and self-deception.

This kind of thinking and self-deception is impregnated with the curse of death upon any potential for glory to God and hopelessness towards the production of any real spiritual fruit. However, if you are living this kind of life and are still breathing air, do not fool yourself into think that God does not care and that you *got by with it.* You did not *get by with it.* This is the reason your life is fruitless. Remember, the Judgment Seat still lies before you in your near future.

"[1] Therefore seeing we have this ministry, as we have received mercy, we faint not; [2] But have renounced the hidden things of dishonesty, not walking in craftiness, nor handling the word of God deceitfully; but by manifestation {*exhibition or living expression*} of the truth commending {*standing beside as a living testimony*} ourselves to every man's conscience {*moral consciousness of what is morally right and morally wrong*} in the sight of {*lit., before the face of*} God" (II Corinthians 4:1-2).

This was where Ananias and Sapphira failed and where many Christians continue to fail daily. We live our little *secrets* as if God is imaginary. Real faith always lives in the light of understanding that our lives are lived before the face of God. He knows! He sees! You will not *get by* with sin. God hates double mindedness.

> When people put the word *little* before any sin, they have just said there is some degree of corruption that God will tolerate. In doing so, they have just created a false god!

DISCUSSION QUESTIONS

1. Discuss why it is so easy for most Christians to justify a façade of pretense for purposes of self-promotion.

2. Expand upon the statement, *"Pretense Christianity* always is accompanied with a *secret sin-life."*

3. The concluding question of II Corinthians 10:7 is critical to our evaluation of the reality of our own filling of the Spirit and our own spirituality. "Do ye look on things after the outward appearance?" Discuss how this manifests itself in your own life and in the lives of others seduced by such a silly measurement of genuine spirituality.

4. As you read Acts 4:32-37, explain why Satan wants to introduce the corruption of spiritual pretense into a local church with the qualities described in the text. If these qualities were evident in the local church you attend, what should you guard against and for what should you *look out*?

5. We cannot correct serious heart issues by merely changing eternal circumstances. Where must the corrupting seed of *spiritual pretense* be dealt with and why?

6. Discuss the ways individual believers enable one another in spiritual pretense.

7. Define and discuss the sin of Ananias and Sapphira. From this context, discuss why "living *fruit* cannot be *born* from the *womb* of dead hypocrisy."

Chapter Thirty-nine
The Outcomes of Pretentious Externalism

In the book of Revelation, in the seven epistles of Christ to the seven local churches, Christ uses the phrase "I know thy works" on seven different occasions (Revelation 2:2, 9, 13, 19; 3:1, 8, and 15). In each case the word "know" is from the Greek word *eido* (i'-do), which literally means *to see with the end result of eyewitness knowledge and in-depth understanding that comes with the knowledge of both the motives and the actions that comes from those motives*. On three of the seven occasions where Christ says "I know thy works," He is speaking of a good testimony (Revelation 2:2, 9, and 3:8). On the other four occasions He is speaking of actions and motives that are a bad testimony (Revelation 2:13, 19; 3:1, and 15). The point is that God knows!

Your testimony before people may be good because it is good. It may be good because they do not know everything there is to know about you (which is true to some degree of almost all of us). Your testimony may be good before men because you have manufactured one and your Christianity is really a façade, a pretense, and a *stench* before God. Your testimony before people may be bad because you live badly. If you live like a *devil*, do not expect people to treat you like a *saint*.

However, your testimony before God is what it is without anything hidden from Him, including the motives of why you do what you do. Your motives are just as important to God as what you do. The point is that God knows! God sees into all your *secret places*. He knows the *thoughts and intents of your heart*. If you believe in that God, you would be wise to remind yourself that all pretenses, and all forms of self-manufactured *spirituality* are immediately reduced to dust and ashes before the *fire* of His eyes.

The manifestation of pseudo-faith is nowhere more evident than it is in the history of the nation of Israel. The history of the nation of Israel, like the history of the Church Age, is a *history of declension* (deterioration or the process of changing to an inferior state). The prophecies of Isaiah come to Israel at the end of this *declension* along with the end of God's longsuffering with national Israel. Church Age believers should read Isaiah and Jeremiah with extreme carefulness, for we of the Church Age have fallen into the same *declension*. The primary characteristic of this *history of declension* is threefold:

1. The children of Israel *forgot* that God *sees all* and *knows all*.
2. The children of Israel took God's blessings for granted and became *ungrateful.*
3. The children of Israel *failed to maintain* doctrinal purity, practical holiness, and began to sacrifice their distinctiveness for varying degrees of worldliness.

"[1] The vision of Isaiah the son of Amoz, which he saw concerning Judah and Jerusalem in the days of Uzziah, Jotham, Ahaz, *and* Hezekiah, kings of Judah. [2] Hear, O heavens, and give ear, O earth: for the LORD hath spoken, I have nourished and brought up children, and they have rebelled against me. [3] The ox knoweth his owner, and the ass his master's crib: *but* Israel doth not know, my people doth not consider. [4] Ah sinful nation, a people laden with iniquity, a seed of evildoers, children that are corrupters: they have forsaken the LORD, they have provoked the Holy One of Israel unto anger, they are gone away backward. [5] Why should ye be stricken any more? ye will revolt more and more: the whole head is sick, and the whole heart faint. [6] From the sole of the foot even unto the head *there is* no soundness in it; *but* wounds, and bruises, and putrifying sores: they have not been closed, neither bound up, neither mollified with ointment. [7] Your country *is* desolate, your cities *are* burned with fire: your land, strangers devour it in your presence, and *it is* desolate, as overthrown by strangers. [8] And the daughter of Zion is left as a cottage in a vineyard, as a lodge in a garden of cucumbers, as a besieged city. [9] Except the LORD of hosts had left unto us a very small remnant, we should have been as Sodom, *and* we should have been like unto Gomorrah. [10] Hear the word of the LORD, ye rulers of Sodom; give ear unto the law of our God, ye people of Gomorrah. [11] To what purpose *is* the multitude of your sacrifices unto me? saith the LORD: I am full of the burnt offerings of rams, and the fat of fed beasts; and I delight not in the blood of bullocks, or of lambs, or of he goats. [12] When ye come to appear before me, who hath required this at your hand, to tread my courts? [13] Bring no more vain oblations; incense is an abomination unto me; the new moons and sabbaths, the calling of assemblies, I cannot away with; *it is* iniquity, even the solemn meeting. [14] Your new moons and your appointed feasts my soul hateth: they are a trouble unto me; I am weary to bear *them*. [15] And when ye spread forth your hands, I will hide mine eyes from you: yea, when ye make many prayers, I will not hear: your hands are full of blood. [16] Wash you, make you clean; put away the evil of your doings from before mine eyes; cease to do evil; [17] Learn to do well; seek judgment, relieve the oppressed, judge the fatherless, plead for the widow. [18] Come now, and let us reason together, saith the LORD: though your sins be as scarlet, they shall be as white as snow; though they be red like crimson, they shall be as wool. [19] If ye be willing and obedient, ye shall eat the good of the land: [20] But if ye refuse and rebel, ye shall be devoured with the sword: for the mouth of the LORD hath spoken *it*" (Isaiah 1:1-20).

The miraculous exodus of Israel from Egypt took place in about 1491 B.C. (Ussher). During the forty years in the Wilderness of Sin, God revealed Himself in many miraculous ways while He purged unbelief from the nation. Israel's entrance into the Promised Land under the leadership of Joshua began in 1451 B.C.

Although Moses brought Israel *out of bondage*, Joshua led them *into the Promised Land*. Both Moses and Joshua are types of Christ; "And he brought us out from thence, that he might bring us in, to give us the land which he sware unto our fathers" (Deuteronomy 6:23). Obviously this physical redemption is typical of the spiritual redemption of Church Age believers. Salvation delivers us from the bondage of a death sentence upon our souls and glorification delivers us into the end of our regeneration in the eternal state of the *New Genesis* "in Christ." The life that we now live in the flesh is to be lived in the power of the indwelling Christ, just as Israel was to live separated from worldliness and unto God. Therefore, the book of Joshua parallels the epistle to the Ephesians and the warfare of the believer with the world and his own carnality.

After Moses' death, for the next twenty-six years God would miraculously lead the children of Israel in victories. He would give victories over hundreds of city-states, ending with Joshua's death and the record of the nation of Israel confirming their faith covenant with God in Joshua chapter twenty-four. Yet, in the very first chapter of the book of Judges, we find the record of the failure of the tribes of Judah, Benjamin, and Manasseh to completely drive out the inhabitants of the Land as God commanded. On two occasions in the book of Judges we find that Israel's problems were directly connected to their failure to maintain doctrinal purity and continuity in their lives. "In those days *there was* no king in Israel, *but* every man did *that which was* right in his own eyes" (Judges 17:6 and 21:25). This began many years of compromise that would lead the nation of Israel into almost complete apostasy. This compromise led to two progressive outcomes:

1. God began to chastise the nation of Israel progressively (by withdrawing His presence) in individual tribes according to their individual compromise. Whatever their compromise was would also become their judgment.

"[1] And an angel of the LORD came up from Gilgal to Bochim, and said, I made you to go up out of Egypt, and have brought you unto the land which I sware unto your fathers; and I said, I will never break my covenant with you. [2] And ye shall make no league with the inhabitants of this land; ye shall throw down their altars: but ye have not obeyed my voice: why have ye done this? [3] Wherefore I also said, I will not drive them out from before you; but they shall be *as thorns* in your sides, and their gods shall be a snare unto you" (Judges 2:1-3).

2. As individual tribes compromised, they became progressively more apostate. After the death of Joshua and the passing of one generation (about twenty years), the vast majority of Israel moved into a four phase sin cycle that was repeated over and over again in the various tribes throughout the nation of Israel.

"[10] And also all that generation were gathered unto their fathers: and there arose another generation after them, which knew not the LORD, nor yet the works which he had done for Israel. [11] And the children of Israel did evil in the sight of the LORD, and served Baalim: [12] And they forsook the LORD God of their fathers, which brought them out of the land of Egypt, and followed other gods, of the gods of the people that *were* round about them, and bowed themselves unto them, and provoked the LORD to anger. [13] And they forsook the LORD, and served Baal and Ashtaroth. [14] And the anger of the LORD was hot against Israel, and he delivered them into the hands of spoilers that spoiled them, and he sold them into the hands of their enemies round about, so that they could not any longer stand before their enemies. [15] Whithersoever they went out, the hand of the LORD was against them for evil, as the LORD had said, and as the LORD had sworn unto them: and they were greatly distressed" (Judges 2:10-15).

Phase One of the Sin Cycle: Judges 2:11-13

This phase begins with apathy and complacency toward the things of God and His expectations of holiness and purity, ending with the intermixing of pagan worship and heathen/worldly practices with the things of God. Eventually this progression would end with "forsaking" the Lord (v. 12) and accepting total paganism and worldliness, as each generation allowed a little more of God's absolutes to *slip through their fingers*.

From where does such obvious and manifest unbelief come? According to what Paul tells us in Romans chapter 1, it begins with failing to glorify God as God and with thanklessness. If you are ungrateful for what you have as a Christian, you have forgotten *from whence you have come.*

"Because that, when they knew God, they glorified *{esteemed/honored/magnified}* him not as God, neither were thankful; but became vain *{morally wicked}* in their imaginations *{thought life}*, and their foolish heart was darkened" (Romans 1:21).

Phase Two of the Sin Cycle: Judges 2:14

Once they began to move away from purity and holiness (separation), God's chastisement would come upon them to the degree necessary to turn them back to Him and His truths (repentance). In this second phase, God's hand of protection and blessing is withdrawn. It was God's intention to prove to His people that they could not survive without His help.

Phase Three of the Sin Cycle: Judges 2:18

Once the people were under the chastisement of God, oppressed, and put into slavery, they would begin to *remember* the God they professed to know and worship. They would begin to cry out to Him in prayerful repentance. God would hear their cries and groanings and have mercy on them.

I always find it amazing to see what God has to do in peoples' lives to get them to remember Him and cry out to Him in prayer for deliverance. When you decline into a life of sin, *remember* God, and then *remember* the only prayer from you He is interested in answering is a prayer of repentance that begins with asking for His forgiveness for *forgetting* Him.

Phase Four of the Sin Cycle: Judges 2:16

In this phase, God would raise up judges to deliver them out of bondage and lead them back to righteousness, holiness, and purity.

According to Judges 2:19, we find the repetition of this four phase sin cycle throughout the book of Judges and throughout the Old Testament. (This cycle is also true of Church Age believers as well.)

"And it came to pass, when the judge was dead, *that* they returned, and corrupted *themselves* more than their fathers, in following other gods to serve them, and to bow down unto them; they ceased not from their own doings, nor from their stubborn way" (Judges 2:19).

The prophecies of Isaiah began around 760 B.C. (about 645 years after Joshua and the end of the book of Judges, about 1406 B.C.). From the end of the book of Judges, Israel's history is one of increasing compromise and God's longsuffering grace. Although there were occasional *flickers* of revival under a few of Israel's kings, the vast majority of Israel's history is that of a corrupt priesthood, false prophets, and selfish monarchies. It is an amazing testimony to God's continuing loving grace that He suffered them as long as He did.

DISCUSSION QUESTIONS

1. In the book of Revelation, in the seven epistles of Christ to the seven local churches, Christ uses the phrase "I know thy works" on seven different occasions (Revelation 2:2, 9, 13, 19; 3:1, 8, and 15). Discuss the significance of this to you personally.

2. Discuss why the history of the nation of Israel, like the history of the Church Age, is a *history of declension*.

3. What are the threefold characteristics of this *history of declension*?

4. Although Moses brought Israel *out of bondage*, Joshua led them *into the Promised Land*. Both Moses and Joshua are types of Christ; "And he brought us out from thence, that he might bring us in, to give us the land which he sware unto our fathers" (Deuteronomy 6:23). Discuss in what ways it is apparent that you have just not been delivered *out of bondage*, but *into the Promised Land* in the spiritual sense.

5. "In those days *there was* no king in Israel, *but* every man did *that which was* right in his own eyes" (Judges 17:6 and 21:25). This began many years of compromise that would lead the nation of Israel into almost complete apostasy. This compromise led to two *progressive outcomes*. List these two *progressive outcomes* and discuss them.

6. Detail and explain the four phase *sin cycle* found in the book of Judges.

7. Discuss how to avoid this four phase *sin cycle*. Discuss what is necessary in a local church so as to avoid this four phase *sin cycle sneaking up* on you.

Chapter Forty
God's Ordinances of Remembrance

"[10] When thou hast eaten and art full, then thou shalt bless the LORD thy God for the good land which he hath given thee. [11] Beware that thou forget not the LORD thy God, in not keeping his commandments, and his judgments, and his statutes, which I command thee this day: [12] Lest when thou hast eaten and art full, and hast built goodly houses, and dwelt therein; [13] And when thy herds and thy flocks multiply, and thy silver and thy gold is multiplied, and all that thou hast is multiplied; [14] Then thine heart be lifted up, and thou forget the LORD thy God, which brought thee forth out of the land of Egypt, from the house of bondage; [15] Who led thee through that great and terrible wilderness, wherein were fiery serpents, and scorpions, and drought, where there was no water; who brought thee forth water out of the rock of flint; [16] Who fed thee in the wilderness with manna, which thy fathers knew not, that he might humble thee, and that he might prove thee, to do thee good at thy latter end; [17] And thou say in thine heart, My power and the might of mine hand hath gotten me this wealth. [18] But thou shalt remember the LORD thy God: for it is he that giveth thee power to get wealth, that he may establish his covenant which he sware unto thy fathers, as it is this day. [19] And it shall be, if thou do at all forget the LORD thy God, and walk after other gods, and serve them, and worship them, I testify against you this day that ye shall surely perish. [20] As the nations which the LORD destroyeth before your face, so shall ye perish; because ye would not be obedient unto the voice of the LORD your God" (Deuteronomy 8:10-20).

Perhaps the greatest spiritual danger any believer faces in this "under the Sun" existence we call *life* is the danger that lies *in* prosperity. It is not that prosperity itself is dangerous. Therefore, the danger is not a danger *of* prosperity, but the danger that lies *in* prosperity. The danger *in* prosperity is the danger of forgetting God and the foolish notion that prosperity is merely the outcome of your own great personal resources. This foolish notion leads foolish people into idol worship, putting themselves upon the idol's pedestal expecting others to give them *respect* (another word for worship) for their accomplishments in life. Only God deserves worship. Although man may receive praise from others, and praise from God Himself, the wise man ALWAYS remembers who and what he is apart from God's gracious workings in his life.

As spiritually wise people grow in prosperity, they also are wise enough to increase their efforts at maintaining their purity of worship and their purity of doctrine. Spiritually wise people also understand the absolute essential to increase involvement in the *mechanisms* God ordains in His Word. God ordains these *mechanisms* to cause believers to remember Him, what He has done, and what He is doing. These *mechanisms of remembrance* that God ordains are called *ordinances*.

In the Old Testament, under the Mosaic Covenant, God had five main offerings/sacrifices and three main feasts, all intent upon calling the believer to *remembrance*. The feasts took place in different times of the year. God gave them to remind Israel of His past workings in bringing them to become a nation. God intended to cause them to remember that all they had and all that they were was inseparably connected to His grace. Sadly, even in all of these *ordinances of remembrance*, the vast majority of the children of Israel reduced these ordinances to rituals and *forgot God*. Reducing the *ordinances of remembrance* to mere rituals is the natural outcome of having forgotten God.

As we look at the five Mosaic Covenant sacrifices and the three feasts of Israel, it is important to point out that none of the sacrifices or feasts were salvific in nature. In other words, participation in any of the sacrifices or any of the feasts did not provide anything for the person's salvation. All the sacrifices and all the feasts were pertinent to a believer's relationship with God. They were physical ways for a believer to show God that he was genuinely concerned about the reality of his spiritual relationship with God and his walk before God's eyes. In other words, participation was a physical acknowledgment before God and others (accountability) that the believer *knew that God knew*. We might go as far as to say that the believer's participation was a public proclamation of faith and call to remembrance that said, "I know God sees all that I am and all that I do." The offerings were offered on an altar to God to signify something done *before God's eyes* and in His presence.

The following outline and general substance of content is from Leon J. Wood.[16]

1. The Burnt Offering or the Offering of Consecration (Leviticus 1:5-17)

The Burnt Offering was made by the Priests for Israel as a nation (national consecration) and at the request of individuals (individual consecration). This was the primary offering for the consecration of Israel as a nation where a lamb was offered every morning and every evening during the days of the week and two lambs morning and evening on Sabbath Days. The numbers of Burnt Offerings increased on feast days. It portrayed complete consecration of the believer's life in that the offering was completely consumed on the altar.

Individuals could bring a Burnt Offering to signify their own individual consecration to God. Consecration always portrayed giving one's life *completely* to the LORD. No one would have considered, or been allowed to consider, bringing a part of the animal as a Burnt Offering or requesting part of the animal to be returned after the offering. Secondly, only animals that were without blemished, or were not maimed in some way, were acceptable (Romans 12:1-2).

In most cases, when individuals brought a Burnt Offering, it was for the purpose of restoration due to ceremonial uncleanness, breaking of a vow and rededication to faithfulness, or when a priest was consecrated to his service before the LORD. An individual could bring a lamb, goat, bullock, or ram as a Burnt Offering.

2. The Meal Offering or the Dedication of Material Possessions (Leviticus 2:1-16 and 6:14-23)

This was a *bloodless* offering and no animal was involved. This was a grain offering usually accompanied with oil, frankincense, and salt. The Meal Offering portrayed the complete dedication of a person's material possessions to be used to the glory of God (I Corinthians 10:31). The Meal Offering accompanied the Burnt Offering and was also completely consumed upon the altar. The intent of this offering was to acknowledge before God that all a person's possessions were from God and that to use those

---

[16] Wood, Leon J. *A Survey of Israel's History Revised & Enlarged Edition.* (Grand Rapids, MI: Academie Books, Zondervan Publishing House, 1978).

possessions for selfish purposes defiled those possessions and manifested that God had been forgotten.

3. The Sin Offering (Leviticus 4:1-35 and 6:24-30)

The Sin Offering was to acknowledge sins of *ignorance* that were not *premeditated* or *deliberate* (sins of deliberation resulted in being cast out of the camp). Although Sin Offerings were regularly offered by the priests for the nation of Israel collectively during various feasts, these offerings were usually intent upon the restoration of individuals to fellowship with God due to an individual's momentary lapse of memory regarding God seeing and knowing all things. *Spontaneous sins* are often emotional responses to people or temptations.

The Sin Offering was intended to be sacrificial on the sinner's part according to a person's economic status. The idea was to reflect the fact that sin always cost more than we can afford and the impact of sin effects a very wide, perhaps immeasurable, realm of influence and even judgment/withdrawal of blessing upon the nation as a whole (compare I Corinthians 11:29; "For he that eateth and drinketh unworthily, eateth and drinketh damnation {*judgment*} to himself, not discerning the Lord's body"). Even in this reality, the Sin Offering could be as insignificant as an ephah of flour for those in extreme poverty. In other words, restoration to fellowship and forgiveness of sin was never outside of anyone's reach.

4. The Trespass Offering or the Offering of Restitution (Leviticus 5:1-6:7 and 7:1-7)

This offering was never made for the nation of Israel collectively. It was always an individual offering. This offering was *required* for various failures involving deceit or abuse of that which was sanctified ("holy") to God. In most cases, the sinner had to restore what he had abused, plus a twenty per cent monetary compensation, and offer a ram for a sacrifice (see Leviticus 5:15, 17; 6:1-2; 14:12; 19:20-22; Numbers 6:12). Again, this offering was for sins of *ignorance* that were not *premeditated* or *deliberate* (sins of deliberation resulted in being cast out of the Camp).

5. The Peace Offering (Leviticus 3:1-17; 7:11-34; 19:5-8; 22:21-25)

There were three types of Peace Offerings:

A. Thank Offering: given when a person received a special blessing from God

B. Votive Offering: given in payment of a vow

C. Freewill Offering: given to express one's love and appreciation to God

A primary aspect of Peace Offerings is that the person giving the sacrificial animal would share in eating portions of the sacrifice to symbolize fellowship with God. To share a meal with someone was the most sincere and highest level of friendship and hospitality.

Obviously, all of these offerings were about the restoration of fellowship with God that was broken due to failure. Or, they were about deepening one's fellowship with God through offerings reflexing one's dedication to the Lord, or one's desire for deeper fellowship with the Lord. None of them had ANYTHING to do with the sinner's salvation. In fact, only believers were allowed to participate. Those who habitually manifested a life of unbelief were either killed or cast out of the congregation (camp).

There were also three main *remembrance* feasts incorporated into Israel's annual calendar. Every male of Israel was *required* to be present either at Shiloh when the Tent of Meeting was set up there, or at Jerusalem after the Temple was built.

1. The Passover along with the Feast of Unleavened Bread (Exodus 12:1-13:10; Deuteronomy 16:1-8)

This feast began the Jewish religious year, represented a new beginning, and was the most significant of all the memorial feasts. On Passover Day, that was followed by the seven day Feast of Unleavened Bread, a memorial meal was eaten commemorating the original Passover Day in God's deliverance (redemption) from Egyptian bondage. On the Day of Passover a perfect, unblemished lamb was killed and eaten by each family. The Passover Day preceded the Sabbath day so that the first day of the Feast of Unleavened Bread and the last day were both Sabbath Days. Numerous sacrifices were offered collectively by the priests for Israel during each day of the Feast of Unleavened Bread.

The Feast of Unleavened Bread is intricately and intimately connected to the Passover. For the seven days of this feast believers were not allowed to eat anything but unleavened bread. Leaven in the Bible is a picture of sin or corruption. These seven days were preoccupied with a complete examination for any leaven in one's household and the removal of that leaven. The emphasis of the

Feast of Unleavened Bread at the beginning of a new Jewish religious year was the careful and extensive examination for any sin within a household or individual's life. Paul applied the word "leaven" in Galatians 5:9 to the adding "works" into the Gospel as a corruption of faith.

The Passover is replaced by the Lord's Supper. The Feast of Unleavened Bread is replaced by careful, deliberate self-examination for any form of worldliness or defilement in one's life. The difference is that eating the Passover preceded the seven days of self-examination. In the Lord's Supper, self-examination precedes *eating and drinking*. Paul refers to this self-examination in I Corinthians 11:27-33. Failure to self-examine and the failure to repent and remove any defilement is what constitutes "eating and drink unworthily."

> "[26] For as often as ye eat this bread, and drink this cup, ye do shew the Lord's death till he come. [27] Wherefore whosoever shall eat this bread, and drink *this* cup of the Lord, unworthily, shall be guilty of the body and blood of the Lord. [28] But let a man examine himself, and so let him eat of *that* bread, and drink of *that* cup. [29] For he that eateth and drinketh unworthily, eateth and drinketh damnation to himself, not discerning the Lord's body. [30] For this cause many *are* weak and sickly among you, and many sleep. [31] For if we would judge ourselves, we should not be judged. [32] But when we are judged, we are chastened of the Lord, that we should not be condemned with the world. [33] Wherefore, my brethren, when ye come together to eat, tarry one for another" (I Corinthians 11:26-33).

The original emphasis of the Passover, in its type, was about securing of the life of the *first-born* by grace through faith. The promise of God in protecting the firstborn by the application of the blood of the Lamb to the lintel and doorposts of the household was not merely a promise to the Jewish household. The Egyptian household that applied the blood and ate the Lamb would also have been protected from the Death Angel as he passed over Egypt. The applied blood signified a household at rest and secured by faith in God's promise.

2. The Feast of Weeks or Feast of Firstfruits culminating with the Day of Pentecost
(Exodus 23:16; Leviticus 23:15-22; Numbers 28:26-31; Deuteronomy 16:9-12)

This was sometimes called the Feast of Pentecost in that the Day of Pentecost was the culmination of the Feast of Weeks and the emphasis of the feast. The Day of Pentecost typified this promised new, everlasting, *eternal Day*. This *eternal Day* initially existing only in the plan and purpose of God through promise of the birth, holy life, death, burial, and resurrection/glorification of the Promised God/Man (the "last Adam"). This *eternal Day* extended from eternity past into eternity future. The original Day of Pentecost fell on the fiftieth day after a seven week period (there are seven Dispensations or Days of New Beginnings revealed throughout Scripture), with each week ending on a Sabbath Day. This was the Day God gave Israel the Law through Moses on Mt. Sinai. The Day of Pentecost, as part of the Feast of Weeks (also called the Feast of Firstfruits), always fell on the first day of a new week after this seven week cycle. It typified the New Eternal/Everlasting Day of "the regeneration." Although all believers of all Ages (Dispensations) have been POSITIONALLY integrated into this *New Genesis*, Christ Jesus was the first human being who ACTUALLY became part of this *Eternal Genesis* through His resurrection/glorification (the "Firstborn").

On the first day of the seven weeks of the Feast of Weeks, the ceremony began by waving a sheaf of grain before the LORD. This typified the first-fruit of the *New Genesis*, which was the resurrected/glorified Messiah (Jesus Christ) and the beginning of "the regeneration." The following seven weeks (see the seven churches of Revelation) typified the harvest of the Church Age of the "church of the firstborn."

The fiftieth day was the Day of Pentecost typifying the culmination of the harvest of souls to God's glory. On the Day of Pentecost two loaves were presented to the LORD made from the new harvest. These two loaves were baked with leaven representing the fact that the Church Age believers still possess a sin nature and throughout the Church Age would still live in corrupt bodies until their glorification. Therefore, a sin offering of a kid of a goat (Leviticus 23:19) was commanded to be offered with the offering of the two loaves. In this sin offering there was a humbling of God's people before Him regarding their own sinfulness and an acknowledgement before God of the need to daily enter into the spiritual struggle against outward temptations and the inward lusts of our own fallen natures.

3. The Feast of Tabernacles (Booths)
(Exodus 23:16; Leviticus 23:34-43; Deuteronomy 16:13-15)

This commemorated Israel's manner of living in tents or temporary tabernacles during their forty year journey through the wilderness under both God's chastisement and God's blessed provisions. The Feast of Tabernacles was one week long in duration. By the end of the week a total of seventy-one bullocks, fifteen rams, one hundred-five lambs, and eight goats were offered collectively for the children of Israel as sacrifices to the LORD.

The one all-encompassing truth of all the sacrifices is that God knows and sees all sin. If a sinner understands that, he will also understand that, since God is holy and righteous, sin must be judged. There are two sides to the judgment of sin.

1. There is the judgment of sin, which is a death sentence upon all sinners that cannot be satisfied by anything or anyone but a perfect, righteous substitute. This is provided in the death, burial, and resurrection/glorification of the Son of God, Jesus the Christ. This finished substitutionary judgment is offered to the sinner as a gift of grace received through faith (repent, believe, confess, call, and receive).

2. There is the self-judgment of sin by believers after they have been saved in order to avoid the chastisement of God upon their lives. This involves confession of sin, repentance from that sin, and seeking forgiveness from God. This, like all the Mosaic Covenant sacrifices, has nothing to do with being saved. This self-examination, self-judgment, repentance, and seeking God's forgiveness through confession is about the believer's *fellowship* with God.

A true New Covenant believer, like the true Old Covenant believer, understands that all the sacrifices were about self-examination and self-judgment in order to avoid God's chastisement. True faith took these issues very seriously.

DISCUSSION QUESTIONS

1. Explain why the greatest spiritual danger any believer faces in this "under the Sun" existence we call *life* is the danger *in* prosperity.

2. Explain the significance of the Burnt Offering or the Offering of Consecration (Leviticus 1:5-17).

3. Explain the significance of the Meal Offering or The Dedication of Material Possessions (Leviticus 2:1-16 and 6:14-23).

4. Explain the significance of the Sin Offering (Leviticus 4:1-35 and 6:24-30).

5. Explain the significance of the Trespass Offering or The Offering of Restitution (Leviticus 5:1-6:7 and 7:1-7).

6. Explain the significance of the Peace Offering (Leviticus 3:1-17; 7:11-34; 19:5-8; 22:21-25).

7. List and explain the three main *remembrance* feasts incorporated into Israel's annual calendar.

Chapter Forty-one

The Consecration of the Priesthood of the Believers

The Priesthood of the believer of the New Covenant is an overwhelming truth. There are few who call themselves Christians that grasp the uniqueness of this position before a holy God and the overwhelming responsibilities that accompany this *vocational calling*, which in every aspect is what really defines the meaning of the word *Christian*. Sadly, even those who profess to believe in the Priesthood of all believers have very little understanding of the doctrine and the depth to which these truths are intended to manifest the grace of God through believer's lives.

All believers of the Church Age live under the scrutinizing gaze of our High Priest, Jesus Christ, who is carefully examining all that we do, the motives of our heart, and the desires of our wills for anything that defiles us. He wants to bless us and use us to His glory and to the glory of the Father if we are simply willing to offer our lives as a burnt offering to Him every moment of every day. This is what defines consecration (Romans 12:1-2). To merely acknowledge that our new life in Christ belongs to Him is not enough. We must actually live every moment of that new life completely to His glory by becoming "doers of the Word" (James 1:22).

"³ For we which have believed do enter into rest, as he said, As I have sworn in my wrath, if they shall enter into my rest: although the works were finished from the foundation of the world. ⁴ For he spake in a certain place of the seventh *day* on this wise, And God did rest the seventh day from all his works. ⁵ And in this *place* again, If they shall enter into my rest. ⁶ Seeing therefore it remaineth that some must enter therein, and they to whom it was first preached entered not in because of unbelief: . . . ¹¹ Let us labour therefore to enter into that rest, lest any man fall after the same example of unbelief. ¹² For the word of God *is* quick, and powerful, and sharper than any twoedged sword, piercing even to the dividing asunder of soul and spirit, and of the joints and marrow, and *is* a discerner of the thoughts and intents of the heart. ¹³ Neither is there any creature that is not manifest in his sight: but all things *are* naked and opened unto the eyes of him with whom we have to do. [14] Seeing then that we have a great high priest, that is passed into the heavens, Jesus the Son of God, let us hold fast *our* profession. [15] For we have not an high priest which cannot be touched with the feeling of our infirmities; but was in all points tempted like as *we are, yet* without sin. [16] Let us therefore come boldly unto the throne of grace, that we may obtain mercy, and find grace to help in time of need" (Hebrews 4:3-6 and 11-16).

The indwelling of the Holy Spirit is unique to believers living after the Day of Pentecost. Another unique aspect of this indwelling is that these New Covenant believers are all priests before God. Under the Mosaic Covenant, only the priests could approach God. After Pentecost and the beginning of the New Covenant every believer became a priest with direct, intimate access to the "throne of grace." The "throne of grace" is the state of existence from which flows God's blessings, fellowship, and spiritual empowerment (anointing) for ministry. Merrill F. Unger provides some insight into "three elements" of the Mosaic Covenant priesthood from Numbers 16:5, which is typical of the New Covenant Priesthood "in Christ."

"And he spake unto Korah and unto all his company, saying, Even to morrow the LORD will shew who *are* his, and *who is* holy; and will cause *him* to come near unto him: even *him* whom he hath chosen will he cause to come near unto him" (Numbers 16:5).

"Moses furnishes us with the key to the idea of OT priesthood in Num. 16:5, which consists of three elements – being chosen or set apart for Jehovah as His own, being holy, and being allowed to come or bring near. The *first* expresses the fundamental condition, the *second* the qualification, the *third* the function of the priesthood."[17]

God initially intended for all of the children of Israel to be a kingdom of priests and to be able to come near and communicate directly with Him. Initially, the children of Israel agreed to this new arrangement that God proposed to them at Sinai.

---

[17] Unger, Merrill F. *The New Unger's Bible Dictionary*, Edited by R.K. Harrison, Contributing Editors Howard F. Vos and Cyril J. Barber. (Chicago, IL: Moody Press, Revised and Updated Edition, 1988).

"[1] In the third month, when the children of Israel were gone forth out of the land of Egypt, the same day came they *into* the wilderness of Sinai. [2] For they were departed from Rephidim, and were come *to* the desert of Sinai, and had pitched in the wilderness; and there Israel camped before the mount. [3] And Moses went up unto God, and the LORD called unto him out of the mountain, saying, Thus shalt thou say to the house of Jacob, and tell the children of Israel; [4] Ye have seen what I did unto the Egyptians, and *how* I bare you on eagles' wings, and brought you unto myself. [5] Now therefore, if ye will obey my voice indeed, and keep my covenant, then ye shall be a peculiar treasure unto me above all people: for all the earth *is* mine: [6] And ye shall be unto me a kingdom of priests, and an holy nation. These *are* the words which thou shalt speak unto the children of Israel. [7] And Moses came and called for the elders of the people, and laid before their faces all these words which the LORD commanded him. [8] And all the people answered together, and said, All that the LORD hath spoken we will do. And Moses returned the words of the people unto the LORD" (Exodus 19:1-8).

This acceptance of God's offer to be a *kingdom of priests* before Him was then followed by God speaking directly to them out of "the thunderings, and the lightnings, and the noise of the trumpet, and the mountain smoking" (Exodus 20:18), giving to these people God's expectations of them in what has come to be known as the Ten Commandments. The context of the giving of the Law to the children of Israel is to this *kingdom of priests* and what would define the qualification of holiness before the LORD in their service before Him.

> After God spoke to the children of Israel, they understood the extreme holiness of God and the extreme responsibilities that would be theirs as priest before Him after which they had second thoughts about their original agreement.

"[18] And all the people saw the thunderings, and the lightnings, and the noise of the trumpet, and the mountain smoking: and when the people saw *it*, they removed, and stood afar off. [19] And they said unto Moses, Speak thou with us, and we will hear: but let not God speak with us, lest we die. [20] And Moses said unto the people, Fear not: for God is come to prove you, and that his fear may be before your faces, that ye sin not. [21] And the people stood afar off, and

Moses drew near unto the thick darkness where God *was*. [22] And the LORD said unto Moses, Thus thou shalt say unto the children of Israel, Ye have seen that I have talked with you from heaven. [23] Ye shall not make with me gods of silver, neither shall ye make unto you gods of gold. [24] An altar of earth thou shalt make unto me, and shalt sacrifice thereon thy burnt offerings, and thy peace offerings, thy sheep, and thine oxen: in all places where I record my name I will come unto thee, and I will bless thee. [25] And if thou wilt make me an altar of stone, thou shalt not build it of hewn stone: for if thou lift up thy tool upon it, thou hast polluted it. [26] Neither shalt thou go up by steps unto mine altar, that thy nakedness be not discovered thereon" (Exodus 20:18-26).

The children of Israel were not wrong in being fearful of God. In fact, according to Exodus 20:20, God showed Himself to the children of Israel in the way He did to cause them to learn to fear Him. They would learn to fear God because they saw awe inspiring things of God that promoted their fear. Only a fool would see these things and hear the extreme expectations regarding personal holiness that God expected from His priests and walk away from that without trembling in fear, especially if they were not willing to serve God under the conditions He defined in the Ten Commandments. Therefore, the Ten Commandments were given especially to define the conditions of holiness that God requires of His priests before they can come before Him in service or ministry, offer sacrifices, offerings, or have fellowship with Him.

As Exodus 20:19 tells us, the children of Israel rescinded their acceptance of the enormous responsibilities of the priesthood and the privilege of direct communication with God. They asked Moses to communicate with God and that God no longer speak with them directly. The children of Israel were asking for a mediator between God and them. As priests, becoming mediators between God and the world is what God wanted of all of them. They were ALL to be God's believer-priests through whom God would communicate to the lost world. Therefore, they were intended to be a nation/kingdom of prophets, priests, and evangelists of the grace of God. Their ministry was supposed to flow from God through an intimate fellowship with him and into the entire world.

Granted, other than the books of Jonah and Nahum, there is little historical evidence that God had much concern with the lost world outside of the Jewish people. However, the books of Jonah and Nahum reveal that was concerned with the city of Nineveh. This alone should be sufficient evidence for us that God still had a burden for the Gentiles. This is evident by the fact that He communicates with them through these two prophets. We must remember that after the Tower of Babel incident and the confounding of languages, the world was divided into warring city-states that sought the destruction of one another. Each city-state would conquer other city-states, progressively and barbarously acquiring real estate, wealth, larger armies, slaves, and a pantheon of pagan gods (Henotheism). The kings of these evolving nations, as their nations grew into empires, began to be considered *descendants of the gods* and the idea of *royal blood* came into existence. The idea of absolute sovereignty of the kings developed in that their thoughts and words were considered *divine*, not merely human. Every word from their mouths was recorded by a scribe as inspired of the gods. This political dynamic made evangelism almost impossible, but that does not mean there were not varying degrees of belief in Jehovah integrated within the pagan idolatry of these nations. This integrationism was common even among the Jews throughout most of their history.

It is clear from Isaiah that part of God's plan in choosing the nation of Israel to be a kingdom of priests was intent upon the redemption of sinners from every nation in the world. However, it is also clear that because of the failure of Israel at Sinai to accept God's commissioning of the nation as a kingdom of priests, God could not commission them to do so. Therefore, the Great Commission was *put on hold* until the beginning of the Church Age. The Great Commission was *put on hold* until the establishment of a New Priesthood in all Church Age believers as the new kingdom of priests. This happens as the Church Age transitions into the Kingdom Age.

"[1] The word that Isaiah the son of Amoz saw concerning Judah and Jerusalem. [2] And it shall come to pass in the last days, *that* the mountain of the LORD'S house shall be established in the top of the mountains, and shall be exalted above the hills; and all nations shall flow unto it. [3] And many people shall go and say, Come ye, and let us go up to the mountain of the LORD, to the house of the God of Jacob; and he will teach us of his ways, and we will walk in his paths: for out of Zion shall go forth the law, and the word of the LORD from Jerusalem. [4] And he shall judge among the nations, and shall rebuke many people: and they shall beat their swords into plowshares, and their spears into pruninghooks: nation shall not lift up sword against nation, neither shall they learn war any more. [5] O house of Jacob, come ye, and let us walk in the light of the LORD" (Isaiah 2:1-5).

"[20] Assemble yourselves and come; draw near together, ye *that are* escaped of the nations: they have no knowledge that set up the wood of their graven image, and pray unto a god *that* cannot save. [21] Tell ye, and bring *them* near; yea, let them take counsel together: who hath declared this from ancient time? *who* hath told it from that time? *have* not I the LORD? and *there is* no God else beside me; a just God and a Saviour; *there is* none beside me. [22] Look unto me, and be ye saved, all the ends of the earth: for I *am* God, and *there is* none else. [23] I have sworn by myself, the word is gone out of my mouth *in* righteousness, and shall not return, That unto me every knee shall bow, every tongue shall swear. [24] Surely, shall *one* say, in the LORD have I righteousness and strength: *even* to him shall *men* come; and all that are incensed against him shall be ashamed. [25] In the LORD shall all the seed of Israel be justified, and shall glory" (Isaiah 45:20-25).

Obviously, as we apply an inductive methodology to interpret these Scriptures from the perspective of God's ultimate purpose through dispensational transitions, we can readily see the *already, not yet* perspective of the fulfillment of these prophecies. They were fulfilled in part by the priesthood of all believers in the Church Age and the giving of the Great Commission by Jesus Christ to all Church Age believers. This is clear from the introductory verses in the Revelation of Jesus Christ.

"[1] The Revelation of Jesus Christ, which God gave unto him, to shew unto his servants things which must shortly come to pass; and he sent and signified *it* by his angel unto his servant John: [2] Who bare record of the word of God, and of the testimony of Jesus Christ, and of all things that he saw. [3] Blessed *is* he that readeth, and they that hear the words of this prophecy, and keep those things which are written therein: for the time *is* at hand. [4] John to the seven churches which are in Asia: Grace *be* unto you, and peace, from him which is, and which was, and which is to come; and from the seven Spirits which are before his throne; [5] And from Jesus Christ, *who is* the faithful witness, *and* the first begotten of the dead, and the prince of the kings of the earth. Unto him that loved us, and washed us from our sins in his own blood, [6] And hath made {*aorist, active, indicative}* us kings and priests unto God and his Father; to him *be* glory and dominion for ever and ever. Amen. [7] Behold, he cometh with clouds; and every eye shall see him, and they *also* which pierced him: and all kindreds of the earth shall wail because of him. Even so, Amen. [8] I am Alpha and Omega, the beginning and the ending, saith the Lord, which is, and which was, and which is to come, the Almighty" (Revelation 1:1-8).

Revelation 1:6 could be translated "hath made us a sovereignty of priests unto God and His Father." The intent is to reflect Christ as High Priest and Supreme Sovereign ("King of kings") over an order of priests who will sovereignly rule directly under Him, but with His sovereign authority delegated to them and through them.

"[26] And he that overcometh, and keepeth my works unto the end, to him will I give power over the nations: [27] And he shall rule them with a rod of iron; as the vessels of a potter shall they be broken to shivers: even as I received of my Father" (Revelation 2:26-27).

This was God's intent in the Age of the Law and the Mosaic Covenant, to establish the nation of Israel as a Theocracy that would conquer the world and then rule the world as a "kingdom of priests" (Exodus 19:5-6). Because the children of Israel rejected their *call* to all be priests before God, then God chose (*elected*) the tribe of Levi to be His priests. Two primary characteristics of God's priesthood are communicated to us in Exodus 19:6 in the words "peculiar treasure" and "holy nation." All of these words are used of Church Age believers in I Peter chapter two.

"[4] To whom coming, *as unto* a living stone, disallowed indeed of men, but chosen of God, *and* precious, [5] Ye also, as lively stones, are built up a spiritual house, an holy priesthood, to offer up spiritual sacrifices, acceptable to God by Jesus Christ. [6] Wherefore also it is contained in the scripture, Behold, I lay in Sion a chief corner stone, elect, precious: and he that believeth on him shall not be confounded. [7] Unto you therefore which believe *he is* precious: but unto them which be disobedient, the stone which the builders disallowed, the same is made the head of the corner, [8] And a stone of stumbling, and a rock of offence, *even to them* which stumble at the word, being disobedient: whereunto also they were appointed. [9] But ye *{Church Age believers}* *are* a chosen *{eklektos, elect}* generation, a royal *{basileios, kingly or sovereign}* priesthood, an holy *{hagios, morally pure, set apart distinctively to serve the*

LORD, and nothing else, and fully consecrated to that purpose} nation, a peculiar *{peripoiesis, a purchased possession}* people; that ye should shew forth the praises of him who hath called you out of darkness into his marvellous light: [10] Which in time past *were* not a people, but *are* now the people of God: which had not obtained mercy, but now have obtained mercy" (I Peter 2:4-10).

One of the transitional issues of the Church Age was that this new priesthood that would become a worldwide sovereignty under the supreme sovereignty of Jesus Christ. This would happen during the Kingdom Age. This would also be a *tested* and *proven* priesthood. This is the substance of what God is doing in believer's lives during the Church Age; i.e., to test and prove believers BEFORE they are installed as a sovereignty of priests during the Kingdom Age. The Levitical priesthood was tried and found guilty of failure in preserving peculiarity and holiness. Therefore, they were disapproved or *cast away*. The Greek word used to translate this concept is *adokimos.*

"[1] This *is* the third *time* I am coming to you. In the mouth of two or three witnesses shall every word be established. [2] I told you before, and foretell you, as if I were present, the second time; and being absent now I write to them which heretofore have sinned, and to all other, that, if I come again, I will not spare: [3] Since ye seek a proof of Christ speaking in me, which to you-ward is not weak, but is mighty in you. [4] For though he was crucified through weakness, yet he liveth by the power of God. For we also are weak in him, but we shall live with him by the power of God toward you. [5] Examine *{peirazo, test or scrutinize}* yourselves, whether ye be in the faith; prove *{dokimazo, to test for genuineness and approval}* your own selves. Know ye not your own selves, how that Jesus Christ is in you, except ye be reprobates *{adokimos, disapproved and rejected due to disingenuousness or pretense}*? [6] But I trust that ye shall know that we are not reprobates *{adokimos, disapproved and rejected due to disingenuousness or pretense}*" (II Corinthians 13:1-6).

"[24] Know ye not that they which run in a race run all, but one receiveth the prize? So run, that ye may obtain. [25] And every man that striveth for the mastery is temperate in all things. Now they *do it* to obtain a corruptible crown; but we an incorruptible. [26] I therefore so run, not as uncertainly; so fight I, not as one that beateth the air: [27] But I keep under my body, and bring *it* into subjection: lest that by any means, when I have preached to others, I myself should be a castaway {*adokimos, disapproved and rejected due to disingenuousness or pretense*}" (I Corinthians 9:24-27).

"[15] Unto the pure all things *are* pure: but unto them that are defiled and unbelieving *is* nothing pure; but even their mind and conscience is defiled. [16] They profess that they know God; but in works they deny *him*, being abominable, and disobedient, and unto every good work reprobate {*adokimos, disapproved and rejected due to disingenuousness or pretense*}" (Titus 1:15-16).

An unfaithful believer will be *cast away* vocationally, as a priest. He will be *cast away* because of failure to maintain his practical sanctification during his lifetime on earth. He will be *cast away* due to failure in being fully consecrated in serving the LORD in the "work of the ministry." He will be *cast away* due to failure in studying to learn the Word of God (II Timothy 2:15). The believer is responsible for knowing how to do the "work of the ministry" as approved by God's instruction book.

However, the outcome of being *cast away* during our lifetimes is that we will have also been *disapproved* for the priesthood of the Kingdom Age and will NOT rule and reign with Christ as a sovereignty of priests. Those who are *disapproved* and *cast away* will be like the unfaithful priests of Levitical priesthood, who will spend the Kingdom Age in shame.

"[10] And the Levites that are gone away far from me, when Israel went astray, which went astray away from me after their idols; they shall even bear their iniquity. [11] Yet they shall be ministers in my sanctuary, *having* charge at the gates of the house, and ministering to the house: they shall slay the burnt offering and the sacrifice for the people, and they shall stand before them to minister unto them {*in shame, see v. 13*}. [12] Because they ministered unto them before their idols, and caused the house of Israel to fall into iniquity; therefore have I lifted up mine hand against them, saith the Lord GOD, and they shall bear their iniquity. [13] And they shall not come near unto me, to do the office of a priest unto me, nor to come near to any of my holy things, in the most holy *place*: but they shall bear their shame, and their abominations which they have committed. [14]

But I will make them keepers of the charge of the house, for all the service thereof, and for all that shall be done therein. [15] But the priests the Levites, the sons of Zadok {*sons of righteousness or the justified ones*}, that kept {*guarded, protected, or preserved*} the charge {*custodial watch*} of my sanctuary {*dedicated or consecrated place or things*} when the children of Israel went astray from me, they shall come near to me to minister unto me, and they shall stand before me to offer unto me the fat and the blood, saith the Lord GOD: [16] They shall enter into my sanctuary, and they shall come near to my table, to minister unto me, and they shall keep my charge" (Ezekiel 44:10-16).

DISCUSSION QUESTIONS

1. Discuss the relationship of Jesus as High Priest and Mediator of the New Covenant as relevant to the priesthood of all Church Age believers, especially from the perspective of Hebrews 4:3-6 and 11-16.

2. List Merrill F. Unger's insight into "three elements" of the Mosaic Covenant priesthood from Numbers 16:5, which is typical of the New Covenant Priesthood "in Christ." Discuss these three elements as they relate to you as a believer priest.

3. Discuss the historical events and give the details of why the children of Israel never became a kingdom of priests as God intended them to be.

4. How do we know that God was concerned with the lost world outside of the Jewish people?

5. Discuss why the Great Commission was put on hold until the beginning of the Church Age.

6. Discuss Revelation 1:1-8 and the pending *sovereignty of priests* that will be installed at the beginning of the Kingdom Age.

7. Discuss the *when* and *how* that this new priesthood would also be a tested and proven priesthood before they become a worldwide sovereignty under the supreme sovereignty of Jesus Christ during the Kingdom Age.

Chapter Forty-two

Substituting Semblance for Substance

As we rapidly advance into the twenty-first century, we celebrate something called *Christmas* where the substance of the celebration in the birth of a Saviour, who is Christ the Lord, has been almost completely removed. Previous to this celebration we have just finished the season of *Thanksgiving* where the substance of the focus is upon what we are thankful *for* rather than the God *to* whom we are thankful. We elected a new President on the basis of a promise of *CHANGE* without any substance for detail as to what that *change* involves. We have an ever evolving religious scene that emphasizes *unity* without any substance to a basis for that *unity*. We have become the *balloon generation* - all puffed up and looking large, while in reality we are full of nothing but *hot air*.

We are a generation with *semblance without substance*. *Semblance* is an outward, token appearance or form that is deliberately misleading. It is a sad day when people are so deceived that they actually are willing to accept *semblance without substance* and actually allow themselves to become involved with this kind of pretentious façade. This is the society that reduces every celebration to a *party*, never mentioning the purpose of the celebration or inventing some silly notion just to *party*. This is what *Christmas* has become. This is the society that turns every Holy Day into a holiday with just another excuse to take a day off from work to get drunk and make fools of themselves. It is difficult to look at all of this and not become a hopeless cynic. The only way to avoid cynicism is to focus on the substance that gives us a purpose for existence beyond just having a *good time* (Hedonism). **Cynicism is living without hope. Hope is living without cynicism.**

When we think of the birth of Messiah, we tend to get bogged down in the miracle of the virgin birth, the drama of Jewish history, and the humble manger scene. Although all of this has substance that is very important and very dramatic, the substance in this historical epic is the fulfillment of thousands of years of prophecy regarding the Promised One that began in Genesis 3:15 and is expanded upon in considerable detail through hundreds of other prophecies through the book of Malachi.

> In all of this there is real substance for us to build our present lives upon and real substance to which we can anchor our futures.

The substance of our celebration of the birth of Messiah, Jesus the Christ, is upon a promise that springs forth from eternity. One day in time, Jehovah would be born through the womb of a woman, He would be born to be a new and last Adam. Through His perfect and sinless life, His substitutionary death, His resurrection/glorification, and His High Priestly intercession, He would become a "door" for "whosoever" to enter into a *New Genesis*. Once there, they would live eternally in the glorious presence of the Heavenly Father. **Here is some real substance for you to build a life and to which you can anchor your future. If we believe in that substance, we should be preoccupied with it.**

Apart from the birth, substitutionary death, burial, resurrection/glorification of Jesus Christ, perhaps one of the greatest truths of the Word of God for present day believers is the Priesthood of all believers that comes to us in our *new birth* relationship with Jesus Christ. This is the substance to which all our future hopes lead. This is the substance to which every believer is intimately and presently connected. We are connected through the indwelling of the Holy Spirit as a direct link to our High Priest at the right hand of our Father in Heaven.

"[17] And if children, then heirs; heirs of God, and joint-heirs with Christ; if so be that we suffer with *him*, that we may be also glorified together. [18] For I reckon that the sufferings of this present time *are* not worthy *to be compared* with the glory which shall be revealed in us. [19] For the earnest expectation of the creature waiteth for the manifestation of the sons of God. [20] For the creature was made subject to vanity, not willingly, but by reason of him who hath subjected *the same* in hope, [21] Because the creature itself also shall be delivered from the bondage of corruption into the glorious liberty of the children of God. [22] For we know that the whole creation groaneth and travaileth in pain together until now. [23] And not only *they*, but ourselves also, which have the firstfruits of the Spirit, even we ourselves groan within ourselves, waiting for the adoption, *to wit*, the redemption of our body. [24] For we are saved by hope: but hope that is seen is not hope: for what a man seeth, why doth he yet hope for? [25] But if we hope for that we see not, *then* do we with patience wait for *it*. [26] Likewise the Spirit also helpeth our infirmities: for we know not what we should pray for as we ought: but the Spirit itself maketh intercession for us with groanings which cannot be uttered. [27] And he that searcheth the hearts knoweth what *is* the mind of the Spirit, because he maketh intercession for the saints according to *the will of* God. [28] And we know that all things work together for good to them that love God, to them who are the called according to *his* purpose" (Romans 8:17-28).

In the few verses of Romans 8:17-28, we are given real substance with which to fill our lives and to which we can anchor our present and future hope. We have some real substance for celebration and some real substance that gives our lives both purpose and worth. In fact, there is so much substance that it is difficult to even know where to begin.

Four different times in Romans 8:19-22 Paul uses the Greek word *ktisis* (ktis'-is), translated "creature" on the first three occasions and "creation" on the last occasion. It is clear that the subject of Romans chapter eight is the future glorification of believers. As already established in Romans 8:10-17, redemption does not remove God's curse upon the first creation. Rather, redemption removes the believing sinner from the cursed first creation and makes him part of the *New Creation* "in Christ." Glorification is the final stage in God's supernatural work of regeneration in a believer's life (although "the regeneration" will not be fully and actually complete until the creation of the New Heaven/Earth after the Kingdom Age).

Secondly, "adoption" refers to *placing believers as adult sons*, giving them their inheritance as "joint heirs with Christ," and refers to a dispensational transition. The first dispensational transition is from the Age of Law to the Age of Grace and happens positionally when the New Covenant believer is indwelled by the Spirit of God. The next dispensational transition is during the transition between the Age of Grace to the Kingdom Age at the time of the Church Age believer's glorification. This inheritance is much more than eternal life. It has to do with the New Covenant believer's new position as "joint heirs with Christ" as a *sovereignty of priests* with Christ as our High Priest" in the Kingdom Age.

"For I reckon that the sufferings of this present time *are* not worthy *to be compared* with the glory which shall be revealed in us" (Romans 8:18). "Sufferings" and "present time" refer to *life within the curse of the fallen creation.* These two things go *hand in hand.* The word "reckon" is from the Greek word *logizomai* (log-id'-zom-ahee). It means to take inventory, accounting, to make a comparative analysis or, to make an evaluation allowing a conclusive decision. It is about *comparative analysis* intent upon putting what we believe into action. It is the same word Paul uses in Romans 6:11 where he says, "Likewise reckon ye also yourselves to be dead indeed unto sin, but alive unto God through Jesus Christ our Lord." The action of faith regarding the reckoning is to count the sufferings of this life incomparable, regardless of how difficult or painful they might be, to the new life we will have in the New Genesis. If what we believe regarding our future glorification and our "so great salvation" "in Christ" is what is going to really happen, death and any difficulties of life that lead to death are really inconsequential.

After our *comparative analysis* of this "present time" compared to our new existence to come is finished and, we have made the necessary decision about the inconsequential difficulties of this life compared to our new existence in the New Genesis, Paul adds, "[19] For the earnest expectation of the creature waiteth for the manifestation of the sons of God. [20] For the creature was made subject to vanity, not willingly, but by reason of him who hath subjected *the same* in hope, [21] Because the creature itself also shall be delivered from the bondage of corruption into the glorious liberty of the children of God. [22] For we know that the whole creation groaneth and travaileth in pain together until now" (Romans 8:19-22).

Notice each new sentence begins with the word "for." Each new sentence adds a *reason* "for" reckoning ". . . the sufferings of this present time . . . not worthy *to be compared* with the glory which shall be revealed in us" (Romans 8:18). The word "for" is from the Greek word *gar* (gar), which assigns a reason for purpose, explaining the argument further or, giving a higher degree of intensity to the facts being presented.

Romans 8:19 advances the comparison of these two existences by the statement, "For the earnest expectation of the creature waiteth for the manifestation of the sons of God." We find the first "creation" personified and involved with two anticipatory preoccupations - *watching* and *waiting*. The words "earnest expectation" are from the Greek word *apokaradokia* (ap-ok-ar-ad-ok-ee'-ah). The Greek word *kara* refers to the *head*. *Apo* means *off from*. *Dokio* (verb form) means *to watch*. I believe the intent here is that the part of creation with rational abilities (humans with understanding) is intensely watching for that which we understand will come about by God's promise; i.e. "the manifestation of the sons of God."

"Waiteth" is from the Greek word *apekdechomai* (ap-ek-dekh'-om-ahee). It means to *fully expect*. Thayer translates, "to wait it out." This translation would align with Paul's previous statement regarding the "sufferings of this present time." The word "manifestation" is from the Greek word *apokalupsis* (ap-ok-al'-oop-sis). This is the same word used of Jesus Christ in Revelation 1:1, there translated "revelation." Included in the second coming, is the revelation of "the sons of God" who are "joint heirs with Christ."

"[2] Beloved, <u>now are we the sons of God</u>, and it doth not yet appear what we shall be: but we know that, when he shall appear, we shall be like him; for we shall see him as he is. [3] And every man that hath this hope in him purifieth himself, even as he is pure" (I John 3:2-3).

"[1] If ye then be risen with Christ, <u>seek those things which are above, where Christ sitteth on the right hand of God</u>. [2] Set your affection on things above, not on things on the earth. [3] For ye are dead, and your life is hid with Christ in God. [4] When Christ, *who is* our life, shall appear, then shall ye also appear with him in glory" (Colossians 3:1-3).

Paul's further expansion on his argument for giving believer's motivation for looking beyond the "sufferings of this present time" is found in Romans 8:20-21 in his personification of "the creation." "[20] For the creature {*creation*} was made subject to vanity, not willingly, but by reason of him who hath subjected *the same* in hope, [21] Because the creature {*creation*} itself also shall be delivered from the bondage of corruption into the glorious liberty of the children of God." Literally it reads, "the creation became subordinate (*hupotasso*, hoop-ot-as'-so) to uselessness (*mataiotes*, mat-ah-yot'-ace)." After the fall, the creation became *subservient to depravity* and could no longer bring glory to God. God initiated this subjection intent upon a higher and nobler outcome; i.e., "hope."

The word "hope" is translated from the Greek word *elpis* (el-pece') and refers to the confident anticipation or expectation of something good or pleasant. The creation could then look forward in confident expectation to the time God would deliver the "creation itself . . . from the bondage of corruption into the glorious liberty [Thayer: "liberty of glory"] of the children of God" (Romans 8:21), referring to "the regeneration" or the creation of the new Heaven/Earth. When the "children of God" by regeneration are finally glorified, they will be liberated from the subservience to the depravity of the fallen creation and once again be able to fully glorify God.

> The main emphasis of the birth of a Saviour and the doctrine of redemption is not upon *from* what we are saved. The main emphasis of the birth of a Saviour and the doctrine of redemption is upon *to* what we are saved.

If our focus is merely upon *from* what we are saved, the hope of our salvation ends with a faith decision to be "born again." When the focus of our salvation is upon *to* what we are saved, not just a place called Heaven, that focus immediately translates us into the realm of the proving of our new lives "in Christ." We prove ourselves to be worthy of the new sovereignty of priesthood that will be given to the faithful. Before God will install Church Age believers in the Kingdom Age as a sovereignty of priests, every individual believer will need to prove himself faithful during his/her lifetime in the Church Age.

"Study to shew thyself approved unto God, a workman that needeth not to be ashamed, rightly dividing the word of truth" (II Timothy 2:15).

DISCUSSION QUESTIONS

1. Why might it be said that we have become the *Balloon Generation*?

2. Discuss the relationship of hope to the promises connected to Genesis 3:15.

3. Read Romans 8:17-28 and describe the real substance for hope for all truly "born again" believers.

4. Explain the significance of each of the four different times in Romans 8:19-22 Paul uses the Greek word *ktisis*, translated "creature" on the first three occasions and "creation" on the last occasion.

5. "Adoption" refers to placing believers as adult sons, giving them their inheritance as "joint heirs with Christ." What is that inheritance? (No one is *adopted* to salvation.)

6. Explain the following verse of Scripture according to your understanding of dispensational transitions: "For I reckon that the sufferings of this present time *are* not worthy *to be compared* with the glory which shall be revealed in us" (Romans 8:18).

7. Thoroughly explain the following Scripture from your understanding of dispensational transitions: "For the earnest expectation of the creature waiteth for the manifestation of the sons of God" (Romans 8:19).

Chapter Forty-three

Preapproving a New Priesthood

"[17] Now in this that I declare *unto you* I praise *you* not, that ye come together not for the better, but for the worse. [18] For first of all, when ye come together in the church, I hear that there be divisions among you; and I partly believe it. [19] For there must be also heresies among you, that they which are approved may be made manifest among you. [20] When ye come together therefore into one place, *this* is not to eat the Lord's supper. [21] For in eating every one taketh before *other* his own supper: and one is hungry, and another is drunken. [22] What? have ye not houses to eat and to drink in? or despise ye the church of God, and shame them that have not? What shall I say to you? shall I praise you in this? I praise *you* not. [23] For I have received of the Lord that which also I delivered unto you, That the Lord Jesus the *same* night in which he was betrayed took bread: [24] And when he had given thanks, he brake *it*, and said, Take, eat: this is my body, which is broken for you: this do in remembrance of me. [25] After the same manner also *he took* the cup, when he had supped, saying, This cup is the new testament in my blood: this do ye, as oft as ye drink *it, in remembrance of me*. [26] For as often as ye eat this bread, and drink this cup, ye do shew the Lord's death till he come. [27] Wherefore whosoever shall eat this bread, and drink *this* cup of the Lord, unworthily, shall be guilty of the body and blood of the Lord. [28] But let a man examine himself, and so let him eat of *that* bread, and drink of *that* cup. [29] For he that eateth and drinketh unworthily, eateth and drinketh damnation to himself, not discerning the Lord's body. [30] For this cause many *are* weak and sickly among you, and many sleep. [31] For if we would judge ourselves, we should not be judged. [32] But when we are judged, we are chastened of the Lord, that we should not be condemned with the world. [33] Wherefore, my brethren, when ye come together to eat, tarry one for another. [34] And if any man hunger, let him eat at home; that ye come not together unto condemnation. And the rest will I set in order when I come" (I Corinthians 11:17-34).

The Lord's Supper is an *ordinance of remembrance* that looks backward to the Cross-work of Jesus Christ and to a "finished" work of redemption. We see this emphasis of *remembrance* in I Corinthians 11:24-25 by the repeated words "in remembrance of me." The Lord's Supper is intent upon bringing the believer-priest back to Calvary to remind him of the cost of his redemption. The Lord's Supper is intent upon reminding him to be thankful for the overwhelming, unsearchable, and unspeakable work of grace in the death, burial, and resurrection/glorification of Jesus Christ. This cross-work was necessary to secure the salvation of the believer's soul for all eternity and to make him a priest before God.

> The Lord's Supper is ONLY for believers. We can go even beyond that basic restriction. The Lord's Supper is ONLY for believer priests who seek to be completely consecrated to the LORD (Romans 12:1-2) and who pursue being morally pure and sanctified as they stand before Him to minister His message of reconciliation (II Corinthians 5:18) and to make disciples for Jesus Christ to the glory of God.

Therefore, it is *ordinance of remembrance* ONLY for those who remember their *purpose of approval* before God and are determined to fulfill that purpose by the grace of God's indwelling power through the filling of the Spirit of God (Ephesians 5:18). The Lord's Supper is an *ordinance of remembrance* ONLY for believer priests who remember, are grateful, and who are obedient (are "doers of the Word, and not hearers only," James 1:22) in all that they know of the Word of God.

In light of all of this, we can also go so far as to say that the Lord's Supper is an *ordinance of consecration* for God's New Covenant believer priests. Participation in the Lord's Supper is intent upon a commitment to have a sanctified local church through which the Holy Spirit might manifest the *Christ-life*, bring forth the fruit of souls to salvation, and supernaturally and progressive transfigure their lives through the discipleship process. Therefore, the Lord's Supper is an *ordinance of remembrance* and an *ordinance of consecration* to achieve the "unity of the Spirit in the bond of peace" (Ephesians 4:3) within the formal membership of a local church so that God might be glorified/magnified through the "work of the ministry" (Ephesians 4:12) of the members of a local church.

To help understand God's expectations in the consecration of His New Covenant believer priests, we must apply a *complimentary hermeneutic*; i.e., looking at the Mosaic Covenant type in the consecration of those Priests and the elements and areas of emphasis in those types that define consecration and sanctification. The consecration of a priest typically involved four areas of his life to be qualified to serve/minister before the LORD.

It must be emphasized that in transitioning these qualifications for ministry from the Mosaic Covenant type to the New Covenant reality, we must be careful that we do not convey an idea that all God was concerned about in the Levitical priesthood was externals. This is certainly not the case.

Although the Levitical priests under the Mosaic Covenant quickly slipped into this deadly externalism, it is clear from many Scriptures that God intended for them to understand these types and translate them into spiritual realities. That is what we need to do in order to understand how these types apply to New Covenant believers and what is required of us to be qualified to serve the LORD that defines the perfection of the saints necessary to doing "the work of the ministry" (Eph. 4:12). Each of the areas listed below were intricately connected one to the other. There was no such nonsense as allowing a priest to serve that was disqualified by failure in any one of these four areas.

1. Jesus was elected by birthright as God's "firstborn" and peculiar possession, with unique privileges and model moral responsibilities. Therefore, the priest's *election* was *vocational*. They had no part in the land distribution of Israel and were totally separated from temporal promises of God, being connected to God's provision for them and to serve before God and to men. In this *vocational calling/election*, each priest was to be totally devoted to serving the LORD through teaching and explaining God's Word, administrating the Law and making judgments regarding the Law, and involving himself in the sacred duties of the Tabernacle/Temple of God.

For the New Covenant priesthood, this qualification type is basically salvation. The New Covenant priest MUST be "born again." All "born again" believers are *called/elected* to be priests before God. However, the next three areas of qualifications will determine *when*, *if*, and *how often* God will be able to bless what they seek to do for Him.

2. God made holiness the indispensable condition before any priest dare stand before Him, the Holy One of Israel. The priests could not have a physical defect or disease of any kind to typify spiritual blamelessness and moral purity. Holiness extended into defining factors of his daily life such as who he could marry or could not marry, the foods he ate, and the things he drank. Almost every detail of his life was defined and had specific moral boundaries that he could not cross lest he be disqualified/disapproved. His life and relationships were under the constant scrutiny of the High Priest, his fellow priests, and by the congregation of Israel. In every aspect of his life, he lived in a *glass house.*

We must be careful here to distinguish between the believer's positional sanctification "in Christ" and his practical sanctification through confession of sin, forgiveness and cleansing by Christ (I John 1:7-9), and the filling of the Spirit of God for spiritual empowerment, discernment, and illumination. The acceptability of a New Covenant believer's priestly service as an Ambassador for Christ is conditioned BOTH upon his positional sanctification "in Christ" (this is salvation) and his practical sanctification through separation from worldliness and through spiritual cleansing.

3. God's consecration of the priest was typified by how the priests approached God. Consecration involves the presentation of what we are to God to be used by God for His purposes. Therefore, consecration involves a commitment to God to serve Him by actually DOING the work He has called us to do.

Under the Mosaic Covenant, consecration involved ceremonial washings, times of purification, and offering of the right sacrifices for himself. When all of these areas of sanctification were in order, the priest would receive his ceremonial clothing that he wore only for service in the Tabernacle/Temple and was anointed with oil (typical of the Holy Spirit) before he began to actually do the work he was ordained to do. To go before the LORD without considerations of meeting the qualifications of both holiness and consecration was a rank manifestation of unbelief. The ceremony of sanctification and consecration was elaborately detailed involving seven days of purification and separation. This is recorded in Exodus 29:1-37.

4. The clothing of the priest as he ministered before the LORD was an outward manifestation of both holiness in the clean white linen garments and consecration. These garments were never to be worn for any other purpose than to serve the LORD in His Temple. These garments were never to be worn by anyone that was not a sanctified and consecrated priest. Therefore, the Mosaic Covenant priest's garments distinguished him as uniquely peculiar. He literally looked different than anyone else merely by his dress. No one but a consecrated and sanctified priest could ever wear the priestly garb. Secondly, the priest never wore shoes/sandals when ministering before the LORD because he walked upon holy ground sanctified by the presence of Jehovah.

The New Covenant priests are equally limited in their requirements to be both sanctified and consecrated before they can be clothed for ministry. However, the New Covenant priest's clothing is not physical. The New Covenant priest's clothing is Jesus Christ (the Christ-life).

"[11] And that, knowing the time, that now *it is* high time to awake out of sleep: for now *is* our salvation nearer than when we believed. [12] The night is far spent, the day is at hand: let us therefore cast off the works of darkness, and let us put on the armour of light. [13] Let us walk honestly, as in the day; not in rioting and drunkenness, not in chambering and wantonness, not in strife and envying. [14] But put ye on the Lord Jesus Christ, and make not provision for the flesh, to *fulfil* the lusts *thereof*" (Romans 13:11-14).

In Ephesians 4:17-32, the Apostle Paul defines what is meant by his statements in Romans 13:12 and 14 respectively in the phrases "put on the armour of light" and "put ye on the Lord Jesus Christ."

"[17] This I say therefore, and testify in the Lord, that ye henceforth walk not as other Gentiles walk, in the vanity of their mind, [18] Having the understanding darkened, being alienated from the life of God through the ignorance that is in them, because of the blindness of their heart: [19] Who being past feeling have given themselves over unto lasciviousness, to work all uncleanness with greediness. [20] But ye have not so learned Christ; [21] If so be that ye have heard him, and have been taught by him, as the truth is in Jesus: [22] That ye put off concerning the former conversation the old man, which is corrupt according to the deceitful lusts; [23] And be renewed in the spirit of your mind; [24] And that ye put on the new man, which after God is created in righteousness and true holiness. [25] Wherefore putting away lying, speak every man truth with his neighbour: for we are members one of another. [26] Be ye angry, and sin not: let not the sun go down upon your wrath: [27] Neither give place to the devil. [28] Let him that stole steal no more: but rather let him labour, working with *his* hands the thing which is good, that he may have to give to him that needeth. [29] Let no corrupt communication proceed out of your mouth, but that which is good to the use of edifying, that it may minister grace unto the hearers. [30] And grieve not the holy Spirit of God, whereby ye are sealed unto the day of redemption. [31] Let all bitterness, and wrath, and anger, and clamour, and evil speaking, be put away from you, with all malice: [32] And be ye kind one to another, tenderhearted, forgiving one another, even as God for Christ's sake hath forgiven you" (Ephesians 4:17-32).

We do not merely "put on" Christ over "the old man." The "old man" must be "put off" first. That is what Paul defines in Ephesians 4:25-32. Paul reiterates this same concept in Colossians chapter three. We cannot, and should not, separate this instruction from the context of the sanctification and consecration of the believer priest of the New Covenant before God. Colossians chapter one lays the foundation for what Paul will say later in Colossians chapter three.

"[21] And you, that were sometime alienated and enemies in *your* mind by wicked works, yet now hath he reconciled [22] In the body of his flesh through death, to present you holy and unblameable and unreproveable in his sight: [23] If ye continue in the faith grounded and settled, and *be* not moved away from the hope of the gospel, which ye have heard, *and* which was preached to every creature which is under heaven; whereof I Paul am made a minister; [24] Who now rejoice in my sufferings for you, and fill up that which is behind of the afflictions of Christ in my flesh for his body's sake, which is the church: [25] Whereof I am made a minister, according to the dispensation of God which is given to me for you, to fulfil the word of God; [26] *Even* the mystery which hath been hid from ages and from generations, but now is made manifest to his saints: [27] To whom God would make known what *is* the riches of the glory of this mystery among the Gentiles; which is Christ in you, the hope of glory: [28] Whom we preach, warning every man, and teaching every man in all wisdom; that we may present every man perfect in Christ Jesus: [29] Whereunto I also labour, striving according to his working, which worketh in me mightily" (Colossians 1:21-29).

DISCUSSION QUESTIONS

1. Discuss the following statement: "The Lord's Supper is ONLY for believer priests who seek to be completely consecrated to the LORD (Romans 12:1-2) and who pursue being morally pure and sanctified as they stand before Him to minister His message of reconciliation (II Corinthians 5:18) and to make disciples for Jesus Christ to the glory of God."

2. Discuss why the Lord's Supper is also an *ordinance of consecration*.

3. Explain how the Mosaic Covenant priest's election was by birthright as God's "firstborn" and God's peculiar possession with unique privileges and model moral responsibilities. Explain how this type is fulfilled by the New Covenant priesthood of all believers.

4. Explain why the Mosaic Covenant priest's holiness was the indispensable condition before any priest dare stand before God, the Holy One of Israel. Explain how this type is fulfilled by the New Covenant priesthood of all believers.

5. God's consecration of the Mosaic Covenant priest was typified by how the priests approached Him. Explain how this type is fulfilled by the New Covenant priesthood of all believers.

6. Explain how the clothing of the Mosaic Covenant priest as he ministered before the LORD was an outward manifestation of both holiness and consecration. Explain how this type is fulfilled by the New Covenant priesthood of all believers.

7. Explain Ephesians 4:17-32 from your answer above.

Chapter Forty-four

Instilling Substance Over Semblance

As we have already discussed, God initially intended for all of the children of Israel to be a *kingdom of priests* and to be able to come near and communicate directly with Him. Initially, the children of Israel agreed to this new arrangement that God proposed to them at Sinai.

"[5] Now therefore, if ye will obey my voice indeed, and keep my covenant, then ye shall be a peculiar treasure unto me above all people: for all the earth *is* mine: [6] <u>And ye shall be unto me a kingdom of priests, and an holy nation</u>. These *are* the words which thou shalt speak unto the children of Israel. [7] And Moses came and called for the elders of the people, and laid before their faces all these words which the LORD commanded him. [8] And all the people answered together, and said, <u>All that the LORD hath spoken we will do</u>. And Moses returned the words of the people unto the LORD" (Exodus 19:5-8).

God's intent in establishing the whole nation of Israel as a "kingdom of priests," or a *sovereignty of priests*, was to establish a theocracy. This would be a theocracy through which He could sovereignly rule the nation of Israel through direct communication to and through the children of Israel as priests. On two different occasions Israel refused the direct theocratic rule of God through their lives as priests. The first occasion is when they asked for another mediator in Moses to speak to God for them and through which God would speak to them.

"[18] And all the people saw the thunderings, and the lightnings, and the noise of the trumpet, and the mountain smoking: and when the people saw *it*, they removed, and stood afar off. [19] And they said unto Moses, <u>Speak thou with us, and we will hear: but let not God speak with us, lest we die</u>. [20] And Moses said unto the people, Fear not: for God is come to prove you, and that his fear may be before your faces, that ye sin not. [21] <u>And the people stood afar off</u>, and Moses drew near unto the thick darkness where God *was*" (Exodus 20:18-21).

After the children of Israel rejected God's offer to speak directly to them and through them, God established the Levitical priesthood for that purpose. The second occasion when Israel refused the theocratic rule of God was just before Samuel's death. Although Samuel told God what the people said and then told the people God's response to their request, "nevertheless," they demanded that Samuel make a king that would judge them like the other nations had.

"[4] Then all the elders of Israel gathered themselves together, and came to Samuel unto Ramah, [5] And said unto him, Behold, thou art old, and thy sons walk not in thy ways: now make us a king to judge us like all the nations. [6] But the thing displeased Samuel, when they said, Give us a king to judge us. And Samuel prayed unto the LORD. [7] And the LORD said unto Samuel, Hearken unto the voice of the people in all that they say unto thee: for they have not rejected thee, but they have rejected me, that I should not reign over them. [8] According to all the works which they have done since the day that I brought them up out of Egypt even unto this day, wherewith they have forsaken me, and served other gods, so do they also unto thee. [9] Now therefore hearken unto their voice: howbeit yet protest solemnly unto them, and shew them the manner of the king that shall reign over them. [10] And Samuel told all the words of the LORD unto the people that asked of him a king. [11] And he said, This will be the manner of the king that shall reign over you: He will take your sons, and appoint *them* for himself, for his chariots, and *to be* his horsemen; and *some* shall run before his chariots. [12] And he will appoint him captains over thousands, and captains over fifties; and *will set them* to ear his ground, and to reap his harvest, and to make his instruments of war, and instruments of his chariots. [13] And he will take your daughters *to be* confectionaries, and *to be* cooks, and *to be* bakers. [14] And he will take your fields, and your vineyards, and your oliveyards, *even* the best *of them*, and give *them* to his servants. [15] And he will take the tenth of your seed, and of your vineyards, and give to his officers, and to his servants. [16] And he will take your menservants, and your maidservants, and your goodliest young men, and your asses, and put *them* to his work. [17] He will take the tenth of your sheep: and ye shall be his servants. [18] And ye shall cry out in that day because of your king which ye shall have chosen you; and the LORD will not hear you in that day. [19] Nevertheless the people refused to obey the voice of Samuel; and they said, Nay; but we will have a king over us; [20] That we also may be like all the nations; and that our king may judge us, and go out before us, and fight our battles" (I Samuel 8:4-20).

The intent of the Theocracy was that God intended to govern His redeemed directly through His Law. When they refused, He continued to pursue this avenue of His sovereignty in the *Rule of Law* through an appointed priesthood. When the nation of Israel added their desire for a king like all of the other nations, they rejected the direct sovereignty of God over them. Instead, they wanted another *in-betweener* between them and. This was not God's will, but He allowed it. He gave them what they demanded along with the just desserts of their demand. At this point, Israel became a Theonomy.

The difference between a Theocracy and a Theonomy is the transition from God's governance of Law *over His redeemed* directly through His Word and through an ordained priesthood. This resulted in changing to God's governance of Law *over a society, nation, or group of nations* through an established government usually through a king, political leader, or developed organization with multilateral input.

Israel evolved into a Theonomy through the progressive rejection of God's will. God allowed this, but He wanted a more intimate and direct relationship with His people.

The restoration of the Theocracy is a major aspect of God's intended sovereign rule over His creation through the lives of His redeemed. The restoration of this Theocracy is also a major part of the incarnation and the coming of the promised Messiah. It is into this context of the *restoration of dominion* through a Theocracy with Jesus as the High Priest, and a new priesthood as His *sovereignty of priests* of all Church Age believers, that God would provide a *new beginning*. This *new beginning* would begin at the second coming of Christ at the beginning of the Kingdom Age.

However, before this *new beginning* for the restoration of the Theocracy could come into existence, Jesus needed to be born of a virgin and live a sinless life. He needed to be substitutionally crucified to bear the sins of the whole world in His body to propitiate God. He needed to be buried, resurrected, and glorified to ascend to the right hand of the Father in Heaven. From that exalted position, our new High Priest lives to mediate between the Father and believers and to examine, test, and qualify Church Age believers as His new *kingdom of priests*. This is the substance of Isaiah 9:1-7 in the prophetic announcement of the birth of Messiah and His ultimate reign as Prophet, High Priest, and King. We must see this restoration of the Theocracy "in Christ" and the *testing/proving/qualifying* of individual believers for a new priesthood as the central purpose of the time span we know as the Church Age.

"[1] Nevertheless the dimness *shall* not *be* such as *was* in her vexation, when at the first he lightly afflicted the land of Zebulun and the land of Naphtali, and afterward did more grievously afflict *her by* the way of the sea, beyond Jordan, in Galilee of the nations. [2] The people that walked in darkness have seen a great light: they that dwell in the land of the shadow of death, upon them hath the light shined. [3] Thou hast multiplied the nation, *and* not increased the joy: they joy before thee according to the joy in harvest, *and* as *men* rejoice when they divide the spoil. [4] For thou hast broken the yoke of his burden, and the staff of his shoulder, the rod of his oppressor, as in the day of Midian. [5] For every battle of the warrior *is* with confused noise, and garments rolled in blood; but *this* shall be with burning *and* fuel of fire. [6] For unto us a child is born, unto us a son is given: and the government {*misrah = empire, referring to a Theocracy; this comes from the Hebrew word sarah, which means to prevail connecting to the power that comes from that prevailing victory*} shall be upon his shoulder: and his name shall be called Wonderful, Counsellor, The mighty God, The everlasting Father, The Prince of Peace. [7] Of the increase of *his* government and peace *there shall be* no end {*infinite or eternal*}, upon the throne of David, and upon his kingdom, to order it, and to establish it with judgment and with justice from henceforth even for ever {*infinite or eternal*}. The zeal of the LORD of hosts will perform this {*i.e., this will not be accomplished by human efforts such as Amillennialism or the political activism of Theonomic Reconstructionism*}" (Isaiah 9:1-7).

When a sinner calls on the Name of the LORD Jesus to save his soul from condemnation, he is immediately and supernaturally connected to the spiritual dynamic of God's glorious purpose detailed in Isaiah 9:1-7. This *spiritual dynamic* to which all true believers are connected through the New Birth does not end with the virgin birth of the promised Messiah. Therefore, although we can celebrate the virgin birth of the Promised One, it is not His birth that opens the *door* to our New Birth. His death, burial, resurrection, and glorification are what make Jesus the "door" into the New Genesis "by grace through faith."

Secondly, for the vast majority who celebrate the birth of the Messiah, most are still lost and on their way to an eternity of hopeless despair and endless torment. This is their destiny because they have never heard or understood the Gospel. They have never responded to God's gracious offer of redemption. They have never repented of sin, believed the objective facts of the Gospel, confessed Jesus as JEHOVAH, called on His Name to save them, and received the impartation of God-kind righteousness by receiving Christ in the person of the indwelling Holy Spirit of God. Although they celebrate the birth of Messiah, they remain disconnected to the *spiritual dynamic* of the hope of salvation and their own future glorification. Many have been deceived and misplaced their faith in their own works (Moralism and/or Ritualism) producing a false hope.

> "[21] Not every one that saith unto me, Lord, Lord, shall enter into the kingdom of heaven; but he that doeth the will of my Father which is in heaven. [22] Many will say to me in that day, Lord, Lord, have we not prophesied in thy name? and in thy name have cast out devils? and in thy name done many wonderful works? [23] And then will I profess unto them, I never knew you: depart from me, ye that work iniquity" (Matthew 7:21-23).

There is no deception more subtle than self-deception, for when we are self-deceived we stop looking for the truth.

The greatest self-deception is to convince ourselves that we have an eternal hope without having laid the foundation for that hope in the objective facts of the Gospel of Jesus Christ and without evaluating whether or not we have made a biblically defined response of faith in those objective facts.

Whatever aspect of the Theocracy that the local church fulfills under the headship of Christ and the priesthood of the believer, we can be confident that this aspect of the theocracy cannot be fulfilled apart from the enabling grace of God and the *filling* of the believer priest by the Spirit of God. The congregational polity of a local church is a Theocracy and a major aspect of the moral responsibility of every person who claims to be "born again" of the Spirit of God.

DISCUSSION QUESTIONS

1. Discuss the details of the Theocracy in the extensive substance of the Priesthood of all Church Age believers over the semblance (type) in the Levitical Priesthood.

2. Explain the difference between a Theocracy and a Theonomy.

3. Read I Samuel 8:4-20 and discuss why and how this text details Israel's transitioning from a Theocracy to a Theonomy.

4. Discuss why establishing a Theocracy is a major part of the incarnational purpose of Jesus Christ as the substance of Isaiah 9:1-7 in the prophetic announcement of the birth of Messiah and His ultimate reign as Prophet, High Priest, and King.

5. Explain the meaning of the words "the government" in Isaiah 9:6.

6. What is the major purpose of the Church Age regarding Jesus as High Priest and all "born again" believers of the Church Age becoming a *sovereignty of priests* in the Kingdom Age?

7. Discuss why *there is no deception more subtle than self-deception.*

Chapter Forty-five
The Incarnation of the Theanthropic Christ

A foundational truth of Scripture is the *two natures* of Jesus. He is both fully God by nature and fully man by nature. That is essentially what the word *theanthropic* means. In the body of Jesus *housed* both the Person of God (Deity) and a New and Last Adam (humanity).

"For it pleased *the Father* that in him should all fulness dwell" (Colossians 1:19).

"For in him dwelleth all the fulness of the Godhead bodily" (Colossians 2:9).

To deny the *theanthropicity* of Christ is to deny the very essence of God's glorious purpose in the redemption of fallen mankind and the restoration of sovereignty ("dominion") to mankind. If either the Deity of Christ or His humanity is not true than all of Christianity falls, for it is upon the reality of the *theanthropicity* of Christ that all of these issues depend.

"[12] For the word of God *is* quick, and powerful, and sharper than any twoedged sword, piercing even to the dividing asunder of soul and spirit, and of the joints and marrow, and *is* a discerner of the thoughts and intents of the heart. [13] Neither is there any creature that is not manifest in his sight: but all things *are* naked and opened unto the eyes of him with whom we have to do. [14] Seeing then that we have a great high priest, that is passed into the heavens, Jesus the Son of God, let us hold fast *our* profession. [15] For we have not an high priest which cannot be touched with the feeling of our infirmities; but was in all points tempted like as *we are, yet* without sin. [16] Let us therefore come boldly unto the throne of grace, that we may obtain mercy, and find grace to help in time of need. [1] For every high priest taken from among men is ordained for men in things *pertaining* to God, that he may offer both gifts and sacrifices for sins: [2] Who can have compassion on the ignorant, and on them that are out of the way; for that he himself also is compassed with infirmity. [3] And by reason hereof he ought, as for the people, so also for himself, to offer for sins. [4] And no man taketh this honour unto himself, but he that is called of God, as *was* Aaron. ⁵ <u>So also Christ</u> <u>glorified not himself to be made an high priest; but he that said unto</u> <u>him, Thou art my Son, to day have I begotten thee</u>. ⁶ As he saith also in another *place*, Thou *art* a priest for ever after the order of Melchisedec. ⁷ Who in the days of his flesh, when he had offered up prayers and supplications with strong crying and tears unto him that was able to save him from death, and was heard in that he feared; ⁸ Though he were a Son, yet learned he obedience by the things which he suffered; ⁹ And being made perfect, he became the author of eternal salvation unto all them that obey him; ¹⁰ Called of God an high priest after the order of Melchisedec. ¹¹ Of whom we have many things to say, and hard to be uttered, seeing ye are dull of hearing" (Hebrews 4:12-5:11).

Both the High Priesthood of Christ and the priesthood of all believers "in Christ" are also dependent upon the reality of the *theanthropicity* of Christ. There is undoubtedly no greater expression of the grace of God and the love of God than the birth of Jehovah through the womb of a virgin woman named Mary. It is also undoubtedly true that it is an *impossibility* for finite man to comprehend the scope of the infinite truth of God's purposes in the incarnation. This is what is referred to in Hebrews 5:11 by the words "hard to be uttered." These things are very difficult to understand. Yet, obviously God wants us to try to understand them and He wants us to try *really hard*. We know this because of the fact He has given us so much detail ("many things to say") in so much Scripture from cover to cover.

We have the four gospels of Jesus Christ emphasizing the *theanthropic* Christ as detailed in the Scofield Reference Bible.

1. The Gospel of Matthew gives us the genealogy from Abraham through David to emphasize Christ's connection and fulfillment of the Abrahamic Covenant and connects Him to the fulfillment of the Davidic Covenant and the Palestinian Covenant as "the Branch of David" (Isaiah 11:1; Jer. 23:5; 33:15) "the seed of David according to the flesh" (Rom. 1:3).

2. The Gospel of Mark emphasizes the servanthood of Christ as Jehovah's "Servant, the Branch" (Zech. 3:8) with "Messiah's humiliation and obedience unto death according to Isa. 52:13-15." Therefore, Mark gives no genealogy of Christ.

3. The Gospel of Luke gives us the genealogy of Christ from the first Adam emphasizing that He is the "man who is the Branch" (Zech. 6:12-13) emphasizing the character of Christ " 'as Son of man,' the 'last Adam,' the 'second Man' (I Cor. 15:45-47), reigning as Priest-King over the earth in the dominion given to and lost by the first Adam."

4. The Gospel of John emphasizes the Deity of Christ as "the Branch of Jehovah" (Isa. 4:2), "that is, the 'Immanuel' character of Christ (Isa. 7:14) to be fully manifested to restored and converted Israel after His return in divine glory (Mt. 25:31)." Since John emphasizes the deity of Christ, he includes no genealogy.[18]

Christ was born to be a new *theanthropic* High Priest and to create a new *theanthropic* priesthood of all New Covenant believers through their indwelling by the Holy Spirit of God. Jesus was not merely born to occupy a human body, with a human soul and a human nature for thirty-three years. When He was resurrected and glorified, He was resurrected and glorified *in that human body*, with a human soul, and a human spirit, and He will live in that glorified human body with its human soul, and human spirit for all of eternity. Although the sinless humanity of Jesus is immeasurably important to His purpose, what He came to accomplish could not have been fulfilled apart from His being truly God, for almost all prophecy speaks of the incarnation of Jehovah and therefore, can only be fulfilled through the incarnation of Jehovah.

The *theanthropic* Christ also connects to five Covenants. The *theanthropic* Christ defines the substance of Christ that dwells within the believer through the *indwelling* of the Spirit of God. The *theanthropic* Christ explains the release of the *Christ-life* through the believer through the *filling* of the Spirit of God thereby creating the *theanthropic* priesthood of all believers through the "unity of the Spirit in the bond of peace" (Ephesians 4:3).

1. The Before Time Covenant (Revelation 13:8, Titus 1:2; II Timothy 1:1 and 9)

2. The Adamic Covenant and therefore to Adam in the Protevangelium (Genesis 3:15)

3. The Abrahamic Covenant in that through the incarnation of Jehovah "shall all families of the earth be blessed" (Genesis 12:3, the Abrahamic Covenant was actually between God the Father and His eternal Son, Galatians 3:6-18)

---

[18] Scofield, C.I. *Scofield Reference Bible.* Edited by Rev. C.I. Scofield. (New York, New York: Oxford University Press, Inc., 1996), pages 716-717

4. The Palestinian Covenant and the restoration of the nation of Israel at His Second Advent

5. The Davidic Covenant as the glorified God/man returns at the Second Advent to occupy the throne of David as Prophet, High Priest, and King of kings

There are four major events in the life of the *theanthropic* Christ that were necessary in fulfilling the Law that was necessary before Christ could be acceptable to propitiate God as a perfect sacrifice for sin. Lewis Sperry Chafer gives us these four fulfilled events:

"There were three appointed events in the life of a male child in Israel – *circumcision* at the time he was eight days old (Lev. 12:3), *presentation* at the time he was forty days old (Lev.12:4-7), and *confirmation* at twelve years of age (Ex. 34:23; 23:17) – and the male children began to be numbered at twelve years of age. In the case of the male child appointed to public service there was a recognition and consecration when the appointed service began, but not until the man was at least thirty years of age (Num. 4:3). . .

Thus the theanthropic Person entered the human family. His advent – the importance of which is knowledge-surpassing – had been anticipated throughout the sacred Scriptures by all the prophets and seers. That expectation traces Him from the Protevangelium of Genesis 3:15 to His return to the earth in glory. He is the blessing of all nations in the Abrahamic Covenant, the Shiloh of the tribe of Judah, the everlasting King on David's throne, and the virgin-born son foreseen by Isaiah. It is the burden of each of the two major passages which predict His birth that He should be born in the Davidic line and sit on David's throne forever (cf. Isa. 9:6-7; Luke 1:31-33). Of the two great divine purposes – one for the earth centered in Israel and one for heaven centered in the Church – Christ is the Executor and Consummator of each. As the everlasting occupant of David's throne, the whole earth shall be filled with His glory. As the Lamb whose blood of redemption was shed and who arose from the dead, He became the First-Born among many brethren, which company He is bringing unto heaven's glory. Now He became a son in a fivefold sense – the Son of Adam, the Son of Abraham, the Son of David, the Son of Mary, and the Son of God."[19]

---

[19] Ibid., page 53.

This leads us to the next event in the life of the *theanthropic* Christ; i.e., His baptism. This event is important to every Church Age believer because it is through His baptism that the *theanthropic* Christ is connected and installed in His new *Melchisedecan Priesthood* as a new heavenly High Priest who would offer Himself to propitiate God for "*the sins* of the whole world" (I John 2:2). We must understand that the baptism of the *theanthropic* Christ was to physically signify the acceptability of His sanctification before God. The baptism of the *theanthropic* Christ was His consecration to present Himself to serve God in the capacity of God's new High Priest. The sinless God/man was God's ONLY acceptable offering for the remission of the penalty of sin to "whosoever" calls "upon the name of the Lord" to be saved.

"[7] But when he saw many of the Pharisees and Sadducees come to his baptism, he said unto them, O generation of vipers, who hath warned you to flee from the wrath to come? [8] Bring forth therefore fruits meet for repentance: [9] And think not to say within yourselves, We have Abraham to *our* father: for I say unto you, that God is able of these stones to raise up children unto Abraham. [10] And now also the axe is laid unto the root of the trees: therefore every tree which bringeth not forth good fruit is hewn down, and cast into the fire. [11] I indeed baptize you with water unto repentance: but he that cometh after me is mightier than I, whose shoes I am not worthy to bear: he shall baptize you with the Holy Ghost, and *with* fire: [12] Whose fan *is* in his hand, and he will throughly purge his floor, and gather his wheat into the garner; but he will burn up the chaff with unquenchable fire. [13] Then cometh Jesus from Galilee to Jordan unto John, to be baptized of him. [14] But John forbad him, saying, I have need to be baptized of thee, and comest thou to me? [15] And Jesus answering said unto him, Suffer *it to be so* now: for thus it becometh us to fulfil all righteousness. Then he suffered him. [16] And Jesus, when he was baptized, went up straightway out of the water: and, lo, the heavens were opened unto him, and he saw the Spirit of God descending like a dove, and lighting upon him: [17] And lo a voice from heaven, saying, This is my beloved Son, in whom I am well pleased" (Matthew 3:7-17).

"[29] The next day John seeth Jesus coming unto him, and saith, Behold the Lamb of God, which taketh away the sin of the world. [30] This is he of whom I said, After me cometh a man which is preferred before me: for he was before me. [31] And I knew him not: but that he should be made manifest to Israel, therefore am I come baptizing with water. [32] And John bare record, saying, <u>I saw the Spirit descending from heaven like a dove, and it abode upon him.</u> [33] And I knew him not: but he that sent me to baptize with water, the same said unto me, <u>Upon whom thou shalt see the Spirit descending, and remaining on him, the same is he which baptizeth with the Holy Ghost.</u> [34] And I saw, and bare record that this is the Son of God. [35] Again the next day after John stood, and two of his disciples; [36] And looking upon Jesus as he walked, he saith, Behold the Lamb of God (John 1:29-36)!

> As we look at John 1:29-36, the believer needs to learn to think *spiritually*. To think *spiritually* is not looking at the text in some *mystical way* or in some *metaphysical way*. Thinking *spiritually* is seeing and understanding what is happening in the invisible spiritual realm of God's existence. We can only comprehend the physical with our physical senses.

For instance, if you would have lived at the time of the crucifixion of Christ and stood before the Cross to see Jesus die, you would have a clear and accurate understanding of the historical crucifixion and the events of that day. You would be able to describe them in detail. However, it would require you to have and understand the inspired Words of God in order to in any way grasp the spiritual accomplishments of the death, burial, and resurrection of Christ. These spiritual accomplishments could not be visibly seen or comprehended in any way through sight, touch, taste, smell, or even your emotions. Although the physical is important in its relationship to the spiritual, we do not understand the spiritual through the physical senses.

"[9] But as it is written, Eye hath not seen, nor ear heard, neither have entered into the heart of man, the things which God hath prepared for them that love him. [10] But God hath revealed *them* unto us by his Spirit: for the Spirit searcheth all things, yea, the deep things of God. [11] For what man knoweth the things of a man, save the spirit of man which is in him? even so the things of God knoweth no man, but the Spirit of God. [12] Now we have received, not the spirit of the world, but the spirit which is of God; that we might know the things that are freely given to us of God. [13] Which things also we speak, not in the words which man's wisdom teacheth, but which the Holy

Ghost teacheth; comparing spiritual things with spiritual. [14] But the natural man receiveth not the things of the Spirit of God: for they are foolishness unto him: neither can he know *them*, because they are spiritually discerned. [15] But he that is spiritual judgeth all things, yet he himself is judged of no man. [16] For who hath known the mind of the Lord, that he may instruct him? But we have the mind of Christ" (I Corinthians 2:9-16).

Therefore, as we look at the historical account of the physical baptism of Jesus, there must be an explanation of what happened in the invisible spiritual realm of God's existence that also accompanied the physical account. If God had not revealed the spiritual aspects of this event somehow, we would not even know that these spiritual events took place. We do not know if everyone saw or heard what John saw when he baptized Jesus. We do know that John saw and heard some miraculous things that happened in the spiritual and, and least to him, became visible and audible to him.

"[16] And Jesus, when he was baptized, went up {*ascended up*} straightway {*at once*} out of the water: and, lo, the heavens were opened {*anoigo*} unto him, and he saw the Spirit of God descending like a dove, and lighting upon him: [17] And lo a voice from heaven, saying, This is my beloved Son, in whom I am well pleased" (Matthew 3:16-17).

Since Matthew records these visible spiritual events at the baptism of Jesus, Matthew was either there and saw these spiritual revelations himself or God simply described the event to him through inspired revelation of the Words of God, and Matthew recorded those Words. The Gospel of Mark uses a different word that gives a different description of what Matthew says "the heavens were opened." The KJV translates the word Mark uses as "opened," but it is actually a different Greek word. Mark also gives us other added details to the spiritual events surrounding the baptism of Jesus. Therefore, John Mark was either at the baptism of Jesus and personally saw these spiritual revelations or he received them by the revelation of God.

"[9] And it came to pass {*as the fulfillment of prophecy*} in those days, that Jesus came from Nazareth of Galilee, and was baptized of John in Jordan. [10] And straightway coming up out of the water, he saw the heavens opened {*schizo, to divide, split, or cleave*}, and the

Spirit like a {*similar to a*} dove descending {*through the opening in the heavens*} upon him {*while He was ascending*}: [11] And there came a voice from heaven, *saying*, Thou art my beloved Son, in whom I am well pleased. [12] And immediately the Spirit driveth {*pluck Him out and transported*} him into the wilderness. [13] And he was there in the wilderness forty days, tempted of Satan; and was with the wild beasts; and the angels ministered unto him" (Mark 1:9-13).

The miraculous events that become apparent to us through the inspired Words of God are not merely intended to amaze us. These miraculous events reveal to us the merging of the material, physical realm of humanity with the eternal, spiritual realm of God's existence. Spiritual beings transcending into the material world has been going on since the beginning of time. Before the fall, these spiritual beings may have been visible to Adam and Eve or they may not have been. God may have been visible to Adam and Eve, or He may not have been visible. We just do not know. However, we do know that throughout history God has visibly manifested Himself in various ways to numerous people.

The transitional issue of the *theanthropic* Christ in the life of a believer is that the manifestation of the merging of the physical with the spiritual is transitioning to a permanent state "in Christ." This happens as the believer transitions through the indwelling of the Holy Spirit, progressive transfiguration through the filling of the Spirit, and ultimately through the glorification of the body of the believer into a new *theanthropic* existence in Christ. This transitioning of all believers into this new state of existence is a major aspect of the High Priesthood of Christ and of the priesthood of all believers. The believer is immediately connected to this dispensational transition through the birth of Messiah and through faith in the theanthropic Christ as the "door" (John 10:7-9) that Jesus becomes through His death, burial, and resurrection/glorification.

"[4] Being made so much better than the angels, as he hath by inheritance obtained a more excellent name than they. [5] For unto which of the angels said he at any time, Thou art my Son, this day have I begotten thee? And again, I will be to him a Father, and he shall be to me a Son? [6] And again, when he bringeth in the firstbegotten into the world, he saith, And let all the angels of God worship him. [7] And of the angels he saith, Who maketh his angels spirits, and his ministers a flame of fire. [8] But unto the Son *he saith*,

Thy throne, O God, *is* for ever and ever: a sceptre of righteousness *is* the sceptre of thy kingdom. [9] Thou hast loved righteousness, and hated iniquity; therefore God, *even* thy God, hath anointed thee with the oil of gladness above thy fellows. [10] And, Thou, Lord, in the beginning hast laid the foundation of the earth; and the heavens are the works of thine hands: [11] They shall perish; but thou remainest; and they all shall wax old as doth a garment; [12] And as a vesture shalt thou fold them up, and they shall be changed: but thou art the same, and thy years shall not fail. [13] But to which of the angels said he at any time, Sit on my right hand, until I make thine enemies thy footstool? [14] Are they not all ministering spirits, sent forth to minister for them who shall be heirs of salvation" (Hebrews 1:5-14)?

In Hebrews 1:5-14, God uses seven Old Testament Scriptures to elaborate on the Deity of Jesus Christ. These statements and corresponding verses are as follows:

1. Hebrews 1:5: "Thou art my Son, this day have I begotten thee?" (Quoted from Psalm 2:7)
2. Hebrews 1:5: "I will be to him a Father, and he shall be to me a Son?" (Quoted from II Samuel 7:14)
3. Hebrews 1:6: "When he bringeth in the firstbegotten into the world, he saith, And let all the angels of God worship him." (Refers to what is said in Psalm 97:7)
4. Hebrews 1:8: "Thy throne, O God, *is* for ever and ever: a sceptre of righteousness *is* the sceptre of thy kingdom." (Quoted from Psalm 45:6)
5. Hebrews 1:9: "Thou hast loved righteousness, and hated iniquity; therefore God, *even* thy God, hath anointed thee with the oil of gladness above thy fellows." (Quoted from Psalm 45:7)
6. Hebrews 1:10-12: "[10] And, Thou, Lord, in the beginning hast laid the foundation of the earth; and the heavens are the works of thine hands: [11] They shall perish; but thou remainest; and they all shall wax old as doth a garment; [12] And as a vesture shalt thou fold them up, and they shall be changed: but thou art the same, and thy years shall not fail." (Quoted from Psalm 102:25-27)
7. Hebrews 1:13: "Sit on my right hand, until I make thine enemies thy footstool?" (Quoted from Psalm 110:1)

The words "this day" in Hebrews 1:5 are from the Greek word *semeron* (say'-mer-on). Alford refers "this day" to the *eternal* generation of the Son - the day in which the Son was begotten by the

Father is an everlasting *to-day*. There never was a yesterday or past time to Him, nor a tomorrow or future time. "Nothing there is to come, and nothing past, but an eternal NOW doth ever last." The communication of the theanthropic essence in its fullness, involves eternal generation, for the divine essence has no beginning.

> "Who hath ascended up into heaven, or descended? who hath gathered the wind in his fists? who hath bound the waters in a garment? who hath established all the ends of the earth? what *is* his name, and what *is* his son's name, if thou canst tell" (Proverbs 30:4)?

Yet the context of Hebrews 1:4 refers to a definite point in time, namely, that of His having entered the *inheritance*. Jesus "obtained a more excellent name than" the angels. Although the Son of God has been who He is eternally (without beginning or end), Jesus obtained, by right of inheritance, a more excellent name than the angels through His incarnation, death, burial, and resurrection from the dead. In doing so, He becomes the new theanthropic Federal Head of Creation, "Lord of lords and King of kings." Therefore, this primarily refers to the "day" of the resurrection of Jesus the Christ.

> "[28] And though they found no cause of death *in him*, yet desired they Pilate that he should be slain. [29] And when they had fulfilled all that was written of him, they took *him* down from the tree, and laid *him* in a sepulchre. [30] But God raised him from the dead: [31] And he was seen many days of them which came up with him from Galilee to Jerusalem, who are his witnesses unto the people. [32] And we declare unto you glad tidings, how that the promise which was made unto the fathers, [33] God hath fulfilled the same unto us their children, in that he hath raised up Jesus again; as it is also written in the second psalm, Thou art my Son, this day have I begotten thee" (Acts 13:28-33).

The third reference is Hebrews 1:6. It refers to what is said in Psalm 97:1-7; specifically verse seven. The context refers to the second coming of Messiah in glory at Armageddon.

> "[1] The LORD reigneth; let the earth rejoice; let the multitude of isles be glad *thereof*. [2] Clouds and darkness *are* round about him: righteousness and judgment *are* the habitation of his throne. [3] A fire goeth before him, and burneth up his enemies round about. [4] His lightnings enlightened the world: the earth saw, and trembled. [5] The hills melted like wax at the presence of the LORD, at the presence of the Lord of the whole earth. [6] The heavens declare his

righteousness, and all the people see his glory. [7] Confounded be all they that serve graven images, that boast themselves of idols: worship him, all *ye* gods" (Psalm 97:1-7).

These verses are written in what is referred to as the *Prophetic Perfect*. That means they refer to a future event as if it has already happened. The word "gods" of Psalm 97:7 is from the Hebrew word *'elohiym* (el-o-heem'). It was used to refer to beings or things that were *godlike*. In this context, and as the New Testament quote in Hebrews 1:6 supports, it was also a word used to refer to angels.

The fourth reference is found in Hebrews 1: 8; "Thy throne, O God, *is* for ever and ever: a sceptre of righteousness *is* the sceptre of thy kingdom." This is quoted from Psalm 45:6:

> "Thy throne, O God, *is* for ever and ever: the sceptre of thy kingdom *is* a right sceptre."

When the verse says "the scepter of thy kingdom is a right scepter," the word "right" is from the Hebrew *miyshor* (mee-shore'). It refers to something that is *level* or *upright*. In this context, it means something that is righteous or just. That is how the inspired writer of Hebrews quotes it.

The fifth reference is found in Hebrews 1:9; "Thou hast loved righteousness, and hated iniquity; therefore God, *even* thy God, hath anointed thee with the oil of gladness above thy fellows." This is quoted from Psalm 45:7:

> "Thou lovest righteousness, and hatest wickedness: therefore God, thy God, hath anointed thee with the oil of gladness above thy fellows."

The anointing referred to here is that which was done to consecrate (prepare and dedicate) a king or priest to his office. In reference to Jesus Christ, it refers to both King and Priest. The fact is further expanded by this anointing in that God raises the office of Jesus' Kingship and High Priesthood above that of every other king or priest that preceded Him. Some say that "above thy fellow" refers to angels. Although the context might support this, the more natural meaning would refer to other kings, rulers, and priests within the new theanthropic existence of the glorified Church Age believers during the Kingdom Age.

The sixth reference is found in Hebrews 1:10-12; "[10] And, Thou, Lord, in the beginning hast laid the foundation of the earth; and the heavens are the works of thine hands: [11] They shall perish; but thou remainest; and they all shall wax old as doth a garment; [12] And as a vesture shalt thou fold them up, and they shall be changed: but thou art the same, and thy years shall not fail." This is quoted from Psalm 102:25-27:

> "[25] Of old hast thou laid the foundation of the earth: and the heavens *are* the work of thy hands. [26] They shall perish, but thou shalt endure: yea, all of them shall wax old like a garment; as a vesture shalt thou change them, and they shall be changed: [27] But thou *art* the same, and thy years shall have no end."

The word "and," which starts Hebrews 1:10, is adding another testimony of Scripture to those already given regarding the superiority of the theanthropic Christ over the prophets and angels. The inspired writer of Hebrews adds the words "thou, Lord" to clarify the meaning of Psalm 102:25.

Clearly, Psalm 102:25-27 is a specific reference to Jehovah. Similarly, the epistle to the Hebrews clearly establishes that Jesus is the incarnate theanthropic Jehovah. This follows the context of Hebrews 1:4-14 as it is intended to establish the exalted character, person, and position of the theanthropic Jesus Christ. There is no character, person, or position higher than that of Jehovah. It is apparent that Psalm 102:25-27 refers to Jehovah and that this was the prevailing interpretation by the Jews at the time of Christ.

The seventh reference establishing the deity of Jesus and the theanthropic Christ is found in Hebrews 1:13; "Sit on my right hand, until I make thine enemies thy footstool?" It is quoted from Psalm 110:1:

> "The LORD said unto my Lord, Sit thou at my right hand, until I make thine enemies thy footstool" (Psalm 110:1).

Jesus uses this verse to challenge the theology of the scribes and Pharisees in Matthew chapter twenty-two.

> "[42] Saying, What think ye of Christ? whose son is he? They say unto him, *The Son* of David. [43] He saith unto them, How then doth David in spirit call him Lord, saying, [44] The LORD said unto my Lord, Sit thou on my right hand, till I make thine enemies thy footstool? [45] If David then call him Lord, how is he his son? [46] And no man was

able to answer him a word, neither durst any *man* from that day forth ask him any more *questions*" (Matthew 22:42-46).

The Apostle Peter used this reference to refer to Jesus in his great message on the day of Pentecost in Acts chapter two.

"[32] This Jesus hath God raised up, whereof we all are witnesses. [33] Therefore being by the right hand of God exalted, and having received of the Father the promise of the Holy Ghost, he hath shed forth this, which ye now see and hear. [34] For David is not ascended into the heavens: but he saith himself, The LORD said unto my Lord, Sit thou on my right hand, [35] Until I make thy foes thy footstool. [36] Therefore let all the house of Israel know assuredly, that God hath made that same Jesus, whom ye have crucified, both Lord and Christ" (Acts 2:32-36).

"[10] For it became him {*it was suitable or fitting*}, for whom *are* all things, and by whom *are* all things, in bringing {*ago; to lead or bring with*} many sons unto glory, to make the captain {*archegos, chief leader referring to His High Priestly work in both the offering of Himself as the propitiatory sacrifice to God and as the Advocate for the redeemed*} of their salvation perfect through sufferings. [11] For both he that sanctifieth and they who are sanctified *are* all of one {*in the sense of a theanthropic family in "the regeneration," Matthew 19:28*}: for which cause he is not ashamed to call them brethren {*adelphos, union of the womb*}, [12] Saying, I will declare thy name unto my brethren, in the midst of the church will I sing praise unto thee. [13] And again, I will put my trust in him. And again, Behold I and the children which God hath given me. [14] Forasmuch then as the children {*who are also spiritual beings after being "born again" of the Spirit*} are partakers of flesh and blood, he {*the eternal Son of God who was pure Spirit*} also himself likewise took part of the same {*becoming a theanthropic Being*}; that through death he might destroy him that had the power of death, that is, the devil; [15] And deliver them {*into a new theanthropic existence*} who through fear of death were all their lifetime subject to bondage. [16] For verily he took not on *him the nature of* angels {*His purpose was not to create a new theanthropic existence for angels.*}; but he took on *him* the seed of Abraham. [17] Wherefore in all things it behoved him to be made like unto *his* brethren, that he might be a merciful and faithful high priest in things *pertaining* to God, to make reconciliation for the sins of the people. [18] For in that he himself hath suffered being tempted, he is able to succour them that are tempted" (Hebrews 2:10-18).

DISCUSSION QUESTIONS

1. Explain the word *theanthropic* as it refers to the humanity of Jesus and the Deity of Jesus uniting the *two natures* of Jesus.

2. Explain why the following statement is true: "If either the deity of Christ or His humanity is not true, then all of Christianity falls, for it is upon the reality of the *theanthropicity* of Christ that all of these issues depend."

3. Explain why the High Priesthood of Christ and the priesthood of all believers "in Christ" are also dependent upon the reality of the *theanthropicity* of Christ.

4. List and define the five covenants of God to which the *theanthropic* Christ connects all believers.

5. List and discuss the four major events in the life of the *theanthropic* Christ. These four events were necessary in fulfilling the Law, which fulfillment was necessary before Christ could be acceptable to propitiate God as a perfect sacrifice for sin.

6. Discuss the significance of the baptism of Jesus as it relates to His new position as High Priest of new *Melchisedecan Priesthood*. Also discuss how this defines the fourth necessity in the life of the *theanthropic* Christ that was necessary in fulfilling the Law before Christ could be acceptable to propitiate God as a perfect sacrifice for sin.

7. The very title Jesus Christ merges the humanity of Jesus with the deity of Jesus. Together these two words exemplify the *theanthropicity* of Jesus. In Hebrews 1:5-14, God uses seven Old Testament Scriptures to elaborate on the deity of Jesus Christ in *theanthropic union* with His humanity. List each of these Old Testament references and discuss how each text establishes the *theanthropicity* of Jesus Christ.

Chapter Forty-six

The Gift of Grace: Seldom Opened and Seldom Used

For centuries Christianity has been progressively reduced to a *pie in the sky* kind of idea with salvation being some kind of *reward* for being one of the *good guys*. Salvation is not a reward. Salvation is a gift given "by grace" and received "through faith." Salvation is not a *pie in the sky* kind of thing either. Salvation is a present reality of a *new existence* "in Christ" that begins the moment a sinner receives God's gift of grace "through faith." Eternal life is much more than life that goes on forever and never ceases. Eternal life is a *new kind of life* lived in a *new existence* called "grace." This is part of a *New Creation* that begins the moment we repent, understand and believe the gospel, confess Jesus to be Jehovah, call on His name to save us, and receive Him (the *Christ-life*) in the indwelling Holy Spirit of God. This *new existence* and *New Creation* moves the believer into a life of unlimited potential through the release of the creative power of God through us.

The vast majority of professing Christians are hoping for a *pie in the sky* reward for being *good boys and girls*. They will enter into eternity with a false hope. There they will discover they have been deceived by false teachers and have misplaced their faith in "another gospel, which is not another." That is a very sad reality that every truly "born again" believer must try to correct by proclaiming the truth of the true Gospel that alone is the "power of God unto salvation."

Those truly "born again" of the Spirit of God have received God's gift of the *New Creation* "in Christ." However, many of these too have been deceived into thinking their salvation gift will not be opened unto them until after they die. Therefore, they presently possess a gift they have never opened. They have a *new existence* in a *New Creation* although they have never really lived in the intended supernatural spiritual dynamic of that *new existence* called *grace*. Until we understand the spiritual dynamic of our *new existence* "in Christ," the gift of salvation that is presently our possession will remain unopened for all of our lifetimes. Because the gift remains unopened, our new lives "in Christ" will be wasted in being able to fulfill the purpose for which they are intended; i.e., to win souls and make disciples in order to bring glory to God through the fruit of His Spirit.

"[1] Therefore <u>being</u> {*lit., having been*} <u>justified by faith, we have peace with God</u> through our Lord Jesus Christ: [2] By whom {*Jesus Christ as our theanthropic High Priest at the right hand of the Father seated upon the Mercy Seat in Heaven*} also <u>we have access by faith into this grace wherein we stand</u>, and rejoice in hope of the glory of God. [3] And not only *so*, but <u>we glory in tribulations also</u>: knowing that tribulation worketh patience; [4] And patience, experience; and experience, hope: [5] And hope maketh not ashamed; because <u>the love of God is shed abroad in our hearts by the Holy Ghost</u> which is given unto us" (Romans 5:1-5).

Romans 5:1-5 gives us a look inside the gift of grace that we know as *salvation*. As we look inside the gift, we immediately see that there are many aspects that are ours that we would never realize unless we actually open the gift. Like the child that finds a bicycle on his birthday with a big bow on it, he is not excited about just *having* the bicycle. He is excited about what he will be able to *do* with the bicycle once he takes off the bow. Most truly "born again" Christians never get excited about their salvation because they have never opened the package to see what is theirs and they never study the Scriptures to find out what they can actually do with the gift that is given to them in this *New Creation*. Notice five *gifts* within the *gift* of salvation (uniquely the number five is the number of grace).

1. "*having been* justified by faith"
2. "we have peace with God"
3. "we have access by faith into this grace wherein we stand"
4. "we glory in tribulations also"
5. "the love of God is shed abroad in our hearts by the Holy Ghost which is given unto us"

From these five gifts within the gift of salvation, the Apostle Paul *begins to open* each of these gifts going throughout the rest of the Epistle to the Romans. As the next eleven chapters of Romans unfold, we find gifts of grace within gifts of grace within gifts of grace. This is also true of Paul's Epistle to the Ephesians.

"[1] Paul, an apostle of Jesus Christ by the will of God, to the saints which are at Ephesus, and to the faithful in Christ Jesus: [2] Grace be to you, and peace, from God our Father, and *from* the Lord Jesus Christ. [3] Blessed *be* the God and Father of our Lord Jesus Christ, who hath blessed us with all spiritual blessings in heavenly *places* in Christ: [4] According as he hath chosen us {*the Church corporately as a new priesthood*} in him before the foundation of the world, that we should be holy and without blame before him in love: [5] Having predestinated us {*the Church corporately as a new priesthood*} unto the adoption of children {*placement as adult sons positionally*} by Jesus Christ to himself, according to the good pleasure of his will, [6] To the praise of the glory of his grace, wherein {*in His grace*} he hath made us accepted in the beloved. [7] In whom we have redemption through his blood, the forgiveness of sins, according to the riches of his grace;" (Ephesians 1:1-7).

God's new priests are to be *spiritual* people. A spiritual person is a person filled with the Spirit of God and overflowing with the *Christ-life* because he is living in a right relationship with Christ ("abiding," John 15:1-8).

> A person filled with the Spirit of God is a NORMAL Christian. Every Christian that is saved and not filled with the Spirit of God is an ABNORMAL or carnal Christian.

Therefore, a *fruitless* Christian is an abnormal Christian who is not sanctified to the degree God intends him to be and not consecrated to the degree God intends him to be. It is not enough to merely control the externals, a person must be filled with the Spirit AND begin to live the Christ-life, DOING what Christ commands.

"[4] But God, who is rich in mercy, for his great love wherewith he loved us, [5] Even when we were dead in sins, hath quickened us together with Christ, (by grace ye are saved;) [6] And hath raised *us* up together, and made *us* sit together in heavenly *places* in Christ Jesus: [7] That in the ages to come he might shew the exceeding riches of his grace in *his* kindness toward us through Christ Jesus. [8] For by grace are ye saved through faith; and that not of yourselves: *it is* the gift of God: [9] Not of works, lest any man should boast. [10] For we are his workmanship {*in the New Creation of being "born again" and continuing in the supernatural enabling of the grace of God through the indwelling Holy Spirit*}, created {*referring to the new man that comes forth from the New Creation*} in Christ Jesus unto {*supernaturally enabled doing*} good works, which God hath before ordained that we should walk in them {*these supernaturally enabled works of righteousness*}" (Ephesians 2:4-10).

All the verbs in Ephesians 2:5 ("hath quickened," "hath raised," and "made us sit together") are in the aorist tense, signifying something beginning at some point in time with continuing results. These continuing results are the present and ongoing realities that are supposed to be part of the normal Spirit-filled believer's *new life* "in Christ." The outcome of this supernaturally created *new life* in Christ is an ongoing work of creation through the Spirit-filled believer in producing the fruit of "good works." These "good works" manifest the *Christ-life* in the "fruit of the Spirit" and "the work of the ministry." Again, this defines NORMAL Christianity. Anything less than this is ABNORMAL and is carnal Christianity. Paul then expands upon this context into what he says in Ephesians chapters three through six. If you miss this context, you will miss the whole purpose of the next four chapters of the Epistle to the Ephesians regarding the ministry of the Church and the New Priesthood of Christ. Paul uses himself as the *model of God's intent* for all believer-priests in the New Covenant.

"[1] For this cause {*because we, the Church, "are builded together for an habitation of God through the Spirit," Ephesians 2:22*} I Paul, the prisoner of Jesus Christ for you Gentiles, [2] If ye have heard of the dispensation of the grace of God which is given me to you-ward: [3] How that by revelation he made known unto me the mystery {*the New Creation and the supernatural enabling of the indwelling Holy Spirit*}; (as I wrote afore in few words, [4] Whereby, when ye read, ye may understand my knowledge in the mystery of Christ) [5] Which in other ages was not made known unto the sons of men, as it is now revealed unto his holy apostles and prophets by the Spirit; [6] That the Gentiles should be fellowheirs {*with the saved of true Israel*}, and of the same body, and partakers of his promise in Christ by the gospel: [7] Whereof I was made a minister, according to the gift of the grace of God given unto me by the effectual working of his power. [8] Unto me, who am less than the least of all saints, is this grace given, that I should preach among the Gentiles the unsearchable riches of Christ; [9] And to make all *men* see what *is* the fellowship of the mystery, which from the beginning of the world hath been hid in God, who created all things by Jesus Christ: [10] To the intent that now unto the principalities and powers in heavenly *places* might be known by the church the manifold wisdom of God, [11] According to the eternal purpose which he purposed in Christ Jesus our Lord: [12] In whom {*referring to the believer's Spirit baptism into the 'body of Christ' and 'the regeneration'*} we {*all believers individually and corporately as the Church*} have boldness and access {*to God's distribution center at His throne of grace, Hebrews 4:16*} with confidence by the faith {*faithfulness or fidelity*} of him {*the resurrected/glorified theanthropic High Priest who is Christ*}. [13] Wherefore I desire that ye faint not at my tribulations for you, which is your glory" (Ephesians 3:1-13).

If every believer truly lives in this new existence and spiritual dynamic that God calls "grace" (Romans 5:2), why is it that we are not seeing the "fruit" that the early Church Age believers saw and that we see in various historical revivals of this spiritual dynamic throughout history? We do not see it because most local churches have accepted standards of holiness and separation from worldliness that are far below how the Word of God defines them. Most local churches do not see revival, and the "fruit" of that revival, because they are carnal to some degree and therefore defiled before God.

There are five commandments regarding the believer's supernatural relationship with the Holy Spirit of God. These are essential to the manifestation of the *Christ-life* through a believer's life. If any one of these five commandments is broken regarding a believer's relationship with the Holy Spirit in the least way, the believer is defiled before God. Then, the "fruit" to the glory of God cannot, and will not, be produced.

Without the spiritual dynamic of the believer's supernatural relationship with the Holy Spirit of God, "fellowship" (a working partnership in "the work of the ministry") is never created, "abiding" (*hypostatic unity*) never takes place, and eternal spiritual "fruit" is never produced.

1. Be filled with the Spirit (Ephesians 5:18)
2. Grieve not the Spirit (Ephesians 4:30)
3. Quench not the Spirit (I Thessalonians 5:19)
4. Walk in the Spirit (Galatians 5:16 and 25)
5. Be transformed/transfigured (Romans 12:2)

It is through the supernatural dynamic of the believer yielding to the indwelling Spirit of God that these five commandments are fulfilled in the life of a believer. These five commandments are what defines walking "worthy of the vocation wherewith ye are called" in Ephesians 4:1 and how a believer keeps "the unity of the Spirit in the bond of peace," as discussed in Ephesians 4:2.

"[1] I therefore, the prisoner of the Lord, beseech you that ye walk worthy of the vocation wherewith ye are called, [2] With all lowliness and meekness, with longsuffering, forbearing one another in love; [3] Endeavouring to keep the unity of the Spirit in the bond of peace. [4] *There is* one body, and one Spirit, even as ye are called in one hope of your calling; [5] One Lord, one faith, one baptism, [6] One God and Father of all, who *is* above all, and through all, and in you all. [7] But unto every one of us is given grace according to the measure of the gift of Christ" (Ephesians 4:1-7).

Undoubtedly, the gift of salvation is the giving of the Holy Spirit of God (the "breath of life"). The giving of the indwelling Holy Spirit of God is the giving of the *Christ-life* (I John 5:11-12). As the believer comes to open this gift, we simply find gifts within gifts within gifts to an infinite, unimaginable, and unsearchable degree. This indwelling Holy Spirit gift is the unlimited resource of the "living water" that Christ spoke of to the Samaritan woman in John chapter four.

"[9] Then saith the woman of Samaria unto him, How is it that thou, being a Jew, askest drink of me, which am a woman of Samaria? for the Jews have no dealings with the Samaritans. [10] Jesus answered and said unto her, If thou knewest the gift of God, and who it is that saith to thee, Give me to drink; thou wouldest have asked of him, and he would have given thee living water. [11] The woman saith unto him, Sir, thou hast nothing to draw with, and the well is deep: from whence then hast thou that living water? [12] Art thou greater than our father Jacob, which gave us the well, and drank thereof himself, and his children, and his cattle? [13] Jesus answered and said unto her, Whosoever drinketh of this water shall thirst again: [14] But whosoever drinketh of the water that I shall give him shall never thirst; but the water that I shall give him shall be in him a well of water springing up into everlasting life" (John 4:9-14).

Clearly this "gift of God" of the "living water" is referring to the indwelling Holy Spirit (John 7:38-39). Paul expands upon this "gift" in Romans chapter five.

"[12] Wherefore, as by one man sin entered into the world, and death by sin; and so death passed upon all men, for that all have sinned: [13] (For until the law sin was in the world: but sin is not imputed when there is no law. [14] Nevertheless death reigned from Adam to Moses, even over them that had not sinned after the similitude of Adam's transgression, who is the figure of him that was to come. [15] But not as the offence, so also is the free gift. For if through the offence of one many be dead, much more the grace of God, and the gift by grace, which is by one man, Jesus Christ, hath abounded unto many {not all, in that the "gift" "by grace" must be received 'through faith'}. [16] And not as it was by one that sinned, so is the gift: for the judgment was by one to condemnation, but the free gift is of many offences unto justification. [17] For if by one man's offence death reigned by one; much more they which receive abundance of grace and of the gift of righteousness shall reign in life by one, Jesus Christ.) [18] Therefore as by the offence of one judgment came upon all men to condemnation; even so by the righteousness of one the free gift came upon all men unto justification of life. [19] For as by one man's disobedience many were made sinners, so by the obedience of one shall many be made righteous. [20] Moreover the law entered, that the offence might abound. But where sin abounded, grace did much more abound: [21] That as sin hath reigned unto death, even so might grace reign through righteousness unto eternal life by Jesus Christ our Lord" (Romans 5:12-21).

The important aspect of the gift of God's grace, both in salvation and in the "river of living water" that flows from the *new man* of the *New Creation* in Christ Jesus, is that God does not want us to merely receive His free gift, or even that we might open that free gift and the many gifts within each gift. God wants us to, and expects us to, *use* each aspect of the gift He has given and we have received in the unlimited depth of its unsearchable riches.

"[7] But the end of all things is at hand: be ye therefore sober, and watch unto prayer. [8] And above all things have fervent charity among yourselves: for charity shall cover the multitude of sins. [9] Use hospitality one to another without grudging. [10] As every man hath received the gift, *even so* minister the same one to another, as good stewards of the manifold grace of God. [11] If any man speak, *let him speak* as the oracles of God; if any man minister, *let him do it as*

400
WWW.DISCIPLEMAKERMINISTRIES.ORG

of the ability which God giveth: that God in all things may be glorified through Jesus Christ, to whom be praise and dominion for ever and ever. Amen" (I Peter 4:7-11).

Many times I have given someone a book I have written as a gift. My intent in giving them the book was to try to help them with a spiritual issue in their life with which they were struggling. Many times I have visited some of those people only to find the book was never opened, let alone read. They continued in the same spiritual struggle they had before I gave them the book and will most probably continue in that struggle and its outcomes for the rest of their lives. It is not enough to *open* God's Book. You will actually need to read it, study it, and learn its truths. Yet, even reading the Book will not be enough. You will also have to begin to apply those truths, live these truths, and incorporate them into your everyday practices of life. Even all of this is not enough if we want to see God produce fruit through our lives. Before this *doing* can be spiritually effective, believers will need to live these truths through the supernatural enabling of the Holy Spirit (the *filling* of the Spirit).

DISCUSSION QUESTIONS

1. Explain why it is essential to understand that salvation is not a *pie in the sky* reward and that your new life in Christ is an open door to unimaginable new potential through the indwelling Holy Spirit.

2. Explain why it can be said of most true Christians that they presently possess a gift they have never opened.

3. From your understanding of your new supernatural life available to all believers in the indwelling of the Holy Spirit, thoroughly explain the practical application of what Paul says in Romans 5:2, "we have access by faith into this grace wherein we stand, and rejoice in hope of the glory of God."

4. In Romans 5:1-5 there are five gifts within the gift of grace (supernatural enabling). List and discuss the practical ramifications of each of these five gifts.

5. Thoroughly define and discuss the *what*, *why*, and *how* of being a *spiritual person*.

6. If every believer truly lives in this *new existence* and spiritual dynamic that God calls "grace" (Romans 5:2), why is it that we are not seeing the "fruit" that the early Church Age believers saw and that we see in various historical revivals of this spiritual dynamic throughout history?

7. List and discuss the five commandments regarding the believer's supernatural relationship with the Holy Spirit of God that are essential to the manifestation of the *Christ-life* through a believer's life.

Chapter Forty-seven

Filled for a Working Fellowship

The filling of the Spirit of God is what brings the believer into a supernaturally enabled partnership with God ("fellowship") in "the work of the ministry." This supernaturally enabled partnership in "the work of the ministry" is energized by the Spirit of God as the believer obeys the five commandments necessary to a right relationship with the Holy Spirit and unity with the Godhead.

1. Be filled with the Spirit (Ephesians 5:18)
2. Grieve not the Spirit (Ephesians 4:30)
3. Quench not the Spirit (I Thessalonians 5:19)
4. Walk in the Spirit (Galatians 5:16 and 25)
5. Be transformed/transfigured (Romans 12:2)

These five commandments must be obeyed in order for God to *generate*, or *create*, a supernaturally enabled partnership with the believer in "the work of the ministry." Being *filled with* the Spirit must be connected to *walking in* the Spirit. Filling is never static or without *spiritual life*. If there is no spiritual *movement* ("walk"), there was no *filling* either. **Whatever God fills God moves!** Spiritual people "obey from the heart" and begin DOING!

God does not leave us guessing as to how these five commandments regarding the believer's relationship with the Holy Spirit are to be fulfilled. In other words, He has not told us to do something that He has not told us *how to do it*. The *how* is defined in detail in Romans 6:1 through 8:28 (as well as a number of other Scriptures). Lewis Sperry Chafer gives us an important point of focus regarding this instruction:

" . . . [R]especting the negative aspect of the spiritual life, it may be restated that each of the three foes – the world, the flesh, and the devil – can outmatch all human ability and the victory over them is gained only by the superior power of the Holy Spirit; and this success, if it is to become a reality in daily life, calls for a peculiar and altogether different plan or principle of living. The change from self-sufficiency to dependence upon the Holy Spirit is a comprehensive one; yet at no time, even when believers are fully enabled, does the Spirit of God work outside the functions of the human will, nor is a consciousness experienced that another than one's own self is acting or determining. The spiritual life does not consist in the withdrawal of self, of initiative, or of the consciousness of responsibility. 'It is God,' the Apostle declares, 'which worketh in you both to will [with your own will] and do [with your own doing] of his good pleasure' (Phil. 2:13)."[20]

Simply stated, the *reckoning* and *yielding* that Paul refers to in Romans 6:11-13 are not intended to bring the believer into a *passive relationship* with the Holy Spirit. They are intended to bring the believer into an *active, cooperative partnership* of two wills and two natures. These two wills and two natures are the Divine and the human. They are to be brought into both *union* and *unity* that will bring forth fruit to glorify God through a supernaturally enabled "work of the ministry."

The believer is filled with the Spirit to *supernaturally energize* a working partnership that the Word of God refers to as "fellowship." Take "the work of the ministry" out of "fellowship" and you have destroyed the purpose of God's supernatural enabling/filling. This is the context of God's instructions that transition through Romans 6:1 to Romans 8:28.

"[1] What shall we say then? Shall we continue in sin, that grace may abound? [2] God forbid. How shall we, that are dead to sin, live any longer therein? [3] Know ye not, that so many of us as were baptized into Jesus Christ were baptized into his death? [4] Therefore we are buried with him by baptism into death: that like as Christ was raised up from the dead by the glory of the Father, even so we also should walk in newness of life. [5] For if we have been planted together in the likeness of his death, we shall be also *in the likeness* of *his*

---

[20] Chafer, Lewis Sperry. *Systematic Theology, Volume VI*. (Dallas Texas: Dallas Seminary Press, Thirteenth Printing, June 1976), page 195.

resurrection: [6] Knowing this, that our old man is crucified with *him*, that the body of sin might be destroyed, that henceforth we should not serve sin. [7] For he that is dead is freed from sin. [8] Now if we be dead with Christ, we believe that we shall also live with him: [9] Knowing that Christ being raised from the dead dieth no more; death hath no more dominion over him. [10] For in that he died, he died unto sin once: but in that he liveth, he liveth unto God. [11] Likewise <u>reckon</u> ye also yourselves to be dead indeed unto sin, but alive unto God through Jesus Christ our Lord. [12] <u>Let not sin therefore reign</u> in your mortal body, that ye should obey it in the lusts thereof. [13] <u>Neither yield ye your members *as* instruments of unrighteousness unto sin</u>: but <u>yield yourselves unto God,</u> as those that are alive from the dead, and <u>your members *as* instruments of righteousness unto God.</u> [14] For sin shall not have dominion over you: for ye are not under the law, but under grace. [15] What then? shall we sin, because we are not under the law, but under grace? God forbid. [16] Know ye not, that to whom ye yield yourselves servants to obey, his servants ye are to whom ye obey; whether of sin unto death, or of obedience unto righteousness. [17] But God be thanked, that ye were the servants of sin, but ye **have obeyed from the heart** that form of doctrine which was delivered you. [18] Being then made free from sin {*through the filling of the Spirit*}, ye became the servants of righteousness {*living, doing, walking in the Spirit's supernatural enabling*}." (Romans 6:1-18; underlining and bolding added).

> The words "obeyed from the heart" in Romans 6:17 give us a simple statement of a new reality made possible through yielding to the indwelling Holy Spirit of God and the conditions necessary to supernatural enabling.

It is not enough to involve our physical bodies in an external form of obedience. There MUST BE a complete involvement of our beings spiritually, emotionally, and physically in this obedience. This answers the questions of Romans 6:1-3. The essence of these questions is this, since the salvation of our souls from eternal separation from God is not dependent in any way on how we live, does that mean God does not care how we live? Are we free to live any way we want to live? The answer is simply, "God forbid."

"[14] For the love of Christ constraineth us {*holds us together or compels us to unity in purpose*}; because we thus judge, that if one died for all, then were all dead: [15] And *that* he died for all, that they

405

which live should not henceforth live unto themselves, but unto him which died for them, and rose again" (II Corinthians 5:14-15).

The *no* answer to the questions of Romans 6:1-3 is expanded upon through chapter eight to include, not only the *no* answer, but the *how to* answer. This *how to* answer involves God's instructions for practical *sanctification* (separation from the world and not serving our sin natures in our separation unto God and serving Him). God did not save us and make us part of the *New Creation* in Christ Jesus only to leave us powerless over our carnal natures. Grace is the supernatural enabling of God available to the believer to bring this "under the sun" existence to live within the *New Creation*.

"[15] If ye love me, keep my commandments. [16] And I will pray the Father, and he shall give you another Comforter, that he may abide with you for ever; [17] *Even* the Spirit of truth; whom the world cannot receive, because it seeth him not, neither knoweth him: but ye know him; for he dwelleth with you, and shall be in you. [18] I will not leave you comfortless: I will come to you. [19] Yet a little while, and the world seeth me no more; but ye see me: because I live, ye shall live also. [20] At that day ye shall know that I *am* in my Father, and ye in me, and I in you. [21] He that hath my commandments, and keepeth them, he it is that loveth me: and he that loveth me shall be loved of my Father, and I will love him, and will manifest myself to him. [22] Judas saith unto him, not Iscariot, Lord, how is it that thou wilt manifest thyself unto us, and not unto the world? [23] Jesus answered and said unto him, If a man love me, he will keep my words: and my Father will love him, and we will come unto him, and make our abode with him" (John 14:15-23).

There is a critical phrase in John 14:20 necessary for the believer to realize the potential in the practicality of presently living as part of the *New Creation* of the Lordship of Christ that is in every believer. We are positionally set apart from the world "in Christ" (the baptism of the Holy Spirit and regeneration). That is what Christ refers to in John 14:20 by the words "ye in me." However, the critical key to the realization of our spiritual potential "in Christ" is revealed by the words "I in you." "Ye in me" refers to the *New Creation* "in Christ." "I in you" refers to the indwelling presence of the Holy Spirit of God who desires to enable the believer to live as *New Creatures*. This is what the phrase "under grace" means in Romans 6:14.

In the Old Covenant, a believer was "under the Law." That means during the Dispensation of the Mosaic Law, the believer was *under* the administration (control) of the Law. In the New Covenant (the Dispensation of the Church Age), the believer is *under* the administration (control) of grace. That means the intent of God in this new Dispensation and New Covenant is to bring the believer to voluntarily yield his will to the indwelling Holy Spirit, who will empower that believer to live a life of righteousness that God can bless with the supernatural production of "much fruit" (John 15:8).

This teaching on practical sanctification is intent to present the means by which the believer can overcome the desires of his own corrupted *sin nature* of the old and cursed first creation. God's purpose in indwelling the believer is that the believer's fallen *sin nature* "shall not have dominion over" him (Romans 6:14). The words "have dominion over" are from the Greek word *kurieuo* (ko-ree-yoo'-o). It is a derivative of the Greek word that we get the word *lord* from. It means to *exercise lordship over* someone. The purpose of the Holy Spirit's indwelling is to provide a means for victory over the dominating lordship of our carnal, fallen, and corrupt *sin nature* and bring our lives practically into the ongoing *New Creation.*

Again, the means God has provided for us to escape the domination of our *sin natures* is the indwelling Person of the Holy Spirit. The indwelling Holy Spirit is what Christ was referring to by the word "Comforter" in John 14:16. The word "Comforter" is from the Greek word *parakletos* (par-ak'-lay-tos). It refers to a person summoned to join another in a *partnership venture.* The idea is joining the strengths of two to function as one. In this case it is the union of the power of the Creator in union with the power of the yielded believer. Therefore, this yielding is not passive, but active (participatory). The realization of the potential that lies in the Lordship of Christ lies in the *union of two wills.* The will of the believer must be yielded to, and become one with, the indwelling Holy Spirit (Romans 6:11-13).

> "[1] I therefore, the prisoner of the Lord, beseech you that ye walk worthy of the vocation wherewith ye are called, [2] With all lowliness and meekness, with longsuffering, forbearing one another in love; [3] Endeavouring to keep the unity of the Spirit in the bond of peace. [4] *There is* one body, and one Spirit, even as ye are called in one hope of your calling; [5] One Lord, one faith, one baptism, [6] One God and

Father of all, who *is* above all, and through all, and in you all. [7] But unto every one of us is given grace according to the measure of the gift of Christ" (Ephesians 4:1-7).

This *hypostatic unity* of two wills (the believer's will with God's will) is what the Word of God refers to as "fellowship" and what Ephesians 4:3 refers to as 'the unity of the Spirit." It is also what Christ refers to in John 14:16 and John 15:4-7 by the word "abide." "Abide" is from the Greek word *meno* (men'-o) and means *to remain* or *to continue in a place or position.* I believe the *place or position* that a believer is commanded to "abide" is *fellowship* with God. Notice the number of times the word "abide" is used in John 15:4-7 and how it directly relates to *bearing fruit* for Christ.

"[4] Abide in me, and I in you. As the branch cannot bear fruit of itself, except it abide in the vine; no more can ye, except ye abide in me. [5] I am the vine, ye *are* the branches: He that abideth in me, and I in him, the same bringeth forth much fruit: for without me ye can do nothing. [6] If a man *abide* not in me, he is cast forth as a branch, and is withered; and men gather them, and cast *them* into the fire, and they are burned. [7] If ye abide in me, and my words abide in you, ye shall ask what ye will, and it shall be done unto you. [8] Herein is my Father glorified, that ye bear much fruit; so shall ye be my disciples" (John 15:4-7).

The work of the believer in maintaining his fellowship with God is to maintain a submissive and broken will to God's will. In doing so, that believer will "abide in" Christ. The words "fellowship" and "abide" are synonyms in the practical application of the doctrine of grace. The practical application of doctrine of grace refers to the indwelling presence of the Holy Spirit in the body of the believer and the *filling* of the Spirit. The word "fellowship" is from the Greek word *koinonia* (koy-nohn-ee'-ah) and refers to a joint participation between the yielded believer and the indwelling Holy Spirit. Notice the number of times the word "fellowship" is used in I John 1:3-7 as it relates to how a believer restores the *relationship* (abiding partnership or "unity of the Spirit") that is broken by sin.

"[3] That which we have seen and heard declare we unto you, that ye also may have fellowship with us: and truly our fellowship *is* with the Father, and with his Son Jesus Christ. [4] And these things write we unto you, that your joy may be full. [5] This then is the message which we have heard of him, and declare unto you, that God is light, and in him is no darkness at all. [6] If we say that we have <u>fellowship</u> with him, and walk in darkness, we lie, and do not the truth: [7] But if we walk in the light, as he is in the light, we have <u>fellowship</u> one with another, and the blood of Jesus Christ his Son cleanseth us from all sin" (I John 1:3-7).

Relationship is another key word for the believer to realize the potential of the Lordship of Christ in his life. The words "under grace" (Romans 6:14-15) bring the believer into a *new relationship* with God within the *New Creation* and frees him from an old relationship ("under Law," Romans 7:1-4). The matter of *maintaining* that *new relationship* with God "under grace" is the subject of the rest of Romans 6:16-23.

"Under Law" the believer's sin nature was in constant servitude to the Law of commandments because it simply brought the believer's attention upon what sin is. Since the believer is a sinner by nature, the believer's focus was constantly on the struggle to overcome his own carnal desires. The Law was powerless to do anything for the believer, but condemn him. The Law could not *redeem* the believer. Neither could the Law *empower* the believer to obey.

Romans chapter six is still dealing with the issue of *abounding grace* (Romans 5:15-21). Does God's *abounding grace* free us to live a life of selfish pursuits? Salvation goes beyond the saving of our soul. It is God's purpose and desire to *save our lives* from being wasted upon the ruins of the cursed first creation. God wants to use our lives to bring "many sons unto glory" (Hebrews 2:10). That is the purpose behind the teaching of the doctrine of sanctification in Romans 6:1-8:39.

> God wants to teach us what we need to do in order to fully realize the potential of a *fruitful* life in the *New Creation* under the Lordship of Jesus Christ. This potential is realized as the believer *cooperatively* yields his life to the indwelling Holy Spirit and *practically* brings his life "under grace."

The word "also" of Romans 6:11 connects the practical aspects of the believer's carnal desires of this life with the death of

Christ (Romans 6:6). These two verses (Romans 6:11 and 6:6) are now connected by Romans 6:14. It is through the practical application of the spiritual realities of these two verses that the "dominion" (lordship) of the sin nature over the life of the believer is removed and the "dominion" of Christ (Lordship") in the *New Creation* is established.

The word "yield" (Romans 6:13, 16, and 19) refers to a *choice of lordship.* If a person chooses the lordship of the Law, he chooses the "dominion" of the sin nature. If a person chooses to be led by his emotions and carnal desires, he again chooses the lordship of the sin nature. Only when the believer chooses to yield "dominion" of his life (his will) to the "dominion" of the indwelling Holy Spirit will he begin to realize the full potential of the power of God in his life and *practically* bring his life into the *New Creation.*

We automatically become the "servants" of our choices (Romans 6:16). When the believer chooses to serve the desires of his carnal nature, he forfeits the *power* (not the *presence*) of the indwelling Holy Spirit in his life. Even though he is still positionally sanctified and his soul is eternally anchored in heaven "in Christ" (the *New Creation*), he moves his life back into the realm of "death" (the old cursed creation), where he is spiritually powerless and helpless. The realm of "death" is the realm of the Adamic curse (Romans 5:12). The realm of "death" is the realm of darkness and broken fellowship with God. The realm of "life" is the realm of "light" and the power of restored fellowship and restored dominion over angels (even the fallen ones).

When we choose to "yield" our will to the indwelling Holy Spirit, we choose a life of supernaturally enabled obedience to God's will. When we choose a Holy Spirit empowered life of obedience to God's will, we choose a life of obedience "unto righteousness;" that life of "righteousness" is a life that lives itself in the "light" of God's fellowship and blessing (I John 1:7). The simple truth of Romans 6:16 is that you choose your *master* (lord) and in that choice you choose to live either in the realm of death, darkness, and the curse (the cursed original creation) or in the realm of life, light, and God's blessings (the *New Creation*).

The impact that living your new Spirit-filled *Christ-life* will have on this world is simply a matter of *choice.* To understand what it means to be "under grace" is to understand the potential that lies in the matter of that *choice.* To say that "under grace" means to be able to live your life any way you want is a complete misunderstanding and misrepresentation of the God's intent. "Under grace" means to live your life under the potential outpouring of God's blessings *through* your Christian service and what the influence your *new life* can be once you learn to habitually yield your will to God's will. The realization of this potential of your new life "in Christ" is simply a matter of choosing to *completely* yield the control of your life to the Lordship of Christ. Sadly, this is a level of commitment very few believers are willing to give to the Lord. Their profession of faith in who Jesus is does not equivocate with a corresponding level of practice. Their lives become a shameful contradiction of what they profess to believe that in fact denies that profession.

"[18] And it came to pass, as he was alone praying, his disciples were with him: and he asked them, saying, Whom say the people that I am? [19] They answering said, John the Baptist; but some *say*, Elias; and others *say*, that one of the old prophets is risen again. [20] He said unto them, But whom say ye that I am? Peter answering said, The Christ of God. [21] And he straitly charged them, and commanded *them* to tell no man that thing; [22] Saying, The Son of man must suffer many things, and be rejected of the elders and chief priests and scribes, and be slain, and be raised the third day. [23] And he said to *them* all, If any *man* will come after me, let him deny himself, and take up his cross daily, and follow me. [24] For whosoever will save his life shall lose it: but whosoever will lose his life for my sake, the same shall save it. [25] For what is a man advantaged, if he gain the whole world, and lose himself, or be cast away? [26] For whosoever shall be ashamed of me and of my words, of him shall the Son of man be ashamed, when he shall come in his own glory, and *in his* Father's, and of the holy angels" (Luke 9:18-26).

DISCUSSION QUESTIONS

1. Explain why being *filled with* the Spirit MUST be connected to *walking in* the Spirit.

2. Discuss the following statement by Lewis Sperry Chafer:

" . . . [R]especting the negative aspect of the spiritual life, it may be restated that each of the three foes – the world, the flesh, and the devil – can outmatch all human ability and the victory over them is gained only by the superior power of the Holy Spirit; and this success, if it is to become a reality in daily life, calls for a peculiar and altogether different plan or principle of living. The change from self-sufficiency to dependence upon the Holy Spirit is a comprehensive one; yet at no time, even when believers are fully enabled, does the Spirit of God work outside the functions of the human will, nor is a consciousness experienced that another than one's own self is acting or determining. The spiritual life does not consist in the withdrawal of self, of initiative, or of the consciousness of responsibility. 'It is God,' the Apostle declares, 'which worketh in you both to will [with your own will] and do [with your own doing] of his good pleasure' (Phil. 2:13)."[21]

3. Discuss and explain the words "obeyed from the heart" in Romans. 6:17.

4. The *no* answer to the questions of Romans 6:1-3 is expanded through chapter eight to include, not only the *no* answer, but the *how to* answer. Briefly discuss the *how to*.

5. Give a simple and practical definition of grace as it defines the operations of the Holy Spirit in the life of a believer during the Church Age. Two words should be sufficient, one of which is *supernatural*.

6. Most Christians think their greatest opposition to living the *Christ-life* is demonic. According to Romans 6:14 define the Christian's greatest opposition and God's simple solution.

7. Practically define the word "abide" as used in John 15:4-7.

---

[21] Ibid., page 195.

Chapter Forty-eight

Obeying from the Heart and the Filling with the Spirit

To define outward conformity to laws or rules as a relationship with God is to somehow personify laws or rules, reducing God to little more than a *tyrant*. Although God is just, God is also merciful and longsuffering in His mercy. God is a Person and all that a believer does should be part of the relationship we have with the Person who is God. The filling of the Spirit is an outcome of a right relationship with God that comes from completely yielding our will to Him. The qualities involved in this relationship are twofold: FAITH/TRUST and LOVE. As we have already emphasized, there are five commands regarding the believer's maintenance of his relationship with the Person of the Holy Spirit.

1. Be filled with the Spirit (Ephesians 5:18)
2. Grieve not the Spirit (Ephesians 4:30)
3. Quench not the Spirit (I Thessalonians 5:19)
4. Walk in the Spirit (Galatians 5:16 and 25)
5. Be transformed/transfigured (Romans 12:2)

In our last chapter, we saw that being filled with the Spirit is connected with walking "in the Spirit" or walking "in the light" (I John 1:7). A person cannot "walk in the Spirit" if he is not "filled with the Spirit." In this chapter, I want to deal with the two negatives: "grieve not the Spirit" and "quench not the Spirit." These negative outcomes happen at any time the believer is not "filled with the Spirit." There is nothing a person can do in the strength of his own flesh that can be pleasing to God. Obedience *from* the flesh is still carnal. Even if your *sepultures are white washed,* they are still "full of dead men's bones" (Matthew 23:27) apart from the supernatural operations of the indwelling Spirit. This is why Christ so emphatically condemned the "scribes and Pharisees" as "hypocrites." His opinion of the *pseudo-spirituality* of externalism has not changed.

"[16] Know ye not, that to whom ye yield yourselves servants to obey, his servants ye are to whom ye obey; whether of sin unto death, or of obedience unto righteousness. [17] But God be thanked, that ye were the servants of sin, but ye have obeyed from the heart that form of doctrine which was delivered you. [18] Being then made free from sin, ye became the servants of righteousness. [19] I speak after the manner of men because of the infirmity of your flesh: for as ye have yielded your members servants to uncleanness and to iniquity unto iniquity; even so now yield your members servants to righteousness unto holiness. [20] For when ye were the servants of sin, ye were free from righteousness. [21] What fruit had ye then in those things whereof ye are now ashamed? for the end of those things *is* death. [22] But now being made free from sin, and become servants to God, ye have your fruit unto holiness, and the end everlasting life. [23] For the wages of sin *is* death; but the gift of God *is* eternal life through Jesus Christ our Lord" (Romans 6:16-23).

"Grieve not the Spirit"

"[26] Be ye angry, and sin not: let not the sun go down upon your wrath: [27] Neither give place to the devil. [28] Let him that stole steal no more: but rather let him labour, working with *his* hands the thing which is good, that he may have to give to him that needeth. [29] Let no corrupt communication proceed out of your mouth, but that which is good to the use of edifying, that it may minister grace unto the hearers. [30] And grieve not {*lit., stop grieving*} the holy Spirit of God, whereby ye are sealed unto the day of redemption. [31] Let all bitterness, and wrath, and anger, and clamour, and evil speaking, be put away from you, with all malice: [32] And be ye kind one to another, tenderhearted, forgiving one another, even as God for Christ's sake hath forgiven you" (Ephesians 4:26-32).

To "grieve" the Holy Spirit is to cause Him to be mournful or sorrowful. A believer grieves the Spirit of God at any time the things in Ephesians 4:26-31 are manifested through the believer's life. These things are a contradiction against the manifestation of the Spirit. A believer grieves the Spirit at any time he yields his will to his fallen nature. This is allowing anything that is contrary to the will of God. Any sinful thought, emotion, or action grieves the Spirit of God because it enjoins Him *to* (not *in*) the sinful act. God hates all sin, but He certainly hates the sin in the life of a believer who professes to love Him. To profess to love God and do the things listed in Ephesians 4:26-31 is a contradiction of that profession and is unfaithfulness to God in spiritual adultery. This spiritual adultery grieves Him.

I find it interesting that only one act of what we call *moral turpitude* is included in Ephesians 4:26-31, i.e., stealing. The rest of the things listed are issues involving the temper and sinful use of language to the spiritual harm of others. Most professing Christians would not even consider their carnality in these areas of life, let alone consider that the failure to yield to the Spirit in these areas would grieve Him. However, it is apparent that even allowing this kind of thinking is to grieve the Holy Spirit in that it is a contradiction against His holiness.

The indwelling presence of the Holy Spirit in the body of the believer is God's *seal* upon that believer's life (Ephesians 4:30). Although the believer forfeits the *power* of God when the Spirit is grieved by manifestations of yielding to the carnal *flesh*, the Spirit never leaves nor "forsakes" the believer. The *presence* of the Spirit is never lost. The *seal* of the indwelling presence of the Holy Spirit is a testimony *in* His presence that the believer is a part of the *body of Christ* and the *bride of Christ*. Therefore, the *seal* of the indwelling Spirit is a supernatural testimony to the world of *spirit beings.* The *seal* of the indwelling Spirit testifies that the believer has willfully made a choice to accept God's redemption payment and has chosen to be His eternal servant.

However, when the believer yields his will to his sin nature, he joins himself in an unfaithful, adulterous relationship with the cursed world that is under the sovereignty of Satan and his emissaries. The great tragedy in this dynamic is that the cursed world that is under the sovereignty of Satan and his emissaries, to which the carnal Christian joins himself in spiritual adultery, is at *enmity* (war) against God and God is at war against the sinful rebellion of this satanic *cosmos* of corruption. When the carnal Christian yields to his carnal flesh, he joins himself to that rebellion against God and becomes part of the *enmity* against God. An aspect of God's grief about this is that God must then war against His own "born again" children who are living in their flesh. The depth of God's grief about this is hard to even comprehend. This reality is expressed in numerous Scriptures.

"[4] Ye adulterers and adulteresses, know ye not that the friendship of the world is enmity with God? whosoever therefore will be a friend of the world is the enemy of God. [5] Do ye think that the scripture

415

saith in vain, The spirit that dwelleth in us lusteth to envy? [6] But he giveth more grace. Wherefore he saith, <u>God resisteth the proud</u>, but giveth grace unto the humble" (James 4:4-6).

"[40] How oft did they provoke him in the wilderness, *and* grieve him in the desert! [41] Yea, they turned back and tempted God, and limited the Holy One of Israel. [42] They remembered not his hand, *nor* the day when he delivered them from the enemy" (Psalm 78:40-42).

"[7] I will mention the lovingkindnesses of the LORD, *and* the praises of the LORD, according to all that the LORD hath bestowed on us, and the great goodness toward the house of Israel, which he hath bestowed on them according to his mercies, and according to the multitude of his lovingkindnesses. [8] For he said, Surely they *are* my people, children *that* will not lie: so he was their Saviour. [9] In all their affliction he was afflicted, and the angel of his presence saved them: in his love and in his pity he redeemed them; and he bare them, and carried them all the days of old. [10] But they rebelled, and vexed his holy Spirit: <u>therefore he was turned to be their enemy, *and* he fought against them</u>" (Isaiah 63:7-10).

"Quench not the Spirit"

"[16] Rejoice evermore. [17] Pray without ceasing. [18] In every thing give thanks: for this is the will of God in Christ Jesus concerning you. [19] <u>Quench not the Spirit</u>. [20] Despise not prophesyings. [21] Prove all things; hold fast that which is good. [22] Abstain from all appearance of evil. [23] And the very God of peace sanctify you wholly; and *I pray God* your whole spirit and soul and body be preserved blameless unto the coming of our Lord Jesus Christ" (I Thessalonians 5:16-23).

Although anything that *grieves* the Holy Spirit would also *quench* the Holy Spirit, the idea of *quenching* has more to do with failing to yield to *doing* what God commands us to do. This is more about the "work of the ministry" than it has to do with sins of moral turpitude. When a believer is filled with the Spirit of God, but fails to do the work that the Spirit filling empowers him to do, the believer *quenches*, or *extinguishes*, the power that is potentially released through the work God has saved him to do.

God's filling of the believer can only be manifested when the yielded believer is in motion (*doing*) according to God's will. We *quench* the potential power of the Spirit of God at any moment we resist the leading of His will as He directs the believer to witness, to speak to someone about Christ, or to initiate conversation that would involve another believer in discipleship. What God loves, the Spirit-filled believer will love and in the same way God loves. The loving compassion, mercy, and the longsuffering of God are intended to be communicable attributes that are manifested through the life of a Spirit-filled believer. These communicable attributes are never intended to be merely possessed by the believer.

> Communicable attributes are only communicable when they are *communicated* through our lives to those to whom God directs us.

To somehow think that we can possess these communicable attributes and never express them in any real or tangible way is the most subtle form of spiritual self-deception imaginable. Yet, this self-deception is common among the vast majority of professing Christians (even evangelicals and fundamentalists). This is undoubtedly the most common way the Spirit of God is *quenched* in his supernatural enabling of the believer's life. We are filled, but never engage our Spirit-filled life with any kind of real ministry.

> *Grieving* the Spirit keeps the believer from being filled. *Quenching* the Spirit is extinguishing the empowering of the Spirit by not using that empowering for its intended purpose of fruit production and disciple making.

Once we understand the five commandments regarding our relationship with the indwelling Spirit of God, we must understand the four conditions necessary to restoration when we *grieve* or *quench* the Holy Spirit. These four conditions are necessary to restore the ongoing inner creative work of the Holy Spirit that progressively transfigures the way a believer lives his life and that brings forth "fruit" to God's glory. **Salvation is presumed**. The first prerequisite to a personal relationship with the indwelling Holy Spirit is salvation "by grace through faith" (Ephesians 2:8-9). The natural, unregenerate man cannot have "fellowship" with God nor the *indwelling* or *filling* of the Spirit of God.

1. Repentance: the saved sinner must live in the ongoing, moment-by-moment, repentance of sin. Repentance simply refers to a complete (180°) change of *mind* and *heart* about sin. This involves more than a mere change of *mind* about selfish acts of sin, but a complete turning away from allowing the Sin Nature to dominate our will. The *turning* must be so radical that we come to hate the very innate desires/lusts of our own fallen natures.

2. Confession (I John 1:9): the saved sinner must live and think within the framework of constant awareness of God's presence, openness with Him regarding our weaknesses and the fragility of our character, and a transparency about ourselves with Him that necessitates constant communication with Him regarding our failures and weaknesses. To "confess our sins" simply means to *have the same mind* as God has about our sins. It *does not* mean to merely tell Him what we have done or have not done that is sin. God already knows what we have done and He knows the thoughts and intents of our hearts. In other words, He knows the sins of the heart as well as those that we perform before His eyes. God is not concerned about *low self-esteem* or *high self-esteem*. God wants us to think of ourselves as He thinks of us. We are sinners that He loves. He knows we are sinners, hates our sin, and loves us enough to establish a partnership with us to overcome that which He hates.

3. Yield: we must completely yield our wills to His will. There is no middle ground here. This is where the vast majority of "born again" people fail miserably. They think that total yielding is only for pastors, evangelists, and missionaries. Total yielding of our wills to God's will is His expectation of all His "born again" children. This yielding involves completely trusting God with every aspect of our lives. We trust as we seek to be filled with His Spirit and obey from the heart. This involves both the things He tells us NOT TO DO and the things he tells us TO DO. We cannot say we are totally yielding if we are not committed/dedicated to both of these aspects of yielding.

4. Dependence or Faith: "the just shall live by faith." We must live every moment of our lives in complete dependence upon the supernatural enabling of the Holy Spirit intent, upon bringing God glory through each and every moment our lives.

At any moment in time that a believer fails to fulfill any one of these four conditions, that believer will break all five of the commandments regarding his relationship ("fellowship" or working partnership) with the indwelling Holy Spirit. Primarily, at the moment when any one of the four conditions is not met, the believer will grieve the Spirit of God, quench the Spirit of God, or both. *Quenching* and *grieving* are two outcomes of two different forms of failure to yield to the indwelling Holy Spirit.

An issue that must be addressed at this point is the false notion that the Mosaic Covenant believer "under the Law" had no other option than mere outward conformity (externalism) to God's moral commands. Although these believers did not have the indwelling of the Spirit, they did have the *filling* of the Spirit and the *anointing* of the Spirit. These operations of the Spirit of God were *with* or *upon* them, not from *within* them.

> "[15] If ye love me, keep my commandments. [16] And I will pray the Father, and he shall give you another Comforter, that he may abide with you for ever; [17] *Even* the Spirit of truth; whom the world cannot receive, because it seeth him not, neither knoweth him: but ye know him; for he dwelleth <u>with you</u>, and <u>shall be in you</u>" (John 14:15-17).

The failure of Israel, both the saved and natural Israel, was the failure of the priesthood. These men were anointed for the purpose of teaching the people and were responsible for teaching them both how to be saved "through faith" and how to live their new lives empowered by the Spirit of God, who was *with them* and *upon them*. Because of this failure of the priesthood of Israel in understanding this dynamic and teaching it to the people, the vast majority of the priesthood and the vast majority of the people of Israel never were saved and regenerated. As a result, they sought to obey the Law through outward conformity through the strength of their own will power ("flesh") rather than through God's supernatural enabling "from the heart."

There are many today who claim that God never expected obedience "from the heart" under the Mosaic Covenant. They make that claim on the false premise (presupposition) that God could not expect of people what they were powerless to do. The fact is that many Scriptures teach us that God did expect obedience "from the heart." Obedience "from the heart" was the emphasis and daily reminder of the *Shema*, recited twice daily at morning and evening prayer (*Shema* is the shortened version of *Sh'ma Yisroel*, which are the two Hebrew words *hear* and *Israel*).

"⁴ Hear, O Israel: The LORD our God *is* one LORD: ⁵ And thou shalt love the LORD thy God with all thine heart, and with all thy soul, and with all thy might. ⁶ And these words, which I command thee this day, shall be in thine heart: ⁷ And thou shalt teach them diligently unto thy children, and shalt talk of them when thou sittest in thine house, and when thou walkest by the way, and when thou liest down, and when thou risest up. ⁸ And thou shalt bind them for a sign upon thine hand, and they shall be as frontlets between thine eyes. ⁹ And thou shalt write them upon the posts of thy house, and on thy gates" (Deuteronomy 6:4-9).

Although the *Shema* was a twice daily reminder of obeying "from the heart," this became little more than a vain repetition and outward conformity where the words were said, but never heeded or obeyed except in a very external way. The Jews lived primarily according to the Pentateuch, or the five books of Moses commonly called the Law (Genesis, Exodus, Leviticus, Numbers, and Deuteronomy). In the book of Deuteronomy alone there are forty-four different verses extending through almost every chapter from beginning to end, warning about *heart obedience* to God and maintaining their relationship with God out of love for Him. By the time of Isaiah, Israel had fallen almost completely into dead ritualism and outward moral conformity.

"¹³ Wherefore the Lord said, Forasmuch as this people draw near *me* with their mouth, and with their lips do honour me, but have removed their heart far from me, and their fear toward me is taught by the precept of men: ¹⁴ Therefore, behold, I will proceed to do a marvellous work among this people, *even* a marvellous work and a wonder: for the wisdom of their wise *men* shall perish, and the understanding of their prudent *men* shall be hid. ¹⁵ Woe unto them that seek deep to hide their counsel from the LORD, and their works are in the dark, and they say, Who seeth us? and who knoweth us? ¹⁶ Surely your turning of things upside down shall be esteemed as the potter's clay: for shall the work say of him that made it, He made me not? or shall the thing framed say of him that framed it, He had no understanding" (Isaiah 29:13-16)?

Christ quotes Isaiah 29:13 to the Pharisees and applies it to them in Matthew 15:8 and Mark 7:6. Neither has Christianity escaped this façade of *outward conformity*. This is what defines the hypocrisy of *Pharicism. Pharicism* is not about expecting people to live by rules or according to God's standards of holiness. *Pharicism* is teaching people that mere outward conformity and *white washed sepulchers* are somehow pleasing to God (Galatians 3:1-4).

The great tragedy of New Covenant Christianity is that the vast majority of people who profess to be believers (however they might define that) have failed in exactly the same way Israel failed. They have trusted their souls to the teaching of priests, pastors, or clergymen who often are not saved themselves and who certainly do not understand the spiritual dynamic of being "filled with the Spirit" and "walking in the Spirit."

Therefore, the vast majority of professing Christianity is doomed to misplaced faith and a false hope of eternal life or being saved but living out their lives in mere externalism to outward conformity to the commandments of God. They will do this thinking that somehow God is pleased with them for such nonsense. This latter failure is not limited merely to the liturgical/sacramental Christianity. The vast majority of both evangelical and fundamental Christianity fall into this subtle deception as well.

Once a person is saved from the condemned *old creation* in Adam and made part of the *New Creation* "in Christ," there ought to be a change in the *way* he lives. Not just an outward change, but an inward change of heart; i.e., motivation and desires. When I refer to a new *way*, I am referring to the supernatural enabling of the indwelling Spirit of God. There ought to be a change from living under the *control* (lordship) of the fallen nature of Pharicism, and under the dominion of a fallen angel called Satan, to living under the *control* (Lordship) of his *new nature* (II Peter 1:4) and within the *New Creation* ("into this grace in which we stand," Romans 5:2) through the indwelling Holy Spirit. That is God's expected transition for the life of every believer. If a person is genuinely saved, God expects that believer to choose to cease being a servant to *sin* (his sin nature) and to choose to become a servant of righteousness "from the heart" through the supernatural enabling ("grace") provided by the indwelling Holy Spirit. There should be a change of *heart*!

DISCUSSION QUESTIONS

1. Discuss the filling of the Spirit as an *outcome* of a right relationship with God. Discuss what defines that right relationship.

2. Thoroughly explain what it means to *grieve* the Spirit of God.

3. Discuss why *grieving* the Holy Spirit is always accompanied with the forfeiture of the power of God in your life.

4. Discuss how believers can be "adulterers and adulteresses" and at enmity against God even after they have been "born again."

5. Discuss what defines *quenching* the Spirit and how this is different than *grieving* the Spirit.

6. Discuss when communicable attributes are communicable and why we seldom see this in the lives of believers.

7. List and discuss the four conditions necessary to restore the ongoing inner creative work of the Holy Spirit that progressively transfigures the way a believer lives his life and that brings forth "fruit" to God's glory.

Chapter Forty-nine
Knowing the Crucifixion of the Old Man Experientially

"[1] What shall we say then? Shall we continue in sin, that grace may abound? [2] God forbid. How shall we, that are dead to sin, live any longer therein? [3] Know ye not, that so many of us as were baptized into Jesus Christ were baptized into his death? [4] Therefore we are buried with him by baptism into death: that like as Christ was raised up from the dead by the glory of the Father, even so we also should walk in newness of life. [5] For if we have been planted together in the likeness of his death, we shall be also *in the likeness* of *his* resurrection: [6] Knowing this, that our old man is crucified with *him*, that the body of sin might be destroyed, that henceforth we should not serve sin. [7] For he that is dead is freed from sin" (Romans 6:1-7).

We all must get away from the foolish notion that we can somehow change ourselves by the mere exercise of the human will in outward conformity. We cannot *will* ourselves to change anymore than we can bring the dead back to life. Only God can revive the dead and only God can change us. Therefore, we need to yield to the indwelling Creator to accomplish a change in our hearts before we can ever expect to see any real change in the practices of our lives that will be pleasing to Him and blessed of Him.

"Can the Ethiopian change his skin, or the leopard his spots? *then* may ye also do good, that are accustomed to do evil" (Jeremiah 13:23).

This new spiritual reality of the ongoing work of *transfiguring creation* (Rom. 12:2) taking place inside a believer, and through the yielded believer, continues to answer the questions of Romans 6:1-3 in the transition from the doctrine of justification into the doctrine of *spiritual growth* (sanctification). *Spiritual growth* (sanctification) is progressive transfiguration through the ongoing creative work of indwelling Holy Spirit. Sanctification means to be *set apart* from worldliness and *set apart* unto God for service ("the work of the ministry," Eph. 4:12). In this case, when a person is saved, God positionally sets that person apart for His peculiar use as a priest before Him.

Water baptism (portraying the Spirit baptism of Romans 6:3-5) is intended to be the time in a believer's life when he recognizes and accepts his responsibilities in this transition from *salvation* to *service* "from the heart" (the "newness of life," Romans 6:4). Part of a believer's recognition and transition into this *renewal* is to accept the fact that he no longer has the right to live any way he wants to live. "What shall we continue in sin that grace may abound? God forbid" (Romans 6:1).

The teaching that salvation is nothing more than to be rescued from Hell and God's eternal wrath is extremely shallow and superficial. The believer's "so great salvation" is the gift of eternal life. However, that eternal life is the divine, supernatural *Christ-life* that becomes available to EVERY believer the moment he receives Christ in the indwelling Holy Spirit of God. That is the transitional issue of Romans 6:1-7 going through Romans 8:39. These few chapters of Romans explain to us three different aspects of the "born again" believer's sanctification from the moment of salvation from Hell to the moment of salvation to glory (glorification). These three aspects of sanctification are three aspects of *perfection.*

1. Positional perfection "in Christ"
2. Practical progressive perfection (transfiguration) through the filling of the Spirit
3. Permanent perfection in glorification

These three aspects of the believer's sanctification also detail three aspects of the believer's salvation. Salvation in Scripture comes to us in three stages or phases.

1. The salvation of the believer's *soul* from Hell and God's wrath
2. The practical salvation of the believer's *life* (spirit or essence) through the filling of the Spirit
3. The salvation of the believer's *body* upon glorification

Because many Christians do not understand how to apply an inductive hermeneutical methodology in understanding the doctrinal context of a particular text, they misapply Scriptures that deal with the three aspects of *perfection.* They fail to see the three stages/phases of salvation and come up with false conclusions such as the *annihilation of the sin nature* or *sinless perfectionism* in a *second blessing.*

There will be an annihilation of the sin nature when the believer is glorified (the salvation of the body). The believer will come to the place of sinless perfection when his sin nature is annihilated. However, neither *sinless perfection* nor annihilation of the sin nature will take place, or ever be experienced in the believer's "under the Sun" existence until glorification.

As we understand the three stages/phases of salvation, we can understand how the word "perfect" is to be understood within those three phases. When we find the word "perfect" in a text, the first things we must understand is the context of that text and to what phase of salvation does it refer. The Greek word usually translated "perfect" in our KJV is the word *teleios* (tel'-i-os, used nineteen times in the New Testament). It basically refers to *completeness*. The applications of use would be *completeness* in physical or spiritual growth, or maturity in thinking or moral character. It is used to speak of a person of full age, fully educated, and able to live and function morally even within a corrupt corporate ethic. It is also used of people who have grown in their spiritual lives to the degree that they could be referred to as *habitually spiritual* people. Ephesians 4:12 refers to this latter idea.

"[43] Ye have heard that it hath been said, Thou shalt love thy neighbour, and hate thine enemy. [44] But I say unto you, Love your enemies, bless them that curse you, do good to them that hate you, and pray for them which despitefully use you, and persecute you; [45] That ye may be the children of your Father which is in heaven: for he maketh his sun to rise on the evil and on the good, and sendeth rain on the just and on the unjust. [46] For if ye love them which love you, what reward have ye? do not even the publicans the same? [47] And if ye salute your brethren only, what do ye more *than others*? do not even the publicans so? [48] Be ye therefore perfect, even as your Father which is in heaven is perfect" (Matthew 5:43-48).

"[11] And he gave some, apostles; and some, prophets; and some, evangelists; and some, pastors and teachers; [12] For the perfecting of the saints, for the work of the ministry, for the edifying of the body of Christ: [13] Till we all come in the unity of the faith, and of the knowledge of the Son of God, unto a perfect man, unto the measure of the stature of the fulness of Christ: [14] That we *henceforth* be no more children, tossed to and fro, and carried about with every wind of doctrine, by the sleight of men, *and* cunning craftiness, whereby they lie in wait to deceive; [15] But speaking the truth in love, may grow up into him in all things, which is the head, *even* Christ: [16]

From whom the whole body fitly joined together and compacted by that which every joint supplieth, according to the effectual working in the measure of every part, maketh increase of the body unto the edifying of itself in love" (Ephesians 4:11-16).

In Philippians 3:12-16, Paul refers to two different aspects of *perfection* in one text. In Philippians 3:12, Paul refers to *permanent perfection* and in Philippians 3:15 he refers to *practical/progressive perfection*.

"[12] Not as though I had already attained {*have a grasp on or possess*}, either were already perfect: but I follow after {*pursue*}, if that I may apprehend {*possess or get hold of*} that for which also I am apprehended of Christ Jesus {*referring to what Christ has already attained for the believer positionally*}. [13] Brethren, I count not myself to have apprehended: but *this* one thing *I do*, forgetting those things which are behind, and reaching forth unto {*stretching one's self toward the goal*} those things which are before, [14] I press {*push forward*} toward the mark for the prize of the high calling of God in Christ Jesus. [15] Let us therefore, as many as be perfect, be thus minded: and if in any thing ye be otherwise minded, God shall reveal even this unto you. [16] Nevertheless, whereto we have already attained {*arrived at or achieved*}, let us walk by the same rule {*standard of faith and practice*}, let us mind {*set affections on*} the same thing" (Philippians 3:12-16).

The fact of the matter is that no believer can ACHIEVE any of the three aspects of *perfection* in the power of his own will. Each aspect of *perfection* requires a supernatural operation of the Holy Spirit upon that believer's life. Paul refers to this spiritual dynamic of the three aspects of *perfection* and the three phases of salvation in the ongoing creative work of the Holy Spirit in I Thessalonians 5:23-24.

"[23] And the very God of peace sanctify you wholly; and *I pray God* your whole spirit and soul and body be preserved blameless unto the coming of our Lord Jesus Christ. [24] Faithful *is* he that calleth you, who also will do *it*" (I Thessalonians 5:23-24).

Romans 6:1-7 transitions in the teaching of God's Word from *positional perfection* "in Christ" to *practical/progressive perfection* through the filling of the Holy Spirit. If the believer does not understand his *positional perfection* in Christ, he will not understand the dynamic of the ongoing creative work of the Holy

Spirit into which he enters when he is "born again" and indwelled by the Spirit of God.

Paul has already established in Romans 5:12 that there is a perpetuation of the corruption of all humans in the passing of the *sin nature* through procreation in the descendants of Adam. It is not that Adam's sin is imputed to his descendants, but that each of his descendants possesses their own *sin nature* that comes from the corrupted seed of Adam. The *sin nature* is procreated through conception and natural birth.

The *divine nature* (I Peter 1:4) is *imparted* to the believer "through faith" and through being "born again" (the spiritual birth of regeneration or the "new creation"). It is the possession of this *sin nature* that condemns all of mankind having human fathers. God's condemnation is on the *sin nature* of man. However, the possession of a *sin nature* corrupts the body in which it dwells and condemns the soul to which it is connected. Therefore, the corruption of the *sin nature* condemns the whole of a person - body, soul, and spirit. Each aspect of that person must be redeemed or *saved*. A thorough understanding of the doctrine of salvation (Soteriology) understands what God *has done* "in Christ," what God *is doing* in Christ in us, and what God *will do* in the believer's glorification that completely saves a person body, soul, and spirit.

The issue before us in Romans 6:1-23 has to do with what is known as *federal headship*. In the text, we have two different *federal headships* before us:

1. The *federal headship* of the first Adam and the condemnation of all those that descend from that federal headship and the complete corruption of the life of every individual that continues to live under that *federal headship*, including the redeemed

2. The new *federal headship* of Jesus Christ, the "last Adam," and the salvation of all those that descend from that new *federal headship* "in Christ" "by grace through faith"

The baptism with the Spirit and the indwelling of the Spirit creates a new *union* under the new *federal headship* of Christ. This union is eternal and is positionally complete "in Christ." Practically, this new *union* makes the production of God-kind righteousness possible through the filling of the Spirit or "the unity of the Spirit" as the saved believer completely yields his will to the indwelling Spirit of God.

These two *federal headships* are the subject matter of the *perfectionism* teaching (positional, progressive, and permanent sanctification/perfection) of the Apostle Paul that begins in Romans 5:1, transitioning from the doctrines of the propitiation of God and the justification of believers and going through Romans chapter eight. The subject matter then is picked up again in Romans chapter twelve and goes through the end of the epistle.

The first aspect of the believer's perfection/sanctification "in Christ" is positional. This means that in the *federal headship* of Christ through the *New Birth* into the *New Creation* every "born again" believer has such an intricate and intimate union with Christ that everything that has already happened to Christ *actually* has happened to the believer *positionally*. Under the *federal headship* of the first Adam through procreation, all of us are sinners by nature, condemned, and hopelessly spiritually dead in trespasses and sin. Under the new *federal headship* of the last Adam, Christ Jesus, all believers through the *New Creation* have positionally been crucified with Him, died with Him, buried with Him, are resurrected/glorified with Him, and are already seated with Him at the right hand of the Father.

"[1] For I would that ye knew what great conflict I have for you, and *for* them at Laodicea, and *for* as many as have not seen my face in the flesh; [2] That their hearts might be comforted, being knit together in love, and unto all riches of the full assurance {*perfect confidence*} of understanding, to the acknowledgement of the mystery of God, and of the Father, and of Christ; [3] **In whom** are hid all the treasures of wisdom and knowledge. [4] And this I say, lest any man should beguile you with enticing words. [5] For though I be absent in the flesh, yet am I with you in the spirit, joying and beholding your order, and the stedfastness of your faith **in Christ**. [6] As ye have therefore received Christ Jesus the Lord, *so* walk ye **in him**: [7] Rooted and built up **in him**, and stablished in the faith, as ye have been taught, abounding therein with thanksgiving. [8] Beware lest any man spoil you through philosophy and vain deceit, after the tradition of men, after the rudiments of the world, and not after Christ. [9] For **in him** dwelleth all the fulness of the Godhead bodily. [10] And ye are complete {*pleroo, another Greek word referring to a full or finished work*} **in him** {*in that you have been positionally immersed into the New Creation and the 'body of Christ' by the baptism with the Holy Spirit*}, which is the head {*new federal headship of the last Adam*} of all principality and power: [11] **In**

whom also ye are circumcised with the circumcision made without hands, in putting off the body of the sins of the flesh by the circumcision of Christ: [12] Buried **with him** in baptism {*Spirit baptism; I Corinthians 12:13*}, wherein {*in that Spirit baptism into the New Creation "'in Christ'*} also ye are risen **with *him*** through the faith of the operation of God, who hath raised him from the dead. [13] And you, being dead in your sins and the uncircumcision of your flesh, hath he quickened {*positionally resurrected and glorified*} together **with him**, having forgiven {*gratuitously pardoned*} you all trespasses; [14] Blotting out the handwriting of ordinances that was against us, which was contrary to us, and took it out of the way, nailing it {*vicariously, I Peter 2:24, 3:18*} to his cross; [15] *And* having spoiled principalities and powers, he made a shew of them openly, triumphing over them in it" (Colossians 2:1-15).

> When we speak of the doctrine of *federal headship*, we often use the term *Lordship*. However, this term is usually understood to refer to the *Lordship* of Christ in that He is God. As the title *Lord* is applied to Jesus the Christ, it is used in relationship to His *theanthropicity* (the union of God and man through the incarnation).

The importance in our understanding this *mystery,* now revealed to us in Paul's epistles, is that this understanding explains the three aspects of *perfectionism* and the three phases of the believer's salvation. What has happened to Jesus *actually* has happened to every believer *positionally.* The end result of what happened to Jesus is His *theanthropic federal headship.* **This is the same ultimate outcome for every believer as "joint heirs with Christ" (Romans 8:17).** It is to this ultimate outcome that the words "Lord of lords and King of kings" (I Timothy 6:17; Revelation 17:14, and 19:16) refers. This phraseology refers to an order of *theanthropic sovereignty* during the Kingdom Age on earth. Church Age believers will rule and reign (Revelation 2:26-27) with Christ in glorified bodies as "joint heirs" of His *theanthropic Federal Headship.* We will be the "lords" of whom He will be "Lord" and the "kings" of whom He will be "King."

What qualifies the believer for this exalted position is the prerequisite of having been "born again," and the last aspect of

Perfectionism; i.e. permanent perfection in glorification. However, no one will be given these positions of *theanthropic federal headship* in the Kingdom Age who are unfaithful in their practical/progressive perfection during the Church Age as manifested by the production of some degree of *fruit* (Matthew 25:14-30) through the "unity of the Spirit" (John 15:1-18 and Ephesians 4:1-16). There are a number of portions of Scripture that would be completely obscure to us if we did not understand the *federal headship* of Christ from this theanthropic perspective.

"[18] And Jesus came and spake unto them, saying, <u>All power is given unto me in heaven and in earth</u>. [19] Go ye therefore, and teach all nations, baptizing them in the name of the Father, and of the Son, and of the Holy Ghost: [20] Teaching them to observe all things whatsoever I have commanded you: and, lo, I am with you alway, *even* unto the end of the world. Amen" (Matthew 28:18-20).

The word "power" in Matthew 28:18 is from the Greek word *exousia* (ex-oo-see'-ah). It means *authority*, particularly in the sense of jurisprudence and governance. The word "all" conveys the idea of *absoluteness* in that "given" authority. In other words, there is nothing or no one that is not directly under that authority, subject to that authority, and accountable to and before that authority. If we do not understand this text from the context of the theanthropic *federal headship* of Jesus as the incarnate Son of God, we could never understand how this "power" was "given" to Him, in that as the Son of God He would have always had this "power."

"[12] Giving thanks unto the Father, which hath made us meet to be partakers of the inheritance of the saints in light: [13] Who hath delivered us from the power of darkness, and hath translated *us* into the kingdom of his dear Son: [14] In whom we have redemption through his blood, *even* the forgiveness of sins: [15] Who is the image of the invisible God, the firstborn of every creature: [16] For by him were all things created, that are in heaven, and that are in earth, visible and invisible, whether *they be* thrones, or dominions, or principalities, or powers: all things were created by him, and for him: [17] And he is before all things, and by him all things consist. [18] And he is the head of the body, the church: who is the beginning, the firstborn from the dead; <u>that in all *things* he might have the preeminence</u>" (Colossians 1:12-18).

The words "might have" in Colossians 1:18 are translated

from the Greek word *ginomai* (ghin'-om-ahee). It simply means *to cause to be*. It is used in the context of the Son of God as the Creator (vs. 16-17). The fact that the Son of God is the Creator is emphatically stated. However verse 18 refers to the theanthropic *federal head*ship of Jesus that He earned through His incarnation, death, burial, resurrection, and glorification.

The Greek word translated "might have" is in the subjunctive mood, which is the mood of possibility. That possibility is realized and assured in His death, burial, resurrection, and glorification. The Greek word is in the aorist tense, meaning it refers to something that begins at some point in time with continuing or unfolding results. The glorified and ascended Jesus the Christ has already received His theanthropic *federal headship* as revealed by His statement in Matthew 28:18. He presently exercises His theanthropic *federal headship* over the Church during the Church Age (Ephesians 1:22 and Colossians 1:18). He will take *absolute Lordship* at His second coming. Then, He will administrate that *theanthropic federal headship* through a worldwide *chain of command* through Church Age believers. These believers will have been given these positions as *under lords* according to their *faithfulness in fellowship* during their lifetimes in the Church Age. Understanding this context gives us an expanded understanding of I Corinthians 15:20-28.

"[20] But now is Christ risen from the dead, *and* become the firstfruits of them that slept. [21] For since by man *came* death, by man *came* also the resurrection of the dead. [22] For as in Adam all die, even so in Christ shall all be made alive. [23] But every man in his own order: Christ the firstfruits; afterward they that are Christ's at his coming. [24] Then *cometh* the end, when he shall have delivered up the kingdom to God, even the Father; when he shall have put down all rule and all authority and power. [25] For he must reign, till he hath put all enemies under his feet. [26] The last enemy *that* shall be destroyed *is* death. [27] For he hath put all things under his feet. But when he saith all things are put under *him, it is* manifest that he is excepted, which did put all things under him. [28] And when all things shall be subdued unto him, then shall the Son also himself be subject unto him that put all things under him, that God may be all in all" (I Corinthians 15:20-28).

DISCUSSION QUESTIONS

1. Discuss why it is a foolish notion that we can somehow change ourselves by the mere exercise of the human will in outward conformity.

2. Explain the ongoing work of *transfiguring creation* (Romans 12:2).

3. List and explain the three aspects of sanctification as the three aspects of *perfection*.

4. Detail the three aspects of the believer's salvation and why it is critical to understand these three aspects.

5. Discuss the *perpetuation of the corruption* of all humans and its only solution after salvation.

6. List and discuss the two *federal headships* and why it is critical to understanding both in order to understand Christ's twofold work of redemption.

7. The end result of what happened to Jesus is His *theanthropic federal headship*. This is the same ultimate outcome for every believer as "joint heirs with Christ" (Romans 8:17). Explain when and how this will become a reality.

Chapter Fifty

Living in Spiritual Adultery and Committing Grand Larceny

Many Christians who have received God's free gift of salvation and have been "born again" of the Spirit of God have been led astray by false teaching on the doctrine of grace into a *pseudo Christian liberty*. They have been taught that since Christ has already "once for all" propitiated God for every sin they have committed (past, present, and future sins), that they have *liberty* to live just about any way they want. They believe they are not governed by the Word of God, but can now live merely according to the dictates of their own *consciences*. However, this kind of false teaching is a serious misrepresentation of the doctrine of Grace and is contrary to the repeated testimony and instruction of the Word of God. In fact, we can go so far as to say this kind of corruption of the doctrine of Grace is to condone *spiritual adultery* and encourage *grand larceny* regarding the redemption of their souls purchased by the shed blood of Jesus Christ. "[14] For the love of Christ constraineth us; because we thus judge, that if one died for all, then were all dead: [15] And *that* he died for all, that they which live should not henceforth live unto themselves, but unto him which died for them, and rose again" (II Corinthians 5:14-15).

I want to look at three texts from I Corinthians and II Corinthians that need to be understood along with Romans chapters six and seven. They emphatically teach us that just because we are saved *freely* by God's grace "through faith," we are not *free* to live any way we want to live. Although we are not "under the Law" for righteousness, the Word of God clearly teaches us that "[14] For sin {*the sin nature*} shall not have dominion over you: for ye are not under the law {*the governance of the Mosaic Covenant*}, but under grace {*the governance of the illuminating, empowering cooperative partnership with the indwelling Holy Spirit in His ongoing supernatural creative work of progressive transfiguration*}. [15] What then? shall we sin, because we are not under the law, but under grace? God forbid" (Romans 6:14-15).

"[1] It is reported commonly *that there is* fornication among you, and such fornication as is not so much as named among the Gentiles, that one should have his father's wife. [2] And ye are puffed up, and have not rather mourned, that he that hath done this deed might be taken away from among you. [3] For I verily, as absent in body, but present in spirit, have judged already, as though I were present, *concerning* him that hath so done this deed, [4] In the name of our Lord Jesus Christ, when ye are gathered together, and my spirit, with the power of our Lord Jesus Christ, [5] To deliver such an one unto Satan for the destruction of the flesh, that the spirit may be saved in the day of the Lord Jesus. [6] Your glorying *is* not good. Know ye not that a little leaven leaveneth the whole lump" (I Corinthians 5:1-6)?

The epistle of I Corinthians is written to deal with the carnality that was being tolerated in the local church at Corinth. Therefore, the "whole lump" that was being *leavened* (corrupted and defiled) was the whole of the local church. The "little leaven" that was defiling the "whole" local church was the carnality of any individual believer living in sin and yielding to the *lordship* of his fallen nature.

This is the context that goes into I Corinthians chapter 6. There were some things that the Law (the first five books of the Bible known as the Pentateuch) did not mention specifically. Paul is addressing a cultural abnormality known as *Antinomianism*. Paul is not saying that "all" practices of life "are lawful" (i.e., alright with God). Paul is quoting a *cultural proverb* that wrongly taught that the desires of a person's body were normal and that it was perfectly normal to satisfy those desires. The culture had accepted the premise that sexual desires were a normal part of a person's humanity and therefore it was not immoral to satisfy those sexual desires.

Paul is dealing with two cultural abnormalities in I Corinthians chapter six - *fornication* (cultural sexual aberrations) and *eating meat that had been sacrificed to idols*. These two practices were common to the Corinthian pagan culture and a culturally accepted norm of idolatry. There were rational and accepted cultural arguments that were justifying aberrations regarding these two cultural abnormalities. Paul is *correcting* these cultural aberrations and rational justifications by his inspired statements in I Corinthians 6:12-20.

"[12] All things are lawful unto me, but all things are not expedient: all things are lawful for me, but I will not be brought under the power of any. [13] Meats for the belly, and the belly for meats: but God shall destroy both it and them. Now the body *is* not for fornication, but for the Lord; and the Lord for the body. [14] And God hath both raised up the Lord, and will also raise up us by his own power. [15] Know ye not that your bodies are the members of Christ? shall I then take the members of Christ, and make *them* the members of an harlot? God forbid. [16] What? know ye not that he which is joined to an harlot is one body? for two, saith he, shall be one flesh. [17] But he that is joined unto the Lord is one spirit. [18] Flee fornication. Every sin that a man doeth is without the body; but he that committeth fornication sinneth against his own body. [19] What? know ye not that your body is the temple of the Holy Ghost *which is* in you, which ye have of God, and ye are not your own? [20] For ye are bought with a price: therefore glorify God in your body, and in your spirit, which are God's" (I Corinthians 6:12-20).

The Greek word translated "expedient" in I Corinthians 6:12 is from the Greek word *sumphero* (soom-fer'-o). It means *profitable* or *conducive*. Although God has been propitiated "for *the sins* of the whole world" (I John 2:2), and there is no sin that can ever condemn a believer once he is "born again" (Romans 8:1), such practices are not *conducive to spirituality* and to *bringing glory to God* (I Corinthians 10:31). Taking liberty in such areas is to give *license* for sin. God does not give that *license* and it would be usurping authority (*grand larceny* of lordship) for the believer to take that *license*.

As Romans 6:18-22 teaches, the believer is "free from sin" (freedom *from* the dominating lordship of the sin nature), but is not free *to* sin (to live any way he wants). Some are teaching that being *free* (Christian liberty under grace) means Christians are no longer governed by the commands of God's Word. That is heresy and leads to what Paul says "God forbid" to in Romans 6:1. Christian liberty has to do with the freedom to choose who will be *Lord of our will*.

The Old Testament believer had the freedom to choose as well. That is proven by Joshua's statement in Joshua 24:15-28. I believe Paul's many uses of the phrase "God forbid" (used on fourteen different occasions in his epistles) is directly related to the original commitment of Israel to what Joshua addressed in this text.

The grand difference *under grace* and the indwelling Holy Spirit is that now, in the New Covenant, the believer has the indwelling power to live in a supernatural *new existence* through the empowering of the Holy Spirit, because the sin nature has been "crucified with Christ" (Romans 6:6). This supernatural *New Creation*, to which every "born again" believer is connected in a theanthropic union with the Godhead, is what enables believers. They are enabled to have the *liberty* to both choose to live for and serve the Lord, and to do what we choose to do if we will completely surrender to the indwelling Spirit.

Christ spoke to the Jews about this transitional issue, but they did not understand what He was saying. They could only see *liberty* as *freemen* in their genealogy from Abraham. They were not (at that point in history) a *slave nation* in captivity. They did not understand or recognize their abject slavery to their own fallen natures. When any person chooses freedom *from* God's will, he chooses to be a slave *to* His own will.

"[31] Then said Jesus to those Jews which believed on him, If ye continue in my word, *then* are ye my disciples indeed; [32] And ye shall know the truth, and the truth shall make you free. [33] They answered him, We be Abraham's seed, and were never in bondage to any man: how sayest thou, Ye shall be made free? [34] Jesus answered them, Verily, verily, I say unto you, Whosoever committeth sin is the servant of sin. [35] And the servant abideth not in the house for ever: *but* the Son abideth ever. [36] If the Son therefore shall make you free, ye shall be free indeed. [37] I know that ye are Abraham's seed; but ye seek to kill me, because my word hath no place in you" (John 8:31-36).

Anytime a person commits an act of sin, that person did so subservient to the lordship of his own *sin nature*. In other words, that person made a decision to let his *sin nature* put a *ring in his nose* and lead him around like a slave. The believer *has been* delivered from the *penalty* of the *sin nature* in the salvation of his soul. He *is being* delivered from the *power* (lordship) of *sin nature* through his progressive transfiguration as he yields to the indwelling Holy Spirit through incremental decisions. He *will be* fully delivered from the *presence* of the *sin nature* (annihilation of the *sin nature*) at his ultimate and predestined glorification.

The salvation of our soul and deliverance from the *penalty* of the *sin nature* is the outcome of a single action of faith in response to the gospel of Jesus Christ (Romans 10:9-13). The salvation of a believer's life and the regular deliverance from the *power* of the *sin nature* is the outcome of the constant and continual life of faith ("the just shall live by faith").

Both of these outcomes are supernaturally produced "by grace through faith." Lewis Sperry Chafer quotes Bishop H. C. G. Moule on this:

"The first case is in its nature one and single: an admission, an incorporation. The second is in its nature progressive and developing: the discovery, advancing with the occasion for it, of the greatness of the resources of Christ for life. The latter *may*, not *must*, thus include one great crisis in consciousness, one particular spiritual act. It is much more certain to include many starting-points, critical developments, marked advances. The act of self-surrendering faith in the power of Christ for inward cleansing of the will and affections may be, and often indeed it is, as it were a new conversion, a new 'effectual calling.'" (for clarity, the believer should understand I John 1:8-10).[22]

"[12] For we commend not ourselves again unto you, but give you occasion to glory on our behalf, that ye may have somewhat to *answer* them which glory in appearance, and not in heart. [13] For whether we be beside ourselves, *it is* to God: or whether we be sober, *it is* for your cause. [14] For the love of Christ constraineth us; because we thus judge, that if one died for all, then were all dead: [15] And *that* he died for all, that they which live should not henceforth live unto themselves, but unto him which died for them, and rose again" (II Corinthians 5:12-15).

There is a *progression* in the emphasis of these two exhortations found in these two epistles to the Church at Corinth. These epistles are written only a year apart from each other. However, the exhortation in the second epistle is on a much higher level of *spiritual walk* with the Lord and another, much higher, level

---

[22] Ibid., page 294

of *spiritual expectation* than the first. The Corinthian believers had listened to Paul's extensive and scathing rebuke in his first epistle and "obeyed from the heart" what the Lord commanded them to do regarding their carnality. In II Corinthians 5:15, Paul introduces this higher, nobler motivation for living in this "new creation" into which every believer has been "born again." It is not merely a *new existence*. It comes with a *new ministry* and some very high expectations of those "born again" and indwelled by the Spirit of God; i.e., "ambassadors for Christ" in doing "the ministry of reconciliation." This cannot be accomplished apart from *spirituality*.

"[17] Therefore if any man *be* in Christ, *he is* a new creature: old things are passed {*aorist, past beginning with continuing results*} away; behold, all things are become {*perfect tense, something once for all completed in the past*} new {*kainos, new of a new/different kind*} . [18] And all things {*pas, everything or every aspect of this New Creation*} *are* of {*proceed from or originate from*} God, who hath reconciled us to himself by Jesus Christ {*in this New Creation; i.e., 'the regeneration'*}, and hath given to us the ministry of reconciliation {*in that the believer is restored to a position of rightness with God in this New Creation, the believer can now minister out of that New Creation in partnership or 'fellowship' with God*}; [19] To wit {*in this manner or even as; showing how this reconciliation was accomplished and how the believer is to minister within and out of this New Creation of reconciliation with God*}, that God was in Christ {*the theanthropic union of the 'fullness of the Godhead' in man; Colossians 2:9 now available to every believer in the indwelling of the Spirit; Ephesians 3:19 and 4:13*}, reconciling the world unto himself, not imputing their trespasses unto them; and hath committed unto us {*made believers responsible for communicating*} the word {*logos, the detailed word or message of this divine communication from God*} of reconciliation. [20] Now then we are ambassadors {*presbeuo, to act as representatives*} for Christ, as though God did beseech *you* by us: we pray *you* in Christ's stead, be ye reconciled to God {*This phrase from the, reflects the pleading and persuading aspect of the believer's ministry as 'ambassadors' for Christ. Therefore, the ministry of reconciliation is not merely the systemic proclamation of a message from God, but must reflect the attributes of God in His love, compassion, and mercy as He reaches out to lost souls through the lives of individual Spirit-filled believers.*}. [21] For he hath made him *to be* sin for us {*in the vicarious judgment of the sin nature in the human body of Jesus the*

Christ}, who knew no sin {*experientially, John 8:46; Hebrews 7:26-28; I Peter 2:22; I John 3:5*}; that we might be made {*the potential of practically becoming through the indwelling and filling of the Holy Spirit*} the righteousness of God in him {*the believer's theanthropic union*}" (II Corinthians 5:17-21).

II Corinthians 5:17-21 defines exactly how we are to live "unto" Christ "which died for them and rose again" as II Corinthians 5:15 tells us. The resurrection of Jesus Christ, along with His glorification and ascension, released His supernatural life into the world through the indwelling of the Holy Spirit. The indwelling of every believer with the Holy Spirit is the *Seed* of the *Christ-life* that will bring forth the fruit that will fill the *New Creation* with "born again" people who will be resurrected, glorified and perfectly transfigured to be exactly like Jesus is presently. With that blessed hope comes enormous responsibilities in this present life.

"[1] Behold, what manner of love the Father hath bestowed upon us, that we should be called the sons of God: therefore the world knoweth us not, because it knew him not. [2] Beloved, now are we the sons of God, and it doth not yet appear what we shall be: but we know that, when he shall appear, we shall be like him; for we shall see him as he is. [3] And every man that hath this hope in him purifieth himself, even as he is pure" (I John 3:1-3).

The phrase "old man" that is used in Romans 6:6 is only used in two other portions of Scripture (Ephesians 4:22-24 and Colossians 3:9). However, the context of each of those texts is important and definitive to our understanding of the doctrine of *perfection*. As we look at these three texts, it is important to see that they refer to two different aspects of the believer's *perfection/sanctification* "in Christ." In Romans 6:6, the text is referring to the believer's *positional perfection* "in Christ" in that the believer's *sin nature* ("old man") was crucified with Christ positionally. This co-crucifixion of the sinless human Jesus and the believer's *sin nature* has to do with the new *federal headship* of Christ that the believer enters into through the "door" of Christ's death, burial, and resurrection/glorification.

From Romans 6:6, it is essential that we understand that the believer's *sin nature* was "crucified with Christ" in that the death of the believer's *sin nature* frees that believer to be *married* (a metaphor for *union*) to another once the *federal headship* (union) of the *sin nature* is broken through the death of that co-crucifixion. It is in this spiritual dynamic between the death of the old *federal headship* in the crucifixion of the believer's *sin nature* in the believer's *positional perfection* "in Christ" that we transition to the believer's *practical/progressive perfection* in Romans 6:11-7:25 under the new *federal headship* of Christ through the indwelling Holy Spirit.

1. Salvation (being "born again") brings the believer **into** this new union of the *federal headship* of Christ.
2. Yielding to the indwelling Holy Spirit brings the believer practically and progressively **under** this new *federal headship* of Christ (His Lordship) and releases the supernatural power of that new *federal headship* into this present world through the believer's life.

"[1] Know ye not, brethren, (for I speak to them that know the law,) how that the law hath dominion over a man as long as he liveth? [2] For the woman which hath an husband is bound by the law to *her* husband so long as he liveth; but if the husband be dead, she is loosed from the law of *her* husband. [3] So then if, while *her* husband liveth, she be married to another man, she shall be called an adulteress: but if her husband be dead, she is free from that law; so that she is no adulteress, though she be married to another man. [4] Wherefore, my brethren, ye also are become dead to the law by the body of Christ; that ye should be married to another, *even* to him who is raised from the dead, that we should bring forth fruit unto God. [5] For when we were in the flesh, the motions of sins, which were by the law, did work in our members to bring forth fruit unto death. [6] But now we are delivered from the law, that being dead wherein we were held; that we should serve in newness of spirit, and not *in* the oldness of the letter" (Romans 7:1-6).

DISCUSSION QUESTIONS

1. Discuss why so many Christians have been led astray by false teaching on the doctrine of grace into a *pseudo Christian liberty*. Discuss *why* this kind of corruption of the doctrine of Grace is really just a way to condone *spiritual adultery* and encourage *grand larceny* regarding the redemption of their souls purchased by the shed blood of Jesus Christ.

2. Explain I Corinthians 6:12-20 from the perspective of the context that Paul is quoting a *cultural proverb* that wrongly taught that the desires of a person's body were normal and that it was perfectly normal to satisfy those desires.

3. Christian liberty has to do with the freedom to choose who will be *Lord of our will*. Explain Romans 6:18-22 from this context.

4. Why couldn't most of the elitists of Israel understand what Christ was saying in John 8:31-36?

5. Discuss and explain the following statement: "The salvation of our soul and deliverance from the *penalty* of the *sin nature* is the outcome of a single action of faith in response to the Gospel of Jesus Christ (Romans 10:9-13). The salvation of a believer's life and the regular deliverance from the *power* of the *sin nature* is the outcome of the constant and continual life of faith ('the just shall live by faith')."

6. Discuss the *spiritual progression* in the exhortations in I Corinthians 6:12-20 compared to the exhortations in II Corinthians 5:12-21.

7. The phrase "old man" that is used in Romans 6:6 is only used in two other portions of Scripture (Ephesians 4:22-24 and Colossians 3:9). Explain how the context of each of these texts is important and definitive to our understanding of the doctrine of *perfection*.

Chapter Fifty-one
Rescuing Those Perishing in Their Ignorance of God

Local churches like the one at Corinth and Ephesus were made up of people saved out of hedonistic, licentious cultures steeped in paganistic ideologies. Almost every kind of sin forbidden by the Word of God was commonly practiced and accepted by these cultures as normal. The *Christian* churches of Europe, Canada, the Netherlands, South America, Africa, and the United States have all become very much like these early churches defined by the Epistle of I Corinthians.

To use a simple phrase, these churches look a lot like a *train wreck*. When people first begin to attend a Bible believing, Bible preaching church out of these kinds of cultures, they come into the church with enormous amounts of *baggage* - false beliefs, misnomers about God, and are culturally induced with ideologies that they have been taught by paganized *Christians* to be acceptable by God. They not only come with *baggage*, they come with *history*. Their *baggage* is really *garbage* and their *history* just makes that *garbage* more rotten and putrid. The *salvation of the soul* cleanses away the penalty of this corruption. However, *the salvation of the life* is the long process of *cleaning out the corruption* by correcting the ignorance of God that generated all the putrid garbage they allowed into their lives in the first place. We cannot merely wash away this *putrid baggage*. It is on the *inside* of us in our desires and character. This *garbage* needs to be *cleaned out* along with the "old man" who keeps accumulating it. This is what Paul addresses in Ephesians 4: 17-24.

Before we look at this text, we need to clearly understand that the believer has no part whatsoever in his *positional perfection* "in Christ." His *positional perfection* "in Christ" (both *imparted* righteousness and sanctification) is part of the gift of salvation given to the believer "by grace through faith." However, it is equally clear that *practical perfection* is *progressive* through a *cooperative partnership* between a believer and the indwelling divine nature of the Holy Spirit. *Practical perfection* is *progressive* because it happens through *incremental decisions* prompted by the working of the Holy Spirit from within the believer. This happens through His *illumination* of the Word of God in personal Bible study and through God's ordained methodology for *progressive transfiguration* in the "foolishness of preaching." This happens through the "renewing" of the believer's mind through those incremental decisions to yield to the Spirit and the Word, repent of sin, and begin to "obey from the heart." This is what Paul teaches us in Ephesians 4:17-24, which is the third text in which the phrase "old man" is used regarding the *sin nature*.

"[17] **This I say therefore, and testify** {*affirm to be true by exhortation and, therefore, the following exhortation is a reality to which every believer will be accountable for doing at the Judgment Seat*} **in the Lord** {*as His 'born again' authorized Ambassador*}, **that ye henceforth walk not as other Gentiles walk, in the vanity of their mind** {*the mind that is empty of any true knowledge of God or His will because of the failure to believe in God and be illuminated by God*}, [18] **Having the understanding darkened** {*not illuminated by the Spirit*}, **being alienated from the life of God** {*the supernatural eternal life practically available to the believer through the empowering of the Holy Spirit*} **through the ignorance that is in them** {*because their understanding of God, His Word, and this new supernatural spiritual dynamic of the New Creation in the believer is not illuminated to them by the Spirit*}, **because of the blindness** {*porosis, hardness or callousness*} **of their heart** {*The word 'heart' was used to express the source of emotions/feelings; the idea is that of being 'past' sensitivity to God's leading.*}: [19] **Who being past feeling** {*no longer any sense of guilt or shame about sin or selfishness and without any feeling of remorse for such carnal actions*} **have given themselves over unto lasciviousness** {*uncleanness, lechery, and debauchery of every kind*}, **to work all uncleanness with greediness** {*such as was common among the pagan Gentiles who lived without knowledge of God and the paganized Jews who live in rebellion against God*}. [20] **But ye have not so learned Christ;** [21] **If so be that ye have heard him, and have been taught by him, as the truth is in Jesus:** [22] **That ye <u>put off concerning the former conversation</u>** {*behavior of*} **<u>the old man</u>** {*sin nature*}, **which is corrupt according to the deceitful lusts;** [23] **And <u>be renewed</u>** {*be ye being renovated; present tense, passive voice*} **<u>in the spirit of your mind</u>;** [24] **And that ye <u>put on</u>** {*clothe yourselves with, aorist tense, the idea is to begin to clothe yourselves and continue to put on items of clothing until you are* *fully dressed}* **the new** *{kainos, not merely new as neos, of the same kind, but new of a different kind}* **man, which after God is created in righteousness and true holiness**" (Ephesians 4:17-24).

This "new man" was created the instant of salvation (Romans 10:9-13) when the believing sinner was immediately *transitioned* from being "dead in trespasses and sin" to being "a living soul" *(the salvation of the soul)*. At that moment of salvation, God breathed into that individual the "breathe of life" in the indwelling of the Holy Spirit (I Peter 1:4). However, there is a *progressive aspect* of this *New Creation* that is ongoing within the believer in the creative work of the Holy Spirit. This goes on as the Holy Spirit *progressively transfigures* the believer as the believer is "renewed in the spirit of your mind" (the salvation of the believer's *life* or *essence of being*).

"[1] If ye then be risen with Christ { *'if' this is positionally a reality in that the believer has been baptized into the 'body of Christ,' i.e., 'the regeneration'}*, seek those things which are above *{spiritual or heavenly things}*, where Christ sitteth on the right hand of God. [2] Set your affection on *{keep your thinking fixed on; we are responsible for our thought life and our fantasy life}* things above, not on things on the earth *{our ambitions and goals in life are not to be earthly}*. [3] For ye are dead, and your life is hid with Christ in God. [4] When Christ, *who is* our life, shall appear, then shall ye also appear with him in glory. [5] Mortify therefore your members which are upon the earth; fornication, uncleanness, inordinate affection, evil concupiscence *{evil longings or desires}*, and covetousness, which is idolatry: [6] For which things' sake the wrath of God cometh on the children of disobedience: [7] In the which ye also walked some time, when ye lived in them. [8] But now ye also *{all the first things listed and now these also}* put off all these; anger, wrath, malice, blasphemy, filthy communication out of your mouth. [9] Lie not one to another, seeing that ye have put off the old man with his deeds; [10] And have put on the new *man*, which is renewed in knowledge after the image of him that created him: [11] Where there is neither Greek nor Jew, circumcision nor uncircumcision, Barbarian, Scythian, bond *nor* free: but Christ *is* all, and in all *{i.e., Christ should occupy every thought, action, and motivation of the Christian's life to the glory of God; to be filled with the Spirit is to have every aspect of our existence filled to overflowing with the Christ-life.}*" (Colossians 3:1-11).

To continue living a life subservient to the *sin nature* is to continue under the corrupted *federal headship* of the first Adam and under the *curse*. The believer does not have that *right* (although he still has that *choice*). The statement of Romans 6:17-18 should be an expectation in the life of every person who understands the consequences of sin and the price Christ paid to redeem him from the bondage of the *sin nature*: "[17] But God be thanked, that ye were the servants of sin, but ye have obeyed from the heart that form of doctrine which was delivered you. [18] Being then made free from sin, ye became the servants of righteousness."

> Knowing the overwhelming price of redemption, and being freed from the fear of death, why would anyone abuse that freedom and the love of God so grossly by continuing to live a life filled with selfish choices and by continuing to choose to be the "servants" of the *sin nature*?

This would certainly define an abuse of God's grace and such carnality cheapens grace in a way that it is a spiritual attack against the very character, nature, and righteousness of God. By living in such wickedness, believers create an abusive relationship through which carnal believers both *grieve* the indwelling Spirit of God and *quench* the supernatural work He seeks to do in us and through us.

Few people see the *sin nature* for what it really is. The *sin nature* is a harsh *slave master and* sin in any form merely manifests the fact that the believer continues to live with these shackles of bondage he puts upon his will. Sin is addictive and life dominating. Sin consumes lives and devours resources. Even though sin provides *pleasure for a season* (Hebrews 11:25), it never satisfies regardless of how much you involve yourself. Give it an *inch* and it will demand a *foot*. Give it a *foot* and it will demand an *arm* and a *leg*. It will never be satisfied until it completely devours your whole life. When God says Satan, like "a roaring lion, walketh about, seeking whom he may devour" (I Peter 5:8), He means that Satan uses sin to devour lives. In this case, it is the "flesh" that he uses to consume our lives by seconds, minutes, and hours at a time. On two occasions Paul admonishes believers to be "redeeming the time"

(Ephesians 5:16 and Colossians 4:5). Once those precious moments are lost on carnality, they can never be reinvested or recovered. Those carnal choices will bear the carnal fruit of eternal consequences.

Sin is like a *caustic acid* that eats away at a person's life, scarring at first, but eventually completely consuming a life when left unrestrained. Every person is scarred to some degree. Some have scars that run all the way to the soul. These scars cannot be repaired by outward conformity. Salvation saves the soul, but it may take a lifetime to clear away the ugliness of those spiritual scars upon a life. The process is slow and painful because the sinner must choose to work with God in overcoming the *addiction* to sin that caused those spiritual scars in the first place. It is to that choice that Paul refers us in Romans 6:17-23. This is the process we call *spiritual growth,* involving an ongoing creative work of God in *progressively transfiguring* a believer from within through a cooperative partnership with the indwelling Spirit of God.

"But God be thanked" for providing the believer with a choice (Romans 6:17).

The omnipresence of the Holy Spirit of God within the old, fallen, and cursed creation provides the omni-influence of God upon all people within that fallen first creation. In other words, even though the first creation is fallen into complete spiritual darkness and Satan has "blinded the minds of them which believe not" (II Corinthians 4:4, the Greek word translated "blinded" means *to obscure with smoke, to obfuscate*), God has not left us alone in the darkness. The Spirit of God is "drawing all men" unto God and to "the regeneration."

Until a person is saved, he really has no power in himself to serve God. He is spiritually depraved. His *sin nature* may be restrained by the moral peer pressure and laws of the society in which he lives (Romans 2:1-16). His *sin nature* may be restrained by the religious peer pressure of the religious community he chooses to live under (Romans 2:17-29). However, these are all externals of outward conformity and cannot produce God-kind righteous in the life of the believer. The *New Creation* provides a divine inner source to produce God-kind righteousness through the person of the indwelling Holy Spirit.

"[10] Jesus answered and said unto her, If thou knewest the gift of God, and who it is that saith to thee, Give me to drink; thou wouldest have asked of him, and he would have given thee living water {*referring to the indwelling Spirit of God*}. [11] The woman saith unto him, Sir, thou hast nothing to draw with, and the well is deep: from whence then hast thou that living water? [12] Art thou greater than our father Jacob, which gave us the well, and drank thereof himself, and his children, and his cattle? [13] Jesus answered and said unto her, Whosoever drinketh of this water shall thirst again: [14] But whosoever drinketh of the water that I shall give him shall never thirst; but the water that I shall give him shall be in him a well {*fount*} of water springing up {*gushing out*} into {*not unto*} everlasting {*perpetual*} life" (John 4:10-14).

"Living water" was water that came from a spring out of the ground. It was clear, pure, and cold compared to the water that came from a well or a standing pool of water. The metaphor refers to the indwelling Holy Spirit of God Who is the righteousness of God and who can produce God-kind righteousness in the yielded believer's life. The idea of this "living water" is not that it merely fills the person who takes it in, but that the person in which it resides becomes the *fount from which it flows*. If the *fount is not flowing*, it is because your carnal nature is *quenching* Him.

"[37] In the last day, that great *day* of the feast, Jesus stood and cried, saying, If any man thirst, let him come unto me, and drink. [38] He that believeth on me, as the scripture hath said, out of his belly shall flow rivers of living water. [39] (But this spake he of the Spirit, which they that believe on him should receive: for the Holy Ghost was not yet *given*; because that Jesus was not yet glorified.) (John 7:37-39).

Just like the Law (Romans 7:12), all of the external restraints upon the *sin nature* within various societies are *good* things (positive peers pressures). These restraints keep a sinner, who is addicted to sin, from running into the *fire* to which he is addicted. These restraints can help keep the damage that sin causes in a life to a minimum. However, the ministry of the indwelling Holy Spirit takes the restraint of the *sin nature* to another level altogether. All the other forms of restraint on sin are external (social peer pressure, moral laws of government, and religious peer pressure). They operate by continually pulling the sinner out of the *fire, hosing him down*, and applying *skin grafts*.

The Holy Spirit works internally. When the believer chooses to yield to the internal promptings of the Holy Spirit, the Holy Spirit takes control of that believer's heart and mind and provides him the power to restrain himself from jumping into the *fire*.

However, even more significant than this, the indwelling Holy Spirit is capable of actually producing God-kind righteousness in the yielded believer's life. The reason God should be thanked is because He has provided the believer with a *choice* and the internal strength for the sinner to say *yes* to God's will and to say *no* to his desire to jump into the *fire*. The order of this is important! We must say *yes* to God before we can say *no* to Sin.

The first step away from a life consumed by sin is to "obey from the heart that form of doctrine" (the Gospel).

This obedience "from the heart" refers to the *Spring of Living Water* in the indwelling Holy Spirit that comes forth from the very core of a believer's being, bringing forth the *Christ-life* "from the heart" of that believer.

When a person obeys the Gospel he believes the judicial outcomes of the death, burial, and resurrection of Christ. This involves God's condemnation of the sinner. In a Biblical response to the Gospel (what Jesus accomplished in His death, burial, and resurrection), in response to the person of Jesus Christ (who Jesus is; i.e. Lord), a person is "born again" into the *New Genesis* and receives the indwelling Holy Spirit (the "impartation of the divine nature." This "divine nature" is the believer's *new nature*, II Peter 1:4) to inwardly empower that believer to live victorious over his "old man" (fallen sin nature).

"[29] Then Peter and the *other* apostles answered and said, We ought to obey God rather than men. [30] The God of our fathers raised up Jesus, whom ye slew and hanged on a tree. [31] Him hath God exalted with his right hand *to be* a Prince and a Saviour, for to give repentance to Israel, and forgiveness of sins. [32] And we are his witnesses of these things; and *so is* also the Holy Ghost, whom God hath given to them that obey him" (Acts 5:29-32).

A person who hears the gospel, but refuses to believe the gospel and confess Jesus as Lord, disobeys the teaching of the gospel, which teaching tells a person he needs to get saved and call on the name of Jesus to save him. That person will suffer both the temporal and eternal consequences of that disobedience as part of the condemned old creation.

"[5] Which is a manifest token of the righteous judgment of God, that ye may be counted worthy of the kingdom of God, for which ye also suffer: [6] Seeing it is a righteous thing with God to recompense tribulation to them that trouble you; [7] And to you who are troubled rest with us, when the Lord Jesus shall be revealed from heaven with his mighty angels, [8] In flaming fire taking vengeance on them that know not God, and that obey not the gospel of our Lord Jesus Christ: [9] Who shall be punished with everlasting destruction from the presence of the Lord, and from the glory of his power; [10] When he shall come to be glorified in his saints, and to be admired in all them that believe (because our testimony among you was believed) in that day" (II Thessalonians 1:5-10).

"[16] Yet if any man suffer as a Christian, let him not be ashamed; but let him glorify God on this behalf. [17] For the time is come that judgment must begin at the house of God: and if it first begin at us, what shall the end be of them that obey not the gospel of God? [18] And if the righteous scarcely be saved, where shall the ungodly and the sinner appear" (I Peter 4:16-18)?

God's deliverance in the Gospel goes beyond delivering the believer from the condemnation of sin in the salvation of the soul. God's deliverance in the Gospel is intent upon delivering the believer from the addictive power the *sin natu*re holds over his life to practically escape the corruption of the first creation and to practically live a righteous life in the *New Creation*. God also wants to save our lives!

The words "was delivered you" (Romans 6:17) are from the Greek word *paradidomi* (par-ad-id'-o-mee); "But God be thanked, that ye were the servants of sin, but ye have obeyed from the heart that form of doctrine which was delivered you." *Paradidomi* means to *deliver over into the authority or power of another*. Before the believer obeyed the gospel by confessing Jesus as the Lord of his life and trusting completely in the finished work of the Cross, he lived his life under the addictive authority of his *sin nature* within the fallen creation. Once a person places faith in Christ, that believer is delivered **into** the *New Creation* by the power of the indwelling Spirit of God and **INTO** the power of God ("into this grace in which we stand," Romans 5:2). The higher truth of this *New Creation* is that the believer is now delivered **into** a *new existence*. Once there, he has unlimited resources of *divine power* available that exponentially increase the believer's *responsibilities and accountability* for the way those unlimited resources are invested through every day living.

> The great truth of this statement is that God has opened the door of opportunity for the believer to practically and presently live the actual life of the resurrected and glorified Christ. This *Christ-life* is within the *New Creation* through the power of the indwelling Holy Spirit. It is just a matter of choice.

"Therefore we are buried with him by baptism into death: that like as Christ was raised up from the dead by the glory of the Father, even so we also should walk in newness of life" (Romans 6:4).

However, before a person can be empowered to live as part of the *New Creation* "in Christ," that believer must willfully "put off" every carnal influence of the *sin nature* ("old man"). This includes all of the desires for the things of the "world" (the corrupt, condemned first creation). The believer must also "put on the new man." The "new man" brings that believer's life to be practically lived within the *New Creation* "in Christ."

"[17] This I say therefore, and testify in the Lord, that ye henceforth walk not as other Gentiles walk, in the vanity of their mind, [18] Having the understanding darkened, being alienated from the life of God through the ignorance that is in them, because of the blindness of their heart: [19] Who being past feeling have given themselves over unto lasciviousness, to work all uncleanness with greediness. [20] But ye have not so learned Christ; [21] If so be that ye have heard him, and have been taught by him, as the truth is in Jesus: [22] That ye put off concerning the former conversation the old man, which is corrupt according to the deceitful lusts; [23] And be renewed in the spirit of your mind; [24] And that ye put on the new man, which after God is created in righteousness and true holiness" (Ephesians 4:17-24).

The word "renewed" in Ephesians 4:23 is translated from the Greek word *ananeoo* (an-an-neh-o'-o). The idea is that of *constantly being renewed to a state of youth*. This was probably God's intent in the original creation. Man would not grow old, decrepit, and die; he would constantly be renewed as his body constantly regenerated itself. This may be a major part of our future glorified bodies in the *New Creation*. Presently, before our glorification, the best we can hope for is the practical renewal of "the spirit" of our "mind." This refers to bringing the human will into alignment with the will of God, thereby creating perfect harmony and fellowship with the *oneness* of the Godhead. Although the believer is positionally part of the *New Creation*, he is not yet glorified. The renewal of "the spirit" of our "mind" is how the yielded believer practically brings his present *life* into the *New Creation* and is how he is being *progressively transfigured* by the indwelling Holy Spirit.

"[1] I therefore, the prisoner of the Lord, beseech you that ye walk worthy of the vocation wherewith ye are called, [2] With all lowliness and meekness, with longsuffering, forbearing one another in love; [3] Endeavouring to keep the unity of the Spirit in the bond of peace. [4] *There is* one body, and one Spirit, even as ye are called in one hope of your calling; [5] One Lord, one faith, one baptism, [6] One God and Father of all, who *is* above all, and through all, and in you all. [7] But unto every one of us is given grace according to the measure of the gift of Christ" (Ephesians 4:1-7).

The **first choice** a person must make to escape the addictive power of sin and the fallen creation of which he is part, is to choose to obey the Gospel. The **second choice** is the moment-by-moment yielding to the Holy Spirit (Romans 6:11-13). Being delivered from the power of the *sin nature* is not available to the person who rejects the finished work of the Cross and refuses to obey the gospel. That person's destiny is sealed in the condemned first creation by his own unbelief. He may live a relatively moral life and escape the effects of sin upon his life to some small degree, but he will not escape the ultimate penalty of sin. He will not escape death and the fires of Hell.

"[1] Therefore we ought to give the more earnest heed to the things which we have heard, lest at any time we should let *them* slip. [2] For if the word spoken by angels was stedfast, and every transgression and disobedience received a just recompence of reward; [3] How shall we escape, if we neglect so great salvation; which at the first began to be spoken by the Lord, and was confirmed unto us by them that heard *him*; [4] God also bearing *them* witness, both with signs and wonders, and with divers miracles, and gifts of the Holy Ghost, according to his own will" (Hebrews 2:1-4)?

"[25] See that ye refuse not him that speaketh. <u>For if they escaped not who refused him that spake on earth, much more *shall not* we escape, if we turn away from him that *speaketh* from heaven</u>: [26] Whose voice then shook the earth: but now he hath promised, saying, Yet once more I shake not the earth only, but also heaven. [27] And this *word*, Yet once more, signifieth the removing of those things that are shaken, as of things that are made, that those things which cannot be shaken may remain. [28] Wherefore we receiving a kingdom which cannot be moved, let us have grace, whereby we may serve God acceptably with reverence and godly fear: [29] For our God *is* a consuming fire" (Hebrews 12:25-29).

DISCUSSION QUESTIONS

1. Discuss why it is critical to understand that simply because a person is "born again" that this does not get rid of all the pagan and false religious *baggage* they have acquired in their lifetimes.

2. Discuss why it is important that the believer has no part whatsoever in his *positional perfection* "in Christ."

3. Discuss the *process of practical perfection* and why it is essential to understand the necessity of the Holy Spirit's enabling grace in the process.

4. Explain Ephesians 4:17-24 from the perspective of what this text teaches regarding the *process of practical perfection*.

5. Explain Colossians 3:1-11 from the perspective of what this text teaches regarding the *process of practical perfection*.

6. Discuss what is necessary to get the *sin nature out of your way* so that the "living water" of the indwelling Spirit can be released through your life and ministry.

7. Discuss the following statement from the threefold perspective of salvation, i.e., the salvation of the *soul*, the *spirit* or *life*, and the *body* of the believer. How is God working from within to *save your life*?

> "God's deliverance in the gospel goes beyond delivering the believer from the condemnation of sin in the salvation of the soul. God's deliverance in the gospel is intent upon delivering the believer from the addictive power the *sin nature* holds over his life to practically escape the corruption of the first creation and to practically live a righteous life in the *New Creation*. God also wants to save our lives!"

Chapter Fifty-two

Why Can't I be Good?
Part of the Good News is that You Can - Now!

There are some very important dispensational transitional issues detailed in Romans chapter six through Romans chapter seven. The spiritual depth of these two chapters transition us from the believer's position "in Christ" (positional sanctification or perfection) to the believer's potential and responsibility for progressive sanctification (progressive transfiguration/perfection) through Christ *in us* in the indwelling Holy Spirit.

The Judaism of the Mosaic Covenant was never intended to be a *religion* of *will power*. Neither is Christianity intended to be a religion of *will power*, at least not *human will power*. Christianity takes the Christian to a higher level of culpability then those under the Law could ever have imagined. Christ said, "[27] Ye have heard that it was said by them of old time, Thou shalt not commit adultery: [28] But I say unto you, That whosoever looketh on a woman to lust after her hath committed adultery with her already in his heart" (Matthew 5:27-28). He then goes on in Matthew chapters five through seven to *raise the bar* regarding spiritual expectations to a level unimaginable by the Jews (especially since they already knew the level of expectation they presently had was completely unattainable). This new level of expectation is what Paul deals with in Romans chapter seven.

"[14] For we know that the law is spiritual: but I am carnal, sold under sin. [15] For that which I do I allow not: for what I would, that do I not; but what I hate, that do I. [16] If then I do that which I would not, I consent unto the law that *it is* good. [17] Now then it is no more I that do it, but sin that dwelleth in me. [18] For I know that in me (that is, in my flesh,) dwelleth no good thing: for to will is present with me; but *how* to perform that which is good I find not. [19] For the good that I would I do not: but the evil which I would not, that I do. [20] Now if I do that I would not, it is no more I that do it, but sin that dwelleth in me. [21] I find then a law, that, when I would do good, evil is present with me. [22] For I delight in the law of God after the inward man: [23]

But I see another law in my members, warring against the law of my mind, and bringing me into captivity to the law of sin which is in my members. [24] O wretched man that I am! who shall deliver me from the body of this death? [25] I thank God through Jesus Christ our Lord. So then with the mind I myself serve the law of God; but with the flesh the law of sin" (Romans 7:14-25).

Judaism had reduced the Law to *spiritual superficiality*. It had become little more than a series of ceremonial rituals that involved individuals in equally superficial externalism in varying degrees of outward conformity. This is what *mere religion* always does with the worship of God. *Mere religion* reduces relationship to rituals and true spirituality to externalism. This was not what the Law was intended to do. The "law is spiritual" (Romans 7:14). The Law was intended to touch mankind at the very core and depth of their being. The Law was intended to bring about deep conviction of sin and the knowledge of God's grace and redemption in the Promised One of whom it was intended to typify.

"[7] The law of the LORD *is* perfect, converting the soul: the testimony of the LORD *is* sure, making wise the simple. [8] The statutes of the LORD *are* right, rejoicing the heart: the commandment of the LORD *is* pure, enlightening the eyes. [9] The fear of the LORD *is* clean, enduring for ever: the judgments of the LORD *are* true *and* righteous altogether. [10] More to be desired *are they* than gold, yea, than much fine gold: sweeter also than honey and the honeycomb. [11] Moreover by them is thy servant warned: *and* in keeping of them *there is* great reward" (Psalm 19:7-11).

As we understand the statement of Hebrews 4:11-13, we must remember that at the time of its writing it referred primarily to the Old Testament Scriptures, and even more primarily to the five books of the Law. The "word of God" was, and is, a book of spiritual truths that are able to touch our souls and move our hearts. There is great significance in the words "the law is spiritual."

"[11] Let us labour therefore to enter into that rest, lest any man fall after the same example of unbelief. [12] For the word of God *is* quick, and powerful, and sharper than any twoedged sword, piercing even to the dividing asunder of soul and spirit, and of the joints and marrow, and *is* a discerner of the thoughts and intents of the heart. [13] Neither is there any creature that is not manifest in his sight: but all things *are* naked and opened unto the eyes of him with whom we have to do" (Hebrews 4:11-13).

The Law, as a spiritual entity, comes from God along with the Spirit of God. Its spirituality goes beyond giving instructions for living and for faith; the Spirit of God remains intrinsically part of the Law. We might go as far as to say God not only inspired His Word, but that God remains in His Word in the person of the Holy Spirit. This is what makes the Word of God "quick, and powerful, and sharper than any twoedged sword, piercing even to the dividing asunder of soul and spirit, and of the joints and marrow, and *is* a discerner of the thoughts and intents of the heart." The Word of God is *alive* spiritually in its synergism with the Holy Spirit.

On the other hand, Paul as an entity was carnal. Paul is using himself as an example of all fallen humanity. Paul is referring to the fact he had a fallen nature and that, apart from unity with the Spirit of God, he was a carnal entity without any possibility of producing *spiritual life*. Paul explains his meaning in Romans 7:18, "For I know that in me (that is, in my flesh,) dwelleth no good thing: for to will is present with me; but *how* to perform that which is good I find not." The subject of the text is the *spiritual warfare* in which the believer is involved. This is about his own carnal nature/heart hindering the production of *spiritual life* through synergism with the indwelling Spirit of God. *Will power* was not going to get the job done.

Paul exemplifies the fact that not only is he "carnal" as an entity, but that the problem goes much deeper; he is "sold under sin." One of a believer's first discoveries after being saved is to discover that salvation is not a *magic wand* waved over his life that takes away his carnal nature and its voracious appetite for sin. Salvation takes away the *penalty* of the *sin nature* (Romans 6:6), but the *power* of the *sin nature* is still very much within us all. The weight of the *penalty* of the *sin nature* is "once for all" lifted from our shoulders. However, the guilt of our continuing desire for sin is still very much with us.

The *power* of the *sin nature* will be a problem in our Christian lives until we die or until our glorification when we will be delivered from both the *power* and *presence* of our sinful natures. Until then, we still live in the *slave market* of sin (the *fall*). The good news is that due to the indwelling of the Holy Spirit, we have been given a choice as to who we *will* to serve. We determine the *outcomes* of carnality or spirituality by choosing to whom we yield our will (Romans 6:11-13). Salvation is choosing God's side in the battle against evil. To understand the doctrine of sanctification is to understand that part of the evil with which we war is our very own *sin nature*.

> To understand the doctrine of sanctification is understanding that the first front of spiritual warfare lies within our own corrupted *hearts*. If we are ever going to be supernaturally enabled to win spiritual victories in the world, we must first learn to be habitually victorious over our own fallen nature.

This inner battle is emphasized by the words of Romans 7:15, "For that which I do I allow not: for what I would, that do I not; but what I hate, that do I." The word translated "allow" in the KJV is the Greek word *ginosko* (ghin-oce'-ko). It means to *know, perceive,* or *be aware* of something. The meaning is that all of humanity, saved and unsaved alike, are not really aware that EVERYTHING we do that finds its source in our fallen natures. This applies to even that which we might think to be good and righteous. It is in fact *carnality*. The words "I allow not" would be better translated "I do not comprehend." Even though Paul was saved, his *sin nature* still hindered him from fully comprehending the problem of producing spiritual life from this "carnal" entity. Although he was saved, he was not yet glorified and not yet fully regenerated. It certainly appeared to be an irresolvable problem and it would continue to be apart from the indwelling Spirit of God.

The phrase "that I do not" within the phrase "what I would, that do I not" is also misleading. The word "do" is from the Greek word *prasso* (pras'-so). It means *to practice, to repeatedly or habitually perform*. This is important in that Paul is saying the difficulty of this spiritual struggle is in being *spiritually consistent*. He wanted to be consistent in his spiritual life, but his *sin nature* constantly hindered him. His *sin nature* constantly led him back to the *pig trough* of the world. If it did not lead him into actual acts of sin, at least it led him in the continuing desire for sin. However, the opposite was even more a dilemma. The things the Law had taught Paul to hate were the things he found himself desiring and doing.

The word "do" in the phrase "what I hate, that do I" is from a different Greek word which greatly impacts what is being said.

Here the word "do" is translated from the Greek word *poieo* (poy-eh'-o), which properly refers to a *single act* or an *occasional act*. The importance in this is that Paul closes the door for the excuse for the habitual sin he has already forbidden in Romans 6:1.

In Romans 7:16, Paul extends the example up one more step. "If then I do that which I would not, I consent unto the law that *it is* good." This is the *second step* towards producing spiritual life through the believer. The first is acknowledging the continuing desire for sin that comes from the still-present *sin nature*. The second is acknowledging that a desire to obey the Law reveals the inner working of the Spirit of God. The very fact that he knows that the sinful things he desires are sinful reveals to his *internal consent* that the Law is "good" (*valuable*). Apart from God's working of grace, the Law merely condemns. However, within God's working of grace in the indwelling of the Holy Spirit, the Law also serves a higher and nobler purpose. The Law not only reveals our sinfulness, once separated from its condemnation of our souls, but it also leads us to what is righteous and defines a righteous life. In this purpose, the Law is "good."

DISCUSSION QUESTIONS

1. Discuss the dispensational transitional issues detailed in Romans chapter six through Romans chapter seven in transitioning from the believer's position "in Christ" (positional sanctification/perfection) to the believer's potential. Explain the believer's responsibility for progressive sanctification (progressive transfiguration/perfection) through Christ *in us* in the indwelling Holy Spirit.

2. Discuss why Christianity is not intended to be a religion of *will power*.

3. Read Psalm 19:7-11 and Hebrews 4:11-13. Discuss why the Law is *spiritual* according to Romans 7:14.

4. Explain what Paul means when he says "I am carnal" in Romans 7:14 and that he is "sold under sin."

5. Explain the meaning of the word "do" in the phrase "what I would, that do I not" in Romans 7:15.

6. Explain the meaning of the word "do" in the phrase "what I hate, that do I" in Romans 7:15.

7. In Romans 7:16, Paul takes the example up *one more step*. What is this next *step* and why is it significant to our understanding of *progressive sanctification*.

Chapter Fifty-three
The Local Church of the New Covenant
and the Strife of the Two Natures

As we study the "unity of the Spirit," or that which is more commonly referred to as the *filling with* the Spirit, we must keep the purposes of God in His provision of this supernatural dynamic at the center of our focus. If we do not keep these purposes at the forefront of our thinking, we will easily, and quickly, slip into externalism and into a kind of false pursuit of holiness. God's purposes are always *practical.* God's purposes are never merely for appearances sake. God's purposes are connected in a line of spiritual outcomes. The believer is practically sanctified before God, allowing that believer to be used of God in two primary ways:

1. To bring glory to God through the supernatural operations of the indwelling Spirit through the overflow of the "fruit of the Spirit" in the production of the *Christ-life* through the believer's body as the believer actively cooperates with the Spirit
2. To bring God glory through producing "fruit" in winning souls to Christ and making those newly "born again" believers disciples of Jesus Christ

True local churches are a composite of individuals whose lives are built upon, and who agree to live within, a covenant relationship with God and with one another. The initial prerequisite to becoming a member of a local church body is being "born again." What actually defines a local church are the biblical Doctrinal Statement and the Church Covenant, which are *binding* on the constituency. No organization can consider itself a true local church apart from these two *binding* documents that must align according to Scriptural criteria.

From the beginning of time, believers have been relationally linked to God by covenants ordained by Him. Every individual within any Dispensation enters into that Dispensation's Covenant with God and is then united in a Covenant relationship with one another. Entering into the covenant that defines a local church, and the ministry that extends from that local church, primarily involves commitment to practical sanctification and the commitment to evangelism (win souls, bring those individuals into a local church to be baptized and commit to practical sanctification and discipleship, and *actually* become accountable to learn the Word of God and engage themselves in evangelism). This is the covenant to which Church age believers are united.

In the last 300 years this definition of the local church has been almost completely lost. Church covenants frequently become nothing but words recited before men with little consciousness of the sovereign Third Party (God) who is the primary focus of the covenant. It is little wonder that most local churches have completely lost their purpose for existence when they have almost completely lost their practical connection to their own responsibilities defined by their local church covenant. Church covenants are *job descriptions* for every member. Every member is to prepare himself to fulfill these *job descriptions* through the teaching/discipleship ministries of the local church.

I would like you to read our local church covenant. As you read it, notice the points of emphasis.

DECLARATION OF PRINCIPLES OF THE COVENANT

"**And they entered in a covenant <u>to seek the Lord God of their fathers with all their heart and with all their soul</u>**" (II Chron. 15:12).

Having been led, as we believe, by the Spirit of God to receive the Lord Jesus Christ, as our Savior, and on profession of our faith having been baptized (Matt. 3:13-17; 28:19; Acts 8:38; 8:12; Col. 2:12) in the Name of the Father, and of the Son and of the Holy Ghost, we do now, in the presence of God, angels, and this assembly, most solemnly and joyfully enter into covenant with one another, as one body in Christ.

We do promise by the aid of the Holy Spirit to forsake the paths of sin, and to walk together in Christian love; to strive for the advancement of this church, in knowledge, holiness, and comfort; to promote its prosperity and spirituality; to sustain its worship, ordinances, discipline, and doctrines; to contribute cheerfully to the support of the ministry, the expenses of the church, the relief of the poor, and the spread of the gospel through all nations.

We also engage to maintain family and personal devotions; to religiously educate our children; to seek the salvation of our kindred and acquaintances; to walk circumspectly in the world, to be just in our dealings, faithful in our engagements, and exemplary in our deportment; to avoid all tattling, backbiting, and excessive anger; to abstain from the sale and use of intoxicating drink as a beverage, and to be zealous in our efforts to advance the work of our Savior.

We further engage to watch over one another in brotherly love; to remember each other in prayer; to aid each other in sickness and distress; to cultivate Christian sympathy in feeling and courtesy in speech; to be slow to take offense, but always ready for reconciliation and mindful of the rules of our Savior, to seek it without delay.

We moreover engage that, when we remove from this place, we will as soon as possible unite with some other church of like precious faith where we can carry out the spirit of this covenant and the principles of God's Word.

It is important for us to remember that Romans chapter seven is contextually connected to what Paul said in Romans 6:1-4: "[1] What shall we say then? Shall we continue in sin, that grace may abound? [2] God forbid. How shall we, that are dead to sin, live any longer therein? [3] Know ye not, that so many of us as were baptized into Jesus Christ were baptized into his death? [4] Therefore we are buried with him by baptism into death: that like as Christ was raised up from the dead by the glory of the Father, <u>even so we also should walk in newness of life</u>." Water baptism, which testifies to the reality of a believer's Spirit baptism, is a *vow of commitment* to seek to habitually "walk in newness of life." Christians need to understand God's view of a *vow*.

"If a man vow a vow unto the Lord, or swear an oath to bind his soul with a bond; he shall not break his word, he shall do according to all that proceedeth out of his mouth" (Numbers 30:2).

A "vow" is a *promise to God* that a person will perform a certain task or maintain the conditions of an agreement or covenant. A "vow" involves the commitment of *personal character* and *personal integrity* to a promise. Vows usually involve the voluntary imposition of self-denial or self-discipline in order to build and prove *personal character* and *personal integrity* to God in order to attain to certain spiritual goals. The Nazarite Vow of Numbers 6 is such a vow. It was a vow of separation and consecration unto God. *Self-denial* is expected of all those who commit to being a disciple of the Lord Jesus (Matt 16:24; Mark 8:34-38; Phil 3:7- 14).

Jehovah is a Covenant God

Throughout the Bible, we discover that our God is a covenant making and covenant keeping God. A covenant is a "vow" to a certain person, or groups of people, detailing the conditions of a relationship and individual responsibilities within that relationship. The New Testament word for this covenant *relationship* with God is "fellowship." Believers are to seek to live in unbroken "fellowship" with God.

One central expectation of God to all people who wish to have this unbroken personal relationship with Him is the necessity of maintaining personal sanctity before Him. Sanctity is the maintenance of personal purity and separation from the world's carnal influences (and customs) so that the believer can live undefiled for God's use.

This sanctity is always a matter of personal choice. It is not the product of a *reflect action*. We will need to make hundreds of choices each day (perhaps more) that will determine our sanctity before God and reveal our desire for that sanctity. The reality is that personal sanctity will not be important to us until we understand its importance to God and until we love Him enough to insure that our lifestyles will not be offensive to His holy character.

The choices we make will involve every aspect of our lives: the things we wear, eat, and drink, and the things we choose to entertain us. We will choose who will be our friends and we will determine to what degree we will allow them to be an influence on us. We will choose where we go, how we will get there, and the speed we will travel. Any error in making any one of these choices *may* defile us before God.

The *God factor* must always be the first consideration when making choices. His will must be the *determining factor* for our *equation* of living life. The *equation* for sanctity must be a *composite of pluses* (righteous choices). Any negative choice (unrighteous choice) in the equation for spiritual sanctity negates the whole. These choices of the will are the determining factors to our personal attitude about sanctity.

The idea of sanctity cannot be separated from service or service from sanctity. The idea of *worship* without *service* is really foreign to the Scriptures. The acceptance of the gift of salvation carries with it the *obligation of service* to the Redeemer. This is the context that begins in Romans 6:1 and continues into Romans chapter seven. We cannot lose the practicality intended in this context regarding what is necessary to the spiritual dynamic of sanctification before God. This spiritual dynamic must exist before God can use the believer and produce *spiritual fruit* through that believer's life.

Romans 7:17 is a critical verse in Paul's transitioning from his "old man" and the *new life* he has "in Christ." "Now then it is no more I that do it, but sin that dwelleth in me." The use of the pronoun "I" down through verse 25 refers to these two identities existing in the believer's life; i.e., the *new man* "in Christ" and the "old man" as part of the *fall*. The *new man* is the person created by yielding to the indwelling Spirit. The context must determine to which of these two entities the "I" refers. Perhaps we can simplify this by using the name *Paul* for the pronoun referring to the *new man* and the name *Saul* for the pronoun referring to the "old man" (*sin nature*).

"[17] Now then it is no more I {*Paul*} that do it, but sin {*Saul*} that dwelleth in me. [18] For I {*Paul*} know that in me {*Saul*} (that is, in my flesh,) dwelleth no good thing: for to will is present with me; but *how* to perform that which is good I {*Saul*} find not. [19] For the good that I {*Paul*} would I {*Saul*} do not: but the evil which I {*Paul*} would not, that I {*Saul*} do. [20] Now if I {*Saul*} do that I {*Paul*} would not, it is no more I {*Paul*} that do it, but sin {*Saul*} that dwelleth in me. [21] I {*Paul*} find then a law, that, when I {*Paul*} would do good, evil {*Saul*} is present with me. [22] For I {*Paul*} delight in the law of God after the inward man {*Paul*}: [23] But I {*Paul*} see another law in my members, warring against the law of my mind, and bringing me into captivity to the law of sin which is in my members. [24] O wretched man that I {*Saul*} am! who shall deliver me {*Paul*} from the body of this death {*Saul*}? [25] I {*Paul*} thank God through Jesus Christ our Lord. So then with the mind I {*Paul*} myself serve the law of God; but with the flesh {*Saul*} the law of sin" (Romans 7:17-25).

Although there will undoubtedly be some disagreement about which of these two entities are being referred to by the pronoun "I," the above rendering should be fairly accurate in representing the meaning of the text. The fact that the believer still possesses a *sin nature* exposes the reality that "evil is present" *with* and *in* us (Romans 7:21, 23). This does not refer to the presence of evil in a *demon* or even to *satanic influence*. This refers to the evil that is part of what we all are as fallen in sin and corrupted in the very essence of what we are (our *nature* or *essence of being*). This "evil" refers to our *sin natures* and our wicked desire for sin.

Paul has already said, "but what I hate, that do I." Paul's *new nature* hated the things his *sin nature* desired and the acts of sin into which his *sin nature* led him. One of the characteristics of a saved person is a love for the Word of God and hatred for anything that contradicts the Word of God.

> "[8] Zion heard, and was glad; and the daughters of Judah rejoiced because of thy judgments, O LORD. [9] For thou, LORD, *art* high above all the earth: thou art exalted far above all gods. [10] Ye that love the LORD, hate evil: he preserveth the souls of his saints; he delivereth them out of the hand of the wicked. [11] Light is sown for the righteous, and gladness for the upright in heart. [12] Rejoice in the LORD, ye righteous; and give thanks at the remembrance of his holiness" (Psalm 97:8-12).

> "[103] How sweet are thy words unto my taste! *yea, sweeter* than honey to my mouth! [104] Through thy precepts I get understanding: therefore I hate every false way" (Psalm 119:103-104).

Now, in Romans 7:22, Paul says, "For I delight in the law of God after the inward man." The word "delight" is translated from the Greek word *sunedomai* (soon-ay'-dom-ahee). This refers to an *inner rejoicing that overflows in outward expressions*. This is an expression of the outcome of the *unity* of the believer with the indwelling Holy Spirit and to the synergism that *unity* creates. True inward joy, rejoicing, and worship of God are produced inwardly. In that *unity*, there is also a rejoicing "in the Law" in that the Law now ("in grace," Romans 5:2) takes on positive spiritual connotations. This could never be said of the unregenerate man.

> "[18] Having the understanding darkened, being alienated from the life of God through the ignorance that is in them, because of the blindness of their heart: [19] Who being past feeling have given themselves over unto lasciviousness, to work all uncleanness with greediness" (Ephesians 4:18-19).

Yet Paul says, "But I see another law in my members, warring against the law of my mind, and bringing me into captivity to the law of sin which is in my members" (Romans 7:23). The word "another" is translated from the Greek word *heteros* (het'-er-os) and refers to *another that is different.*

> Paul is aware of a *different* "law" within his *inner man* that opposes his *new nature* "in Christ." This *different* "law" (inner evil influence) is actively *waging war* to bring the *new man*, created through the "new creation" and the *unity* of the Spirit in the indwelling, back into "captivity" (present active participle) to itself ("the law of sin").

The Law of God (personified in the person of the indwelling Spirit of God), acting in synergism with the yielded believer (Romans 6:11-13), was warring against the "law of sin" in synergism with the "old man" (the *sin nature*) that is still within every believer "warring" to bring the regenerated believer back into "captivity" (functionally into the slave market of sin; i.e., the *fall*).

Romans 7:24 is the helpless cry that comes from the heart of every soul that desires to live for Christ; "O wretched man that I am! who shall deliver me from the body of this death?" The "body of death" refers to the *internal force of evil* (Romans 7:21; "the law of sin") of the "old man" still living within our bodies. It is this *internal force of evil* that condemns our soul to "death" and corrupts the *fountain of spiritual life.* There is only one avenue of deliverance from this "body of death" - the indwelling Christ (Romans 7:25).

"3 Grace *be* to you and peace from God the Father, and *from* our Lord Jesus Christ, 4 Who gave himself for our sins, that he might deliver us from this present evil world, according to the will of God and our Father: 5 To whom *be* glory for ever and ever. Amen" (Galatians 1:3-5).

Paul ends the chapter with this ongoing spiritual struggle of progressive sanctification and the production of spiritual life. "So then with the mind I myself serve the law of God; but with the flesh the law of sin" (Romans 7:25). Only God is able to *practically* deliver us from this "body of death." He has already done so *positionally* in the death, burial, resurrection, and glorification of Christ. He wants to deliver us *practically* through His indwelling Spirit. This deliverance is readily available, not by *will power*, but by yielding our wills to the indwelling Holy Spirit. This must be a cooperative and participatory work *with* the indwelling Holy Spirit. This "work of the ministry" is *passive* in the sense that the Spirit of God does all the *supernatural* and *spiritual* work, but the yielded believer must be *participatory* in obeying the Word of God and actually doing the *natural* and *physical* work that we are commanded to do.

"[8] But now ye also put off all these; anger, wrath, malice, blasphemy, filthy communication out of your mouth. [9] Lie not one to another, seeing that ye have put off the old man with his deeds; [10] And have put on the new *man*, which is renewed in knowledge after the image of him that created him: [11] Where there is neither Greek nor Jew, circumcision nor uncircumcision, Barbarian, Scythian, bond *nor* free: but Christ *is* all, and in all. [12] Put on therefore, as the elect of God, holy and beloved, bowels of mercies, kindness, humbleness of mind, meekness, longsuffering; [13] Forbearing one another, and forgiving one another, if any man have a quarrel against any: even as Christ forgave you, so also *do* ye. [14] And above all these things *put on* charity, which is the bond of perfectness. [15] And let the peace of God rule in your hearts, to the which also ye are called in one body; and be ye thankful. [16] Let the word of Christ dwell in you richly in all wisdom; teaching and admonishing one another in psalms and hymns and spiritual songs, singing with grace in your hearts to the Lord. [17] And whatsoever ye do in word or deed, *do* all in the name of the Lord Jesus, giving thanks to God and the Father by him" (Colossians 3:8-17).

DISCUSSION QUESTIONS

1. Discuss why it is critical to our progressive sanctification to keep the purposes of God in His provision of this *supernatural dynamic* of the filling of the Spirit at the center of our focus.

2. List and discuss the two primary ways practical sanctification allows the believer to be used of God.

3. Discuss what is meant by the fact that the biblical Doctrinal Statement and the Church Covenant must be *binding* on the constituency of a local church.

4. Discuss the ordinance of water baptism as a *vow of commitment* to seek to habitually "walk in newness of life."

5. Discuss a "vow" as it involves the commitment of *personal character* and *personal integrity* in a promise to God.

6. Discuss the local church as a group of people *covenantally* bound together to live in unbroken "fellowship" with God.

7. Discuss why sanctity cannot be separated from service and why service cannot be separated from sanctity.

Chapter Fifty-four
The Local Church as the New Covenant Theanthropic Priesthood

"¹ Behold, what manner of love the Father hath bestowed upon us, that we should be called the sons of God: therefore the world knoweth us not, because it knew him not. ² Beloved, now are we the sons of God, and it doth not yet appear what we shall be: but we know that, when he shall appear, we shall be like him; for we shall see him as he is. ³ And every man that hath this hope in him purifieth himself, even as he is pure" (I John 3:1-3).

As we seek to understand the *theanthropic* Christ before His death, burial, and resurrection, we must understand that the *theanthropic* Christ after His resurrection and glorification became *another kind of being* that never existed ever before, except in the plan of God. Although there are many similarities in the pre-resurrected Christ and the glorified Christ, there are also many things that are unique. There is a permanent supernatural aspect in the union of God and man in glorification that is part of every believer's future and eternal existence "in Christ."

"³⁶ And as they thus spake, Jesus himself <u>stood in the midst of them,</u> and saith unto them, Peace *be* unto you. ³⁷ But they were terrified and affrighted, and supposed that they had seen a spirit. ³⁸ And he said unto them, Why are ye troubled? and why do <u>thoughts arise in your hearts</u>? ³⁹ Behold my hands and my feet, that it is I myself: <u>handle me, and see; for a spirit hath not flesh and bones,</u> as ye see me have. ⁴⁰ And when he had thus spoken, he shewed them *his* hands and *his* feet. ⁴¹ And while they yet believed not for joy, and wondered, he said unto them, <u>Have ye here any meat?</u> ⁴² And they gave him a piece of a broiled fish, and of an honeycomb. ⁴³ And he took *it*, and did eat before them" (Luke 24:36-43).

The baptism of Jesus by John the Baptist was not the same as John's baptism of Jewish believers. John the Baptist's ministry was ordained for two primary purposes:

1. To sanctify Jewish believers for the coming of the Messiah. This was accomplished through his baptism of repentance (Mark 1:4; Luke 3:3; Acts 13:24) as a preparation for those believers to recognize and believe on (Acts 19:4) the One who John would reveal as the promised Messiah.

2. A central aspect of John the Baptist's prophetic message to the people of Israel was that God would reveal to him who was actually the Messiah. This revealing was his proclamation to the people of Israel through which he called them to repentance with the understanding that the promised Messiah was alive and living in their midst.

"[29] The next day John seeth Jesus coming unto him, and saith, Behold the Lamb of God, which taketh away the sin of the world. [30] This is he of whom I said, After me cometh a man which is preferred before me: for he was before me. [31] And I knew him not: but that he should be made manifest to Israel, therefore am I come baptizing with water. [32] And John bare record, saying, I saw the Spirit descending from heaven like a dove, and it abode upon him. [33] And I knew him not: but he that sent me to baptize with water, the same said unto me, Upon whom thou shalt see the Spirit descending, and remaining on him, the same is he which baptizeth with the Holy Ghost. [34] And I saw, and bare record that this is the Son of God. [35] Again the next day after John stood, and two of his disciples; [36] And looking upon Jesus as he walked, he saith, Behold the Lamb of God" (John 1:29-36)!

The Word of God prophesied of a new coming order of Priesthood that was not connected tribally to the nation of Israel. As High Priest of this new order of Priesthood, Jesus and His faithful disciples of the Church Age, would rule as judging prophets, priests, and kings during the Kingdom Age on earth.

"[1] A Psalm of David. The LORD {*Jehovah*} said unto my Lord {*Adoni, referring to the sovereignty of God in the theanthropic union in the incarnate Son of God as also the resurrected and glorified "Son of man;" the Jews would have understood this to refer to the promised Messiah*}, Sit thou at my right hand {*upon His ascension and throughout the Church Age*}, until I make thine enemies thy footstool {*which will take place during the seven year Tribulation*}. [2] The LORD shall send the rod {*the second coming of Jesus to earth at Armageddon*} of thy strength out of Zion {*Zion is true Israel 'born again' of the Spirit of God that is presently embodied in all Church Age believers made up of saved Jews and Gentiles as the true theanthropic spiritual Temple of God, who will be resurrected, glorified, and will return to earth to reign with Jesus during the Kingdom Age.*}: rule thou in the midst of thine enemies. [3] Thy people *shall be* willing in the day of thy power, in the beauties of holiness from the womb of the morning: thou hast the dew of thy youth. [4] The LORD hath sworn, and will not repent, <u>Thou *art* a priest for ever after the order</u> {*similitude, Hebrews 7:15*} <u>of Melchizedek</u> {*He was a prophet, priest and king; therefore, the similitude of this priesthood is a priesthood of prophets, priests, and kings with the LORD Jesus as the High Priest and 'King of kings and LORD of lords.'*}. [5] The Lord at thy right hand shall strike through kings in the day of his wrath. [6] He shall judge among the heathen, he shall fill *the places* with the dead bodies; he shall wound the heads over many countries. [7] He shall drink of the brook in the way: therefore shall he lift up the head" (Psalm 110:1-7).

Christ Jesus' baptism had nothing to do with sanctifying Him in that He was perfectly sanctified in His own sinlessness. However, Jesus was consecrated by the Father into this new High Priestly office of the Melchisedecan priesthood through His baptism by John the Baptist. It was not John who consecrated Jesus as this new High Priest. It was God the Father. The consecration of this new High Priest by the Father had to take place before His sacrifice could be accepted by God.

"[13] Then cometh Jesus from Galilee to Jordan unto John, to be baptized of him. [14] But John forbad him, saying, I have need to be baptized of thee, and comest thou to me? [15] And Jesus answering said unto him, Suffer *it to be so* now: for thus it becometh us <u>to fulfil all righteousness.</u> Then he suffered him. [16] And Jesus, when he was baptized, went up straightway out of the water: and, lo, the heavens were opened unto him, and he {*John the Baptist; there is no Scriptural testimony that anyone else saw or heard*} saw the Spirit of God descending like a dove, and lighting upon him: [17] And lo a voice from heaven, saying, This is my beloved Son, in whom I am well pleased" (Matthew 3:13-17).

The fact that this baptism of Jesus was His consecration as the new High Priest of the Melchisedecan priesthood is substantiated by the fulfillment of its Aaronic type. Priests could not be consecrated into their office until they were thirty years of age.

"[46] All those that were numbered of the Levites, whom Moses and Aaron and the chief of Israel numbered, after their families, and after the house of their fathers, [47] From thirty years old and upward even unto fifty years old, every one that came to do the service of the ministry, and the service of the burden in the tabernacle of the congregation, [48] Even those that were numbered of them, were eight thousand and five hundred and fourscore. [49] According to the commandment of the LORD they were numbered by the hand of Moses, every one according to his service, and according to his burden: thus were they numbered of him, as the LORD commanded Moses" (Numbers 4:46-49).

"[21] Now when all the people were baptized, it came to pass, that Jesus also being baptized, and praying, the heaven was opened, [22] And the Holy Ghost descended in a bodily shape like a dove upon him, and a voice came from heaven, which said, Thou art my beloved Son; in thee I am well pleased. [23] And Jesus himself began to be about thirty years of age . . ." (Luke 3:21-23a).

> Christ offered Himself as the vicarious sacrifice for sin, as both the High Priest and the sacrifice, as both the *Offerer* and the *Offering*, so that all believers in the New Covenant could be positionally sanctified before God "by grace through faith" as a New Order of Priesthood.

However, the New Covenant believer-priest must still present his own body to the Father as a "living sacrifice" before God can, and will, consecrate that believer-priest for the service to which he is ordained. It is not enough to be a saved and positionally sanctified believer-priest. Consecration is also essential before God can accept that believer's service and before God can produce "fruit" through that believer's life. Once consecrated, it is the believer-priest's responsibility to maintain sanctity through practical sanctification in separation from sin and from worldliness.

It is extremely important to note that the consecration of a priest by the Lord can NEVER be separated from their "service of ministry." This is to what Paul speaks in Ephesians 4:12 regarding the purpose of God in giving *gifted men* to local churches so that *every* New Covenant (Church Age) believer-priest can be perfected "for the work of the ministry." The **Scofield Study Bible** gives us the following note:

"The New Testament priesthood, Summary:

(1) Until the law was given the head of each family was the family priest (Gen. 8:20; 26:25; 31:54).

(2) When the law was proposed, the promise to perfect obedience was that Israel would be unto God 'a kingdom of priests' (Ex. 19:6). But Israel violated the law, and God shut up the priestly office to the Aaronic family, appointing the tribe of Levi to minister to them, thus constituting the typical priesthood (Ex. 28:1).

(3) In the dispensation of grace, all believers are unconditionally constituted a 'kingdom of priests' (1Pet. 2:9; Rev. 1:6) the distinction which Israel failed to achieve by works. The priesthood of the believer is, therefore, a birthright; just as every descendant of Aaron was born to the priesthood (Heb. 5:1).

(4) The chief privilege of a priest is access to God. Under law the high priest only could enter 'the holiest of all,' and that but once a year (Heb. 9:7), but when Christ died, the veil, type of Christ's human body (Heb. 10:20) was rent, so that now the believer-priests, equally with Christ the High Priest, have access to God in the holiest (Heb. 10:19-22). The high Priest is corporeally there (Heb. 4:14-16; 9:24; 10:19-22).

(5) In the exercise of his office the New Testament believer-priest is

   (1) a sacrificer who offers a threefold sacrifice:
      (*a*) his own living body. (Rom. 12:1; Phil. 2:17; 2 Tim. 4:6; 1 John 3:16; Jas. 1:27)
      (*b*) praise to God, 'the fruit of the lips that make mention of His name' (R.V.), to be offered 'continually' (Heb. 13:15; Ex. 25:22) 'I will commune with thee from above the mercy seat');
      (*c*) his substance (Heb. 13:16; Rom. 12:13; Gal. 6:6; 3 John 1:5-8; Heb. 13:2; Gal. 6:10; Tit. 3:14).
   (2) The N.T. priest is also an intercessor (1 Tim. 2:1; Col. 4:12)"[23]

---

[23] Scofield, C. I., ed. *The Scofield Study Bible,* 1996 edition. (new York, New York: Oxford University Press), pages 1313-1314.

From the context of the baptism of Christ, we can understand that the believer's baptism *portrays* a similar level of commitment to sanctification and consecration to *serve* God as believer-priests serve in "Christ's stead" (II Corinthians 5:20). Through the *filling* of the *indwelling* Christ, the believer becomes a living and practical continuation of the *theanthropic union* of Christ as a believer-priest after the order of Melchisedec. This is the *union* or *oneness* referred to in Ephesians 4:1-7 to which every believer-priest is commanded to enter into through the "unity of the Spirit" or more commonly referred to as the *filling, fellowship,* or the outcome of being *spiritual.*

In Exodus 28:1-4, there is a critical statement to our understanding the priesthood of the believer "in Christ" and why the believer-priest of the New Covenant does everything in the name of Jesus.

"[1] And take thou unto thee Aaron thy brother, and his sons with him, from among the children of Israel, that he may minister unto me in the priest's office, *even* Aaron, Nadab and Abihu, Eleazar and Ithamar, Aaron's sons. [2] And thou shalt make holy garments for Aaron thy brother for glory and for beauty. [3] And thou shalt speak unto all *that are* wise hearted, whom I have filled with the spirit of wisdom, that they may make Aaron's garments to consecrate him, that he may minister unto me in the priest's office. [4] And these *are* the garments which they shall make; a breastplate, and an ephod, and a robe, and a broidered coat, a mitre, and a girdle: and they shall make holy garments for Aaron thy brother, and his sons, that he may minister unto me in the priest's office" (Exodus 28:1-4).

Henry W. Soltau comments on this text:

"The wording of the first verse is remarkable: 'take thou unto thee Aaron [. . .], and his sons with him [. . .], that *he* may minister." Aaron and his sons formed but one ministry in the priest's office: and Aaron could not exercise his service, unless his sons were taken with him. Is there not in this, an intimation of the union in priesthood of Christ and [H]is house; and that one great object of [H]is priesthood is, that He may minister to God respecting [H]is house?"[24] ([ ] corrected)

---

[24] Soltau, Henry W. *The Tabernacle; The Priesthood and the Offerings.* (Grand Rapids, Michigan: Kregel Publications, 1974), page 190.

Christ Jesus, as the High Priest of all Church Age believers, is our *Intercessor* and *Advocate* before the Father in the literal Holy of Holies on the basis of His perfect, finished sacrifice. The New Covenant believer-priests minister on earth to one another and to the lost as theanthropic Ambassadors for Christ. The supernatural dynamic involved in the *synergism* of this New Covenant priesthood is the *union* created through the indwelling of the Spirit and the *unity* of the Spirit through the filling of the Spirit. If the *union* and *unity* do not exist, the supernatural *ministry* of Christ through the believer-priest cannot take place.

However, also of great importance is the fact that the ministry of any individual believer-priest is only *acceptable* to God AFTER that believer-priest is supernaturally sanctified. Sanctification is both positionally and practically. Then Jesus, our High Priest, consecrates that sanctified believer to service. This leads us to Hebrews chapter seven.

"[1] For this Melchisedec, king of Salem, priest of the most high God, who met Abraham returning from the slaughter of the kings, and blessed him; [2] To whom also Abraham gave a tenth part of all; first being by interpretation King of righteousness, and after that also King of Salem, which is, King of peace; [3] Without father, without mother, without descent, having neither beginning of days, nor end of life; but made like unto the Son of God; abideth a priest continually. [4] Now consider how great this man *was*, unto whom even the patriarch Abraham gave the tenth of the spoils. [5] And verily they that are of the sons of Levi, who receive the office of the priesthood, have a commandment to take tithes of the people according to the law, that is, of their brethren, though they come out of the loins of Abraham: [6] But he whose descent is not counted from them received tithes of Abraham, and blessed him that had the promises. [7] And without all contradiction the less is blessed of the better. [8] And here men that die receive tithes; but there he *receiveth them*, of whom it is witnessed that he liveth. [9] And as I may so say, Levi also, who receiveth tithes, payed tithes in Abraham. [10] For he was yet in the loins of his father, when Melchisedec met him. [11] If therefore perfection were by the Levitical priesthood, (for under it the people received the law,) what further need *was there* that another priest should rise after the order of Melchisedec, and not be called after the order of Aaron? [12] <u>For the priesthood being changed, there is made of necessity a change also of the law.</u> [13] For he of whom these things are spoken pertaineth to another tribe, of which no man gave attendance at the altar. [14] For *it is* evident that our Lord sprang out of Juda; of which tribe Moses spake nothing concerning priesthood. [15] And it is yet far more evident: for that after the similitude of Melchisedec there ariseth another priest, [16] Who is made, not after the law of a carnal commandment, but after <u>the power of an endless life.</u> [17] For he testifieth, Thou *art* a priest for ever after the order of Melchisedec. [18] For there is verily a disannulling of the commandment going before for the weakness and unprofitableness thereof. [19] For the law made nothing perfect, but the bringing in of a better hope *did*; by the which we {*all believers*} draw nigh unto God. [20] And inasmuch as not without an oath *he was made priest*: [21] (For those priests were made without an oath; but this with an oath by him that said unto him, The Lord sware and will not repent, Thou *art* a priest for ever after the order of Melchisedec:) [22] By so much was Jesus made a surety of a better testament" (Hebrews 7:1-22).

One of the great superiorities of the New Covenant over the Mosaic Covenant is the superiority and "surety" of the New Covenant priesthood and the priesthood of all believers in the New Covenant. God told Moses to tell the children of Israel, "And ye shall be unto me a kingdom of priests, and an holy nation" (Exodus 19:6). This promise was intended to show Israel a future relationship and position that did not exist for them in the Old (Mosaic) Covenant. This promise was intended to look forward to what would come into existence after Messiah's coming and the establishment of His Kingdom on earth. Therefore, the Epistle to the Hebrews is detailing the New Covenant as the means by which that new kingdom/sovereignty of theanthropic priests is elect "in Christ."

This new priesthood is the "bride of Christ," commonly (but errantly) called the *Universal* or *Mystical Church*. This new priesthood "in Christ" is a present reality with a missional purpose, but will not become a *functional entity* in its relationship to national Israel until after the *rapture* (resurrection/translation and glorification of Church Age believers) and the second coming of

Christ to the earth to establish his Kingdom on earth. Jesus is the King and High Priest of this "kingdom of priests" on earth. That is the *prophetic type* that Melchisedec portrays to us as fulfilled "in Christ" in Hebrews 7:1-3. All those born again of the Spirit of God from Pentecost until the *rapture* are a new *theanthropic* servant-priesthood of Christ now and will take on added responsibilities in the coming Kingdom Age.

In Hebrews 7:1-10, God takes the Jewish/Hebrew believer back into their own history in order to bring them forward to reveal to them that Jesus is the *theanthropic* fulfillment of the New Covenant promises in relation to the Kingdom. This differentiation is intended to show them that they have no hope of being part of the Kingdom if they abandon the *already, not yet* dispensational transition regarding the New Covenant in Jesus Christ. They were wrongly being persuaded that the hope of their Kingdom blessings still lay in the Old Covenant and in the connection with national Israel and its Aaronic priesthood. This was false doctrine.

Hebrews reveals directly that the priesthood of Jesus, after the order of Melchisedec as prophesied by Psalm 110 and spoken of in Hebrews 5:6, is the literal fulfillment of those prophecies. Therefore, to abandon the *theanthropic* Jesus, in His literal fulfillment of the Melchisedecan type in order to continue claiming the inferior Old Covenant promises and beliefs regarding the Kingdom, is to abandon the real spiritual hope for believers in the Kingdom. The reality of this *Kingdom hope* lies in the New Covenant *theanthropic* priesthood, not the inferior Old Covenant or its inferior and typical Aaronic Priesthood.

"^{2} And it shall come to pass in the last days {*Kingdom Age*}, *that* the mountain of the LORD'S house shall be established in the top of the mountains, and shall be exalted above the hills; and all nations shall flow unto it. ^{3} And many people shall go and say, Come ye, and let us go up to the mountain of the LORD, to the house of the God of Jacob; and he will teach us of his ways, and we will walk in his paths: for out of Zion shall go forth the law, and the word of the LORD from Jerusalem. ^{4} And he shall judge among the nations, and shall rebuke many people: and they shall beat their swords into plowshares, and their spears into pruninghooks: nation shall not lift up sword against nation, neither shall they learn war any more" (Isaiah 2:2-4).

Israel's future position in the Kingdom was prophesied over and over again (Zechariah alone: 2:10-13, 8:3 and 8, 9:9 as quoted in Matthew 21:5). The greatest of all these is Zechariah 14:9.

"And the LORD shall be king over all the earth: in that day shall there be one LORD, and his name one."

Melchisedec was the King/Priest of Zion. Messiah came to fulfill the *theanthropic* Melchisedecan type and to establish a new *theanthropic* priesthood of the Melchisedecan order. All of this ties the promise of God regarding the Kingdom to the New Covenant, not to the Old. "In that day shall there be one Lord, and his name one" (Zechariah 14:9). It is by the fulfillment of this prophetic type in Melchisedec that Jesus is the "surety of a better covenant."

"By so much was Jesus made a surety of a better testament" (Hebrews 7:22).

The word "perfection" in Hebrews 7:11 is from the Greek word *teleiosis* (tel-i'-o-sis). It means *to complete* or *fulfill*. It can refer to an *event* that verifies or consummates a promise. The *Levitical priesthood,* with all of its sacrifices, holy days, and rituals, could never bring the believing sinner to the place of completion because none of the practices (sacrifices and rituals) could propitiate God for the participator's sins. The abrogation of the Mosaic (Old) Covenant priesthood in itself is evidence of the inadequacy of the whole Mosaic Covenant in bringing sinners to completion (justification) before God. The sacrifices of the Mosaic Covenant were never intended to propitiate God or justify sinners. If any sacrifice could have propitiated God's wrath or justified even one sinner, all sacrifices would have ceased after that perfect sacrifice was offered.

"[9] For in him dwelleth all the fulness of the Godhead bodily. [10] And ye are complete in him, which is the head of all principality and power: [11] In whom also ye are circumcised with the circumcision made without hands, in putting off the body of the sins of the flesh by the circumcision of Christ: [12] Buried with him in baptism, wherein also ye are risen with *him* through the faith of the operation of God, who hath raised him from the dead. [13] And you, being dead in your sins and the uncircumcision of your flesh, hath he quickened together with him, having forgiven you all trespasses; [14] Blotting out the handwriting of ordinances that was against us, which was contrary to us, and took it out of the way, nailing it to his cross; [15] *And* having spoiled principalities and powers, he made a shew of them openly, triumphing over them in it" (Colossians 2:9-15).

Therefore, Hebrews 7:11-22 continues to provide evidence of the superiority of the New Covenant over the Old (Mosaic) Covenant. The basis of this superior priesthood is in the *theanthropic* Christ Jesus as the *theanthropic* High Priest after the order of Melchisedec. "If therefore perfection were by the Levitical priesthood" (v 11), why did another priest (Jesus) rise up after another "order?" The answer of course is that the Levitical priesthood could not offer *completion* or *perfection*. In fact, the constant repetition of sacrifices and yearly Day of Atonement cried out to God for completion, but never found completion or satisfaction in what they did. The very fact of constant repetition denied any *satisfaction* or *perfection*.

"For the law made nothing perfect" (v. 19); the Law was never satisfied. The Law with all of its rituals, priesthood, and continual sacrifices never made anyone *complete*. It never propitiated anyone, let alone God. The Law was no one's *redeemer* or *justifier*. Instead, the Law became everyone's *accuser* and *judge*.

"[9] Now we know that what things soever the law saith, it saith to them who are under the law: that every mouth may be stopped, and all the world may become guilty before God. [20] Therefore by the deeds of the law there shall no flesh be justified in his sight: for by the law *is* the knowledge of sin" (Romans 3:19-20)

There was no justification in the Mosaic Covenant (the Law-ceremonial rituals, sacrifices, and priesthood), only condemnation. "But now the righteousness of God without the law is manifested, being witnessed by the law and the prophets" (Romans 3:21). In other words, "the righteousness of God without the law is manifested" now that Jesus has come. "The righteousness of God without the law is manifested" now that the Gospel details a finished work of redemption. "The righteousness of God without the law is manifested" now that the work of the Messiah is "finished." "The righteousness of God without the law is manifested" now that the righteousness of God is available through impartation (II Peter 1:4) to the believer through faith in what Christ has done. "The righteousness of God without the law is manifested" now that God's righteousness is openly and publicly visible in the sinless life of Jesus, His substitutionary death at Calvary, His burial, and His resurrection/glorification.

> "Even the righteousness of God *which is* by faith of Jesus Christ unto all and upon all them that believe: for there is no difference" (Romans 3:22).

This "perfection" of Hebrews 7:11 (the idea in the word "perfection" is *completion*) is something the Old or Mosaic Covenant, with all its sacrifices and elaborate priesthood, could never do. The very existence of the practices of the Old Covenant was an ongoing testimony to *imperfection* and *incompletion* in that they needed to be repeated over and over again. The reason for this *incompleteness* was that the rituals, sacrifices, and priesthood of the Mosaic Covenant cover never satisfy the single demand of the Law upon sin; i.e., justice must be executed. The sentence of eternal death (someone must satisfy the sentence of *eternal death* by the sacrifice of an *eternal life*), which is God's wrath upon sin, must be satisfied for God to be propitiated.

Secondly, the Law (Mosaic Covenant) had no power to redeem because it had no desire for personal redemption. The Law was an *impersonal body of truth* that a person only could try to be obedient to, but to no avail. No one could *keep* the Law. There is no passion, love, or mercy in the Law. It has no concern for frailty, weakness, and mankind's innate propensity for sin. The Law has no *personality* or *compassion* for sinners. The Law simply points its unforgiving, merciless finger of guilt at the sinner.

> "⁶ Now when these things were thus ordained, the priests went always into the first tabernacle, accomplishing the service *of God*. ⁷ But into the second *went* the high priest alone once every year, not without blood, which he offered for himself, and *for* the errors of the people: ⁸ The Holy Ghost this signifying, that the way {*see John 14:6*} into the holiest of all was not yet made manifest, while as the first tabernacle was yet standing: ⁹ Which *was* a figure {*or type*} for the time then present, in which were offered both gifts and sacrifices, that could not make him that did the service perfect, as pertaining to the conscience; ¹⁰ *Which stood* only in meats and drinks, and divers washings, and carnal ordinances, imposed *on them* until the time of reformation. ¹¹ But Christ being come an high priest of good things to come, by a greater and more perfect tabernacle, not made with hands, that is to

say, not of this building; [12] Neither by the blood of goats and calves, but by his own blood he entered in once into the holy place, having obtained eternal redemption *for us*" (Hebrews 9:6-12).

The word "reformation" in Hebrews 9:10 is from the Greek word *diorthosis* (dee-or'-tho-sis). It means *to straighten out that which is bent or crooked*, like the idea of setting a broken bone and putting it back into its natural and intended line.

What was it that confused everything regarding God's plan of redemption? Hebrews 9:10 tells us that everything was *messed up* due to the distortion of the purpose of the Mosaic Law's "carnal ordinances." The Jewish priesthood had perverted the purpose of the Law by making it salvific. All the sacrifices and rituals in the world could never satisfy God righteousness when it comes to man's sin. The rituals, sacrifices, and priesthood of the Mosaic Covenant were external types and were hopeless when it came to providing salvation. The Mosaic Covenant was never intended for that purpose. The intent of the Mosaic Covenant and its constant sacrifices, repetitious rituals, and its sinful priesthood was to cause every Jew to see the *evident hopelessness* of it all and cry out to God for completion - for perfection or *propitiation*. It was to this *perfection* or *propitiation* to which Christ's last words on the Cross refer: "it is finished" (John 19:30).

The Law was "a carnal commandment" (Hebrews 7:16). In other words, it could only speak to the fleshly desires of man, condemning them; but Jesus, who was not made after the "carnal commandment" or the Levitical Priesthood, provided *completeness*. Jesus "was made after "the order of Melchisedec" (Hebrews 7:11). He "had the power of an endless life" (Hebrews 7:16). The Levitical priesthood and the Law could offer no such hope (Hebrews 7:19).

Jesus not only offers perfection, completion and propitiation, He gives it (Colossians 2:9-10). "In Christ," the believer's New Covenant High Priest, we have *perfection* in God's eyes (positionally in our theanthropic union with our new High Priest, Jesus the Christ). The believing sinner has been raised to the highest state of *theanthropic* existence "in Christ." Christ was able to do (Hebrews 7:11) what the Levitical Old Covenant priesthood could never do in all of its dead rituals. The Old Covenant rituals, sacrifices, and priesthood could never take away sin (Hebrews 10:4); all rituals, all empty liturgies, are absolutely powerless when it comes to sin.

DISCUSSION QUESTIONS

1. We must understand that the *theanthropic* Christ after His resurrection and glorification became *another kind of being* that never existed ever before, except in the plan of God. Discuss why it is essential to understand this truth.

2. Read Luke 24:36-43. Define and discuss four characteristics of the new *theanthropic* Christ after His resurrection and glorification that are revealed in this text.

3. List and discuss the two primary purposes for John the Baptist's ministry of baptism of Jewish believers.

4. Discuss how all of Israel should have known about the new coming order of Priesthood that was not connected tribally to the nation of Israel

5. Discuss the significance of Christ's baptism in its relationship to the new Melchisedecan priesthood.

6. Discuss the significance of Christ's consecration as the High Priest of the new Melchisedecan priesthood as both the Offerer and the Offering for sin.

7. Discuss how every New Covenant believer's baptism relates to the priesthood of all Church Age believers as a new order of *theanthropic* priests.

Chapter Fifty-five
The Local Church as a Microcosm of Kingdom Living

"[1] And seeing the multitudes, he went up into a mountain: and when he was set, his disciples came unto him: [2] And he opened his mouth, and taught them, saying, [3] Blessed *are* the <u>poor in spirit</u>: for theirs is the kingdom of heaven. [4] Blessed *are* <u>they that mourn</u>: for they shall be comforted. [5] Blessed *are* <u>the meek</u>: for they shall inherit the earth. [6] Blessed *are* <u>they which do hunger and thirst after righteousness</u>: for they shall be filled. [7] Blessed *are* <u>the merciful</u>: for they shall obtain mercy. [8] Blessed *are* <u>the pure in heart</u>: for they shall see God. [9] Blessed *are* <u>the peacemakers</u>: for they shall be called the children of God. [10] Blessed *are* <u>they which are persecuted for righteousness' sake</u>: for theirs is the kingdom of heaven. [11] Blessed are ye, <u>when *men* shall revile you, and persecute *you*, and shall say all manner of evil against you falsely, for my sake.</u> [12] Rejoice, and be exceeding glad: for great *is* your reward in heaven: for so persecuted they the prophets which were before you. [13] Ye are the salt of the earth: but if the salt have lost his savour, wherewith shall it be salted? it is thenceforth good for nothing, but to be cast out, and to be trodden under foot of men. [14] Ye are the light of the world. A city that is set on an hill cannot be hid. [15] Neither do men light a candle, and put it under a bushel, but on a candlestick; and it giveth light unto all that are in the house. [16] Let your light so shine before men, that they may see your good works, and glorify your Father which is in heaven" (Matthew 5:1-16).

Matthew chapters five, six, and seven give us the truths that define the *Christ-life* that is produced through the supernatural enabling of the Holy Spirit of God. Matthew chapters five, six, and seven are very important in that the teachings of Jesus in these texts practically define a *spiritually mature local church*. There are many today who say that these three chapters are intended only for the glorified Church during the Kingdom Age because they present *impossible standards* that no individual could live during the Church Age. This is nothing but rationalization and is certainly not consistent with God's expectations of believers in any Dispensation. In every Dispensation God has given *impossible* expectations to believers. The very fact that the expectations are *impossible* is intended to reveal to believers the necessity of God's supernatural workings *within* the lives of believers individually and within the context of a local church. Only the operations of God in the person of the Holy Spirit working *upon* and *within* believers make these *impossibilities possible*. Making *impossibilities possible* seems like an *oxymoron*. The statement is an *oxymoron* if we see life merely from an "under the sun" perspective. We cannot look at this apart from the supernatural workings of God *through* the lives of believers. God delights in doing impossible things through the lives of obedient believers in order to magnify Himself to the lost. He magnifies himself to allow believers to bring glory to His name through their lives of faithfulness. He has been doing this for thousands of years.

"A Song of degrees for Solomon. Except the LORD build the house, they labour in vain that build it: except the LORD keep the city, the watchman waketh *but* in vain" (Psalm 127:1).

"[1] And the angel that talked with me came again, and waked me, as a man that is wakened out of his sleep, [2] And said unto me, What seest thou? And I said, I have looked, and behold a candlestick all *of* gold, with a bowl upon the top of it, and his seven lamps thereon, and seven pipes to the seven lamps, which *are* upon the top thereof: [3] And two olive trees by it, one upon the right *side* of the bowl, and the other upon the left *side* thereof. [4] So I answered and spake to the angel that talked with me, saying, What *are* these, my lord? [5] Then the angel that talked with me answered and said unto me, Knowest thou not what these be? And I said, No, my lord. [6] Then he answered and spake unto me, saying, This *is* the word of the LORD unto Zerubbabel, saying, Not by might, nor by power, but by my spirit, saith the LORD of hosts" (Zechariah 4:1-9).

Zechariah 4:1-9 is another very important text for Church Age believers. This text puts us in the context of the restoration of the nation of Israel at the second coming of Christ and at the beginning of the Kingdom Age. Most Church Age believers fail to see the panoramic of the judgments of God surrounding the second coming in the judgment of the unbelieving nations of the world, the cataclysmic destruction of the earth's eco-system, and the Judgment Seat of Christ where the faithfulness of Church Age believers will be judged. All of these judgments are part of the eight visions of Zechariah.

We can be sure that Zechariah 4:1-9 refers to the true Zion and Church Age believers according to the seven epistles of Christ to the seven churches of Revelation. Zechariah chapter four is the fifth in the middle of this series of eight visions revealing the events of the "last days" of the "times of the Gentiles." These visions all reveal the events in the fulfillment of the Palestinian Covenant and the Davidic Covenant. The eight visions of Zechariah are as follows:

Vision one (1:7-17): Red Horse in midst of the Myrtle Trees

This vision reveals the worldwide Kingdom of Messiah established with worldwide peace. The rider on the "red horse" is Christ and the "Myrtle trees" (vs. 13-14) is Israel during the times of the Gentiles. God has allowed Israel to go into captivity and be dispersed throughout the Gentile nations because of their unfaithfulness to the Mosaic Covenant. He has allowed this because of their unbelief. Nonetheless, He is displeased with the Gentile nation's brutal treatment of Israel and promises the future restoration of national Israel (v. 15).

Vision two (1:18-24): Four Horns and the Four Smiths

The "four horns" are four Gentile world powers that rule over and persecute Israel. These "four horns" are Babylon, Medo-Persia, Macedonian Greece, and the Roman Empire. The "four smiths" are the empires God used to overthrow and punish the previous empire for their mistreatment of Israel. Therefore Medo-Persia is the "smith" that God uses to judge Babylon. Macedonian-Greece is the "smith" God uses to judge Medo-Persia. The Roman Empire is the "smith" God used to judge Macedonian-Greece. The Roman Empire continues to exist in Romanism and will be revived during the "last days" prior to the second coming of Christ. Christ will be the "smith" that God will use to judge the Roman Empire.

Rome was considered the center of the Mother of the Earth (Cybele; *Magda Mater* or Mother Earth/Nature – this extends itself into the Neo-Paganism of Ecological Pantheism today in extreme environmentalism and the evolutionary theory that man evolved from the *primordial ooze* of Mother Earth/Nature).

Vision three (2:1-13): the Man with the Measuring Line (compare Heb. 2:5-17)

This vision reveals the restoration of Jerusalem during the days of Zechariah. This vision prophetically reveals the rebuilding of Jerusalem and the Millennial Temple at the second coming of Christ. Jesus will return as the *new federal head* of God's original, but fallen creation. The "man" is the theanthropic Christ (Zechariah 6:12), who will build/architect the Millennial Temple (compare Ezekiel 40:2-3). This prophecy is intended to comfort Israel during her times of chastisement in the "times of the Gentiles." Church Age believers as Priests of the Melchisedecan order are very much part of this prophecy under their Prophet/Priest/King Jesus.

"[5] For unto the angels hath he not put in subjection the world to come, whereof we speak. [6] But one in a certain place testified, saying, What is man, that thou art mindful of him? or the son of man, that thou visitest him? [7] Thou madest him a little lower than the angels; thou crownedst him with glory and honour, and didst set him over the works of thy hands: [8] Thou hast put all things in subjection under his feet. For in that he put all in subjection under him, he left nothing *that is* not put under him. But now we see not yet all things put under him. [9] But we see Jesus, who was made a little lower than the angels for the suffering of death, crowned with glory and honour; that he by the grace of God should taste death for every man. [10] For it became him, for whom *are* all things, and by whom *are* all things, in bringing many sons unto glory, to make the captain of their salvation perfect through sufferings. [11] For both he that sanctifieth and they who are sanctified *are* all of one: for which cause he is not ashamed to call them brethren, [12] Saying, I will declare thy name unto my brethren, in the midst of the church will I sing praise unto thee. [13] And again, I will put my trust in him. And again, Behold I and the children which God hath given me. [14] Forasmuch then as the children are partakers of flesh and blood, he also himself likewise took part of the same; that through death he might destroy him that had the power of death, that is, the devil; [15] And deliver them who through fear of death were all their lifetime subject to bondage. [16] For verily he took not on *him the nature of* angels; but he took on *him* the seed of Abraham. [17] Wherefore in all things it behoved him to be made like unto *his* brethren, that he might be a merciful and faithful high priest in things *pertaining* to God, to make reconciliation for the sins of the people. [18] For in that he himself hath suffered being tempted, he is able to succour them that are tempted" (Hebrews 2:5-18).

Vision four: (3:1-10): the Cleansing of Joshua the High Priest

"Joshua" is a *dualistic* prophecy of the purging/cleansing of the Levitical priesthood. This purging will be through the transformation of the "new creation" (glorification) and the establishment of a new theanthropic High Priest in Jesus Christ. There will be a new theanthropic order of priesthood after the similitude of Melchisedec. Jesus is the Greek counterpart to the Hebrew name Joshua. This also portrays the transformation of national Israel as they repent of their unbelief in Jesus as Messiah, repent of their self-righteousness (Romans 3:22 and 10:1-4), and receive the impartation of God-kind righteousness "by grace through faith" in the Person of Jesus Christ and His death, burial, resurrection, and glorification (Romans 10:9-13).

Vision five (4:1-14): the Golden Candlestick and the Two Olive Trees

Although this vision reveals the restoration of national Israel as a "kingdom of priests" during the Kingdom Age, it also includes Church Age believers after the "casting away" of the Levitical priesthood. Church Age believers will be *grafted into* national Israel (Romans 11:14-32) as a new theanthropic Melchisedecan priesthood to rule and reign with Christ. Glorified Church Age believers are the *primary focus* of this vision. They will exist in the Kingdom Age in sinless perfection having been delivered from the penalty of sin in salvation, the power of sin in their perfect sanctification, and the presence of the inward desire for sin in their glorification. This is especially important as we come to see the meaning of the "flying scroll" of the sixth vision in Zechariah 5:1-4.

The Jews, to which Zechariah's fifth vision is directed, would have understood the "candlestick" as the Temple Menorah. They would have understood the "olive trees" to be direct supernatural sources of the filling with oil of the seven bowls that are on top of the Temple Menorah. The "two olives trees" are the theanthropic Christ in the eternal union of the "fullness of the Godhead bodily" in the humanity of Jesus and the indwelling of the Holy Spirit. Although there will be an *eternal distinction* between the human and the divine, these two essences are united in the body of believers in the "new creation." In the glorified state of existence, this new priesthood will be continually and supernaturally filled with the Spirit of God and the Spirit of Christ. The explanation of these things in Revelation 1:9-20 is critical to understanding the intercessory ministry of the High Priesthood of Christ during the Church Age and to Church Age believers in local churches. The vast majority of the Revelation of Jesus Christ cannot be understood apart from the explanation of this "mystery" hidden to national Israel until its fulfillment at the second coming of Messiah.

"For I would not, brethren, that ye should be ignorant of this mystery, lest ye should be wise in your own conceits; that blindness in part is happened to Israel, until the fulness of the Gentiles be come in" (Romans 11:25).

"[25] Now to him that is of power to stablish you according to my gospel, and the preaching of Jesus Christ, according to the revelation of the mystery, which was kept secret since the world began, [26] But now is made manifest, and by the scriptures of the prophets, according to the commandment of the everlasting God, made known to all nations for the obedience of faith: [27] To God only wise, *be* glory through Jesus Christ for ever. Amen" (Romans 16:25-27).

"[6] Howbeit we speak wisdom among them that are perfect: yet not the wisdom of this world, nor of the princes of this world, that come to nought: [7] But we speak the wisdom of God in a mystery, *even* the hidden *wisdom*, which God ordained before the world unto our glory: [8] Which none of the princes of this world knew: for had they known *it*, they would not have crucified the Lord of glory" (I Corinthians 2:6-8).

"[51] Behold, I shew you a mystery; We shall not all sleep, but we shall all be changed, [52] In a moment, in the twinkling of an eye, at the last trump: for the trumpet shall sound, and the dead shall be raised incorruptible, and we shall be changed. [53] For this corruptible must put on incorruption, and this mortal *must* put on immortality. [54] So when this corruptible shall have put on incorruption, and this mortal shall have put on immortality, then shall be brought to pass the saying that is written, Death is swallowed up in victory. [55] O death, where *is* thy sting? O grave, where *is* thy victory? [56] The sting of death *is* sin; and the strength of sin *is* the law. [57] But thanks *be* to God, <u>which giveth us the victory through our Lord Jesus Christ</u>. [58] Therefore, <u>my beloved brethren</u>, be ye stedfast, unmoveable, always abounding in the work of the Lord, forasmuch as ye know that your labour is not in vain in the Lord" (I Corinthians 15:51-58).

"[3] Blessed *be* the God and Father of our Lord Jesus Christ, who hath blessed us {*Church Age believers*} with all spiritual blessings in heavenly *places* in Christ: [4] According as he hath chosen us {*Church Age believers*} in him before the foundation of the world, that we should be holy and without blame before him in love: [5] Having predestinated us {*Church Age believers*} unto the adoption of children by Jesus Christ to himself, according to the good pleasure of his will, [6] To the praise of the glory of his grace, wherein he hath made us {*Church Age believers*} accepted in the beloved. [7] In whom we {*Church Age believers*} have redemption through his blood, the forgiveness of sins, according to the riches of his grace; [8] Wherein he hath abounded toward us {*Church Age believers*} in all wisdom and prudence; [9] Having made known unto us {*Church Age believers*} the mystery of his will, according to his good pleasure which he hath purposed in himself: [10] That in the dispensation of the fulness of times he might gather together in one all things in Christ, both which are in heaven, and which are on earth; *even* in him: [11] In whom also we {*Church Age believers*} have obtained an inheritance, being predestinated according to the purpose of him who worketh all things after the counsel of his own will: [12] That we {*Church Age believers*} should be to the praise of his glory, who first trusted in Christ. [13] In whom ye also *trusted*, after that ye heard the word of truth, the gospel of your salvation: in whom also after that ye believed, ye were sealed with that holy Spirit of promise, [14] Which is the earnest of our {*Church Age believers*} inheritance until the redemption of the purchased possession, unto the praise of his glory" (Ephesians 1:3-14).

"[1] For this cause I Paul, the prisoner of Jesus Christ for you Gentiles, [2] If ye have heard of the dispensation of the grace of God which is given me to you-ward: [3] How that by revelation he made known unto me the mystery; (as I wrote afore in few words, [4] Whereby, when ye read, ye may understand my knowledge in the mystery of Christ) [5] Which in other ages was not made known unto the sons of men, as it is now revealed unto his holy apostles and prophets by the Spirit; [6] That the Gentiles should be fellowheirs, and of the same body, and partakers of his promise in Christ by the gospel: [7] Whereof I was made a minister, according to the gift of the grace of God given unto me by the effectual working of his power. [8] Unto me, who am less than the least of all saints, is this grace given, that I should preach among the Gentiles the unsearchable riches of Christ; [9] And to make all *men* see what *is* the fellowship of the mystery, which from the beginning of the world hath been hid in God, who created all things by Jesus Christ: [10] To the intent that now unto the principalities and powers in heavenly *places* might be known by the church the manifold wisdom of God, [11] According to the eternal purpose which he purposed in Christ Jesus our Lord: [12] In whom we have boldness and access with confidence by the faith of him. [13] Wherefore I desire that ye faint not at my tribulations for you, which is your glory" (Ephesians 3:3-9).

"[21] Submitting yourselves one to another in the fear of God. [22] Wives, submit yourselves unto your own husbands, as unto the Lord. [23] For the husband is the head of the wife, even as Christ is the head of the church: and he is the saviour of the body. [24] Therefore as the church is subject unto Christ, so *let* the wives *be* to their own husbands in every thing. [25] Husbands, love your wives, even as Christ also loved the church, and gave himself for it; [26] That he might sanctify and cleanse it with the washing of water by the word, [27] That he might present it to himself a glorious church, not having spot, or wrinkle, or any such thing; but that it should be holy and without blemish. [28] So ought men to love their wives as their own bodies. He that loveth his wife loveth himself. [29] For no man ever yet hated his own flesh; but nourisheth and cherisheth it, even as the Lord the church: [30] For we are members of his body, of his flesh, and of his bones. [31] For this cause shall a man leave his father and mother, and shall be joined unto his wife, and they two shall be one flesh. [32] This is a great mystery: but I speak concerning Christ and the church" (Ephesians 5:21-32).

"[9] For this cause { *'fruit'*} we also, since the day we heard *it*, do not cease to pray for you, and to desire that ye might be filled with the knowledge of his will in all wisdom and spiritual understanding; [10] That ye might walk worthy of the Lord unto all pleasing, being fruitful in every good work, and increasing in the knowledge of God; [11] Strengthened with all might, according to his glorious power, unto all patience and longsuffering with joyfulness; [12] Giving thanks unto the Father, which hath made us meet to be partakers of the inheritance of the saints in light: [13] Who hath delivered us from the power of darkness, and hath translated *us* into the kingdom of his dear Son: [14] In whom we have redemption through his blood, *even* the forgiveness of sins: [15] Who is the image of the invisible God, the firstborn of every creature: [16] For by him were all things created, that are in heaven, and that are in earth, visible and invisible, whether *they be* thrones, or dominions, or principalities, or powers: all things were created by him, and for him: [17] And he is before all things, and by him all things consist. [18] And he is the head of the body, the church: who is the beginning, the firstborn from the dead; that in all *things* he might have the preeminence. [19] For it pleased *the Father* that in him should all fulness dwell; [20] And, having made peace through the blood of his cross, by him to reconcile all things unto himself; by him, *I say*, whether *they be* things in earth, or things in heaven. [21] And you, that were sometime alienated and enemies in *your* mind by wicked works, yet now hath he reconciled [22] In the body of his flesh through death, to present you {*in consecration*} holy and unblameable and unreproveable in his sight {*as a theanthropic priesthood*}: [23] If ye continue in the faith grounded and settled, and *be* not moved away from the hope of the gospel, which ye have heard, *and* which was preached to every creature which is under heaven; whereof I Paul am made a minister; [24] Who now rejoice in my sufferings for you, and fill up that which is behind of the afflictions of Christ in my flesh for his body's sake, which is the church: [25] Whereof I am made a minister, according to the dispensation of God which is given to me for you, to fulfil the word of God; [26] *Even the mystery which hath been hid from ages and from generations, but now is made manifest to his saints:* [27] To whom God would make known what *is* the riches of the glory of this mystery among the Gentiles; which is Christ in you, the hope of glory: [28] Whom we preach, warning every man, and teaching every man in all wisdom; that we may present every man perfect in Christ Jesus: [29] Whereunto I also labour, striving according to his working, which worketh in me mightily" (Colossians 1:26-27).

DISCUSSION QUESTIONS

1. As you read John 15:5 and Matthew 5:1-16 together, discuss why understanding that the expectations of Christ in Matthew chapters five through seven are *impossible* is critical to understanding the implementation of the doctrine of Grace-enablement.

2. Explain the vision in Zechariah 1:7-17: the Red Horse in midst of the Myrtle Trees.

3. Explain the vision in Zechariah 1:18-24: the Four Horns and the Four Smiths.

4. Explain the vision in Zechariah 2:1-13: the Man with the Measuring Line (compare Hebrews 2:5-17).

5. Explain the vision in Zechariah 3:1-10: the Cleansing of Joshua the High Priest.

6. Explain the vision in Zechariah 4:1-14: the Golden Candlestick and the Two Olive Trees.

7. The vast majority of the Revelation of Jesus Christ cannot be understood apart from the explanation of this "mystery" hidden to national Israel until its fulfillment at the second coming of Messiah. Explain the "mystery."

Chapter Fifty-six

The Local Church as the Light of the World

The fifth vision of Zechariah (4:1-14) is partially fulfilled by local churches during the Church Age. Each local church is an independent, self-governing *republic* of believer priests working in synergism with the Holy Spirit and with each individual member of that local body. Therefore, during the Church Age, we find Christ addressing seven individual epistles to seven individual local churches, which are referred to as seven individual "candlesticks" in Revelation chapters two and three. These local churches cannot be the spiritual "light" they are ordained to be apart from the supernatural workings of the Holy Spirit. This working is through the indwelling and filling of individual members of those local churches as they live the Word of God and fulfill their obligations as ministering priests of their theanthropic High Priest, Jesus Christ.

It is in the fulfillment of practical sanctification/perfection and progressive transfiguration during the Church Age that individual local churches and individual believers, as part of local churches, fulfill this Menorah type as the 'light of the world." During the Church Age this type cannot be fulfilled apart from the "unity of the Spirit" of believers as priests before God within the *working partnership* ("fellowship") of a local church (Ephesians 4:1-16). The "unity of the Spirit" cannot be separated from its context of the local church and the *vocational* election *collectively* of all believers as priests before God. This *collective* is what Christ referred to in Matthew 5:14 as "a city that is set on a hill."

"[14] Ye are the light of the world. A city that is set on an hill cannot be hid. [15] Neither do men light a candle, and put it under a bushel, but on a candlestick; and it giveth light unto all that are in the house. [16] Let your light so shine before men, that they may see your good works, and glorify your Father which is in heaven" (Matthew 5:14-16).

Revelation 1:9-20 reveals Jesus as the Melchisedecan High Priest ministering in the midst of local churches, which are His Melchisedecan priesthood of all believers. It is amazing that people could believe that fallen creatures could do supernatural work apart from a *partnership in faith* with the LORD of hosts. This is the way we see God work throughout the books of the Old Testament. In fact, we NEVER see Him work in any other way! Any local church begins to fail the moment they leave their "first love" (Revelation 2:4). Their "first love" defines the intimacy of a love motivated relationship with the person of Christ in the person of the indwelling Spirit. Leaving their "first love" was failing to maintain their "unity of the Spirit."

"[9] I John, who also am your brother, and companion in tribulation, and in the kingdom and patience of Jesus Christ, was in the isle that is called Patmos, for the word of God, and for the testimony of Jesus Christ. [10] I was in the Spirit on the Lord's day, and heard behind me a great voice, as of a trumpet, [11] Saying, I am Alpha and Omega, the first and the last: and, What thou seest, write in a book, and send *it* unto the seven churches which are in Asia; unto Ephesus, and unto Smyrna, and unto Pergamos, and unto Thyatira, and unto Sardis, and unto Philadelphia, and unto Laodicea. [12] And I turned to see the voice that spake with me. And being turned, I saw seven golden candlesticks; [13] And in the midst of the seven candlesticks *one* like unto the Son of man, clothed with a garment down to the foot, and girt about the paps with a golden girdle. [14] His head and *his* hairs *were* white like wool, as white as snow; and his eyes *were* as a flame of fire; [15] And his feet like unto fine brass, as if they burned in a furnace; and his voice as the sound of many waters. [16] And he had in his right hand seven stars: and out of his mouth went a sharp twoedged sword: and his countenance *was* as the sun shineth in his strength. [17] And when I saw him, I fell at his feet as dead. And he laid his right hand upon me, saying unto me, Fear not; I am the first and the last: [18] I *am* he that liveth, and was dead; and, behold, I am alive for evermore, Amen; and have the keys of hell and of death. [19] Write the things which thou hast seen, and the things which are, and the things which shall be hereafter; [20] The mystery of the seven stars which thou sawest in my right hand, and the seven golden candlesticks. The seven stars are the angels of the seven churches: and the seven candlesticks which thou sawest are the seven churches" (Revelation 1:9-20).

Every individual local church throughout the Church Age is a "candlestick." Every individual believer, when united to a local church and when filled with the Spirit, becomes part of the "unity of the Spirit" and contributes to *the collective* of the *light* that local church is intended to be in the world.

When each believer is filled with the Spirit of God and living the *Christ-life*, each local church is intended to be a microcosm of God's ideal *culture of spirituality*. Each local church then becomes a counterculture within, and to, the larger corrupted and worldly culture. In order for any local church to have the kind of *testimony* that will actually *counter* the darkness of the evil of the world, every individual believer that is part of that local church must live the *Christ-life* as defined by the teachings of Jesus, as patterned in the book of Acts, and as defined by the epistles of the New Covenant.

Understanding this, we can certainly agree that *Emergent Church* philosophies, which teach that local churches should be as much like the world and their surrounding cultures as possible, is an extreme contradiction of God's definitive truths: "[4] *There is* one body, and one Spirit, even as ye are called in one hope of your calling; [5] One Lord, one faith, one baptism, [6] One God and Father of all, who *is* above all, and through all, and in you all" (Ephesians 4:4-6).

It is from the context of Christ ministering as High Priest in the midst of and throughout the Church Age that the continual call to "repent" comes to His priesthood in all of His seven epistles to local churches of the Church Age (Revelation 2:5, 16, 21, 22, 3:3, and 19). It is the ministry of the High Priest to keep His priesthood within local churches pure and undefiled in their "work of the ministry." He accomplishes this accountability through our mutual accountability to one another, doctrinal purity in the teaching of the Word of God. He accomplishes this accountability through pastoral administration, practical purity through mature modeling of the Spirit filled *Christ-life* by local church leadership, and church discipline. He accomplishes this accountability through separation from worldliness and ecclesiastical corruption. Jesus is the "Light of the world" who manifests the glory of God *through* the Spirit-filled individuals that make up a local church, which local churches then become "the light of the world and "a city that is set on an hill" (Matthew 5:14).

> "Then spake Jesus again unto them, saying, I am the light of the world: he that followeth me shall not walk in darkness, but shall have the light of life" (John 8:12).

> "As long as I am in the world, I am the light of the world" (John 9:5).

There is a dispensational transition stated in these two verses. When Jesus ascended and the Spirit of God indwelled the priesthood of all believers of the Church Age, beginning on the Day of Pentecost, those individuals *when united to local churches* became the "light of the world" through the filling of the Spirit. God accomplishes this transition as the Spirit-filled priesthood of all believers unites together in local churches. This unites the Lordship, or Kingship, of Christ and His High Priesthood lived out during the Church Age through His priesthood in local churches. Merrill F. Unger comments on the two olives trees in Zechariah's fifth vision:

> "As the golden candlestick symbolizes Israel in full fellowship with God as a light-bearer to the nations as she was divinely intended to be in Old testament times and as she will actually be in her millennial restoration, *so the two olive trees represent the two offices of the kingship and priesthood* through which the blessings of God was to flow (and will yet do so) to the nation and through the nation in witness to all the nations of the world."[25]

Therefore, in Zechariah's fourth vision, we see the purging of the priesthood by Christ as both the *Offerer* and the *Offering* for sin. In the fifth vision, we see Christ establishing Himself as both the new High Priest of Israel, after the eternal Melchisedecan order, and as the King of Israel upon the Davidic throne. Clearly in Zechariah 4:6-9, king Zerubbabel typifies the Lord Jesus Christ in His restoration of the Davidic throne.

> "[6] Then he {*the angel*} answered and spake unto me, saying, This *is* the word of the LORD unto Zerubbabel, saying, Not by might, nor by power, but by my spirit, saith the LORD of hosts. [7] Who *art* thou, O great mountain? before Zerubbabel *thou shalt become* a plain: and he shall bring forth the headstone *thereof with* shoutings, crying, Grace, grace unto it. [8] Moreover the word of the LORD came unto me, saying, [9] The hands of Zerubbabel have laid the foundation of this house; his hands shall also finish it; and thou shalt know that the LORD of hosts hath sent me unto you. [10] For who hath despised the day of small things? for they shall rejoice, and shall see the plummet in the hand of Zerubbabel *with* those seven; they *are* the eyes of the LORD, which run to and fro through the whole earth" (Zechariah 4:6-10; compare 14:1-11).

---

[25] Unger, Merrill F. *ZECHARIAH: Prophet of Messiah's Glory*. (Grand Rapids, Michigan: Zondervan Publishing House, 1982), page 80.

In Zechariah 4:7, we find the final fulfillment of Messianic prophecies. Jesus came to be the "cornerstone." Instead, His death on the Cross became a "stumbling stone" to Israel. In His second coming, He becomes the "headstone" or *capstone* of the Millennial Temple.

This leads us to the sixth vision of Zechariah. This vision is particularly important to our understanding of the roll of glorified Church Age believers as a "kingdom of priests" (Exodus 19:6, in Revelation1:6 and 5:10 this is "kings and priests") during the Kingdom Age. It is especially important in that it defines the objective of the Spirit-filled life during the Church Age. During the Church Age, believers are commanded to "be filled with the Spirit" (Ephesians 5:18; literally reads "be ye being filled"). This filling will be continuous in the glorification of these believer priests during the Kingdom Age. Then they will experience the constant fullness of the Spirit and all which that entails. The sixth vision of Zechariah gives us an important vision into what this will be like.

Vision six (5:1-4): the Flying Scroll

"[1] Then I turned, and lifted up mine eyes, and looked, and behold a flying roll. [2] And he said unto me, What seest thou? And I answered, I see a flying roll; the length thereof *is* twenty cubits, and the breadth thereof ten cubits. [3] Then said he unto me, This *is* the curse that goeth forth over the face of the whole earth: for every one that stealeth shall be cut off *as* on this side according to it; and every one that sweareth shall be cut off *as* on that side according to it. [4] I will bring it forth, saith the LORD of hosts, and it shall enter into the house of the thief, and into the house of him that sweareth falsely by my name: and it shall remain in the midst of his house, and shall consume it with the timber thereof and the stones thereof" (Zechariah 5:1-4).

This Flying Scroll represents the restoration of the Mosaic Covenant (the Law) during the Kingdom Age. However, the institution and administration of the Mosaic Covenant will be through the New Covenant priesthood. Christ will live as High Priest and glorified believers from the Church Age will serve as His *administrative priesthood* through which the Mosaic Covenant is restored and instituted. Again, Merrill F. Unger gives us some insight into this text.

"The scroll of Zechariah's vision was not wound up but unrolled or spread open, like a huge sheet. This appears from the circumstances that it is a flying scroll (*megillah 'aphah*) the participle denoting a continuous verbal action of 'floating' since the scroll itself was inanimate, but evidently graphically described as animate to symbolize the active energy of the Word of God it represents. 'for the Word of God is living and active, sharper than a two-edged sword, piercing to the dividing asunder of soul and spirit, of joints and marrow, and is a discerner of the thoughts and intentions of the heart' (Heb. 4:12)."[26]

The Flying Scroll vision is the Law now *animated in a practical way* through the glorification of the new eternal Melchisedecan theanthropic priesthood. This new priesthood literally becomes an *animate and practical extension* of the living *Logos* as they rule and reign with Christ during the Kingdom Age. They will become *living translations* of the Word of God through the fullness of the Spirit. This fullness of the Spirit, which is related to the believer's complete transfiguration to Christ-likeness once glorified, is referred to in the epistle to the Ephesians as the "fullness of God."

"[15] Wherefore I also, after I heard of your faith in the Lord Jesus, and love unto all the saints, [16] Cease not to give thanks for you, making mention of you in my prayers; [17] That the God of our Lord Jesus Christ, the Father of glory, may give unto you the spirit of wisdom and revelation in the knowledge of him: [18] The eyes of your understanding being enlightened; that ye may know what is the hope of his calling, and what the riches of the glory of his inheritance in the saints, [19] And what *is* the exceeding greatness of his power to us-ward who believe, according to the working of his mighty power, [20] Which he wrought in Christ, when he raised him from the dead, and set *him* at his own right hand in the heavenly *places*, [21] Far above all principality, and power, and might, and dominion, and every name that is named, not only in this world, but also in that which is to come: [22] And hath put all *things* under his feet, and gave him *to be* the head over all *things* to the church, [23] Which is his body, the fulness of him that filleth all in all" (Ephesians 1:15-23).

"[14] For this cause I bow my knees unto the Father of our Lord Jesus Christ, [15] Of whom the whole family in heaven and earth is named, [16] That he would grant you, according to the riches of his glory, to be

---

[26] Ibid., page 84.

strengthened with might by his Spirit in the inner man; [17] That Christ may dwell in your hearts by faith; that ye, being rooted and grounded in love, [18] May be able to comprehend with all saints what *is* the breadth, and length, and depth, and height; [19] And to know the love of Christ, which passeth knowledge, <u>that ye might be filled with all the fulness of God</u>. [20] Now unto him that is able to do exceeding abundantly above all that we ask or think, according to the power that worketh in us, [21] Unto him *be* glory in the church by Christ Jesus throughout all ages, world without end. Amen" (Ephesians 3:14-21).

This Flying Scroll typifies the glorified Church Age Priesthood of all believers during the Kingdom Age. They will serve as the *Living Law* and the *Living Tabernacle* of God in their relationship and theanthropic union with their High Priest, Jesus Christ. The *Living Tabernacle* is revealed by the dimensions of the Flying Scroll.

"[1] Then I turned, and lifted up mine eyes, and looked, and behold a flying roll. [2] And he said unto me, What seest thou? And I answered, I see a flying roll; the length thereof *is* twenty cubits, and the breadth thereof ten cubits" (Zechariah 5:1-2).

Merrill F. Unger comments on this text:

"Since these measurements are the exact size of the tabernacle in the wilderness, as may be computed from the boards used to build it (Exod. 26:15-25), the indication is that the judgments proceeding were in accordance with the holiness of the Lord's habitation in the midst of Israel."[27]

The second aspect of this vision is found in Zechariah 5:3-5. This refers to the *Living Law* existing in its enforcement through Jesus Christ and His theanthropic priesthood of glorified Church Age believers. Uniquely, the "blessing and curse" of the Mosaic Covenant will no longer be limited merely to the nation of Israel, but will extend "over the face of the whole earth" (all nations).

"[3] Then said he unto me, This *is* the curse that goeth forth over the face of the whole earth: for every one that stealeth shall be cut off *as* on this side according to it; and every one that sweareth shall be cut off *as* on that side according to it. [4] I will bring it forth, saith the LORD of hosts, and it shall enter into the house of the thief, and into the house of him that sweareth falsely by my name: and it shall

---

[27] Ibid., page 85.

remain in the midst of his house, and shall consume it with the timber thereof and the stones thereof" (Zechariah 5:3-4).

> The "curse" of Zechariah 5:3 is not the *original curse* of God upon His *original creation*. That curse is already *universal*. The curse of the sixth vision of the Flying Scroll is curse of the "blessing and a curse" for obedience and disobedience within the Mosaic Covenant that was to be enforced by the priesthood of Israel.

When the priesthood *kept*, or *enforced*, the "statutes and judgments" given by God in the Mosaic Covenant, God promised to prosper the nation of Israel. When the priesthood failed to keep, or enforced, the "statutes and judgments" given by God in the Mosaic Covenant, God promised to withdraw His material blessings upon the nation of Israel in chastisement.

"[26] Behold, I set before you this day a blessing and a curse; [27] A blessing, if ye obey the commandments of the LORD your God, which I command you this day: [28] And a curse, if ye will not obey the commandments of the LORD your God, but turn aside out of the way which I command you this day, to go after other gods, which ye have not known" (Deuteronomy 11:26-28).

If chastisement did not result in national repentance, God said He would bring the children of Israel into captivity. That is where Israel is today. They remain there while God calls and prepares a New Priesthood to teach and enforce the Mosaic Covenant upon all nations during the Kingdom Age. Very early in the life of the Exodus Jews, God spoke of a future day of restoration of national Israel in Deuteronomy 30:1-10. God's foreknowledge of Israel's failure as a nation to keep the Mosaic Covenant is revealed in the first few words "and it shall come to pass" in Deuteronomy 30:1.

We must remember that although the whole nation of Israel was accountable to keep the Mosaic Covenant, the responsibility for teaching the Law and enforcing the Law fell upon the priesthood of Israel. God's message through Malachi was primarily to this corrupt and corrupting Levitical priesthood.

"[1] And now, O ye priests, this commandment *is* for you. [2] If ye will not hear, and if ye will not lay *it* to heart, to give glory unto my name, saith the LORD of hosts, I will even send a curse upon you, and I will curse your blessings: yea, I have cursed them already, because ye do not lay *it* to heart. [3] Behold, I will corrupt your seed, and spread dung upon your faces, *even* the dung of your solemn feasts; and *one* shall take you away with it. [4] And ye shall know that I have sent this commandment unto you, that my covenant might be with Levi, saith the LORD of hosts. [5] My covenant was with him of life and peace; and I gave them to him *for* the fear wherewith he feared me, and was afraid before my name. [6] The law of truth was in his mouth, and iniquity was not found in his lips: he walked with me in peace and equity, and did turn many away from iniquity. [7] For the priest's lips should keep knowledge, and they should seek the law at his mouth: for he *is* the messenger of the LORD of hosts. [8] But ye are departed out of the way; ye have caused many to stumble at the law; ye have corrupted the covenant of Levi, saith the LORD of hosts. [9] Therefore have I also made you contemptible and base before all the people, according as ye have not kept my ways, but have been partial in the law" (Malachi 2:1-5).

Because of this corruption and defilement of the Levitical Covenant by the descendants of Levi, the Mosaic Covenant was put on Sabbath (*shabath or cease,* Hosea 2:11). This will continue until God could call, ordain, and consecrate a new priesthood. He will do this before He would reinstitute the Mosaic Covenant during the Kingdom Age. The Mosaic Covenant will then be taught and enforced by that new priesthood. This new priesthood would not be like the Levitical priesthood that possessed a sin nature, corruption, and personal ambitions. This new priesthood will be glorified Church Age believers in theanthropic union with their High Priest, Jesus Christ. They will live their new lives in the fullness of the Spirit of God in perfect unity with the Godhead.

The Flying Scroll as the representation of the restoration of the Mosaic Covenant (the Law) during the Kingdom Age is a reference to both the Palestinian Covenant and the Davidic Covenant. Church Age believers are connected to these two Covenants through their connection to the Abrahamic Covenant in the "Seed." Both Galatians chapter three and Deuteronomy 30:1-10 reveal this connection.

"[1] And it shall come to pass, when all these things are come upon thee, the blessing and the curse, which I have set before thee, and thou shalt call *them* to mind among all the nations, whither the

LORD thy God hath driven thee, [2] And shalt return unto the LORD thy God, and shalt obey his voice according to all that I command thee this day, thou and thy children, with all thine heart, and with all thy soul; [3] That then the LORD thy God will turn thy captivity, and have compassion upon thee, and will return and gather thee from all the nations, whither the LORD thy God hath scattered thee. [4] If *any* of thine be driven out unto the outmost *parts* of heaven, from thence will the LORD thy God gather thee, and from thence will he fetch thee: [5] And the LORD thy God will bring thee into the land which thy fathers possessed, and thou shalt possess it; and he will do thee good, and multiply thee above thy fathers. [6] And the LORD thy God will circumcise thine heart, and the heart of thy seed, to love the LORD thy God with all thine heart, and with all thy soul, that thou mayest live. [7] And the LORD thy God will put all these curses upon thine enemies, and on them that hate thee, which persecuted thee. [8] And thou shalt return and obey the voice of the LORD, and do all his commandments which I command thee this day. [9] And the LORD thy God will make thee plenteous in every work of thine hand, in the fruit of thy body, and in the fruit of thy cattle, and in the fruit of thy land, for good: for the LORD will again rejoice over thee for good, as he rejoiced over thy fathers: [10] If thou shalt hearken unto the voice of the LORD thy God, to keep his commandments and his statutes which are written in this book of the law, *and* if thou turn unto the LORD thy God with all thine heart, and with all thy soul" (Deuteronomy 30:1-10).

"[13] Christ hath redeemed us from the curse of the law, being made a curse for us: for it is written, Cursed *is* every one that hangeth on a tree: [14] That the blessing of Abraham might come on the Gentiles through Jesus Christ; that we might receive the promise of the Spirit through faith. [15] Brethren, I speak after the manner of men; Though *it be* but a man's covenant, yet *if it be* confirmed, no man disannulleth, or addeth thereto. [16] Now to Abraham and his seed were the promises made. He saith not, And to seeds, as of many; but as of one, And to thy seed, which is Christ. . . [26] For ye are all the children of God by faith in Christ Jesus. [27] For as many of you as have been baptized into Christ have put on Christ. [28] There is neither Jew nor Greek, there is neither bond nor free, there is neither male nor female: for ye are all one in Christ Jesus. [29] And if ye *be* Christ's, then are ye Abraham's seed, and heirs according to the promise" (Galatians 3:13-16, 26-29).

Although the Palestinian Covenant and the Davidic Covenant are primarily applied to the nation of Israel and the

Promised Land, Christ's Kingdom will extend throughout the whole earth. Also, Christ's Kingdom "rod of iron" rule will be *administrated* by His Kingdom of priests on a worldwide scale. It is the Kingdom of priests of Church Age believers who will enforce the Mosaic Covenant upon all nations and people groups. It is to this Kingdom "rod of iron" rule that Galatians 2:29 refers with the words "heirs according to the promise." Although national Israel has her promises in the Abrahamic Covenant, the Church has her own promises within the Abrahamic Covenant relating to the theanthropic priesthood and shared "rod of iron" rule with Christ.

DISCUSSION QUESTIONS

1. Describe how the fifth vision of Zechariah (4:1-14) is partially fulfilled by local churches during the Church Age.

2. Explain the *office* and *purpose* of Christ in Revelation 1:9-20 as He ministers in the midst of these seven local churches.

3. Explain the metaphor of the seven golden candlesticks in Revelation chapters two and three as they relate to the church as the "light of the world."

4. Explain Christ's continue call to "repent" throughout the Church Age, represented in the seven local churches of Revelation chapters two through three, as this relates to their being the "light of the world."

5. Discuss the *dispensational transition* revealed in John 8:12 and John 9:5 and how this transition *takes place*.

6. Explain the fifth vision of Zechariah 4:6-9.

7. Thoroughly explain the sixth vision of Zechariah 5:1-4, the Flying Scroll as the *Living Law* and the *Living Tabernacle* of God.

Chapter Fifty-seven
The Local Church as the Pillar and Ground of the Truth

Jesus said, "I am the Way, the Truth, and the Life, no man cometh unto the Father, but by me" (John 14:6). Salvation (the "Way") is in a Person. "Truth" is not merely systematic theology developed through detailed study of the Word of God. "Truth" is personified in the theanthropicity of the Person of Jesus Christ (John 1:1, the *Logos*). Eternal "Life" is not merely living forever. Eternal "Life" is the Person of Jesus Christ (I John 5:11-13) living His "Life" through theanthropic union within the body of the yielded "born again" and Spirit-filled believer (Romans 6:11-13). The significance of all this is that Christianity is not just about the truths we know and believe. Christianity is about the truths we know, believe, and LIVE. Christianity is the *Christ-life* lived through Spirit-filled believers. Truths that do not transform/transfigure our lives are truths that are not being lived. That is a duplicity that promotes pseudo-Christianity.

"[1] This *is* a true saying, If a man desire the office of a bishop, he desireth a good work. [2] A bishop then must be blameless, the husband of one wife, vigilant, sober, of good behaviour, given to hospitality, apt to teach; [3] Not given to wine, no striker, not greedy of filthy lucre; but patient, not a brawler, not covetous; [4] One that ruleth well his own house, having his children in subjection with all gravity; [5] (For if a man know not how to rule his own house, how shall he take care of the church of God?) [6] Not a novice, lest being lifted up with pride he fall into the condemnation of the devil. [7] Moreover he must have a good report of them which are without; lest he fall into reproach and the snare of the devil. [8] Likewise *must* the deacons *be* grave, not doubletongued, not given to much wine, not greedy of filthy lucre; [9] Holding the mystery of the faith in a pure conscience. [10] And let these also first be proved; then let them use the office of a deacon, being *found* blameless. [11] Even so *must* *their* wives *be* grave, not slanderers, sober, faithful in all things. [12] Let the deacons be the husbands of one wife, ruling their children and their own houses well. [13] For they that have used the office of a deacon well purchase to themselves a good degree, and great boldness in the faith which is in Christ Jesus. [14] These things write I unto thee, hoping to come unto thee shortly: [15] But if I tarry long, that thou mayest know how thou oughtest to behave thyself in the house of God, which is the church of the living God, the pillar and ground of the truth. [16] And without controversy great is the mystery of godliness: God was manifest in the flesh, justified in the Spirit, seen of angels, preached unto the Gentiles, believed on in the world, received up into glory" (I Timothy 3:1-16).

I Timothy 3:1-16 and Titus chapter one are often referred to as the *qualifications* for pastors and deacons. These men must meet *specific qualifications* before they can be installed into their working ministries in local church leadership through congregational polity. However, notice that almost every *qualification* is defined by a *testimony* (history) of *living* the truth, not just *knowing* the truth. These men are the *models of ministry* within local churches. They are the *living standard* for living the truth for other believers in a local congregation. They set this standard of leadership by literally being followers of Jesus Christ; i.e., seeking to live exactly the way Jesus lived. This is the admonition of spiritual leadership as these men literally live the *Christ-life* in their appeal to others to follow them in doing the same thing. Congregational polity works when local congregations hold their leadership to the high standards that God defines for them. They do so understanding that the lowest standard allowed will be the standard to which most people will gravitate. Therefore, the standards to which they hold their leaders are the same standards they expect of all members of the local church. This was the appeal of Paul to the carnal Corinthian church.

"[14] I write not these things to shame you, but as my beloved sons I warn *you*. [15] For though ye have ten thousand instructors in Christ, yet *have ye* not many fathers: for in Christ Jesus I have begotten you through the gospel. [16] Wherefore I beseech you, be ye followers of me" (I Corinthians 4:14-16).

"Be ye followers of me, even as I also *am* of Christ" (I Corinthians 11:1).

"[17] Brethren, be followers together of me, and mark them which walk so as ye have us for an ensample. [18] (For many walk, of whom I have told you often, and now tell you even weeping, *that they are* the enemies of the cross of Christ: [19] Whose end *is* destruction, whose God *is their* belly, and *whose* glory *is* in their shame, who mind earthly things.) [20] For our conversation {*citizenship or communal loyalty}* is in heaven; from whence also we look for the Saviour, the Lord Jesus Christ: [21] Who shall change our vile body, that it may be fashioned like unto his glorious body, according to the working whereby he is able even to subdue all things unto himself" (Philippians 3:17-21).

I want to focus our attention on the statement in I Timothy 3:15-16: "[15] But if I tarry long, that thou mayest know how thou oughtest to <u>behave</u> thyself in the house of God, which is the church of the living God, the pillar and ground of the truth. [16] And without controversy great is the mystery of godliness: God was manifest in the flesh, justified in the Spirit, seen of angels, preached unto the Gentiles, believed on in the world, received up into glory." Paul is talking about the *unified collective* of believers in a given locality known as a local church. In the next three chapters of I Timothy, Paul gives considerable detail regarding how Christians are to "behave" themselves "in the house of God" and lays upon Timothy (and all future generations of spiritual leaders) the responsibility for teaching and living these details that define local church polity (or *congregational polity*).

Although the qualifications for spiritual leadership are extremely important and cannot be minimized in any way, once a man meets these qualifications and is installed into the position as a pastor or deacon, he is required to *model* and *teach* the congregational polity taught in I Timothy chapters four through six. God cannot, and will not, bless a local church that does not operate within the spiritual definitions of the polity defined in these three chapters of Scripture. This doctrine (orthodoxy) and practices (orthopraxy) is expanded upon considerably in the rest of the books of the New Testament, but we have a *nutshell view* in I Timothy chapters four through six. Although there are ordained offices or positions of spiritual leadership in every local church, the issue of spiritual leadership is intended to *model* a lifestyle of the *Christ-life* for every individual believer priest within a local church. The model is found in Christ first, His ordained spiritual leaders second, and in every believer within a local church giving us the levels of accountability in a *chain of command* (i.e., accountability).

"[1] Be ye followers of me, even as I also *am* of Christ. [2] Now I praise you, brethren, that ye remember me in all things, and keep the ordinances, as I delivered *them* to you. [3] But I would have you know, that the head of every man is Christ; and the head of the woman *is* the man; and the head of Christ *is* God" (I Corinthians 11:1-3).

We find this *modeling* of the *Christ-life* extending out of the *church house* and into every facet of the believer's life in Ephesians chapters five and six. There is considerable detail given defining how believers in a local church are to "behave" themselves as the "church," or the *living spiritual house* of the "Living God."

"[21] Submitting yourselves one to another in the fear of God. [22] Wives, submit yourselves unto your own husbands, as unto the Lord. [23] For the husband is the head of the wife, even as Christ is the head of the church: and he is the saviour of the body. [24] Therefore as the church is subject unto Christ, so *let* the wives *be* to their own husbands in every thing. [25] Husbands, love your wives, even as Christ also loved the church, and gave himself for it; [26] That he might sanctify and cleanse it with the washing of water by the word, [27] That he might present it to himself a glorious church, not having spot, or wrinkle, or any such thing; but that it should be holy and without blemish" (Ephesians 5:21-27).

Paul then defines this *living or animate spiritual house* of the "living God" as "the pillar and ground of the truth." The "Cornerstone" of the *living spiritual house* of God is the theanthropic Christ. Upon that "Cornerstone" is laid the lives and teaching of the theanthropic Apostles of Jesus Christ. Upon the foundation of testimony and doctrine of the theanthropic Apostles is built the individual "pillars," which are made up of the lives of generation after generation of faithful theanthropic Spirit-filled believers living the truth. As their numbers grow, these generations move through history, their testimony expands through soul winning and discipleship. As these living "pillars" are built and shaped with each new "living stone," the truth is raised to a more exalted position, like the roof of a *living temple* to the glory of God.

"[1] Wherefore laying aside all malice, and all guile, and hypocrisies, and envies, and all evil speakings, [2] As newborn babes, desire the sincere milk of the word, that ye may grow thereby: [3] If so be ye have tasted that the Lord *is* gracious. [4] To whom {*the theanthropic Jesus Christ*} coming, *as unto* a living stone, disallowed indeed of men, but chosen of God, *and* precious, [5] Ye also, as lively stones, are built up a spiritual house, an holy priesthood, to offer up spiritual sacrifices, acceptable to God by Jesus Christ. [6] Wherefore also it is contained in the scripture, Behold, I lay in Sion a chief corner stone, elect, precious: and he that believeth on him shall not be confounded. [7] Unto you therefore which believe *he is* precious: but unto them which be disobedient, the stone which the builders disallowed, the same is made the head of the corner, [8] And a stone of stumbling, and a rock of offence, *even to them* which stumble at the word, being disobedient: whereunto also they were appointed. [9] But ye *are* a chosen generation, a royal priesthood, an holy nation, a peculiar people; that ye should shew forth the praises of him who hath called you out of darkness into his marvellous light: [10] Which in time past *were* not a people, but *are* now the people of God: which had not obtained mercy, but now have obtained mercy. [11] Dearly beloved, I beseech *you* as strangers and pilgrims, abstain from fleshly lusts, which war against the soul; [12] Having your conversation honest among the Gentiles: that, whereas they speak against you as evildoers, they may by *your* good works, which they shall behold, glorify God in the day of visitation" (I Peter 2:1-12).

The *living house* of the *Living God* is built upon the foundation of the *New Creation* in the theanthropicity of Christ. The church is a *living house* because every individual stone in that *living house* is a theanthropic "living stone" through regeneration.

"[11] Behold, I come quickly: hold that fast which thou hast, that no man take thy crown. [12] Him that overcometh will I make a pillar in the temple of my God, and he shall go no more out: and I will write upon him the name of my God, and the name of the city of my God, *which is* new Jerusalem, which cometh down out of heaven from my God: and *I will write upon him* my new name" (Revelation 3:11-12).

"[9] For we are labourers together with God: ye are God's husbandry, *ye are* God's building. [10] According to the grace of God which is given unto me, as a wise masterbuilder, I have laid the foundation, and another buildeth thereon. But let every man take heed how he buildeth thereupon. [11] For other foundation can no man lay than that is laid, which is Jesus Christ. [12] Now if any man build upon this foundation gold, silver, precious stones, wood, hay, stubble; [13] Every man's work shall be made manifest: for the day shall declare it, because it shall be revealed by fire; and the fire shall try every man's work of what sort it is. [14] If any man's work abide which he hath built thereupon, he shall receive a reward. [15] If any man's work shall be burned, he shall suffer loss: but he himself shall be saved; yet so as by fire" (I Corinthians 3:9-15).

Although the theanthropic Christ is the Chief Cornerstone of the *living temple* of the "Living God," the Apostles are the secondary foundation of this eternal *living temple*. Upon that foundation, the "pillars" are built of "gold, silver, and precious stones." These are individual faithful believers throughout the generations of the Church Age.

"[19] Now therefore ye {*Church Age believers as the new theanthropic priesthood 'in Christ'*} are no more strangers and foreigners, but fellowcitizens with the saints, and of the household of God {*the truly saved 'by grace through faith' of Israel*}; [20] And are built upon the foundation of the apostles and prophets, Jesus Christ himself being the chief corner *stone*; [21] In whom all the building fitly framed together groweth unto an holy temple in the Lord: [22] In whom ye also are builded together for an habitation of God through the Spirit" (Ephesians 2:19-22).

The reason we can say this is the *eternal position* of the Apostles is because we see this eternal *living temple* in the description of the *New Heaven/Earth* of Revelation chapter twenty-one. This is the final state of existence in the complete unfolding of "the regeneration" (Matthew 19:28). "The regeneration" is the believer's eternal theanthropic existence "in Christ."

"[9] And there came unto me one of the seven angels which had the seven vials full of the seven last plagues, and talked with me, saying, Come hither, I will shew thee the bride, the Lamb's wife. [10] And he carried me away in the spirit to a great and high mountain, and shewed me that great city, the holy Jerusalem, descending out of heaven from God, [11] Having the glory of God: and her light *was* like unto a stone most precious, even like a jasper stone, clear as crystal; [12] And had a wall great and high, *and* had twelve gates, and at the gates twelve angels, and names written thereon, which are *the names* of the twelve tribes of the children of Israel: [13] On the east three gates; on the north three gates; on the south three gates; and on the west three gates. [14] And the wall of the city had twelve foundations, and in them the names of the twelve apostles of the Lamb. . . [18] And the building of the wall of it was *of* jasper: and the city *was* pure gold, like unto clear glass. [19] And the foundations of the wall of the city *were* garnished with all manner of precious stones. The first foundation *was* jasper; the second, sapphire; the third, a chalcedony; the fourth, an emerald; [20] The fifth, sardonyx; the sixth, sardius; the seventh, chrysolite; the eighth, beryl; the ninth, a topaz; the tenth, a chrysoprasus; the eleventh, a jacinth; the twelfth, an amethyst. [21] And the twelve gates *were* twelve pearls; every several gate was of one pearl: and the street of the city *was* pure gold, as it were transparent glass. [22] And I saw no temple therein: for the Lord God Almighty and the Lamb are the temple of it." (Revelation 21:9-14 and 18-22).

When we think of this "truth" that the *living church* of the Living God is the "pillar and ground of the truth," we tend to think of "truth" as the inspired words on the pages of our Bible. The written Word of God or the spoken Word of God is indeed *truth*. However, these two forms of "truth" are merely expressions of the revelations of God's will in all matters of temporal and eternal realities. The ultimate expression of "truth" is God Himself. Truth is what God is (John 14:6). *Truth* is the living, communicable attributes that God is. This *Living Truth* is what the Greek word *Logos* refers to in John 1:1 and 14, regarding the person of Jesus Christ in His theanthropic union in His incarnation. The *Logos* is the Word of God that was living before the incarnation became a living entity in the theanthropic union of the Son of God and the Son of man.

It is through the theanthropic union of the indwelling Holy Spirit of God that individual believers are progressively being transfigured into living *Logos* beings. A person can *tell* the truth. A person can *live* the truth (that is what believers are commanded to do during the Church Age). However, there is a new day coming in the believer's glorification when every believer will become the *living embodiment* of *truth* in the final fullness of the Spirit "full of grace and truth." This is outcome of Christ's resurrection and glorification and will be the outcome of every believer's glorification.

"[10] He was in the world, and the world was made by him, and the world knew him not. [11] He came unto his own, and his own received him not. [12] But as many as received him, to them gave he power to become the sons of God, *even* to them that believe on his name: [13] Which were born, not of blood, nor of the will of the flesh, nor of the will of man, but of God. [14] And the Word was made flesh, and dwelt among us, (and we beheld his glory, the glory as of the only begotten of the Father,) full of grace and truth" (John 1:10-14).

The believer's glorification goes far beyond a mere physical transformation. Every believer that is "born again" of the Spirit of God will be completely transfigured to be like the glorified Jesus in His theanthropic union as the *living Logos*. In other words, every believer will be "full of grace and truth." Christ Jesus is both God and man. All believers, beginning on the Day of Pentecost, are God *in* man. In this *theanthropic union*, all believers become responsible to be separate from sin, worldliness, and false doctrine, just as God is separate from these things. In other words, those believers who want to live in the "unity of the Spirit" must live in a way completely different from the rest of the world as defined by the Word of God. We cannot be *living Logos* if our lives are lived in contradiction to the *written Logos*. If a local church is to be "the pillar and ground of the truth," as God intends every local church to be, that local church constituency must be separate from worldliness and false doctrine in both its practices and affiliations.

The *living church* of the *Living God* was created by *recreating* believers by indwelling them with the Holy Spirit of God. Every believer is intended to become a *living translation* of the *living Logos*. The progressive revelation of God is now literally written on the hearts of God's "born again" children.

The process of discipleship is not merely *head-work*. The process of discipleship also involves *heart-work* and *foot-work*. We see this in the training of the twelve in the Gospels. Discipleship in the *heart-work* and the *foot-work* were the most difficult areas in that these two areas required believers to live under enormous trials, difficulties, and the willingness to live completely outside of their comfort zones.

The easiest of the three is to get people to do the *head-work* (although few will truly do it). The great failure of the Church Age is that a very small minority of believers have been willing to do the *heart-work* resulting in genuine Spirit-filled *foot-work*.

"[1] Do we begin again to commend ourselves? or need we, as some *others*, epistles of commendation to you, or *letters* of commendation from you? [2] <u>Ye are our epistle written in our hearts, known and read of all men:</u> [3] *Forasmuch as ye are* <u>manifestly declared to be the epistle of Christ ministered by us, written not with ink, but with the Spirit of the living God; not in tables of stone, but in fleshy tables of the heart.</u> [4] And such trust have we through Christ to God-ward: [5] Not that we are sufficient of ourselves to think any thing as of ourselves; but our sufficiency *is* of God; [6] <u>Who also hath made us able ministers of the new testament; not of the letter, but of the spirit: for the letter killeth, but the spirit giveth life.</u> [7] But if the ministration of death, written *and* engraven in stones, was glorious, so that the children of Israel could not stedfastly behold the face of Moses for the glory of his countenance; which *glory* was to be done away: [8] How shall not the ministration of the spirit be rather glorious? [9] For if the ministration of condemnation *be* glory, much more doth the ministration of righteousness exceed in glory. [10] For even that which was made glorious had no glory in this respect, by reason of the glory that excelleth. [11] For if that which is done away *was* glorious, much more that which remaineth *is* glorious. [12] Seeing then that we have such hope, we use great plainness of speech: [13] And not as Moses, *which* put a vail over his face, that the children of Israel could not stedfastly look to the end of that which is abolished: [14] But their minds were blinded: for until this day remaineth the same vail untaken away in the reading of the old testament; which *vail* is done away in Christ. [15] But even unto this day, when Moses is read, the vail is upon their heart. [16] Nevertheless when it shall turn to the Lord, the vail shall be taken away. [17] Now the Lord is that Spirit: and where the Spirit of the Lord *is*, there *is* liberty. [18] But we all, with open face beholding as in a glass the glory of the Lord, are changed {*present tense and passive voice; lit, are being transfigured from one form of existence into another form of existence*} into the same image from glory to glory, *even* as by the Spirit of the Lord" (II Corinthians 3:1-18).

Throughout the Gospels, we see Jesus teaching the truth to His disciples. However, if all that was needed to disciple them was *head-work*, He could have written it down, told them to memorize it, and have them quote it back to Him. That is not Christ's *model of discipleship*. He taught them (*head-work*). He brought them into situations of life where they needed to apply those truths in passion, compassion, faithfulness, mercy, and love (*heart-work*). Then He sent them out into the world to do the same with others (*the foot-work*). A person is not discipled until the *head-work, heart-work,* and *foot-work* are all Spirit-filled realities of that believer's everyday existence of living.

Jesus, the incarnate, eternal Son of God is the Creator. Many New Testament Scriptures assure us of that truth. John 1:3 and 1:10 are only a few of those Scriptures. The word "made" from the Greek word *ginomai* (ghin'-om-ahee) in John 1:3 and 1:10 means *to bring something into existence*. The "world" and all that is in it was brought into existence by the eternal Son of God, who then became incarnate as Jesus.

Yet, when the Creator became part of His creation, the creation did not recognize Him. Due to mankind's fall into the darkness of sin, the creation lost knowledge of its Creator. They lost this knowledge to the degree that when Deity was united with humanity in the incarnation, the creation could not even recognize Him.

A *central* purpose of the Scriptures is the continuing and progressive revelation of God to fallen mankind. God, down through the centuries, continually sought to make Himself known ("Light") to His spiritually blinded and fallen creation ("darkness"). Even with an inner testimony to God's existence (Romans 1:19) instilled within every person, the knowledge of God was further lost with each succeeding generation. Each generation lost something. Each succeeding generation failed to teach the next generation until the knowledge of their Creator was almost completely lost or perverted.

Progressive revelation means that throughout the history of the world, God chose certain individuals to *restore* knowledge of Him that had been lost by previous generations. They were *commissioned* by Him to work to *restore* that knowledge in their generation. Abraham, the father of Israel was one such individual. The nation of Israel became the chosen nation, *commissioned* to *restore* a true knowledge of the Creator to the creation. Due to a failed priesthood and the compromise and apathy of the children of Israel, Israel miserably failed to fulfill their *commission*.

However, God had another plan in His progressive revelation. He would become part of humanity by becoming one of His chosen nation of Israel. Jesus would die on a Cross to bear the wrath of God and the penalty of sin for the whole world. He would rise victorious over death and personally become a *door* into a *New Creation* for anyone willing to believe what He did and trust in Him for their salvation.

However, what He came to do *just begins with salvation.* He said He would build His Church and the "gates of hell" would not prevail against it. As the new High Priest who is already resurrected, glorified, and ascended to the right hand of the Father, He guarantees the same for every true believer. That is why the church, as the "body of Christ," can be the "pillar and ground of the truth."

What is meant by "His own" in John 1:11? The word "own" is from the Greek word *idios* (id'-ee-os). It refers to something or someone pertaining to one's self, one's own, belonging to one's self. According to R. V. G. Tasker, "His own" is in the neuter (*ta idia*) in the first use in John 1:11 and masculine (*hoi idioi*) in its second use."[28] From the context, the first use would appear to refer to His incarnation into His creation in general (*some believe it refers to the Temple*). However, the second use means the Word became flesh in the specific form of a Jewish child as promised to the nation of Israel. The people of Israel were His chosen people. Therefore, the second use of "his own" in John 1:11 refers to His *own chosen people.* The most accurate meaning of this statement is that *the Creator came home, but was not welcomed there by His chosen family.*

Once again, the progressive revelation and knowledge of God was lost. It was lost due to the apathy of succeeding generations as they failed to *learn* and *teach* their children the truth about God. It was lost to the degree that when Messiah finally came, they not only failed to recognize Him as a nation, but they rejected Him as a nation. This was a great failure on their part with overwhelming consequences upon the nation of Israel for thousands of years.

The word "received" in John 1:11 is from the Greek word *paralambano* (par-al-am-ban'-o). It means *to take with one's self* or *to join to one's self to something or someone.* Metaphorically, it means to accept or acknowledge someone to be what he professes to be. In the sense of receiving someone who comes claiming

---

[28] Tasker, R. V. G. The *Gospel According to St. John, Tyndale N.T. Commentaries, Vol. 4* (Grand Rapids, Michigan: Wm. B. Eerdmans Publishing Co., 1980), page 47.

authority, it means to acknowledge their authority and submit to them by obeying what they say.

The word "received" in John 1:12 is from a different Greek word. It is from the word *lambano* (lam-ban'-o), which means *to take something with the hand with the intent of using it*. When used regarding another person, it means *to associate one's self with that person as a companion or attendant*. The context would determine that the intent of "receive" in John 1:12 is the recognition of Jesus as the incarnate Creator (Lord), *enjoining* yourself to Him and the recognition and submission to His absolute sovereign authority over your life. *Enjoining* is the key word here. The believer does not merely intellectually acknowledge Jesus to be the sovereign Creator and Lord. The believer *enjoins* himself to all that the Person Jesus is in His character and purposes. This *enjoining* or *receiving* Christ is to enter into the spiritual dynamic of Christ's purpose with *head*, *heart*, and *feet*.

The promise of the Sovereign to the submissive believer (John 1:12)

Anyone receiving Jesus, fully recognizing Him as the ultimate revelation of the righteousness of God and as his only means of salvation, and submitting to His sovereignty as God, is given the "power to become the sons of God." "Power" is from the Greek word *exousia* (ex-oo-see'-ah). In this context it means the *power of authority* and the *right of privilege as sons*.

"Sons" is from the Greek word *teknon* (tek'-non) and refers to the offspring or children of someone. Literally becoming "the sons of God" was promised to anyone ("as many") "that believe on His Name."

The word "believe" is from the Greek word *pisteuo* (pist-yoo'-o), which means *to commit one's trust to something or someone based upon a conviction of truth*. The application in the context is that once Jesus is recognized as the incarnate revelation of the righteousness of God in coming to redeem fallen mankind from the condemnation of sin, the believing sinner would recognize Him as God, trust completely in Him for salvation, and submit to His sovereignty.

To believe "on His Name" (Greek: *onoma,* on'-om-ah) is *to understand, trust in, and submit to everything for which the name is used, everything which the name covers, and every thought or feeling which the name arouses when it is mentioned, heard, or comes to mind.* The name *Jesus* cannot be separated from all that His name represents. It cannot be separated from all with which His name connects the believer in the progressive revelation of the righteousness of God and His only means of salvation. To believe on the name of Jesus is to believe:

1. Jesus is God incarnate.

2. Jesus is the Creator and sovereign Lord of His Creation.

3. Jesus is the promised Savior and Redeemer of His fallen Creation.

4. Jesus is the resurrected, glorified, new theanthropic High Priest offering a new theanthropic existence to all believers as a new priesthood of the "sons of God."

DISCUSSION QUESTIONS

1. Explain the following statement, "Christianity is about the Truths we know, believe, and LIVE."

2. Discuss why God gives us the *living models of ministry* in I Timothy 3:1-16.

3. Discuss how your answer the previous question should reflect itself in congregational polity.

4. Read I Timothy 3:15-16 and explain how this defines the *unified collective* of believers in a given locality known as a local church.

5. In I Corinthians 11:1-3, Paul establishes his life as a model of living the Christ-life. How does Paul expect this model to be *fleshed out* in all believers in and through a local church?

6. Thoroughly discuss the *living or animate spiritual house* of the "living God," embodied today in local churches, as "the pillar and ground of the truth." Discuss how you will *put flesh* on this truth.

7. Thoroughly discuss the following statement:

"The *living house* of the *Living God* is built upon the foundation of the New Creation in the theanthropicity of Christ. The church is a *living house* because every individual stone in that *living house* is a theanthropic "living stone" through regeneration."

Chapter Fifty-eight
The New Covenant Necessitates a New Priesthood

There are many Dispensationalists that reject that the Church Age believer is presently part of the New Covenant. I believe this is because they do not see the *already, not yet* aspect of prophetic fulfillment regarding this promise of the Abrahamic Covenant. This fulfillment relates to all believers in the "Seed, which is Christ" (Galatians 3:16 and 29). The Church Age believer is a partial fulfillment prophetically (*already, not yet*) of the unfolding nature of the Abrahamic Covenant. The initiation of the beginning of this unfolding of the New Covenant took place on the Day of Pentecost with the two primary works of the Holy Spirit:

1. The baptism with the Holy Spirit into the "body of Christ" or the New Genesis (New Creation)
2. The indwelling of the believer with the person of the Holy Spirit creating new *theanthropic beings* from every "born again" believer "in Christ"

The Church Age believer has more of God's promises fulfilled than did the believer during the Dispensation of the Law. The Church Age believer is *actually* part of the New Creation presently through the baptism with the Holy Spirit and the indwelling of the Holy Spirit. Christ has fulfilled the prophecies regarding His substitutionary death and the propitiation of God's wrath upon sin (Romans 6:23a). He has been buried, and is resurrected and glorified. Therefore, the New Covenant believer has literally entered the New Creation ("the regeneration") through the baptism with the Holy Spirit into the "body of Christ." This is not a positional issue as it was for believers prior to the Day of Pentecost. Believers after the Day of Pentecost, and all believers that WERE in "Abraham's bosom," ARE now *ACTUALLY* in the New Creation "in Christ." The unfolding nature of the New Covenant will not be completely fulfilled until the literal creation of the New Heaven/Earth, but that New Creation is finished and complete already in the person of Jesus Christ and all believers have entered into the *actuality* of the New Creation "in Christ."

"[14] For the love of Christ constraineth us; because we thus judge, that if one died for all, then were all dead: [15] And *that* he died for all, that they which live should not henceforth live unto themselves, but unto him which died for them, and rose again. [16] Wherefore henceforth know we no man after the flesh: yea, though we have known Christ after the flesh, yet now henceforth know we *him* no more. [17] Therefore if any man *be* in Christ, *he is* a new creature {*creation*}: old things are passed {*aorist tense*} away; behold, all things are become {*perfect tense, finished and once for all*} new" (II Corinthians 5:14-17).

As Hebrews 7:12 reveals, the "priesthood" of Israel is "being changed." The verb "changed" is a present, passive participle. This means that the "priesthood" of Israel is presently, during the Church Age, in the *process of being created.* This change in the "priesthood" will also necessitate a change in the Mosaic Covenant (the "Law").

"[12] <u>For the priesthood being changed</u> {*present, passive, participle*}, <u>there is made of necessity a change also of the law.</u> [13] For he of whom these things are spoken pertaineth to another tribe, of which no man gave attendance at the altar. [14] For *it is* evident that our Lord sprang out of Juda; of which tribe Moses spake nothing concerning priesthood. [15] And it is yet far more evident: for that after the similitude of Melchisedec there ariseth another priest, [16] Who is made, not after the law of a carnal commandment, but after <u>the power of an endless life.</u> [17] For he testifieth, Thou *art* a priest for ever after the order of Melchisedec. [18] For there is verily a disannulling of the commandment going before for the weakness and unprofitableness thereof. [19] For the law made nothing perfect, but the bringing in of a better hope *did*; by the which we {*all believers*} draw nigh unto God. [20] And inasmuch as not without an oath *he was made priest*: [21] (For those priests were made without an oath; but this with an oath by him that said unto him, The Lord sware and will not repent, Thou *art* a priest for ever after the order of Melchisedec:) [22] By so much was Jesus made a surety of a better testament. [23] And they truly were many priests, because they were not suffered to continue by reason of death: [24] But this *man*, because he continueth ever, hath an unchangeable priesthood. [25] <u>Wherefore he is able also to save them to the uttermost that come unto God by him, seeing he ever liveth to make intercession for them.</u> [26] For such an high priest became us, *who is* holy, harmless, undefiled, separate from sinners, and made higher than the heavens; [27] Who needeth not daily, as those high priests, to offer up sacrifice, first for his own sins, and then for the people's: for this he did once, when he offered up himself. [28] For the law maketh men high priests which have infirmity; but the word of the oath, which was since the law, *maketh* the Son, who is consecrated for evermore" (Hebrews 7:12-28).

Hebrews 7:12-28 details the *changes* in the Law, beginning with a *change* in "the priesthood." The Law had three aspects:

1. The High Priest and his various levels of priests, all descendants of Levi

2. The moral aspects of the Law detailed in abbreviation in the Ten Commandments and in the "statutes and judgments" (The priesthood was responsible for *preserving* these moral laws through teaching them, enforcing them as judges, and administrating them.)

3. The Sacrifices, Holy Days, Sabbath Days, and Feast Days

The priesthood of Israel miserably failed in their responsibilities regarding the Law. They allowed the moral aspects of the Law to become an avenue of self-righteousness and self-justification. They perverted the purpose and meaning of the sacrifices, allowing the sacrifices to become efficacious for "the remission of sin." Since they were materially enriched by the offering of sacrifices (they kept portions of meat that was not offered), they became greedy and self-serving. They grew proud and self-righteous in their exalted position as mediators between God and the people. They used their positions as judges and administrators of the "statutes and judgments" to advance themselves in society by taking bribes. They did this to the extent that graft and injustice became their true nomenclatures in the eyes of God and in their reputation among the children of Israel.

In short, the Levitical Priesthood defiled themselves before God in every way imaginable and God completely detested what they did to His Law and to the children of Israel. God had appointed the priesthood to *shepherd* these children. Because of the Priesthood's corruption, God would cast away the Levitical Priesthood of Israel and replace it with a new eternal, sinless, glorified, theanthropic *High Priest* and *Chief Shepherd* and a new eternal, perfected, glorified, theanthropic *priesthood of shepherds*. This is what God is doing during the Dispensation of the Church Age. God is calling a new priesthood out of the world from all nations. This calling is from the "whosoever will call on the name of the Lord" Jesus to be their Saviour. These are those referred to as the "whosoever will confess Him to be Lord (Jehovah incarnate). These will be "born again" of the Spirit of God, become sons of God, and become priests after the order of Melchisedec to be "grafted" into Israel (Romans 11:15-32) at the second coming of Jesus Christ.

Clearly, according to the prophecy of Ezekiel 34:1-16, God was justified in casting away the Levitical Priesthood and replacing that priesthood with a new, better, eternal, and perfect priesthood. The Levitical Priesthood had completely perverted the trust God gave them in their responsibilities in shepherding the children of Israel. Literally thousands, perhaps millions, of souls are in eternal Hell right now because of their failure. Millions of others down through the centuries have died in captivity, torture, and brutalization by the nations into which God scattered the nation of Israel. All of this happened because a group of men, who were elected to be God's priests and mediators, failed and began to make *merchandise* out of God's people.

Christ warned His disciples about their responsibilities in Luke 12:22-53. In verse 47-48, Christ responds to Peter's question in verse 41: "Lord, speakest thou this parable unto us, or even to all?" The parable applies to all Church Age believers; "[47] And that servant, which knew his lord's will, and prepared not *himself*, neither did according to his will, shall be beaten with many *stripes*. [48] But he that knew not, and did commit things worthy of stripes, shall be beaten with few *stripes*. <u>For unto whomsoever much is given, of him shall be much required: and to whom men have committed much, of him they will ask the more</u>."

Look at the detail of God's condemnation of the Levitical Priesthood and see His promise of another Shepherd and a new priesthood in Ezekiel 34:1-16. It is a solemn prophecy in that we have already seen about 3,000 years of God's judgment upon the Levitical Priesthood and the children of Israel. This judgment happened because the Priesthood failed to shepherd as God commanded them. It is a solemn warning to Church Age believers because we are given similar responsibilities during the Church Age in the evangelization of the world and in making disciples of the Lord Jesus Christ. It is solemn to us because we are failing too!

"[1] And the word of the LORD came unto me, saying, [2] Son of man, prophesy against the shepherds of Israel, prophesy, and say unto them, Thus saith the Lord GOD unto the shepherds; Woe *be* to the shepherds of Israel that do feed themselves! should not the shepherds feed the flocks? [3] Ye eat the fat, and ye clothe you with the wool, ye kill them that are fed: *but* ye feed not the flock. [4] The diseased have ye not strengthened, neither have ye healed that which was sick, neither have ye bound up *that which was* broken, neither have ye brought again that which was driven away, neither have ye sought that which was lost; but with force and with cruelty have ye ruled them. [5] And they were scattered, because *there is* no shepherd: and they became meat to all the beasts of the field, when they were scattered. [6] My sheep wandered through all the mountains, and upon every high hill: yea, my flock was scattered upon all the face of the earth, and none did search or seek *after them.* [7] Therefore, ye shepherds, hear the word of the LORD; [8] *As* I live, saith the Lord GOD, surely because my flock became a prey, and my flock became meat to every beast of the field, because *there was* no shepherd, neither did my shepherds search for my flock, but the shepherds fed themselves, and fed not my flock; [9] Therefore, O ye shepherds, hear the word of the LORD; [10] Thus saith the Lord GOD; Behold, I *am* against the shepherds; and I will require my flock at their hand, and cause them to cease from feeding the flock; neither shall the shepherds feed themselves any more; for I will deliver my flock from their mouth, that they may not be meat for them. [11] For thus saith the Lord GOD; Behold, I, *even* I, will both search my sheep, and seek them out. [12] As a shepherd seeketh out his flock in the day that he is among his sheep *that are* scattered; so will I seek out my sheep, and will deliver them out of all places where they have been scattered in the cloudy and dark day. [13] And I will bring them out from the people, and gather them from the countries, and will bring them to their own land, and feed them upon the mountains of Israel by the rivers, and in all the inhabited places of the country. [14] I will feed them in a good pasture, and upon the high mountains of Israel shall their fold be: there shall they lie in a good fold, and *in* a fat pasture shall they feed upon the mountains of Israel. [15] I will feed my flock, and I will cause them to lie down, saith the Lord GOD. [16] I will seek that which was lost, and bring again that which was driven away, and will bind up *that which was* broken, and will strengthen that which was sick: but I will destroy the fat and the strong; I will feed them with judgment" (Ezekiel 34:1-16).

Because of the failure of the Levitical Priesthood of Israel, God would put the Mosaic Covenant and the Dispensation of the Law on *Sabbath* until He could call, ordain, and consecrate His New

Covenant theanthropic Priesthood during the Church Age. In Hosea chapter two, God promises this *Sabbath* from the Law, the future restoration of the Law, and the restoration of the nation of Israel with certain changes in the Law that are also spoken of in Hebrews chapter seven.

"[1] Say ye unto your brethren, Ammi {*my Brethren*}; and to your sisters, Ruhamah {*Favoured*}. [2] Plead with your mother, plead: for she *is* not my wife, neither *am* I her husband: let her therefore put away her whoredoms out of her sight, and her adulteries from between her breasts; [3] Lest I strip her naked, and set her as in the day that she was born, and make her as a wilderness, and set her like a dry land, and slay her with thirst. [4] And I will not have mercy upon her children; for they *be* the children of whoredoms. [5] For their mother hath played the harlot: she that conceived them hath done shamefully: for she said, I will go after my lovers, that give *me* my bread and my water, my wool and my flax, mine oil and my drink. [6] Therefore, behold, I will hedge up thy way with thorns, and make a wall, that she shall not find her paths. [7] And she shall follow after her lovers, but she shall not overtake them; and she shall seek them, but shall not find *them*: then shall she say, I will go and return to my first husband; for then *was it* better with me than now. [8] For she did not know that I gave her corn, and wine, and oil, and multiplied her silver and gold, *which* they prepared for Baal. [9] Therefore will I return, and take away my corn in the time thereof, and my wine in the season thereof, and will recover my wool and my flax *given* to cover her nakedness. [10] And now will I discover her lewdness in the sight of her lovers, and none shall deliver her out of mine hand. [11] I will also cause all her mirth to cease, her feast days, her new moons, and her sabbaths, and all her solemn feasts. [12] And I will destroy her vines and her fig trees, whereof she hath said, These *are* my rewards that my lovers have given me: and I will make them a forest, and the beasts of the field shall eat them. [13] And I will visit upon her the days of Baalim, wherein she burned incense to them, and she decked herself with her earrings and her jewels, and she went after her lovers, and forgat me, saith the LORD" (Hosea 2:1-13).

Throughout the Church Age, God is calling, sanctifying, proving/testing, qualifying, and consecrating a New Covenant Priesthood by the faithfulness of every believer to the Great Commission in winning souls to Christ and making disciples of Jesus Christ. The changes in the Mosaic Covenant and the Dispensation of the Law is what defines the New Covenant, which is a New Mosaic Covenant that will govern the nation of Israel and all nations of the world during the Kingdom Age through this new theanthropic Priesthood of Church Age believers. ONLY those believers of the Church Age that prove themselves faithful will qualify to be this new "kingdom of priests" (Matthew 25:14-30). This also is perhaps the best explanation of Christ's statement in Matthew 20:16: "So the last shall be first, and the first last: for many be called, but few chosen."

Many of the parables and metaphors that Christ used spoke of this new theanthropic Priesthood that could not be merely added to the Mosaic Covenant and the Dispensation of the Law. The Priesthood of the Mosaic Covenant needed to be changed and this change in the Priesthood would radically change how the Mosaic Covenant would be reinstituted, administrated, and enforced in the world. Christ used two metaphors to teach that the *new* could not be merely added to the *old,* lest the *old* be completely destroyed by the *new*. Both the priesthood and the Mosaic Covenant needed to be changed in order for the New Covenant to be fully effective. This is what Christ was referring to in His three metaphors of the "new cloth," "new wine," and "new *skins*" of Matthew 9:16-17.

"[9] And as Jesus passed forth from thence, he saw a man, named Matthew, sitting at the receipt of custom: and he saith unto him, Follow me. And he arose, and followed him. [10] And it came to pass, as Jesus sat at meat in the house, behold, many publicans and sinners came and sat down with him and his disciples. [11] And when the Pharisees saw *it*, they said unto his disciples, Why eateth your Master with publicans and sinners? [12] But when Jesus heard *that*, he said unto them, They that be whole need not a physician, but they that are sick. [13] But go ye and learn what *that* meaneth, I will have mercy, and not sacrifice: for I am not come to call the righteous, but sinners to repentance. [14] Then came to him the disciples of John, saying, Why do we and the Pharisees fast oft, but thy disciples fast not? [15] And Jesus said unto them, Can the children of the bridechamber mourn, as long as the bridegroom is with them? but the days will come, when the bridegroom shall be taken from them, and then shall they fast. [16] No man putteth a piece of new cloth unto an old garment, for that which is put in to fill it up taketh from the garment, and the rent is made worse. [17] Neither do men put new wine into old bottles {*skins*}: else the bottles {*skins*} break {*burst*}, and the wine runneth out, and the bottles {*skins*} perish: but they put new wine into new bottles {*skins*}, and both are preserved" (Matthew 9:9-17).

> The "new wine" is the regenerated, or "born again," Church Age believer. The new *skin* is the new body of the glorified believer. Together the "new wine" and the new "*skins*" are a new theanthropic priesthood "in Christ" that constitutes the Church. This new priesthood of theanthropic priests constitutes the radical change in both the Law and the Mosaic Covenant as these are reinstituted during the Kingdom Age. For the Mosaic Covenant to be administrated and preserved perfectly, this would require a perfect and eternal High Priest and a perfect and eternal priesthood. These two requirements are perfectly met in the New Covenant theanthropic Melchisedecan priesthood fulfilled and elect "in Christ."

As we return to Hebrews 7:12-28, it is important to see that the text continues from the previous context (Hebrews 7:1-11) of the superiority of the New Covenant in the new Melchisedecan Priesthood of Jesus Christ. The superiority of the New Covenant High Priesthood of Jesus Christ rests on four unshakeable superiorities over the Levitical Priesthood.

1. Jesus lives forever. Therefore, His High Priesthood and the new theanthropic Priesthood that is elect/chosen "in Him" is eternally unchangeable (vs. 23-24).
2. Jesus is able to guarantee salvation (eternal security), because "He ever liveth to make intercession for them" (v. 25).
3. Jesus is holy, harmless, separate from sinners (the old Priesthood). Therefore, He is a perfect representative High Priest in that He never needs to offer a sacrifice for His own sins. Secondly in this argument, He has offered one sacrifice for the "people;" i.e., Himself (vs. 26-27), which one sacrifice (Hebrews 10:10, 12, 14, and 18) completely propitiates the wrath of God upon sin.
4. The Old Covenant made sinners High Priests, but the "word of oath" (v. 21; i.e., the New Covenant) makes Jesus the

theanthropic Son of God the High Priest, who is perfected forever more never needing sacrifice for His sin (v. 28).

Look at these four superiorities individually. **First (v. 24)**, Jesus lives forever. Therefore, His New Covenant Melchisedecan Priesthood is unchangeable. In the Old Covenant, the High Priest came into position and represented the people until he died or until he grew old and could no longer function. According to Hebrews 7:23, there were many high priests in the Old Covenant. That in itself shows the weakness and insufficiency of that Priesthood and a major weakness in the Mosaic Covenant.

Due to the death of High Priests (v. 23), there were "many" successors to the High Priesthood. With these continual transferences of the High Priesthood of the Old Covenant from one man to another, doubt and fear came. This fear was due to the fact that this one man's relationship with God represented the whole nation's relationship with God. What the High Priest was ethically, morally, and spiritually is what the congregation of Israel was in God's eyes. This continual transference of the office of High Priest from one man to another was intended to portray the weakness of the Mosaic Covenant Priesthood. At the same time it motivated the Old Covenant believer to cry out to God for the New Covenant and a new Messianic High Priest. The promise of a new High Priest after the order of Melchisedec was clearly Messianic.

"[1] A Psalm of David. The LORD said unto my Lord, Sit thou at my right hand, until I make thine enemies thy footstool. [2] The LORD shall send the rod of thy strength out of Zion: rule thou in the midst of thine enemies. [3] Thy people *shall be* willing in the day of thy power, in the beauties of holiness from the womb of the morning: thou hast the dew of thy youth. [4] The LORD hath sworn, and will not repent, Thou *art* a priest for ever after the order of Melchizedek. [5] The Lord at thy right hand shall strike through kings in the day of his wrath {*the Tribulation, judgment of the nations, and second coming of Messiah*}. [6] He shall judge among the heathen, he shall fill *the places* with the dead bodies; he shall wound the heads over many countries. [7] He shall drink of the brook in the way: therefore shall he lift up the head" (Psalm 110:1-7).

Unlike the Mosaic Covenant Priesthood, the New Covenant Priesthood of Jesus is unchangeable, or literally *non-transferable*, because Jesus "continueth forever" (Hebrews 7:24). This truth provides great security based upon the *unchangeableness* of Jesus Himself. He is the same yesterday, today and forever. Therefore, He is a perfect representative and, in God's eyes, all believers are what He is. He is an eternal theanthropic High Priest and all Church Age believers are eternal theanthropic priests "in Christ" as "sons of God" (John 1:12).

Superiority Two: (v. 25) the New Covenant Priesthood of Jesus Christ is superior because he is able to "save to . . . the uttermost."

The word "save" is from the Greek word *sozo* (sode'-zo). In the grammatical sense the word "save" means *to rescue from danger or destruction* and *to keep safe and sound.* To "save" technically, in the biblical sense, is *to deliver from the penalties of Messianic judgment* or *to save from the influences of evil forces that attempt to obstruct individuals from receiving their Messianic deliverance.* That is how the Jew would have understood the word "save."

The Mosaic Covenant High Priesthood could not offer this kind of salvation. None of these individuals, regardless of how great they were individually, had any power to do such a tremendous thing. However, Jesus did, does, could, and will. He can "save them to the uttermost that come unto God by him." The word "uttermost" is from the Greek word *panteles* (pan-tel-ace'). It means *perfectly* or *completely.* It refers back in contradistinction to the statement of Hebrews 7:11: "If therefore perfection were by the Levitical priesthood, (for under it the people received the law,) what further need *was there* that another priest should rise after the order of Melchisedec, and not be called after the order of Aaron?" This marks a major paradigm in change from the Mosaic Covenant priesthood to the New Covenant priesthood "in Christ."

The Mosaic Covenant saint "came unto God" in their representative man, the High Priest. By the very nature of that Old Covenant High Priesthood, the High Priest came fearfully before the veil of the Holy of Holies once a year because of his own sin. The very nature of that fearful inadequacy proves the Mosaic Covenant High Priesthood inferior. Therefore, a believer's rightness before God was always in the same degree of doubt as was the rightness of the High Priest before God. However, regarding the new High Priest of the New Covenant, Jesus lives in the *literal* (not *typical*) Holy of Holies forever, constantly representing the believer in sinless perfection before God.

What does "uttermost," or completely, mean? Was the Mosaic Covenant believer saved *incompletely*? They were saved just as *completely* as we are, but they could yet not come unto God because God was not yet propitiated. The word that is translated *atonement* simply referred to the *covering* of the Old Covenant believer's sin, not the removal of sin's penalty (remission).

> "[25] Whom God hath set forth *to be* a propitiation through faith in his blood, to declare his righteousness for the remission of sins that are past, through the forbearance of God; [26] To declare, *I say*, at this time his righteousness: that he might be just, and the justifier of him which believeth in Jesus" (Romans 3:25-26).

The word "remission" in Rom. 3:25 is from the Greek word *paresis* (par'-es-is). It does not refer to *forgiveness*. It means *to pass over*. It referred to what God did in the Old Covenant in setting aside the consequences/judgment of sin until Jesus came. Then the consequences of sin was adjudicated and paid for in His substitutionary sacrifice. This refers to all the sins of the world from Adam forward that had been just "covered over" with the blood of animals (typifying the blood of the Lamb of God; Revelation 13:8). Jesus did not cover over sin. He propitiated God. Sin was not covered over with His blood. God's sentence upon sin ("death") was executed and the "wages of sin" were paid for. This marks a major transitional change between the Mosaic Covenant and the New Covenant in Christ's blood. Although the Mosaic Covenant will be reinstituted in the Kingdom Age, from the day of the death of Christ at Calvary, never again can it be said that sin was merely *atoned* (covered over). This was a major "change also of the Law" (Hebrews 7:12). To refer to the sacrifice of Christ as the *Atonement* is to deny this radical "change also of the Law."

> "And for this cause he is the mediator of the new testament, that by means of death, for the redemption of the transgressions *that were* under the first testament, they which are called might receive the promise of eternal inheritance" (Hebrews 9:15).

> "[25] Nor yet that he should offer himself often, as the high priest entereth into the holy place every year with blood of others; [26] For then must he often have suffered since the foundation of the world: but now once in the end of the world hath he appeared to put away sin by the sacrifice of himself. [27] And as it is appointed unto men once to die, but after this the judgment: [28] So Christ was once

offered to bear the sins of many; and unto them that look for him shall he appear the second time without sin unto salvation" (Hebrews 9:25-28).

> What does this all mean? The Mosaic Covenant believer could not enter into God's presence when they died. Up until the death, burial, resurrection, and ascension of Jesus Christ, all believers were merely *saved on credit and put on lay-away.*

"[22] And it came to pass, that the beggar died, and was carried by the angels into Abraham's bosom: the rich man also died, and was buried; [23] And in hell he lift up his eyes, being in torments, and seeth Abraham afar off, and Lazarus in his bosom" (Luke 16:22-23).

This portion of Scripture reveals what Old Covenant salvation was. Hell, or Hades, (Old Testament word was *Sheol*) existed in two separate *compartments* or *holding areas*. The human bodies of the dead were not in these two places. These two compartments held the spirits/souls of the lost and those saved "by grace through faith." One area was called "Abraham's bosom" or "paradise." The place of torment (v. 26) was separated from this by a "great gulf." While Christ was on the Cross, He told the believing thief that "today" he would be with Him "in paradise."

"[39] And one of the malefactors which were hanged railed on him, saying, If thou be Christ, save thyself and us. [40] But the other answering rebuked him, saying, Dost not thou fear God, seeing thou art in the same condemnation? [41] And we indeed justly; for we receive the due reward of our deeds: but this man hath done nothing amiss. [42] And he said unto Jesus, Lord, remember me when thou comest into thy kingdom. [43] And Jesus said unto him, Verily I say unto thee, To day shalt thou be with me in paradise" (Luke 23:39-43).

After Christ's ascension, *Abraham's Bosom* no longer exists. New Covenant salvation brought the believer into the very presence of God. Although the spirits/souls of these believers are with Christ in the presence of God, they still await the redemption of their bodies (Romans 8:23).

"[8] Wherefore he saith, When he ascended up on high, he led captivity captive, and gave gifts unto men. [9] (Now that he ascended, what is it but that he also descended first into the lower parts of the earth? [10] He that descended is the same also that ascended up far above all heavens, that he might fill all things.)" (Ephesians 4:8-10).

"[8] We are confident, *I say*, and willing rather to be absent from the body, and to be present with the Lord. [9] Wherefore we labour, that, whether present or absent, we may be accepted of him" (II Corinthians 5:8-9).

Third Superiority: the New Covenant High Priesthood of Christ is superior because Jesus requires no sacrifice for Himself because He was sinless (II Corinthians 5:21). One sacrifice was sufficient to satisfy God's justice by adjudicating His death sentence vicariously upon sin in a sinless substitute - the Messiah.

"[1] For the law having a shadow of good things to come, *and* not the very image of the things, can never with those sacrifices which they offered year by year continually make the comers thereunto perfect. [2] For then would they not have ceased to be offered? because that the worshippers once purged should have had no more conscience of sins. [3] But in those *sacrifices there is* a remembrance again *made* of sins every year. [4] For *it is* not possible that the blood of bulls and of goats should take away sins" (Hebrews 10:1-4).

The Old Covenant, by the very nature of a High Priest that required sacrifice to cover over his own sin, is inferior and necessitated change. This was not true of Christ and the New Covenant in His Blood. This is why the sinlessness and Deity of Christ is critical to the Gospel message and the New Covenant believer's faith. "Who needeth not daily, as those high priests, to offer up sacrifice, first for his own sins, and then for the people's: for this he did once, when he offered up himself" (Hebrews 7:27). Jesus "knew no sin" (II Corinthians 5:21).

"[14] Nevertheless death reigned from Adam to Moses, even over them that had not sinned after the similitude of Adam's transgression, who is the figure of him that was to come. [15] But not as the offence, so also *is* the free gift. For if through the offence of one many be dead, much more the grace of God, and the gift by grace, *which is* by one man, Jesus Christ, hath abounded unto many. [16] And not as *it was* by one that sinned, *so is* the gift: for the judgment *was* by one to condemnation, but the free gift *is* of many offences unto justification. [17] For if by one man's offence death reigned by one; much more they which receive abundance of grace and of the gift of righteousness shall reign in life by one, Jesus

Christ.) [18] Therefore as by the offence of one *judgment came* upon all men to condemnation; even so by the righteousness of one *the free gift came* upon all men unto justification of life. [19] For as by one man's disobedience many were made sinners, so by the obedience of one shall many be made righteous. [20] Moreover the law entered, that the offence might abound. But where sin abounded, grace did much more abound: [21] That as sin hath reigned unto death, even so might grace reign through righteousness unto eternal life by Jesus Christ our Lord" (Romans 5:15-21).

The Mosaic Covenant priesthood was born after the "similitude "of Adam (Romans 5:14). Jesus was not born through the seed of man. He was supernaturally implanted into the womb of Mary. On the other hand (Hebrews 7:27), the Old Covenant Priesthood had to daily offer sacrifices for their own sins before they could ever offer sacrifices for the sins of the people. This shows an inferior Priesthood and the necessity for change.

Fourth Superiority: (Hebrews 7:28) Jesus is a perfect High Priest in that He is always (eternally) consecrated to God. There can never be any fault or imperfection found in our new High Priest. There is constant and perfect union in the new theanthropic existence created in Christ Jesus through His incarnation, death, burial, resurrection, and glorification. Jesus is eternally theanthropic. This is a High Priest on which we can trust in and rely. The High Priesthood of Christ is a High Priesthood of sinless perfection and perfect consecration, providing full and bold (fearless) access to the "throne of grace" to every believer "born again" of the Spirit of God.

"[1] Now of the things which we have spoken *this is* the sum: We have such an high priest, who is set on the right hand of the throne of the Majesty in the heavens; [2] A minister of the sanctuary, and of the true tabernacle, which the Lord pitched, and not man. [3] For every high priest is ordained to offer gifts and sacrifices: wherefore *it is* of necessity that this man have somewhat also to offer. [4] For if he were on earth, he should not be a priest, seeing that there are priests that offer gifts according to the law: [5] Who serve unto the example and shadow of heavenly things, as Moses was admonished of God when he was about to make the tabernacle: for, See, saith he, *that* thou make all things according to the pattern shewed to thee in the mount. [6] But now hath he obtained a more excellent ministry, by how much also he is the mediator of a better covenant, which was established upon better promises" (Hebrew 8:1-6).

Now, here in Hebrews chapter eight through Hebrews 10:18, we have the summary of what has been said thus far. We now begin to establish the application of what has been established doctrinally. In this *contextual continuity*, we now see the sum of what we have learned. In the next few chapters, God will interweave all believers into this truth regarding the ministry of Jesus Christ as our great High Priest. He will show us exactly how the High Priesthood affects the New Covenant believer and draws each believer into the mediatory work of Christ. Jesus ministers both on Earth and in Heaven for man to God, and He does so day and night. The believer becomes part of this ministry as we become the new *theanthropic human agents* through which Christ ministers here on earth.

DISCUSSION QUESTIONS

1. The initiation of the beginning of the *unfolding* of the New Covenant took place on the Day of Pentecost with the two primary works of the Holy Spirit. List and discuss these two works of the Spirit and why each reveals an *already, not yet* aspect of the beginning of the New Covenant.

2. Discuss the differences between *position* and *actuality* that took place on the Day of Pentecost regarding "the regeneration." Also discuss why understanding this is critical to practical Pneumatology.

3. Read Hebrews 7:12-28 and discuss what God means when He says, "For the priesthood being changed {*present, passive, participle*}, there is made of necessity a change also of the law." Since this truth relates specifically to your ministry now and in the Kingdom Age, be specific.

4. Discuss why God *cast away* the Mosaic Covenant Priesthood. Discuss why understanding this is critical to the seriousness to which you should take your present responsibilities as a Believer Priest before God and to the world.

5. Read Luke 12:22-53. In vs. 47-48, Christ responds to Peter's question in verse 41; "Lord, speakest thou this parable unto us, or even to all?" What is Christ's answer to Peter and how does that answer apply to you personally?

6. Read Ezekiel 34:1-16 and discuss why Israel should have known God was going to establish a new Shepherd (High Priest) and a new Priesthood (of under-shepherds).

7. We find from Hebrews 7:12-28 that the superiority of the New Covenant High Priesthood of Jesus Christ rests on four unshakeable superiorities over the Levitical Priesthood. List and discuss each of these four superiorities as each relates to the new *theanthropic Priesthood* that is elect/chosen "in Him."

Chapter Fifty-nine
Sin has Consequences

Someone has said that insanity is defined as a person who repeatedly does the same thing while expected different results. If this does not define mental insanity, it certainly defines moral depravity. Christians live their lives repeating the same sins thinking that simply because God forgives sin that there are no lingering or continuing consequences to their sins. Thinking like that is either a matter of complete ignorance or complete idiocy.

> "[7] Then said he {*John the Baptist*} to the multitude that came forth to be baptized of him, O generation of vipers, who hath warned you to flee from the wrath to come? [8] <u>Bring forth therefore fruits worthy of repentance</u>, and begin not to say within yourselves, We have Abraham to *our* father: for I say unto you, That God is able of these stones to raise up children unto Abraham" (Luke 3:7-8).

John the Baptist fulfilled the prophecy of the forerunner of the promised Jewish Messiah (Isaiah 40:3-8). His ministry was especially to prepare the nation of Israel for the coming of Messiah to Zion. As far as Israel was concerned, they viewed the coming of Messiah as the fulfillment of all the prophecies regarding the judgment of the nations and the restoration of the nation of Israel for the Kingdom on Earth. John the Baptist had a simple message: REPENT! Over seven-hundred years had gone by since the prophecies of Isaiah. Although Israel had abandoned the idolatry of its previous years, she had become deeply *Hellenized* by the Greek and Roman cultures. Although the vast majority of Jews did not worship Rome's idols, the vast majority of Jews were very much influenced by the worldliness of the Roman culture. The Jews practiced all their *God-stuff* in the legalistic externalism of the Pharisees, but were far from God in their love for Him. Christ spoke of another prophecy of Isaiah in Matthew 15:7-9, "[7] *Ye* hypocrites, well did Esaias prophesy of you, saying, [8] This people draweth nigh unto me with their mouth, and honoureth me with *their* lips; but their heart is far from me. [9] But in vain they do worship me, teaching *for* doctrines the commandments of men."

The pathway to real faith will always lead us to unscalable *mountains of trials*. Reason will try to persuade us to find an easier pathway around the *mountain*. God wants us to trust Him to move those *mountains*. Then, and only then, does our faith become bigger than the trials and failures we face each day. Sadly, for most professing Christians, life is just a series of *inconveniences* that they must endure on the journey to a place called Heaven. They are completely missing God's purpose in the journey, which is the *trying of their faith* (James 1:3).

In Israel's legalistic externalism, they did all the *God-stuff* they were expected to do, but without any real cognizance of God's presence, any real thoughts about Him, or any real acknowledgement of their need for Him. Isaiah spoke of this as well in Isaiah 40:27-31, as God promised His presence to be with the truly repentant, humble, and dependent believer.

> Only those who come to the end of themselves will be able to find the strength of the Lord there waiting for them. Those that take the *pathway of reason* around the *mountain of trials* will never find the omnipotent resources of God waiting to provide them the victory they need to experience. They must find this victory before their lives will ever be enabled to bring God glory and bear eternal fruit. Real faith is forged on the *mountainside*, not in the *Jacuzzi*. The very first sin the Christian must repent of is the sin of *unbelief*.

"²⁷ Why sayest thou, O Jacob, and speakest, O Israel, My way is hid from the LORD, and my judgment is passed over from my God? ²⁸ Hast thou not known? hast thou not heard, *that* the everlasting God, the LORD, the Creator of the ends of the earth, fainteth not, neither is weary? *there is* no searching of his understanding. ²⁹ He giveth power to the faint; and to *them that have* no might he increaseth strength. ³⁰ Even the youths shall faint and be weary, and the young men shall utterly fall: ³¹ But they that wait upon the LORD shall renew *their* strength; they shall mount up with wings as eagles; they shall run, and not be weary; *and* they shall walk, and not faint" (Isaiah 40:27-31).

There is a serious failure among most Christians in their

understanding of the doctrine of repentance. Repentance is much more than telling God you are sorry for something, asking for His forgiveness, and just going on in life like it never happened. Repentance is a turning away from sin with a commitment to not go there again. Repentance comes with a broken heart about the sin and a remorseful grief that comes from an understanding we have grieved a holy God who genuinely loves us. Repentance comes with an understanding that *sin does not happen in a vacuum.* Repentance understands that any sin ALWAYS impacts hundreds of other lives and certainly understands that any sin impacts God's blessing on individual lives, the sinner's family, and the sinner's local church. Repentance understands that the sin of any moment continues in its impact far beyond that moment and into eternity. People may reject Christ, reject Christianity, and spend eternity in Hell because of that one moment a professed believer commits a selfish act of self-gratification.

Genuine repentance understands that if you always do what you always did, you'll always get what you always got. Without genuine repentance a believer will NEVER see lasting fruit from the testimony of his life.

As we have read in Luke 3:8, John the Baptist said, "Bring forth therefore fruits worthy of repentance." With genuine repentance there is expectation by God of *change* in our lifestyle, *change* in our thought life, *change* in our preoccupation with the things of this world, and a *change* in our occupation with the things of God. Genuine faith is nonexistent apart genuine repentance. God watches for these "fruits."

However, Paul speaks of a *godly sorrow* and a *worldly sorrow.* *Godly sorrow* is genuine repentance that is life changing for the right reasons. *Worldly sorrow* is an outward conformity that lacks an inward and relational motivation due to a lack of genuine faith in the living God. The *godly sorrow* that Paul speaks of manifests itself in real *lifestyle change*, real *thought-life change*, which leads to real *living faith change.*

"[5] For, when we were come into Macedonia, our flesh had no rest, but we were troubled on every side; without *were* fightings, within *were* fears. [6] Nevertheless God, that comforteth those that are cast down, comforted us by the coming of Titus; [7] And not by his coming only, but by the consolation wherewith he was comforted in you, when he told us your earnest desire, your mourning, your fervent mind toward me; so that I rejoiced the more. [8] For though I made you sorry with a letter, I do not repent, though I did repent: for I perceive that the same epistle hath made you sorry, though *it were* but for a season. [9] Now I rejoice, not that ye were made sorry, but that ye sorrowed to repentance: for ye were made sorry after a godly manner, that ye might receive damage by us in nothing. [10] For godly sorrow worketh repentance to salvation not to be repented of: but the sorrow of the world worketh death. [11] For behold this selfsame thing, that ye sorrowed after a godly sort, what **carefulnes**s {*caution in life decisions and earnestness in correcting failures*} it wrought in you, yea, *what* **clearing of yourselves** {*confession with the desire to set things right or to vindicate one's self*}, yea, *what* **indignation** {*much grief to the place it moves one to do what is right*}, yea, *what* **fear** {*of repeating the same failure*}, yea, *what* **vehement desire** {*the desire to not fail again*}, yea, *what* **zeal** {*in dealing with the sin in the local church through congregational polity*}, yea, *what* **revenge** {*the local church was willing to justly apply penalties for sins committed by a congregational member*}! In all *things ye have approved yourselves to be clear* {*literally; pure; the idea is that they had cleared themselves of any accusation of tolerating sin amongst their membership*} in this matter" (II Corinthians 7:5-11).

Worldly sorrow is a sorrow for hurting your own image in the eyes of others. This is a sorrow that brings shame, but a shame that is born out of pride. When sorrow is about the destruction of our own image in the eyes of others, it is nothing more than another form of idolatry. *Godly sorrow* is a sorrow about marring, defiling, or corrupting the testimony of God's work of grace in our lives. The only image the world has of God is the image restored through the salvation of a sinner's soul and the progressive transfiguration of a believer's life through the "renewing" of that believer's mind. *Godly sorrow* is broken about any practice that is hypocritical to the restoration of the image of God in our lives.

Faith and repentance are both *life changing commitments.* Neither can be said to truly exist apart from these life changes that manifest themselves in very real, tangible ways. Faith, in any real sense of its meaning, is a commitment to live the Word of God to the glory of God.

Repentance, in any real sense of its meaning, is a

commitment to stop living for self, to stop living like the world lives, and to stop thinking temporally. Genuine repentance always results in genuine change manifesting genuine faith. Repentance is expressed when we turn from our own selfishness, worldliness, and mortality to live like the eternal sons of God that we have been "born again" to be. Repentance is an ongoing decision that progressively and completely changes the direction of one's life. Repentance turns our focus from the things of this world to refocus our intentions upon *doing* the will of God. Therefore, genuine repentance is always accompanied with death to the *old man* and the production of multiplied spiritual fruit.

> "[20] And there were certain Greeks among them that came up to worship at the feast: [21] The same came therefore to Philip, which was of Bethsaida of Galilee, and desired him, saying, Sir, we would see Jesus. [22] Philip cometh and telleth Andrew: and again Andrew and Philip tell Jesus. [23] And Jesus answered them, saying, The hour is come, that the Son of man should be glorified. [24] Verily, verily, I say unto you, Except a corn of wheat fall into the ground and die, it abideth alone: but if it die, it bringeth forth much fruit. [25] He that loveth his life shall lose it; and he that hateth his life in this world shall keep it unto life eternal. [26] If any man serve me, let him follow me; and where I am, there shall also my servant be: if any man serve me, him will *my* Father honour" (John 12:20-26).

Yes, there is real sorrow for sin and real regret for its consequences when genuine repentance exists. However, whenever real repentance exists, there is also a real change in a person's existence. Repentance is primarily a commitment to change one's existence by the supernatural enabling of God.

> If the commitment to change one's existence is not accompanied with a real change in existence, that person is spiritually delusional about both the reality of repentance and the reality of faith. False decisions always result is a false hope of productivity; i.e., NO FRUIT!

Christ frequently used the parable of the fruitless fig tree to reveal to the Jews that Israel was delusional about their professed faith in God. They had all the semblance of being able to bear fruit. The tree was there (structure). The leaves were there (life). Where was the fruit? A fig tree full of leaves, but empty of fruit reveals a serious failure in the purpose for that fig tree's existence. It wasn't a fig tree after all. In fact, it was a *hypocritical tree*.

God does not want Christians to be *shade trees*. God wants us to be *fruit trees*. Only genuine repentance resulting in genuine faith will change us from *shade trees* to *fruit trees*. If all you are producing is *shade*, you are delusional about God's purpose in your salvation and in your change in existence.

Yes, genuine repentance is being sorry enough about your selfishness, worldliness, and sinfulness that you stop these sins. However, repentance is not just a turn away *from* these practices. Repentance is a turning *to* live to the glory of God through the indwelling power of God.

> "[6] And ye became followers of us, and of the Lord, having received the word in much affliction, with joy of the Holy Ghost: [7] So that ye were ensamples to all that believe in Macedonia and Achaia. [8] For from you sounded out the word of the Lord not only in Macedonia and Achaia, but also in every place your faith to God-ward is spread abroad; so that we need not to speak any thing. [9] For they themselves shew of us what manner of entering in we had unto you, and how ye turned to God from idols to serve the living and true God" (I Thessalonians 1:6-9).

Notice in I Thessalonians 1:9 that there was a both a turning *from* and a turning *to*. Genuine repentance ALWAYS has both of those two characteristics. The defining issue is who and what we *serve*. The vast majority of Old Testament uses of the Hebrew word translated "repent" is turning *from* evil *to* righteousness or turning *from* idols *to* God. In every case, repentance carries with it a commitment *to* a life of living faith and the turning away *from* a previous lifestyle and its practices.

Perhaps the most foolish of all notions is that once we repent of a sinful practice and God forgives that sin, that somehow there are no more outcomes or consequences in life or eternity for that transgression. This is certainly not the overwhelming biblical example. However, although we have thousands of years of biblical history to the contrary, it would seem that most Christians still cannot grasp the fact that any sin we commit has ongoing and eternal consequences. These consequences continue even after we repent of a sin, turned from the sin, and the sin has been forgiven by God.

Adam and Eve are our first examples. Their sin was

forgiven by God. However, every human being born as their descendants were born spiritually corrupt and spiritually blind.

Abraham and Sarah sinned in unbelief against God's promise of a son and took the matter into their own control. Abraham sinned with Hagar, the handmaiden of Sarah, and bore Ishmael. Abraham repented of his sin, God forgave him, but Ishmael lived on to father the Arab nations and the nation of Islam (the Muslim religion). Millions have died, and millions more will die in corruption because Abraham sinned

> Sins of which we repent, from which we turn, even those have been forgiven by God, continue to bear eternal consequences.

David committed adultery with his comrade's wife in one weak moment of carnality. He compounded that sin by having Bathsheba's husband, Uriah the Hittite, murdered to cover his sin. A child is born and dies. David cries out to God in repentance and God forgives him. However, sexual sin had infected the household of David. His daughter Tamar, by one of David's wives, was raped by her half-brother Ammon, from another of David's wives. Absalom, Tamar's full brother, has his servants execute Ammon. Absalom, having lost all respect for David's unwillingness to deal with Ammon, later rises upon in insurrection against David and Absalom is killed in a freak accident while riding his mule. Sins of which we repent, from which we turn, even those have been forgiven by God, continue to bear eternal consequences.

Solomon then becomes king and becomes a sexual addict, leading the nation of Israel into idolatry. God forgives his sin. But sins of which we repent, from which we turn, even those have been forgiven by God, continue to bear eternal consequences. Over and over again we see this same thing throughout the Word of God. For the next three-hundred years, the nation of Israel lived in idolatry to the place the Book of the Law was lost. It was later found in the dust of the now defiled Temple that was built and dedicated to God by Solomon three-hundred years earlier. Yes indeed, insanity is defined as a person who repeatedly does the same thing while expecting different results. Sin has consequences!

DISCUSSION QUESTIONS

1. Christians live their lives repeating the same sins thinking that simply because God forgives sin that there are no lingering or continuing consequences to their sins. Discuss why this kind of thinking is an overwhelming spiritual anomaly.

2. In Luke 3:8, John the Baptist said, "Bring forth therefore fruits worthy of repentance." Explain why this needs to be preached and why it should be a beginning place for evaluating genuine spiritual decisions.

3. In Matthew 15:7-9 Christ said, "[7] Ye hypocrites, well did Esaias prophesy of you, saying, [8] This people draweth nigh unto me with their mouth, and honoureth me with *their* lips; but their heart is far from me. [9] But in vain they do worship me, teaching *for* doctrines the commandments of men." Explain this statement as an explanation of where genuine repentance finds its *fountainhead* and what genuine repentance looks like when it comes forth from that *fountainhead*.

4. "Those that take the *pathway of reason* around the *mountain of trials* will never find the omnipotent resources of God waiting to provide them the victory they need to experience before their lives will ever be enabled to bring God glory and bear eternal fruit. Real faith is forged on the *mountainside*, not in the *Jacuzzi*." Explain Isaiah 40:27-31 from the context of the above statement.

5. Thoroughly explain the differences between *godly sorrow* and a *worldly sorrow*.

6. According to II Corinthians 7:5-11, what does *godly sorrow* look like?

7. "Perhaps the most foolish of all notions is that once we repent of a sinful practice and God forgives that sin, that somehow there are no more outcomes or consequences in life or eternity for that transgression. This is certainly not the overwhelming biblical example. However, although we have thousands of years of biblical history to the contrary, it would seem that most Christians still cannot grasp the fact that any sin we commit has ongoing and eternal consequences. These consequences continue even after we repent of a sin, turned from the sin, and the sin has been forgiven by God." List and discuss the four examples that are given of this.

Chapter Sixty
The Necessity of Separation to the Ministry of Reconciliation

Repentance is the changing of one's thinking, beliefs, and practices to the degree that one's thinking, beliefs, and practices correspond with God's thinking, beliefs, and practices. We know what God thinks, believes, and practices by the revelation of His inspired Word. Therefore, true repentance does not exist apart from a *turning* to the Word of God with the intention of knowing and doing the will of God that is revealed in the Word of God. This is also a simple definition of genuine faith. Repentance is an integral part of faith. Faith and repentance are not the same things, but genuine faith cannot be accurately defined apart from genuine repentance. Like the word *believe*, the command to repent is a *verb*. That means it is a word that describes an *action*. Repentance is one of the actions that define the words *faith* and *believe*.

Perhaps the best word that describes the ongoing action and attitude of repentance is the word *separation*. The repentant believer separates from sin, from worldliness, from theological error (false teaching and false teachers), and from any co-operation with others, even if they profess to be Christians, who fail the tests of correct *doctrine* and correct *practice*. The simple principle is that a person cannot be separated if he is not separated from those who fail to practice biblical repentance or who hold to false doctrine.

Critical to our understanding of the necessity of all this is the doctrine of the priesthood of the believer under the New Covenant (the Dispensation of Grace). Every believer from the Day of Pentecost to the end of the Church Age is a *ministering priest* before God and to men. One of the sacrifices that the New Covenant believer/priest makes to God today is the sacrifice of his life as a servant of God to men through ministry. God cannot accept the ministry of any believer/priest who is defiled by sin, by false doctrine, and/or by the failure to be separate.

Since every individual believer/priest is an individual *Temple* of the Holy Spirit, and every local church is corporately a "living"

Temple made up of "living stones," separation on these two levels, individual and corporate, is essential to sanctity and to God's blessings of supernatural enabling at these two levels.

1. Person separation

2. Local church (Ecclesiastical) separation

The issue of separation from sin, heresy, and false teachers, both individually and corporately, is the issue that defines the *militant terms* that God has chosen in His inspired Words to describe how individual believers and local churches are to "stand" in their fight against Satan, sin, and worldliness.

"[10] Finally, my brethren, be strong in the Lord, and in the power of his might. [11] Put on the whole armour of God, that ye may be able to stand against the wiles of the devil. [12] For we wrestle {*Greco-Roman style, legs may not be used in any way to obtain a fall, and no holds may be taken below the waist; the opponent was to be thrown to the ground by the pure power and finesse of upper body strength and coordination*} not against flesh and blood, but against principalities, against powers, against the rulers of the darkness of this world, against spiritual wickedness in high *places*. [13] Wherefore take unto you the whole armour of God, that ye may be able to withstand in the evil day, and having done all, to stand. [14] Stand therefore, having your loins girt about with truth, and having on the breastplate of righteousness; [15] And your feet shod with the preparation of the gospel of peace; [16] Above all, taking the shield of faith, wherewith ye shall be able to quench all the fiery darts of the wicked. [17] And take the helmet of salvation, and the sword of the Spirit, which is the word of God: [18] Praying always with all prayer and supplication in the Spirit, and watching thereunto with all perseverance and supplication for all saints; [19] And for me, that utterance may be given unto me, that I may open my mouth boldly, to make known the mystery of the gospel, [20] For which I am an ambassador in bonds: that therein I may speak boldly, as I ought to speak" (Ephesians 6:10-20).

Therefore, even the ideas of Ecumenicism, the Emergent Church philosophy (cultural relativism), and/or the pragmatism of the Purpose Driven church growth philosophy are a complete contradiction against the essential of separation. Separation is essential to sanctity before God in order to "stand" against opposition to God's supernatural work and eternal purpose. Any *fruit* (church growth) that is produced apart from sanctity and God's supernatural enabling (grace) is counterfeit and is artificially *manufactured fruit* - not supernaturally produced *fruit*. Artificially *manufactured fruit* will never stand the test of time in that it is *manufactured* out of compromise. The priesthood of the New Covenant believer carries with it a *militancy* regarding standing for truth and against doctrinal error.

> "[27] Only let your conversation {*a manner of living that corresponds with loyalty to a citizen of Heaven*} be as it becometh {*axios, appropriate or worthy of*} the gospel of Christ: that whether I come and see you, or else be absent, I may hear of your affairs, that ye stand fast {*are unmoving or persevering*} in one spirit, with one mind striving together {*wrestle in company with or jointly*} for the faith of the gospel; [28] And in nothing terrified by your adversaries: which is to them an evident token of perdition, but to you of salvation, and that of God. [29] For unto you it is given in the behalf of Christ, not only to believe on him, but also to suffer for his sake; [30] Having the same conflict which ye saw in me, and now hear *to be* in me" (Philippians 1:27-30).

II Corinthians 5:14-6:18 is an excellent example of why context is so important to the proper interpretation of Scripture. One of the weaknesses of verse-by-verse exposition is that it often disconnects *contextual continuity*. Notice that the context of II Corinthians 5:14-6:18 is about ministry "in Christ's stead."

> "[14] For the love of Christ constraineth us; because we thus judge, that if one died for all, then were all dead: [15] And *that* he died for all, that they which live should not henceforth live unto themselves, but unto him which died for them, and rose again. [16] Wherefore henceforth know we no man after the flesh: yea, though we have known Christ after the flesh, yet now henceforth know we *him* no more. [17] Therefore if any man *be* in Christ, *he is* a new creature: old things are passed away; behold, all things are become new. [18] And all things *are* of God, who hath reconciled us to himself by Jesus Christ, and hath given to us the ministry of reconciliation; [19] To wit, that God was in Christ, reconciling the world unto himself, not imputing their trespasses unto them; and hath committed unto us the word of reconciliation. [20] Now then we are ambassadors for Christ, as though God did beseech *you* by us: we pray *you* in Christ's stead, be ye reconciled to God. [21] For he hath made him *to be* sin for us, who knew no sin; that we might be made the righteousness of God in him. [1] We then, *as* workers together *with him*, beseech *you* also that ye receive not the grace of God in vain. [2] (For he saith, I have

heard thee in a time accepted, and in the day of salvation have I succoured thee: behold, now *is* the accepted time; behold, now *is* the day of salvation.) [3] Giving no offence in any thing, that the ministry be not blamed: [4] <u>But in all *things* approving ourselves as the ministers of God</u>, in much patience, in afflictions, in necessities, in distresses, [5] In stripes, in imprisonments, in tumults, in labours, in watchings, in fastings; [6] By pureness, by knowledge, by longsuffering, by kindness, by the Holy Ghost, by love unfeigned, [7] By the word of truth, by the power of God, by the armour of righteousness on the right hand and on the left, [8] By honour and dishonour, by evil report and good report: as deceivers, and *yet* true; [9] As unknown, and *yet* well known; as dying, and, behold, we live; as chastened, and not killed; [10] As sorrowful, yet alway rejoicing; as poor, yet making many rich; as having nothing, and *yet* possessing all things. [11] O *ye* Corinthians, our mouth is open unto you, our heart is enlarged. [12] Ye are not straitened in us, but ye are straitened in your own bowels. [13]Now for a recompence in the same, (I speak as unto *my* children,) be ye also enlarged. [14] Be ye not unequally yoked together with unbelievers: for what fellowship hath righteousness with unrighteousness? and what communion hath light with darkness? [15] And what concord hath Christ with Belial? or what part hath he that believeth with an infidel? [16] And what agreement hath the temple of God with idols? for ye {*collectively and individually*} are the temple of the living God; as God hath said, I will dwell in them, and walk in *them*; and I will be their God, and they shall be my people. [17] Wherefore {*because we are "the temple of the living God"*} come out from among them, and be ye separate, saith the Lord, and touch not the unclean *thing*; and I will receive you, [18] And will be a Father unto you, and ye shall be my sons and daughters, saith the Lord Almighty" (II Corinthians 5:14-6:18).

The application of II Corinthians 5:14-6:18 is that *of military responsibilities in warfare.* To fail to be obedient to God's command regarding separation is to become a traitor to the warfare of the believer against apostasy and Antichristism.

In II Corinthians 6:14, the word "unbelievers" is used of anyone whose life or teaching is contrary to biblical truth. It is not used in the salvational sense. Anyone who says they are a believer, but continues to *practice* or *live* contrary to what the Word of God says, is in fact, manifesting "unbelief."

The rhetorical question of II Corinthians 6:14 is essentially asking what spiritual partnership can righteousness and lawlessness have together? This is the same principle as, "Thou shalt not plow with an ox and an ass together" (Deuteronomy 22:10).

The second rhetorical question in II Corinthians 6:14 is, what does light and darkness have in common? *Light* refers to walking in truth and *darkness* to walking in the ways of the world.

> "And hereby we do know that we know him, if we keep his commandments. He that saith, I know him, and keepeth not his commandments, is a liar, and the truth is not in him" (I John 2:3-4, to keep His Word or commandments is to be governed by them).

A third rhetorical question is found in II Corinthians 6:15. What kind of symphony ("concord") can Christ, who is perfect in order and obedience and always walks in harmony with His Word, have with Belial? Belial is a transliteration of a Hebrew word meaning *worthlessness,* and here it refers to Satan.

The fourth rhetorical question is found in II Corinthians 6:15. "Unbelief" and "belief" - how can anyone continue professing to be a Christian, and by doing so, state they are under the direction and complete influence of God's Word. How can they do this while continuing to disobey the Word in everyday practices by association with "infidels"? How can they do this while disregarding those who overtly disobey what the Word of God says, manifesting their unbelief in the Word?

The fifth rhetorical question is found in II Corinthians 6:16. What can be more abominable than an idol in God's Temple? In this contradiction there is absolutely no "agreement" or right of compromise. The worship of the two is wholly and totally incompatible in the eyes of God. The believer's heart/body is the temple of God. Therefore, to compromise your heart's allegiances and your body's associations to anything but a distinctive, separated, and peculiar service to God is a paradox. This is the exact same kind of failure committed by the Priesthood of Israel at the time of Ezekiel's prophecy.

> "[1] And it came to pass in the sixth year {*of the four-hundred and thirty years of prophesized captivity beginning with the captivity of Jehoiachin; Ezekiel 4:5-6*}, in the sixth *month*, in the fifth *day* of the month, *as* I sat in mine house, and the elders of Judah {*the seventy elders that came to be known as the Sanhedrin that were now in captivity at Chebar*} sat before me, that the hand of the Lord GOD fell {*with full force and power*} there upon me. [2] Then I beheld, and

lo a likeness {*the same "likeness as the appearance of a man" in Ezekiel 1:26; refers to the pre-incarnate Messiah*} as the appearance of fire {*manifesting the wrath and judgment of God's holiness now kindled against the apostasy of Israel*}: from the appearance of his loins even downward, fire; and from his loins even upward, as the appearance of brightness, as the colour of amber. [3] And he put forth the form of an hand, and took me by a lock of mine head; and the spirit lifted me up between the earth and the heaven, and brought me in the visions of God {*to see what God had seen that prompted and required God's judgment upon Israel in their captivity; God was revealing why the captivity took place*} to Jerusalem, to the door of the inner gate that looketh toward the north; where *was* the seat of the image of jealousy {*the image of the so called Queen of Heaven; Ishtar or Astarte, that was accompanied by all kinds of vile, licentious sexual fertility rites*}, which provoketh to jealousy. [4] And, behold, the glory of the God of Israel *was* there {*they did what they did in the presence of God somehow thinking that integrating paganism into the worship of God was somehow acceptable*}, according to the vision that I saw in the plain. [5] Then said he unto me, Son of man, lift up thine eyes now the way toward the north. So I lifted up mine eyes the way toward the north, and behold northward at the gate of the altar {*The altar gate opened into the inner sanctuary of the Temple where the altar of burnt offerings was. The inner court was the court of the priests and the outer court, from which the altar gate entered, was the court of the people.*} this image of jealousy in the entry {*The idol was set up right before the Brazen Altar of burnt offerings signifying the worship of Jehovah through pagan rituals.*}. [6] He said furthermore unto me, <u>Son of man, seest thou what they do</u>? *even* the great abominations that the house of Israel committeth here, that I should go far off from my sanctuary {*intimating that if God abandoned Israel, the abandonment would result in the utter destruction of Israel*}? but turn thee yet again, *and* thou shalt see greater abominations. [7] And he brought me to the door of the court {*within the Inner Court there was an inner sanctum called the Court of the Priests where only priests and Levites were allowed to enter*}; and when I looked, behold a hole {*an opening or window*} in the wall. [8] Then said he unto me, Son of man, dig now in the wall: and when I had digged in the wall {*forced a larger opening that exposes what was on the inside*}, behold a door {*into the Court of the Priests signifying that the main culpability for Israel's chastisement was upon the heads of the priests*}. [9] And he said unto me, Go in, and behold the wicked abominations that they {*the priests*} do here. [10] So I went in and saw; and behold every form of creeping things, and abominable beasts, and all the idols of the house of Israel, pourtrayed {*painted and carved*} upon the wall round about. [11] And there stood before them seventy men of the ancients of the house of Israel {*signifying that the Sanhedrin, as representatives of all the tribes, were aware of these atrocities and condoned them*}, and in the midst of them stood Jaazaniah {*most probably as the Chief of the Seventy*} the son of Shaphan {*Shaphan was the scribe that read the book of the Law that had been lost in the three-hundred years of the idolatry that king Solomon led the nation of Israel into and was later found during the reign of king Josiah; II Kings 22:10-14.*}, with every man {*revealing that the elders of Israel had usurped the authority of the priests in that only the priests were allowed to offer incense to God, but this incense was offered to idols*} his censer in his hand; and a thick cloud of incense went up. [12] Then said he unto me, Son of man, hast thou seen what the ancients of the house of Israel do in the dark {*The elders of Israel were involved in the pagan mysteries and were the Initiates of the mysteries who then led the children of Israel into this pagan integrationism.*}, every man in the chambers of his imagery {*each had his own secret chamber where the licentiousness of paganism was practiced*}? for they say, The LORD seeth us not; the LORD hath forsaken the earth {*because God had forsaken Israel due to her failure to keep/preserve the Mosaic Covenant, the leaders of Israel mistakenly interpreted this to mean God had completely forsaken the whole earth*}. [13] He said also unto me, Turn thee yet again, *and* thou shalt see greater abominations that they do. [14] Then he brought me to the door of the gate {*the North Gate of the Outer Court of the people; women were not allowed into the Outer Court*} of the LORD'S house which *was* toward the north; and, behold, there sat women weeping for Tammuz {*Tammuz was fabled to spend half the year in the underworld and, at the beginning of the other half, he would return to the Earth and bless it with fertility; the women of Israel were weeping and crying out for his return*}. [15] Then said he unto me, Hast thou seen *this*, O son of man? turn thee yet again, *and* thou shalt see greater abominations than these. [16] And he brought me into the inner court of the LORD'S house, and, behold, at the door of the temple of the LORD, between the porch and the altar, *were* about five and twenty men {*these twenty-five were the High Priest and the leaders of the twenty-four orders of priests, also known as 'the princes of the sanctuary'; I Chronicles 24:18-19 and Isaiah 43:28*}, with their backs toward the temple of the LORD {*having turned away from worship of Jehovah*}, and their faces toward the east {*where the Sun rose each morning*}; and they worshipped {*bowed down or prostrated themselves*} the sun toward the east. [17] Then he said unto me, Hast thou seen *this*, O son of man? Is it a light thing to the house of Judah that they commit the abominations which they commit here? for they have filled the land with violence, and have returned to provoke me to anger: and, lo, they put the branch to their nose {*to turn up the nose in scorn and rejection*}. [18] Therefore will I also deal in fury: mine eye shall not spare, neither will I have pity: and though they cry in mine ears with a loud voice, *yet* will I not hear them" (Ezekiel 8:1-18).

DISCUSSION QUESTIONS

1. Discuss the relationship of genuine repentance to genuine faith.

2. The repentant believer separates from sin, from worldliness, from theological error (false teaching and false teachers), and from any co-operation with others, even if they profess to be Christians, who fail the tests of correct *doctrine* and correct *practice*. Discuss how this *two tests* are to be applied in the life of every Christian and why.

3. Discuss why the ideas of Ecumenicism, the Emergent Church philosophy (cultural relativism), and/or the pragmatism of the Purpose Driven church growth philosophy are a complete contradiction against the essential of separation.

4. Discuss and define the *contextual continuity* of II Corinthians 5:14 through 6:18.

5. List and explain each of the four rhetorical questions of II Corinthians 6:14-16.

6. As you read Ezekiel 8:1-18, discuss how what God describes in this text parallels much of what is going on today in the Contemporary Christianity Church Growth movement.

7. Read and explain what happened in Ezekiel 8:1-18 and why it is absolutely critical for you as a believer-priest before God to understand this.

Chapter Sixty-one
Our High Priest's Model of the
Ministry of Reconciliation

"[11] O *ye* Corinthians, our mouth is open unto you, our heart is enlarged. [12] Ye are not straitened in us, but ye are straitened in your own bowels. [13]Now for a recompence in the same, (I speak as unto *my* children,) be ye also enlarged. [14] Be ye not unequally yoked together with unbelievers: for what fellowship hath righteousness with unrighteousness? and what communion hath light with darkness? [15] And what concord hath Christ with Belial? or what part hath he that believeth with an infidel? [16] And what agreement hath the temple of God with idols? for ye {*collectively and individually*} are the temple of the living God; as God hath said, I will dwell in them, and walk in *them*; and I will be their God, and they shall be my people. [17] Wherefore {*because we are 'the temple of the living God'*} come out from among them, and be ye separate, saith the Lord, and touch not the unclean *thing*; and I will receive you, [18] And will be a Father unto you, and ye shall be my sons and daughters, saith the Lord Almighty" (II Corinthians 6:11-18).

II Corinthians 6:16 is a summary statement regarding God's covenant promise to faithful believers of the Church Age. It is an all-inclusive "whoever will" statement regarding those who are truly saved by being "born again." It could be paraphrased, "If people will take Me for their God (their supreme and eternal Lord), I will take them for My people; I will instruct them, enlighten them, defend them, provide for them, support them, and bless them as if they were the only ones who existed in all of creation."

In the seven epistles of Christ in Revelation chapters one through three we see Jesus, as the High Priest of the New Covenant and as the "head of the body" (Ephesians 5:23, Colossians 1:18) of Christ, working through His admonition to the pastors of local churches to keep His local churches pure from false doctrine, false practices, and false alignments. This leads us to the *already, not yet* implementation of the New Covenant. As we understand the *already, not yet* fulfillment of the implementation of the New

Covenant during the Church age, we must understand that a dispensation is defined by principles of the covenant for that dispensation. Faithfulness is determined by how believers within a dispensation live, according to the governing principles of the covenant of that dispensation. That is why a dispensation is often simply defined as a *stewardship*. The *stewardship* of the New Covenant in the Church Age is defined by the congregational polity of a local church, evangelism/discipleship, the sanctification and consecration of the priesthood of all believers, and the practices of holiness, separation, and local church discipline in maintaining congregational accountability to the principles of the New Covenant.

It is critically important to understand that the theanthropic Christ administrates His theanthropic Church as a Priesthood through the indwelling of the Holy Spirit, the preaching of His inspired Word through God called pastors and evangelists, and through congregational polity. The connecting link to the heavenly ministry of our High Priest, who is in Heaven, is through the indwelling and filling of all believers by the Holy Spirit of God. This is why we must understand the critical necessity of the command of Christ to "be filled with the Spirit" (Ephesians 5:18). The *indwelling* of the Holy Spirit is universal to all believers the instant they are "born again." The *indwelling* is what makes all believers *theanthropic beings* and is what brings us into *union* with our High Priest in Heaven. The *filling* of the Spirit of God releases the supernatural, creative power of the Lord Jesus Christ through the believer-priest's "work of the ministry, for the edifying of the body of Christ" (Ephesians 4:12). *Union* (Ephesians 4:4-8, the *indwelling*) and *unity* (Ephesians 4:3, the *filling*) are essential for the spiritual dynamic of Christ's creative work to take place in the winning of souls and the progressive transfiguration of lives through Spirit-filled discipleship of newly "born again" souls. This leads us to Hebrews chapter eight and the High Priesthood of Christ.

"[1] Now of the things which we have spoken *this is* the sum: We have such an high priest, who is set on the right hand of the throne of the Majesty in the heavens; [2] A minister of the sanctuary, and of the true tabernacle, which the Lord pitched, and not man. [3] For every high priest is ordained to offer gifts and sacrifices: wherefore *it is* of necessity that this man have somewhat also to offer. [4] For if he were on earth, he should not be a priest, seeing that there are priests that offer gifts according to the law: [5] Who serve unto the example and shadow of heavenly things, as Moses was admonished of God when he was about to make the tabernacle: for, See, saith he, *that* thou make all things according to the pattern shewed to thee in the mount. [6] But now hath he obtained a more excellent ministry, by how much also he is the mediator of a better covenant, which was established upon better promises. [7] For if that first *covenant* had been faultless, then should no place have been sought for the second. [8] For finding fault with them, he saith, Behold, the days come, saith the Lord, when I will make a new covenant with the house of Israel and with the house of Judah: [9] Not according to the covenant that I made with their fathers in the day when I took them by the hand to lead them out of the land of Egypt; because they continued not in my covenant, and I regarded them not, saith the Lord. [10] For this *is* the covenant that I will make with the house of Israel after those days, saith the Lord; I will put my laws into their mind, and write them in their hearts: and I will be to them a God, and they shall be to me a people: [11] And they shall not teach every man his neighbour, and every man his brother, saying, Know the Lord: for all shall know me, from the least to the greatest" (Hebrews 8:1-11).

As our High Priest, Jesus is the ultimate and typical minister by whom the faithfulness of every New Covenant believer-priest connects through "unity of the Spirit" (Ephesians 4:3) and to which our ministry will be compared and measured. This is the summational emphasis of the High Priest of Christ - *ministry*. Therefore, *ministry* should be the major thrust of the Priesthood to which all believers are a part. You can easily delineate between a real, functioning local church and a group of people *playing church* simply by measuring their involvement in *ministry*.

How does Jesus minister? Jesus ministers through those He has indwelled with His Holy Spirit. Our High Priest Jesus, as the "Chief Shepherd" (*archipoimen*, I Peter 5:4) supernaturally ministers to His *sheep* through *under-shepherds* (pastors). The intent of this is the spiritual maturing and the spiritual equipping of all *sheep* through the preaching/teaching of the Word of God. Then, all *sheep* can then involve themselves in the *supernatural flow* of the ongoing creative work of Christ in the New Genesis ("the regeneration") from Heaven to Earth.

The epistle to the Hebrews gives us the summary of the High Priestly ministry of Jesus up to this point in Hebrews 8:1.

1. Hebrews 2:17: Jesus, who is now in Heaven, was made exactly like those to whom, and for whom, He ministers.
2. Hebrews 2:18: Jesus "suffered" the same trials and temptations that we all do while having the same needs as we all have.
3. Hebrews 4:14-15: Jesus can identify personally with the "feeling" of our weaknesses, for He shared them in the frailties of a human body.
4. Hebrews 5:5-6: Jesus has been ordained by God to represent believers in Heaven as our High Priest.
5. Hebrews 5:9: Jesus is the *author* (originator) of eternal salvation.
6. Hebrews 6:19-20: Jesus is our *fore runner* and the *anchor* of our soul (security or surety) in Heaven itself.
7. Hebrews 7:16-17: Jesus has the power of an endless life and therefore, an eternal High Priesthood, "ever living to make intercession" for all believers (Hebrews 7:25).
8. Hebrews 7:26 and 8:1: Jesus is exalted to the highest position in all of creation, to the right hand of God as "Lord of lords and King of kings" (I Timothy 6:15) and, at His second coming, will restore the "dominion" to mankind that God gave to Adam before he sinned.

Jesus Christ alone qualifies to meet both God's requirements and man's needs. He has become the *Supreme Minister*. Therefore, this is more than a position of pomp and glory, but a position that Jesus has chosen for himself - the servant of God and the *model for all believers*. Jesus is the *reproduction model* that is designed to reach the world through a network of millions of theanthropic disciples all following, emulating, and reproducing the model that Christ is.

"[23] And Jesus answered them, saying, The hour is come, that the Son of man should be glorified. [24] Verily, verily, I say unto you, Except a corn {*kokkos, grain or seed*} of wheat fall into the ground and die, it abideth alone: but if it die, it bringeth forth much fruit. [25] He that loveth his life shall lose it; and he that hateth his life in this world shall keep it unto life eternal. [26] If any man serve me, let him follow me; and where I am, there shall also my servant be: if any man serve me, him will *my* Father honour" (John 12:23-26).

No farmer plants a seed in the ground expecting only to get one more seed in return. A seed is planted with the expectation of exponential return in multiplied growth. We often make the focus of the death of Christ in this text as that which "bringeth forth much fruit." This is part of the focus. However, Christ is stating a universal principle of *plant biology*. Seed is produced when a plant dies, providing opportunity for life/germination to be *multiplied on an expansive scale*. Then, when all the plants die and the multiplied seeds from those plants are *planted*, each succeeding generation then multiplies itself exponentially. Verses twenty-five and twenty-six of John chapter twelve are the emphasis of the text. To follow Christ is to follow Him in our *death to self.* The spiritual *fruit* of souls who are won to Christ and who are then discipled become the production of multiplied seed for another generation.

According to Hebrews 8:2, Jesus is in Heaven. He is also on Earth in "the true tabernacle" (the Temple of God made up of "living stones," i.e. individual, "born again" believers of local churches). He is on Earth in believers through the indwelling of His Holy Spirit, ministering, serving, and meeting needs through *human agents* (believer-priests). Christ is the believer's model of ministry.

"[25] But Jesus called them *unto him*, and said, Ye know that the princes of the Gentiles exercise dominion over them, and they that are great exercise authority upon them. [26] But it shall not be so among you: but whosoever will be great among you, let him be your minister; [27] And whosoever will be chief among you, let him be your servant: [28] Even as the Son of man came not to be ministered unto, but to minister, and to give his life a ransom for many" (Matthew 20:25-28).

If the Creator of the Heaven and the Earth is willing to submit Himself to serve mankind, why do we think ministry is beneath us? The believer that fails in this model of ministry fails in his/her test of faithfulness. This test of faithfulness is the substance of the *stewardship* of the Church Age Dispensation. The phrase "dispensation of the grace" in Ephesians 3:2 is a *stewardship* of the supernatural enabling of the Spirit-indwelled believer through the filling of the Spirit. Anytime we think of a stewardship, we must understand that God holds us *accountable* for the things of which we are stewards.

"[7] But the end of all things is at hand: be ye therefore sober, and watch unto prayer. [8] And above all things have fervent charity among yourselves: for charity shall cover the multitude of sins. [9] Use hospitality one to another without grudging. [10] As every man hath received the gift, *even so* minister the same one to another, as good stewards of the manifold grace of God. [11] If any man speak, *let him speak* as the oracles of God; if any man minister, *let him do it* as of the ability which God giveth: that God in all things may be glorified through Jesus Christ, to whom be praise and dominion for ever and ever. Amen" (I Peter 4:7-11).

The words "stewards of . . . grace" in I Peter 4:10 translates into the practical reality of **accountability** for this supernatural spiritual endowment of power that is given to all true believers "born again" of the Spirit of God.

> The eyes of faith see every task or difficulty in life through the possibility of grace enablement.

This translates into two great spiritual realities that we MUST understand (indwelling and filling). What does this ministry of Christ as the believer's High Priest involve?

1. To receive us as we come to God
2. To hear our cries for mercy and grace in time of need and to help us
3. To save us to the "uttermost;" that means to keep us safe and secure
4. To represent us before God as the propitiating sacrifice for our sins (I John 1:7-9)
5. To deliver us through all the trials and temptations of this corrupt and dying world
6. To minister the Word of God *to* our hearts and *through* our hearts to others

In doing so, Jesus is the "minister of true sanctuary" (Hebrews 8:2), which is the *living Temple* (II Corinthians 6:16) made up of *living stones* (I Peter 2:5). He is the minister of "the true tabernacle," or the place where all of a believer-priest's worship, ministry, and fruit is actually offered and accepted by God in and through Jesus as the believer's High Priest. Everything the Church Age believer-priest does, he does through the theanthropic union he has with his High Priest, Jesus Christ. This is the spiritual significance of praying in Jesus' name. We live and minister *in His stead.* Only ministry done through this *union* (indwelling) and *unity* (filling) is done in Jesus' name. Prayer is a central form of ministry in the name of Jesus as our High Priest.

"[13] And whatsoever ye shall <u>ask in my name</u>, that will I do, that the Father may be glorified in the Son. [14] If ye shall ask any thing in my name, I will do *it*" (John 14:13-14).

"Ye have not chosen me, but I have chosen you, and ordained you, that ye should go and bring forth fruit, and *that* your fruit should remain: that <u>whatsoever ye shall ask of the Father in my name</u>, he may give it you" (John 15:16).

"[23] And in that day ye shall ask me nothing. Verily, verily, I say unto you, <u>Whatsoever ye shall ask the Father in my name</u>, he will give *it* you. [24] Hitherto have ye asked nothing in my name: ask, and ye shall receive, that your joy may be full" (John 16:23-24).

Therefore, prayer is first and foremost a *declaration of dependence* upon Jesus as our High Priest. NOTHING a believer does apart from *union* (the indwelling) and *unity* (the filling) can be said to be done in Jesus' name. No fruit can be produced apart from the supernatural *union* (the indwelling) and *unity* (the filling) of the Holy Spirit. Therefore, neither can the believer expect God's blessing upon any ministry that is not done in Jesus' name and to His glory. This is the meaning of *abiding in Christ.*

"[1] I am the true vine, and my Father is the husbandman. [2] Every branch in me that beareth not fruit he taketh away: and every *branch* that beareth fruit, he purgeth it, that it may bring forth more fruit. [3] Now ye are clean through the word which I have spoken unto you. [4] Abide in me, and I in you. As the branch cannot bear fruit of itself, except it abide in the vine; no more can ye, except ye abide in me. [5] I am the vine, ye *are* the branches: He that abideth in me, and I in him, the same bringeth forth much fruit: for <u>without me ye can do nothing</u>" (John 15:1-5).

"[15] For we have not an high priest which cannot be touched with the feeling of our infirmities; but was in all points tempted like as *we are, yet* without sin. [16] Let us therefore come boldly unto the throne of grace, that we may obtain mercy, and <u>find grace to help in time of need</u>" (Hebrews 4:15-16).

DISCUSSION QUESTIONS

1. As we understand the *already, not yet* fulfillment of the implementation of the New Covenant during the Church age, we must understand that a dispensation is defined by principles of the covenant for that dispensation. Faithfulness is determined by how believers within a dispensation live according to the governing principles of the covenant of that dispensation. Discuss stewardship in the context of Dispensationalism and how stewardship is *defined* and *measured*.

2. Discuss how the theanthropic Christ administrates His theanthropic Church as a Priesthood.

3. Discuss the difference between *union* and *unity* as they relate to Christ ministering through a believer-priest.

4. The epistle to the Hebrews gives us the summary of the High Priestly ministry of Jesus. List the verse given for these distinguishing characteristics of Christ's High Priestly ministry and explain each of the eight that are given.

5. Read John 12:23-26. Discuss the *Supreme Production Model* that Jesus is and what is necessary to reproduce this *model* in your life.

6. According to Hebrews 8:2, Jesus is there in Heaven, and on earth in "the true tabernacle." Define what this "true tabernacle" on earth is as it defines the local church.

7. From the context of the High Priesthood of Jesus and the *believer-priesthood* of all believers, explain the deep spiritual significance of praying *in Jesus' name*.

Chapter Sixty-two

Christ's Ministry as High Priest of the New Covenant

"[6] But now hath he obtained a more excellent ministry, by how much also he is the mediator of a better covenant, which was established upon better promises. [7] For if that first *covenant* had been faultless, then should no place have been sought for the second. [8] For finding fault with them, he saith, Behold, the days come, saith the Lord, when I will make a new covenant with the house of Israel and with the house of Judah: [9] Not according to the covenant that I made with their fathers in the day when I took them by the hand to lead them out of the land of Egypt; because they continued not in my covenant, and I regarded them not, saith the Lord. [10] For this *is* the covenant that I will make with the house of Israel after those days, saith the Lord; I will put my laws into their mind, and write them in their hearts: and I will be to them a God, and they shall be to me a people: [11] And they shall not teach every man his neighbour, and every man his brother, saying, Know the Lord: for all shall know me, from the least to the greatest. [12] For I will be merciful to their unrighteousness, and their sins and their iniquities will I remember no more. [13] In that he saith, A new *covenant*, he hath made the first old. Now that which decayeth and waxeth old *is* ready to vanish away" (Hebrews 8:6-13).

The High Priesthood of Christ is the position Christ holds in the *progressive unfolding* (*already, not yet*) of the New Covenant. The "ministry" is the function or work of that position (vs. two and six). "Ministry" here is from the Greek word *leitourgia* (li-toorg-ee'-ah). This word referred to all the work of a priest in his service ("ministry") to people as he offered prayer and sacrifices for them. Christ ministers on the basis of His "finished" sacrifice. He intercedes in prayer to the Father on behalf of the saved of the Church Age. He mediates, and is the *connecting link*, between the Father and the ministering believer through the filling of the Spirit. The only Spirit-empowered ministry is that ministry done through our Mediator through the filling of the Spirit.

The predominant "ministry" of Christ's High Priesthood is defined by the word "mediator." The word "mediator" is from the

Greek word *mesites* (mes-ee'-tace). It refers to the person who intervenes between two people or arbitrates an agreement or ratifies a "covenant" between two people or groups. This new "covenant" of *grace enabling* is ratified between God and believers trusting in the efficaciousness of the blood sacrifice of Christ to propitiate God for the sins of the world. Individuals enter into this newly ratified covenant "by grace through faith" in the objective details of the Gospel of Jesus Christ. The entry into this New Covenant is accomplished by the baptism with the Holy Spirit. Living as a faithful steward of the New Covenant is accomplished through the indwelling and filling of the believer with Holy Spirit. Jesus, as High Priest, is the *Mediator* of this New Covenant through which God's Power is released into the world through the Spirit-filled believer.

First, we need to understand what a "covenant" is. The word "covenant is from the Greek word *diatheke* (dee-ath-ay'-kay). The word "covenant" was used to describe a *disposition* or an *arrangement/agreement* of any sort. It also referred to as the last disposition that a person made of his earthly possessions after his death - a *testament,* or what we call a *will* today. There are basically two kinds of covenants recorded in the Bible.

1. There is a covenant where two parties or groups sit down and work out the terms and conditions, and then all parties agree to be bound by them. For instance, this is what many local churches have in their Church Covenants. A marriage covenant is also such a covenant and the vows are the promises. The marriage covenant is a covenant between the two people getting married, God, and the witnesses of the covenant vows.

2. There is also a covenant where one party sets the terms and then both parties orally agree to abide by them. This kind of covenant is called a *Last Will* or a *Testament.*

The latter kind of covenant is the New Covenant made by God (Hebrews 8:8). It is not a covenant made by man. In fact, man has absolutely nothing to do with the terms of this covenant. God sets the terms and conditions and man accepts the covenant as a whole, or rejects it as a whole. God compares this to a *last will and testament* of a person. We cannot change the terms. We can only receive or reject the *inheritance* it offers.

> **The New Covenant is essentially the conditions that are necessary in the life of a believer for the release of the supernatural enabling of God. This release is through the believer's life as a believer seeks to live the *Christ-life* and do the "work of the ministry."**

"Now" (Hebrews 8:6), in the establishment of this New Covenant of God, the conditions and terms clearly distinguish Jesus to be both the *Testator* and the *Mediator*.

"[15] And for this cause he is {*present tense*} the mediator of the new testament {*literally, 'new covenant,' therefore the New Covenant must be in existence if Jesus is presently its Mediator*}, that by means of death, for the redemption of the transgressions *that were* under the first testament, they which are called might receive the promise of eternal inheritance. [16] For where a testament *is*, there must also of necessity be the death of the testator. [17] For a testament *is* of force after men are dead: otherwise it is of no strength at all while the testator liveth" (Hebrews 9:15-17).

The great misnomer of the believer's "eternal inheritance" is that this is something the believer receives when the believer dies. In reality, the believer's "eternal inheritance" is received the moment he is "born again." Yes, there will be a fuller sense of the realization of the believer's "eternal inheritance" once he is glorified, but the *union* of the Spirit (indwelling) and *unity* with the Spirit (filling) provides an extensive release of the "eternal inheritance" during our present lifetimes.

In the usual application of this kind of *last will* or *testament*, the *testator* is the person who defined the conditions of the *will*, was dead, and so the mediation/administration of the Covenant would fall into the hands of another person previously appointed to that task. However, in the New Covenant, both the *testator* and *mediator* are one in that the *testator* (Jesus) "continueth ever" (7:24) and "ever liveth" (7:25). Therefore, Jesus is both the *initiator* of the New Covenant and the *mediator* of all of its conditional requirements. It is important to understand that God's covenants are His *governing principles* for any given dispensation and are *only for the believers* within the time span of that dispensation. The New Covenant is a not new set of conditions for salvation. Covenants define how God will bless and administrate the lives of *believers*.

"[23] And they truly were many priests, because they were not suffered to continue by reason of death: [24] But this *man {Jesus}*, because he continueth ever, hath an unchangeable priesthood. [25] Wherefore he is able also to save them to the uttermost {*because believers are 'complete' in the efficacy of Christ's once for all sacrifice*} that come unto God by him, seeing he ever liveth to make intercession for them" (Hebrews 7:23-25).

Therefore, the reality of Christ's death and resurrection makes for both a perfect New Covenant and a perfect Mediator. Jesus Christ Himself mediates/administrates the conditions of the covenant perfectly as the Chief Shepherd of His Church. He does not lie, deceive, misrepresent, change, add to, or take away from the Covenant's original terms.

I was asked by my wife's uncle to administrate his will for him before he died. I agreed, not knowing about anything his will said. In his will, he stipulated that his estate was to be divided between four of his five nieces and nephews. One was excluded from receiving any funds. After his death and after the reading of the will, his sister thought this was unfair and asked that the estate be divided between all five of the nieces and nephews. I told her the estate would be divided exactly the way her brother defined according to his last will and testament. That was my responsibility. It was not my responsibility to make any moral judgments or to amend the will in any way. It was not my responsibility to make everyone *happy* or see to it that there were not any rifts created between family members. I was simply entrusted with carrying out his wishes according to the exact specifications of his will.

According to Hebrews 9:15, a mediator is a person who stands between two parties to *unify* them. A perfect mediator has no personal agenda, only the agenda of the covenant that he mediates. Since Christ mediates His own covenant and the intent of that covenant is the good of all mankind in redemption through the "ministry of reconciliation" (this is the purpose of the New Covenant), we can be absolutely confident that He will mediate according to that purpose (Romans 8:28).

"For God sent not his Son into the world to condemn the world; but that the world through him might be saved" (John 3:17).

"[51] And it came to pass, when the time was come that he should be received up, he stedfastly set his face to go to Jerusalem, [52] And sent messengers before his face: and they went, and entered into a village of the Samaritans, to make ready for him. [53] And they did not receive him, because his face was as though he would go to Jerusalem. [54] And when his disciples James and John saw *this*, they said, Lord, wilt thou that we command fire to come down from heaven, and consume them, even as Elias did? [55] But he turned, and rebuked them, and said, Ye know not what manner of spirit ye are of. [56] For the Son of man is not come to destroy men's lives, but to save *them*. And they went to another village" (Luke 9:51-56).

"For Christ is not entered into the holy places made with hands, *which are* the figures of the true; but into heaven itself, now to appear in the presence of God for us" (Hebrews 9:24).

"For us" (Hebrews 9:24) means that Christ is not against believers, but that He ministers on behalf of believers. For that believer who is in *union* and *unity* with Christ, Jesus is mediating between him and the Father for the supernatural enabling of the indwelling Spirit. Jesus is the *conduit* through which the power of God *flows* to the Spirit-filled believer. The Spirit-filled believer is the *conduit* through which God's creative power *flows* into the world through the preaching of the Gospel and the teaching of God's Word. We not only have a better Mediator, we have better promises.

The Law (Mosaic Covenant) was a testimony against man, not for him. What is meant by that statement? The Law did not testify on behalf of the sinner (and all of us are still sinners in nature even after we are "born again"), but *against us*. The Law *points the finger* of condemnation at us.

"[19] Now we know that what things soever the law saith, it saith to them who are under the law: that every mouth may be stopped, and all the world may become guilty before God. [20] Therefore by the deeds of the law there shall no flesh be justified in his sight: for by the law *is* the knowledge of sin" (Romans 3:19-20).

God promised in the Old (Mosaic) Covenant that He would accept, bless, and fellowship with the people of the *nation* of Israel, *if* they would *keep the Law*. The people agreed to those conditions, but then found out something. They found out that the Law (Mosaic Covenant) made enormous demands, but did not, and could not, provide the inner strength and power to obey those demands. The Mosaic Covenant simply stated the conditions of *fellowship* with God, but yet, because of the nature of man, denied him access to God because the Law could not make anyone perfect.

"[1] For the law {*Mosaic Covenant*} having a shadow of good things to come, *and* not the very image of the things, can never with those sacrifices which they offered year by year continually make the comers thereunto perfect {*regarding positional sanctification*}. [2] For then would they not have ceased to be offered? because that the worshippers once purged should have had no more conscience of sins. [3] But in those *sacrifices there is* a remembrance again *made* of sins every year. [4] For *it is* not possible that the blood of bulls and of goats should take away sins" (Hebrews 10:1-4).

The substance of Hebrews chapter ten is not about salvation, but the purification of a believer's sins for *fellowship* with God. The word "perfect" in Hebrews 10:1 is translated from the Greek word *teleioo* (tel-i-o'-o). In this context, it simply means that the Mosaic Covenant could not produce a *finished product*. The New Covenant, through *union* with our heavenly High Priest and the "unity of the Spirit," can produce a *finished product* in the spiritual maturity of a believer supernaturally enabled to reproduce *fruit*. Herein lays the great superiority of the New Covenant on the basis of its better *promises*.

1. Hebrews 8:10a: Although the New Covenant is not yet fully implemented, the Word of God would become an indwelling, inner force aiding the believer to obey, rather than an outward demand without any aid. Aiding the believer from within is the primary meaning of the promised *Parakletos* (par-ak'-lay-tos) - someone called to another's side to comfort or provide aid. The contextual meaning of this word would better render it *Partner* or *Helper* than "Comforter." The word refers to the Holy Spirit as the believer's divine *Partner* in ministry; i.e., doing God's will.

"[15] If ye love me, keep my commandments. [16] And I will pray the Father, and he shall give you another Comforter, that he may abide with you for ever; [17] *Even* the Spirit of truth; whom the world cannot receive, because it seeth him not, neither knoweth him: but ye know him; for he dwelleth with you, and shall be in you. [18] I will not leave you comfortless {*helpless*}: I will come to you. [19] Yet a little while, and the world seeth me no more; but ye see me: because I live, ye shall live also. [20] At that day ye shall know that I *am* in my Father, and ye in me, and I in you. [21] He that hath my commandments, and keepeth them, he it is that loveth me: and he that loveth me shall be loved of my Father, and I will love him, and will manifest myself to him. . . [26] But the Comforter, *which is* the Holy Ghost, whom the Father will send in my name, he shall teach you all things, and bring all things to your remembrance, whatsoever I have said unto you" (John 14:15-21 and 26).

2. Hebrews 8:10b: The New Covenant, although it is not yet fully implemented, provides the believer-priest complete personal acceptance by God and direct access to Him in our High Priest, Jesus Christ.

3. Hebrews 8:11: The New Covenant, although it is not yet fully implemented, provides the believer-priest personal knowledge (intimacy) and fellowship with God through our High Priest, Jesus Christ.

4. Hebrews 8:12: The New Covenant, although it is not yet fully implemented, provides the believer-priest perfect, ongoing forgiveness for fellowship with God, and absolute mercy through the blood sacrifice of our High Priest, Jesus Christ (I John 1:7-9).

"For the law made nothing perfect, but the bringing in of a better hope *did*; by the which we draw nigh unto God" (Hebrew 7:19).

The Mosaic Law (the Old Covenant) made nothing perfect; i.e., it could not produce a *finished product* in the maturing/equipping of a believer. However, the New Covenant can and does make the believer "perfect" regarding both positional and practical sanctification for fellowship with God. This is needed for the release of God's supernatural enabling in the filling of the Spirit through the "unity of the Spirit." As far as salvation is concerned, the believer is already eternally prefect in sanctification before God "in Christ" through the baptism with the Spirit (*union*). As far as service or ministry is concerned, perfect sanctification is available to the believer upon the believer's genuine repentance of sin, confession of sin, and restoration to fellowship with God through the filling of the Spirit (*unity* of the Spirit). *Union* is about the believer's *position* "in Christ." *Unity* is about the believer's *practices* or ministry "in Christ."

"[9] For in him dwelleth all the fulness of the Godhead bodily. [10] And ye are complete in him, which is the head of all principality and power: [11] In whom also ye are circumcised with the circumcision made without hands, in putting off the body of the sins of the flesh by the circumcision of Christ: [12] Buried with him in baptism, wherein also ye are risen with *him* through the faith of the operation of God, who hath raised him from the dead" (Colossians 2:9-12).

"Complete in" Christ - this is our position in Jesus Christ in the New Covenant. The word translated "complete" in Colossians 2:10 is in the perfect tense and passive voice. That means it is a *finished reality* accomplished sometime in the past and continues in that accomplished reality through the Spirit-filled life of the believer. The believer was completed "in Christ," continues to be complete in Christ in the present, and will continue to be complete in Christ in the future.

Why was the Mosaic Covenant faulty (Hebrews 8:7-8)? It was faulty because it could reveal sin to man, but could not remove the guilt of that sin. "For the law having a shadow of good things to come, *and* not the very image of the things, can never with those sacrifices which they offered year by year continually make the comers thereunto perfect" (Hebrews 10:1). The only thing the sacrifices of the Mosaic Covenant could do was *cover over* sin from the eyes of the Cherubim (the vindicators of God's righteousness/holiness, II Thessalonians 1:8). The Law had no power to redeem, justify, or save guilty sinners from condemnation. In fact, the Law had nothing to do with a person's salvation and never was intended for that purpose. "For *it is* not possible that the blood of bulls and of goats should take away sins" (Hebrews 10:4). The Mosaic Covenant was given to believers for *fellowship* with God. It was not given to lost people as a condition for salvation.

The New Covenant in Christ's blood has no such faults. The New Covenant not only reveals what sin is and the consequences of sin, but the New Covenant in Christ's blood also completely remits the punishment of sin by satisfying God's condemnation and death sentence upon the sinner in the perfect Substitute, Jesus Christ. Secondly, once a sinner is "born again," the New Covenant in Christ's Blood establishes the believer as a priest before God and provides everything that believer-priest needs for "life and godliness" (II Peter 1:3).

"[13] And you, being dead in your sins and the uncircumcision of your flesh, hath he quickened together with him, having forgiven you all trespasses; [14] Blotting out the handwriting of ordinances that was against us, which was contrary to us, and took it out of the way, nailing it to his cross; [15] *And* having spoiled principalities and powers, he made a shew of them openly, triumphing over them in it" (Colossians 2:14).

According to Hebrew 8:13, by comparison to the New Covenant, the Mosaic Covenant was decaying, broken down, and about ready to crumble into nonexistence. The Mosaic Covenant was already obsolete and no longer of any use by the time of the coming of Messiah (Hosea 2:11). So why does *Replacement Theology* try to hold on to it? Why try to make over the ordinances of the New Covenant after the "dead works" of the Old? Why reduce the great truths of the ordinances of the New Covenant, as they testify to *completeness* and *perfection* in Jesus Christ, to a dead *Sacramentalism* that denies that New Covenant *completeness* and denies the complete provision of the New Covenant promises?

I'll never understand the loyalties that people have to churches that for years have misrepresented the great promise of the New Covenant. They misrepresent these promises by continuing in the abrogated practices of the Old Covenant with all of its inadequacies thinking these abrogated practices of *dead sacrifices* are merely replaced with dead *sacraments*. "Dead works" will always be "dead works" (Hebrews 6:1).

I will never understand why people continue trusting in these "dead works" when their Moms and Dads, and their grandparents and great grandparents have died and gone to Hell because of a misrepresentation of the New Covenant of grace and salvation as a free gift.

> I will never understand why people will constantly return to drink from "broken cisterns" (Jeremiah 2:13) when the spiritual *living waters* of Christ can literally flow through them personally

"[37] In the last day, that great *day* of the feast, Jesus stood and cried, saying, If any man thirst, let him come unto me, and drink. [38] He that believeth on me, as the scripture hath said, <u>out of his belly shall flow rivers of living water</u>. [39] (But this spake he of the Spirit, which they that believe on him should receive: for the Holy Ghost was not yet *given*; because that Jesus was not yet glorified.)" (John 7:37-39)

"[17] Wherefore come out from among them, and be ye separate, said the Lord, and touch not the unclean *thing*; and I will receive you, [18] And will be a Father unto you, and ye shall be my sons and daughters, saith the Lord Almighty" (II Corinthians 6:17-18).

DISCUSSION QUESTIONS

1. The High Priesthood of Christ is the position Christ holds in the *progressive unfolding* (*already, not yet*) of the New Covenant. The "ministry" is the function or work of that position (vs. two and six). Discuss Christ's *mediatorial ministry* as High Priest of the New Covenant and the practical purposes of that ministry throughout the Church Age.

2. Define the two different kinds of Covenants found in the Word of God. Discuss the New Covenant as the *last will* or a *testament* of Christ.

3. Discuss why it is critical to understand that Jesus is both the *testator* and the *mediator* of the New Covenant.

4. What is the great misnomer regarding the believer's "eternal inheritance" and what is the proper *expression* of this "inheritance" as it works itself out in your everyday life?

5. Describe what it is about Jesus Christ that makes Him a perfect *mediator*.

6. Explain the significance of the words "for us" in Hebrews 9:24.

7. List and discuss the four superiorities of the New Covenant on the basis of its better *promises* from Hebrews 8:10-12.

Chapter Sixty-three

Inadequate Old Covenant Approaches to God

"[1] Then verily the first *covenant* had also ordinances of divine service, and a worldly sanctuary. [2] For there was a tabernacle made; the first, wherein *was* the candlestick, and the table, and the shewbread; which is called the sanctuary. [3] And after the second veil, the tabernacle which is called the Holiest of all; [4] Which had the golden censer, and the ark of the covenant overlaid round about with gold, wherein *was* the golden pot that had manna, and Aaron's rod that budded, and the tables of the covenant; [5] And over it the cherubims of glory shadowing the mercyseat; of which we cannot now speak particularly. [6] Now when these things were thus ordained, the priests went always into the first tabernacle, accomplishing the service *of God.* [7] But into the second *went* the high priest alone once every year, not without blood, which he offered for himself, and *for* the errors of the people: [8] The Holy Ghost this signifying, that the way into the holiest of all was not yet made manifest, while as the first tabernacle was yet standing: [9] Which *was* a figure for the time then present, in which were offered both gifts and sacrifices, that could not make him that did the service perfect, as pertaining to the conscience; [10] *Which stood* only in meats and drinks, and divers washings, and carnal ordinances, imposed *on them* until the time of reformation" (Hebrews 9:1-10).

We now move from the superiority of the High Priesthood of Jesus Christ that is detailed in Hebrews 7:1 through 8:13 to the inferiority of Mosaic Covenant worship types. Since the Mosaic Covenant worship types were so inferior, why is it that so much of professing *Christianity* continues to pattern its worship practices and styles after the Old Covenant? The reason is the failure to eradicate the influx of Covenant Theology (*Replacement* or *Reformed Theology*) in its early development. What were some of the inadequate Old Covenant ways that people tried to approach God?

1. Earthly Sanctuaries: sanctuaries of worship, physical buildings (Hebrews 9:1-5, God's Shekinah does not dwell in temples of wood and stone today. God's Shekinah dwells in Temples made with "living stones.")

2. Earthly Priests: specially ordained men of God (Sacerdotalism; Hebrews 9:6-7: There are no *clergy* in the Body of Christ. All believers are priests before God and God governs the local church through congregational polity of believer priests.)
3. Gifts and sacrifices: participatory works misunderstood to bring favor with God (Hebrews 9:9)
4. Carnal (physical) ordinances (Sacramentalism, Hebrews 9:10)

All these things were completely inadequate to bring anyone one step closer to God, or to make man's worship of God acceptable. These things were *earthly* (Hebrews 9:1). They were "worldly." That means they were practices that were bound to this physical world. They could not touch the spiritual realm of God. Man is earth bound.

Somehow man's worship would need to be moved to Heaven before it could escape being earth bound. The only way that could happen was to move man, who desires to worship God, to Heaven. This is the main emphasis of praying, serving, and worshipping in the name of Jesus. All that the Spirit-filled believer does on earth is channeled through Jesus to the Father in the literal Heaven.

"[11] But Christ being come an high priest of good things to come, by a greater and more perfect tabernacle, not made with hands, that is to say, not of this building; [12] Neither by the blood of goats and calves, but by his own blood he entered in once into the holy place, having obtained eternal redemption *for us*" (Hebrews 9:11-12).

Are buildings intended to be physical aids to help us approach God? Are the beautiful edifices designed by the minds of great architecture and made by the hands of gifted craftsman the houses where God dwells?

"[44] Our fathers had the tabernacle of witness in the wilderness, as he had appointed, speaking unto Moses, that he should make it according to the fashion that he had seen. [45] Which also our fathers that came after brought in with Jesus into the possession of the Gentiles, whom God drave out before the face of our fathers, unto the days of David; [46] Who found favour before God, and desired to find a tabernacle for the God of Jacob. [47] But Solomon built him an house. [48] Howbeit the most High dwelleth not in temples made with hands; as saith the prophet, [49] Heaven *is* my throne, and earth *is* my footstool: what house will ye build me? saith the Lord: or what *is* the place of my rest? [50] Hath not my hand made all these things" (Acts 7:44-50).

"[22] Then Paul stood in the midst of Mars' hill, and said, *Ye* men of Athens, I perceive that in all things ye are too superstitious. [23] For as I passed by, and beheld your devotions, I found an altar with this inscription, TO THE UNKNOWN GOD. Whom therefore ye ignorantly worship, him declare I unto you. [24] God that made the world and all things therein, seeing that he is Lord of heaven and earth, dwelleth not in temples made with hands; [25] Neither is worshipped with men's hands, as though he needed any thing, seeing he giveth to all life, and breath, and all things;" (Acts 17:22- 25).

Worshipping God is not limited to some *religious edifice* dedicated for that purpose. Buildings are not vehicles for us to have a place to meet with God. God meets you wherever you are. This fact does not mean you can justify forsaking the assembly of Christians (the local church). God commands the assembly of His children on the Lord's Day.

"[24] And let us consider one another to provoke unto love and to good works: [25] Not forsaking the assembling of ourselves together, as the manner of some *is*; but exhorting *one another*: and so much the more, as ye see the day approaching" (Hebrews 10:24-25).

"[1] Now concerning the collection for the saints, as I have given order to the churches of Galatia, even so do ye. [2] Upon the first *day* of the week let every one of you lay by him in store, as *God* hath prospered him, that there be no gatherings when I come" (I Corinthians 16:1-2).

Where ever a true local church assembles, there you will find the *Living Temple* of the Living God.

"[6] Know ye not that ye are the temple of God, and *that* the Spirit of God dwelleth in you? [17] If any man defile the temple of God, him shall God destroy; for the temple of God is holy, which *temple* ye are" (I Corinthians 3:16-17; this portion of Scripture is referring to the corporate body of Christ or a local church).

"[9] What? know ye not that your body is the temple of the Holy Ghost *which is* in you, which ye have of God, and ye are not your own? [20] For ye are bought with a price: therefore glorify God in your body, and in your spirit, which are God's" (I Corinthians 6:19-20; this portion of Scripture refers to the individual believer).

A common term used of the large room in a church building that is used for worship is the word *sanctuary*. This is a term carried over from the Old Covenant. I never call the room used for worship in a *church house* the *sanctuary*. In the Old Covenant, *Sanctuary* was a word used to refer to the Holy of Holies and the most sacred part of the Temple where only the Priests were allowed, sacrifices were offered, and where the Altar of sacrifice was. True New Covenant *church houses* do not have an *Altar*. An *Altar* is **any place** you meet God and offer sacrifice.

"[10] We have an altar, whereof they have no right to eat which serve the tabernacle. . . [15] By him therefore let us offer the sacrifice of praise to God continually, that is, the fruit of *our* lips giving thanks to his name. [16] But to do good and to communicate forget not: for with such sacrifices God is well pleased" (Hebrew 13:10 and 15-16).

An Altar in the New Covenant exists anyplace we "present our bodies a living sacrifice, holy and acceptable unto God" (Romans 12:1). There are no earthly buildings that can claim to be the *sanctuary* where men meet God. We do not need to travel to some building to pray or confess sin. Church buildings are not *heavenly portals* to God's presence. Nor do we need some man, or *earthly priest*, or a pastor (or whatever else you want to call them) to help us to talk to God or be a vehicle that God's *grace can be transferred* to us (Hebrews 9:6-7). This is known as Sacerdotalism. It ended with the Old Covenant.

This is about the perversion of the *sacrament of ordination* (not to be confused with the biblical ordination of "elders in every church," Titus 1:5). The perverted *sacrament of ordination* is the belief that God's grace is transferred from the hands of one ordained clergyman to another ordained clergyman (*Successionism*) so as that person can confer God's grace (regeneration, forgiveness of sin, etc.) to participants in the Sacraments.

"The Catholic Church teaches that ordination can be performed validly only by a bishop, who is a successor of the Apostles, and that it can be received validly only by a baptized male. It is the episcopate which is the means of the transmission of grace in ordination."[29]

Is there any hint of such nonsense in the New Covenant? What the *sacrament of ordination* translates into is that the "ordained" individual can then administer the *Sacraments* and transfer the *grace* that is in his hands through the *Sacraments* to the participants. It is easy to see how Sacerdotalism is a complete distortion of almost everything that the New Covenant is.

It is also easy to see how salvation by grace is totally misrepresented in the way a Sacerdotalist quotes Ephesians 2:8-9. For them it obviously means something totally different than what the Scriptures intend. "For by grace" (that comes from the hands of the priest through the *Sacrament*) "are ye saved through faith" (in those *Sacraments*) "and not of yourselves" (it comes through the hands of God through the priest to you).

Neither are you personally made acceptable to God, nor is your worship made acceptable to God, because of the earthly/material gifts or sacrifices you make (Hebrews 9:9). There is no gift or sacrifice that is acceptable to God except those offered through our High Priest Jesus Christ and offered in His name.

"[4] To whom coming, *as unto* a living stone, disallowed indeed of men, but chosen of God, *and* precious, [5] Ye also, as lively stones, are built up a spiritual house, an holy priesthood, to offer up spiritual sacrifices, acceptable to God by Jesus Christ" (I Peter 2:4-5).

Neither can carnal or physical ordinances make our worship acceptable to God (Hebrews 9:10).

"[1] For the law having a shadow of good things to come, *and* not the very image of the things, can never with those sacrifices which they offered year by year continually make the comers thereunto perfect. [2] For then would they not have ceased to be offered? because that the worshippers once purged should have had no more conscience of sins. [3] But in those *sacrifices there is* a remembrance again *made* of sins every year. [4] For *it is* not possible that the blood of bulls and of goats should take away sins. [5] Wherefore when he cometh into the world, he saith, Sacrifice and offering thou wouldest not, but a body hast thou prepared me: [6] In burnt offerings and *sacrifices* for sin thou hast had no pleasure" (Hebrews 10:1-5).

---

[29] Stravinskas, Peter M.J. *Our Sunday Visitor's Catholic Encyclopedia.* (Huntington, IN: Our Sunday Visitor Publishing Division, 1991), page 705

When someone changes the New Covenant ordinances from their original intent and make them *doorways* to salvation (baptismal regeneration) or vehicles to receive forgiveness of sins (Transubstantiation or Consubstantiation in the Lord's Supper), we pervert those ordinances into *carnal ordinances* in the same class as the Old Covenant's "carnal ordinances."

These are the reasons why Covenant Theology, Replacement Theology, and/or Reformed Theology are such abominations. Covenant Theology brings item after item from the Old Covenant and imposes those practices upon the New Covenant, *Christianizing* them. However, in doing this, Covenant Theology completely destroys the uniqueness of the believer's New Covenant position "in Christ" as our High Priest and the uniqueness of the priesthood of the believer "in Christ."

Hebrews 9:10 tells us the Old Covenant was an imposition "until the time of reformation." This does not refer to *thee* Reformation. The word "reformation" is translated from the Greek word *diorthosis* (dee-or'-tho-sis). It means to *thoroughly straighten*, like setting a broken bone. The Old Covenant was imperfect in its types. People were easily led astray from its intended purposes. The New Covenant "in Christ" is intended to *straighten out* all the Old Covenant imperfections.

Dispelling the Shadows for the Reality of Christ

"[11] But Christ being come an high priest of good things to come, by a greater and more perfect tabernacle, not made with hands, that is to say, not of this building; [12] Neither by the blood of goats and calves, but by his own blood he entered in once into the holy place, having obtained eternal redemption *for us*. [13] For if the blood of bulls and of goats, and the ashes of an heifer sprinkling the unclean, sanctifieth to the purifying of the flesh: [14] How much more shall the blood of Christ, who through the eternal Spirit offered himself without spot to God, purge your conscience from dead works to serve the living God? [15] And for this cause he is the mediator of the new testament, that by means of death, for the redemption of the transgressions *that were* under the first testament, they which are called might receive the promise of eternal inheritance" (Hebrew 9:11-15).

New Covenant worship and ministry is not about *types* and *shadows*. The ministry of new priesthood of the New Covenant is not about endless sacrifices, rituals, liturgies, and holy days. The

New Covenant is not about a small piece of real estate in the Mid-East, about political controls, or about Theonomically ushering in a utopian kingdom on earth where God rules through an Ecclesiastical body.

> The New Covenant is about the supernatural and *enabling grace* of God released into the world through the propitiation of God and regeneration of lost sinners. Sinners are saved "by grace through faith" in a finished work of Christ, which grace is manifested to the world through the lives of believer priests as they are "filled" with the Spirit of God. Upon the filling of the believer with the Spirit of God, He overflows through their lives producing the "fruit of the Spirit." This results in souls being won to Christ and discipled to the glory of God.

"Being come" and "of good things to come" (Hebrews 9:11) shows the *intermediary state* of the Church Age. It is not the Old Covenant of Mosaic Law with its Sacerdotalism and unending sacrifices and Holy Days, but neither is it yet the Kingdom Age where Christ rules on earth from the throne of David. The Church Age is an *intermediary stage* of the *already, not yet* implementation of the New Covenant. Christ is the High Priest of things that have already come into practice in the Church Age and He is High Priest of other "good things to come" in the Kingdom Age. All of these things are part of the New Covenant promises that are part of a New Covenant believer's "so great salvation."

The benefits of the New Covenant believer's position "in Christ" as a believer priest are unfolding in nature and will increase dramatically in the historical paradigms of the Rapture, Marriage Supper of the Lamb, second Coming of Christ to earth at Armageddon with His Bride, and the establishment of His Kingdom on earth, where His glorified Bride will rule and reign with Him as a *kingdom of priests.* The New Covenant has "come" in our High Priest Jesus Christ and His finished work of redemption (*are already*), but all of its benefits are *yet to come.*

The point of "being come" and "of good things to come" (Hebrews 9:11) is that Christ *already* is part of this literal and heavenly existence as the victorious God/man. This is a testimony to the "surety" that belongs to all believers that are "in Christ." Although there is an *already* aspect of the New Covenant that is *already* in place, the *not yet* aspect that is to come is a "surety."

"[17] For he testifieth, Thou *art* a priest for ever after the order of Melchisedec. [18] For there is verily a disannulling of the commandment going before for the weakness and unprofitableness thereof. [19] For the law made nothing perfect, but the bringing in of a better hope *did*; by the which we draw nigh unto God. [20] And inasmuch as not without an oath *he was made priest*: [21] (For those priests were made without an oath; but this with an oath by him that said unto him, The Lord sware and will not repent, Thou *art* a priest for ever after the order of Melchisedec:) [22] <u>By so much was Jesus made a surety of a better testament</u>. [23] And they truly were many priests, because they were not suffered to continue by reason of death: [24] But this *man*, because he continueth ever, hath an unchangeable priesthood. [25] Wherefore he is able also to save them to the uttermost that come unto God by him, seeing he ever liveth to make intercession for them. [26] For such an high priest became us, *who is* holy, harmless, undefiled, separate from sinners, and made higher than the heavens; [27] Who needeth not daily, as those high priests, to offer up sacrifice, first for his own sins, and then for the people's: for this he did once, when he offered up himself" (Hebrews 7:17-27).

In Hebrews 9:11, we step completely out of the Old Covenant (*the shadows*) as described in vs. 1-10 of chapter nine and we step into the glories of the relation of the New Covenant in Christ. In the New Covenant, there are no more types and no more shadows. Christ Jesus is portrayed as the actual and literal fulfillment of all of which the Old Covenant was merely a shadow.

"[11] And every priest standeth daily ministering and offering oftentimes the same sacrifices, which can never take away sins: [12] But this man, after he had offered one sacrifice for sins for ever, sat down on the right hand of God; [13] From henceforth expecting till his enemies be made his footstool. [14] For by one offering he hath perfected for ever them that are sanctified" (Hebrews 10:11-14).

According to Hebrews 8:5, the Old Covenant Tabernacle was just a "shadow of heavenly things." Shadows are not realities. The analogy is that no one walks into a room and talks to the shadows of people on the wall. Yet, there are so many professing

Christians who still live in the *shadows* of the Old Covenant practices still worshipping, or trying to worship, in types and through symbols. That kind of "worship" is no longer acceptable in that the real thing is here.

"²¹ Jesus saith unto her, Woman, believe me, the hour cometh, when ye shall neither in this mountain, nor yet at Jerusalem, worship the Father. ²² Ye worship ye know not what: we know what we worship: for salvation is of the Jews. ²³ But the hour cometh, and now is, when the true worshippers shall worship the Father in spirit and in truth: for the Father seeketh such to worship him. ²⁴ God *is* a Spirit: and they that worship him <u>must</u> worship *him* in spirit and in truth" (John 4:21-24).

The Old Covenant looked forward in great anticipation and expectation to the literal *fulfillment* of all the *shadows* of heavenly things. The Old Covenant had only an earthly calling. The New Covenant has a heavenly calling (3:1). The reality of the New Covenant is that the promised Messiah of the Old Covenant has come in the person of Jesus. He was crucified for the judicial payment of all sin (a death sentence). He is risen from the dead as proof of the acceptability of His sacrifice before God, His victory over death itself, is glorified and ascended to the heavenly (*literal* or *real* tabernacle, Hebrews 9:11, "not made with hands"), and is not part of this earthly creation.

Once the resurrection and ascension happened, Jesus sent forth the Holy Spirit as He promised He would and baptized all believers into Him (I Corinthians 12:13). In doing so, each believer positionally shares in a heavenly fellowship with the Father, presently having the eternal life of Jesus and positionally lives with Him in His heavenly place. One day we will actually live with Him in Heaven (John 14:1-3). After the Millennial Kingdom and the creation of a new Heaven and new Earth, the whole heavenly Jerusalem will descend out of Heaven to the new Heaven/Earth (Revelations 21:9-22:5). This new Heaven/Earth is part of every believer's eternal inheritance. It is the reality of which the Old Covenant was merely a type. The Kingdom Age is only a partial fulfillment of that type.

Eternal life is more than just the life God possesses. Eternal life is another existence generated by God's presence. In the book of Hebrews, Old Covenant believers are told to step out of the *shadows* of the Old Covenant types and into the light of the New

Covenant reality. If the truth of the New Covenant reality is hidden, it is hidden only to those who remain lost in shadows of the Old Covenant.

"[3] But if our gospel be hid, it is hid to them that are lost: [4] In whom the god of this world hath blinded the minds of them which believe not, lest the light of the glorious gospel of Christ, who is the image of God, should shine unto them" (II Corinthians 4:3-4).

Hebrews 9:12 tells us that the blood of Christ provides access to the presence of God for all believers. Jesus does not enter heaven by virtue of His Sonship alone. Jesus does not enter the heavenly Tabernacle by virtue of being the Creator of all things. He enters the heavenly Tabernacle as our personal High Priest, having offered one final, never to be repeated, and never needing repetition sacrifice.

Jesus did not enter the heavenly Holy of Holies with the "blood of goats and calves," but "His own blood." The theological implication is that this He has done "once" for all, making complete redemption available to "whosoever will." Note the finality of this offering (Hebrews 9:12). He has entered "once." That one sacrifice offered on the Cross of Calvary over two-thousand years ago made all those once separated from God by sin "nigh by the blood of Christ" (Ephesians 2:13).

The only way to the *heavenly promise land* of God, the Heavenly Jerusalem, and the Heavenly Tabernacle is through the blood of Christ. The "once for all" Cross-work of Christ takes all of our past failures and sins and delivers us cleansed into the eternal redemption that is ours in Christ. That redemption has already been obtained and is our present possession in Jesus Christ (v. 12).

Hebrews 9:13 tells us the Old Covenant types pointed to Christ, but there was never any real consciousness in those "shadows" that sin was ever really removed in any final sense. It was only a ceremonial cleansing of the "flesh" (externalism). It could never touch the heart where real sin condemned the conscience. The Cross-work of Christ cleanses the conscience (Hebrews 9:14).

The cleansing of the conscience was for a purpose. If a person can understand the completeness of the adjudication of the "wages of sin" in the crucifixion of Jesus Christ, that person can then understand the complete forgiveness that is available to the believer in Christ. The paradox of verse nineteen is that this cleansing should also cleanse our conscience, alleviating the need for the endless and hopeless dead works of the Old Covenant in the constant and "perpetual" sacrifices. This is the great heresy of the Roman Catholic Eucharist (the Sacrament of Holy Communion). It propagates a "perpetual sacrifice."

> "The celebration of the Eucharist is the action of both Christ and His Church. 'For in it Christ **perpetuates** (emphasis mine) in an unbloody manner the sacrifice offered on the cross, offering himself to the Father for the world's salvation through the ministry of priests. The Church, the spouse and minister of Christ, performs together with him the role priest and victim, offers him to the Father and at the same time makes a total offering of herself with him.' (*Eucharisticum Mysterium, Instruction on the Worship of the Eucharistic Mystery*)"[30]

"Dead works" were the vain efforts of those under the perversion of the Old Covenant to relieve a troubled conscience by legal obedience to a system that only condemned them. When we serve out of "duty," or because it is our *cross to bear*, we serve out of the carnality of "dead works." Only in an understanding of the complete propitiation that is ours in Christ can we truly "serve the living God." Why do you think that so many Christian martyrs of early Christianity gloried in being able to die for Christ? They did so because they viewed themselves as God's *sheep*.

> "[35] Who shall separate us from the love of Christ? *shall* tribulation, or distress, or persecution, or famine, or nakedness, or peril, or sword? [36] As it is written, For thy sake we are killed all the day long; we are accounted as sheep for the slaughter. [37] Nay, in all these things we are more than conquerors through him that loved us. [38] For I am persuaded, that neither death, nor life, nor angels, nor principalities, nor powers, nor things present, nor things to come, [39] Nor height, nor depth, nor any other creature, shall be able to separate us from the love of God, which is in Christ Jesus our Lord (Romans 8:35-37).

The persecutors could not *threaten* Christians with Heaven. A threat of Heaven was all that death was to them. Death was deliverance unto glory and into the presence of God.

---

[30] Ibid., page 369.

DISCUSSION QUESTIONS

1. List and define the four inadequate Old Covenant ways that people tried to approach God in worship.

2. List some of the *replacements* modern *Christianity* has invented to approach God in worship.

3. Read Acts 7:44-50 and Acts 17:22- 25. Discuss why *buildings* or *church houses* are not places where God *dwells*.

4. Read I Corinthians 3:16-17 and I Corinthians 6:19-20. List and define the two different entities that are referred to as God's Temple in these two texts.

5. Explain the *sacrament of ordination* and why it is a great contradiction against the priesthood of all believers "in Christ."

6. Read Hebrew 9:11-15. Compare this to the statement of Christ in John 4:24, "God *is* a Spirit: and they that worship him must worship *him* in spirit and in truth" and discuss the differences between worshipping *shadows* and worshipping the reality of Christ.

7. Discuss the Theological implications and ramifications of the fact that Jesus did not enter the heavenly Holy of Holies with the "blood of goats and calves," but "His own blood" as this relates to the cleansing of the believer's conscience before God.

Chapter Sixty-four
Local Church Discipline:
The Ananias and Sapphira Phenomenon

"[1] But a certain man named Ananias, with Sapphira his wife, sold a possession, [2] And kept back *part* of the price, his wife also being privy *to it*, and brought a certain part, and laid *it* at the apostles' feet. [3] But Peter said, Ananias, why hath Satan filled thine heart to lie to the Holy Ghost, and to keep back *part* of the price of the land? [4] Whiles it remained, was it not thine own? and after it was sold, was it not in thine own power? why hast thou conceived this thing in thine heart? thou hast not lied unto men, but unto God. [5] And Ananias hearing these words fell down, and gave up the ghost: and great fear came on all them that heard these things. [6] And the young men arose, wound him up, and carried *him* out, and buried *him*. [7] And it was about the space of three hours after, when his wife, not knowing what was done, came in. [8] And Peter answered unto her, Tell me whether ye sold the land for so much? And she said, Yea, for so much. [9] Then Peter said unto her, How is it that ye have agreed together to tempt the Spirit of the Lord? behold, the feet of them which have buried thy husband *are* at the door, and shall carry thee out. [10] Then fell she down straightway at his feet, and yielded up the ghost: and the young men came in, and found her dead, and, carrying *her* forth, buried *her* by her husband. [11] And great fear came upon all the church, and upon as many as heard these things. [12] And by the hands of the apostles were many signs and wonders wrought among the people; (and they were all with one accord in Solomon's porch. [13] And of the rest durst no man join himself to them: but the people magnified them. [14] And believers were the more added to the Lord, multitudes both of men and women.)" (Acts 5:1-14).

We might entitle these few verses of Scripture *A Conspiracy in Spiritual Deception*. Much of what we find in the fifth Gospel (the Book of Acts) is transitional in nature. It transitions from the Dispensation of the Law and the Mosaic Covenant to the Dispensation of the Church and the initiation of the New Covenant. We must understand that what we see in Acts two and Acts five were essentially signs to the Jews showing the radical differences between God's heightened expectations for New Covenant believers. This is compared to His lesser expectations of believers under the Mosaic Covenant. Because of the distortion of the doctrine of Grace, most evangelicals see the New Covenant as just the opposite; i.e., a lowering of God's expectations under the New Covenant of Grace.

Acts 5:1-14 give us God's perspective of how the New Covenant is to be administrated in a cooperative venture of joint participation between God and local congregations of Spirit-filled believers. Central to our understanding of this cooperative venture of joint participation with God in the administration of the local church is the overwhelming reality that *God sees*. In other words, there may be things that get by the *eyes of justice* in congregational polity. Nonetheless, these kinds of things will not get beyond the eyes of the *God who sees*. God may choose to act directly in the matters of spiritual deception as He did in the case of Ananias and Sapphira.

The Word of God commands believers to obey the Lord out of "fear of the LORD" on numerous occasions and under many different situations. A proper understanding of the righteousness of God, His hatred of any kind of iniquity, and His complete unwillingness to show *inequality* in His dealing with sinners generates a sincere and real fear of God. A lack of fear of God reveals ignorance of God regarding these aspects of His holy character. Even when a believer genuinely loves the Lord, there still should be a reverential fear and awe of who He is and the absolute power He has to deal with our lives according to His will.

"[5] And he set judges in the land throughout all the fenced cities of Judah, city by city, [6] And said to the judges, Take heed what ye do: for ye judge not for man, but for the LORD, who *is* with you in the judgment. [7] Wherefore now let the fear of the LORD be upon you; take heed and do *it*: for *there is* no iniquity with the LORD our God, nor respect of persons, nor taking of gifts. [8] Moreover in Jerusalem did Jehoshaphat set of the Levites, and *of* the priests, and of the chief of the fathers of Israel, for the judgment of the LORD, and for controversies, when they returned to Jerusalem. [9] And he charged them, saying, Thus shall ye do in the fear of the LORD, faithfully, and with a perfect heart. [10] And what cause soever shall come to you of your brethren that dwell in their cities, between blood and blood, between law and commandment, statutes and judgments, <u>ye shall even warn them that they trespass not against the LORD, and <i>so</i> wrath come upon you, and upon your brethren: this do, and ye shall not trespass.</u> [11] And, behold, Amariah the chief priest <i>is</i> over you in all matters of the LORD; and Zebadiah the son of Ishmael, the ruler of the house of Judah, for all the king's matters: also the Levites <i>shall be</i> officers before you. Deal courageously, and the LORD shall be with the good" (II Chronicles 19:5-11).

Under previous kings of Israel, the matters of justice and righteousness had fallen into the hands of corruption. The nation of Israel was divided after the death of Solomon into the Northern Kingdom, which came to be known as Israel. The Southern Kingdom was comprised of the tribes of Judah and Benjamin, which came to be known simply as Judah. Solomon had led the people of Israel into almost total idolatry. Although he repented of his foolishness at the end of his life, the spiritual damage he caused would take generations to repair. Some would go as far as to say that Israel never recovered from Solomon's failures.

The Jehoshaphat of II Chronicles 19:8 was the son of king Asa and, in most part, followed in the footsteps of his righteous father. Other than political alliances with two kings of the paganized Northern Kingdom, king Ahab (II Chronicles 19:2) and king Ahaziah (II Chronicles 20:35), Jehoshaphat brought great spiritual reforms to Judah and the restoration of the Law and the administration of the Mosaic Covenant. II Chronicles 19:5-11 details the way God intended the administration/stewardship of the Mosaic Covenant under the Dispensation of the Law. Throughout the nation of Israel and, in every major city ("fenced cities," v. 5), God ordained that "judges" be put into office to adjudicate the matters of the statutes of God's Law in both civil matters and criminal matters. In Jerusalem, we might say there was a <i>Supreme Court</i> of Chief priests that ruled over the city of Jerusalem and appeals from other areas.

It is not my intent to get bogged down in the details of the administration of the Mosaic Covenant under the Dispensation of the Law. My intent is to show three specifics regarding polity in the administration of the Law that transition into the Church Age and the administration of the New Covenant in Congregational Polity.

1. The administration/adjudication of the Mosaic Covenant was performed by the priesthood in every locality.

585

2. Both civil matters and criminal matters were adjudicated.

3. There is the need to maintain the *God sees* perspective.

The emphasis in II Chronicles 19:5-11 is upon the administration of the Mosaic Covenant in restoring justice and righteousness before God. Those involved in the administration were to maintain the *God sees* perspective and the resulting fear of God's judgment upon them should they fail to be faithful in their responsibilities. All three of these matters transition into the administration of the New Covenant through local churches and through Congregational Polity of the priesthood of all Church Age believers.

The spiritual dynamic involved in the administration of the New Covenant through local churches and through Congregational Polity of the Priesthood of all Church Age believers is critical to the definition of a local church. If the *Church* is merely a *physical organization*, rather than a *spiritual organism*, then the definition of the *Church* is misdirected to an emphasis upon *organizational structure* rather than upon the *spiritual qualifications for membership* and *involvement* in the administrational responsibilities of the New Covenant. Before Congregational Polity can function according to its defined and intended spiritual dynamic of Holy Spirit-filled and guided membership, there must be some qualifications met by individuals. These must be met before they are united in formal membership within the *spiritual organism* that constitutes any local church. Each individual should be carefully examined by the officers of the local church and then by the congregation of the local church to insure they are qualified to become part of the *spiritual organism* of a local church. Every individual should be carefully examined for two basic evidences of the "new creation":

1. Every person should be examined regarding a genuine testimony of salvation that is marked by a historical event when he repented of sin and dead works, understood and believed the Gospel of a finished work of redemption through the blood of Jesus Christ, confessed Jesus to be God (Jehovah), called on the name of Jesus to be saved, and received the person of the Lord Jesus into their body in the person of the indwelling Holy Spirit of God.

2. Every person should be examined regarding his understanding of water baptism, his determination to "die daily" to the "old man" and live each day to the glory of God in the supernatural enabling of the indwelling Spirit of God through yielding to Him (Romans 6:11-13), and becoming "doers of the Word" (James 1:22).

As these two matters of the *spiritual dynamic* of local church membership are considered, other points of emphasis also become important. There also needs to be some kind of assurance that doctrinal purity is maintained. According to the New Covenant epistles, we see that doctrinal error entered into Christianity in the very first century of its birth. The vast majority of the teachings of the Apostles in the epistles to local churches were for the purpose of correcting false doctrine and for maintaining purity of doctrine among the membership of local churches. Those holding false doctrine were to be excluded from the assembly just as were those who refused to be separated from sin and worldliness. The congregation (formal membership) was responsible for maintaining doctrinal purity and practical purity among their own constituency.

"[17] Now I beseech you, brethren, mark them which cause divisions and offences <u>contrary to **the** doctrine</u> which ye have learned; and avoid them. [18] For they that are such serve not our Lord Jesus Christ, but their own belly; and by good words and fair speeches deceive the hearts of the simple. [19] For your obedience is come abroad unto all *men*. I am glad therefore on your behalf: but yet I would have you wise unto that which is good, and simple concerning evil. [20] And the God of peace shall bruise Satan under your feet shortly. The grace of our Lord Jesus Christ *be* with you. Amen." (Romans 16:17-20).

"[7] For many deceivers are entered into the world, who confess not that Jesus Christ is come in the flesh. This is a deceiver and an antichrist. [8] <u>Look to yourselves,</u> that we lose not those things which we have wrought, but that we receive a full reward. [9] <u>Whosoever transgresseth, and abideth not in the doctrine of Christ, hath not God. He that abideth in the doctrine of Christ, he hath both the Father and the Son.</u> [10] If there come any unto you, and bring not this doctrine, receive him not into *your* house {*the churches at this time met in households of members*}, neither bid him God speed: [11] For he that biddeth him God speed is partaker of his evil deeds" (II John 1:7-10).

Maintaining purity of doctrine was not just the responsibility of the pastors. Every individual member within a local congregation was responsible to deal with false doctrine should it arise in the local church through one of the members. Visiting preachers were to be carefully examined to insure they held to orthodox doctrine (the teaching or "the doctrine of Christ"). The "doctrine of Christ" was not merely the teachings of Jesus in the Gospels, but all that the Scriptures revealed about the Promised One from Genesis 3:15 to Revelation 22:21. This included all that the Apostles taught regarding Christ in all of the epistles. Every member was responsible to know doctrine, to be able to discern false doctrine when it was being taught, and address that false teaching.

Another part of the Congregation Polity as a responsibility of the Priesthood of all Church Age believers is the responsibility to maintain moral purity among the formal membership (those who have agreed to be held accountable within the context of formal membership that began initially at the time of their water baptism). Both the doctrinal and moral purity of a local church are of utmost importance to God.

"[1] From whence *come* wars and fightings among you? *come they* not hence, *even* of your lusts that war in your members? [2] Ye lust, and have not: ye kill, and desire to have, and cannot obtain: ye fight and war, yet ye have not, because ye ask not. [3] Ye ask, and receive not, because ye ask amiss, that ye may consume *it* upon your lusts. [4] Ye adulterers and adulteresses, know ye not that the friendship {*philia, fondness*} of the world is enmity with God? whosoever therefore will be {*is inclined or disposed to be*} a friend of the world is the enemy of God. [5] Do ye think that the scripture saith in vain, The spirit that dwelleth in us lusteth to envy? [6] But he giveth more grace. Wherefore he saith, God resisteth the proud, but giveth grace unto the humble. [7] Submit yourselves therefore to God. Resist the devil, and he will flee from you. [8] Draw nigh to God, and he will draw nigh to you. Cleanse *your* hands, *ye* sinners; and purify *your* hearts, *ye* double minded. [9] Be afflicted, and mourn, and weep: let your laughter be turned to mourning, and *your* joy to heaviness. [10] Humble yourselves in the sight of the Lord, and he shall lift you up" (James 4:1-10).

James was the senior pastor of the local church of Jerusalem. Although this local church had membership in the thousands, they probably met in numerous households with an associate pastor assigned to that *household church.* James' epistle is a *general epistle* written to the Jewish believers and addressed "to the twelve tribes which are scattered abroad." Other than the two epistles to the Thessalonians, written in about 54 A.D., the epistle of James is the second earliest epistle, written about 60 A.D. Yet even in these first few decades of Christianity and the beginnings of the New Covenant governance of local churches in Congregational Polity, we find that there were issues of both doctrinal error and moral impurity going on.

The address to "adulterers and adulteresses" in James 4:4 addresses the issue of *spiritual fornication* in the issues of *worldliness.* The admonition addresses the definitive nature of even flirting with *worldliness* or wanting to look *like,* live *like,* or be *like* paganized people.

A Christian's priorities should not be the same as a worldly person, should not be temporal in life's focuses, and should not even lean in the direction of being *like* the world. In other words, there should be a complete and distinct peculiarity about everything a Christian does in the way we dress, invest our money and resources, and our time (Titus 2:14; I Peter 2:9). This peculiarity defines a Spirit-filled life and should be obvious and easily apparent to everyone.

No one can rejoice over the wonderfulness of the Saviour until he is repulsed by the horribleness of his own sin. The quest for moral purity touches upon and exposes many avenues and levels of worldliness. Paganism perverted cultures on a wide scale and at numerous levels of corruption. The most predominant perversion was sexual perversion. Worldliness is not merely an undefined concept, nor is the term ambiguous. Within the pagan Roman culture, some of the predominant forms of *worldliness* were:

1. Avarice or Covetousness: the insatiable desire for wealth and power leading to unrestrained excesses in living in luxury and extravagance

2. Lusts: consumed with fulfilling personal passions (lusts) in pursuit of pleasure and recreation. This person *lives to play*. The common name for this is Hedonism.

3. Apathy or Indifference: today this is expressed in the reply to serious inquiry with the phrase *Whatever*. Nothing is to be taken too seriously and the matters of God are usually at the top of the list regarding indifference.

4. Pessimism or Depression: this usually results from chronic narcissism and cynicism. It is a hopeless view of personal existence often resulting in suicide.

5. Sloth: this is the hatred of work to the point of avoiding anything that comes close to doing something one does not enjoy or in which one finds pleasure. Sloth goes beyond laziness. It is the failure, in varying degrees, of working to fully realize and utilize one's abilities and talents to the glory of God.

6. Wrath: varying degrees of unrestrained anger resulting in varying degrees of warfare and personal animosity towards those with which a person is angry.

7. Pride: this is the exalted view of one's self that desires worship or glory from others. Pride is the ultimate form of idolatry in that it exalts one's own image to a place deserved only by God. Pride is the opposite of humility and is willing to go to enormous extremes to protect the image created by pride and for the purposes of glory seeking. This was Satan's sin; "I will be like the most High" (Isaiah 14:14).

Throughout the Scriptures, believers are admonished to rebuke and reprove one another for worldliness, false doctrine, and for wrong attitudes and actions regarding sin. In I Corinthians 5:1-13, the Apostle Paul admonishes and rebukes the whole local church at Corinth for their failure to deal with ongoing sin within their formal membership. Such failures are common among many local churches of today. The failures are justified by a rationalization that dealing *harshly* with unrepentant sinners is *unloving*. This is the same rational of those who object to capital punishment in the judicial system of our government with satirical statement: *how are they going to learn if you don't kill them*? Local church discipline is a judicial matter that God has put in the hands of the local church to be administrated through Congregational Polity. Local churches cannot merely shirk that responsibility because it is unpleasant and sometimes seems harsh.

"[1] It is reported {*present, passive, it is being heard*} commonly {*it is general knowledge everywhere*} *that there is* fornication {*porneia, a word used to describe a wide range of sexual immorality*} among you, and such fornication as is not so much as named among the Gentiles, that one {*the type of porneia is now specified*} should have his father's wife. [2] And ye are puffed up {*haughty, the idea is putting one's own rational above God's commands; there were some justifying the inaction of the church and the action of the sinner*}, and have not rather mourned {*lament over the shamefulness of it all*}, that he that hath done this deed might be taken away {*removed or put away by God's chastisement in such a manner as to reflect God's hatred for the corruption of the spiritual dynamic of a Spirit-filled congregation*} from among you. [3] For I verily, as absent in body, but present in spirit, have judged already {*made a conclusive decision regarding the case and the sentence*}, as though I were present, *concerning* him that hath so done this deed, [4] In the name of our Lord Jesus Christ {*the word 'name' expresses the idea of the transposition of authority of our High Priest, Jesus Christ, to the local church acting as a priesthood of believers through congregational polity with the authority to take extreme action regarding the unrepentant sinner*}, when ye are gathered together {*as part of their regular times of assembly*}, and my spirit {*as an Apostle, Paul had the authority to command the action in himself, however he wants the local church to act and fulfill their responsibilities in Congregational polity*}, with the power {*dunamis, the supernatural enabling power and authority*} of our Lord Jesus Christ, [5] To deliver {*see I Timothy 1:20, the context refers to expulsion from local church membership so that the whole 'body' is not chastised; I Corinthians 11:29-33*} such an one unto Satan for the destruction of the flesh {*for whatever remedial punishment that God releases into Satan's distribution*}, that the spirit may be saved in the day of the Lord Jesus {*the issue is not one of eternal damnation, but of remedial punishment within time; the ultimate goal is the reformation of the sinner to self-discipline rather than his ultimate destruction*}. [6] Your glorying *is* not good. Know ye not that a little leaven leaveneth the whole lump? [7] Purge out therefore the old leaven, that ye may be a new lump, as ye are unleavened. For even Christ our passover is sacrificed for us: [8] Therefore let us keep the feast, not with old leaven, neither with the leaven of malice and wickedness; but with the unleavened *bread* of sincerity and truth. [9] I wrote unto you in an epistle not to company

591
WWW.DISCIPLEMAKERMINISTRIES.ORG

with fornicators: [10] Yet not altogether with the fornicators of this world {*lost people*}, or with the covetous, or extortioners, or with idolaters; for then must ye needs go out of the world. [11] But now I have written unto you not to keep company, if any man that is called a brother {*the idea is in the context of local church membership*} be a fornicator, or covetous, or an idolater, or a railer, or a drunkard, or an extortioner; with such an one no not to eat. [12] For what have I to do to judge them also that are without? do not ye judge them that are within? [13] But them that are without God judgeth. <u>Therefore put away from among yourselves that wicked person</u>" (I Corinthians 5:1-13).

I Corinthians 5:5 details a transitional issue from the Mosaic Covenant under the Dispensation of the Law to the New Covenant under the Dispensation of Grace (the Church Age). This transitional issue is exemplified in the Ananias and Sapphira phenomenon found in Acts chapter five. If local churches were still administrated under the Law, there would be a big pile of very large rocks out behind every *church house*. When someone would refuse to repent and continue to bring disgrace to the name of Christ through false doctrine or through an immoral lifestyle, that person would simply be taken out behind the *church house* and stoned to death by every member of the local church. Local churches do not deal with unrepentant members in this way during the New Covenant and through Congregational Polity. When another member refuses to repent of false doctrine or immorality, that person is to be *excommunicated* from the local church. This *excommunication* is a judicial action ordained by God and is done through Congregational Polity.

> A great misnomer regarding the transition between the administration of the Mosaic Covenant and the New Covenant is that God deals more *graciously* with unrepentant sinners during the Dispensation of Grace than he did during the Dispensation of the Law. The only difference is in the actual execution of the judicial sentence upon the unrepentant sinner.

Under the Dispensation of Law the execution of the judicial sentence prescribed by God or by an ordained judge was to be executed by the people of the city and particularly those who were the victims of the offender.

"[1] And the LORD spake unto Moses, saying, [2] Again, thou shalt say to the children of Israel, Whosoever *he be* of the children of Israel, or of the strangers that sojourn in Israel, that giveth *any* of his seed unto Molech; he shall surely be put to death: the people of the land shall stone him with stones" (Leviticus 20:1-2).

"[10] And the son of an Israelitish woman, whose father *was* an Egyptian, went out among the children of Israel: and this son of the Israelitish *woman* and a man of Israel strove together in the camp; [11] And the Israelitish woman's son blasphemed the name *of the LORD*, and cursed. And they brought him unto Moses: (and his mother's name *was* Shelomith, the daughter of Dibri, of the tribe of Dan:) [12] And they put him in ward {*under guard*}, that the mind of the LORD might be shewed them. [13] And the LORD spake unto Moses, saying, [14] Bring forth him that hath cursed without the camp; and let all that heard *him* lay their hands upon his head, and let all the congregation stone him. [15] And thou shalt speak unto the children of Israel, saying, Whosoever curseth his God shall bear his sin. [16] And he that blasphemeth the name of the LORD, he shall surely be put to death, *and* all the congregation shall certainly stone him: as well the stranger, as he that is born in the land, when he blasphemeth the name *of the LORD*, shall be put to death" (Leviticus 24:10-16).

Under the administration of the New Covenant, and during the Church Age, the individual members become the judges and remove the unrepentant sinner from church membership through Congregational Polity. This puts the matter in God's hands where He removes His *protective custody* upon Satan's forces of destruction. Then the forces of evil are released by degrees against the unrepentant sinner according to God's will. Sometimes this results in the premature death of the unrepentant sinner. Sometimes it may result in some *catastrophe of chastisement*. It may become a health issue, loss of a job, or any means God might use to *turn the heart* of the unrepentant sinner.

The responsibility of the local church and Congregational Polity is to act in fear of God for themselves should they fail to act decisively according to God's will and in the fear of God for the sinner who refuses to repent. In order for Congregational Polity to work, the congregation MUST ACT according to God's will, trusting that God will know exactly what is necessary in the sinner's life to *turn the sinner's heart.*

However, the primary concern of any decision regarding local church discipline is that God is not blasphemed or that reproach is not brought upon the name of the Lord by failure to act. In the instance of Ananias and Sapphira, the deception may never have been discovered and God's power and blessing upon the ministry of the local church at Jerusalem would have been lost just as it was in the case of Achan in Joshua chapter seven. God needed to expose the sin and the sinner, and He did!

Congregations that do not take the matters of unrepentant sin within their membership seriously, become passive in their role as priests before God. Then they fail in their judicial responsibilities of the Priesthood of all believers to keep the local church, their own order of the priesthood, pure from false doctrine and worldliness. The true spiritual growth of a local church membership is not measured by numbers, but by faithfulness to their responsibilities as defined by the Word of God. Failure in the responsibilities of local church discipline manifests a lack of love for God and a complete misunderstanding of the spiritual dynamic involved in God's supernatural enabling and blessing upon the work of the ministry of individuals within a local church. In the case of the circumstances of I Corinthians 5:1, "It is reported commonly *that there is* fornication among you, and such fornication as is not so much as named among the Gentiles, that one should have his father's wife." Here we have a local church trying to bring their pagan community to faith in Christ. They try to do so while allowing someone to be part of their testimony that is living in a way that would repulse even most of the pagans.

> Church discipline is like *gardening.* Everyone likes to *garden*, but nobody likes *to pull the weeds.*

Is there a "Blessing and Curse" in the New Covenant?

The "blessing and curse" of the Mosaic Covenant (Deuteronomy 11:26-32) had nothing to do with the salvation of individuals within the nation of Israel. The "blessing and curse" of the Mosaic Covenant was the means that God used to keep the nation of Israel accountable in *policing* themselves and individuals within their congregation. This applied to doctrinal purity, sin, and separation from the paganism of their surrounding nations. An important question that believers should answer is if the "blessing and curse" is unique to the Mosaic covenant. In other words, is there a "blessing and curse" included within other covenants and especially within the New Covenant?

Under the Dispensation of Innocence (Genesis 1:28-3:13), God had one governing commandment. In that one governing commandment of the Edenic Covenant we find both the "blessing and curse."

> "[15] And the LORD God took the man, and put him into the garden of Eden to dress it and to keep it. [16] And the LORD God commanded the man, saying, Of every tree of the garden thou mayest freely eat: [17] But of the tree of the knowledge of good and evil, thou shalt not eat of it: for in the day that thou eatest thereof thou shalt surely die" (Genesis 2:15-17).

Surely we can understand that this was not a condition for salvation, because Adam was not yet lost in that he had not yet sinned. God provided him with almost unlimited and renewable resources in the "garden of Eden." All Adam had to do was "dress it and keep it." Of course, the *curse* in this instance is the ultimate curse of eternal damnation. In order to be restored to fellowship with God, Adam and Eve needed to get saved and "born again" "by grace through faith," according to the Protevangelium of Genesis 3:15.

Under the Dispensation of Conscience (Genesis 3:23-7:23), God instituted the "blessing and curse" of the Adamic Covenant. Although we may not easily see the "blessing" of the Adamic Covenant, it exists in the mere fact that God allowed them to be redeemed, and that He continued to provide for them in the ecosystem of His creation. They could have merely been eternally condemned and God could have just created a new creation that excluded Satan, fallen angels, and fallen humans. The important thing to see here is that we are created as eternal beings and God's loving and gracious continuation within the fallen creation is an overwhelming action of "blessing" in grace. That does not mean that there would not be remedial consequences for sin. Those remedial consequences have fallen upon all of the fallen creation and continue into eternity. Only the redeemed will escape the eternal remedial consequences of the Adamic Covenant.

"[14] And the LORD God said unto the serpent, Because thou hast done this, thou *art* cursed above all cattle, and above every beast of the field; upon thy belly shalt thou go, and dust shalt thou eat all the days of thy life: [15] And I will put enmity between thee and the woman, and between thy seed and her seed; it shall bruise thy head, and thou shalt bruise his heel. [16] Unto the woman he said, I will greatly multiply thy sorrow and thy conception; in sorrow thou shalt bring forth children; and thy desire *shall be* to thy husband, and he shall rule over thee. [17] And unto Adam he said, Because thou hast hearkened unto the voice of thy wife, and hast eaten of the tree, of which I commanded thee, saying, Thou shalt not eat of it: cursed *is* the ground for thy sake; in sorrow shalt thou eat *of* it all the days of thy life; [18] Thorns also and thistles shall it bring forth to thee; and thou shalt eat the herb of the field; [19] In the sweat of thy face shalt thou eat bread, till thou return unto the ground; for out of it wast thou taken: for dust thou *art*, and unto dust shalt thou return" (Genesis 3:14-19).

Under the Dispensation of Human Government (Genesis 8:20-11:9), God instituted the governance of the "blessing and curse" of the Noahic Covenant. The "blessing" of the Noahic Covenant is that God would never again destroy mankind with a flood as He did in the Noahic Flood. However, God now made mankind (all descendants of Noah and his sons) accountable for governing themselves in the taking of a life (murder) of another human being. Humans became accountable for justice and adjudication of the injustice of murder.

"[1] And God blessed Noah and his sons, and said unto them, Be fruitful, and multiply, and replenish the earth. [2] And the fear of you and the dread of you shall be upon every beast of the earth, and upon every fowl of the air, upon all that moveth *upon* the earth, and upon all the fishes of the sea; into your hand are they delivered. [3] Every moving thing that liveth shall be meat for you; even as the green herb have I given you all things. [4] But flesh with the life thereof, *which is* the blood thereof, shall ye not eat. [5] And surely your blood of your lives will I require; at the hand of every beast will I require it, and at the hand of man; at the hand of every man's brother will I require the life of man. [6] Whoso sheddeth man's blood, by man shall his blood be shed: for in the image of God made he man. [7] And you, be ye fruitful, and multiply; bring forth abundantly in the earth, and multiply therein. [8] And God spake unto Noah, and to his sons with him, saying, [9] And I, behold, I establish my covenant with you, and with your seed after you; [10] And with every living creature that *is* with you, of the fowl, of the cattle, and of every beast of the earth with you; from all that go out of the ark, to every beast of the earth. [11] And I will establish my covenant with you; neither shall all flesh be cut off any more by the waters of a flood; neither shall there any more be a flood to destroy the earth. [12] And God said, This *is* the token of the covenant which I make between me and you and every living creature that *is* with you, for perpetual generations: [13] I do set my bow in the cloud, and it shall be for a token of a covenant between me and the earth. [14] And it shall come to pass, when I bring a cloud over the earth, that the bow shall be seen in the cloud: [15] And I will remember my covenant, which *is* between me and you and every living creature of all flesh; and the waters shall no more become a flood to destroy all flesh. [16] And the bow shall be in the cloud; and I will look upon it, that I may remember the everlasting covenant between God and every living creature of all flesh that *is* upon the earth. [17] And God said unto Noah, This *is* the token of the covenant, which I have established between me and all flesh that *is* upon the earth" (Genesis 9:1-17).

The "blessing and curse" of the Mosaic Covenant was added to the Abrahamic Covenant "because of transgressions" (Galatians 3:19). We must understand that the New Covenant is merely a *change* in the Abrahamic Covenant and a *dispensational upgrade* of the Mosaic Covenant. The "blessing and curse" continues in the New Covenant. God *blesses* His children when they are faithful and *withdraws* His blessings (defining the "curse") when they are unfaithful. Although there is an individual aspect of this "blessing and curse" for faithfulness, the primary impact during the Church Age relates to God's spiritual blessings upon the ministry of any given local church.

"[29] For he that eateth and drinketh unworthily {*living in disobedience to the commands of Scripture in unrepentant sin*}, eateth and drinketh damnation {*the idea is chastisement, not eternal damnation*} to himself {*personally*}, not discerning the {*impact of his sin upon the*} Lord's body {*the local church*}. [30] For this cause many {*within the local church as the result of the withdrawal of God's protective custody and blessings*} *are* weak and sickly among you, and many sleep. [31] For if we {*not ye individually, but we corporately*} would judge ourselves, we should not be judged. [32]

But when we are judged, <u>we are chastened of the Lord</u>, that we should not be condemned with the world. [33] Wherefore, my brethren, when ye come together to eat, tarry one for another {*The issue of tarrying for one another is connected to the self-examination aspect of the Lord's Supper in its intended purpose of remembering what it cost to redeem our souls insuring reverence for God through maintaining internal purity within the body of Christ. In other words, the Lord's Supper should not be tacked onto the end of a service, but should be the primary focus insuring that there is regular time spent in self-examination of one's life before the eyes of the God who sees.*}" (I Corinthians 11:29-33).

From the context of I Corinthians 11:1-28, the admonitions for discernment regarding the "Lord's body" (I Corinthians 11:29) is clearly referring to the impact of an individual believer's sinful lifestyle upon God's blessing upon the work of the ministry of those formally united to a local church. This "curse" upon "eating and drinking" in participation in the local church ordinance of the Lord's Supper with unconfessed sin in one's life would manifest itself through God's withdrawal of His protective custody over the membership of a local church. The withdrawal of God's protective custody resulted in "many" becoming "weak and sickly among you" (I Corinthians 11:30). God's curse upon the failure to maintain personal and local church purity through self-examination, confession, repentance, and God's restoration through the cleansing of *familial forgiveness* extended beyond the individual committing the sin into the whole congregation.

We can go as far as to say that Christ's instructions in Matthew chapters five, six, and seven define the "blessing and curse" expectations of the New Covenant that began on the Day of Pentecost and continues throughout the Church age.

DISCUSSION QUESTIONS

1. Discuss why Acts 5:1-14 might be entitled *A Conspiracy in Spiritual Deception.*

2. Central to our understanding of this cooperative venture of joint participation with God in the administration of the local church is the overwhelming reality of the fact that *God sees.* Discuss why this is critical to understanding Congregational Polity.

3. Define the three specifics regarding polity in the administration of the Law that transition into the Church Age and the administration of the New Covenant in Congregational Polity.

4. If the *Church* is merely a *physical organization*, rather than a *spiritual organism*, then the definition the *Church* focuses upon the *organizational structure.* The focus should be upon the *spiritual qualifications for membership* and *involvement* in the administrational responsibilities of the New Covenant. From the context of this statement, discuss these *spiritual qualifications for membership* and the level of *involvement* of each member necessary for Congregational Polity to really work.

5. What are the two basic evidences of the "new creation" for which every person applying for formal membership in a local church should be examined?

6. Discuss the maintenance of purity of doctrine among the formal membership of a local church as a major responsibility of Congregational Polity.

7. Discuss Congregation Polity as a responsibility of the Priesthood of all Church Age believers as the responsibility to maintain moral purity among the formal membership. Discuss how this is to be accomplished or administrated.

Chapter Sixty-five
Four Failures that Should Result in Excommunication

If there is one thing we learn from the Scriptural testimony of hundreds of believers throughout the Scriptures it is that people have two lives - the one with which God uses to teach us and the one with which we have to live after we have learned from our own failures. The life with which we have to live is often more difficult than the life with which God used to teach us. The consequences of a person's sin continue in their influence into numerous generations after the sin itself has long descended over the horizon of that person's lifetime. No one knows this better than the person who lives long enough to see his children, grandchildren, and great-grandchildren grow to adulthood. It seems like every failure is magnified in the lives of succeeding generations.

The local church, as ordained of God, is intended to be a *living, spiritual organism* in corporate "fellowship" with God. The only way the spiritual dynamic of corporate "fellowship" can exist within a local church is when each person in the formal membership of that local church is genuinely "born again" and living each moment of their lives filled to overflowing with the supernatural energizing (grace) of the indwelling Spirit of God. To insure that a local church maintains unbroken "fellowship" with God, a local church MUST maintain internal purity among its formal membership. When a single believer in the formal membership of a local church lives in unrepentant sin, worldliness, or carnality, the spiritual *unity* ("fellowship") with God is broken. The blessings of God upon the "work of the ministry" of the whole local church are lost until internal purity is restored. Restoration is either through genuine repentance of the sinner or through excommunication of the sinner from formal membership. This is what Paul addressed in I Corinthians 5:6-7: "[6] Your glorying *is* not good. Know ye not that a little leaven leaveneth the whole lump? [7] Purge out therefore the old leaven, that ye may be a new lump, as ye are unleavened." Excommunication is to *disfellowship* someone.

The first qualification for formal local church membership is a testimony of being a "born again" Christian. Initially, such a testimony is mainly verbal. A believer's life should begin to manifest the genuineness of *progressive transformation* as that believer *grows in grace* (II Peter 3:18). *Growing in grace* is visible in the *progressive transfiguration* of a believer's life as that believer begins to live the truths he learns from Scripture (Rom. 12:1-2). Orthodoxy (right doctrine) becomes orthopraxy (righteous practice) and a life is progressively transfigured. Therefore, there are four main failures that necessitate the *disfellowshipping* of an individual from a local church:

1. False profession of faith
2. Refusal to genuinely repent of moral turpitude
3. Doctrinal heresy
4. Unwillingness to resolve personal offenses

As I have previously stated, everyone likes to garden, but nobody likes to put the weeds. Church discipline is about evaluating who are genuine Christians and those who are either *false* Christians or *pretending* Christians. If there has been *life transference* (salvation), there should be some visible progressive *life transfiguration* (practical spiritual growth, I John 5:11-12). There will always be people who profess to be "born again" children of God, but who live like children of the Devil. This is an anomaly that cannot be allowed within a local church.

"[9] The Lord is not slack concerning his promise, as some men count slackness; but is longsuffering to us-ward, not willing that any should perish, but that all should come to repentance {*and the accompanying genuine salvation*}. [10] But the day of the Lord <u>will come</u> as a thief in the night; in the which the heavens shall pass away with a great noise, and the elements shall melt with fervent heat, the earth also and the works that are therein shall be burned up. [11] <u>*Seeing* then *that* all these things shall be</u> dissolved, what manner *of persons* <u>ought ye to be in *all* holy conversation and godliness</u> {*internal moral purity within the local church*}, [12] Looking for and hasting unto the coming of the day of God, wherein the heavens being on fire shall be dissolved, and the elements shall melt with fervent heat? [13] Nevertheless we, according to his promise, look for new heavens and a new earth, wherein dwelleth righteousness. [14] <u>Wherefore, beloved, seeing that ye look for such things, be diligent that ye may be found of him in peace, without spot, and blameless</u>

{living in repentance, confession of sin, and cleansed by the blood of Christ, I John 1:7-9}. [15] And account *that* the longsuffering of our Lord *is* salvation; even as our beloved brother Paul also according to the wisdom given unto him hath written unto you; [16] As also in all *his* epistles, speaking in them of these things; in which are some things hard to be understood, which they that are unlearned and unstable wrest, as *they do* also the other scriptures, unto their own destruction. [17] Ye therefore, beloved, seeing ye know *these things* before, beware lest ye also, being led away with the error of the wicked *{false doctrine}*, fall from your own stedfastness *{in the practice of truth}*. [18] But grow in grace *{progressive supernatural transfiguration}*, and *in* the knowledge of our Lord and Saviour Jesus Christ. To him *be* glory both now and for ever. Amen" (II Peter 3:9-18).

II Peter 3:9-18 addresses the four realities that should be evident in the life and in the living of a genuinely "born again" person. God commands purity and accountability in all four of these areas. According to II Peter 3:9-18, there should be the expectation of some real practices of life that correspond with the expectations of a real faith as true believers look to their futures as those futures relate to the second coming of Christ.

A FALSE PROFESSION OF FAITH IN CHRIST

Perhaps the most difficult area of discernment in evaluating a person for formal membership in a local church is that of the genuineness of having been "born again." It is difficult because church members are not able to *know the heart* of another person.

When a person expresses a desire for formal church membership, he should be carefully examined regarding his understanding of the gospel, repentance of sin (as a whole and in general, not specific sins) and "dead works," belief/rest/trust in the "finish" work of redemption, belief in and confession of the Deity of Jesus, calling on His name to save him (signifying a moment in *time* or an *event* when they trusted in Christ), and having received the Lord Jesus in the person of the indwelling Holy Spirit. The significance of salvation being an *event* (even if the date and specific time cannot be remembered) is of extreme significance to a genuine testimony of salvation.

A preliminary examination of a formal membership candidate should be made by the pastor and deacons prior to the time the individual is questioned and approved by the congregation for formal membership. If there appears to be some area where the person lacks understanding or some issue that might be in question, those things should be dealt with at this time.

> There should be extreme caution in this examination in that if a person is allowed to come into formal church membership under a false assumption of salvation, there is a very high probability that such a person will go through the rest of his life living under a *delusion of salvation* when it is not real.

This should be explained at the time of the private questioning so that the membership candidate can understand that the questioning is being done out of genuine concern. Secondly, the person that is not "born again" does not have the indwelling of the Holy Spirit and such a person cannot live the *Christ-life* no matter how hard he tries. Such a person is doomed to an existence of legalism and a life of continual failures. When salvation is a delusion, the *Christ-life* can never be anything more than an illusion. Sadly, the person with a delusion of salvation lives under that delusion, never recognizing it as a delusion because he thinks that his Christian life is like every other Christian's life. When two delusional Christians get together, they tend to reinforce each other's delusion with the commonality of never experiencing the Spirit-filled *Christ-life* and its accompanying *progressive transfiguration*. As a result, they think that what they know experientially as *Christianity* is normal Christianity. The delusion then reinforces the illusion.

It is important to note that the genuineness of a person's salvation may be QUESTIONED, but no one should be removed from formal church membership because of another person's doubt or even because a person may doubt his own salvation. A person must admit to a false profession of salvation before that person should be removed from formal church membership or give evidence of trusting in something other than the "finished" work and person of the Lord Jesus Christ. If a person states he is now trusting in either some degree of Moralism or some form of Ritualism for salvation, that must be corrected or that person must be removed from membership.

REFUSAL TO GENUINELY REPENT OF MORAL TURPITUDE

The only sin that would cause a local church to *disfellowship* another believer is a sin that is accompanied with the refusal to genuinely repent (to sincerely turn from that sin in remorse). When we understand *moral turpitude*, we see this kind of sin in such a way as to see it as more than just an offense against a holy God. *Moral turpitude* is essentially a judicial term describing action that is criminal in that the impact of the act goes beyond the individual to affect a group or a society. This is what defines the unrepentant sinner who lives in *secret sin* and *deception* of his fellow local church members. His unrepentant lifestyle causes the whole of the formal membership of a local church to lose the supernatural enabling of the Spirit of God upon their ministry. It is to the unrepented sin in the life of the unrepentant sinner that Paul refers to in I Corinthians 5:6 by the phrase, "a little leaven leaveneth the whole lump." Moral turpitude as a judicial term is defined as:

> "act of baseness, vileness or depravity in the private and social duties which a man owes to his fellowmen, or to society in general, contrary to the accepted and customary rule of right and duty between man and man."[31]

The heinousness of secret *moral turpitude* is that God acts upon the secret sin by withdrawing Himself and His blessings from the fellowship. This is what happened in Joshua chapter seven in the sin of Achan's moral turpitude.

> "[1] But the children of Israel committed a trespass in the accursed thing: for Achan, the son of Carmi, the son of Zabdi, the son of Zerah, of the tribe of Judah, took of the accursed thing: and the anger of the LORD was kindled against the children of Israel. [2] And Joshua sent men from Jericho to Ai, which *is* beside Bethaven, on the east side of Bethel, and spake unto them, saying, Go up and view the country. And the men went up and viewed Ai. [3] And they returned to Joshua, and said unto him, Let not all the people go up; but let about two or three thousand men go up and smite Ai; *and* make not all the people to labour thither; for they *are but* few. [4] So there went up thither of the people about three thousand men: and they fled before the men of Ai. [5] And the men of Ai smote of them about thirty and six men: for they chased them *from* before the gate *even* unto

---

[31] Chadwick v. State Bar, 49 Cal. 3d 103, 110, 776 P.2d 240, 260 Cal.Rptr. 538 (1989); Sosa-Martinez v. United States AG, 420 F.3d 1338, 1341 (11th Cir. 2005).

Shebarim, and smote them in the going down: wherefore the hearts of the people melted, and became as water" (Joshua 7:1-5).

Because of one man's selfish act of secret *moral turpitude*, thirty-six innocent men were killed when God withdrew His blessing and protective custody upon the nation of Israel. That which defines the *criminal action* in *moral turpitude* is revealed in the extensive levels of its impact upon the nation of Israel as a whole.

1. Joshua, the leader of Israel, was discouraged and began to wrongly accuse God of being unfaithful to His covenant promise (Joshua 7:6-7).
2. An open door was provided for God's name and God's abilities to be blasphemed among the heathen and the congregation of Israel to be mocked by their enemies (Joshua 7:8-9).
3. Thirty-six innocent men died (Joshua 7:5). These men had fathers, mothers, brothers, sisters, wives, children, and other extended family members who became victims of the consequences of the moral turpitude of Achan and his family as they concealed his sin.
4. The whole congregation of Israel was defiled and accursed before God (Joshua 7:11) until they corporately dealt with the problem judicially and were once again sanctified before God (Joshua 7:13-26).
5. God established a memorial in the "great heap of stones" (Joshua 7:26) and, from that day forward, the valley where this stoning took place "was called, the Valley of Achor." Achor means *trouble*. This was to be an ongoing historical testimony to the infamy of one man who brought so much trouble upon the congregation of Israel because of his own carnal selfishness.

It should be noted that the whole immediate family of Achan were required to be present at his stoning and it appears that they were stoned along with Achan, which would require their complicity in concealing of the sin. This complicity of family members, or anyone, to conceal sin is a level of moral turpitude that must as well be dealt with during church discipline through congregational polity. It should also be noted that in order for the defilement to be removed from the congregation of Israel and God's blessing restored through sanctification, the whole congregation was required to take part in the stoning and the burning of all the bodies and belongings of the family of Achan (Joshua 7:24-26).

REFUSAL TO REPENT OF DOCTRINAL HERESY

Ephesians 4:2 emphatically states that there is but "one faith." Since "faith *cometh* by hearing, and hearing by the Word of God" (Romans 10:17), we should understand that the "one faith" Paul refers to is one correct interpretation of Scripture that is defined as right doctrine. The word "doctrine" in the New Testament is translated from the Greek word *didache* (did-akh-ay'). The Greek word simply means *instruction*. Doctrine is the *teaching* that explains the meaning of the inspired Words of Scripture. Our modern term for doctrine is the word *theology*. Right doctrine (orthodoxy) provides the correct foundation for righteous, God-pleasing practice (orthopraxy).

Heresy is any wrong interpretation of Scripture *that creates disunity*. The word heresy means *disunion*. It is false teaching of false doctrine that breaks the ". . . unity of the Spirit in the bond of peace. [4] *There is* one body, and one Spirit, even as ye are called in one hope of your calling; [5] One Lord, one faith, one baptism, [6] One God and Father of all, who *is* above all, and through all, and in you all" (Ephesians 4:3b-6). The word *heresy* actually refers to the creation of another *sect* or *division* of people that breaks away from the original *fellowship* by teaching things contrary to that right doctrine and its practice or the *unity* that existed in right doctrine and right practice.

> "[17] Now I beseech you, brethren, mark them which cause divisions and offences contrary to the doctrine which ye have learned; and avoid them. [18] For they that are such serve not our Lord Jesus Christ, but their own belly; and by good words and fair speeches deceive the hearts of the simple" (Romans 16:17-18).

The word "mark" in Romans 16:17 is from the Greek word *skopeo* (skop-eh'-o). It means to *focus upon, point out,* or *take aim*. People, both within a local church membership and without, who teach false interpretations of Scripture that lead to *disunion* should be singled out and publicly acknowledged. If they are members of a local church and refuse to repent of their false teachings, they must be removed from the formal membership of the church and not allowed to have any position of leadership. Since they will continue to teach their false interpretation of Scripture even after they have been excommunicated, it becomes the responsibility of the leadership and the formal members of a local church to constantly warn new believers about them and maintain a public *mark* upon them through continual warnings.

UNWILLINGNESS TO RESOLVE PERSONAL OFFENSES

In most cases, Matthew 18:15-20 is used for the foundation of church discipline in dealing with issues of moral turpitude. That is not the context of the instruction of Matthew chapter eighteen. The context is about lifestyles that lead little children astray (Matthew 18:1-6) by living in contradiction to the practice of right doctrine. Contextually, the instruction of Matthew eighteen is about how believers should treat one another and resolve personal problems in a God-honoring way. Sadly, dealing with the issues of false professions of salvation, moral turpitude, and heresy get all mixed together. According to the teaching of the Word of God, we have separate instructions regarding the way these various issues are to be dealt with by individual believers and within the context of formal local church membership. Matthew 18:15-20 gives us instructions regarding how God wants individuals to deal with personal offenses that they might *cause* or *receive*.

> "[15] Moreover if thy brother shall trespass against thee, go and tell him his fault between thee and him alone: if he shall hear thee, thou hast gained thy brother. [16] But if he will not hear *thee, then* take with thee one or two more, that in the mouth of two or three witnesses every word may be established. [17] And if he shall neglect to hear them, tell *it* unto the church: but if he neglect to hear the church, let him be unto thee as an heathen man and a publican. [18] Verily I say unto you, Whatsoever ye shall bind on earth shall be bound in heaven: and whatsoever ye shall loose on earth shall be loosed in heaven. [19] Again I say unto you, That if two of you shall agree on earth as touching any thing that they shall ask, it shall be done for them of my Father which is in heaven. [20] For where two or three are gathered together in my name, there am I in the midst of them" (Matthew 18:15-20).

The word "trespass" is from the Greek word *hamartano* (ham-ar-tan'-o). It simply means to *miss the mark*. It is usually translated *sin*, but in this case the better translation is "trespass." It means to err or make a serious mistake in judgment or to say or do something that causes another person grief because of that wrong statement. What is usually the case is that one person says something wrong or makes a false speculation about another person to a friend or acquaintance. Then that person goes to the person that the statement was made about and repeats it or asks that person if the statement is true. The latter person is the person offended by the statement. Both the person who made the original offending statement and the person who repeated the offending statement become party to the offense and become accountable to try to resolve the offense. The false statement is *gossip*. The person, who listened to the *gossip* and repeated the *gossip*, even bringing the *gossip* to the person in question, becomes party to the *gossip*. *Gossip* is a secret assault upon the character of another person. If a person has a concern or question about an action of another person, the only appropriate person to discuss the issue with is the person in question. ALL PARTIES INVOLVED IN THE DISCUSSION NEED TO BE INVOLVED IN THE RESOLUTION.

The context of Matthew chapter eighteen is the bad example that adults establish before children that lead those children into similar practices. One of the most basic principles of parenting, in teaching children self-discipline, is the principle: WHAT YOU MESS UP, YOU STRAIGHTEN UP! In Matthew chapter eighteen, the mess up is the question, "Who is the greatest in the kingdom of heaven?" This question was asked in almost complete ignorance of those *little ears* and *little eyes* that hear everything and see everything and record those things they hear and see. These *little ears* have gossiping endorsed by the actions of the adults from which they learn. The question raised the issue of WHAT is important in life by raising a false example of WHO is important in life. Christ brings those invisible *ears* and *eyes* into the midst of those disciples and in the midst of the theological debate and shows these adults the perspective of their discussion. Congregational polity holds formal church members accountable to resolve the offenses created by misstatements and bad examples.

The testimony of any local church will never be any better than the testimony of any individual who is allowed to live in contradiction to his profession of salvation or in contradiction to his commitment to die to the "old man" and live in the indwelling power of the resurrected and indwelling Christ. The basic responsibility of Congregational Polity is the protection and maintenance of a testimony that will bring glory to God and His power to completely transfigure the lives of sinners.

DISCUSSION QUESTIONS

1. Discuss what is meant by the statement, "that in Scripture everyone is presented as having two lives."

2. The local church, as ordained of God, is intended to be a *living, spiritual organism* in corporate "fellowship" with God. Discuss how the spiritual dynamic of every member living a Spirit-filled life before corporate "fellowship" with God can ever be experienced.

3. Explain what *excommunication* is and why it is critical for corporate "fellowship" with God to go unhindered.

4. List and define the four main failures that necessitate the *disfellowshipping* of an individual from a local church.

5. Define *moral turpitude* and why it is such a heinous problem.

6. Discuss the five outcomes that were given regarding Achan's sin in Joshua chapter seven and how this correlates with Church discipline for moral turpitude.

7. Discuss the distinct purpose of Matthew 18:15-20 in giving directions for dealing with personal issues in a local church rather than as it is commonly and errantly applied to dealing with the sins of moral turpitude.

Chapter Sixty-six
Spirit-Filled Communication in Speaking and Hearing

"A word fitly spoken *is like* apples of gold in pictures of silver" (Proverbs 25:11).

Imagine, God says that one single word, when spoken at just the right time and in just the right way, is as pleasing to the ear as is the ascetic image of golden apples presented in a delicately constructed filigree silver basket. The idea is that such a word will be desired and received with gladness by the hearer. Understanding and waiting for the exact moment in time to speak that word and having exactly the right word to say requires the spiritual discernment of a Spirit-filled life. This also requires the wisdom that comes from a Spirit-filled life.

The Word of God has much instruction regarding verbal communication. The words that come out of our mouths can edify, encourage, instruct, bless, correct, and rebuke. The words of our mouth can also destroy, deceive, discourage, defeat, curse, and abuse. An unjustified insinuation, gossip, or a lie about another person can be destructive. False words can be used as weapons of character assassination. A person's integrity and character can be attacked by merely making a suggestion of the possibility of inappropriate behavior. I call this *assassination by innuendo*. The hatred of murder does not have to be directed at the body. Words can be directed to hurt, maim, or murder another person's spirit as well.

"A man that beareth false witness against his neighbour *is* a maul, and a sword, and a sharp arrow" (Proverbs 25:18).

Communication Central is the *brain*, but Communication Central's *operator* is the *heart*. The believer must yield his will to the indwelling Spirit in order to control the heart (emotions) in communication. The heart is corrupted by our sin natures and a corrupt heart will corrupt our speech if a believer is not Spirit-filled. Christ spoke regarding this on numerous occasions. We should understand that the corrupted heart, as that which motivated corrupted speech, was a subject Christ spoke of regularly.

"[43] For a good tree bringeth not forth corrupt fruit; neither doth a corrupt tree bring forth good fruit. [44] For every tree is known by his own fruit. For of thorns men do not gather figs, nor of a bramble bush gather they grapes. [45] A good man out of the good treasure of his heart bringeth forth that which is good; and an evil man out of the evil treasure of his heart bringeth forth that which is evil: for of the abundance of the heart his mouth speaketh" (Luke 6:43-45).

"[34] O generation of vipers, how can ye, being evil, speak good things? for out of the abundance of the heart the mouth speaketh. [35] A good man out of the good treasure of the heart bringeth forth good things: and an evil man out of the evil treasure bringeth forth evil things. [36] But I say unto you, That every idle word {*This refers to a word that does not minister; i.e., instruct, encourage, edify, reprove, or rebuke. Injurious words or words used merely for manipulation, flattery, or for selfish reasons would be included in this condemnation.*} that men shall speak, they shall give account thereof in the day of judgment. [37] For by thy words thou shalt be justified, and by thy words thou shalt be condemned {*Every word we have ever said, and the motives behind those words, have been recorded by God. Those words will provide evidence for or against the reality of our salvation.*}" (Matthew 12:34-37).

Communicating ideas and feelings with words is perhaps one of the most difficult aspects of a person's life. We are told by God that controlling our communication will require a level of spiritual maturity and self-discipline that is supernatural. "The tongue can no man tame" (James 3:8). The facts of James 3:1-18 become very apparent very early in life.

"[1] My brethren, be not many masters, knowing that we shall receive the greater condemnation. [2] For in many things we offend all. If any man offend not in word, the same *is* a perfect man, *and* able also to bridle the whole body. [3] Behold, we put bits in the horses' mouths, that they may obey us; and we turn about their whole body. [4] Behold also the ships, which though *they be* so great, and *are* driven of fierce winds, yet are they turned about with a very small helm, whithersoever the governor listeth. [5] Even so the tongue is a little member, and boasteth great things. Behold, how great a matter a little fire kindleth! [6] And the tongue *is* a fire, a world of iniquity: so is the tongue among our members, that it defileth the whole body, and setteth on fire the course of nature; and it is set on fire of hell. [7]

For every kind of beasts, and of birds, and of serpents, and of things in the sea, is tamed, and hath been tamed of mankind: [8] But the tongue can no man tame; *it is* an unruly evil, full of deadly poison. [9] Therewith bless we God, even the Father; and therewith curse we men, which are made after the similitude of God. [10] Out of the same mouth proceedeth blessing and cursing. My brethren, these things ought not so to be. [11] Doth a fountain send forth at the same place sweet *water* and bitter? [12] Can the fig tree, my brethren, bear olive berries? either a vine, figs? so *can* no fountain both yield salt water and fresh. [13] Who *is* a wise man and endued with knowledge among you? let him shew out of a good conversation his works with meekness of wisdom. [14] But if ye have bitter envying and strife in your hearts, glory not, and lie not against the truth {*do not decieve yourself by denying these corruptions of your hearts*}. [15] This wisdom descendeth not from above {*does not come from God*}, but *is* earthly {*worldly*}, sensual {*animalistic*}, devilish {*demonically influenced*}. [16] For where envying and strife *is*, there *is* confusion and every evil work. [17] But the wisdom that is from above is first pure, then peaceable, gentle, *and* easy to be intreated, full of mercy and good fruits, without partiality, and without hypocrisy. [18] And the fruit of righteousness is sown in peace of them that make peace" (James 3:1-18).

Perhaps the most difficult area of our communication to control and evaluate is to deal with what motivates us to say the words that we say. In order to evaluate *what* is being said, sometimes it is important to ask *why* it is being said. What is the motivation behind the communication? Motives are often communicated by *emotions* and reflected by *moods*. *Looking behind* the words being said is very important. Are you, or the person that is speaking, angry, defensive, justifying, joking around, serious, trying to teach, trying to sell something or manipulate, or trying to correct something said or done? The best way to answer these kinds of questions is to simply ask the person, are you angry? Are you joking? Speak at the level of your concern.

A basic fact of life is that eventually we will say something that will offend someone, or others will say something that will offend us. This can happen because we say something out of anger, jealousy, and pride, even with purposeful intent to hurt because we allow our carnality to reign in our hearts for a moment, or for an extended period of time. Another problem is that we cannot control how a person receives what we say, even if what we say was not intended to hurt. Angry people, scorners, and cynics hear what is said in a very negative and critical way because that is the way they think. Their Communication Central is totally *cross wired* somewhere.

Learning to humbly, submissively, and apologetically deal with things we say that are offensive to others is very much a part of the Spirit-filled life. Obviously, God hates communication that is purposely offensive and that simply comes forth from the mouth unrestrained with little or no consideration about how it might hurt someone or purposefully intent upon hurting someone.

> "The fear of the LORD *is* to hate evil: {*evil manifested through*} pride, and arrogancy, and the evil way, and the froward mouth, do I hate" (Proverbs 8:13).

To say we fear the LORD and do not hate the evils of pride, arrogance, the evil way, and the froward mouth" is a sure sign of self-deception regarding our own spirituality. The word "froward" refers to speaking about perverted things, trying to deceive, or saying things that are intent upon fraud. This can refer to discussing worldly things that might lead a person to desire what is being discussed. It can refer to false doctrine. It can refer to flattery intent upon gaining the favor or friendship of another for selfish reasons. If we fear the LORD, we will hate this kind of speech. It is not enough that we merely dislike this kind of speech. We must determine to hate it. That means we must hate it to the degree that we *kill it* in our thought-life and in our *hearts* before it ever comes forth from our mouths. In order to do that, it will require a constant, conscious awareness of others around us and the necessity of keeping our attitudes in check, especially in our response to others.

> "[23] Burning lips and a wicked heart *are like* a potsherd covered with silver dross. [24] He that hateth dissembleth { *'pretends love and kindness'[32]*} with his lips, and layeth up deceit within him {*referring to his real, but hidden agenda*}; [25] When he speaketh fair {*the idea is flattering words*}, believe him not {*do not trust what the unrepentant, carnal person says*}: for *there are* seven {*as an expression of fullness or completeness, not necessarily this specific number of evil attitudes*} abominations in his heart. [26] *Whose* hatred is covered by deceit, his wickedness shall be shewed before the

---

[32] Poole, Matthew. *Matthew Poole's Commentary on the Whole Bible*; Sword Searcher Software 6.2.

whole congregation {*will eventually expose itself and expose the deception*}. [27] Whoso diggeth a pit shall fall therein: and he that rolleth a stone, it will return upon him. [28] A lying tongue hateth *those that are* afflicted by it; and a flattering mouth worketh ruin" (Proverbs 26:23-28).

"Burning lips" refer to the deception of outward appearances and flattering words. "Burning lips" coupled with "a wicked heart" are nothing but earthenware (carnality) covered with silver to make it appear valuable. The idea is that of a woman who paints her lips red to sexually attract a man while her inward motives are wicked, selfish, or carnal. *"Warm professions* can no more give value to insincerity than silver coating to rude earthenware."[33] The idea here is that the hearer must give careful consideration to the motives of the person communicating. We can never truly know a person's motives through mere outward observances, but we should know a person well enough to be able evaluate the sincerity of his words and the purpose of the communication.

The Spirit-filled believer will consciously and purposefully maintain certain attitudes that impact what we say, how we say it, and how we hear what is said to us. These attitudes must be "put on" in the sense of dressing one's self with spiritual clothing. When the believer is filled with the Spirit, that believer *puts o*n attitudes that reflect the character and nature of God. It is a spiritual contradiction to profess spirituality and not manifest the qualities of character that reflect that spirituality.

"[12] Put on therefore, as the elect of God {*referring to the believer's vocational priesthood*}, holy and beloved, bowels of mercies, kindness, humbleness of mind, meekness, longsuffering; [13] Forbearing one another, and forgiving one another, if any man have a quarrel against any: even as Christ forgave you, so also *do* ye. [14] And above all these things *put on* charity, which is the bond of perfectness. [15] And let the peace of God rule in your hearts, to the which also ye are called in one body; and be ye thankful. [16] Let the word of Christ dwell in you richly in all wisdom; teaching and admonishing one another in psalms and hymns and spiritual songs, singing with grace in your hearts to the Lord. [17] And whatsoever ye

---

[33] Jamieson, Robert, Fausset, A.R., and Brown, David. *Jamieson-Fausset-Brown Commentary Critical and Explanatory on the Whole Bible.* SwordSearcher Software 6.2, 1871.

do in word or deed, *do* all in the name of the Lord Jesus, giving thanks to God and the Father by him" (Colossians 3:12-17).

> The spiritual person not only speaks with the character and nature of God, he hears with the character and nature of God. God's character and nature is exemplified by the words "holy and beloved, bowels of mercies, kindness, humbleness of mind, meekness, longsuffering." The Spirit-filled believer *predetermines* to "forbear" and "forgive."

The word "forbear" simply means we have *predetermined* to *put up with* one another. We know, like God knows us, that we are all going to eventually *fail*. The more immature the child, the more messes we can expect him to make. The predetermination to "forbear" means you will *work through it all* together. When (not *if*) a person fails and says something or does something that offends, we are *predetermined* to resolve the issue and forgive the offense. Sins are against God. An offense is the way a sin or act of carelessness impacts someone's life.

The word "offence" is usually translated from the Greek word *skandalon* (skan'-dal-on), from which we get our English word *scandal*. The Greek word refers to a *snare* or a *trip-stick*. The idea is doing something wrong that might cause another person to fail spiritually or lead someone astray in making wrong choices. Every one of us will eventually do something that is offensive in nature. The spiritual believer lives *en guarde* - on guard with sword drawn in *defense* as opposed to *attack*. That means we are prepared by *predetermining* our actions according to biblical mandates for an offence when the offence arises.

There are always those it seems that open their mouths and everything in their minds and hearts floods forth without any restraint. There is great wisdom in careful speech and in the *weighing of words* before they are said. God tells us to do so. There are times that silence is the best response.

"He that is void of wisdom despiseth his neighbour: but a man of understanding holdeth his peace" (Proverbs 11:12).

"He that reproveth a scorner {*the person who mocks or ridicules sacred things or righteous acts*} getteth to himself shame {*will receive in return dishonor and accusations from the one reproved*}: and he that rebuketh a wicked *man getteth* himself a blot {*a bruise; the idea is that a wicked person will respond in anger and violence*}" (Proverbs 9:7).

"*If* a wise man contendeth with a foolish man, whether he rage or laugh, *there is* no rest" (Proverbs 29:9).

"A fool uttereth all his mind: but a wise *man* keepeth it in till afterwards" (Proverbs 29:11).

"[1] The preparations of the heart in man, and the answer of the tongue, *is* from the LORD. [2] All the ways of a man *are* clean in his own eyes; but the LORD weigheth the spirits" (Proverbs 16:1-2).

SPIRIT-FILLED HEARING

Equally important as Spirit-filled speech is Spirit-filled hearing or listening. In each of the seven epistles of Christ to the seven local churches of Revelation chapters one and two, Christ says: "He that hath an ear, let him hear what the Spirit saith unto the churches" (Revelation 2:7, 11, 17, 29, 3:6, 13, and 22). The Spirit of God communicates to individuals through the inspired Scriptures and primarily through the *organism* of the local church (one person to another person). The local church is a *living organism* made up of *living stones* all proclaiming and living the inspired Words of Scripture. Christ used the phrase "he that hath ears to hear, let him hear" on numerous occasions as recorded in the synoptic Gospels (Matthew 11:15, 13:9, 43, Mark 4:9, 23, and Luke 8:8, 14:35). The implication of having "ears to hear" refers to those who are open to communication from God, believing God desires to communicate His will regarding salvation, condemnation, judgment, blessings, and instructions for living so as to bring glory to His name. This must be the inclination of a person's heart before God's communication can be heard and understood.

Christ spoke to the hardened Pharisees of Israel giving them a spiritual requisite before God would supernaturally give someone understanding of His inspired Scriptures. This simple statement made by Jesus defines what is meant by the phrase "he that hath ears to hear, let him hear."

"[14] Now about the midst of the feast Jesus went up into the temple, and taught. [15] And the Jews marvelled, saying, How knoweth this man letters, having never learned? [16] Jesus answered them, and said, My doctrine is not mine, but his that sent me. [17] If any man will do his will, he shall know of the doctrine, whether it be of God, or *whether* I speak of myself" (John 7:14-17).

Before God will reveal His will to anyone, that person must decide beforehand to obey whatever God's will is for that person. Decisions regarding doing God's will should take place BEFORE reading Scripture or listening to preaching, not afterwards. This *predetermination* is an act of faith in God that defines the "ear to hear" of the man inclined to hear and obey what God has to say. The mental picture before us is of a person seeking to get as close as possible so as to eliminate any interference or misunderstanding regarding what is being communicated.

> For most people, including most Christians, they want to *hear before they make a decision.* They treat God like some *huckster* selling some commodity. If they like what God has to offer, then they will *join the club* or *buy the product.* The person with an "ear to hear" always listens in reverential fear and trembling for the voice of God to speak.

"[12] Wherefore, my beloved, as ye have always obeyed, not as in my presence only, but now much more in my absence, work out your own salvation with fear and trembling. [13] For it is God which worketh in you both to will and to do of *his* good pleasure" (Philippians 2:12-13).

Isaiah chapter 49 is a Messianic prophecy of the coming of Messiah. There is an interesting phrase in Isaiah 49:2 about the Messiah and His communication to the nation of Israel now hardened in their hearts to the communication from God. We can learn from this much about what God will do to persuade and condition people to have an "ear to hear" what He has to say.

"[1] Listen, O isles, unto me; and hearken, ye people, from far; The LORD hath called me {*referring to the Messiah*} from the womb; from the bowels of my mother hath he made mention of my name. [2] And he hath made my mouth like a sharp sword; in the shadow of his hand hath he hid me, and made me a polished shaft; in his quiver hath he hid me; [3] And said unto me, Thou *art* my servant, O Israel *{Jesus is the true personification of Israel, which literally means, 'he shall rule as God'}*, in whom I will be glorified. [4] Then I said, I have laboured in vain, I have spent my strength for nought, and in vain: *yet* surely my judgment *is* with the LORD, and my work with my God. [5] And now, saith the LORD that formed me from the womb *to be* his servant, to bring Jacob again to him, Though Israel be not gathered, yet shall I be glorious in the eyes of the LORD, and my God shall be my strength. [6] And he said, It is a light thing that thou shouldest be my servant to raise up the tribes of Jacob, and to restore the preserved of Israel: I will also give thee for a light to the Gentiles, that thou mayest be my salvation unto the end of the earth" (Isaiah 49:1-6).

How *sharp* does God have to bring forth His Word before it is able to pierce the hardened heart of a willful sinner? How sharp does the arrow's tip of truth need to be and how polished the arrow's shaft before it is able to reach the depth of a heart hardened to God's will? Notice the loving and longsuffering of God with the people of Israel, who for most part had lived in spiritual adultery, idolatry, and willful disobedience to God's commands. Yet, His chastisements continued year after year and century after century in seeking to pierce their hardened hearts with conviction of sin, righteousness, and judgment. This is God's action upon those who profess to believe but do not have "an ear to hear" - CHASTISEMENT. The chastisement of a true believer causes that believer to incline his hearing to the voice of the Spirit of God.

Hearing that is accompanied with the predetermined decision to obey what God says will also be accompanied with understanding or illumination that comes from being Spirit-filled. This is the fulfillment of the second part of the phrase, "he who hath ears to hear, let him hear." The idea is "let him hear" with understanding or supernatural illumination.

"[18] Hear ye *{with understanding}* therefore the *{explanation of}* parable of the sower. [19] When any one heareth the word of the kingdom *{the coming Kingdom of Christ on earth}*, and understandeth *it* not, then cometh the wicked *one*, and catcheth away that which was sown in his heart. This is he which received seed by the way side. [20] But he that received the seed into stony places, the same is he that heareth the word *{of the coming Kingdom of Christ on earth}*, and anon *{at once or immediately}* with joy

618
WWW.DISCIPLEMAKERMINISTRIES.ORG

receiveth it; [21] Yet hath he not root in himself, but dureth for a while: for when tribulation or persecution ariseth because of the word {*of the Kingdom of Christ resulting in the loss of vision of that reality because of a preoccupation with temporal things in this life*}, by and by he is offended. [22] He also that received seed among the thorns is he that heareth the word {*of the coming Kingdom of Christ on earth*}; and the care of this world, and the deceitfulness of riches, choke the word, and he becometh unfruitful. [23] But he that received seed into the good ground is he that heareth the word {*of the coming Kingdom of Christ on earth*}, and understandeth *it*; which also beareth fruit, and bringeth forth, some an hundredfold, some sixty, some thirty" (Matthew 13:18-23).

The implication is that *hearing* the truths of the coming Kingdom of Christ on earth *with understanding* will so radically change our lives and our priorities that we will begin to invest all that we are and possess in persuading people of their need of salvation through Christ and escaping the wrath to come in God's preceding judgment of the nations. Anything less and we have either not heard or not understood the message of the coming Kingdom of Christ on earth and what will precede it.

DISCUSSION QUESTIONS

1. Explain Proverbs 25:11.

2. Communication Central is the *brain*, but Communication Central's *operator* is the *heart*. Expand upon this statement.

3. Discuss why it is so difficult to communicate ideas and feelings with words.

4. Motives are often communicated by *emotions* and reflected by *moods*. *Looking behind* the words being said is very important. Discuss why evaluating a communicator's motives is important while differentiating between evaluating and judging motives.

5. Practically explain Proverbs 8:13.

6. Practically explain Proverbs 26:23-28.

7. Discuss what is involved in Spirit-filled hearing by explaining the phrase "he that hath and ear, let him hear what the Spirit saith."

Chapter Sixty-seven

The Priesthood of the Home and Reproducing a Godly Seed

Since the fall of some angels and all of mankind into sin, world history is the record of the never ending battles of *wants* and *wills*. It all began when one fallen angel put his will above the will of God and, through deception, led the father of all mankind down the same pathway of corruption. Since then, every conflict between individuals, groups, and nations has been the product of putting someone else's *want* or *will* above that of another.

In this *battle of the ages*, those who battle for truth, or "the faith," do not battle directly with fallen angels. We battle against those deceived by them and who are being led by them through ongoing deception, false doctrines about God, and in varying degrees of unbelief regarding the person and work of God. The Christian should not lose this perspective of the battle between good and evil. Although satanic opposition comes to us in the bodies of human beings, the human beings are only instruments in their power, controlled and manipulated through demonic deception. The spiritual struggle is that of innumerable individual battles fought against false philosophies, mythologies, distortions and perversions of truth, lies, manipulations, selfishness, greed, lusts, and a million other battle fronts of variations and combinations of corruption.

"[10] Finally, my brethren, be strong in the Lord, and in the power of his might. [11] Put on the whole armour of God, that ye may be able to stand against the wiles of the devil. [12] For we wrestle not against flesh and blood, but against principalities, against powers, against the rulers of the darkness of this world, against spiritual wickedness in high *places*. [13] Wherefore take unto you the whole armour of God, that ye may be able to withstand in the evil day, and having done all, to stand" (Ephesians 6:10-13).

The primary focus of this onslaught of evil is directed against the home and especially against the God appointed spiritual guardian of the home - the FATHER.

It is an operation in human vanity to think that a man can win this never ending, unrelenting onslaught, waged by supernatural beings with powers beyond our imagination against the home and family. The spiritual man lives each moment in an ongoing *declaration of dependence* upon God and in his understanding of the absolute necessity of living in unbroken fellowship with God.

There is only one will in existence that deserves to be fought for within such levels of conflict - the will of God. It is to this seemingly never ending struggle that the Word of God directs us in the short epistle of Jude, the half-brother of our Lord Jesus Christ, centering on the statement in verse three, "that ye should earnestly contend for the faith which was once delivered unto the saints." The Word of God reveals the will of God, which defines "the faith."

"[1] Jude, the servant of Jesus Christ, and brother of James, to them that are sanctified by God the Father, and preserved in Jesus Christ, *and* called: [2] Mercy unto you, and peace, and love, be multiplied. [3] Beloved, when I gave all diligence to write unto you of the common salvation, it was needful for me to write unto you, and exhort *you* that ye should earnestly contend for the faith which was once delivered unto the saints. [4] For there are certain men crept in unawares, who were before of old ordained to this condemnation, ungodly men, turning the grace of our God into lasciviousness, and denying the only Lord God, and our Lord Jesus Christ. [5] I will therefore put you in remembrance, though ye once knew this, how that the Lord, having saved the people out of the land of Egypt, afterward destroyed them that believed not. [6] And the angels which kept not their first estate, but left their own habitation, he hath reserved in everlasting chains under darkness unto the judgment of the great day. [7] Even as Sodom and Gomorrha, and the cities about them in like manner, giving themselves over to fornication, and going after strange flesh, are set forth for an example, suffering the vengeance of eternal fire. [8] Likewise also these *filthy* dreamers defile the flesh, despise dominion, and speak evil of dignities. [9] Yet Michael the archangel, when contending with the devil he disputed about the body of Moses, durst not bring against him a railing accusation, but said, The Lord rebuke thee. [10] But these speak evil of those things which they know not: but what they know naturally, as brute beasts, in those things they corrupt themselves. [11] Woe unto them! for they have gone in the way of Cain, and ran greedily after the error of Balaam for reward, and perished in the gainsaying of Core. [12] These are spots in your feasts of charity, when they feast with you, feeding themselves without fear: clouds *they are* without water, carried about of winds; trees whose fruit withereth, without fruit, twice dead, plucked up by the roots; [13] Raging waves of the sea, foaming out their own shame; wandering stars, to whom is reserved the blackness of darkness for ever. [14] And Enoch also, the seventh from Adam, prophesied of these, saying, Behold, the Lord cometh with ten thousands of his saints, [15] To execute judgment upon all, and to convince all that are ungodly among them of all their ungodly deeds which they have ungodly committed, and of all their hard *speeches* which ungodly sinners have spoken against him. [16] These are murmurers, complainers, walking after their own lusts; and their mouth speaketh great swelling *words*, having men's persons in admiration because of advantage. [17] But, beloved, remember ye the words which were spoken before of the apostles of our Lord Jesus Christ; [18] How that they told you there should be mockers in the last time, who should walk after their own ungodly lusts. [19] These be they who separate themselves, sensual, having not the Spirit. [20] But ye, beloved, building up yourselves on your most holy faith, praying in the Holy Ghost, [21] Keep yourselves in the love of God, looking for the mercy of our Lord Jesus Christ unto eternal life. [22] And of some have compassion, making a difference: [23] And others save with fear, pulling *them* out of the fire; hating even the garment spotted by the flesh. [24] Now unto him that is able to keep you from falling, and to present *you* faultless before the presence of his glory with exceeding joy, [25] To the only wise God our Saviour, *be* glory and majesty, dominion and power, both now and ever. Amen" (Jude 1:1-25).

Defining what is meant by the words "the faith" that we are commanded to "contend for" is a critical aspect of what defines the struggle of the Christian life and the primary ministry of the father as the guardian of his home. No man will take the responsibilities of the spiritual guardianship of his home seriously until he understands the wicked purposes of the enemy and the cost of failure.

Men have difficulty dealing with intangible probabilities. Men tend to deal only with things they can see, touch, hear, and smell.

However, if a man knew there was an invader coming who would steal all that he had worked for, rape his wife and daughters, and then sell them with his sons into slavery, he would do everything in his power and intellect to provide for their protection. Why then is it that most men are apathetic about spiritual things, about church going, about Bible study, and about prayer? They are apathetic because they do not really believe there is any real danger to them or their families.

We also find the phrase "the common salvation" in verse three of Jude. The *soteriological reductionism* of *Post-modern evangelicalism* defines this "common salvation" as merely the salvation of the soul from condemnation and deliverance from Hell. The salvation of the Bible has three levels of deliverance of the body, soul, and spirit of a person (I Thessalonians 5:23). There are times when the word *salvation* is used to refer to all three of these aspects of salvation (such as in the case of Jude 1:3). There are also times when the context determines to which aspect of salvation the text is referring. The three aspects of a person's salvation are:

1. The salvation of the soul through propitiation and justification
2. The salvation of the spirit (*one's life*) through practical sanctification
3. The salvation of the body through glorification

The phrase "common salvation" in Jude 1:3 refers to all three aspects of a person's salvation. In fact, perhaps we can go so far as to say that the words "common salvation" embody all that defines Christianity as a whole. Although any phase of a person's ongoing salvation (he *has been* saved, *is being* saved, and *will be* saved) is an operation of God, He has numerous human partners in this "work of the ministry."

God has commanded all believers to preach the gospel and make disciples. God has called all believers to work together through the local church towards spiritual growth (practical sanctification). However, God has but one person that He has put in charge of the home and with whom He wants to work in a formal partnership so as to protect the family members of that home against the unrelenting onslaught of satanic deception and corruption. God calls him the *father*. Wives call him *honey*. Children call him *dad*. That man's primary *line of defense* is to maintain unbroken fellowship with God so that His family is never left unguarded against the supernatural onslaught of evil that only God can protect against.

Secondly, understanding the numerous levels of personalities, individuals, and *forces* we battle is also critical. The primary enemy is the corrupting influence of demonic forces. In defining that corrupting influence, we must include our own corrupted nature with its corrupted, selfish desires and all of our *idols of the heart*. Because each of us, including fathers, has a corrupted nature, we are a potential danger to our own families. In most cases, corrupted individuals become the tools with which demonic corruption is advanced in families, cultures, and nations. Warning about these corrupted individuals is what the epistle of Jude is all about and the primary focus of the command to "earnestly contend for the faith which was once delivered unto the saints."

There is no escaping this warfare in this life. A new battle is always looming on the horizon of the next moment. The *army of enemy* is constantly being refreshed with new deceived souls willing to evangelize the world with their deceptions and mock all that contradict their heresies. There is nothing sacred to them. The most difficult aspect of "contending for the faith" is that those individuals we contend with are also those that we are trying to evangelize. At that level, our enemies become our ministry.

False doctrine is an attack against "the faith." False doctrine is the most significant enemy of the family in the arsenal of satanic opposition to the will of God. Right doctrine determines right practice. Fathers who do not make learning doctrine a priority of their lives will never be able to transfer right doctrine into the practice of the lives of their families.

According to Jude 1:4, not all of the enemies of the family are demons. Some of them are false teachers who have been deceived and corrupted by demons. These people enter the local church under the guise of orthodoxy with a covert agenda to take control. Once they have gained positions of favor, they begin to sow their seeds of corruption.

We might ask why this is so easily accomplished. There is a simple reason. When a genuine man of God labors "in word and doctrine" (I Timothy 5:17), his work is often resisted by degrees. Some people resist his teaching/preaching because they think it is too restrictive on their lifestyles and practices, and they quickly shut their ears to anything he says regarding these issues. Others may resist the laborious detail in which truth is presented. Others simply resist because they really do not want to labor in learning and they allow their minds to wonder towards more interesting things of the world. These individuals will welcome someone who will remove the restrictions, make church going *fun or entertaining*, and not require any effort of their parts to learn and live the truth. Another dynamic is that a pastor eventually just gets so discouraged in *trying to get a dead horse to run*, he just gives up and starts bringing *cotton candy* sermons.

For those individuals who would so easily follow one of these teachers of false doctrine, they are admonished to remember where those false teachers are headed, because when they follow them, they follow them to the same destiny. Jude 1:5-7 details three instances of God's *predetermined* judgment upon similar circumstances:

1. God delivered all of Israel out of Egyptian bondage. All those over the age of twenty that followed the advice ("unbelief") of the ten spies who gave a discouraging report regarding being able to conquer the Promised Land died in the next thirty-eight years in the wilderness. They died because of their own unfaithfulness in unbelief.
2. The fallen angels were judged, who followed Satan in his insurrection and rebellion against God's divine order in giving mankind "dominion" over the creation, including angels.
3. The cities of "Sodom and Gomorrah" were judged as they gave themselves permission against God's will to live in sexual licentiousness and homosexuality. God "set forth for an example" (Jude 1:7) the judgment on the people and cities of "Sodom and Gomorrah."

Do we think that we can minimize the importance of doctrine and not suffer similar consequences at the hand of God? Do we somehow think that we are excluded from this for ordained judgment warning of which we have hundreds of similar examples in the Scriptures?

Doctrine is what defines the Church as the "pillar and ground {*foundation*} of the truth" (I Timothy 3:15). Take away doctrine from the Church and you remove its foundations. Take away doctrine from the home and you remove its foundations. If false doctrine is Satan's main weapon in his arsenal against the family, right doctrine is the primary weapon of opposition against him. Show me a father who does not think that learning doctrine and teaching doctrine to his family is not a priority and I will show you a household destined for destruction in one way or another. That is the warning of Jude 1:3 in the command to "earnestly contend for the faith." Christ gave a similar warning.

> "[46] And why call ye me, Lord, Lord, and do not the things which I say? [47] Whosoever cometh to me, and heareth my sayings, and doeth them, I will shew you to whom he is like: [48] He is like a man which built an house, and digged deep, and laid the foundation on a rock: and when the flood arose, the stream beat vehemently upon that house, and could not shake it: for it was founded upon a rock. [49] But he that heareth, and doeth not, is like a man that without a foundation built an house upon the earth; against which the stream did beat vehemently, and immediately it fell; and the ruin of that house was great" (Luke 6:46-49).

The words "earnestly contend" in Jude 1:3 are from one Greek word, *epagonizomai* (ep-ag-o-nid'-zom-ahee). The *epi* prefix raises the issue of the struggle to its highest level. In other words, contending "for the faith" must be at the highest level of priorities. We are to use everything at our disposal in contending "for the faith."

A central aspect of contending "for the faith" is teaching doctrine to our children so as to transpose it to another generation who will do the same. This has been the responsibility of fathers since the beginning of time and God has never removed that responsibility from their shoulders. A father who is successful in everything else in life, but who fails to definitively teach his children about the character and attributes of God and how He wants us to live is a failure. However, as Christ said in Luke 6:47; "Whosoever cometh to me, and heareth my sayings, and doeth them" is about living truth. Living the truths that are learned intellectually is the primary way those truths will be transferred into the lives, not just the heads, of our children.

> "[1] Now these *are* the commandments, the statutes, and the judgments, which the LORD your God commanded to teach you, that ye might do *them* in the land whither ye go to possess it: [2] That thou mightest fear the LORD thy God, to keep all his statutes and his

commandments, which I command thee, thou, and thy son, and thy son's son, all the days of thy life; and that thy days may be prolonged. [3] Hear therefore, O Israel, and observe to do *it*; that it may be well with thee, and that ye may increase mightily, as the LORD God of thy fathers hath promised thee, in the land that floweth with milk and honey. [4] Hear, O Israel: The LORD our God *is* one LORD: [5] And thou shalt love the LORD thy God with all thine heart, and with all thy soul, and with all thy might. [6] And these words, which I command thee this day, shall be in thine heart: [7] And thou shalt teach them diligently unto thy children, and shalt talk of them when thou sittest in thine house, and when thou walkest by the way, and when thou liest down, and when thou risest up. [8] And thou shalt bind them for a sign upon thine hand, and they shall be as frontlets between thine eyes. [9] And thou shalt write them upon the posts of thy house, and on thy gates. [10] And it shall be, when the LORD thy God shall have brought thee into the land which he sware unto thy fathers, to Abraham, to Isaac, and to Jacob, to give thee great and goodly cities, which thou buildedst not, [11] And houses full of all good *things*, which thou filledst not, and wells digged, which thou diggedst not, vineyards and olive trees, which thou plantedst not; when thou shalt have eaten and be full; [12] *Then* beware lest thou forget the LORD, which brought thee forth out of the land of Egypt, from the house of bondage" (Deuteronomy 6:1-12).

Read Deuteronomy 6:5 again. The *Shema* of the Old Testament was repeated twice daily, every morning and every evening. The expectation of God is the total commitment of all that we are to Him - body (might or physical strength), soul (will and personality), and spirit (desires and attitudes). Loving God (sacrificially putting Him first) involves this kind of commitment.

Read Deuteronomy 6:6 again. Truth must be in the heart, not just in the head. *Imprinting absolutes* on the psyche refers to convictions of truth that stimulate our conscience to act upon what we believe to be right and wrong. This means we accept that there is reality to what we claim to believe. That reality is evident by our moment by moment attitude about truth. Our love for God is also evident by our work at integrating God's truth into our lives and into our relationships with others. We cannot honestly claim to love others if we fail to work at integrating God's truths into our lives and into theirs. We cannot love others and at the same time sacrifice truth, or compromise truth.

Read Deuteronomy 6:7-9 again. These three verses detail

the transfer of our love for God into the three other areas of relationships (husband/wife relationship, family relationship, and career or non-intimate relationships). God's emphasis on loving Him seems to be centrally concerned with our *attitudes* and *actions* in obeying truth. God's emphasis in loving others seems to be centrally concerned with the *integration* and *implementation* of truth into their lives (becoming *doers of the truth*).

Deuteronomy 6:7 shows the integration of truth into our children's lives (Action + Attitude = Loving God). The emphasis is upon the INCREMENTAL IMPLEMENTATION of truth as it is INTEGRATED into every aspect of living (not just memorization). Incremental means piece by piece by piece by piece - a little here, a little there.

> A fortress of biblical convictions is built one brick at a time. Each brick of truth must be carefully laid in place so that when the next truth is built upon it, the underlying structure is solid enough to support the additional stress of that new truth.

"For precept must be upon precept, precept upon precept; line upon line, line upon line; here a little, and there a little" (Isaiah 28:10).

Building truth into the lives of our children is the predominant factor in their education. Like the weaving of a basket, biblical truth *must* be interwoven into the everyday education of our children. It is not something that can be done as an add-on to their education. Neither is it something that can be done separately from their education. It must be integrated into and with their education.

We must learn to use every opportunity in life (successes and failures) to incrementally integrate truth in the lives of our children. The surest way to accomplish this is through the continual application of truth in our own lives and in the lives of our children. There must be consistency. The surest way to destroy this is by allowing duplicity in our lives. Duplicity is the *erasure of absolutes imprinted upon the psyche.*

Read Deuteronomy 6:8 again. The best way to incrementally integrate truth into the lives of our children is to live truth before them (by example). Can we honestly, or even intelligently, expect our children to love the Lord any more than we do? If God's truth is not important enough for you to work at translating it into the *language of living*, do not expect your children to make the attempt. The spiritual REALITY that is evident in your life will become evident in theirs.

Deuteronomy 6:8 is referring to being a living testimony to a reality that God's truths are important enough to you that you will make every effort to live those truths (not just an exhibition of spiritual piety). When our lives are a living testimony of God's truths, it brings glory to God. When our lives are just an exhibition of personal piety, it only brings glory to us. Our goal is to have our children's lives bring glory to God by restoring God's image in their lives.

Read Deuteronomy 6:9 again. God's truths need to be integrated into our external relationships. There is a lesser degree of influence and control in external relationships. Again the emphasis is about a *testimony of a living example*. The intent of living truth as a public testimony is to reveal a way of living that manifests what you hold valuable by what you are willing to stand for, with, or against. Your whole world is watching your attitude and actions. You are a living testimony to the reality of Christianity. Our public testimony is what we have established as a public standard. It is defined by the priorities of our lives and the truths by which we have determined to live.

1. Do you love the Lord? This is measured by your attitude (*God's commands are not a burden*) and actions (you obey God's commands).

2. What is your level of commitment to keeping God first in everything you do?

3. What efforts are you making to incrementally integrate God's truths into your own life and the lives of others (especially your children)?

DISCUSSION QUESTIONS

1. Discuss all that is involved in the never ending battles of *wants* and *wills*.

2. Read Ephesians 6:10-13. Explain the statement, "In the *battle of the ages*, those who battle for truth, or "the faith," do not battle directly with fallen angels. We battle against those deceived by them and who are being led by them through ongoing deception, false doctrines about God, and in varying degrees of unbelief regarding the person and work of God."

3. Discuss why the father in a home is a primary target in the *battle of the ages*.

4. Read Jude 1:1-25. Discuss the *will* of God as it relates to "the faith."

5. List and discuss the three aspects of a person's salvation and why understanding these three aspects of salvation is critical to "rightly dividing the word of truth."

6. Explain the phrase "common salvation" in Jude 1:3 and what is involved in contending for it.

7. Read Deuteronomy 6:1-12. Expand upon each of the practical applications given in verses five, six, seven, eight, and nine.

Chapter Sixty-eight
Understanding the Supernatural
Nature of Chastisement

When we ask God to act, we should be willing to wait upon Him for a supernatural response. True Christianity is living in such total *yieldedness* to the indwelling Holy Spirit that the supernatural aspect of that relationship becomes evident in our continence, demeanor, and attitudes. In this supernatural relationship with God that has come to be known as Christianity, a totally yielded believer occupies more than just a material/physical existence in this world. The totally yielded believer now operates within a supernatural *partnership* with God, as God seeks to miraculously save souls and teach those saved how to live to His glory.

Yet, a vast majority of that which professes to be *Christian* lacks any real manifestation of the *supernaturalness* of genuine Christianity. I am not talking about all the *pseudo-spirituality* of the Charismatic Movement. I am referring to the reality of the "fruit of the Spirit" manifested through the lives of those who profess to be "born again" believers. These are they that are baptized with the Spirit into the New Creation "in Christ," indwelled, and filled with the Spirit of God. When this genuine kind of Christian prays, he moves the *heart* and *hand* of God. When this kind of Christian walks through the world, people's lives are *moved* and *touched* by the *heart* and *hand* of God. When this kind of Christian speaks, the sinners of this world will either *get glad or get mad.*

The testimony of a genuine Christian is a history of God's supernatural activity. Sadly, the only supernatural activity most professing Christians have ever experienced is the conviction of sin, righteousness and judgment, and the supernatural work of the Holy Spirit in bringing them to faith in Christ and to salvation. This reality has to be a concern lest people live their lives with a false sense of security in a false reality. Granted, there will always be real Christians who regularly fail and fall into sin. The question we should ask though is, can a truly "born again" Christ habitually live in sin and not find the chastisement of a loving heavenly Father at his doorstep? The Word of God emphatically says, NO! Chastisement is a supernatural work of God in believers' lives.

"⁴ Ye have not yet resisted unto blood, striving against sin. ⁵ And ye have forgotten the exhortation which speaketh unto you as unto children, My son, despise not thou the chastening of the Lord, nor faint when thou art rebuked of him: ⁶ For whom the Lord loveth he chasteneth, and scourgeth every son whom he receiveth. ⁷ If ye endure chastening, God dealeth with you as with sons; for what son is he whom the father chasteneth not? ⁸ But if ye be without chastisement, whereof all are partakers, then are ye bastards, and not sons. ⁹ Furthermore we have had fathers of our flesh which corrected *us*, and we gave *them* reverence: shall we not much rather be in subjection unto the Father of spirits, and live? ¹⁰ For they verily for a few days chastened *us* after their own pleasure; but he for *our* profit, that *we* might be partakers of his holiness. ¹¹ Now no chastening for the present seemeth to be joyous, but grievous: nevertheless afterward it yieldeth the peaceable fruit of righteousness unto them which are exercised thereby" (Hebrews 12:4-11).

Many Christians have a strange and negative view of chastisement and local church-administrated discipline. Chastisement is an action of love according to Hebrews 12:6. This is even true when chastisement comes to an individual through congregational polity in a local church. Chastisement is intended to be *remedial*, not *punitive*. Although there is some unpleasantness involved in chastisement, whether it comes directly from God or through congregational polity, the primary purpose of chastisement is *remedial instruction in self-discipline*.

The word "chastisement" in Hebrews chapter six is translated from the Greek word *paideia* (pahee-di'-ah). It is a derivative of the Greek word *paideuo* (pahee-dyoo'-o), which means to *train up a child*. The idea is to train a child through discipline so that child can be self-disciplined. This training does not have to be in the form of the *rod*, or *scolding*. Any instruction and guidance regarding self-discipline can be considered chastisement. Biblical counseling is a form of chastisement. Preaching is a form of chastisement. Even personal Bible study can be a form of chastisement in that it trains one's self in self-discipline.

Although the primary meaning of the word "chastisement" is *disciplinary instruction*, most people have come to see the meaning to be *disciplinary correction through punitive actions*. This is the meaning only in extreme cases of *hard-heartedness* and unrepentance, but the primary meaning is a *nurturing kind of gentle instruction*. This kind of chastisement is exemplified by the Apostle Paul in I Thessalonians 2:7-12. The extreme of *disciplinary correction through punitive actions* is usually the necessity because of parental failures in the *nurturing instruction* of the Word of God, although even the best raised child is capable of hardness of the heart and unbelief.

"[7] But we were gentle among you, even as a nurse cherisheth her children: [8] So being affectionately desirous of you, we were willing to have imparted unto you, not the gospel of God only, but also our own souls, because ye were dear unto us. [9] For ye remember, brethren, our labour and travail: for labouring night and day, because we would not be chargeable unto any of you, we preached unto you the gospel of God. [10] Ye *are* witnesses, and God *also*, how holily and justly and unblameably we behaved ourselves among you that believe: [11] As ye know how we exhorted and comforted and charged every one of you, as a father *doth* his children, [12] That ye would walk worthy of God, who hath called you unto his kingdom and glory" (I Thessalonians 2:7-12).

"[24] And the servant of the Lord must not strive; but be gentle unto all *men*, apt to teach, patient, [25] In meekness instructing those that oppose themselves; if God peradventure will give them repentance to the acknowledging of the truth; [26] And *that* they may recover themselves out of the snare of the devil, who are taken captive by him at his will" (II Timothy 2:24-26).

> Wisdom in the Word of God does not merely know what is righteous. Wisdom is *knowing* the mind of God (God's will) through the Word of God and then *doing* what is righteous (or right).

This is the emphasis of the book of James and is the defining factor in a genuine life of *faith*. Knowing, without doing, is a subtle form of self-deception involving the issues of self-discipline.

"[19] Wherefore, my beloved brethren, let every man be swift to hear, slow to speak, slow to wrath: [20] For the wrath of man worketh not the righteousness of God. [21] Wherefore lay apart all filthiness and superfluity {*overflowing abundance*} of naughtiness, and receive with meekness the engrafted word, which is able to save your souls. [22] But be ye doers of the word, and not hearers only, deceiving your own selves" (James 1:19-22).

"[13] Who *is* a wise man *{in the knowing, application of, and living of truth}* and endued with knowledge *{having full comprehension}* among you? let him shew *{manifest that full comprehension}* out of a good conversation *{behavior}* his works *{doing}* with meekness of wisdom. [14] But if ye have bitter envying and strife in your hearts, glory not, and lie not against the truth. [15] This wisdom descendeth not from above, but *is* earthly, sensual, devilish. [16] For where envying and strife *is*, there *is* confusion and every evil work. [17] But the wisdom that is from above is first pure, then peaceable, gentle, *and* easy to be intreated, full of mercy and good fruits, without partiality, and without hypocrisy. [18] And the fruit of righteousness is sown in peace of them that make peace" (James 3:13-18).

Doing, or applying knowledge, is a manifestation that chastisement has accomplished its intent - SELF DISCIPLINE. This is the context of Proverbs 3 from which we find the quote in Hebrews 12:6. What the Father begins in the governance of his son's life, the son continues in his own governance of his life and practice.

"[1] My son, forget not my law; but let thine heart keep my commandments: [2] For length of days, and long life, and peace, shall they add to thee. [3] Let not mercy and truth forsake thee: bind them about thy neck; write them upon the table of thine heart: [4] So shalt thou find favour and good understanding in the sight of God and man. [5] Trust in the LORD with all thine heart; and lean not unto thine own understanding. [6] In all thy ways acknowledge him, and he shall direct thy paths. [7] Be not wise in thine own eyes: fear the LORD, and depart from evil. [8] It shall be health to thy navel, and marrow to thy bones. [9] Honour the LORD with thy substance, and with the firstfruits of all thine increase: [10] So shall thy barns be filled with plenty, and thy presses shall burst out with new wine. [11] My son, despise not the chastening of the LORD; neither be weary of his correction: [12] For whom the LORD loveth he correcteth; even as a father the son *in whom* he delighteth" (Proverbs 3:1-12).

Obviously, according to Hebrews 12:8, we cannot overemphasize the importance of chastisement in a believer's life when that believer commits a willful act of sin against God. Although a believer may stop God's chastisement with genuine repentance, things do not always happen that way. David's chastisement for his adulterous relationship with Bathsheba, and his murder of Bathsheba's husband Uriah to cover his sin, still resulted in the death of the child. Psalm 51 reflects the heart of David's repentance, but the child still died and David's testimony before the people of Israel and his children was greatly marred.

"[1] To the chief Musician, A Psalm of David, when Nathan the prophet came unto him, after he had gone in to Bathsheba. Have mercy upon me, O God, according to thy lovingkindness: according unto the multitude of thy tender mercies blot out my transgressions. [2] Wash me throughly from mine iniquity, and cleanse me from my sin. [3] For I acknowledge my transgressions: and my sin *is* ever before me. [4] Against thee, thee only, have I sinned, and done *this* evil in thy sight: that thou mightest be justified when thou speakest, *and* be clear when thou judgest. [5] Behold, I was shapen in iniquity; and in sin did my mother conceive me. [6] Behold, thou desirest truth in the inward parts: and in the hidden *part* thou shalt make me to know wisdom. [7] Purge me with hyssop, and I shall be clean: wash me, and I shall be whiter than snow. [8] Make me to hear joy and gladness; *that* the bones *which* thou hast broken may rejoice. [9] Hide thy face from my sins, and blot out all mine iniquities. [10] Create in me a clean heart, O God; and renew a right spirit within me. [11] Cast me not away from thy presence; and take not thy holy spirit from me. [12] Restore unto me the joy of thy salvation; and uphold me *with thy* free spirit. [13] *Then* will I teach transgressors thy ways; and sinners shall be converted unto thee" (Psalm 51:1-13).

Show me a *professing* Christian that habitually lives in sin and does not experience the supernatural chastisement of God upon his life and I will show you a person who has never been saved. According to Hebrews 12:8, that person has an *illegitimate birth*. The idea is that God is not that person's supernatural Father.

Some professing Christian's lifestyles are nothing more than a mockery of supernatural Christianity. These people profess to be Christians while living like "brute beasts." Both Peter and Jude warn of these kinds of professing Christians who enter the Church as "false teachers."

"But these speak evil of those things which they know not {*the supernatural or spiritual things*}: but what they know naturally {*as fallen beings*}, as brute {*irrational or unreasonable*} beasts {*that live by natural instincts*}, in those things they corrupt themselves" (Jude 1:10).

Peter and Jude almost *parrot* one another in their warning regarding false teachers and the false *Christianity* that comes from the mouths and lives of false teachers. There are characteristics of the supernatural life that is genuine Christianity and there are characteristics of the "natural" life of the carnal Christian and the false Christian. The significance of these ongoing "natural" characteristics is that the reality of having been "born again" is in question. The reality may be that a person has never been "born again" and that is why he cannot live the Christian life regardless of how hard he tries. Because this *pseudo-Christian* lacks the supernatural resources for a supernatural life (genuine Christianity), he will usually resort to various forms of legalism or asceticism to control his natural tendencies toward carnality. These solutions will equally prove unfruitful as he begins to encircle himself and his life in a constantly narrowing system of isolation from the world and restraints upon himself.

> "[12] But these, as natural brute beasts, made to be taken and destroyed, speak evil of the things that they understand not; and shall utterly perish in their own corruption; [13] And shall receive the reward of unrighteousness, *as* they that count it pleasure to riot in the day time. Spots *they are* and blemishes, sporting themselves with their own deceivings while they feast with you; [14] Having eyes full of adultery, and that cannot cease from sin; beguiling unstable souls: an heart they have exercised with covetous practices; cursed children: [15] Which have forsaken the right way, and are gone astray, following the way of Balaam *the son* of Bosor, who loved the wages of unrighteousness; [16] But was rebuked for his iniquity: the dumb ass speaking with man's voice forbad the madness of the prophet. [17] These are wells without water, clouds that are carried with a tempest; to whom the mist of darkness is reserved for ever" (II Peter 2:12-17).

In trying to counteract the constant carnality of pseudo-Christians, pastors often contribute to these individuals' self-deception. First, they never raise the question of the reality of a false profession of faith and the possibility of never having been "born again." Second, they reinforce the false profession by teaching these people eternal security. Third, they instruct the person to live in higher levels of isolation and a more stringent list of self-restraints. Higher levels of isolation and a more stringent list of self-restraints may be effective in the areas of self-discipline, but what they really do is merely take the person out of the circumstances of life that require a supernatural Christianity. Although a genuine Christian should never purposefully put himself in situations or places that would contradict a testimony of holiness and separation, there is nothing spiritual or supernatural about a Christianity that merely avoids *life in general* and the daily temptations and difficulties of the interpersonal relationships that come with *life in general.*

> "[17] But, beloved, remember ye the words which were spoken before of the apostles of our Lord Jesus Christ; [18] How that they told you there should be mockers in the last time, who should walk after their own ungodly lusts. [19] These be they who separate themselves, sensual, having not the Spirit. [20] But ye, beloved, building up yourselves on your most holy faith, praying in the Holy Ghost, [21] Keep yourselves in the love of God, looking for the mercy of our Lord Jesus Christ unto eternal life. [22] And of some have compassion, making a difference: [23] And others save with fear, pulling *them* out of the fire; hating even the garment spotted by the flesh. [24] Now unto him that is able to keep you from falling, and to present *you* faultless before the presence of his glory with exceeding joy, [25] To the only wise God our Saviour, *be* glory and majesty, dominion and power, both now and ever. Amen" (Jude 1:17-25).

In Jude 1:18, the Word of God directs our attention to the "mockers in the last time." When God gives a backslidden Christian a *wake-up call* of chastisement, do not hit the *snooze button* by rescuing the sinner from God's supernatural operations in his life. The word "mockers" is from the Greek word *empaiktes* (emp-aheek-tace'). It refers to a person who derides something or someone verbally or by actions. This deriding is defined by the words "who should walk after their own ungodly lusts. These are "they who separate themselves, sensual, having not the Spirit." This false lifestyle is the by-product of false beliefs and false teaching regarding *Christian liberty* and a false teaching regarding *freedom from the Law.* The most critical part of Jude's statement regarding these individuals is that they have "not the Spirit." In other words, they are not saved.

It is a sad state of affairs when a professing Christian lives in such outward contradiction to the Word of God - in sensuality and carnality. However, these false teachers mock God's holiness and the distinctive, "peculiar" lifestyle of genuine Christianity by justifying *sensuality* and *carnality*. "Sensual" refers to allowing the free expression of the fallen nature. This is often argued as justifiable as long as there is a degree of *moderation*. However, that degree of *moderation* seems to be increasing with every generation of this pseudo-Christianity.

Another characteristic of these undisciplined and *pseudo-Christians* is given to us by the words "who separate themselves." This is not referring to what is commanded in other portions of Scripture about being separated from worldliness. It is not referring to God's command to separate ourselves from allegiances with other ecclesiastical bodies that hold to false doctrine or involve themselves in sinful practices. The word "separate" in Jude 1:19 is from the Greek word *apodiorizo* (ap-od-ee-or-id'-zo). It simply means to *disjoin*. This refers to being disconnected from formal local church membership and the spiritual vitality of that communion and its accountability. The idea is that these individuals live independently of local church accountability and the auspices of the chastisement (*growth towards self-discipline*) that comes through the spiritual dynamic of the local church. Although they profess to be in union with Christ through salvation, they choose to *disjoin* or *remain disconnected* from the local *body* of which Jesus is the "head." This is a serious act of disobedience that reflects an almost complete misunderstanding of the ongoing, nurturing process of chastisement through local church involvement.

Although God gave Israel a formal vehicle for their *nurturing growth* (chastisement) in the Priesthood of Israel, God continued to intercede within the nation of Israel as *Father*. God has appointed the Priesthood of Israel to be the means through which He would work in His teaching, nurturing ministry from generation to generation. Sadly, the Priesthood of Israel failed as did the priesthood of the family under the patriarchal system of truth transference. Yet, through all those many centuries of failure by those God had appointed to the work of nurturing and chastisement, God never relinquished His interceding work of chastisement upon individuals, families, the Priesthood, and the nation as a whole. God speaks to this in Malachi chapter two at the close of Israel's failure in *preserving* the Mosaic Covenant.

"[10] Have we not all one father? hath not one God created us? why do we deal treacherously every man against his brother, by profaning the covenant of our fathers? [11] Judah hath dealt treacherously, and an abomination is committed in Israel and in Jerusalem; for Judah hath profaned the holiness of the LORD which he loved, and hath married the daughter of a strange god. [12] The LORD will cut off the man that doeth this, the master and the scholar, out of the tabernacles of Jacob, and him that offereth an offering unto the LORD of hosts. [13] And this have ye done again, covering the altar of the LORD with tears, with weeping, and with crying out, insomuch that he regardeth not the offering any more, or receiveth *it* with good will at your hand. [14] Yet ye say, Wherefore? Because the LORD hath been witness between thee and the wife of thy youth, against whom thou hast dealt treacherously: yet *is* she thy companion, and the wife of thy covenant. [15] And did not he make one? Yet had he the residue of the spirit. And wherefore one? <u>That he might seek a godly seed</u>. Therefore take heed to your spirit, and let none deal treacherously against the wife of his youth. [16] For the LORD, the God of Israel, saith that he hateth putting away: for *one* covereth violence with his garment, saith the LORD of hosts: therefore take heed to your spirit, that ye deal not treacherously. [17] Ye have wearied the LORD with your words. Yet ye say, Wherein have we wearied *him*? When ye say, Every one that doeth evil *is* good in the sight of the LORD, and he delighteth in them; or, Where *is* the God of judgment" (Malachi 2:10-17)?

The priesthood of the father in the home is the earliest leadership role God gave to believers. It is a responsibility that transcends all dispensations. After the fall of mankind into sin and the corruption of man with a sin nature, the priesthood of the father in the home became a critical responsibility in order for a man to reproduce a "godly seed."

Since the "seed" of the man was corrupted by the fall, procreation could no longer reproduce in the "image of God" in which man was originally created. Yet, even in this corruption, God sought a "godly seed" by covenanting with fathers as priests of their homes in raising their children in such a manner as to regenerate godliness in their lives. Salvation and regeneration were not just about a *fire escape* from the condemnation of eternal Hell. Salvation and regeneration are about the restoration of the *God-life*. Salvation and regeneration are about the supernatural restoration of the image of God in all the lives of true believers through the work of the Holy Spirit in the world. Godly fathers, who had this supernatural work done in their lives, could reproduce it in their children by the priestly leadership of instruction, modeling, and devotional dedication to live for the LORD. Before the fall, procreation would have resulted in the reproduction of the image of God in our children naturally. After the fall, reproducing the image of God in our children would require a supernatural relationship with God in parenting and a supernatural involvement of God in the lives of children through a faith relationship with Him.

"[21] And the LORD God caused a deep sleep to fall upon Adam, and he slept: and he took one of his ribs, and closed up the flesh instead thereof; [22] And the rib, which the LORD God had taken from man, made he a woman, and brought her unto the man. [23] And Adam said, This *is* now bone of my bones, and flesh of my flesh: she shall be called Woman, because she was taken out of Man. [24] Therefore shall a man leave his father and his mother, and shall cleave unto his wife: and they shall be one flesh. [25] And they were both naked, the man and his wife, and were not ashamed" (Genesis 2:21-25).

"[25] Husbands, love your wives, even as Christ also loved the church, and gave himself for it; [26] That he might sanctify and cleanse it with the washing of water by the word, [27] That he might present it to himself a glorious church, not having spot, or wrinkle, or any such thing; but that it should be holy and without blemish. [28] So ought men to love their wives as their own bodies. He that loveth his wife loveth himself. [29] For no man ever yet hated his own flesh; but nourisheth and cherisheth it, even as the Lord the church: [30] For we are members of his body, of his flesh, and of his bones. [31] For this cause shall a man leave his father and mother, and shall be joined unto his wife, and they two shall be one flesh. [32] This is a great mystery: but I speak concerning Christ and the church. [33] Nevertheless let every one of you in particular so love his wife even as himself; and the wife *see* that she reverence *her* husband" (Ephesians 5:25-33).

The *union* of two cooperative individuals, as husband and wife, involving themselves in *unity* with God to raise a "godly seed" is said to also portray the spiritual dynamic of the *union* and *unity* of the Spirit in His operations within the context of the local church. The individual that lives disjoined from formal local church membership is like the man who wants *union* with his girlfriend but refuses to marry her. He wants *union* without formally *uniting* with her. It is like the woman that says to her boyfriend, "yes, you are the only one I love, but I still want to date other men." Salvation is your formal union and formal church membership is living in faithfulness and accountability to that union with Christ.

DISCUSSION QUESTIONS

1. Why do you think that the vast majority of that which professes to be *Christian* lacks any real manifestation of the supernaturalness of genuine Christianity?

2. Can a truly "born again" Christian habitually live in sin and not find the chastisement of a loving heavenly Father at his doorstep? If not, explain why not.

3. Explain the purpose in the spiritual dynamic of chastisement translated from the Greek word *paideia* (pahee-di'-ah) in Hebrews 12:8.

4. Read I Thessalonians 2:7-12 and II Timothy 2:24-26. The primary meaning of chastisement is a *nurturing* kind of gentle instruction. Discuss how this definition is practically manifested in the ministry of the Apostle Paul in the above two texts.

5. Define biblical *wisdom* from James 1:19-22 and 3:13-18. Discuss how this is the outcome of true chastisement.

6. "What the Father begins in the governance of his son's life, the son continues in his own governance of his life and practice." Read Proverbs 3:1-12 and discuss this statement from the context of these verses of Scripture.

7. A number of issues arise concerning Hebrews 12:8.

   A. If a professing Christian continues to live in habitual unrepentance of sin, what should be your conclusion about that person's salvation?
   B. How would you deal with such a person?
   C. Often this kind of person responds to an invitation under the guilt of sin, resulting in doubts about salvation. How would you deal with such a person and what questions should you ask?
   D. Why should eternal security be the last thing you consider?

Chapter Sixty-nine
Assurance of Salvation and Eternal Security

Which came first, the chicken or the egg? We can only know the answer from the speculation that since God created Adam as a mature adult that the chicken came before the egg. As I prepared this study on the two related doctrines of eternal security and assurance of salvation, I had to ask myself which of the two should be taught first. Should I teach eternal security first and risk the possibility of giving someone with a false conversion a false security? In order to avoid that possibility, I thought it best to first teach regarding the issue of assurance of salvation. If a person is genuinely "born again," God will not *un-birth* him if he lives in sin. Therefore, the *if* becomes the first question that must be answered.

"[1] Behold, what manner of love the Father hath bestowed upon us, that we should be called the sons of God: therefore the world knoweth us not, because it knew him not. [2] Beloved, now are we the sons of God, and it doth not yet appear what we shall be: but we know that, when he shall appear, we shall be like him; for we shall see him as he is. [3] And every man that hath this hope in him purifieth himself, even as he is pure. [4] Whosoever {*habitually*} committeth sin {*habitually*} transgresseth also the law: for sin is the transgression of the law. [5] And ye know that he was manifested to take away our sins; and in him is no sin. [6] Whosoever abideth in him {*habitually*} sinneth {*linear present active indicative*} not: whosoever {*habitually*} sinneth {*linear present active articular participle*} hath not seen him, neither known him. [7] Little children, let no man {*habitually*} deceive {*present active imperative*} you: he that {*habitually*} doeth {*present active participle*} righteousness is righteous, even as he is righteous. [8] He that {*habitually*} committeth sin is of the devil; for the devil sinneth {*linear progressive present active indicative*, "he has been sinning from the beginning"} from the beginning. For this purpose the Son of God was manifested, that he might destroy the works of the devil. [9] Whosoever is born of God doth not {*habitually*} commit sin; for his seed remaineth in him: and he cannot sin, because he is born of God. [10] In this the children of God are manifest {*revealed*}, and the children of the devil:

whosoever {*habitually*} doeth {*linear present participle*} not righteousness is not of God, neither he that {*habitually*} loveth {*present active participle*} not his brother" (I John 3:1-10).

The word "committeth" in I John 3:4 and 8 is a *present active participle*. The words "transgresseth" in I John 3:4, "sinneth" in I John 3:6, and "commit" in I John 3:9 are all *present active indicative*. What this means is that we can insert the word *habitually* before each of these words to clarify the meaning. Although the believer will commit occasional acts of sin, if he *habitually* lives in sin *and is not repentant*, his salvation should questioned. *Habitual* sin is not a question of carnality. *Habitual* sin is a question of salvation. *Robertson's Word Pictures in the New Testament* says the following on I John 3:9.

> "Doeth no sin (*hamartian ou poiei*). Linear present active indicative as in verse 1Jo 3:4 like *hamartanei* in verse 1Jo 3:8. The child of God does not have the habit of sin. His seed (*sperma autou*). God's seed, 'the divine principle of life' (Vincent). Cf. Joh 1:1-51. And he cannot sin (*kai ou dunatai hamartanein*). This is a wrong translation, for this English naturally means 'and he cannot commit sin' as if it were *kai ou dunatai hamartein* or *hamartêsai* (second aorist or first aorist active infinitive). The present active infinitive *hamartanein* can only mean '**and he cannot go on sinning**,' as is true of *hamartanei* in verse 1Jo 3:8 and *hamartanôn* in verse 1Jo 3:6. For the aorist subjunctive to commit a sin see *hamartête* and *hamartêi* in 1Jo 2:1. A great deal of false theology has grown out of a misunderstanding of the tense of *hamartanein* here. Paul has precisely John's idea in Ro 6:1 *epimenômen têi hamartiâi* (shall we continue in sin, present active linear subjunctive) in contrast with *hamartêsômen* in Ro 6:15 (shall we commit a sin, first aorist active subjunctive)."[34] **Bolding added**

Eternal security is a doctrine that finds its foundations in the work of Christ for our salvation. It is God who saves us "by grace through faith," and it is God who *keeps* us (*preserves* us) in that salvation. Once a person has been regenerated ("born again") that person is eternally secure in that position.

On the other hand, assurance of salvation "assures the heart" (I John 3:19) that regeneration has taken place. In other words, assurance has to do with the *empirical evidences* that a "new

---

[34] Robertson, A.T. *Word Pictures in the New Testament. SwordSearcher Software 6.2.*

creation" has happened in a person's life and that he has been "born again."

Eternal security and assurance of salvation are separate doctrines in their view of salvation (although assurance can come through fully understanding the basis of eternal security). Eternal security looks at salvation from God's perspective. Assurance of salvation looks at salvation from man's perspective and asks the question; have I really been *born again* and if so, how can I know this has taken place? Because these two doctrines are not separated into and viewed from these two perspectives, many people mix them together and end up offering more confusion than comfort.

Assurance of Salvation

Warren Wiersbe says in his book *Be Real*:

"A counterfeit Christian - and they are common - is something like a counterfeit ten-dollar bill. Suppose you have a counterfeit bill and actually think it is genuine. You use it to pay for a tank of gas. The gas station manager uses it to buy supplies. The supplier uses the bill to pay the grocer. The grocer bundles the bill up with 49 other ten-dollar bills and takes it to the bank. And the teller says, 'I'm sorry, but this bill is counterfeit.'

That ten-dollar bill may have done a lot of good while it was in circulation, but when it arrived at the bank it was exposed for what it really was, and put out of circulation.

So with a counterfeit Christian. He may do many good things in this life, but when he faces the final judgment he will be rejected. 'Many will say to me in that day, Lord, Lord, have we not prophesied in thy name? and in thy name have cast out devils? and in thy name done many wonderful works? And then will I profess unto them, I never knew you: depart from me, ye that work iniquity.' (Matthew 7:22-23). Each of us must ask himself honestly, 'Am I a true child of God or am I a counterfeit Christian? Have I truly been born of God?'"[35]

---

[35] Wiersbe, Warren W. *Be Real*. (Wheaton, Illinois: Victor Books, 1978) pages 17-18.

If we have placed saving faith in the finished work of Christ, then we are "born again." If that is the case, there should be *empirical evidences* of that regeneration. The two issues with which assurance of salvation is involved are:

1. Have I understood the gospel and trusted in Christ and what He has accomplished? (repented, believed, confessed, called, and received)

2. If you have trusted in "another gospel, which is not another" (Galatians 1:6-7), the reason you do not, and cannot, have assurance is because you are not saved. For any real assurance, you must begin there.

A wise person should ask himself, "What evidence is there in my life to show that I am a "new creation" (II Corinthians 5:17)?" Assurance answers the hypothetical *if* of salvation. Many today are teaching that salvation is based upon *commitment* to Christ. There are many who are saved who have little, if any, *commitment* to Christ. However, without *commitment*, if they are saved they are eternally secure in that salvation, but they can never really have assurance of salvation. Their lack of *commitment* will continually cause them to question the reality and genuineness of their new birth "in Christ." As a result, they will constantly doubt their salvation. The epistle of I John was written to give assurance of salvation (see I John 3:19 and 5:13). People who question their salvation almost always have a sin problem or a lack of genuine interest in spiritual things.

The epistle of I John is the epistle of assurance. I often refer to it as the *if epistle*. The word "if" is used twenty-one times in this little epistle and is the emphasis in each of its five chapters. The many *ifs* draw your attention to the evidences that salvation is real so that you "might know that ye have eternal life." Notice the repeated use of the word "if" in the five sentences in I John 1:5-10.

"[5] This then is the message which we have heard of him, and declare unto you, that God is light, and in him is no darkness at all. [6] **If** we say that we have fellowship {a *working partnership in union and unity*} with him, and walk in darkness, we lie, and do not the truth: [7] But **if** we walk in the light, as he is in the light, we have fellowship {a *working partnership in union and unity*} one with another, and the blood of Jesus Christ his Son cleanseth {*this is familial forgiveness, not judicial*} us from all sin. [8] **If** we say that we have no sin, we deceive ourselves, and the truth is not in us. [9] **If** we confess our sins, he is faithful and just to forgive us *our* sins, and to cleanse us from all unrighteousness. [10] **If** we say that we have not sinned, we make him a liar, and his word is not in us" (I John 1:5-10)

According to I John 1:8 and 10, a person is deceiving himself if he claims to be sinless. We are sinners even after salvation. In fact, if we claim not to be a sinner we call God a liar (Romans 3:23). Every one of us sins in some way every day. That sin needs to be daily repented of *moment-by-moment* and confessed *moment-by-moment* for the maintenance of a working partnership with God in ministry to supernaturally occur. However, that sin never affects our salvation in any way. God's wrath upon all sin has universally been satisfied in the death of Jesus Christ. A person still needs to repent, believe, confess, call, and receive Jesus Christ to be saved, but God has been propitiated for all sin from all ages, past, present, and future.

"[1] My little children, these things write I unto you, that ye sin not. And **if** any man sin, we have an advocate {*parakletos, intercessor, consoler, or comforter*} with the Father, Jesus Christ the righteous: [2] And he is the propitiation for our sins: and not for ours only, but also for *the sins of* the whole world. [3] And hereby we do know that we know him, **if** we keep {*watch over, as in guarding something precious; the emphasis is the value we put upon the teachings of Jesus to the degree that we observe*} his commandments {*the revealed will of God in the teachings of Jesus*}. [4] He that saith, I know him, and keepeth not his commandments, is a liar, and the truth is not in him. [5] But whoso keepeth his word, in him verily is the love of God perfected: hereby know we that we are in him. [6] He that saith he abideth in him ought himself also so to walk, even as he walked" (I John 2:1-6).

The genuinely "born again" believer understands that if he seeks to obey God's commands, doing so will require spiritual warfare. To profess to be a Christian and not hold precious the Word of God is an overwhelming contradiction to the definition of faith, which means to believe something so deeply that it commands our life actions in conformity to the truth we believe. To say we are saved and not have this *value* in our lives is a contradiction against the reality of salvation and having been "born again." Sadly, many people can give themselves false assurance when they overlook this testimony against "being born" again.

I John 2:1-6 is not talking about living sinlessly. That has already been established in I John 1:8, "**If** we say that we have no sin, we deceive ourselves, and the truth is not in us." The assurance is found in the reality of the *desire to obey* and in the spiritual *struggle* with our own sin nature to actually live the *Christ-life*. Spiritual growth is simply measured upon a scale of the degree of submission of the believer's will to God's will as revealed by God's Word. Therefore, spiritual growth is not merely growth in the knowledge of God's Word. Lost people can acquire tremendous amounts of Scriptural knowledge through reading, teaching, and preaching. However, if that Scriptural knowledge does not move a person to love the LORD and obey Him from the heart, knowledge then is nothing more than knowledge. That is what is meant by the phrase, "[3] And hereby we do know that we know him, **if** we keep {*watch over, as in guarding something precious; the emphasis is the value we put upon the teachings of Jesus to the degree that we we observe*} his commandments {*the revealed will of God in the teachings of Jesus*}. [4] He that saith, I know him, and keepeth not his commandments, is a liar, and the truth is not in him. [5] But whoso keepeth his word, in him verily is the love of God perfected: hereby know we that we are in him. [6] He that saith he abideth in him ought himself also so to walk, even as he walked" (I John 2:1-6).

I will never understand why people want to give themselves a false assurance of salvation when the evidence to the contrary seems so obvious. God is not finished in I John with bringing those looking for assurance before the *mirror of reality*.

"[7] Brethren, I write no new commandment unto you, but an old commandment which ye had from the beginning. The old commandment is the word which ye have heard from the beginning. [8] Again, a new commandment I write unto you, which thing is true in him and in you: because the darkness is past, and the true light now shineth {*referring to the indwelling Shekinah*}. [9] He that saith he is in the light {*is 'born again' into the supernatural realm of union and unity with Christ*}, and hateth his brother, is in darkness {*the natural realm of spiritual powerlessness*} even until now. [10] He that loveth his brother abideth {*in this action of loving, he continues, stays, or remains; the idea is that through this act of supernatural loving he generates this permanent residency*} in the light {*not in the sense of keeping one's own salvation, but in the sense of the manifestation of the reality of that salvation*}, and there is none occasion of stumbling in him. [11] But he that hateth his brother is in darkness, and walketh in darkness, and knoweth not whither he goeth, because that darkness hath blinded his eyes" (I John 2:7-11).

When we look at the historical account of Cain's murder of his brother Abel, we can obviously see that Abel was saved because he brought the substitutionary lamb sacrifice and we can see that Cain was lost in that Cain brought the work of his own hands. However, there is another level to this account. Cain's jealousy and hatred of Abel's righteous standing before God, because of Abel's correct understanding of the *gospel in the sacrifice* and Abel's faith in that sacrifice, manifested the reality of Cain's degenerate heart. Cain hated and murdered as a result. The truly regenerate person keeps the *chains of spiritual restraint* upon his heart through the moment by moment yielding of emotions to the Lord. The truly regenerate person understands his depravity and knows he cannot allow that depravity to find release in any form. He also understands that he has little power over his depraved nature and declares his dependence upon God for help through each moment of his life.

In I John 2:18-19, God addresses the issue of departure from the practice of the faith as evidence that regeneration has never taken place. This is parallel teaching to Christ's parable of the *Sower, the Seed, and the Soils* in Matthew chapter thirteen.

> "[18] Little children, it is the last time: and as ye have heard that antichrist shall come, even now are there many antichrists; whereby we know that it is the last time. [19]They went out from us, but they were not of us; for if they had been of us, they would *no doubt* have continued with us: but *they went out*, that they might be made manifest that they were not all of us" (I John 2:18-19).

In Christ's parable of the *Sower, the Seed, and the Soils*, we are given three forms of departure revealing that the *Seed* never produced true salvation. There may be a semblance of salvation, but that salvation was not genuine. The key word to genuine conversion in the heart is the word "understandeth." It is the condition of the *Soil* that determines if a *plant* comes to maturity and actually produces *fruit*. The person whose professed spiritual life never produces *fruit* should question the reality of his salvation.

> "[18] Hear ye therefore the parable of the sower. [19] When any one heareth the word of the kingdom, and understandeth *it* not, then cometh the wicked *one*, and catcheth away that which was sown in

his heart. This is he which received seed by the way side. [20] But he that received the seed into stony places, the same is he that heareth the word, and anon with joy receiveth it; [21] Yet hath he not root in himself, but dureth for a while: for when tribulation or persecution ariseth because of the word, by and by he is offended. [22] He also that received seed among the thorns is he that heareth the word; and the care of this world, and the deceitfulness of riches, choke the word, and he becometh unfruitful. [23] But he that received seed into the good ground is he that heareth the word, and understandeth it; which also beareth fruit, and bringeth forth, some an hundredfold, some sixty, some thirty" (Matthew 13:18-23).

1. He that "received seed by the way side": The "kingdom" is "the regeneration" or the final eternal existence of the "new creation" in the New Heaven/Earth. We enter into "the regeneration" by being "born again." We are "born again" when we understand our condemnation, understand the death, burial, and resurrection of Christ and what it accomplishes for those that understand and believe it. Those that do not understand do not biblically respond to God's offered gift and their faith is misplaced or misdirected.

2. "He that received the seed into stony places": Here again, there is no depth of understanding of the Gospel. Many today are honestly searching for God's way, but Satan has erected hundreds and thousands of *misdirection signs*. Satan does not need to get you living in the depth of sin to deceive you. He simply needs to misdirect your faith into trusting your own morals. He simply needs to get you to trust in some religious ritual in order to misplace your faith in something other than the finished work of Christ.

3. "He also that received seed among the thorns": There are some who say this type of person may be saved. That is certainly possible. However, here the purpose of life is completely misdirected. This person may be saved, but will NEVER see *fruit* in his life because is life is invested in the material things of this world. Notice that this is not referring to a person living in outrageous acts of moral turpitude. This person is concerned more about what the people of the world think of him than in being faithful to his new citizenship in "the regeneration." His life then becomes preoccupied with pursuing *status*.

The Works of the Holy Spirit that Confirm Eternal Security and Give Assurance of Salvation

"[22] And it was at Jerusalem the feast of the dedication, and it was winter. [23] And Jesus walked in the temple in Solomon's porch. [24] Then came the Jews round about him, and said unto him, How long dost thou make us to doubt? If thou be the Christ, tell us plainly. [25] Jesus answered them, I told you, and ye believed not: the works that I do in my Father's name, they bear witness of me. [26] But ye believe not, because ye are not of my sheep, as I said unto you. [27] My sheep hear my voice, and I know them, and they follow me: [28] And I give unto them eternal life; and they shall never perish, neither shall any *man* pluck them out of my hand. [29] My Father, which gave *them* me, is greater than all; and no *man* is able to pluck *them* out of my Father's hand. [30] I and *my* Father are one" (John 10:22-30).

> Salvation is a supernatural work of God given to the believer as a gift. It cannot be earned, purchased, or retained through human "works." Salvation is a work of God and is provided to "whosoever" by the loving grace of God through the death, burial, and resurrection of Jesus Christ. Once a person has been supernaturally "born again" "by grace through faith" that person is kept, or preserved, in that salvation by the *works* of God, not by the *works* of man.

There are four main works of the Holy Spirit of God that secure the believer in salvation. Each of these four *works* is connected to many other *works* of the Spirit. None of these four *works* of the Spirit of God can be undone. They are permanent.

Regeneration or being "born again"

If a person has been "born again," and could lose his salvation, he would also need to be *un-born again* to somehow lose his salvation. The "born again" person's salvation is already "complete" positionally as far as God is concerned.

"[4] And this I say, lest any man should beguile you with enticing words. [5] For though I be absent in the flesh, yet am I with you in the spirit, joying and beholding your order, and the stedfastness of your faith in Christ. [6] As ye have therefore received Christ Jesus the

Lord, *so* walk ye in him: [7] Rooted and built up in him, and stablished in the faith, as ye have been taught, abounding therein with thanksgiving. [8] Beware lest any man spoil you through philosophy and vain deceit, after the tradition of men, after the rudiments of the world, and not after Christ. [9] For in him dwelleth all the fulness of the Godhead bodily. [10] And ye are complete in him, which is the head of all principality and power: [11] In whom also ye are circumcised with the circumcision made without hands, in putting off the body of the sins of the flesh by the circumcision of Christ: [12] Buried with him in baptism, wherein also ye are risen with *him* through the faith of the operation of God, who hath raised him from the dead. [13] And you, being dead in your sins and the uncircumcision of your flesh, hath he quickened together with him, having forgiven you all trespasses; [14] Blotting out the handwriting of ordinances that was against us, which was contrary to us, and took it out of the way, nailing it to his cross; [15] *And* having spoiled principalities and powers, he made a shew of them openly, triumphing over them in it" (Colossians 2:4-15).

If a person has been genuinely "born again," that person's eternal destiny is *predestined to glorification.* In other words, God is going to insure the final outcome. The context of Romans chapter eight is the doctrine of glorification, which is the final act of God in a person's regeneration that begins with salvation. The person who genuinely has been "born again" is predestined to this ultimate outcome by God's assurance.

"[29] For whom he did foreknow, he also did predestinate _to be conformed to the image of his Son_, that he {*Jesus*} might be the firstborn among many brethren. [30] Moreover whom he did predestinate, them he also called: and whom he called, them he also justified: and whom he justified, them he also glorified. [31] What shall we then say to these things? If God *be* for us, who *can be* against us? [32] He that spared not his own Son, but delivered him up for us all, how shall he not with him also freely give us all things? [33] Who shall lay any thing to the charge of God's elect? *It is* God that justifieth. [34] Who *is* he that condemneth? *It is* Christ that died, yea rather, that is risen again, who is even at the right hand of God, who also maketh intercession for us. [35] Who shall separate us from the love of Christ? *shall* tribulation, or distress, or persecution, or famine, or nakedness, or peril, or sword? [36] As it is written, For thy sake we are killed all the day long; we are accounted as sheep for the slaughter. [37] Nay, in all these things we are more than conquerors through him that loved us. [38] For I am persuaded, that neither death, nor life, nor angels, nor principalities, nor powers, nor things present, nor things to come, [39] Nor height, nor depth, nor any other creature, shall be able to separate us from the love of God, which is <u>in Christ Jesus</u> our Lord (Romans 8:29-39).

The "love of God" is "in Christ Jesus." This love extends into the cursed creation through revelation of God, the offering of salvation to "whosoever" "by grace through faith," and the procuring of salvation through the death, burial, and resurrection of Jesus Christ as "the firstborn from the dead." This is the *New Genesis* into which the believer is "born again" at the moment of salvation. The ultimate outcome of that *delivery* is guaranteed by God. This is what *predestined* means.

Indwelling

The instant a person puts faith in Jesus Christ for salvation the Holy Spirit of God indwells him. If he could lose his salvation, the Holy Spirit would have to *un-indwell* him. Hebrews 13:5 promises that He will never do that.

"[5]*Let your* conversation *be* without covetousness; *and be* content with such things as ye have: for he hath said, I will never leave thee {*referring to His abiding presen*ce}, nor forsake thee {*referring to His works in our lives; Romans 8:28*}. [6] So that we may boldly say, The Lord *is* my helper, and I will not fear what man shall do unto me" (Hebrews 13:5-6).

Although the "born again" believer is commanded to "abide in" Christ, this has nothing to do with the believer's salvation. Abiding in Christ is seeking to live in unbroken "fellowship" with Christ.

The indwelling of the Holy Spirit is the *abiding* or *living presence* of the Holy Spirit within the body of the "born again" Christian. The indwelling of the Spirit is a permanent *union*. Abiding "in Christ" is bringing our actions, thought life, and emotions into a *unity* with the Spirit of God. The indwelling *union* defines the security of the "born again" believer's position "in Christ." The sinning believer can break the "unity of the Spirit" but never the *union*.

The Baptism with the Spirit

The instant a person puts faith in Jesus Christ for salvation the Holy Spirit *positionally* removes the believer from the cursed first creation and places that believer *into* the *New Creation* ("the regeneration," Matthew 19:28) as a part of the "body of Christ" (I

Corinthians 12:13, i.e., the *New Creation*). If we could lose our salvation, the Holy Spirit would have to un-join us from the "body of Christ."

"¹² For as the body is one, and hath many members, and all the members of that one body, being many, are one body: so also *is* Christ. ¹³ For by one Spirit are we all baptized into one body, whether *we be* Jews or Gentiles, whether *we be* bond or free; and have been all made to drink into one Spirit" (I Corinthians 12:12-13).

"¹⁶ Wherefore henceforth know we no man after the flesh: yea, though we have known Christ after the flesh, yet now henceforth know we *him* no more. ¹⁷ Therefore if any man *be* in Christ, *he is* a new creature: old things are passed away; behold, all things are become new" (II Corinthians 5:16-17).

The Sealing of the Holy Spirit

The Holy Spirit is said to be the believer's *seal of redemption* (Ephesians 4:30). If a believer could lose his salvation, he would have to be *un-sealed*. This would deny Ephesians 1:13-13 and 4:30 (compare Romans 8:14-23).

"³ Blessed *be* the God and Father of our Lord Jesus Christ, who hath blessed us with all spiritual blessings in heavenly *places* in Christ: ⁴ According as he hath chosen us {*the Church collectively as an eternal priesthood of all believers*} in him before the foundation of the world, that we should be holy and without blame before him in love: ⁵ Having predestinated us {*the Church collectively as an eternal priesthood of all believers*} unto the adoption of {*the placement in position as adult*} children by Jesus Christ to himself, according to the good pleasure of his will, ⁶ To the praise of the glory of his grace, wherein he hath made us accepted in the beloved. ⁷ In whom we have redemption through his blood, the forgiveness of sins, according to the riches of his grace; ⁸ Wherein he hath abounded toward us in all wisdom and prudence; ⁹ Having made known unto us the mystery of his will, according to his good pleasure which he hath purposed in himself: ¹⁰ That in the dispensation of the fulness of times he might gather together in one all things in Christ, both which are in heaven, and which are on earth; *even* in him: ¹¹ In whom also we have obtained an inheritance, being predestinated according to the purpose of him who worketh all things after the counsel of his own will: ¹² That we should be to the praise of his glory, who first trusted in Christ. ¹³ In whom ye also *trusted*, after that ye heard the word of truth, the gospel of your salvation: in whom also <u>after that ye believed, ye were sealed with that holy Spirit of promise,</u> [14] Which is the earnest of our inheritance *{the Holy Spirit's indwelling is God's signature of possession upon the believer's soul and the surety of the promises of God connected to His gift of salvation}* until the redemption of the purchased possession, unto the praise of his glory" (Ephesians 1:3-14).

"[30] And grieve not the holy Spirit of God, whereby ye are <u>sealed unto the day of redemption.</u> [31] Let all bitterness, and wrath, and anger, and clamour, and evil speaking, be put away from you, with all malice: [32] And be ye kind one to another, tenderhearted, forgiving one another, even as God for Christ's sake hath forgiven you" (Ephesians 4:30-32).

Eternal Security

Central to our understanding of the doctrine of eternal security is our understanding that salvation is a covenant between the Father and the Son. Any person is able to enter into this covenant by simple faith in the finished work of the Son (Jesus Christ), who has already fulfilled all the conditions of that covenant on mankind's behalf.

"[7] And he said unto him, I *am* the LORD that brought thee out of Ur of the Chaldees, to give thee this land to inherit it. [8] And he said, Lord GOD, whereby shall I know that I shall inherit it? [9] And he said unto him, Take me an heifer of three years old, and a she goat of three years old, and a ram of three years old, and a turtledove, and a young pigeon. [10] And he took unto him all these, and divided them in the midst, and laid each piece one against another: but the birds divided he not. [11] And when the fowls came down upon the carcases, Abram drove them away. [12] And when the sun was going down, a deep sleep fell upon Abram; and, lo, an horror of great darkness fell upon him. [13] And he said unto Abram, Know of a surety that thy seed shall be a stranger in a land *that is* not theirs, and shall serve them; and they shall afflict them four hundred years; [14] And also that nation, whom they shall serve, will I judge: and afterward shall they come out with great substance. [15] And thou shalt go to thy fathers in peace; thou shalt be buried in a good old age. [16] But in the fourth generation they shall come hither again: for the iniquity of the Amorites *is* not yet full. [17] <u>And it came to pass, that, when the sun went down, and it was dark, behold a smoking furnace, and a burning lamp that passed between those pieces.</u> [18] In the same day the LORD made a covenant with Abram, saying, Unto thy seed <u>have I given</u> this land, from the river of Egypt unto the great river, the river Euphrates:" (Genesis 15:7-18).

Historically in the making of a covenant between two people, an animal would be killed and divided in half. The parties involved would stand before the divided parts of the animals and state their individual parts in the covenant promises. Then they would pass together between the divided parts of the animal(s), signifying their acceptance of death should they break their covenant promises to one another.

Notice that this is not what took place in Genesis 15:7-18. God brought a deep sleep upon Abram. God alone states the conditions of the covenant and God alone passes between the divided parts. The covenant of God with Abraham was not based upon Abraham's faith or conditioned on Abraham's performance, but solely on the basis of God's purpose. The *covenant of salvation* is between the Father and the Son. Every aspect of this covenant is fulfilled by Jesus Christ and then offers salvation as a gift given to believers received "through faith."

By the "one offering" of the sacrifice of Jesus Christ, He has completely fulfilled all the conditions of the *covenant of salvation* (the Abrahamic Covenant), and the expectations of God for any one, and every one, to be saved. That is why "whosoever shall call upon the name of the Lord shall be saved" (Romans 10:13) is possible. Salvation has nothing to do with what man accomplishes and everything to do with what Christ has accomplished on our behalf. The complete fulfillment of the conditions of the Abrahamic Covenant by Jesus Christ in His death, burial, and resurrection is the basis for the offering of the *paid for* gift of redemption and salvation in Jesus Christ. However, we must emphasis that although the "gift" is universally offered, it is beneficial ONLY to those who receive it "through faith," not "works."

"[4] But God, who is rich in mercy, for his great love wherewith he loved us, [5] Even when we were dead in sins, hath quickened us together with Christ, (by grace ye are saved;) [6] And hath raised *us* up together, and made *us* sit together in heavenly *places* in Christ Jesus: [7] That in the ages to come he might shew the exceeding riches of his grace in *his* kindness toward us through Christ Jesus. [8] For by grace are ye saved through faith; and that not of yourselves: *it is* the gift of God: [9] Not of works, lest any man should boast. [10] For we are his workmanship, created in Christ Jesus unto good works, which God hath before ordained that we should walk in them" (Ephesians 2:4-10).

DISCUSSION QUESTIONS

1. Discuss why, when dealing with a person regarding doubts about salvation, it is wise to deal with assurance of salvation before dealing with eternal security.

2. Thoroughly explain I John 3:1-10, especially explaining the significance of understanding the Greek verb tenses.

3. Discuss the *difference* between the issues of assurance of salvation and eternal security. Include in your discussion God's view of salvation and man's view of salvation as these two views relate to these two doctrines.

4. List and discuss the two issues with which assurance of salvation is involved.

5. Explain I John 2:7-11 in light of John bringing the professing believer before the *mirror of reality* regarding the issue of assurance of salvation.

6. List and discuss the four *works* of the Spirit of God in a person's salvation and why each of these *works* provide the genuine believer with eternal security.

7. Discuss why understanding that the Abrahamic Covenant is a covenant between the Father and the Son is critical to our understanding eternal security.

Chapter Seventy
Discipleship and the Aquila and Priscilla Phenomenon

"[18] And Paul *after this* tarried *there* yet a good while, and then took his leave of the brethren, and sailed thence into Syria, and with him Priscilla and Aquila; having shorn *his* head in Cenchrea: for he had a vow. [19] And he came to Ephesus, and left them there: but he himself entered into the synagogue, and reasoned with the Jews. [20] When they desired *him* to tarry longer time with them, he consented not; [21] But bade them farewell, saying, I must by all means keep this feast that cometh in Jerusalem: but I will return again unto you, if God will. And he sailed from Ephesus. [22] And when he had landed at Caesarea, and gone up, and saluted the church, he went down to Antioch. [23] And after he had spent some time *there*, he departed, and went over *all* the country of Galatia and Phrygia in order, strengthening all the disciples. [24] And a certain Jew named Apollos, born at Alexandria, an eloquent man, *and* mighty in the scriptures, came to Ephesus. [25] This man was instructed in the way of the Lord; and being fervent in the spirit, he spake and taught diligently the things of the Lord, knowing only the baptism of John. [26] And he began to speak boldly in the synagogue: whom when Aquila and Priscilla had heard, they took him unto *them*, and expounded unto him the way of God more perfectly. [27] And when he was disposed to pass into Achaia, the brethren wrote, exhorting the disciples to receive him: who, when he was come, helped them much which had believed through grace: [28] For he mightily convinced the Jews, *and that* publickly, shewing by the scriptures that Jesus was Christ" (Acts 18:18-28).

This text deals with a transition from the Dispensation of the Law and the Mosaic Covenant into the Dispensation of Grace and the New Covenant. Apollos was what many would call a *layman* in today's terminology. He was a saved Jew with extensive knowledge of the Old Testament Scriptures and "eloquent" in his ability to stand in the synagogues expounding these truths that he knew deeply. However, he did not yet know of Jesus as the Christ. He knew "the baptism of John" and was prepared for, and looking toward, the soon appearing of the Messiah. He did not know that

Jesus was the Messiah or that the death, burial, and resurrection of Jesus was "the way" to which the Old Testament Scriptures referred. Apollos understood that "the way" was through faith, but he did not understand that after the death, burial, and resurrection of Jesus, his faith needed to rest in the objective facts accomplished through the "finished" work of redemption.

However, there is another important issue before us. Before we can look at this other important principle of New Covenant responsibilities for all believers modeled by Priscilla and Aquilla, we will need to have a little historical background about them and understand the *gift of prophecy*.

In the book of Acts, the Spirit of God is the means through which God would speak *to* and *through* New Covenant believers. The words *to* and *through* are critical to understanding the dispensational transition in the giving of the gift of "prophecy" (Romans 12:6). The *to* aspect of the gift of prophecy ceased with the completion of the New Testament Scriptures (I Corinthians 13:8). The *through* aspect of the gift of prophecy would continue. In this ministry, the Holy Spirit is known as the *Spirit of prophecy*. When the Holy Spirit spoke *to* an individual to reveal God's will, that individual became the *conduit* of direct revelation from God with the responsibility of communicating that inspired revelation word for word. The direct revelation from God is what is known as *inspiration* (II Timothy 3:16 and II Peter 1:21).

The *through* aspect of the gift of prophecy is more commonly referred to as *preaching*. True spiritual preaching is the Spirit of God moving and speaking through the life and mouth of His host - the "born again" and yielded believer. Preaching is the proclamation of what had been previously revealed, recorded, and communicated. Therefore, true preaching is ALWAYS the *proclamation* or *explanation* of Scripture. Because most people do not distinguish between these two different aspects of the gift of prophecy, many people are greatly confused. Any teaching/preaching ministry that is focused on *proclaiming* or *explaining* the inspired words of God through the Spirit's illumination of those inspired words, can be considered part of this latter aspect of the gift of prophecy. This too is a supernatural operation of God.

The reality of our faith in God is also what Luke is dealing with in his introduction to his continuation of the Gospel of Luke that we have come to call the Acts of the Apostles. The title *Acts of the Apostles* is a man-made title and not really accurate to the scope of the intent of this historical account of the first generation of the Age of Grace. This purpose is given to us in the first two verses of Acts chapter one; "[1b] all that Jesus began both to do and teach, [2] Until the day in which he was taken up, after that he through the Holy Ghost had given commandments unto the apostles whom he had chosen."

Do not rush by this statement. In this statement, we have the whole Church Age defined. In this statement, we have the scope of the "work of the ministry" as a continuum of the Christ-life *through* every Spirit enabled believer throughout the Church Age. This historical account would be better entitled the *Acts of Jesus Christ Lived through the Priesthood of All Believers*.

David Thomas gives us the following note on the statement "all that Jesus began both to do and teach:"

". . . from the arrangement of these words in the original Greek, two things are plain which escape the English reader: First, there is an emphasis on the verb '*began*;' secondly, there is none on the word '*Jesus*.' The contrast is not that the former treatise related what *Jesus* began, and this relates what some other person or persons continued; but it is that the former treatise related what Jesus *began* to do and teach: and this relates what He, the same Jesus, *continued* to do and teach."[36]

The question immediately then is raised, how could Jesus continue to "do and teach" after He was dead? Answering this question gives us the supernatural nature of God's intent beyond salvation from Hell and what we see *fleshed out* in the lives of those recorded in the book of Acts. The answer is simple: Christ lives supernaturally through the yielded life of the believer indwelled and "filled" with the Spirit of God. What Jesus began to do on the Day of Pentecost was something the world had never seen before. Jesus

---

[36] Thomas, David. *Acts of the Apostle: Expository and Homiletical.* (Grand Rapids, Michigan: Kregal Publications, 1980), page 2.

would supernaturally live THROUGH those "born again" of the Spirit of God and those who were completely yielded to Him. This is the spiritual dynamic that is going on in the lives of Priscilla and Aquilla in the discipleship of Apollos.

Although there are biblical restrictions on the use of this *through* gift of prophecy within the local church, women can also have this gift. They cannot be pastors, teachers of men in the church, or be deacons, but they can teach and proclaim the Truth to anyone outside of the local church's formal teaching/preaching ministry. Women can proclaim the Gospel to men and lead them to Christ and they can teach other women and children (Titus 2:4).

Who then was this *husband and wife team* who were so greatly used of God in the use of their *through* gift of prophecy (proclamation/teaching)? (This gift is available to all believers during the Church Age through the indwelling and filling of the Holy Spirit.) They are mentioned six times in Scripture (Acts 18:2, 18, 26; Romans 6:3; I Corinthians 16:19; II Timothy 4:19).

When the Apostle Paul arrives in Corinth, he *finds* Aquila and Pricilla. They had been expelled from Rome in about 49-50 A.D., along with all other Jews, by Emperor Claudius (Acts 18:2). The probable reason Paul and this couple became friends was because Paul was a tent maker like they were (Acts 18:3) and he became a partner in their business while he was at Corinth. They may have already been Christians as well, but we do not know this for sure. We do know that at some point they became Christians and were foundational in the establishment of the church at Corinth and later at Ephesus (Acts 18:18-19).

Although the local church at Corinth began with God leading the Apostle Paul to Corinth to evangelize the city and make disciples out of those who received Christ, the local church at Corinth was *established* through the commitment of people like Aquila and Priscilla.

Initially, the church probably met in their home and most of the discipleship that was done was in that location. They were probably involved with Paul in teaching the same foundational truths over and over again to the many souls that came to trust in Christ and were "born again" of the Spirit of God. The home and lives of Aquila and Priscilla literally became the *distribution center* of God's grace in the city of Corinth.

We learn a great deal about missions and *church planting* from the example given us in Acts 18. Although souls need to be won to Christ before a local church can be constituted and a constituency formed, the foundations of a local church are laid in the lives of people committed to the establishment of a Christ-honoring and God-glorifying *truth center*. The church planting missionary may be the initial foundation layer, but if a new local church is going to be successful and continue over any length of time, there MUST be a group of people who are whole heartedly committed to insuring the continuum of soul winning and disciple making in that locality.

The spirit of the *missional vision* of the *church planter* must become the *missional vision* of every individual that becomes part of the "work of the ministry" of any local church. There are no *spectators* in the "body of Christ." Allowing believers in a local church to become *spectators* is a contradiction against the very nature of a local church's *mission purpose* and where the decline and death of a church begins. The fact that Aquila and Priscilla were just as involved in making disciples of those saved as was the Apostle Paul was, and is, what defines the *Aquila and Priscilla Phenomena*.

I refer to this as the *Aquila and Priscilla Phenomena* because of the exceptional nature of the character and commitment of people like Aquila and Priscilla. I do not use the term in the sense that they were *abnormal*. The kind of commitment and dedication to winning souls and making disciples *should be* the norm that defines Christianity for every truly "born again" and Spirit-filled believer. The fact that this kind of commitment and dedication is rare or unusual today only defines the degree to which Christianity has evolved into the abstract of the norm. For most professing Christians today, *church* is a place we attend a few hours a week.

The Scriptural definition of a church is defined by the "work of the ministry" that the members of a local church do during the everyday aspects of their daily routines. Each person and each Christian home becomes an extension of their local church as a *distribution center* of God's grace. Every life and every home becomes a *ministry center*. This is what defines the *Aquila and Priscilla Phenomena*.

Local churches are not built upon the backs of great pastors. Great local churches are built when those saved and discipled become the "living stones" of a living, working organism that literally infects a community with the grace of God. In abnormal Christianity, pastors measure Christian faithfulness by attendance at the assembly times of the local church. This is an aberration of normalcy. Pastors need to begin measuring the maturity of individuals and their faithfulness to Christ by the *Aquila and Priscilla Phenomena*. What is this *Phenomena* again? It is every member moving toward and being trained for being *distribution centers* of the supernatural operations of the Holy Spirit *through* their lives. Until the *Aquila and Priscilla Phenomena* is achieved, an individual is nothing more than a *babe* in Christ. In modern Christianity there are few who ever come to "full age" and begin to manifest the *Aquila and Priscilla Phenomena* through their lives. This is ABNORMAL!

"[12] For when for the time ye ought to be teachers, ye have need that one teach you again which *be* the first principles of the oracles of God; and are become such as have need of milk, and not of strong meat. [13] For every one that useth milk *is* unskilful in the word of righteousness: for he is a babe. [14] But strong meat belongeth to them that are of full age, *even* those who by reason of use have their senses exercised to discern both good and evil" (Hebrews 5:12-14).

Why were Aquila and Priscilla so greatly used of God and so effective in their ministry? First of all, they were well trained disciples themselves. Their knowledge of the Word of God did not come through *osmosis* because they lived and worked in close proximity to the Apostle Paul. Discipleship takes place when a person is willing to invest enormous amounts of time, energy, and resources in learning to USE, not just *know*, the *tools* of truth. Modern day Christians are not willing to engage their corporate ethic in discussion of theological truths because they are insecure about what they know and because they are ill-equipped to communicate what they know. As Hebrews 5:14 says, this all comes "by reason of use." People learn to *witness by witnessing.* People learn to *teach by teaching.* People learn to *love by loving.* Men learn to *preach by preaching.* People learn to BE disciples by MAKING disciples!

I also find it extremely interesting that the two cities in which God used Aquila and Priscilla were the two most pagan cities in the Roman Empire - Corinth and Ephesus. Corinth had a *Temple of Aphrodite* and Ephesus had the *Temple of Diana.* Aphrodite was the Greek *god* of love, or fertility. There were one-thousand priestesses at the Temple of Aphrodite in Corinth, who each night would go down into the city as ritual prostitutes. The Greeks developed the term *Corinthiazesthar* to mean a person who has been *Corinthianize* through gross immorality, debauchery, drunkenness, and moral depravity. The city of Ephesus was almost equally wicked and immoral. It was into the midst of these two cities that God moved the Apostle Paul along with Aquila and Priscilla to start local churches.

"[18] And Paul *after this* tarried *there* yet a good while, and then took his leave of the brethren, and sailed thence into Syria, and with him Priscilla and Aquila; having shorn *his* head in Cenchrea: for he had a vow. [19] And he came to Ephesus, and left them there: but he himself entered into the synagogue, and reasoned with the Jews. [20] When they {*Priscilla and Aquila*} desired *him* to tarry longer time with them, he consented not; [21] But bade them farewell, saying, I must by all means keep this feast that cometh in Jerusalem: but I will return again unto you, if God will. And he sailed from Ephesus" (Acts 18:18-21).

The tent making business venture between the Apostle Paul and Aquila and Priscilla was a successful partnership. However, I doubt very much they continued their business relationship merely because of the monetary gain that the business partnership brought to them. Their business, like their home, became a *ministry center*. They would meet numerous clients each day from both the Jewish community and the pagan communities. These contacts provided them numerous opportunities to present Christ and to engage these cultures with the Gospel of Jesus Christ.

Another remarkable event in the history of the Church took place when God brought a man by the name of Apollos together with Aquila and Priscilla. In this encounter, we see the *Aquila and Priscilla Phenomena* taken to an extreme we might never imagine. Aquila and Priscilla would be used of God in the discipleship of one of the greatest men of God in early Church history. Remember, every great Christian begins at the foot of the Cross of Jesus and grows upward towards Christ-likeness from that point. At some point in their life, every greatly used Christian needed to be saved and discipled. There are no exceptions!

Apollos was already very knowledgeable in the Old Testament Scriptures. He was knowledgeable enough to stand in the synagogue at Ephesus and expound upon his depth of understanding.

> "[24] And a certain Jew named Apollos, born at Alexandria, an eloquent man, *and* mighty in the scriptures, came to Ephesus. [25] This man was instructed in the way of the Lord; and being fervent in the spirit, he spake and taught diligently the things of the Lord, knowing only the baptism of John. [26] And he began to speak boldly in the synagogue: whom when Aquila and Priscilla had heard, they took him unto *them*, and expounded unto him the way of God more perfectly" (Acts 18:24-26).

Acts 18:26 says that Aquila and Priscilla took Apollos to their home "and expounded unto him the way of God more perfectly." The Greek word translated "perfectly" simply means they taught him "more accurately" in that they filled in the details regarding the fulfillment of the prophecies of the Old Testament Scriptures in the person and redemptive work of Christ Jesus in His death, burial, and resurrection/glorification.

As a disciple of John the Baptist (Acts 18:25), Apollos was already a saved Jew in the Old Testament sense of salvation. He understood and believed *the gospel in the Law* as it pointed to the coming of Messiah as detailed in Psalm twenty-two and Isaiah fifty-three. This was most probably the substance of his expounding of the Old Testament Scriptures in the synagogue at Ephesus. He was a long way from his home in Alexandria. However, he understood the priorities of his *missional purpose* even before he understood that Messiah had come and fulfilled His work of redemption. Like John the Baptist, he was already an *evangelist* in the O.T. sense of the word. Although he was not yet a pastor, he was already an itinerant preacher (evangelist).

The *Aquila and Priscilla Phenomena* was the norm and model for all local churches everywhere. It certainly was not unique to the local churches at Corinth and Ephesus. In Paul's epistle to the local church at Thessalonica, he commended them for their faithfulness in modeling the *Christ-life* and being biblical "ensamples." Perhaps we can contribute the failure of the vast majority of modern day Christianity in the *Aquila and Priscilla*

Phenomena to the fact we have allowed faithfulness to the Great Commission to be defined merely as faithful church attendance rather than faithfulness to publicly engage our culture with the Gospel of Jesus Christ and working to make disciplined Christians (disciples) out of those who profess to be saved.

> "[2] We give thanks to God always for you all, making mention of you in our prayers; [3] Remembering without ceasing your work of faith, and labour of love, and patience of hope in our Lord Jesus Christ, in the sight of God and our Father; [4] Knowing, brethren beloved, your election of God. [5] For our gospel came not unto you in word only, but also in power, and in the Holy Ghost, and in much assurance; as ye know what manner of men we were among you for your sake. [6] And ye became followers of us, and of the Lord, having received the word in much affliction, with joy of the Holy Ghost: [7] So that ye were ensamples to all that believe in Macedonia and Achaia. [8] For from you sounded out the word of the Lord not only in Macedonia and Achaia, but also in every place your faith to God-ward is spread abroad; so that we need not to speak any thing. [9] For they themselves shew of us what manner of entering in we had unto you, and how ye turned to God from idols to serve the living and true God; [10] And to wait for his Son from heaven, whom he raised from the dead, *even* Jesus, which delivered us from the wrath to come" (I Thessalonians 1:2-10).

Although the Word of God provides only the basic *chain of command* and qualifications for spiritual leaders within a local church context, the principals for qualifications for leadership establish a very high level for those given leadership roles within a local church. The ministry of a local church has two primary places of expression:

1. Within the *Church-house* walls within the assembly
2. Within the world in the forms of evangelism/discipleship and the manifestation of the *Christ-life* in all we do and say

As people are won to Christ and come into the local church to hear preaching, teaching, and to worship and be discipled, their *models of Christianity* are every other person they see within the congregation of a local church. In most cases, they are not aware of who is an accountable *formal member* and who are merely *feeding at the Master's Table* without any accountability to what they are receiving. There is a general assumption that all *attendees* of a local church are also *attending* to the truth the local church teaches and promotes as defining factors of true Christianity. That is a *false assumption*, but it is in fact a *general assumption*. That *general assumption* needs to be addressed to new attendees.

Just because a man or a woman stands at the door of the Church-house smoking a cigarette, does not mean that person represents the convictions of the rest of those in attendance. However, because such a practice is permitted and perhaps the individual committing the misrepresentation is never spoken to about it, the general public viewing the misrepresentation instead views it as a general representation of the values of that local church. In most cases, a person's perception of reality becomes his reality even if his perception is wrong.

The first issue is where do we draw the lines regarding these misrepresentations of values? Secondly, how do we draw the lines when there are often many people who attend a local church's services who are not saved, not committed to Christ, or merely *casual Christians? This is* manifested by their casualness regarding living the truth and the casual way in which they involve themselves in *ministry*; at best only ambiguously defined. Do we make up little name cards that might say something like: ACCOUNTIBLE MEMBER, or DON'T FOLLOW ME, I AM NOT RESPONSIBLE, I AM JUST HERE BECAUSE MY DAD/MOM MADE ME COME.

Of course, doing something like this would be nonsensical. The way visitors know who the committed members of a local church are (and are not) is by the peculiarity of dress, by how people interact with them, and by looking at who are given leadership positions as models within the structure of a church. This extends to all levels of leadership with a local church context. They identify real disciples by seeing the *Aquila and Priscilla Phenomena* reproduced in those claiming to be disciples. If the *Aquila and Priscilla Phenomena* is not evident in any Christian's life, that Christian has a counterfeit Christianity and is a counterfeit disciple of Jesus Christ.

DISCUSSION QUESTIONS

1. Discuss the transitional issue from the Dispensation of the Law and the Mosaic Covenant into the Dispensation of Grace and the New Covenant regarding what is commonly referred to as the *gift of prophecy*. Especially discuss the differences between the *to* and *through* aspects of the gift.

2. Thoroughly explain the deep significance of Luke's statement in Acts 1:1-2; "[1b] all that Jesus began both to do and teach, [2] Until the day in which he was taken up, after that he through the Holy Ghost had given commandments unto the apostles whom he had chosen." Explain how you personally become an extension of this ministry of Jesus Christ.

3. Discuss how women can have the *through* gift of prophecy as well as the biblical restrictions on that gift.

4. Although the local church at Corinth began with God leading the Apostle Paul to Corinth to evangelize the city and make disciples out of those who received Christ, the church was actually established through the commitment of people like Aquila and Priscilla. Discuss why it is absolutely critical to understand this about the church at Corinth.

5. Discuss what is necessary for your home and life to become a *distribution center of God's Grace*. Discuss what steps you need to take in your own spiritual growth to insure this reality.

6. Practically define the *Aquila and Priscilla Phenomena*.

7. Read Hebrews 5:12-14 and explain why there is such a sharp and harsh rebuke for failure to become serious about learning and teaching the truths of God's Word. Do you think such people as rebuked in this text will ever realize the *Aquila and Priscilla Phenomena* in their lives?

Chapter Seventy-one
Filling: the Outpouring of the Indwelling Spirit

"[1] And when the day of Pentecost was fully come {*being completely fulfilled in its type*}, they were all with one accord in one place. [2] And suddenly {*in such a manner as to be startling*} there came a sound from heaven as {*like the sound*} of a rushing mighty wind, and it filled all the house where they were sitting. [3] And there appeared unto them cloven tongues like as of fire {*so that they could know this more than just a rushing wind*}, and it sat upon each of them. [4] And they were all filled with the Holy Ghost, and began to speak with other tongues, as the Spirit gave them utterance" (Acts 2:1-4).

In a previous chapter, I introduced the term *Pneumatological Kinesis.* Kinesis is *the movement of an organism or cell in response to a stimulus, the rate of movement being dependent on the strength of the stimulus.* The stimulus is the *filling* with the Spirit of God conditioned on total yielding (Romans 6:11-13 and 12:1-2). Although the illustration of the *light switch* and the availability of the electrical power at the *flip of a switch* are used to illustrate the *trigger* for *Pneumatological Kinesis,* there is considerably more involved in the necessity for the release of the supernatural creative power dwelling within us in the person of the Spirit of God. In other words, although being *filled* to overflowing with the indwelling Holy Spirit of God is simply conditioned upon yielding our lives and wills to Him, what defines that yielding is very specific and detailed.

The first statement in Acts 2:1 tells us a great deal about the work Christ had accomplished in the lives of His disciples prior to this *New Beginning* in this *new ministration* of the Spirit of God. Acts 2:1 tells us "they were all with one accord in one place." This statement reveals two essentials regarding those who witnessed this *New Beginning* and why they were part of this very small privileged few. First, they were obedient to Jesus' command to wait for the ten days between His ascension and the Day of Pentecost for this coming of the Holy Spirit. Granted all believers, wherever they were in the world at the time of the coming of the Holy Spirit, were baptized into the *New Creation* and indwelled by the Spirit of God. However, only those that obeyed Jesus' command to wait in the same place at which they were in Acts chapter one, were filled with the Spirit. **Filling is conditioned upon obedience to the Word of God.** If there is any single area of your life in which you are disobedient to the known will of God, you cannot be filled with the Spirit of God or blessed of God.

Second, Acts 2:1 tells us "they were all with one accord." This refers to the "unity of the Spirit in the bond of peace" that Paul speaks of in Ephesians 4:3. Acts 2:42-47 gives us specific details defining this "one accord" and the "unity of the Spirit in the bond of peace." **The filling of the Spirit is conditioned upon maintaining this "one accord" within the local church.**

> "[42] And they continued stedfastly in the apostles' doctrine and fellowship, and in breaking of bread, and in prayers. [43] And fear came upon every soul: and many wonders and signs were done by the apostles. [44] And all that believed were together, and had all things common; [45] And sold their possessions and goods, and parted them to all *men*, as every man had need. [46] And they, continuing daily with one accord in the temple, and breaking bread from house to house, did eat their meat with gladness and singleness of heart, [47] Praising God, and having favour with all the people. And the Lord added to the church daily such as should be saved" (Acts 2:42-47).

What we find in these few verses of Scripture is the basic essentials necessary before any local church will ever see a genuine manifestation of the Spirit of God in the "fruit of the Spirit" in believers' lives. This is manifested by believers experiencing growth in their in-depth knowledge of the Word of God and in their personal devotion to the God of the Word. This is manifested by people getting saved and discipled through the bold proclamation of those known truths through the everyday lives of those Spirit-filled believers. Notice six essential conditions and four outcomes:

1. (*Condition*) "they continued stedfastly in the apostles' doctrine and fellowship"
2. (*Condition*) "they continued stedfastly . . . in breaking of bread, and in prayers."
3. (*Condition*) "fear {*of God*} came upon every soul: and many wonders and signs were done by the apostles {*outcome*}."

4. (*Condition*) "and all that believed were together, and had all things common; And sold their possessions and goods, and parted them to all *men*, as every man had need {*outcome*}."
5. (*Condition*) "they continuing daily with one accord in the temple"
6. (*Condition*) "they continuing daily . . . breaking bread from house to house, did eat their meat with gladness and singleness of heart, Praising God, and" . . . "having favour with all the people {*outcome*}."
7. {*Outcome*} "and the Lord added to the church daily such as should be saved"

The great tragedy of "lukewarm" Evangelicalism is that we want to see the *outcomes* without meeting the *conditions* for those *outcomes*. We live a façade of faith, and *manufacture* a façade of blessing (*outcomes*). We fill the church houses with crowds of carnal people through carnal methodologies and tell the world to come see what God is doing. The fact is that God is not doing that. The fact is that this *pseudo-evangelicalism* is nothing more than the *outcome* of human/carnal manufacture.

By a simple evaluation of biblical criteria for the operations of the Spirit through the lives of the Redeemed, we can easily see that if God is even present in these kinds of assemblies, He is there with a *bad taste* in His mouth and is disgusted by this *performance, entertainment, ear-tickling based* pseudo-spirituality (Revelation 3:16).

"[16] So then because thou art lukewarm, and neither cold nor hot, I will spue thee out of my mouth. [17] Because thou sayest, I am rich, and increased with goods, and have need of nothing; and knowest not that thou art wretched, and miserable, and poor, and blind, and naked: [18] I counsel thee to buy of me gold tried in the fire, that thou mayest be rich; and white raiment, that thou mayest be clothed, and *that* the shame of thy nakedness do not appear; and anoint thine eyes with eyesalve, that thou mayest see" (Revelation 3:16-18).

What does it mean to be *filled* with the Holy Spirit? The *filling* with the Holy Spirit is so thorough that no room is left for anything in our practices, emotions, or thoughts that are contrary to the will of God. We literally become *little Christs* (anointed ones). The *Christ-life* flows from our practices, emotions, and thought life as if we were Christ Himself. The "fruit" of the filling overflows from our every action, emotion, and thought as defined by Galatians 5:22-26: "[22] But the fruit of the Spirit is love, joy, peace, longsuffering, gentleness, goodness, faith, [23] Meekness, temperance:

against such there is no law. [24] And they that are Christ's have crucified the flesh with the affections and lusts. [25] If we live in the Spirit, let us also walk in the Spirit. [26] Let us not be desirous of vain glory, provoking one another, envying one another."

When we are filled with the Holy Spirit, our minds think His thoughts and our emotions are driven by His compassion, mercies, burdens, and empathies. Our mouths speak His promptings without hesitation. Our feet simply move in the direction of His leading and the touch of our hands communicate both His power and His gentleness, similarly to the little boy's grasp upon a butterfly; he has the power to crush, but touches with the gentleness of a *whispered caress.*

When a believer is filled with the Spirit of God, there are no thoughts that are allowed to occupy the mind that would contradict the holy character of God or to which He could not be enjoined. The life of the Spirit-filled believer is a living inspiration of the *breath* of God walking and moving through humanity. All that the Spirit-filled believer touches is touched by the hand of God. The Spirit-filled believer is the Temple of God with *legs on it,* supernaturally enabled to transport this new link of direct communication with God to anyone or anywhere to which the believer travels.

The Spirit-filled believer has no ambitions that supersede or contradict God's purposes as recorded in John 20:21-22; "[21] Then said Jesus to them again, Peace *be* unto you: as *my* Father hath sent me, even so send I you. [22] And when he had said this, he breathed on *them*, and saith unto them, Receive ye the Holy Ghost."

Granted, this is a *mountain top Christianity* experienced by only a very few. However, that is not because it is available to only a few. It is available to everyone "born again" of the Spirit of God. The journey to the *mountain top* with God is not long and arduous. It is not another *twelve step program* to spiritual victory. The journey to the *mountain top* with God is **one step**: total, absolute surrender/yielding that is without reservations or restrictions. This complete and total surrender of the *living sacrifice* is defined in very specific terms in Romans chapter twelve:

"[1] **I beseech** {*parakaleo, lit., to call near*} **you therefore, brethren, by the mercies** {*empathetic compassion*} **of God, that ye present your bodies a living sacrifice, holy** {*morally purity being a necessity before the sacrifice can be*}, **acceptable unto God, *which*** *is* your reasonable *{rational or logical}* service *{as an expression of genuine worship; understanding that no other form of worship is acceptable to God until the conditions for accepting worship are met}*. [2] And be not conformed *{present, passive, imperative; stop being fashioned/shaped by worldly association or influence}* to this world *{aion, referring to the cultural and immoral influences of whatever time period you live in}*: but be ye transformed *{metamorphoo, present, passive, imperative; referring to progressive transfiguration/glorification through progressive sanctification}* by the renewing *{anakainosis, referring to the process of the new creation in progressive life transfiguration beginning inwardly through the changing of our thought-life}* of your mind *{thinking or understanding of reality}*, that ye may prove *{dokimazo, to prove what is right regarding the will of God thereby having discernment}* what *is* that good *{agathos, the idea is good to spiritually benefit yourself and others}*, and acceptable *{right and pleasing}*, and perfect *{teleios, complete carrying the idea of moral and spiritual maturity regarding knowing and living the . . .}*, will of God" (Romans 12:1-2).

We cannot rush passed God's definition of the complete and absolute surrender of our wills to Him that is communicated to us by this simple term "living sacrifice." The Greek verb "present" is critical to our understanding of God's expectation regarding the believer's degree of surrender necessary to the filling of the Holy Spirit. "Present" is translated from the Greek word *paristemi* (par-is'-tay-mee). The Greek word basically means *to stand beside* or *to stand with* in the sense of giving of one's self and one's resources in support of a cause. Therefore, there is the implication of yielding all that a person has to benefit the cause of another.

Another important aspect of the verb "present" is that it is in the Aorist tense. The perfect tense conveys the idea of a completed action in the past with FINISHED results in the present. The aorist tense conveys the idea of an action from the point in time, usually the past, with CONTINUING results in the present. Therefore, we might say that the presenting our bodies a living sacrifice to God is truly *the gift that just keeps on giving.*

"[3] For I say, through {*dia, denoting the channel of an action, i.e. grace*} the grace {*charis, contextually the supernatural influence of God upon the life and through one's life in the indwelling of the Holy Spirit*} given unto me, {*the Spirit of God speaking through him*} to every man that is among you, not to think *of himself* more highly than he ought to think {*regarding the progress of spiritual growth*}; but to think soberly {*accurately regarding the 'renewing of the mind'*}, according as God hath dealt to every man the measure of faith {*the living of the truths we profess to believe that have renewed our minds; the idea is that all believer's are at different levels of spiritual growth measured by the degree they live the new reality of the New Creation revealed by the Word of God*}. [4] For as we have many members in one body, and all members have not the same office: [5] So we, *being* many, are one body in Christ, and every one members one of another. [6] Having then gifts differing according to the grace that is given to us, whether prophecy, *let us prophesy* according to the proportion of faith; [7] Or ministry, *let us wait* on *our* ministering: or he that teacheth, on teaching; [8] Or he that exhorteth, on exhortation: he that giveth, *let him do it* with simplicity; he that ruleth, with diligence; he that sheweth mercy, with cheerfulness. [9] *Let* love be without dissimulation. Abhor that which is evil; cleave to that which is good. [10] *Be* kindly affectioned one to another with brotherly love; in honour preferring one another; [11] Not slothful in business; fervent in spirit; serving the Lord; [12] Rejoicing in hope; patient in tribulation; continuing instant in prayer; [13] Distributing to the necessity of saints; given to hospitality. [14] Bless them which persecute you: bless, and curse not. [15] Rejoice with them that do rejoice, and weep with them that weep. [16] *Be* of the same mind one toward another. Mind not high things, but condescend to men of low estate. Be not wise in your own conceits. [17] Recompense to no man evil for evil. Provide things honest in the sight of all men. [18] If it be possible, as much as lieth in you, live peaceably with all men. [19] Dearly beloved, avenge not yourselves, but *rather* give place unto wrath: for it is written, Vengeance *is* mine; I will repay, saith the Lord. [20] Therefore if thine enemy hunger, feed him; if he thirst, give him drink: for in so doing thou shalt heap coals of fire on his head. [21] Be not overcome of evil, but overcome evil with good" (Romans 12:3-20).

The sad truth is that this "living sacrifice" is just not something very many have been willing to give to the LORD down through the years.

DISCUSSION QUESTIONS

1. Discuss what is meant by the term *Pneumatological Kinesis* and how the term is related to the filling of the Holy Spirit.

2. Read Acts 2:42-47 and list the six basic essentials necessary before any local church will ever see a genuine manifestation of the Spirit of God in the "fruit of the Spirit" in believers' lives. This refers to believers experiencing growth in their in-depth knowledge of the Word of God and in their personal devotion to the God of the Word. This refers to people getting saved and discipled through the bold proclamation of those known truths through the everyday lives of those Spirit filled believers.

3. List also the four outcomes of this Spirit-filled local church.

4. Explain what it means to be *filled* with the Holy Spirit.

5. Read Galatians 5:22-26 and state what a Spirit-filled believer *looks like*.

6. How would you describe a Spirit-filled believer?

7. Read Romans 12:1-2 and thoroughly explain the one condition for being filled with the Spirit and then discuss why so few Christian ever habitually live a Spirit-filled life.

Chapter Seventy-two
The High Expectations Defining New Covenant Faithfulness

The "crown" rewards given to faithful Church Age believers at the Judgment Seat of Christ will determine the positions of those faithful believers for the one-thousand year Kingdom Age as they (only the faithful) will rule and reign with Christ as "kings and priests." As we return to Matthew chapters five, six, and seven, we are immediately confronted with the Christ's high expectations defining faithfulness and *grace-living* (the *Christ-life*).

"[21] **Ye have heard** that it was said by them of old time, Thou shalt not kill; and whosoever shall kill shall be in danger of the judgment: [22] **But I say unto you**, That whosoever is angry with his brother without a cause shall be in danger of the judgment: and whosoever shall say to his brother, Raca, shall be in danger of the council: but whosoever shall say, Thou fool, shall be in danger of hell fire. . . [27] **Ye have heard** that it was said by them of old time, Thou shalt not commit adultery: [28] **But I say unto you**, That whosoever looketh on a woman to lust after her hath committed adultery with her already in his heart. [29] And if thy right eye offend thee, pluck it out, and cast *it* from thee: for it is profitable for thee that one of thy members should perish, and not *that* thy whole body should be cast into hell. [30] And if thy right hand offend thee, cut it off, and cast *it* from thee: for it is profitable for thee that one of thy members should perish, and not *that* thy whole body should be cast into hell. [31] **It hath been said**, Whosoever shall put away his wife, let him give her a writing of divorcement: [32] **But I say unto you**, That whosoever shall put away his wife, saving for the cause of fornication, causeth her to commit adultery: and whosoever shall marry her that is divorced committeth adultery. [33] **Again, ye have heard** that it hath been said by them of old time, Thou shalt not forswear thyself, but shalt perform unto the Lord thine oaths: [34] **But I say unto you**, Swear not at all; neither by heaven; for it is God's throne: [35] Nor by the earth; for it is his footstool: neither by Jerusalem; for it is the city of the great King. [36] Neither shalt thou swear by thy head, because thou canst not make one hair white or black. [37] But let your communication be, Yea, yea; Nay, nay: for whatsoever is more than these cometh of evil. [38] **Ye have heard** that it hath been said, An eye for an eye, and a tooth for a tooth: [39] **But I say unto you**, That ye resist not evil: but whosoever shall smite thee on thy right cheek, turn to him the other also. [40] And if any man will sue thee at the law, and take away thy coat, let him have *thy* cloke also. [41] And whosoever shall compel thee to go a mile, go with him twain. [42] Give to him that asketh thee, and from him that would borrow of thee turn not thou away. [43] **Ye have heard** that it hath been said, Thou shalt love thy neighbour, and hate thine enemy. [44] **But I say unto you**, Love your enemies, bless them that curse you, do good to them that hate you, and pray for them which despitefully use you, and persecute you; [45] That ye may be the children of your Father which is in heaven: for he maketh his sun to rise on the evil and on the good, and sendeth rain on the just and on the unjust. [46] For if ye love them which love you, what reward have ye? do not even the publicans the same? [47] And if ye salute your brethren only, what do ye more *than others*? do not even the publicans so? [48] Be ye therefore perfect, even as your Father which is in heaven is perfect" (Matthew 5:21-22 and 27-48).

The silly notion that somehow anyone can live in a way that would be pleasing to God or righteous before God apart from the supernatural enabling of the indwelling Holy Spirit of God must be the result of complete ignorance of who God is and the standard of holiness by which He measures righteousness. Matthew 5:48 gives us a very simple qualifier for God's standard of expectation for what defines righteousness. "Be ye therefore perfect, even as your Father which is in heaven is perfect." The word "perfect" is from the Greek word *teleios* (tel'-i-os). In this context, it refers to a person that is fully matured regarding spiritual, mental, and moral character. The qualifier goes one step further, this person is to be fully matured regarding spiritual, mental, and moral character "even as your Father which is in heaven."

For centuries, the believers in the nation of Israel were taught that God's standard of righteousness could be met in perfect Law keeping. They were falsely taught by the Priesthood that if someone *failed* and broke one of commandments, that person needed to bring the appropriate sacrifice to the Temple and in offering that sacrifice to God, he could be forgiven and restored to perfect righteousness before God. The fact of the matter is that once something is *broken* it is always *broken*. The only way to restore a *broken thing* to perfection is through *re-creation*. Perfection can never be restored through *reformation*. The Apostle Paul sought to correct this false notion of righteousness by the

Law by stating God's new standard of righteousness in the person of Jesus Christ and the Gospel of the *New Creation* in Him.

"[16] For I am not ashamed of the gospel of Christ: for it is the power of God unto salvation to every one that believeth; to the Jew first, and also to the Greek. [17] For therein is the righteousness of God revealed from faith to faith: as it is written, The just shall live by faith" (Romans 1:16-17).

"[20] Therefore by the deeds of the law there shall no flesh be justified in his sight: for by the law *is* the knowledge of sin. [21] But now the righteousness of God without the law is manifested, being witnessed by the law and the prophets; [22] Even the righteousness of God *which is* by faith of Jesus Christ unto all and upon all them that believe: for there is no difference: [23] For all have sinned, and come short of the glory of God" (Romans 3:20-23).

"[19] For I through the law am dead to the law, that I might live unto God. [20] I am crucified with Christ: nevertheless I live; yet not I, but Christ liveth in me: and the life which I now live in the flesh I live by the faith of the Son of God, who loved me, and gave himself for me. [21] I do not frustrate the grace of God: for if righteousness *come* by the law, then Christ is dead in vain" (Galatians 2:19-21).

"[21] *Is* the law then against the promises of God? God forbid: for if there had been a law given which could have given life, verily righteousness should have been by the law. [22] But the scripture hath concluded all under sin, that the promise by faith of Jesus Christ might be given to them that believe. [23] But before faith came, we were kept under the law, shut up unto the faith which should afterwards be revealed. [24] Wherefore the law was our schoolmaster *to bring us* unto Christ, that we might be justified by faith" (Galatians 3:21-24).

"Therefore if any man *be* in Christ, *he is* a new creature: old things are passed away; behold, all things are become new" (II Corinthians 5:17).

Therefore, the notion that righteousness before God could somehow come "by the Law" (by *Law keeping*) is ridiculous. However, the false teaching regarding the doctrine of Grace that says God is no longer concerned about holy living and that the Christian of the Church Age is *liberated* from any moral standard of right and wrong is even more ridiculous. The ridiculousness of such heretical teaching is exemplified by the teachings of Jesus Christ in Matthew chapters five, six, and seven and in Luke 6:20-49.

Christ's teachings on grace enablement are not a freedom *from* rules and the standards of right and wrong. Christ's teachings on grace enablement is that, for the first time since the fall of mankind, a believer can live in *partnership* with the indwelling Holy Spirit of God through the filling of the Spirit to actually be "made the righteousness of God in him" (II Corinthians 5:21).

According to Christ's teaching on grace, the indwelled believer who is filled with the Spirit is supernaturally freed from the weakness of carnal flesh and supernaturally enabled and liberated to live righteously in ways far beyond the *thou shalt nots* of the Law to live in the *thou shalt commands* of God. All of this was, and is, an impossibility in the power of carnal flesh, but praise God we no longer live in bondage to the powerlessness of carnal flesh. Church Age believers are empowered and freed to live spiritual lives supernaturally enabled by the indwelling Holy Spirit of God. This *miracle* is available to every "born again" Christian by simply yielding to the indwelling Holy Spirit and beginning to simply "live by faith." God will do in us and through us exactly what Christ promised He would do.

II Corinthians 5:21 refers to *practical* God-kind righteousness supernaturally produced by the Spirit of God through the regenerated believer. Christ having been "made . . . sin for us" opens the *spiritual door* for the Spirit of God to indwell the believer. "Made" in II Corinthians 5:21 is from the Greek word *ginomai* (ghin'-om-ahee). The idea is *to become*. This goes beyond the impartation of righteousness "in Christ" to the potential of practical God-kind righteousness, supernaturally produced through the believer's life by the indwelling Spirit of God.

This is exactly what Paul is saying in Romans 8:4; "That the righteousness of the law might be fulfilled in us, who walk not after the flesh, but after the Spirit." This was never even a possibility prior to the indwelling of the Holy Spirit and the Age of Grace. "Now . . . in Christ Jesus" the fulfillment of "the righteousness of the law" is a possibility in the regenerated believer's life if that believer will "walk not after the flesh, but after the Spirit." This, of course, refers back to what Paul has already said in Romans 6:11-13.

How many times have you heard someone say to you, "well that is your interpretation"? What they usually mean by those words is that what you say the Word of God means is just too *strict* an interpretation. A strict interpretation and application of the Word of God is considered *legalistic* in today's New Evangelical and Pluralistic religious world of compromise and spiritual confusion.

In Matthew 5:21-48, Jesus begins each of five different definitions and applications of God's intent in His commandments with the words, "Ye have heard that," and then exponentially increases the strictness of the interpretation and application with the words, "But I say unto you." He does this in Matthew 5:21-22; 27-28, 31-32, 33-34, 38-39, and 43-44. The strictness of Christ's expectations regarding the proper interpretation and application of the Law is not restricted merely to these five areas mentioned. It is intended to be applied consistently in the same way in all of God's expectations of those who call Him Lord.

Just as the Mosaic Covenant had its conditions for "blessing and curse" (Deuteronomy 11:26 and 30:1), Matthew chapters five, six, seven and Luke 6:20-49 give us the conditions of the *blessing and curse* ("woe") of the New Covenant for the Church Age believers. These are not conditions for salvation any more than the "blessing and curse" conditions of the Mosaic Covenant were salvational. These are conditions for God's blessings upon the lives of saved BELIEVERS.

To imply that these conditions for *blessing and curse* are only for the Kingdom Age is a major misrepresentation of these texts in that they were taught to the disciples and are expanded upon in detail in almost all of the epistles. In other words, the disciples believed these *blessing and curse* conditions were for them and taught these principles to the believers at the beginning of the Church age.

Secondly, to argue that these conditions cannot be for Church Age believers because they are presently *impossible* conditions is ridiculous. If they are intended only for glorified believers, they are not needed in that glorified believers will be delivered from the corruption of the flesh in their glorified bodies. If they are intended only for Kingdom Age believers living in fleshly (non-glorified) bodies, what would be the difference between those Kingdom Age believers and Church Age believers? It would be just as impossible for them to live up to these conditions as it is for Church age believers. In fact, this *impossibility* is the main emphasis of the understanding of the doctrine of Grace (God's supernatural enabling through the indwelling and filling of the Holy Spirit).

"[1] I am the true vine, and my Father is the husbandman. [2] Every branch in me that beareth not fruit he taketh away: and every *branch* that beareth fruit, he purgeth it, that it may bring forth more fruit. [3] Now ye are clean through the word which I have spoken unto you. [4] Abide in me, and I in you. As the branch cannot bear fruit of itself, except it abide in the vine; no more can ye, except ye abide in me. [5] I am the vine, ye *are* the branches: He that abideth in me, and I in him, the same bringeth forth much fruit: for without me ye can do nothing. [6] If a man abide not in me, he is cast forth as a branch, and is withered; and men gather them, and cast *them* into the fire, and they are burned. [7] If ye abide in me, and my words abide in you, ye shall ask what ye will, and it shall be done unto you. [8] Herein is my Father glorified, that ye bear much fruit; so shall ye be my disciples" (John 15:1-8).

If we could (and would) grasp the *impossibility* of producing *spiritual fruit* apart from the blessing of *unity* with Jesus Christ through the filling of the Spirit of God, then perhaps Church Age believers could (and would) finally try to grasp the essential essence of the total yieldedness (Romans 6:11-13). Total yieldedness is necessary before the Priesthood of every believer can be used of God so that we can be consecrated by our High Priest, Jesus Christ, to be used in the "work of the ministry" to which we are perfected (Ephesians 4:12). It is a matter of fact, without the supernatural enabling of the indwelling Christ, the believer "can do nothing."

The conditions of the *blessing and curse* of the New Covenant are not based upon perfection in sinlessness. These conditions of the *blessing and curse* of the New Covenant are intended to reflect that being right with God. Being right with God is conditioned upon a proper understanding of what we are and who we are apart from the supernatural operations of the indwelling Spirit of God from within us through our lives. Once a believer understands the depth of his own degradation in corruption, only then can he understand that what God merely wants is for that fallen sinner, now saved by grace, to have a complete *change of heart* regarding what he wants God to do through his life. Even if he could somehow never commit an act of sin again for the rest of his life, every believer still thinks about sin, is tempted by certain sinful desires, and is emotionally corrupted. These are the issues with which Matthew chapters five, six, seven and Luke 6:20-49 deal. God simply wants us to WANT what He wants and depend upon Him to accomplish what He wants through us. Yes there must be a *turning from* our corrupted emotions, our perverse desires, and outward acts of sin, but there also needs to be *turning to* God in a *declaration of dependence*. This defines the *altar work* that needs to be done before the Throne of Grace by the broken sinner.

1. There must a declaration of the sinner's understanding of his spiritual brokenness.

2. There must a declaration of the sinner's understanding of his spiritual helplessness to meet God's expectations.

3. There must a declaration of the sinner's dependency upon the indwelling Spirit to supernaturally work through the yielded believer's life.

4. There must be a determination to live in unbroken fellowship with Christ through the continual communication of the above three things during each moment of the day.

5. There must be a determination to be a vocal witness for Christ and a willingness to present the Gospel of Jesus Christ at the first moment an opportunity arises.

In Matthew 5:3-11, Jesus details nine conditions for being "blessed." On nine occasions Jesus uses the Greek word *makarios* (mak-ar'-ee-os), which most translations render as "blessed" and a few translate it "happy." Neither of these two renderings are really adequate. In most cases the Jew thought of God's blessing in the sense of material prosperity. Most Christians have adopted the same meaning regarding God's blessings. When most people think of being blessed of God, they think in terms of *health* and *wealth*. However Christ's use of the word is intent upon reflecting the spiritual nature of God's blessing. The greatest of all forms of wealth is the sense of understanding one's purpose in life and being used of God to see that purpose realized. Therefore, I believe the central meaning of Christ's nine uses of *makarios* (mak-ar'-ee-os) refers to being *spiritually fulfilled* and then gives the conditions of the heart necessary to realize that *spiritual fulfillment* in this life. This *spiritual fulfillment* is the result of right spiritual attitudes and having God's blessing upon our ministry. Read these verses with *makarios* (mak-ar'-ee-os) translated as "*spiritually fulfilled.*"

1. Spiritually fulfilled *are* the poor in spirit: for theirs is the kingdom of heaven (v.3).

2. Spiritually fulfilled *are* they that mourn: for they shall be comforted (v.4).

3. Spiritually fulfilled *are* the meek: for they shall inherit the earth (v.5).

4. Spiritually fulfilled *are* they which do hunger and thirst after righteousness: for they shall be filled (v.6).

5. Spiritually fulfilled *are* the merciful: for they shall obtain mercy (v.7).

6. Spiritually fulfilled *are* the pure in heart: for they shall see God (v.8).

7. Spiritually fulfilled *are* the peacemakers: for they shall be called the children of God (v.9).

8. Spiritually fulfilled *are* they which are persecuted for righteousness' sake: for theirs is the kingdom of heaven (v.10).

9. Spiritually fulfilled are ye, when *men* shall revile you, and persecute *you*, and shall say all manner of evil against you falsely, for my sake. Rejoice, and be exceeding glad: for great *is* your reward in heaven: for so persecuted they the prophets which were before you (vs. 11-12).

The nine conditions listed reflect a radically different set of priorities for life than what the world tells us will bring us *happiness* or *fulfillment*. These nine conditions are intent upon reflecting a people who see this life as temporal and who see that temporal existence through the eyes of God and compared to our eternal destinies.

Three realities must exist in a believer's life before revival can happen.

1. The believer must know the truth. God's truth reveals what sin is. God's truth reveals how God wants us to live. We cannot *do* what is right until we *know* what is right. God's purpose in teaching us truth is his restoration of His image in man in the creation that was distorted by the fall so that we might once again have proper worship of Him (doxologically) and a relationship with Him in holiness.

"Study to shew thyself approved unto God, a workman that needeth not to be ashamed, rightly dividing the word of truth" (II Timothy 2:15).

"[16] All scripture *is* given by inspiration of God, and *is* profitable for doctrine, for reproof, for correction, for instruction in righteousness: [17] That the man of God may be perfect, throughly furnished unto all good works" (II Timothy 3:16-17).

2. The believer must translate that truth into *doing* (obedience from the heart, James 1:22-25). No matter how much truth you know, unless you put *flesh* on that truth by doing it, nothing is accomplished through that truth. No one will ever get saved by you knowing the Gospel. People get saved by hearing and heeding the teaching and preaching of the Gospel.

"[22] But be ye doers of the word, and not hearers only, deceiving your own selves. [23] For if any be a hearer of the word, and not a doer, he is like unto a man beholding his natural face in a glass: [24] For he beholdeth himself, and goeth his way, and straightway forgetteth what manner of man he was. [25] But whoso looketh into the perfect law of liberty, and continueth *therein*, he being not a forgetful hearer, but a doer of the work, this man shall be blessed in his deed" (James 1:22-25).

3. The believer must be right with God through the confession and repentance of sin and yielded to a *cooperative partnership* with the indwelling Holy Spirit (I John 1:3-9). "Fellowship" is the biblical word for this *cooperative partnership* with the indwelling Holy Spirit. When a group of believers come together in this cooperative "fellowship" a synergy is created and their combined "light . . . cannot be hid."

"[3] That which we have seen and heard declare we unto you, that ye also may have fellowship with us: and truly our fellowship *is* with the Father, and with his Son Jesus Christ. [4] And these things write we unto you, that your joy may be full. [5] This then is the message which we have heard of him, and declare unto you, that God is light, and in him is no darkness at all. [6] If we say that we have fellowship with him, and walk in darkness, we lie, and do not the truth: [7] But if we walk in the light, as he is in the light, we have fellowship one with another, and the blood of Jesus Christ his Son cleanseth us from all sin [8] If we say that we have no sin, we deceive ourselves, and the truth is not in us. [9] If we confess our sins, he is faithful and just to forgive us *our* sins, and to cleanse us from all unrighteousness" (I John 1:3-9).

Understanding this *trilogy for revival* helps us to understand why revival is a rare commodity in many churches. It is rare in many churches because this trilogy rarely exists consistently in the lives of believers. Knowing truth will not produce "fruit" or *spiritual fulfillment* until the believer lives that truth. He cannot live that truth until he is right with God and allows the indwelling Holy Spirit to live through his body (Romans 6:11-13).

The first issue dealt with in Matthew 5:21-26 is very strict and definitive regarding God's expectation of His children within interpersonal relationships. The warnings regarding failure in these expectations are equally sobering. This blessing and curse condition defines when a person's *emotions* move out of control and become sinful.

"[21] **Ye have heard** that it was said by them of old time, Thou shalt not kill; and whosoever shall kill shall be in danger of the judgment: [22] **But I say unto you**, That whosoever is angry with his brother <u>without a cause</u> shall be in danger of the judgment: and whosoever shall say to his brother, Raca, shall be in danger of the council: but whosoever shall say, Thou fool, shall be in danger of hell fire. [23] Therefore if thou bring thy gift to the altar, and there rememberest that thy brother hath ought against thee; [24] Leave there thy gift before the altar, and go thy way; first be reconciled to thy brother, and then come and offer thy gift. [25] Agree with thine adversary quickly, whiles thou art in the way with him; lest at any time the adversary deliver thee to the judge, and the judge deliver thee to the officer, and thou be cast into prison. [26] Verily I say unto thee, Thou shalt by no means come out thence, till thou hast paid the uttermost farthing" (Matthew 5:21-26).

The words "ye have heard" reflect the mere "letter of the Law." The words "but I say" reflect the underlying *spirit of the Law* (see Romans 2:27 and 7:6), which carries with it a much higher expectation than does the "letter of the Law."

We do not need to commit an act in order to sin. An improper thought or a hurtful word said in anger is enough to confirm the condemnation of God upon our fallen natures. This is the *spirit of the Law*. The intent of distinguishing between the *spirit of the Law* and the *letter of the Law* is that the *spirit of the Law* carries with it a higher expectation and a more strict application than does the *letter of the Law*. What we find being taught regarding *grace liberty* today is just the exact opposite of that intent and meaning.

Christ's instruction regarding the spirit of the Law does not end with these five stricter interpretations and applications. In Matthew chapter six, He goes on and gives a stricter, narrower application regarding giving "alms" (6:1-4), prayer (6:5-15), fasting (6:16-18), and accumulating wealth rather than trusting in God's *daily bread* provision (6:19-34).

"[27] **Ye have heard** that it was said by them of old time, Thou shalt not commit adultery: [28] **But I say** unto you, That whosoever looketh on a woman to lust after her hath committed adultery with her already in his heart. [29] And if thy right eye offend thee, pluck it out, and cast *it* from thee: for it is profitable for thee that one of thy members should perish, and not *that* thy whole body should be cast into hell. [30] And if thy right hand offend thee, cut it off, and cast *it* from thee: for it is profitable for thee that one of thy members should perish, and not *that* thy whole body should be cast into hell" (Matthew 5:27-30).

"[31] **It hath been said**, Whosoever shall put away his wife, let him give her a writing of divorcement: [32] **But I say** unto you, That whosoever shall put away his wife, saving for the cause of fornication, causeth her to commit adultery: and whosoever shall marry her that is divorced committeth adultery" (Matthew 5:31-32).

"[33] Again, **ye have heard** that it hath been said by them of old time, Thou shalt not forswear thyself, but shalt perform unto the Lord thine oaths: [34] **But I say** unto you, Swear not at all; neither by heaven; for it is God's throne: [35] Nor by the earth; for it is his footstool: neither by Jerusalem; for it is the city of the great King. [36] Neither shalt thou swear by thy head, because thou canst not make one hair white or black. [37] But let your communication be, Yea, yea; Nay, nay: for whatsoever is more than these cometh of evil" (Matthew 5:33-37).

"[38] **Ye have heard** that it hath been said, An eye for an eye, and a tooth for a tooth: [39] **But I say** unto you, That ye resist not evil: but whosoever shall smite thee on thy right cheek, turn to him the other also. [40] And if any man will sue thee at the law, and take away thy coat, let him have *thy* cloke also. [41] And whosoever shall compel thee to go a mile, go with him twain. [42] Give to him that asketh thee, and from him that would borrow of thee turn not thou away" (Matthew 5:38-42).

"[43] **Ye have heard** that it hath been said, Thou shalt love thy neighbour, and hate thine enemy. [44] **But I say** unto you, Love your enemies, bless them that curse you, do good to them that hate you, and pray for them which despitefully use you, and persecute you; [45] That ye may be the children of your Father which is in heaven: for he maketh his sun to rise on the evil and on the good, and sendeth rain on the just and on the unjust. [46] For if ye love them which love you, what reward have ye? do not even the publicans the same? [47] And if ye salute your brethren only, what do ye more *than others*? do not even the publicans so? [48] Be ye therefore perfect, even as your Father which is in heaven is perfect" (Matthew 5:43-48).

DISCUSSION QUESTIONS

1. Explain Matthew 5:48 as a very simple qualifier for God's standard of what defines righteousness.

2. What is the only way to restore something that is *broken* to an *unbroken* state of existence?

3. The notion that righteousness before God could somehow come "by the Law" (by Law keeping) is ridiculous. However, the false teaching about the doctrine of Grace that says God is no longer concerned about holy living and that the Christian of the Church Age is *liberated* from any moral standard of right and wrong is even more ridiculous. How do the things Christ teaches in Matthew five, six, and seven exemplify the ridiculousness of such heretical teaching?

4. Discuss why it is important to understand that II Corinthians 5:21 refers to *practical* God-kind righteousness supernaturally produced by the Spirit of God through the regenerated believer. Discuss the importance of this understanding rather than the wrong emphasis upon the mere imputation of God-kind righteousness in the gift of salvation.

5. Have you heard someone say to you, "well that is your interpretation"? What is the usual reason for making such a statement?

6. Explain why it is critical to understand that Matthew chapters five, six, seven, and Luke 6:20-49 give us the conditions of the *blessing and curse* ("woe") of the New Covenant for the Church Age believers. Discuss how this relates to culpability at the Judgment Seat of Christ for each of us in our stewardship of grace.

7. List and discuss each of the five *Declarations of Dependence* that define the believer's *Altar work* before the Throne of Grace.

Bibliography

Alford, Henry
Alford's Greek Testament
Baker Book House; reprinted 1980

Angus, S.
The Mystery Religions
New York: Dover Publications, 1975.

Barnes, Albert
Barnes' Notes on the New Testament
Baker Book House, twentieth printing 1981

Barton, George A.
Archaeology and the Bible
American Sunday School Union, Sixth Ed., Jan. 1933

Baumgartner, Anne S.
A Comprehensive Dictionary of the Gods
Wings Books, 1995 Edition

Boer, Harry R.
A Short History of the Early Church
Wm. B. Eerdmans Pub. Co., 5th Printing, April 1981

Bruce, F.F.
Jesus: Lord and Savior
Intervarsity Press, 1966

Bullinger, E.W.
Number In Scripture
Kregal Publications, Reprinted 1980

Chafer, Lewis Sperry
Systematic Theology
Dallas Seminary Press, Thirteenth Printing, June, 1976

Garrison, R. Benjamin
Creeds In Collision
Abington Books

Garraty, John A. and Gay, Peter (Editors)
The Columbia History of the World
Harper and Row Publishers

Getz, Gene A.
The Measure of a Church
G.L. Regal Books, 7th Printing, 1979

Green, Michael
Evangelism in the Early Church
Wm. B. Eerdmans Pub. Co., Reprinted Jan. 1985

Hunt, Dave and McMahon, T.A.
The Seduction of Christianity
Harvest House Publishers, 6th Printing, Feb., 1986

Jackson, Jeremy C.
No Other Foundation, The Church Through Twenty Centuries
Cornerstone Books, 1980

Jamieson, Robert, Fausset, A.R., and Brown, David
Jamieson-Fausset-Brown Commentary Critical and Explanatory on the Whole Bible
SwordSearcher Software 6.2, 1871.

Kuen, Alfred F.
I Will Build My Church
Moody Press, Translated from original French Edition in 1971

Lightfoot, J.B. (and Harner, J.R.)
The Apostalic Fathers (Second Edition)
Baker Book House Co., second printing, Aug. 1990

Lindsey, Hal
The Late Great Planet Earth
Zondervan Publishing House, 27th Printing, Feb. 1974

MacArthur, John
God, Satan and Angels
Moody Press, 6th Printing, 1993

The Charismatics
Zondervan Publishing House

Body Dynamics
Victor Books, 1982

Machen, J. Gresham
The Origen of Paul's Religion
Wm. B. Eerdmans Pub. Co.

Maynard, Michael
A History of the Debate Over I John 5:7-8
Tempe, AZ: Comma Publications, 1995

McLachlan, Douglas R.
Reclaiming Authentic Fundamentalism
American Association of Christian Schools, 1993

Moffatt, James
The Expositor's Greek Testament, ed. by W. R. Nicoll
Wm. B. Eerdmans Publishing Co., November 1980 printing

Morris, Leon
Tyndale New Testament Commentaries, ed. R.V.G. Tasker
Wm. B. Eerdmans Publishing Co., November 1980 printing

Murry, Alexander S.
Who's Who in Mythology
Bonanza Books, Second Edition
Nash, Ronald H.
Christian Faith and Historical Understanding
Zondervan Publishing House, 1984

Newell, William R.
Romans Verse by Verse
Moody Press, SwordSearcher Software 6.2.

Poole, Matthew
Matthew Poole's Commentary on the Whole Bible
Sword Searcher Software 6.2

Radmacher, Earl D.
What the Church Is All About
Moody Press, 1978 Edition

Robertson, Archibald T.
Word Pictures In The New Testament
Baker Book House, 1933

Schaff, Philip
History of the Christian Church (8 Volumes)
Eerdmans Printing Co., Reprinted July 1980

Scofield, C.I.
Scofield Reference Bible
Edited by Rev. C.I. Scofield
New York, New York: Oxford University Press, Inc., 1996

Sottau, Henry W.
The Holy Vessels and Furniture of the Tabernacle
Kregal Publications, Reprinted 1975

The Tabernacle, the Priesthood and the Offerings
Kregal Publications, Second Printing, 1974

Stravinskas, Peter M.J.
Our Sunday Visitor's Catholic Encyclopedia
Huntington, IN: Our Sunday Visitor Publishing Division, 1991

Thomas, David
Acts of the Apostles Expository and Homiletical
Grand Rapids, MI: Kregel Publications.
(Reprint of the 1870 ed. published by R.D. Dickinson, London, under title:
Homiletic Commentary on the Acts of the Apostles.)

Thomson, William M.
The Land and the Book
Baker Book House Co., Second printing, 1955

Unger, Merrill F.
Unger's Survey of the Bible
Harvest House Publishers, Reprinted 1981, 3rd printing, March 1985

ZECHARIAH: Prophet of Messiah's Glory
Grand Rapids, Michigan: Zondervan Publishing House, 1982

Vincent, Marvin R.
Word Studies in the New Testament
Wm. B. Eerdman's Publishing Co., seventh printing, 1980

Wiersbe, Warren W.
Be Real
Wheaton, Illinois: Victor Books, 1978

Wood, Leon J.
A Survey of Israel's History Revised and Enlarged Edition
Grand Rapids, MI: Zondervan Publishing House, 1978

Lexcons and Dictionaries

Theological Dictionary of the New Testament, Ten Volumes
Edited by Gerhard Kittel and Gerhard Friedrich. Translated and edited by Geoffrey W. Bromiley.
Wm. B. Eerdmans Publishing Co., reprinted September 1983

Richards, Lawrence O.
Expository Dictionary of Bible Words
Regency Reference Library
Zondervan Publishing House, 1985

Thayer, Joseph H.
Thayer's Greek English Lexicon of the New Testament
Baker Book House, Fifth Printing March 1980

Unger, Merrill F.
The New Unger's Bible Dictionary
Edited by R.K. Harrison, Howard F. Vos and Cyril J. Barber contributing editors.
Moody Press, Revised and updated 1988

Vine, W. E.
An Expository Dictionary of New Testament Words
Fleming H. Revell Company , Seventeenth impression, 1966

The Zondervan Pictoral Encyclopedia of the Bible, Five Volumes
General Editor: Merrill C. Tenney
Associate Editor: Steven Barabas
Zondervan Publishing House; Fifth Printing 1982

Strong, James
Strong's Exhaustive Concordance of the Bible
Riverside Book and Bible House; 1890

CPSIA information can be obtained at www.ICGtesting.com
Printed in the USA
BVOW010026020512

289178BV00006B/1/P

9 780986 011304